MARK

THE NIV
APPLICATION
COMMENTARY

From biblical text . . . to contemporary life

The NIV Application Commentary Series

When complete, the NIV Application Commentary
will include the following volumes:

To see which titles are available,
visit our web site at www.zondervan.com

MARK

THE NIV APPLICATION COMMENTARY

From biblical text . . . to contemporary life

DAVID E. GARLAND

ZONDERVAN™

GRAND RAPIDS, MICHIGAN 49530

The NIV Application Commentary: Mark
Copyright © 1996 by David E. Garland

Requests for information should be addressed to:

Zondervan, *Grand Rapids, Michigan 49530*

Library of Congress Cataloging-in-Publication Data

Garland, David E.
    Mark / David E. Garland.
        p.   cm.—(The NIV application commentary)
      Includes bibliographical references and index.
      ISBN: 0–310–49350-1 (alk. paper)
      1. Bible. N.T. Mark—Commentaries.   I. Title.   II. Series.
  BS2585.3.G37 1966
  226.3'077—dc20   96–9486

This edition printed on acid-free paper.

Printed in the United States of America

01 02 03 04 05 06 07/ ❖ DC / 20 19 18 17 16 15 14 13 12 11 10

Contents

NIV Application Commentary
Series Introduction

THE NIV APPLICATION COMMENTARY SERIES is unique. Most commentaries help us make the journey from the twentieth century back to the first century. They enable us to cross the barriers of time, culture, language, and geography that separate us from the biblical world. Yet they only offer a one-way ticket to the past and assume that we can somehow make the return journey on our own. Once they have explained the *original meaning* of a book or passage, these commentaries give us little or no help in exploring its *contemporary significance*. The information they offer is valuable, but the job is only half done.

Recently, a few commentaries have included some contemporary application as *one* of their goals. Yet that application is often sketchy or moralistic, and some volumes sound more like printed sermons than commentaries.

The primary goal of The NIV Application Commentary Series is to help you with the difficult but vital task of bringing an ancient message into a modern context. The series not only focuses on application as a finished product but also helps you think through the *process* of moving from the original meaning of a passage to its contemporary significance. These are commentaries, not popular expositions. They are works of reference, not devotional literature.

The format of the series is designed to achieve the goals of the series. Each passage is treated in three sections: *Original Meaning, Bridging Contexts,* and *Contemporary Significance.*

THIS SECTION HELPS you understand the meaning of the biblical text in its first-century context. All of the elements of traditional exegesis—in concise form—are discussed here. These include the historical, literary, and cultural context of the passage. The authors discuss matters related to grammar and syntax, and the meaning of biblical words. They also seek to explore the main ideas of the passage and how the biblical author develops those ideas.[1]

---

1. Please note that when the author discusses words in the original biblical languages, this series uses the general rather than the scholarly method of transliteration.

After reading this section, you will understand the problems, questions, and concerns of the *original audience* and how the biblical author addressed those issues. This understanding is foundational to any legitimate application of the text today.

THIS SECTION BUILDS a bridge between the world of the Bible and the world of today, between the original context and the contemporary context, by focusing on both the timely and timeless aspects of the text.

God's Word is *timely*. The authors of Scripture spoke to specific situations, problems, and questions. Paul warned the Galatians about the consequences of circumcision and the dangers of trying to be justified by law (Gal. 5:2–5). The author of Hebrews tried to convince his readers that Christ is superior to Moses, the Aaronic priests, and the Old Testament sacrifices. John urged his readers to "test the spirits" of those who taught a form of incipient Gnosticism (1 John 4:1–6). In each of these cases, the timely nature of Scripture enables us to hear God's Word in situations that were *concrete* rather than abstract.

Yet the timely nature of Scripture also creates problems. Our situations, difficulties, and questions are not always directly related to those faced by the people in the Bible. Therefore, God's word to them does not always seem relevant to us. For example, when was the last time someone urged you to be circumcised, claiming that it was a necessary part of justification? How many people today care whether Christ is superior to the Aaronic priests? And how can a "test" designed to expose incipient Gnosticism be of any value in a modern culture?

Fortunately, Scripture is not only timely but *timeless*. Just as God spoke to the original audience, so he still speaks to us through the pages of Scripture. Because we share a common humanity with the people of the Bible, we discover a *universal dimension* in the problems they faced and the solutions God gave them. The timeless nature of Scripture enables it to speak with power in every time and in every culture.

Those who fail to recognize that Scripture is both timely and timeless run into a host of problems. For example, those who are intimidated by timely books such as Hebrews or Galatians might avoid reading them because they seem meaningless today. At the other extreme, those who are convinced of the timeless nature of Scripture, but who fail to discern its timely element, may "wax eloquent" about the Melchizedekian priesthood to a sleeping congregation.

The purpose of this section, therefore, is to help you discern what is timeless in the timely pages of the New Testament—and what is not. For example, if Paul's primary concern is not circumcision (as he tells us in Gal. 5:6), what *is* he concerned about? If discussions about the Aaronic priesthood or Melchizedek seem irrelevant today, what is of abiding value in these passages? If people try to "test the spirits" today with a test designed for a specific first-century heresy, what other biblical test might be more appropriate?

Yet this section does not merely uncover that which is timeless in a passage but also helps you to see *how* it is uncovered. The author of the commentary seeks to take what is implicit in the text and make it explicit, to take a process that normally is intuitive and explain it in a logical, orderly fashion. How do we know that circumcision is not Paul's primary concern? What clues in the text or its context help us realize that Paul's real concern is at a deeper level?

Of course, those passages in which the historical distance between us and the original readers is greatest require a longer treatment. Conversely, those passages in which the historical distance is smaller or seemingly nonexistent require less attention.

One final clarification. Because this section prepares the way for discussing the contemporary significance of the passage, there is not always a sharp distinction or a clear break between this section and the one that follows. Yet when both sections are read together, you should have a strong sense of moving from the world of the Bible to the world of today.

THIS SECTION ALLOWS the biblical message to speak with as much power today as it did when it was first written. How can you apply what you learned about Jerusalem, Ephesus, or Corinth to our present-day needs in Chicago, Los Angeles, or London? How can you take a message originally spoken in Greek and Aramaic and communicate it clearly in our own language? How can you take the eternal truths originally spoken in a different time and culture and apply them to the similar-yet-different needs of our culture?

In order to achieve these goals, this section gives you help in several key areas.

First, it helps you identify contemporary situations, problems, or questions that are truly comparable to those faced by the original audience. Because contemporary situations are seldom identical to those faced in the first century, you must seek situations that are analogous if your applications are to be relevant.

Second, this section explores a variety of contexts in which the passage might be applied today. You will look at personal applications, but you will also be encouraged to think beyond private concerns to the society and culture at large.

Third, this section will alert you to any problems or difficulties you might encounter in seeking to apply the passage. And if there are several legitimate ways to apply a passage (areas in which Christians disagree), the author will bring these to your attention and help you think through the issues involved.

In seeking to achieve these goals, the contributors to this series attempt to avoid two extremes. They avoid making such specific applications that the commentary might quickly become dated. They also avoid discussing the significance of the passage in such a general way that it fails to engage contemporary life and culture.

Above all, contributors to this series have made a diligent effort not to sound moralistic or preachy. The NIV Application Commentary Series does not seek to provide ready-made sermon materials but rather tools, ideas, and insights that will help you communicate God's Word with power. If we help you to achieve that goal, then we have fulfilled the purpose for this series.

—The Editors

General Editor's Preface

WHEN IT COMES TO LIVING THE CHRISTIAN LIFE, beginnings are better than endings. That may be one of the most important lessons that the Gospel of Mark, by its very structure, teaches us.

We live, unfortunately, in a society more interested in endings than in beginnings. Sporting contests, business profits, and personal résumés exalt final scores, bank accounts, and individual achievement. Endings are more important, it seems, than beginnings.

At first this seems right. Winning, money, and success make life a whole lot easier than losing, debt, and failure. Everyone concerned with raising a family and navigating through the difficult roadblocks of life needs to pay attention to endings. Although reasonable and attractive, however (especially when the Bulls win and our bank account is healthy because of a good job), placing too much emphasis on endings actually creates a climate in which it is impossible ever to be satisfied or whole. The "endings" turn out to be illusory. They are not really endings after all but merely penultimate resting places that lead to new goals and more endings, stages, and levels that go on and on and never really get us to a satisfactory end.

Thus, describing life in terms of endings may not be the best way to do it. It may lead not to the best worldview or philosophy or theology. In fact, it more often than not leads to discontent, neuroses, and despair. We always want to win *more*, make *more*, succeed *more*. *More* is an insatiable taskmaster. Is there another way?

Yes. As Professor David Garland shows in this commentary on the Gospel of Mark, the better way is focusing on beginnings rather than endings. Why? For one reason, it is a better way of describing reality. It gives answers, or hints at answers, to some of the more difficult problems of life. It gives meaning to suffering—although I suffer now, in the Christian life tomorrow is always a new beginning. It makes perseverance sensible—why stick it out? Because life in Jesus Christ promises eternal life. It restores hope to its rightful place as queen of virtues.

One of the geniuses of this Gospel is that it shows how the coming of Jesus Christ helps us focus on beginnings, leaving the endings to God. How? Primarily by showing that Jesus Christ is the New Beginning to end all new beginnings. In one sense, the whole story of the Bible is the story of God's giving first his chosen people and then the whole creation chance after chance to start over again and get their relationship right with God. Jesus Christ represents the culmination of that process, not by saving everyone once for all, but by giving everyone the chance, forever and ever, to start over again at any time. We can never lose hope because there is always another chance, as offered by the life, death, and resurrection of Jesus Christ.

One of the interesting features of Mark's Gospel is that it starts abruptly and really has no ending. Scholars speculate on the reason for this unique feature. I lean toward the idea that this was intentional on Mark's part—one more way of showing that Jesus, the New Beginning, did not end anything but made it possible for the story of God, working in human history and in the church, to go on and on. The Story is never finished, never ended. We are living the salvation offered in Christ right now, and more and more people are beginning to experience the reality of this each and every day.

The ultimate new beginning, of course, is the Resurrection. Death, the ultimate ending, has been defeated by Jesus Christ. Faith ceases to be faith when it is wedded to endings. It is the Resurrection that symbolizes all the new beginnings of the Gospel of Mark, and it is the Resurrection that teaches us that after Jesus Christ, there is no ending, only the hopeful promise of eternal life.

—Terry C. Muck

Author's Preface

THIRTY YEARS AGO Paul Scherer outlined issues one needs to struggle with when interpreting the Scripture—issues that this commentary series consciously tries to address. He wrote that as one ponders the text one tries to determine:

(a) Both what happened here . . . and what the God whose deed is his living Word is saying in and through what happened . . . to you and your people.

(b) What the central thrust of the passage is, that which gathers up all its concerns and gives them direction.

(c) The theological significance of what is being said or done, its place in the systematic thinking which the church has done about her faith.

(d) Its point of immediacy or relevance, where it sits closest and most urgently to our situation, not as an "answer" to our questions so much as questioning of our answers.

(e) The problems of communication that have to be faced, the hazards of thought and experience which stand in the way as we try to hear the Word that is being addressed to us.[1]

Wrestling with this task is far from easy but incredibly rewarding. It has its risks, however, because one is consciously trying to apply a first-century text to the religious interests of the present. Albert Schweitzer underscored the dangers in his renowned critique of the German lives of Jesus. He wrote:

As of old Jacob wrestled with the angel, so German theology wrestles with Jesus of Nazareth and will not let Him go until He bless it—that is, until He will consent to serve it and will suffer Himself to be drawn by the Germanic spirit into the midst of our time and our civilisation. But when the day breaks, the wrestler must let Him go. He will not cross the ford with us. Jesus of Nazareth will not suffer Himself to be modernised. As an historic figure He refuses to be detached from his own time. He has no answer for the question, "Tell us Thy name in our speech and for our day!" But He does bless those who have wrestled with Him, so that, though they cannot take Him with them, yet, like men who have seen God face to face and received strength

---

1. Paul Scherer, "A Gauntlet with a Gift in It," *Int* 20 (1966): 388.

in their souls, they go on their way with renewed courage, ready to do battle with the world and its powers.[2]

Schweitzer perhaps has exaggerated the danger but has clearly pointed out the pitfalls of trying to draw out the contemporary significance of the text. So often, we make Jesus into our image. For this reason, I have employed ancient literature outside the Scriptures to try to understand the Jesus we meet in Mark in his own historical context before building the bridge to bring him into our contemporary world. These tasks—and it is like wrestling—must be completed if Jesus' story will speak to and challenge each generation and culture afresh.

I wish to thank many for helping in the completion of this commentary. I was especially appreciative of the encouragement and advice of Jack Kuhatschek, Verlyn D. Verbrugge, and Scot McKnight, who read and commented on the entire manuscript. Klyne Snodgrass and Terry Muck offered helpful counsel early on. I would also like to thank a list of students who read through a rough draft in an M.Div. seminar: Bruce Allen, Vicky Belcher, Jeff Elieff, Michael Elliott, Terré Jasper, O. H. Nipper, Jr., Ronald L. Mercer, Guillermina Deneb de Montalvo Podgaisky, Thom Thornton, Sean White, and Yin Xu. Our cultural differences made for interesting discussions on the meaning and application of the text. My graduate fellow Sam Pelletier also offered helpful insights, and David Drinnon helped me immensely in the final stages. Of course, they bear no responsibility for any errors and saved me from many.

I also wish to express my appreciation to three churches I served as interim pastor during the writing of this commentary: Crescent Hill Baptist Church in Louisville, Kentucky; First Baptist Church in Crothersville, Indiana; and Immanuel Baptist Church in Lexington, Kentucky. They heard more than their fair share of sermons from Mark, and the task of preaching each week helped make me sensitive to the need of bridging contexts and drawing out the contemporary significance of the text. They were very loving, supportive, and encouraging.

I wish to thank my children, Sarah and John, for bringing so much joy, fun, and love to my life. I dedicate this book to my wife, Diana, who read many drafts and allowed me to include her piece reflecting on marriage in the commentary. She is an extraordinary model of integrity, courage, and love.

—David E. Garland
Louisville, Kentucky
April, 1996

---

2. Albert Schweitzer, *The Quest for the Historical Jesus: A Critical Study of Its Progress from Reimarus to Wrede* (New York: Macmillan, 1968), 312.

Abbreviations

AB	Anchor Bible
ABD	*The Anchor Bible Dictionary*
ANRW	*Aufstieg und Niedergang der römischen Welt*
BETL	Bibliotheca ephemeridum theologicarum lovaniensium
Bib	*Biblica*
BibRev	*Bible Review*
BibTrans	*Biblical Translator*
BJRL	*Bulletin of John Rylands Library*
BR	*Biblical Research*
BTB	*Biblical Theological Bulletin*
CBQ	*Catholic Biblical Quarterly*
CD	*Church Dogmatics*
ExpT	*Expository Times*
HTR	*Harvard Theological Review*
ICC	International Critical Commentary
Int	*Interpretation*
JAAR	*Journal of the American Academy of Religion*
JBL	*Journal of Biblical Literature*
JJS	*Journal of Jewish Studies*
JSNT	*Journal for the Study of the New Testament*
JSNTSup	Journal for the Study of the New Testament Supplement Series
JTS	*Journal of Theological Studies*
KJV	King James Version
MT	Masoretic Text
NASB	New American Standard Version
NICNT	New International Commentary on the New Testament
NIV	New International Version
NovT	*Novum Testamentum*
NovTSup	Novum Testamentum Supplements
NRSV	New Revised Standard Version
NTS	*New Testament Studies*
PGM	*Papyri graecae magicae*
REB	Revised English Bible
RevExp	*The Review and Expositor*

Abbreviations

RSV	Revised Standard Version
RTR	*Reformed Theological Review*
SBT	Studies in Biblical Theology
SBLDS	Society of Biblical Literature Dissertation Series
SNTSMS	Society for New Testament Studies Monograph Series
TDNT	*Theological Dictionary of the New Testament*
TNTC	Tyndale New Testament Commentary
WUNT	Wissenschaftliche Untersuchungen zum Neuen Testament
ZNW	*Zeitschrift für die neutestamentliche Wissenschaft*
ZTK	*Zeitschrift für Theologie und Kirche*

Introduction

IN THE GLARE of the Jerusalem sun, Jews from every nation jostle each other to get a closer look and to hear twelve men speak about God's most recent display of power. One man named Peter raises his voice to address a crowd some fifty days after his Master was crucified in this very city. He solemnly declares that the Holy Spirit has come upon them, inaugurating the new age.

> "Men of Israel, listen to this: Jesus of Nazareth was a man accredited by God to you by miracles, wonders and signs, which God did among you through him, as you yourselves know. This man was handed over to you by God's set purpose and foreknowledge; and you, with the help of wicked men, put him to death by nailing him to the cross. But God raised him from the dead, freeing him from the agony of death, because it was impossible for death to keep its hold on him." (Acts 2:22–24)

In this speech we have the basic outline of Mark's Gospel, which tells more fully the story of what happened. What was hidden during Jesus' public ministry can now be made public to clarify the basis of the Christian faith in Jesus.

The Title of the Gospel

THE OPENING OF Mark's Gospel (1:1) is as abrupt as its ending (16:8). Does this first verse function as a subtitle introducing the subject matter of the first few verses? Is it the beginning of a clause that ends in verse 3? Or is it the title of the whole work? If the first option is correct, then it simply announces that what follows in the next verses launches the story of Jesus' ministry, death, and resurrection. In this case, the story this Gospel tells has its beginning with the preaching of John the Baptizer and Jesus' baptism and temptation in the wilderness. No other subtitles appear in the Gospel, however, which makes this interpretation less likely. The second option takes this opening line as the beginning of a sentence that concludes with the scriptural citation in verses 2–3: "The beginning of the gospel of Jesus Christ, Son of God, as written by Isaiah the prophet ...", this interpretation affirms that the beginning of the gospel story accords with Isaiah's promise of long ago, thus matching the apostles' preaching in Acts, which traced the beginning of the story to the baptism of John (Acts 1:22; 10:37; 13:24–25).

The third option for interpreting this opening line reads it as the title of the whole Gospel (1:2–16:8): "The beginning of the proclamation of the good news about Jesus Christ, the Son of God" (full stop). Modern readers are accustomed to books with attractive dust jackets trumpeting the title of the work and the name of the author, appealing graphics designed to grab the attention of potential buyers, and a snappy blurb summarizing its contents and recommending its purchase. The opening pages of modern books include a title page, a foreword, a preface, and an introduction to provide the reader with some background information before they begin to read. Ancient writers did not have such luxuries, but they did try to alert the reader to the scope of the work with a title or introductory phrase. The opening line, "the beginning of the good news about Jesus Christ, the Son of God," tells us what this work is about.[1] It immediately informs the reader that the story this book recounts is no typical one.

If this interpretation is correct, then the whole Gospel of Mark is about a beginning. One advantage of this reading is that it sheds light on the perplexing ending, where Mark abruptly quits his story: The women flee from the tomb, trembling with fright, and say nothing to anyone (16:8). Mark does not finish the story because the announcement of Jesus' resurrection and his going before his disciples to Galilee is not the final stage. The reader cannot put the book down at the closing line and chalk it up as a good read. The story of the gospel about Jesus Christ continues. On the one hand, the reader knows that the fearful silence of these women could not have been the end of the matter. Something else must have happened, or else we would not be hearing or reading this Gospel. On the other hand, the reader must ask questions: How will the fear of the women be vanquished? How will their mouths be opened? How will the word of good news get out? The answers to such questions can only be found by returning to the beginning "where the reader is reminded that it is all a beginning." Mark must now be reread and reheard "with 20/20 hindsight."[2] The conclusion to this story is only the beginning of the proclamation of good news about Jesus Christ that goes on to the end of time and to the ends of the earth (13:10; 14:9).[3] The Greek word

---

1. The absence of a verb makes it more likely that this opening line serves as a title rather than a verbless sentence (compare the beginnings of Prov. 1:1; Song 1:1; Eccl. 1:1 without predicates, and Rev. 1:1). The result is that verse 2 continues awkwardly in Greek: "Just as it is written by the prophet Isaiah . . . ," but Mark is not known for grammatical deftness.

2. Elizabeth Struthers Malbon, "Echoes and Foreshadowings in Mark 4–8: Reading and Rereading," *JBL* 112 (1993): 229.

3. C. H. Giblin, "The Beginning of the Ongoing Gospel, Mk 1,2–16,8," *The Four Gospels 1992: Festschrift Frans Neirynck,* ed. F. Van Segbroeck, et al. (BETL; Leuven: Peeters, 1992), 2:975–85.

arche ("beginning") can also indicate the basis or foundation of something, as in the sentence, "The fear of the LORD is the beginning of wisdom" (Ps. 111:10). This Gospel is more than just a chronicle of the genesis of God's good news. It is the ground of the church's proclamation of that good news.[4]

The Gospel

THE TITLE CONTAINS three key terms that are vital for understanding what this work is about: *the gospel*, *Christ*, and *Son of God*. The first term, *the gospel*, did not yet refer to a literary genre (a book telling the story of the life and teaching of Jesus) when Mark wrote. The word appears in 1:14, 15; 8:35; 10:29; 13:10; 14:9 and refers to what is preached about God or about Jesus as the Christ, the Son of God. It refers to the whole story about Jesus that not only is narrated in the text but is also told in oral tradition and must supplement the text—the words, deeds, death, and resurrection of Jesus and what it all means as God's act to save humankind.

While the term *gospel* is as familiar as water to most modern readers, it had a variety of associations in the first century. In calling the story of Jesus Christ "the gospel," Mark gives the term a twist that would have surprised first-century readers, particularly in Rome. In the Greek translation of the Old Testament, the verb from which this noun is derived (*euangelizo*) was used for the proclamation of the news of victory from the battlefield. Cranfield notes, however, that most of the inhabitants of the Roman empire would have associated the word with the emperor cult, which represented the announcements of such events as the birth of an heir to the emperor, his coming of age, and his accession to the throne as glad tidings or gospels.[5] These imperial glad tidings "represent the pretentious claims of self-important men" and the fawning flattery of their vassals. A frequently cited inscription from the Roman province of Asia decrees that the birthday of the emperor Augustus (September 23) would now mark the beginning of the year when persons assumed civil office. It was filled with exaggerated praise:

> . . . it is a day which we may justly count as equivalent to the beginning of everything—if not in itself and in its own nature, at any rate in the benefits it brings—inasmuch as it has restored the shape of everything that was failing and turning into misfortune, and has given a new look to the Universe at a time when it would gladly

---

4. Pesch, *Das Markusevangelium*, 1:76. The preaching and activity of John the Baptizer up to the death and resurrection of Jesus is the foundation of the church's preaching about Jesus.

5. C. E. B. Cranfield, *A Critical and Exegetical Commentary on the Epistle to the Romans* (ICC; Edinburgh: T. & T. Clark, 1975), 1:55.

have welcomed destruction if Caesar had not been born to be the common blessing of all men.

The decree resolves that:

> Whereas the Providence which has ordered the whole of our life, showing concern and zeal has ordained the most perfect consummation for human life by giving to it Augustus, by filling him with virtue for doing the work of a benefactor among men, and by sending in him, as it were, a saviour for us and those who come after us, to make war to cease, to create order everywhere ... and whereas the birthday of the God [Augustus] was the beginning for the world of the glad tidings that have come to men through him ... Paulus Fabius Maximus, the proconsul of the province ... has devised a way of honouring Augustus hitherto unknown to the Greeks, which is that the reckoning of time for the course of human life should begin with his birth.[6]

What constitutes good news in this edict is the cessation of wars and the bringing of benefits and social order. Succeeding emperors became even more enamored with themselves and claimed to bring new and greater benefits. Those who profited were the usual recipients of favor, the privileged and powerful. The glad tidings about Jesus, by contrast, are significantly different. (1) It has its origins in God (Rom. 1:1; 15:16; 2 Cor. 11:7; 1 Thess. 2:2, 8; 1 Peter 4:17), who is the beginning and end of all things and the true source of blessing for humankind. (2) The good news cannot be separated from what Jesus said and did as the one who came to give his life as a ransom for many (Mark 10:45). The emperors of Rome belong to the dim past, and we do not think of them in any way as a present reality. One is more likely to ask, "Who was Augustus?" than "Who is Augustus?" By contrast, Jesus' work abides in the present because we ask, "Who is Jesus who continues to reign in the hearts of his subjects?"[7] (3) The peace and the benefits that Jesus brings do not come from crushing resistance with military terror but from his death on the cross. Consequently, Christianity does not offer a series of gospels with each succeeding ruler but only one, *the* gospel. (4) The benefits are universal and bestowed on everyone. They are offered to the outcast, the sinner, and the poor, Jew and Gentile alike, not just to the privileged few. This story is truly good news for the entire world.

---

6. Ernest Barker, *From Alexander to Constantine: Passages and Documents Illustrating the History of the Social and Political Ideas 336 B.C.–A.D. 337* (Oxford: Clarendon, 1956), 211–12.

7. George W. MacRae, "Whom Heaven Must Receive Until the Time," *Int* 27 (1973): 151.

The Christ

THE GOSPEL IS about "Jesus Christ." The term *Christ* means "anointed one" and would have sounded strange to Greek ears.[8] Mark offers no further explanation about the meaning of the word, which suggests that his intended audience was already familiar with it as well as with much of the story. Many characters in the Gospel, however, will use the title but have no idea of what it means for Jesus of Nazareth to be the Christ. As the story unfolds, it becomes plain that one must throw out all preconceptions of what *Christ* means. Only after Jesus' death and resurrection can one understand the momentous nature of the news that he is God's Christ.

The title *Christ* quickly assumed the force of a proper name and has completely lost its original force for the modern reader. Some today may even assume that "Christ" is Jesus' surname, as the son of Joseph and Mary Christ. Others may consider it to be some foreign, generic title of lordship: the holy Christ (like Shah, Rajah, or Kaiser). Christians may simply presume that it refers to the one and only Christ, in whom we believe. For the Greek-speaking Jews of Jesus' day, however, Christ (= Messiah) was a title of the one anointed by God to carry out specific tasks related to the liberation of Israel. The term probably evoked a constellation of hopes for different Jews.

Views about the role of the Christ, when he would come, how he would be recognized, and what precisely he would do, varied.[9] A few well-situated Jews were quite satisfied with the status quo and probably cared less about such speculation except as it threatened their power base. Among the rest, there was general agreement that the Messiah would be Moses-like in delivering the nation of Israel, that he would establish his throne in Jerusalem like David, that he would smash those who made the people suffer, as did the saviors of old (Neh. 9:27), and that he would rule with justice and restore the lost fortunes of the nation. Like Cyrus, also identified as God's anointed (Isa. 45:1), the Messiah would subdue nations before him and make kings run in his service. No longer would Israel be the footstool of heathen overlords but would take its proper place of ascendancy in the world. The author of the *Psalms of Solomon* voiced this dream in the first century B.C.

See, Lord, and raise up for them their king,
   the son of David, to rule over your servant Israel
   in the time known to you, O God.

---

8. See further L. W. Hurtado, "Christ," in *Dictionary of Jesus and the Gospels*, ed. Joel B. Green, Scot McKnight, and I. Howard Marshall (Downers Grove, Ill.: InterVarsity, 1992), 106–17.

9. See further Jacob Neusner, William Scott Green, and Ernest S. Frerichs, eds., *Judaisms and Their Messiahs at the Turn of the Christian Era* (Cambridge: Cambridge Univ. Press, 1987).

> Undergird him with the strength to destroy the unrighteous rulers,
>> to purge Jerusalem from gentiles
>> who trample her to destruction;
>> in wisdom and in righteousness to drive out
>> the sinners from the inheritance;
> to smash the arrogance of sinners
>> like a potter's jar;
> To shatter all their substance with an iron rod;
> to destroy the unlawful nations with the word of his mouth;
> At his warning the nations will flee from his presence;
>> and he will condemn sinners by the thoughts of their hearts
>> (17:21–25).[10]

This kind of false hope helped spark the disastrous revolt against Rome in A.D. 66. The first-century Jewish historian, Josephus, contends that the Jewish rebels were provoked to war by their misunderstanding of an "ambiguous oracle in their sacred scriptures, to the effect that at that time one from their country would become king of the world."[11]

Obviously, proclaiming one who was crucified to be the Christ must have created a severe case of cognitive dissonance for both the early Christians and their Jewish counterparts, whom they were trying to convince. Jesus won no decisive victories worthy of historical mention anywhere but in the Gospels, and these were spiritual triumphs. John the Baptist gets more press in Josephus's account of Jewish history of this era than Jesus does. What little he did write about Jesus has been heavily edited by later Christian copyists. Jesus established no earthly reign. Rome still ruled the world with an iron hand. When Mark wrote, the Roman juggernaut was either about to or had already exacted severe retribution for Israel's rebellion by sacking Jerusalem and burning the temple. Jesus the Messiah had come and gone, and the golden age had not arrived. Consequently, it was easy for many Jews to dismiss him as another dismal failure.

What was even more absurd, Jesus had been crucified like a criminal. Paul himself cites the theological hitch that a crucified Messiah created: "Cursed is everyone who is hung on a tree" (Gal. 3:13; cf. Deut. 21:23). Justin Martyr, in his record of an exchange with Rabbi Trypho about the Christian

---

10. Trans. by R. B. Wright, "Psalms of Solomon," in *The Old Testament Pseudepigrapha*, ed. James H. Charlesworth (Garden City, NY: Doubleday, 1985), 2: 667.

11. Josephus contends that the correct interpretation was that it "signified the sovereignty of Vespasian, who was proclaimed emperor on Jewish soil" (*J.W.* 6.5.4 §§ 312–13; see Tacitus, *Histories* 5.13).

faith, cites Daniel 7 in an attempt to prove that Jesus was the Messiah. Trypho remains unpersuaded and responds: "Sir, these and suchlike passages of scripture compel us to await One who is great and glorious, and takes the everlasting Kingdom from the Ancient of Days as Son of Man. But this your so-called Christ is without honour and glory, so that He has even fallen into the uttermost curse that is in the Law of God, for he was crucified."[12] From a Jewish standpoint, a crucified Messiah was an oxymoron, like calling a prisoner on death row, "Mr. President."

For Mark to say without apology that Jesus was the Christ, the fulfillment of Israel's hopes, her liberator, the one who ushered in the reign of God and who reigns triumphantly at the right hand of God, was and should still be startling if not incredible. The Christian gospel is, as Paul said, a stumbling block to Jews and sheer nonsense to Gentiles (1 Cor. 1:23). From a pagan standpoint, it could be taken as further evidence of Jewish delusions. Years before, Cicero mocked Israel's faith and hope by declaring that it has "made it clear how far it enjoys divine protection by the fact that it has been conquered, scattered, enslaved."[13] In bridging the context to our contemporary situation, we need to recapture the scandal of Jesus as the Christ, the Son of God, who exposes our false hopes and selfish expectations.

The Son of God

THE PHRASE "SON of God" does not appear in all early copies of Mark. Jesus as God's Son, however, is an important theme in Mark's Gospel. The inclusion of this title in the opening line could be the original reading that a scribe accidentally omitted.[14] The title emerges at pivotal junctures in the story: the baptism (1:11), the transfiguration (9:7), and the crucifixion (15:39). Jittery demons also shout out this title (3:11; 5:7), and it appears on the lips of the outraged high priest when he asks point blank if Jesus is the "Christ, the Son of the Blessed One" (14:61). Jesus responds unambiguously, "I am." (14:62). For Mark, being the Christ and the Son of God is one and the same thing.

---

12. Justin Martyr, *Dialogue with the Jew Trypho*, 31–32.

13. Cicero, *Pro Flacco* 28.67.

14. Copyists were tempted to expand the titles of books and also to give full confessional titles, and the title "Son of God" thus may have been added. On the other hand, Christian copyists employed abbreviations for sacred names (*nomina sacra*) by using the first and last letter of the word. The similarities of the endings, which would have been written ΙΥΧΥΥΥΘΥ, may have played tricks on the eye of a copyist and caused the omission of the title.

The Beginning

GOD IS A God of beginnings. The good news of Mark is that God begins again with the chosen people by sending his Son. At the end of the Gospel, however, things look far more gloomy. The women slink away from the empty tomb and are mute from fear. Failure, denial, and fear are not the end of the story, however. When things seem to end, there is a new beginning. The gospel is good news because one can begin again. One may wonder how these discredited disciples could ever emerge as leaders of a growing church and fulfill their mission, but we know that their failure was not fatal. Neither is ours. God is the one who consistently makes something out of nothing. What seems like the end, and a pathetic one at that, is only a new beginning. God will continue to work with and revive the people. Mark makes it clear that "the church exists because of what God has done in Christ, not because of any outstanding abilities in its first members."[15] The gospel proclaims that the one "who began a good work in [us] will carry it on to completion until the day of Christ Jesus" (Phil. 1:6).

As far as Mark is concerned, the story cannot end when the women tell the news or when the disciples rendezvous with Jesus in Galilee. This explains why he does not report either event, as do the other Evangelists. Christianity is not a closed book, and Christian readers are the latest chapter in a continuing story of God's good news. The question for us is, therefore, the same as it was for those early disciples, "Where do we go from here?" The next stage is up to us. How will we continue the story? Will we cower in fear or boldly proclaim the glad tidings of Jesus to the world?

Contemporary Significance

IN PROCLAIMING THE glad tidings, one should reexamine what is good news about our message concerning Jesus Christ. False gospels still abound. In the secular world, politicians promise, like the emperors of old, that happy days will be here again with their offer of a New Deal, a New Frontier, the Great Society, or a New World Order. Tyrants inaugurate such things as the Thousand-Year Reich and the Great Leap Forward, but life seems to remain pretty much the same. The oppressed remain oppressed, and the poor are still downtrodden. Hatred and prejudice are still at home in our communities. In the religious world, the good news about Jesus Christ is watered down to good advice. People are told to be kind, to smile a lot, to love all creatures,

---

15. Leon Morris, "Disciples of Jesus," in *Jesus of Nazareth: Essays on the Historical Jesus and New Testament Christology*, ed. Joel B. Green and Max Turner (Grand Rapids: Eerdmans, 1994), 124.

---

to think positively, and to feel good about themselves. But the true gospel about Jesus Christ is something far more radical and explosive. It has to do with God's redemptive action in Jesus, which reveals God's love for humans and judgment on human sin and satanic evil.

Albert Einstein once said, "I believe in Spinoza's God who reveals himself in the orderly harmony of what exists, not in a God who concerns himself with the fates and actions of human beings."[16] The gospel proclaims, however, that God is involved with the very depths of human trouble and shame and allows the Son of God to be treated ingloriously on the cross to effect our redemption. It reveals that God comes to us in the din of huge crowds, soldiers shooting dice, and priests raging, and in the great darkness when the Son of God drinks the cup of suffering on a cross. In the crown of thorns and the shame of death, we can see the crown of majesty and the victory of God. The gospel also furnishes a new basis for our relationship to God and our relationship to each other. Our relationship to God is based on unmerited forgiveness. Even disobedient disciples, who abandon Jesus in Gethsemane, deny him with curses, and are muzzled by fear, find forgiveness and the chance to begin again through God's power. Jesus' death calls into being a new humanity based on faith in him, not on the biological limitations of clans and tribes. It creates a community based on compassion and a new inclusive sense of family.

The shock that the crucified Jesus is the Messiah, God's Son, makes clear that God cannot and will not be confined by finite human expectations. This is the God who made the platypus, a mammal so unmammal-like that expert scientists declared it a hoax when it was first sent to the British Museum. The religious experts of Jesus' day rejected him because he did not fit any preconceived notions of what the Jewish Messiah would be or do. We today are little different from first-century Jews and the disciples in wanting a Messiah who does our bidding, wins our wars, destroys our enemies, and exalts us. Throughout Mark, the disciples display a delight in power, glorious achievements, and personal ambition; they want a Messiah who is above suffering and who will give them their heart's desires. We too want a Messiah who graciously adapts his will to our desires and needs and is dedicated to serve us rather than all humankind. The Messiah we meet in Mark is a rude awakening to those who are more interested in themselves and in ensuring their personal salvation and entrance to eternal life (10:17) than in God or the fate of God's world. Michael Card captures this reality in his lyrics to "Scandalon."

---

16. W. Russell Hindmarsh, "They Changed Our Thinking: IV Albert Einstein (1879–1955)," *ExpT* 84 (1973): 199, citing a quotation in the *New York Times*.

Along the path of life there lies this stubborn Scandalon
And all who come this way must be offended.
To some He is a barrier; to others He's the way,
For all should know the scandal of believing.[17]

As was the case during Jesus' ministry, so today many will not believe or will try to mold Christ into their own images by telling him who he is and what he is to do. They want glamourous, gimmicky, short-term solutions to their own problems. Many try to domesticate the scandal, turn the cross into jewelry, and turn the Christ into a teacher of self-actualization. The Gospel of Mark is the antidote to this distortion as it presents the foundation story of the gospel about Jesus Christ, who suffers and dies on a cross.

Authorship

MODERN AUTHORS USUALLY want full credit for their work, but the anonymous author of this Gospel wanted only to present the good news about Jesus, the Christ, the Son of God. He had no desire to reap accolades from the church for his work. The power and authority of this Gospel do not derive from the prestige or credentials of its human author. Nevertheless, we are curious about the one who first took pen in hand and wove together the oral traditions about Jesus into a connected narrative. The earliest testimony connects Mark's name to the Gospel. It comes from Papias, Bishop of Hierapolis in Asia Minor, who wrote the *Interpretation of the Lord's Oracles* (written sometime between 110 and 130). His work is lost, but the early church historian Eusebius cites portions of it, including this curious comment about Mark's Gospel:

> And the Elder said this also: "Mark, having become the interpreter of Peter, wrote down accurately whatever he remembered of the things said and done by the Lord, but not however in order." For neither did he hear the Lord, nor did he follow him, but afterwards, as I said, Peter, who adapted his teachings to the needs of his hearers, but not as though he were drawing up a connected account of the Lord's oracles. So then Mark made no mistake in thus recording some things just as he remembered them. For he took forethought for one thing, not to omit any of the things that he had heard nor to state them falsely.[18]

---

17. Michael Card, *The Name of the Promise Is Jesus: Reflections on the Life of Christ* (Nashville: Thomas Nelson, 1993), 81.
18. Eusebuis, *Ecclesiastical History*, 3.39.15.

Most other patristic comments about Mark are variants of this statement. We will look briefly at Mark as the author, the relationship of this Gospel to Peter, and the statement that he did not write "in order."

Although some modern scholars question whether Papias knew what he was talking about,[19] the early attribution of this Gospel to Mark is credible. Why would the church want to credit someone who was not one of the Twelve for writing this work if it were not so? Hengel argues convincingly that the title "The Gospel According to ..." would not have been some late addition but derives from the time when the Gospels were distributed to other communities. They needed a title for hearers to know what was being read and to know what it was that was on the bookshelf.[20] Had the Gospels been sent anonymously, each community would probably have given them a different title.

Modern scholarship also challenges Papias's statement about Mark's relationship to Peter. But that too may be accepted (see 1 Peter 5:13). Hengel argues that the writing of this Gospel would not have been entrusted to a Mr. Nobody but to a recognized teacher in the church who could appeal to an even greater authority.[21] To think that just anyone could write a Gospel that early Christians would accept as authoritative stretches credibility. Matthew and Luke testify to Mark's authority since they allowed themselves to be guided by him when they wrote their own Gospels. Matthew confers even greater prominence to Peter in his Gospel, which reveals the authority he invests in this apostle. It is not unreasonable to assume that Mark's Gospel, therefore, reflects the teaching of the apostle Peter, just as Papias reported.

This relationship to Peter does not mean that the author of this Gospel is the same John Mark that we meet in Acts (12:12, 25; 13:4, 13) and the fellow worker of Paul (Col. 4:10; Philem. 24; 2 Tim. 4:11). Mark was one of the most common names in the Roman world, both in Greek (*Markos*) and in Latin (*Marcus*), and there were probably several Marks in the early church. One should therefore refrain from any fanciful recreations of the Evangelist's career on the basis of the disparate New Testament references to Mark. Mark writes so that Jesus will be the center of attention, not himself.

Papias's comment that Mark "wrote down accurately whatever he remembered of the things said and done by the Lord, but not however in order" is

---

19. See the summary of extensive scholarship about Papias in Black, *Mark*, 82–94, 104–11. The extant fragments from Papias are conveniently collected and translated in William Schoedel, *The Apostolic Fathers, Vol. 5: Polycarp, Martyrdom of Polycarp, Fragments of Papias* (London: Thomas Nelson and Sons, 1967), 89–123.

20. Hengel, *Studies in the Gospel of Mark*, 74–81.

21. Ibid., 52. See further the arguments of Martin, *Mark: Evangelist and Theologian*, 52–61, and the critique in Black, *Mark*, 201–9.

difficult. What did he mean by "in order"? Papias may be comparing Mark unfavorably to Matthew's more ordered arrangement or the three-year chronological arrangement of Jesus' life in the Fourth Gospel.[22] He does not intend to criticize Mark but to defend the Gospel in spite of presumed inadequacies.

Setting

THE TRADITIONAL VIEW that Mark was written in Rome toward the end of or shortly after the Jewish war is still the most probable setting for this Gospel.[23] Wherever it was composed, Mark should be read as a pastoral response to stressful times. The church faced major crises in the 60s. Christians had to cope with the death of eyewitnesses, which created the need to conserve and stabilize the traditions about Jesus. We learn from Tacitus (cited below) that the church in Rome was subject to vicious gossip and hostility (see also 1 Peter 2:15; 3:13–16; 4:12) and needed to fend off attacks from various quarters. Christians had to deflect government suspicion of them as a potentially subversive group. They also had to defend themselves against religious rivals who would foil the church's growth. What did Christians know of the origin of their faith? How could they respond confidently to the misrepresentations without knowing or having an account of what happened to their Founder, who was executed by sentence of a Roman magistrate?[24] Mark compiled a written record of the preaching of Peter and perhaps others to edify the church and to aid it in the task of proclaiming the gospel in the Greco-Roman world.

Mark also composed his Gospel to encourage Christians facing increasingly trying conditions and to remind them of the foundation of their faith. Except for isolated local confrontations, Christians were relatively ignored until A.D. 64. Things changed dramatically, however, after a disastrous fire swept Rome that year. Ten of the city's fourteen wards were destroyed. After the initial shock, rumors began to fill the still smoky air that the fire had been part of Nero's urban renewal scheme. Nero attempted to squelch the rumors with a program of tax relief, food giveaways, and rebuilding. When the gossip persisted, he found a scapegoat in the Christians. Tacitus reports:

> Neither all human endeavor, nor all imperial largess, nor all the modes of placating the gods, could stifle the scandal or banish the

---

22. Ibid., 48–49.

23. For the technical discussion establishing the case, see Hengel, *Studies in the Gospel of Mark*, 1–28; Black, *Mark*, 224–50; Joel Marcus, "The Jewish War and the *Sitz im Leben* of Mark," *JBL* 111 (1992): 441–62.

24. F. F. Bruce, "The Date and Character of Mark," in *Jesus and the Politics of His Day*, ed. Ernst Bammel and C. F. D. Moule (Cambridge: Cambridge Univ. Press, 1984), 78.

belief that the [great Roman] fire had taken place by order. Therefore to scotch the rumor, Nero substituted as culprits, and punished with the utmost exquisite cruelty, a class loathed for their abominations, whom the crowd styled Christians. Christus, from whom the name is derived, had undergone the death penalty in the reign of Tiberius, by sentence of the procurator Pontius Pilate. Checked for the moment, this pernicious superstition again broke out, not only in Judea, the home of the disease, but in the capital itself—that receptacle for everything hideous and degraded from every quarter of the globe, which there finds a vogue. Accordingly, arrest was first made of those who confessed [to being Christians]; next, on their disclosures, vast numbers were convicted, not so much on the charge of arson as for hatred of the human race. Every sort of derision was added to their deaths: they were wrapped in the skins of wild beasts and dismembered by dogs, others were nailed to crosses; others when daylight failed, were set afire to serve as lamps by night. Nero had offered his gardens for the spectacle and gave an exhibition in the circus, mingling with the people in the costume of a charioteer or mounted on a car. Hence even for criminals who merited extreme and exemplary punishment, there arose a feeling of pity, due to the impression that they were being destroyed, not for the public good, but to gratify the cruelty of a single man.[25]

The mass arrest of Christians changed things. Admission to being a Christian led to death. This unparalleled suffering resulted in a brave martyrdom for some and a panicked collapse for others. To undergird Christians in their faith, Mark showed the similarity between what Jesus faced and what they were facing. They could hear of how their Lord had been driven into the desert to do battle with Satan (1:12). Mark is the only Gospel to record that Jesus was with the wild beasts in the desert (1:13). As Christians were misrepresented as atheists and haters of humankind, so Jesus was falsely accused of being in league with the devil (3:21, 30). As they were framed by trumped-up charges, so Jesus was framed by false witnesses (14:56–59). As they were betrayed by intimates, so Jesus was betrayed by an intimate friend, one of the Twelve (14:43–46).

Mark also reminds his readers that Jesus predicted that persecution would come (13:1–13). He spoke openly of his own suffering and death and warned his disciples that they would not escape tribulation. Conditions would go from bad to worse. Cross-bearing was an integral part of discipleship (8:34–39); and for some, it had become a literal reality. Mark records that Jesus

---

25. Tacitus, *Annals* 15.44.

promised his followers rewards but only "with . . . persecutions" (10:29–30). He warned that those who have no root in themselves endure for a while and then immediately fall away at the first sign of persecution on account of the word (4:17). He also warned that they would be salted with fire and that salt that loses its savor could not be resalted (9:49). Mark vividly records Jesus' suffering and his complete abandonment in his moment of trial. One learns from this Gospel, however, that Jesus never abandons his followers, though, at times, he may seem to be absent. The disciples in a boat tossed by the waves may panic in fear and think that Jesus does not care that they are perishing, but he is with them. When he speaks, the winds cease, demons flee, and the dead rise.

Jesus' presence not only brings peace, his behavior under the most severe persecution sets an example for his followers, who must be conformed to him. He made his bold confession before the authorities (14:62; 15:2). He endured the bone-tipped flagellum of the guards in silence. At the end, a Roman soldier, seeing how he died, confesses, "Surely this man was the Son of God" (15:39).

The church in Rome not only faced virulent persecution, the whole world seemed to be coming apart at the seams with the tumult of civil and international wars as well. People faced danger from within—from false fears, false hopes, and false prophets. Tacitus gravely describes the chaotic times of the late 60s:

> The history on which I am entering is that of a period rich in disasters, terrible with battles, torn by civil struggles, horrible even in peace. Four emperors fell by the sword; there were three civil wars, more foreign wars, and often both at the same time. . . . Italy was distressed by disasters unknown before or returning after the lapse of the ages. . . . Beside the manifold misfortunes that befell mankind there were prodigies in the sky and on the earth, warnings given by thunderbolts, and prophecies of the future, both joyful and gloomy, uncertain and clear.[26]

Not only did Christians have to contend with the civil unrest in Rome, they also had to make sense of the disastrous revolt in Judea against Rome. The Jewish rebellion against Rome in A.D. 66 met with initial success, but inevitably the tide turned. The formidable Roman army made its way through Galilee with its scorched earth policy and by the time Mark wrote, had either besieged Jerusalem (A.D. 69) or recently sacked the city and burned the temple to the ground (A.D. 70). Paul's letter to the Romans suggests that the Roman Christian community had close ties with the Jerusalem community,

---

26. Tacitus, *Histories* 1.2.3.

and the imminent destruction of the city or its recent destruction would strike most believers as a sign of the end of this world. Mark flashes across the screen Jesus' warning about wars and rumors of wars and the destruction of the temple in chapter 13. Jesus predicts tumults and the destruction of the temple and warns that the end is not yet (13:7, 20, 27). Disciples must keep a constant spiritual vigil and must continue to proclaim the gospel in the face of brutal hostility. The Son of Man's return to gather his elect awaits an unknown day and hour. In the meantime, Jesus calls disciples to overcome their fear and to bear witness in and through their sufferings. Mark does not complain about the inhumane suffering that Christians undergo but shows that persecution should lead to confession—the confession by Christians that leads to the confession of others (15:39).

Outline of Mark

I. Prologue (1:1–13)
   A. Title of the Gospel: The Beginning of the Good News About Jesus Christ, the Son of God (1:1)
   B. The Ministry of John the Baptizer (1:2–8)
   C. Jesus' Baptism (1:9–11)
   D. Testing in the Desert (1:12–13)
II. Jesus' Ministry in Galilee (1:14–8:21)
   A. Jesus' Ministry in Galilee (1:14–3:6)
      1. Commencement of Jesus' Ministry in Galilee (1:14–45)
         a. Summary of Jesus' Preaching (1:14–15)
         b. Calling of First Disciples (1:16–20)
         c. A New Teaching: Casting out an Unclean Spirit in the Synagogue (1:21–28)
         d. Healing of Simon's Mother-in-Law and Many Others (1:29–34)
         e. Prayer in a Lonely Place Before Going out to the Whole of Galilee (1:35–39)
         f. Healing of a Leper (1:40–45)
      2. Controversies Settled by Jesus' Pronouncements (2:1–3:6)
         a. Over Forgiveness of Sins: Healing of a Paralytic (2:1–12)
         b. Over Sinners: Calling a Toll Collector and Eating with Sinners (2:13–17)
         c. Over Fasting: Jesus Defends His Disciples (2:18–22)
         d. Over Sabbath Observance: Plucking Grain (2:23–28)
         e. Over Sabbath Observance: Healing and the Plot to Destroy Jesus (3:1–6)
   B. Jesus' Ministry Around the Sea of Galilee and Rejection in Nazareth (3:7–6:6a)
      1. Summary Statement of Jesus' Ministry (3:7–12)
      2. Choosing Twelve Disciples to Be With Him (3:13–19)
      3. Accusation by Jesus' Family That He Is Beside Himself (3:20–21)
      4. Accusation by Scribes That Jesus Works by Beelzebub (3:22–29)

      a. Departure to the Mount of Olives and Prediction of Temple' Destruction (13:1–4)

      b. Warnings Connected to the Temple's Destruction (13:5–23)

         i. About Deceivers (13:5–6)

           ii. About International Wars, Earthquakes, and Famines (13:7–8)

           iii. About Persecution of Christians (13:9–13)

           ii'. About the Abomination of Desolation and War in Judea (13:14–20)

         i'. About Deceivers (13:21–23)

      c. Warning About the Coming of the Son of Man (13:24–27)

      d. Warnings That No One Knows the Timing of the End (13:28–37)

         i. Parable of the Fig Tree (13:28–31)

         ii. Announcement About the Unknown Day or Hour (13:32)

         iii. Parable of the Watchful and Indifferent Doorkeepers (13:33–37)

B. Passion of Jesus (14:1–15:41)

  1. Plot by High Priests and Scribes to Kill Jesus (14:1–2)

  2. Anonymous Woman Anoints Jesus for Burial (14:3–9)

  3. Plot by Judas to Betray Jesus (14:10–11)

  4. The Last Supper (14:12–26)

      a. Preparation for the Supper (14:12–16)

      b. Prediction of Betrayal by One of the Twelve and the Disciples' Response (14:17–21)

      c. Interpretation of His Death Through the Bread and Cup (14:22–26)

  5. On the Mount of Olives (14:27–52)

      a. Jesus' Prediction of Disciples' Scattering and Their Response (14:27–31)

      b. Jesus' Anguished Prayer in Gethsemane While Disciples Sleep (14:32–42)

      c. Judas' Betrayal, Jesus' Arrest, and Disciples' Flight (14:43–52)

  6. Jesus on Trial (14:53–15:15)

      a. Jesus Before the Sanhedrin (14:53–72)

         i. Peter Follows Jesus from a Distance to High Priest's Courtyard (14:53–54)

Bibliography

Commentaries

Anderson, Hugh. *The Gospel of Mark*. New Century Bible. London: Oliphants, 1976.

Cranfield, C. E. B. *The Gospel According to St. Mark*. Cambridge Greek Testament Commentary. Cambridge: Cambridge Univ. Press, 1966.

Derrett, J. Duncan M. *The Making of Mark: The Scriptural Bases of the Earliest Gospel*. Shipston on Stour: P. Drinkwater, 1984.

Gnilka, Joachim. *Das Evangelium nach Markus*. Evangelish-katholischer Kommentar zum Neuen Testament. Zurich: Benziger / Neukirchener, 1979.

Guelich, Robert A. *Mark 1–8:26*. Word Biblical Commentary. Dallas: Word, 1989.

Gundry, Robert. *Mark: A Commentary on His Apology for the Cross*. Grand Rapids: Eerdmans, 1993.

Heil, John Paul. *The Gospel of Mark as a Model for Action: A Reader-Response Commentary*. New York / Mahwah, N.J.: Paulist, 1992.

Hooker, Morna D. *The Gospel According to Saint Mark*. Black's New Testament Commentary. Peabody, Mass.: Hendrickson, 1991.

Iersel van, Bas. *Reading Mark*. Collegeville, Minn.: Liturgical Press 1988.

Juel, Donald H. *Mark*. Augsburg Commentary on the New Testament. Minneapolis: Augsburg, 1990.

Lane, William L. *Commentary on the Gospel of Mark*. New International Commentary on the New Testament. Grand Rapids: Eerdmans, 1974.

Lightfoot, R. H. *The Gospel Message of St. Mark*. Oxford: Clarendon, 1950.

Luccock, Halford E. "The Gospel According to Saint Mark: Exposition." *The Interpreter's Bible*, ed. George Arthur Buttrick, 7:629–917. New York / Nashville: Abingdon, 1951.

Minear, Paul S. *Saint Mark*. Layman's Bible Commentary. London: SCM, 1962.

Mitton, C. Leslie. *The Gospel According to St. Mark*. London: Epworth, 1957.

Moule, C. F. D. *The Gospel According to Mark*. Cambridge Bible Commentary. Cambridge: Cambridge Univ. Press, 1965.

Myers, Ched. *Binding the Strong Man: A Political Reading of Mark's Story of Jesus*. Maryknoll, N.Y.: Orbis, 1988.

Pesch, Rudolf. *Das Markusevangelium*. Herders theologischer Kommentar zum Neuen Testament. Freiburg/Basel/Vienna: Herder, 1984.

Schweizer, Eduard. *The Good News According to Mark*. Richmond: John Knox, 1970.

Stock, Augustine. *The Method and Message of Mark*. Wilmington, Del.: Michael Glazier, 1989.

Swete, Henry Barclay. *The Gospel According to Mark*. London: Macmillan, 1913.

Taylor, Vincent. *The Gospel According to St. Mark*. 2d ed. London: Macmillan, 1966.

Waetjen, H. C. *A Reordering of Power: A Socio-political Reading of Mark's Gospel*. Minneapolis: Fortress, 1989.

Special Studies

Achtemeier, Paul J. *Mark*. 2d ed. Proclamation Commentaries. Philadelphia: Fortress, 1986.

_____. "Mark, Gospel of." *The Anchor Bible Dictionary*, ed. David Noel Freedman, 4:541–57. New York: Doubleday, 1992.

Beasley-Murray, George R. *Jesus and the Last Days: The Interpretation of the Olivet Discourse*. Peabody, Mass.: Hendrickson, 1993.

Best, Ernest. *Disciples and Discipleship*. Edinburgh: T. & T. Clark, 1986.

_____. *Following Jesus*. JSNTSup 4. Sheffield: JSOT, 1981.

_____. *Mark: The Gospel As Story*. Studies of the New Testament and Its World. Edinburgh: T. & T. Clark, 1983.

_____. *The Temptation and the Passion*. 2d ed. SNTSMS 2. Cambridge: Cambridge Univ. Press, 1990.

Bilezikian, Gilbert G. *The Liberated Gospel: A Comparison of the Gospel of Mark and Greek Tragedy*. Grand Rapids: Baker, 1977.

Black, C. Clifton. *The Disciples According to Mark*. JSNTSup 27. Sheffield: JSOT, 1989.

_____. *Mark: Images of an Apostolic Interpreter*. Columbia, S.C.: Univ. of South Carolina Press, 1994.

Brown, Raymond E. *The Death of the Messiah*. 2 vols. New York: Doubleday, 1994.

Bryan, Christopher. *A Preface to Mark: Notes on the Gospel in Its Literary and Cultural Settings*. New York / Oxford: Oxford Univ. Press, 1993.

Camery-Hoggatt, Jerry. *Irony in Mark's Gospel: Text and Subtext*. SNTSMS 72. Cambridge: Cambridge Univ. Press, 1991.

Chapman, D. W. *The Orphan Gospel: Mark's Perspective on Jesus*. The Biblical Seminar 16. Sheffield: JSOT, 1993.

Donahue, John R. *Are You the Christ?* SBLDS 10. Missoula, Mont.: Scholars, 1973.

Dowd, Sharon E. *Prayer, Power, and the Problem of Suffering*. SBLDS 105. Atlanta: Scholars, 1988.

France, R. T. *Divine Government: God's Kingship in the Gospel of Mark*. London: SPCK, 1990.

Geddert, Timothy J. *Watchwords: Mark 13 in Markan Eschatology*. JSNTSup 26. Sheffield: JSOT, 1989.

Hengel, Martin. *Studies in the Gospel of Mark*. London: SCM, 1985.

Juel, Donald. *A Master of Surprise*. Minneapolis: Fortress, 1994.

_____. *Messiah and Temple*. SBLDS 31. Missoula, Mont.: Scholars, 1977.

Kelber, Werner H. *Mark's Story of Jesus*. Philadelphia: Fortress, 1979.

Kingsbury, Jack Dean. *The Christology of Mark's Gospel*. Philadelphia: Fortress, 1983.

_____. *Conflict in Mark*. Minneapolis: Fortress, 1989.

Malbon, Elizabeth Struthers. *Narrative Space and Mythic Meaning in Mark*. San Francisco: Harper and Row, 1986.

Marcus, Joel. *The Mystery of the Kingdom of God*. SBLDS 90. Atlanta: Scholars, 1986.

_____. *The Way of the Lord: Christological Exegesis of the Old Testament in the Gospel of Mark*. Louisville: Westminster/John Knos, 1992.

Marshall, Christopher D. *Faith as a Theme in Mark's Narrative*. SNTSMS 64. Cambridge: Cambridge Univ. Press, 1989.

Martin, Ralph P. *Mark: Evangelist and Theologian*. Grand Rapids: Zondervan, 1972.

Matera, Frank J. *The Kingship of Jesus*. SBLDS 66. Chico, Calif.: Scholars, 1982.

Rhoads, David, and Donald Michie. *Mark As Story*. Philadelphia: Fortress, 1982.

Senior, Donald P. *The Passion of Jesus in the Gospel of Mark*. Wilmington, Del.: Michael Glazier, 1984.

Telford, William R. *The Barren Temple and the Withered Fig Tree*. JSNTSup 1. Sheffield: JSOT, 1980.

Tolbert, Mary Ann. *Sowing the Word: Mark's World in Literary-Historical Perspective*. Minneapolis: Fortress, 1989.

Twelftree, Graham. *Jesus the Exorcist: A Contribution to the Study of the Historical Jesus*. Peabody, Mass.: Hendrickson, 1993.

Via, Dan O. Jr. *The Ethics of Mark's Gospel—In the Middle of Time*. Philadelphia: Fortress, 1985.

Willliams, Joel F. *Other Followers of Jesus: Minor Characters As Major Figures in Mark's Gospel*. JSNTSup 102. Sheffield: JSOT, 1994.

Mark 1:1–13

THE BEGINNING OF the gospel about Jesus Christ, the Son of God. ²It is written in Isaiah the prophet:

"I will send my messenger ahead of you,
who will prepare your way"—
³ "a voice of one calling in the desert,
'Prepare the way for the Lord,
make straight paths for him.'"

⁴And so John came, baptizing in the desert region and preaching a baptism of repentance for the forgiveness of sins. ⁵The whole Judean countryside and all the people of Jerusalem went out to him. Confessing their sins, they were baptized by him in the Jordan River. ⁶John wore clothing made of camel's hair, with a leather belt around his waist, and he ate locusts and wild honey. ⁷And this was his message: "After me will come one more powerful than I, the thongs of whose sandals I am not worthy to stoop down and untie. ⁸I baptize you with water, but he will baptize you with the Holy Spirit."

⁹At that time Jesus came from Nazareth in Galilee and was baptized by John in the Jordan. ¹⁰As Jesus was coming up out of the water, he saw heaven being torn open and the Spirit descending on him like a dove. ¹¹And a voice came from heaven: "You are my Son, whom I love; with you I am well pleased."

¹²At once the Spirit sent him out into the desert, ¹³and he was in the desert forty days, being tempted by Satan. He was with the wild animals, and angels attended him.

THE FIRST VERSE of Mark's Gospel, as already argued in the introduction, functions as the title to the entire work. The next twelve verses function as a prologue to this work and divide into three parts: (1) the citation of Scripture and the introduction of John the Baptizer (1:2–8); (2) the baptism of Jesus of Nazareth (1:9–11); and (3) the temptation of Jesus in the desert (1:12–13).

The Structure of Prologue

SOME SCHOLARS EXTEND the prologue to include the preaching of Jesus in Galilee in 1:14–15. The following arguments, however, favor treating 1:14–15 as the beginning of a new unit. (1) Each incident in 1:2–13 takes place in the same locality, the desert and the Jordan River, while what is reported in 1:14–15 takes place in Galilee, and the Sea of Galilee is mentioned in 1:16. (2) Each incident in 1:2–13 contains a reference to the Spirit (1:8, 10, 12), which is mentioned only three other times in the Gospel (3:29; 12:36; 13:11). (3) Most important, each of the three scenes in 1:2–13 presents the reader with privileged information unavailable to the characters in the story other than Jesus.[1] The first scene (1:1–8) emphasizes that John the Baptizer's ministry in the desert was the fulfillment of divine prophecy. A transcendent voice from offstage recites the Scripture and sets what follows in the perspective of salvation history. The reader now knows who John is from the divine perspective. He is the one who comes to bear witness to the more powerful one who comes after him, and Jesus must be that more powerful one promised in Scripture. A transcendent voice from the heavens identifies Jesus as the beloved Son and the conveyor of the Spirit in the second scene (1:9–11). The third scene (1:12–13) gives the reader a transcendent ringside seat of Jesus' confrontation and defeat of Satan, his living at peace with the wild beasts, and his being served by angels. By contrast, the announcement that Jesus preaches the gospel of God in Galilee (1:14–15) brings the readers back down to earth. His public proclamation is not something shrouded in mystery but goes out for all to hear.

The prologue briefly lets the readers in on what are otherwise secrets that will remain hidden in various degrees to all of the characters in the drama that follows. It contains what Mark knows and believes about Jesus[2] as he allows his readers a fleeting glimpse into Jesus' identity and mission from a "heavenly vantage point."[3] Even those devoted to God are in the dark about who Jesus is. We also learn that God is the one who is directing things behind the scenes. Since the verb "he saw" (v. 10) is singular and can refer only to Jesus, not even John the Baptizer witnesses the heavens being torn open and the Spirit's descent on Jesus like a dove when he came up from the water. Did

---

1. Frank Matera, "The Prologue As the Interpretive Key to Mark's Gospel," *JSNT* 34 (1988): 5–6, argues from a literary-critical perspective that a shift in narrative point of view occurs in 1:14. Verses 2–13 provide privileged information solely for the reader; 1:14 begins to relate public events that characters in the story observe or participate in.

2. Lightfoot, *The Gospel Message of St. Mark*, 17, writes: "We find placed in our hands at the outset the key which the evangelist wishes us to have, in order that we may understand the person and office of the central Figure of the book."

3. Hooker, *Mark*, 31–32.

John even know that he was fulfilling Isaiah 40:3? The crowds are certainly unable to distinguish Jesus from any other penitent coming to be baptized. And during the temptation in the desert, no bystanders are present to observe the battle with Satan. Only the reader has this information, which is vital for evaluating Jesus' identity. The point of these opening scenes is, therefore, to let the reader know from the start who Jesus is and to stress that he comes to fulfill divine promises and his divine commission. Because we who read know who Jesus is, our failure to follow and obey makes us more culpable than the characters in the story.

The Promise of Scripture Fulfilled and the Ministry of John the Baptizer (1:2–8)

THE PROMISE OF Scripture fulfilled (1:2–3). The story begins with a voice off-stage, reading from Scripture. While John and Jesus may seem to appear out of the blue, this citation of Scripture makes it clear that they appear out of the blueprint of God's plan. This story is the beginning of the good news, but every beginning is a consequence. By cross-referencing Scripture Mark makes it clear that the gospel is bound fast to the promise of God in the Old Testament and is a continuation of the story of God's saving activity. Long before the promise-filled preaching of John the Baptizer, there was the promise-filled preaching of Isaiah, which shows that God had planned things out long before John appeared on the scene and was the one who initiated the action.[4] The prophets' hope was not a pipe dream; their prophecy still rings forth, and it will be fulfilled by God.

This passage is the only place in Mark where the *narrator* tells us that Scripture is being fulfilled (the others are spoken only by Jesus). It comprises a mixture of texts from Exodus 23:20; Malachi 3:1; and Isaiah 40:3. Exodus 23:20 contains God's promise to send his messenger before the Israelites on their exodus through the desert to Canaan. Isaiah 40:3 speaks of a second exodus through the desert to the final deliverance prepared for God's people. Malachi 3:1 warns that God will send a messenger to prepare the way before him prior to the coming of the day of judgment. Using a familiar technique in postbiblical Judaism, Mark blends these texts that originally had nothing to do with each other.[5] With modern printing conventions, which were

---

4. Gundry, *Mark*, 34.

5. Joel Marcus (*The Way of the Lord*, 12–17) notes that it is characteristic of Qumran exegesis to juxtapose Scriptures; and Ex. 23:20 and Mal. 3:1 are conflated in rabbinic literature in *Ex. Rab.* 32:9 and *Deut. Rab.* 11:9. Marcus argues that if Mark has fused Ex. 23:20/Mal. 3:1 with Isa. 40:3, he has a knowledge of the Hebrew or Aramaic text found in the MT and the Targum. Mark fuses Scripture in 1:11 (Isa. 42:1/Ps. 2:7); 11:17 (Isa. 56:7/Jer. 7:11); 13:24–26

unavailable to Mark, we would put the references to these texts in the margins or in footnotes for the reader to look up and to reflect upon. By quoting these verses, Mark certifies that the Torah (Exodus), the Major Prophets (Isaiah), and the Minor Prophets (Malachi) confirm what he is about to tell.[6] Mark probably ascribes the entire quotation to Isaiah not to identify its source but because that prophet had special importance for him. It is a hint that "his whole story of 'the beginning of the gospel' is to be understood against the backdrop of Isaian themes."[7]

Three individuals are mentioned in Mark 1:2: the one who will send the messenger, the messenger who will construct the way, and the one whose way is prepared ("your way"). Three individuals are also in view in 1:3: the one who is crying in the wilderness, the Lord whose way is made straight, and the one, or ones, who are addressed. The narrative that follows clarifies who the referents are. "I [God] will send my messenger [John/Elijah] ahead of you [Jesus], who will prepare your way." What is novel is that the messenger no longer is paving the way for God as in Malachi, but for another powerful one, Jesus, who is now to be acknowledged as the Lord. This means that God's coming in salvation and judgment, promised in Scripture, "takes place in Jesus."[8] But Mark is elusive, and the citation allows for another meaning. He does not make it explicit that the messenger in the cited Scripture is John the Baptizer; one can only infer it from what follows. The citation could also be interpreted to mean, "I [God] will send my messenger [Jesus] before

---

(Isa. 13:10/34:4/Joel 2:10/Ezek. 32:7–8); and 14:62 (Dan. 7:13/Ps. 110:1). See also Howard Clark Kee, "The Function of Quotations and Allusion in Mark 11–16," in *Jesus und Paulus: Festschrift für Werner Georg Kümmel zum 70. Geburtstag*, ed. E. E. Ellis and E. Grässer (Göttingen: Vandenhoeck & Ruprecht, 1975), 175–78.

6. Derrett, *Mark*, 46–47.

7. Marcus, *The Way of the Lord*, 20; see also R. Guelich, "'The Beginning of the Gospel': Mark 1:1–15," *BR* 27 (1982): 8–10. Isaiah forms an important backdrop for understanding Mark's story. In Isa. 40:9–10, the context of Isa. 40:3 cited in Mark 1:3, there is a reference to preaching the gospel and the Lord God coming with might. The splitting of heavens (Mark 1:10) is mentioned in Isa. 64:1. The heavenly voice (Mark 1:11) echoes Isa. 42:1. Living at peace with animals (Mark 1:13b) can be found in Isa. 11:6–8 and 65:25. The forgiveness of sins is prominent throughout Isaiah. Isaiah is also cited as the explanation for the people's incomprehension of the kingdom of God appearing in Jesus' ministry (Mark 4:12, citing Isa. 6:9–10) and provides the key details of the end time (Mark 13:24–25, citing Isa. 13:10; 34:4). Perhaps the chief reason for naming Isaiah as the source of the quotation is that Isaiah speaks of the desert while Malachi speaks of coming to the temple. Mark does not revere the temple. It is not to be the place of preparation of the people, only the place where treacherous leaders prepare the death of Jesus. The way is the way through suffering prepared by John in the desert. The purification work envisioned by Mal. 3:3 prepares for God's presence in a different temple altogether (see Geddert, *Watchwords*, 156).

8. Hooker, *Mark*, 36.

you [disciples/audience], who will prepare your way." As the story unfolds, Jesus leads the disciples on the way to Jerusalem and death (10:32), and he goes before them to Galilee (14:28; 16:7). It is only on the second and third reading that we begin to realize that Jesus has come to prepare the way for us to follow him.

Marcus argues that mention of the way carries with it apocalyptic expectations. He contends that in Isaiah "the way of the Lord" refers to God's "victory march" and is a mighty demonstration of his power. In the whole story of Mark the way refers to the triumphal way Jesus will lead his people.

The ministry of John the Baptizer (1:4–8). Mark has no interest in John except as the forerunner of Jesus. We get no information about his origin, parents, marvelous birth, or the contents of his ethical teaching—all details that the reader can find in Luke. In Mark, he is simply John the Baptizer,[9] who comes preaching and whose baptizing has to do with the forgiveness of sins.[10] His preaching has to do with the promise of a more powerful one, who will soon immerse them in the Holy Spirit. John can only announce his coming and try to prepare the hearts of the people so that they will be responsive when he arrives. He knows that it will take more than the splash of the muddy Jordan on their bodies to create in them a new heart and spirit. He acknowledges that his water baptism is preparatory; the Spirit baptism will be definitive.

(1) *The host of baptisands.* John apparently demands that all come for his baptism. No one will get a bye in the judgment. It is a remarkable demand because Jews believed that only gentile proselytes and those who were defiled needed to be immersed to cleanse themselves of their impurity (see 2 Kings 5:13, where Elisha tells Naaman the leper to cleanse himself in the Jordan: "Wash and be cleansed!"). To call *all Israel* to baptism implies that in some way all Israel is defiled. Mark tells us that for whatever reason they come to John in droves—"the whole Judean countryside and all the people of Jerusalem"— to get this cleansing in the desert. They are, in effect, backtracking to the place where Israel had so many beginnings.

(2) *John's clothing and diet.* Mark fully describes John's wardrobe (camel's hair and leather belt) and his diet (locusts and wild honey). Why does he fill

---

9. Mark uses the title John the Baptizer (*baptizon*, a participle) in 6:14, 24, 25.

10. One need not interpret 1:4 to mean that baptism effects the forgiveness of sins. One can translate it, "a baptism of repentance on the basis of the forgiveness of sins." The divine action of forgiveness of sins would precede any human action (see Isa. 40:2; Jer. 31:34; Mic. 7:18). Swete (*Mark*, 4) comments that baptism is "the expression and pledge of repentance," which responds to this forgiveness. The baptism purified the faithful (Isa. 4:4; Zech. 13:1) and marked them out as members of the faithful Israel. It also prepared them to receive the Holy Spirit (Ezek. 36:25–27; see also 1QS 1:21–25; 4 :20–21).

us in on these seemingly minor details while ignoring more important background information? Is it to tell us that John is not "mainstream"—hardly a welcomed guest at the Jerusalem Hilton? These descriptions suggest two things. (a) To go out to someone like this in the desert requires a break with the institutions and culture of Jerusalem.[11] The way that is prepared will not be a comfortable path; it will require forgoing pleasures long taken for granted. (b) John is an Elijah-type prophet (2 Kings 1:8; see Zech. 13:4). The clothing imagery derives from Scripture. Note how Elijah intercepted the messengers of King Ahaziah, whom the king had sent to inquire of the god of Ekron whether he would recover from a bad fall, and the prophet told them to inform the king he would die. When the messengers dutifully notified the king of the dire prediction, the king wanted to know who this provocateur was. They could only describe him as a man wearing a hairy garment and with a leather girdle about his loins. The king wailed: "Oh, it's Elijah the Tishbite."

The original auditors of Mark's Gospel were schooled to recognize symbolism. In our culture, we would pick up the allusions if a character were wearing Daniel Boone's coonskin cap or Abraham Lincoln's stovepipe hat and beard. This description of John is reminiscent of Elijah, which may explain his huge success. The crowds presumably believed that he was Elijah reappearing for his second career, to prepare for the imminent coming of God (Mal. 4:5–6; see Mark 9:11–13). A certified prophet had appeared as they used to do with regularity in the good old days, which could only mean that the beginning of the end was about to take shape. The people came out to him to get themselves ready. A rabbi from a later time is reported to have said: "If Israel repents for one day, forthwith the son of David will come" (*y. Ta'an.* 1:1, 64a). The question in Mark is, Will they truly repent? and, When the Son of David comes, will they recognize him and receive him with open arms or with clenched fists?

(3) *John's message.* John has only two small speaking parts in the Gospel (1:7–8; 6:13). The only thing that interests Mark in John's preaching is his announcement that one who is more powerful than he is coming, who will baptize with the Spirit. What is remarkable about this statement is that John hardly seems to rank with those normally deemed to be powerful or mighty. He will end up a prisoner in Herod's dungeon and will be summarily executed, his head handed to the besotted king on a platter (6:14–29). If he is to be regarded as powerful, then the conventional understanding of power must be completely recast. In John's case, he is powerful by dint of his mighty proclamation of God's will and of what God is about to do. The more power-

---

11. Minear, *Mark*, 48.

ful one who is to come is powerful because he will be the one who executes God's will. John comes as a voice crying, a lowly servant. Jesus comes as the beloved Son, who also will serve. The more powerful one is not an invincible warrior who vanquishes his foes with the sword. He will die a powerless death on a cross. The baptism in the Holy Spirit occurs either after this death (which presupposes some knowledge of Pentecost) or during his ministry as he uses the Spirit, rather than gives it, to heal the sick, teach with authority, and cast out demons (see 3:22–30).[12]

Jesus' Baptism (1:9–11)

FROM THE THRONG that goes out to John from Judea and Jerusalem, the focus shifts in verse 9 to one who comes from Galilee. Mark tells us nothing about when this occurs, nothing about Jesus' background, pedigree, or birth (miraculous or otherwise), nothing about heavenly portents, strange callers at the baby shower, or childhood incidents that make it clear that he is no ordinary child prodigy. It is not that Mark is uninformed of the circumstances of Jesus' birth and background, but providing a chronicle of such things is not his purpose. Consequently, all Mark tells is that Jesus comes from Nazareth, the only one mentioned as coming to John from Galilee. This detail creates a sharp contrast. Unlike the urban sophisticates who come from the city of Zion, Jesus comes from a town that did not even rate a mention in the Old Testament. The story will unfold another contrast: Many go out, but only one understands what it all means.

Jesus' arrival is an anticlimactic entrance for one so rousingly introduced. Although the introduction, "It came to pass in those days" (NIV "at the time"), is a phrase that has a scriptural ring to it (Judg. 19:1; 1 Sam. 28:1), one might expect a more eye-catching appearance for the greater successor to John. Jesus appeared as unpowerful as a powerful one could get. One might also assume that the Messiah, the Son of God, would cut a more imposing figure, who would immediately capture the attention of the crowds. Instead, this Messiah, the one who comes from No-wheres-ville in rustic Galilee, seems indistinguishable from the rest of the crowds. He does not come with some special aura or halo.

Mark also does not tell us why Jesus went to be baptized. There is no protest on John's part that he is unworthy to baptize him (see Matt. 3:14). Mark apparently is untroubled by the theological problem of why Jesus would submit to a baptism of repentance. He is only interested in telling what occurs at that baptism.

---

12. Gundry, *Mark*, 38–39, 45.

(1) *The ripping of the heavens.* The opening of the heavens occurs in the calling of Ezekiel in exile: "The heavens were opened and I saw visions of God" (Ezek. 1:1).[13] It is usually a sign that God is about to speak or act and that one will get a quick peek at God's purposes. But Mark does not use the word "open" (*anoigo*), as some translations render it. Instead, he describes that the heavens are torn (*schizo*),[14] as one might imagine a bolt of lightning tearing its fabric. It is a significant difference. What is opened may be closed; what is ripped cannot easily return to its former state. When Jesus comes out of the water, Mark tells us, all heaven breaks loose.[15] It is also significant that Joshua (Josh. 3:7–17; 4:14–17), Elijah (2 Kings 2:8), and Elisha (2:14) each parted the Jordan river as symbol of their power; and the messianic insurrectionist Theudas (Acts 5:36) promised to do it.[16] Jesus, however, does not stand by the Jordan and part it; instead, something far greater is parted—the dome of heaven. It may be a sign of our access to God, but Juel comments: "More accurate than referring to our access to God would be to speak of God's access to us. God comes whether we choose or not."[17] The barriers are torn down and torn open, and God is now in our midst and on the loose. The hope of Isaiah, "Oh, that you would rend the heavens and come down, that the mountains would tremble before you!" (Isa. 64:1) has come to pass.

(2) *The descent of the Spirit.* The Messiah was said to possess the Spirit of God (Isa. 11:1–2; *Tg. Isa.* 42:1–4; *Pss. Sol.* 17:37; 18:7), and the Spirit comes fluttering down on Jesus *"like a dove"* (not *"as a dove"*). It is a dovelike descent, not a dovelike Spirit.[18] The descent of power from heaven that inaugurates God's reign does not swoop down like an eagle or a falcon but comes quietly and gently like a hovering dove. The same Spirit that once hovered over the primeval waters in the beginning of time (Gen. 1:2) now descends on Jesus "to liberate the earth from the stranglehold of chaos, and a voice unheard for age upon age sounds forth, announcing a decision made long ago in the eternal council."[19] Many thought the end time would be like the beginning. Creation would be renewed and Paradise restored. The hovering of

---

13. See John 1:51; Acts 7:56; Rev. 4:1; 11:19; 19:11; *Job. As.* 14:2; *2 Apoc. Bar.* 22:1; *T. Levi* 2:6; 5:1; 18:6; *T. Judah* 24:2.

14. This verb is used again in 15:38 to describe the temple curtain torn from top to bottom at Jesus' death.

15. Minear, *Mark*, 50.

16. Josephus *Ant.* 20.5.1 §§ 97–99.

17. Juel, *Mark*, 34. Juel writes (*A Master of Surprise*, 34–35): "Viewed from another perspective, the image may suggest that the protecting barriers are gone and that God, unwilling to be confined to sacred spaces, is on the loose in our own realm."

18. Leander Keck, "Spirit and Dove," *NTS* 17 (1970–71): 63.

19. Marcus, *The Way of the Lord*, 74.

God's Spirit on Jesus like a dove was a sign that this new creation had begun. The beginning of the gospel is then also the beginning of a new creation. This time, however, the Spirit hovers over a human being, not over a formless void, which suggests that God intends to transform humanity.

(3) *The declaration of the voice from heaven.* A voice from the sundered heavens sounds forth: "You are my Son, whom I love; with you I am well pleased." Mark relates that only Jesus saw the rending of the heavens, and one can assume that the voice was also audible only to Jesus since it speaks in the second person, "You are," not in the third person, "This is" (contrast Mark 9:7). It is therefore directed to Jesus (and to Mark's readers, who are privileged to overhear), not to his contemporaries. The veil of the heavens may be rent, but the revelation is still veiled to those without eyes to see or ears to hear.

The announcement conveys several things to a reader attuned to the Old Testament. (a) In the Old Testament, God is delighted in Israel when Israel is obedient. What the Scriptures ascribe to Israel, Mark transfers to Jesus. The divine good pleasure does not mean that Jesus is an object of God's proud love but signifies God's delight in Jesus as an "agent of a special mission."[20]

(b) Some suggest that this phrase may be an allusion to another biblical "beloved son"—Isaac, whom Abraham offered up (Gen. 22:3, 18). The beloved son reappears in the parable of the vineyard (12:6) and this time is killed.

(c) Mark's language recalls Psalm 2:7 and Isaiah 42:1. Psalm 2 is an enthronement psalm, which celebrates the enthronement of the king to rule over God's people. "My son" is a title for the Davidic kings of Israel (see 2 Sam. 7:12–16). One can interpret the voice at Jesus' baptism as God's announcement that Jesus has been chosen to rule over his people and that he assumes royal power as king. This enthronement, however, is private; and the reader may wonder when others will recognize and accept him as king. The Gentiles will try him and mock and crucify him as the king of the Jews (15:2, 9, 18). The Jewish leaders will taunt him as the king of Israel (15:32). Jesus therefore ascends his throne when they hang him on the cross, but there is only an ironic recognition of him as king. The next time the voice speaks from a cloud announcing that "This is my Son, whom I love" (9:7), Jesus tells his disciples not to make it known until after the resurrection (9:9). Jesus, therefore, is not a triumphant Davidic king but one who will suffer. One can only fathom his kingship after his death and resurrection.

(d) The text does not tell us how Jesus is God's Son or exactly why God is pleased with him. What has he done except to come in obedience with many others to pass through the waters of John's baptism? When God is

---

20. Gustav Dalman, *The Words of Jesus* (Edinburgh: T. & T. Clark, 1902), 280.

said to be "well pleased" or expresses "good pleasure," however, it refers to God's "inscrutable decree," what is otherwise "unaccountable," the sovereignty and mystery of God's choice.[21] The announcement reflects God's divine choice of Jesus "for an eschatological work."[22]

Testing in the Desert (1:12–13)

THE SPIRIT'S DESCENT on Jesus does not induce a state of inner tranquillity. It drives him deeper into the desolate desert and into the clutches of Satan and the wild beasts for forty days, a biblical round number. Mark does not present the testing as a succession of temptations with specific content, as do Matthew and Luke, but as one major clash. One can only assume that Satan has prepared for him another path and will try to coax him to go in a different direction.

The mention of the wild beasts with Jesus in the desert could convey a couple of ideas. It might conjure up the image of Adam, who started with the beasts when the Lord formed every animal of the field and every bird of the air and brought them to the man to see what he would call them (Gen. 2:19). Soon, however, Adam is forced out of Paradise and must toil in land that has been cursed. The testing in the desert with the beasts at peace with Jesus may point to the restoration of Paradise (Isa. 11:6–9).[23] The desert, however, remains a barren place and is not transformed into a garden.[24] Thus it is better to interpret the reference to the wild beasts as conveying the idea of desolation and danger (see Lev. 26:21–23; Ps. 22:12–21; Isa. 13:21–22; Ezek. 34:5, 8; Dan. 7:1–8). The beasts are malevolent and are the natural confederates of evil powers (Ps. 91:11–13).[25] The desert represents the unculti-

---

21. B. W. Bacon, "Notes on New Testament Passages," *JBL* 16 (1897): 136–39; "Supplementary Note on the Aorist εὐδόκησα, Mark i.11," *JBL* 20 (1901): 28–30 (see Luke 12:32; 1 Cor. 1:21; Gal. 1:15; Eph. 1:4–9; Col. 1:19; 2 Peter 1:17; cf. Matt. 17:5).

22. Marcus, *The Way of the Lord*, 74.

23. Richard J. Bauckham, "Jesus and the Wild Animals (Mark 1:13): A Christological Image for an Ecological Age," in *Jesus of Nazareth: Essays on the Historical Jesus and New Testament Christology*, ed. Joel B. Green and Max Turner (Grand Rapids: Eerdmans, 1994), 3–21.

24. Gundry, *Mark*, 58.

25. In an ancient Jewish work, *Books of Adam and Eve* 37:1–3, Seth and Eve went to the gates of Paradise, and "a serpent, a beast, attacked and bit Seth." Eve rebuked it in a loud voice: "Cursed beast! How is it that you were not afraid to throw yourself at the image of God, but have dared to attack it? And how were your teeth made strong?" Jeffrey B. Gibson (in "Jesus' Wilderness Temptation According to Mark," *JSNT* 53 [1994]: 21–23) argues that being with the beasts does not indicate communion with them but their subordination to Jesus. In *T. Ben.* 5:2; *T. Iss.* 7:7; *T. Naph.* 8:4, 6, the imagery of God's watchcare in Ps. 91 is used to argue that those who are faithful will be protected by the angels, and the beasts will become subject to them. According to *T. Iss.* 7:3, the wild beasts have power only over those who sin.

---

vated place of the curse, Paradise lost, and the realm of Satan. Now Satan must contend with a new Adam, who has the power of heaven at his side and angels as his cornermen. Mark does not report the outcome of this harrowing ordeal but does say that angels served him.[26]

ROBERT STEIN INCLUDES in his book on interpreting the Bible a dialogue from a home Bible study. The group read from the opening verses of Mark and then shared their thoughts on what it meant. The first offered, "What this passage means to me is that everyone needs to be baptized, and I believe that it should be by immersion." A second responded, "I think it means that everyone needs to be baptized by the Holy Spirit." A third reacted honestly, "I am not exactly sure what I should be doing." A fourth suggested that the passage meant that if one is to meet God, one needs to get away and commune with nature in the desert.[27] These Bible students were sharing what the passage meant to them, but Mark is not talking about us—what can happen to us or what we should do. His emphasis is on the one who comes who is more powerful than John, who will baptize with the Holy Spirit, who is announced from heaven, and who is tested by Satan in the desert. Jesus is the long-promised one, the Messiah, the Son of God, the bearer of the Spirit, and the victor over Satan. The passage is *not* about John, the nature or mode of baptism, meeting God, or fighting off Satan. Mark introduces us here to Jesus, the central character in all that follows. Our interpretation must stay centered on him and what his coming means.

If the focus is on Jesus, Mark leaves out of his prologue all the details of Jesus' background that most moderns are interested in. We want to know all that has happened in his life to this point, his high school career, what he looked like, how old he was—all of which are things that would divert us from the point. Not until chapter 6 does Mark provide any background information about Jesus' family and hometown. He does, however, sprinkle the text with scriptural allusions to give us the background he thinks is essential for evaluating Jesus. They tip off the reader that unseen forces are working within history to accomplish God's redemptive purpose.

---

26. This same verb (*diakoneo*) means "to serve food" in Mark 1:31. In 1 Kings 19:5–8 Elijah fled into the desert, ready to quit and die, and an angel came to him in a dream and twice said: "Get up and eat." When he ate and drank, he went to Horeb on the strength of that food forty days and nights. According to Ex. 14:19, an angel of God went before and behind Israel in the desert (see also 23:20, 23; 32:34; 33:2).

27. Robert H. Stein, *Playing by the Rules: A Basic Guide to Interpreting the Bible* (Grand Rapids: Baker, 1994), 11–12.

The problem is that we may miss these allusions because of our ignorance of the Scripture. Sometimes we may wonder how a first-century audience might have known the Old Testament so intimately that they were able to pick up on subtle hints, because we project our ignorance of Scripture on to them. Literary allusions are generally lost on modern audiences. Surveys have shown that many cannot name the first book of the Bible, list more than three of the Ten Commandments, or identify more than two of Jesus' disciples. One must remember, however, that the Scripture was the only textbook for the education of a devout Jew and was studied intensely by Christians, including Gentiles. If one were to whistle only a bar of a theme song of a popular TV show in years of syndication, such as the *Andy Griffith Show*, a modern audience would catch it immediately. They would also probably appreciate any allusions to characters or incidents in the show. The explanation for these phenomena is the pervasive influence of the visual media in our culture. Why should it surprise us that the Scriptures, which so pervaded Jewish culture, should be as well known? It was read Sabbath after Sabbath (Acts 14:27). Life centered around it and was ordered by it.

Moreover, authors normally do not write to the lowest common denominator and often include subtle allusions even though they realize that not everyone in the audience will catch them. They know, however, that some will gain increased enjoyment and understanding from their extra knowledge. Therefore, it is important to help modern listeners see these biblical allusions. It reminds them this story has a much broader setting in God's purposes for Israel's and all creation's redemption.

For example, the story starts in the wilderness (NIV, desert), not in the holy temple of the holy city (as in Luke) or with the heavenly council of God before creation (as in John). The wilderness image would evoke all kinds of memories for those grounded in the Old Testament. For those reading from translations that refer to "the wilderness" (e.g., NRSV, REB), that word might rouse a picture from a Wilderness Society poster with a lush forest, sparkling streams, snow-capped mountains, and wild animals (buffalo roaming and antelope playing), which cause tourists excitedly to stop their cars on the highway to take snapshots. For Jews, however, the wilderness/desert called forth a host of different images. It was more than just a place on the margins of civilization; it evoked a variety of powerful biblical memories and expectations. For one, it marked the place of beginnings. It was the region where God led the people out and from which they crossed over Jordan and seized the land promised to them. It was the place to which God allured the people to win them back (Hos. 2:14). It was also the place where one went to flee iniquity. According to 2 Maccabees 5:27, Judas Maccabeus fled with nine others to the wilderness and lived off what grew wild "so that they might not share in the defilement." According to the *Martyrdom of Isaiah* 2:7–11, the prophets Isaiah, Micah, Ananias, Joel, Habbakuk, and Josab, his son, all abandoned the corruption of Judah for the mountainous wilderness, where they clothed themselves in sackcloth, lamented bitterly over straying Israel, and ate wild herbs.

The wilderness was also considered to be "the staging ground for Yahweh's future victory over the power of evil."[28] It was the place where some thought that the final holy war would be fought and won (1QM 1:2–3). The Christ was thought to appear in the wilderness (Matt. 26:24), and it was the haunt of messianic diviners, such as the Egyptian false prophet (Acts 21:38). The wilderness was not only God's staging grounds for the eschatological victory, it was also God's proving grounds for testing the people. Consequently, it was remembered as the place of disobedience, judgment, and grace.

The Jordan River was also evocative. It was more than simply a river to Jews; it represented the border between the desert and the Promised Land. When John refers to a more powerful one who is coming, his audience would naturally understand it to refer to God, since God is the Mighty One in the Old Testament, who comes in judgment and pours out the Spirit. This biblical imagery evokes the expectation that God is about to liberate Israel again. But Mark emphasizes that God now acts through his beloved Son.

The arrival of Jesus to be baptized with the mass of people has perplexed many because it might imply that he was an evildoer who was now reforming his ways or was in some way subordinate to John. But one should not understand repentance only as a turning away from something evil; it can also be understood positively as a turning toward God. Jesus' repentance here represents an openness to God. Mark does not connect Jesus' baptism by John to the later Christian practice of baptism. John was calling Israel to acknowledge God's judgment on Israel. Passing through the waters of the promise again, a new, forgiven Israel would emerge. When Jesus comes to John for baptism, therefore, he is consenting to this calling of Israel. He is not seeking salvation for himself or fleeing from the wrath to come; rather, he is joining in the renewal of Israel and in the march of God's unfolding purpose for the world. Like Moses, who gave up his regal status to identify with his people to deliver them, Jesus humbles himself by entering the ranks of sinners and taking his stand with them, just as later he will die for them, isolated and

---

28. Marcus, *The Way of the Lord*, 22. The wilderness is the place where it was expected that a second exodus would occur (Isa. 40:3; Ezek. 20:35–38), one that would surpass the first—there would be no haste and no flight in fear (Isa. 52:1–12), and the wilderness would be changed into a paradise (51:3). See Ulrich W. Mauser, *Christ in the Wilderness: The Wilderness Theme in the Second Gospel and Its Basis in the Biblical Tradition* (SBT 39; Naperville, Ill.: Alec R. Allenson, 1963), 51.

alone. His baptism, therefore, launches him on the servant road of obedience, which ultimately leads to his death (10:38).

In Jesus' baptism, we also glimpse the mysterious balance between the human and the more-than-human Jesus. The thundering approval from heaven discloses Jesus' divine identity, but it is linked to his humble subjection to human conditions.[29] Jesus does not come as a powerful, conquering Messiah, an irresistible force, but as a submissive Messiah, who yields in obedience to the baptism of John. For first-century readers, this unexceptional arrival gives a clue that this Messiah, Son of God, is not like the divine men they might have been familiar with from Hellenistic religions. One should not expect sensational public displays during Jesus' ministry. The kingdom of God does not come with sirens blaring and bombs bursting in air, but quietly and inconspicuously.

Mark also may frustrate us in telling nothing about Jesus' victory over Satan in the desert. He simply reports that Jesus is among the beasts and that angels come and attend to him. Jesus does not order Satan to leave, and the devil does not run off, tail between his legs. This could signify that the desert sojourn is only the first round in Jesus' struggle with evil. The battle is not over; the decisive victory is yet to come. The confrontation with the foremost of the demonic forces will therefore extend throughout his ministry. At the same time, however, Satan never reappears in the story, and Mark probably intends to depict a decisive defeat of evil. Jesus drubs Satan in a single combat. What ensues in the story is a mopping-up action, the release of Satan's hostages.

Whichever option may be correct, clearly the appearance of the Son of God is a direct onslaught on Satan's realm. All of the unclean spirits recognize him and cower before him. The exorcisms are proof that the powerful one, Satan, has been bound by a more powerful one (Mark 3:22–7), and that his house can now be cleaned out. When Jesus grapples with demons, the outcome is never in doubt.

The temptation scene also reinforces Jesus' distinction as the Son of God. Gundry comments:

> His being tempted by none less than Satan, the archdemon, carries an acknowledgment of Jesus' stature as the very Son of God. The wildness of the beasts with which Jesus is present without harmful consequence bears witness to his being God's Son, the stronger one of whom John the Baptizer spoke. That even the angels serve Jesus adds a final touch to Mark's portrayal of him as no less a personage than the Spirit-endued Son of God.[30]

---

29. Bilezikian, *The Liberated Gospel*, 58.
30. Gundry, *Mark*, 59.

The devil, the beasts, and the angels all acknowledge in their own way that Jesus is the one who brings God's victory.

MARK SHOWS NO interest in listing Jesus' human credentials (as do Matthew and Luke) because those things might cause the reader to miss the divine dimension of who Jesus is. Jesus' status does not derive from his family pedigree but from God. The narrator gives us access to this divine dimension in the prologue so that we know in advance the answers to the questions raised by a variety of baffled characters in the story. A stunned synagogue crowd asks, "What is this? A new teaching—and with authority!" (Mark 1:27). Livid theological experts ask themselves, "Why does this fellow talk like that? He's blaspheming! Who can forgive sins but God alone?" (2:7). Spooked disciples ask, "Who is this? Even the wind and the waves obey him!" (4:41). A resentful hometown crowd asks, "Where did this man get these things? . . . What's this wisdom that has been given him, that he even does miracles!" (6:2). Vexed priests ask, "By what authority are you doing these things? . . . And who gave you authority to do this?" (11:28).

The truth suddenly hits a centurion in the execution squad when he sees how Jesus died: "Surely this man was the Son of God!" (15:39). The Pharisees think he is in league with Satan. Herod's best guess is that he is John the Baptizer come back to life to haunt him for his sins. Some think he is Elijah; others, one of the prophets (6:14–16; 8:27–28). The disciples are captivated by his powers but are baffled as to who he is for much of the opening chapters. Only Peter, James, and John are let in on this mystery at the Transfiguration. They hear the voice from the clouds proclaim that Jesus is God's beloved Son and learn on the way down from the mountain that Elijah has already come and gone (9:2–13). Even so, this experience does not spare them from failure.

We readers and listeners of this Gospel know far more than the characters in the story. We know that John the Baptizer, the messenger sent before the more powerful one, must be referring to Jesus when he confesses that he is unworthy to stoop down to loosen the thongs of that person's sandals. We see the heavens rip open at his baptism and the Spirit descending on him, and we hear the voice proclaim that he is God's beloved Son. This is why we might become exasperated with the disciples who, as the story progresses, sometimes are as thick as a brick. We know more than they do. The coming of the Son of God, who makes a claim on everyone's life, has made an irreparable breach in the fabric of reality. Perhaps for the first disciples, the light was too bright for their eyes to behold. Perhaps it was not too obscure, but too full of meaning for their minds to grasp. But knowing what we know about Jesus, are we any more faithful, any more discerning, any more willing to give our lives?

The opening section of Mark is frequently used as an Advent text in lectionaries. Most Christians consequently associate it with preparing the way for a babe in a manger and assume that it has something to do with getting ready for the coming of the Christ by catching the Christmas spirit. It is questionable, however, whether this text calls for us to do anything to prepare the way for the Christ. Certainly, that way does not lead us to a manger with angels singing, shepherds bowing, and a little drummer boy tapping out the beat. John the Baptizer does prepare the way by leveling the ground, so to speak, in calling all Israel to repentance. He humbly confesses that the gifts of salvation and of the Spirit are not his to give but another's—a good model for modern-day preachers. His arrest, however, makes it clear that the way made ready for Jesus is not going to be a smooth path.

The "way" (*hodos;* 1:2) appears again as a theme in 8:27; 9:33–34; 10:32, 52. In these sections, Jesus speaks frankly (8:32)—the way for him will end in Jerusalem and in a solitary death. The disciples do help somewhat in preparing for his death. They throw clothes on the road as he enters Jerusalem (11:8–10). They prepare the Passover (14:15–16). A woman prepares him for burial (14:8–9). Joseph of Arimathea buries his body in a tomb on the Day of Preparation (15:42–47). But most play their parts without a clue as to what is really happening. This makes it doubtful whether the followers of Christ can prepare or construct the way if they are so often blind to God's purposes. Throughout the story, the disciples spend most of their time getting in the way or trying to lead the way themselves, but always in the wrong direction. The same holds true for modern disciples.

When one reads Mark again, it becomes more clear who it is who needs to prepare the way: Jesus is the one who must be out in front, blazing the trail (10:32, 52) and leading (14:28; 16:7). Disciples are those who follow in his way (8:34–10:52). When Jesus' disciples try to precede him on their own to the other side of the Sea of Galilee (6:45), they do not make it. They are helpless until he comes to their rescue. Jesus must go before them (6:48). Schweizer uses the illustration of a heavy snowfall that strands a young boy in the home of a friend after school. He cannot get home

> until his father comes, with his strong shoulders, and breaks the way through three feet of snow. The boy "follows him" in his footsteps and yet walks in a totally different way. Father is not merely his teacher or example—or otherwise the boy would have to break his own way, only copying the action of the father—nor is it a vicarious act of the

father—otherwise the boy would just remain in the warm room of his friend and think that his father would go home instead of himself.[31]

The problem is that the way that Jesus prepares for us to go home is not the one we want to travel. It is arduous and paved with suffering, but it is one that we must journey to get home. If the church prepares the way for anything, it is for his return by following in the path he has laid out and in the world-wide proclamation of the gospel (13:10).

In following the way that Jesus has prepared, disciples will encounter many enemies, just as Jesus did. Mark does not tell us the specific content of the temptation that Jesus faced in the desert. Did he fast or not? How did he parry Satan's wiles? Mark does not let us in on any internal conflict. Today, we are far more interested in the psychological drama: Jesus' struggle with doubt, with his sense of purpose, with his commitment to his task laid out for him by God[32]—all things that we might identify with from our own pilgrimage. The emphasis in Mark, however, is that Jesus does battle with Satan. The temptation, like the baptism, has cosmic significance. It is not so much a temptation scene in the moral sense as a titanic power struggle between the more powerful one and the prince of the forces of evil. The battle to put the evil genie that crushes the hopes of humanity back into the bottle has begun. It is not enough for God to win over human hearts and for them to repent and to confess their sins. Evil forces organized under the prince of the power of the air (see Phil. 2:9–10) must be defeated before the kingdom of God can be established. The power of God as long promised breaks into the world to conquer the powers of evil that imprison, maim, and distort human life.

If the battle takes place on the cosmic stage, we also learn that God has a cosmic plan discernible from the Scriptures. Few today bother reading or studying the script, yet it is vital because the kingdom of God manifests itself in disarming ways. The power of God appears in the desert, in weakness, in ones who come out of nowhere and will be handed over. God's activity has been hidden from human beings, and even when it is revealed through Jesus, many will be unable to see. Those who do see will take comfort when they pass through the desert. They will know that Jesus has already been there and knows the way. All they have to do is follow.

---

31. Eduard Schweizer, "The Portrayal of the Life of Faith in the Gospel of Mark," *Interpreting the Gospels*, ed. James Luther Mays (Philadelphia: Fortress, 1981), 175.

32. Juel, *Mark*, 37.

Mark 1:14–15

❦

AFTER JOHN WAS put in prison, Jesus went into Galilee, proclaiming the good news of God. ¹⁵"The time has come," he said. "The kingdom of God is near. Repent and believe the good news!"

JOHN'S ARREST. THE work of the forerunner is completed when he is arrested, and the ministry of Jesus must now begin. John's arrest hardly makes this an auspicious beginning and forebodes that Jesus, as John's successor, will also not fare well with the powers of this world. The NIV translation, "after John was put in prison," may cause readers to miss the subtle connection to Jesus' own fate. It reads literally, "after John was handed over" (*paradidomi*). Jesus also will be "handed over" (3:19 ["the one who betrayed him" lit. reads, "the one who handed him over"], 9:31; 10:33; 14:10, 11, 21, 41, 42, 44; 15:1, 15). If one already knows the story or when one reads the Gospel again, the connection between the two becomes clearer. One recognizes that John is more than a town crier who precedes Jesus. He is Jesus' forerunner in his ministry to Israel, in his fateful conflict with earthly authorities, and in his brutal death (6:7–13; 9:13).

The ambiguity of the verb "handed over" without the phrase "to prison" also prods the reader to ask, "Whose hand is really behind this?" Is this being handed over the result of wicked human schemes or is it part of some divine plan?¹ A second reading allows one to see that, unbeknownst to the earthly powers, who are blind to anything that is happening on the spiritual plane, John's arrest sets the stage for the proclamation of the gospel. Herod Antipas may have thought he was getting his prophetic nemesis out of the way; but, in reality, it is all part of preparing the way for the coming of the kingdom of God.

Jesus' message. Jesus returns triumphantly from the combat in the desert to Galilee and joyously announces the good news of God. John was described as simply "preaching" (1:7), but Jesus is said to preach "the good news of God."² This is not routine revival preaching. Marcus comments that the word

---

1. See Cranfield, *Mark,* 62.

2. The word "gospel" is used only by the narrator (1:1, 14) and by Jesus (1:15; 8:35; 10:29; 13:10; 14:9). "Of God " in the phrase "the gospel of God" (see Rom. 1:1; 15:16; 2 Cor. 11:7; 1 Thess. 2:2, 8–9) may be taken as a subjective genitive, meaning "the gospel that

of the gospel is not the proclamation of "timeless spiritual realities." "Rather, it is a word that announces an event, the coming of God's new world, which is even now breaking into the present."[3] The coming of the kingdom of God is central theme in the Gospel (4:11, 26, 30; 9:1, 47; 10:14–15, 23–24; 12:34; 14:25; 15:43).

Jesus makes his appearance when the time (*kairos*) is fulfilled (see Gal. 4:4). Luke fixes that time chronologically in "the fifteenth year of the reign of Tiberius Caesar—when Pontius Pilate was governor of Judea, Herod tetrarch of Galilee ... [and] during the high priesthood of Annas and Caiaphas" (Luke 3:1–2). Mark is not interested in telling us when precisely this occurred on the human calendar. The only thing that counts for him is "the time seen from the divine side."[4] Jesus announces that the time of waiting for God's intervention is over, which means that all that God had said and done in history is reaching its denouement. If Jesus is indeed the Christ, the Son of God, then the kingdom of God is at hand. But when God steps onto the stage of human history, it always comes as a surprise and as a scandal to those whose field of vision is limited only to finite human possibilities and whose time is measured only by the tenure of transient human kings. In the midst of the present moment, one can easily forget that God bestrides time and history and works by a different clock.

When Jesus proclaims the kingdom of God, he announces that the decisive display of God's ruling power over the world is about to be unfurled. The reign of God is not a spatial category but a dynamic event in which God intervenes powerfully in human affairs to achieve his unfading purposes.[5] Jesus' listeners would have been familiar with the idea of God's reign, and his

---

comes from God," or as an objective genitive, meaning "the gospel about God" that has been committed to Jesus to proclaim. In 8:35 and 10:29, Jesus and the gospel are synonymous.

"The gospel of God" does not form an inclusio with the opening phrase in 1:1, "the gospel of Jesus Christ, Son of God," to mark off 1:1–15 as a unit. The two refer to different things. The first is the gospel about Jesus; the second is what Jesus preaches about God.

3. Marcus, *The Mystery of the Kingdom of God*, 152.

4. The phrase is Anderson's definition of *kairos* (in *Mark*, 84).

5. George Eldon Ladd, *The Presence of the Future: The Eschatology of Biblical Realism* (New York: Harper & Row, 1974), 218, defines the kingdom of God as "the redemptive reign of God dynamically active to establish his rule among men, and that this Kingdom, which will appear as an apocalyptic act at the end of the age, has already come into human history in the person and mission of Jesus to overcome evil, to deliver men from its power, and to bring them into the blessings of God's reign. The Kingdom of God involves two great moments: fulfillment within history and consummation at the end of history." See further, C. C. Caragounis, "Kingdom of God/Kingdom of Heaven," in *Dictionary of Jesus and the Gospels*, ed. Joel B. Green, Scot McKnight, and I. Howard Marshall (Downers Grove, Ill.: InterVarsity, 1992), 416–30; and Bruce Chilton, ed., *The Kingdom of God in the Teaching of Jesus* (Philadelphia: Fortress, 1984).

---

announcement would have awakened in their minds all sorts of images, motifs, and hopes. Many would have understood the arrival of the kingdom of God to mean that God was visiting the people to bring grace and judgment, to put things right in the world, to vanquish evil and the malevolent powers, to oust the rulers of this world, to establish the kingdom of Israel, to conquer sin and eradicate sickness, and to vindicate the righteous.[6] That Jesus will spend so much time telling people what the kingdom is like suggests that his view is different from the familiar one, and he must correct their understanding. Now, however, he only heralds its arrival.

The dominion of God has come near—so near that Mark believes you can touch it in Jesus. The future created by God is no longer a flickering hope light years away; it has become available in the present. No minister of an earthly sovereign would ever announce, "So and so has become king! If it pleases you, accept him as your king!" Such a blasé, noncommittal declaration certainly did not characterize the news of a Roman emperor's ascension to the throne. The very announcement that so and so is king contains an implicit demand for submission. Jesus' announcement that God is king contains the same absolute demand. The divine rule blazed abroad by Jesus, therefore, requires immediate human decision and commitment: repentance, submission to God's reign, and trust that the incredible is taking place.

ISRAEL CONFESSED THAT God alone is king. Yet this belief led to the painful question: If God is king, why are his people in such a pitiable condition? Today, after two thousand years of praying "Thy kingdom come," Christians might ask, "If the kingdom of God has come near, why is it that God's purposes still seem to be eclipsed? Why does our world still groan under satanic tyranny (Rom. 8:22; Rev. 6:10), and why is the power of the wicked to oppress the righteous unabated?" These are pressing questions to Christians who are persecuted. Many others, however, have become too comfortable and settled in this world and have lost any sense of the immediacy of God's reign.

Apocalyptic writings during the Second Temple period tried to answer similar kinds of questions by providing a new interpretation of history that made sense of what was happening in a world where God's enemies desecrated his temple and where many Jews buckled under the domination and

---

6. Marshall, *Faith As a Theme*, 34. See the Old Testament confessions of God as king: 1 Sam. 12:12; 1 Chron. 29:11; Pss. 47; 93; 96; 97; 99; 103:19; 145:10–13; Isa. 43:15; Jer. 10:7; Mal. 1:14.

the lure of foreign culture and committed apostasy. These writings and the perspective they represented sought to encourage and comfort the faithful in what seemed to be a hopeless situation (2 Macc. 6:4). They provided answers to such questions as: Why does evil hold sway over the world? Why are God's faithful persecuted? The solution was to view things from the broader perspective of history, past and future, in order to see things from the vantage point of the unseen realm of the divine. The apocalyptic outlook affirmed that while the nations and even some of God's people might not acknowledge God's reign, their failure to pay homage to him did not diminish his power.

(1) They affirmed that God was not an indifferent spectator of human affairs but was over all things, directing them to a specific end that would soon be realized. Zechariah proclaimed, "The LORD will be king over the whole earth. On that day there will be one LORD, and his name the only name" (Zech. 14:9). God had a plan, hidden from humans, that was working itself out in spite of the seeming triumph of evil powers. God was in heaven, and, while all was not right with the world, it soon would be. God had already determined the destiny of the world.

(2) Different elements of the divine plan are worked out in distinct periods of history. Accordingly, history can be arranged into different categories in which God's plan manifests itself. It is assuring to know that time has been measured out and is under God's control. Only God truly knows what time it is, and those who are close to God have been let in on this wisdom.

(3) The world is beset by a kind of spiritual entropy. Human empires rise and seem unshakably established, only to fall and give rise to another human empire. Nothing human has any permanence. Everything is dependent on God, and when all human resources have failed and the faithful look as if they are on the verge of extinction, God will step into the breach to bring salvation. The new age does not come from human activity of any kind, positive or negative, nor does it evolve from this present age. It comes through the direct intervention of God. Human actions determine a person's own particular fate, but they do not affect the fate of the world. That destiny is entirely in the hands of God. H. H. Rowley has noted the difference between the prophets and the apocalyptists: "The prophets foretold the future that should arise *out of* the present, while the apocalyptists foretold the future that should *break into* the present."[7]

The Gospels show that Jesus shared some of this apocalyptic perspective when he announced the good news of God, that the kingdom of God is near. The Gospel of Mark affirms that secular and sacred time intersect with

---

7. H. H. Rowley, *The Relevance of Apocalyptic*, 2d ed. (London: Lutterworth, 1944), 36.

the advent of Jesus, but the power of God's reign that has broken into history remains hidden and is not easily perceived. The announcement that the kingdom of God is near, coming hard on the heels of the announcement that John, God's messenger, has been handed over, makes it plain that we must still live with ambiguity. John is a victim of state violence, yet Jesus announces good news. Jesus will also be handed over, yet this brings the defeat of the powers of evil and the forgiveness of sins and unleashes a new power in the lives of his followers, who may suffer the same fate (13:9, 11, 12). People will have to reevaluate their expectations of God's reign and how it becomes manifest because Mark presents its coming veiled in mystery. The symbol of God's sovereignty is not a scepter or a mace that God uses to break the bones of his opponents, but the cross, on which the blood of the Son of God is shed. Victory is hidden in the cross. Power is to be found in powerlessness. One will live only by giving one's life. Many will be unable to change their accustomed ways of thinking and accept these paradoxes. Consequently, they will be unable to recognize who Jesus is or submit to God's reign. When it is fully revealed in its glory, however, it will be too late.

PREACHING THE GOSPEL today is not simply giving testimony to timeless truths, providing tips on successful living from pop psychology, or regaling congregations with entertaining stories designed to make them feel good about themselves and the preacher. Walter Brueggemann argues that preaching the gospel is a drama in three acts. It consists of (1) the proclamation of God's decisive victory in the struggle with the forces of chaos and death, (2) the announcement of victory by a witness to the combat, and (3) the appropriate response by those who hear.[8]

(1) *The proclamation of victory.* Jesus' clash with Satan in the desert clearly did not end in a tie because the preaching of the good news of God that immediately follows is the proclamation of victory. God has entered the fray; the world is under a new governance.[9] And Jesus came to Galilee, where Herod Antipas reigned and menaced God's messengers, to proclaim the new reality that the transcendent God, who speaks from heaven, is on the loose, giving his Spirit, the authority to forgive sins, and the power both to destroy the bondage of demons and to heal every malady. The victory peals through-

---

8. Walter Brueggemann, *Biblical Perspectives on Evangelism: Living in a Three-Storied Universe* (Louisville: Westminster, 1993), 16–19.

9. See R. T. France, *Divine Government: God's Kingship in the Gospel of Mark* (London: SPCK, 1990).

out Jesus' ministry in many ways in commands and announcements. "Be quiet!" "Come out of him!" "Be clean!" "Your sins are forgiven!" "Your faith has made you well!" "Be opened!" "He has risen! He is not here." Christians are not to be defeatist but confident in their proclamation that the victory has already been won.

(2) *The announcement of victory.* Jesus is confident that God has prepared the end of the age of this world. The kingdom of God has come near and is about to foreclose on the bankrupt kingdoms of this world. Christians need to give evidence of the victories that are being won. Peter Wagner, for example, writes in correspondence with Walter Wink that the small city of Almolonga, Guatemala, was transformed by the gospel from a "center of human misery: disease, poverty, strife, alcoholism, marital infidelity and violence" into a "community of prosperity, health, harmony and peace with over 90% of the inhabitants born again Christians and with churches instead of bar rooms on every street."[10]

(3) *Response by those who hear.* Many an offertory prayer has dedicated the gifts for the building of the kingdom. The truth is that we do not build the kingdom with our paltry offerings, nor can we advance it with our programs. We are not the ones who have crowned Jesus as Christ and Lord; God did, and God's reign on earth does not depend on the feeble obedience of God's people. Human beings do not bring in God's reign; God does. Human actions do not create the actions of God; rather, God's actions create and transform human actions—or at least those persons who look to the actions of God with wholehearted expectancy.[11] All we can do is decide to take our stand for or against God, for or against Satan, and to repent or not to repent in response to God's initiative toward us. The community lives by repentance and faith since, as the story reveals, it consists of people who are far from perfect. The church needs to continue Jesus' appeal for repentance both inside and outside the church.

The preaching of repentance, however, encounters at least four obstacles today. (a) People tend to wince when they hear talk of repentance because that cry has so often been used to harangue others. Grim defenders of a godly lifestyle—one that happens to conform to their own—have tended to pronounce others guilty and to heap reproaches on them. This negative attack tends more often than not to repel people from the gospel rather than draw them to it. The situation is much like what would have happened had the elder brother in Jesus' parable, who slaved faithfully but bitterly in the

---

10. Walter Wink, "Demons and DMINs: The Church's Response to the Demonic," *RevExp* 89 (1992): 508.

11. John Bowker, *Jesus and the Pharisees* (Cambridge: Cambridge Univ. Press, 1973), 44.

fields, met his prodigal brother first as he was coming down the road. The prodigal would have hit such a buzz saw of scolding from this supposedly upright brother that he probably would have made a quick U-turn to go back to the far country and his pigsty rather than proceed any further into the waiting arms of his father. In contrast, Jesus' call to repent is not a caustic reprimand but an invitation to switch allegiances. He offers a summons, welcoming people to respond to God's initiative. God is unleashing a new power that makes repentance possible.[12]

(b) Another problem in preaching repentance to our generation is created by the human penchant to become infuriated at anyone who would dare to tell us we need to change. This is compounded by a stubborn refusal to take our sinful state seriously. We would like to pin the blame on someone or something else, and everybody today seems to qualify as a member of some victim group.

We are too much like Aaron, who tried to duck taking any responsibility for the incident with the golden calf. When Moses asked him why he did such a thing, he did not confess, "I have sinned and brought great sin upon the people! Let God blot my name out of the book of life, but do not hold this sin against the people." Instead, he tried to wriggle out of any personal guilt with a lame excuse: "They brought me their gold, and all I did was toss it into the fire and, would you believe, out came that calf" (cf. Ex. 32:21–24). In other words, the furnace must be to blame. Aaron passed over in silence his agency in collecting the gold, fashioning it with a graving tool, watching over it in the furnace, setting it up on the pedestal, and declaring a feast day for all the people to worship (32:1–6). Perhaps our innate human pride causes us to try to elude our guilt and pass the buck.

This pride first reared its ugly head with Adam. Adam tried to blame both Eve and God for his sin: "The woman you put here with me—she gave me some fruit from the tree, and I ate it" (Gen. 3:12). And Eve tried to shift blame to the serpent: "The serpent deceived me, and I ate" (3:13). The problem is that when we lose any sense of sin and responsibility, we also lose any burning desire for pardon. If we do not admit that we have a problem, then we do not get down on our knees and come to God for the solution.

---

12. A late rabbinic tradition (y. *Mak.* 2:6, 31d) draws out the contrast between the harsh, judgmental approach to sinners and the goodness of a God who "instructs sinners in his ways" (Ps. 25:8) and who "teaches them the way to repentance." "They asked wisdom, 'As to a sinner, what is his punishment?' She said to them, 'Evil pursues sinners' [Prov. 13:21]. They asked prophecy, 'As to a sinner, what is his punishment?' She said to them, 'The soul that sins, shall die' [Ezek. 18:4]. They asked the Holy One, blessed be he, 'As to a sinner, what is his punishment?' He answered, 'Let the sinner repent, and his sin shall be forgiven for him.'"

(c) Our contemporary culture has a shallow view of sin. Many have no sense that they have rebelled against God. Some even argue that there is no such thing as sin, and they are perplexed and dismayed by how so many Christians in history have been tormented by their sin. This superficial attitude is satirized in a rewriting of the "Prayer of General Confession" from the *Old Book of Common Prayer*:

> Benevolent and easy-going Father: we have occasionally been guilty of errors of judgment. We have lived under the deprivations of heredity and the disadvantages of environment. We have sometimes failed to act in accordance with common sense. We have done the best we could in the circumstances; and have been careful not to ignore the common standards of decency; and we are glad to think that we are fairly normal. Do thou, O Lord, deal lightly with our infrequent lapses. Be thy own sweet Self with those who admit they are not perfect; According to the unlimited tolerances which we have a right to expect from thee. And grant us as indulgent Parent that we may hereafter continue to live a harmless and happy life and keep our self-respect.[13]

(d) Finally, our contemporary culture has a shallow view of repentance. The call to repent has been heard so many times before that many have had enough inoculations of repentance to keep from getting the real thing. Many have washed, deodorized, and perfumed their spiritual lives through a variety of religious rituals and believe that they have done their duty before God while countless unconfessed sins lurk within. They are like King Claudius in *Hamlet* who asks, "May one be pardon'd and retain the offense?" (the murderous ambition, the crown, the queen; Act 3, Scene 3); or like King Herod in Auden's *For the Time Being*, who boasts: "I like committing crimes; God likes forgiving them. Really, the world is admirably arranged." Or we may have become a little cynical about it all. We have seen people get teary-eyed and walk the aisle, but it doesn't seem to take—like Huck Finn's alcoholic pappy:

> The old drunk cried and cried when Judge Thatcher talked to him about temperance and such things. Said he'd been a fool and was agoing to turn over a new leaf. And everyone hugged him and cried and said it was the holiest time on record. And that night he got drunker than he had ever been before.

---

13. David Head, *He Sent Leanness* (New York: Macmillan, 1959), 19, cited by William H. Willimon, *Remember Who You Are: Baptism, A Model for Christian Life* (Nashville: The Upper Room, 1980), 53.

Schweizer comments that repentance does not refer to changing the characteristics or the actions of the person but the total direction of life.[14] One needs to turn around, which requires more than a catharsis of tears and a little firecracker pop in one's life. Something internal needs to happen that can be infinitely costly to self-esteem. It means being willing to get down low and become as a slave (Mark 9:35–36; 10:42–44) or as a little child (10:15–16), and being willing to give up trusting in oneself to allow God to take control. For some, it only requires that they open a "clenched fist a little and turn it, empty, toward God."[15] For all, it requires a change of outlook, expectations, and commitments.

The call also "to believe in the gospel" indicates that repentance is not an end in itself but the first step of faith. Where faith is absent in the characters in the story, it must be because repentance is absent. Only those who have turned their lives toward God will be able to see and believe what is not self-evident to others, because the evidence is not compelling but veiled and paradoxical. Marshall notes the difference between rational belief and trust:

> Rational belief is essentially involuntary; a person cannot arbitrarily choose to believe on the spot; it is something that happens to him or her in light of the evidence. Trust, however, is voluntary, an act of the will. Or, again, belief can exist without it immediately affecting one's conduct, whereas trust requires certain consequent actions in order to exist.[16]

Rational belief is sterile and powerless if it does not lead to trust that affects the way one lives. We see this trusting belief in the next episode—the call of the disciples.

---

14. Schweizer, *Mark*, 32.

15. William Peatman, *The Beginning of the Gospel: Mark's Story of Jesus* (Collegeville: Liturgical Press, 1992), 15.

16. Marshall, *Faith As a Theme*, 56 (see the discussion in 51–56).

Mark 1:16–45

AS JESUS WALKED beside the Sea of Galilee, he saw Simon and his brother Andrew casting a net into the lake, for they were fishermen. ¹⁷"Come, follow me," Jesus said, "and I will make you fishers of men." ¹⁸At once they left their nets and followed him.

¹⁹When he had gone a little farther, he saw James son of Zebedee and his brother John in a boat, preparing their nets. ²⁰Without delay he called them, and they left their father Zebedee in the boat with the hired men and followed him.

²¹They went to Capernaum, and when the Sabbath came, Jesus went into the synagogue and began to teach. ²²The people were amazed at his teaching, because he taught them as one who had authority, not as the teachers of the law. ²³Just then a man in their synagogue who was possessed by an evil spirit cried out, ²⁴"What do you want with us, Jesus of Nazareth? Have you come to destroy us? I know who you are—the Holy One of God!"

²⁵"Be quiet!" said Jesus sternly. "Come out of him!" ²⁶The evil spirit shook the man violently and came out of him with a shriek.

²⁷The people were all so amazed that they asked each other, "What is this? A new teaching—and with authority! He even gives orders to evil spirits and they obey him." ²⁸News about him spread quickly over the whole region of Galilee.

²⁹As soon as they left the synagogue, they went with James and John to the home of Simon and Andrew. ³⁰Simon's mother-in-law was in bed with a fever, and they told Jesus about her. ³¹So he went to her, took her hand and helped her up. The fever left her and she began to wait on them.

³²That evening after sunset the people brought to Jesus all the sick and demon-possessed. ³³The whole town gathered at the door, ³⁴and Jesus healed many who had various diseases. He also drove out many demons, but he would not let the demons speak because they knew who he was.

³⁵Very early in the morning, while it was still dark, Jesus got up, left the house and went off to a solitary place, where he prayed. ³⁶Simon and his companions went to look for him,

³⁷and when they found him, they exclaimed: "Everyone is looking for you!"

³⁸Jesus replied, "Let us go somewhere else—to the nearby villages—so I can preach there also. That is why I have come." ³⁹So he traveled throughout Galilee, preaching in their synagogues and driving out demons.

⁴⁰A man with leprosy came to him and begged him on his knees, "If you are willing, you can make me clean."

⁴¹Filled with compassion, Jesus reached out his hand and touched the man. "I am willing," he said. "Be clean!" ⁴²Immediately the leprosy left him and he was cured.

⁴³Jesus sent him away at once with a strong warning: ⁴⁴"See that you don't tell this to anyone. But go, show yourself to the priest and offer the sacrifices that Moses commanded for your cleansing, as a testimony to them." ⁴⁵Instead he went out and began to talk freely, spreading the news. As a result, Jesus could no longer enter a town openly but stayed outside in lonely places. Yet the people still came to him from everywhere.

THIS SECTION CONSISTS of five scenes. With the authority of God, Jesus calls four fishermen (1:16–20). He then teaches with authority in the synagogue and works miracles as the Holy One of God, who has come to destroy the demonic reign of terror (1:21–28). Next, he heals Simon's mother-in-law and many others who flock to him for healing that evening (1:29–34). The cures cause a sensation, and the next morning he retreats for prayer. When the disciples track him down, he informs them of the need to move out from Capernaum into all Galilee to proclaim the good news of God's reign (1:35–39). The next scene shows him healing a leper whose refusal to keep silent results in Jesus' fame stretching far and wide.

After the call of the first disciples, the next scenes form a unit bracketed by the exorcism of an unclean spirit in the synagogue while he is teaching (1:21–28) and the healing of a paralyzed man in the house while he is preaching (2:1–12).[1] Both occur in Capernaum (1:21; 2:2). In both passages, a group of persons questions what Jesus says or does among themselves (1:27;

---

1. The next unit begins with Jesus' returning to the sea and calling another to follow him (2:13–14).

2:6), and the issue of authority comes to the fore. The scribes figure in both scenes. The crowd applauds Jesus as one who teaches with authority and not as the scribes (1:22); he responds to the scribes' questioning by announcing (2:10) that the Son of Man has authority to forgive sins. Both passages conclude with the crowd's responding with amazement (1:22, 27; 2:12), which underscores the point of the newness of his authoritative teaching, for "he even gives orders to evil spirits and they obey him" (1:27). The crowd's amazement in 2:12 leads to glorifying God because they have never seen anything like this. This section does not simply report highlights in Jesus' initial ministry but reveals the new, Spirit-empowered reality that has burst forth from heaven.

Jesus' Call to Discipleship (1:16–20)

JESUS ABRUPTLY APPEARS by the Sea of Galilee and without warning calls unsuspecting fishermen to be disciples. Jesus is not going to be a lone prophet wandering in the desert but a leader, whose task as Messiah is to create a community of followers. Since Peter and Andrew cast nets from the shoreline, they are possibly too poor to own a boat while the Zebedees are more upscale, with a boat that can take them anywhere on the lake and hired hands to help with the labor.[2] Whatever their circumstances, these men show their repentance, their desire "to turn," by dropping everything to heed Jesus' call. Their repentance is more than just a matter of an internal transformation; they turn into something that they are not now, from fishermen to fishers of men.

Jesus does not call them to be shepherds, gathering in the lost sheep of the house of Israel, or to be laborers, bringing in the sheaves (Matt 9:36–38), but to be fishers. Old Testament prophets used this metaphor for gathering people for judgment (Jer. 16:14–16; Ezek. 29:4; 47:10; Amos 4:2; Hab. 1:14–17), and one should not assume that Jesus uses fishing as a benign reference to mission. When the fisherman hooks a fish, it has fatal consequences for the fish; life cannot go on as before. This image fits the transforming power of God's rule that brings judgment and death to the old, yet promises a new creation (see Rom. 6:1–11). The disciples are called to be agents who will bring a compelling message to others that will change their lives beyond recognition. Jesus' call has the same effect on them.

What is striking is that Jesus calls them to "follow *me*." Prophets did not call people to follow themselves but to follow God (compare 1 Kings 19:19–21). The sages of Jesus' day never called people to follow them, only to learn

---

2. So Waetjen, *A Reordering of Power*, 78.

Torah from them. Jesus' call of the disciples is therefore dramatically author-itative and matches the biblical pattern of God's calling of humans: a com-mand with a promise, which is followed by obedience (see Gen. 12:1–4).[3] The call so overpowers these disciples that their lives will never be the same again.

Teaching with Authority (1:21–28)

ONE WHO CALLS with such astounding spiritual power also teaches with power. The next scene, depicting Jesus teaching in a synagogue, concludes with a stunned crowd extolling him as one who teaches with authority and with the news of his feats rocketing through the Galilean countryside. Mark emphasizes the power of Jesus' teaching, not its content. Jesus rarely gives lengthy, sagelike discourses in Mark's Gospel but instead offers pithy state-ments and dramatic action. In this scene Jesus' teaching consists of "an over-powering word of exorcism."[4]

The readers already know that Jesus' authority derives from the Spirit of God, who came on him at the baptism, but even the crowds detect that one is in their midst who speaks for God and not simply about God, as the scribes do. Judaism had become a book religion, and the scribe had authority because of his erudition in sacred Scripture and tradition. He did not claim direct rev-elation from God but was an interpreter and had influence only as a learned man. Mark does not tell us precisely what feature of Jesus' teaching exhibits authority in contrast to that of the scribes. Nevertheless, the narrative reveals that Jesus couples his teaching with mighty deeds—certainly one key dif-ference. The scribes simply make theological pronouncements (2:6–7; 9:11; 12:35); Jesus comes with the authority of God to dismantle the tyranny of Satan. He confronts demons with destruction and Judaism with a new teach-ing.[5] Consequently, both demons and the religious authorities will be threat-ened by him.

An outburst from a man with an unclean spirit interrupts Jesus' teaching. Most would take steps to remove the troublemaker from a place of worship, but Jesus moves to deliver the troubled man. Those who suffer from unclean spirits/demons in Mark are victims who are entirely helpless. Unlike the sick in body, they are too helpless to ask for aid. The demon controlling the man

---

3. Gundry, *Mark,* 70.

4. As Gundry aptly titles this incident (*Mark,* 73). On Mark's presentation of Jesus as a teacher, see R. T. France, "Mark and the Teaching of Jesus," in *Gospel Perspectives Volume I,* ed. R. T. France and David Wenham (Sheffield: JSOT, 1980), 101–36.

5. Geddert, *Watchwords,* 266 n.55. William Manson (*Jesus the Messiah* [London: Hodder and Stoughton, 1961], 35) writes: 'The rabbis taught, and nothing happened, Jesus taught, and all kind of things happened."

("*they* knew who [Jesus] was," 1:34) sees Jesus as a threat and speaks. Only demons and angels fathom the mysteries of the unseen world at this point in the narrative. They recognize that Jesus is not just another exorcist, but the one God has anointed to break the rule of Satan.

The unclean spirit's noisy recognition of Jesus may be viewed as a panicked defensive stratagem or as a reverent acknowledgment of his power. Knowledge is power, and the unclean spirit may be attempting to fend off its impending defeat with the classic exorcist's trick of pronouncing the name of the opponent.[6] He shouts out both an earthly name, Jesus of Nazareth, and a divine name, the Holy One of God, and hints that he has plenty of reserves in his camp, "Have you come to destroy us?" Gundry argues that the Hellenistic audience who hears the unclean spirit will think that it has gained the upper hand by identifying Jesus, but Jesus moves aggressively to silence it.[7] On the other hand, the unclean spirit may be conceding submissively that Jesus is its opposite. He is holy, pure, and close to God, and it has met its match.[8]

Whichever is the case, Jesus tells the spirit to shut up. One might think that Jesus would appreciate the free advertising before the synagogue crowd. The unclean spirit is right, but Jesus does not want testimony that is demonic. He will not accept the hollow confessions of spirits that are not cleansed and transformed. The demons' recognition of Jesus also can only mislead others. Jesus' healing miracles do not simply remedy human physical maladies; they represent a war against demonic forces. Jesus disarms Satan's power that has been pirating human souls and sets the victims free one by one. The demons therefore know him as the victorious Son of God, not as one who must undergo suffering and death.[9] Consequently, Jesus orders their silence. Demons, however, rarely go quietly. This one exits "with a shriek," a death roar not dissimilar to the one Jesus cries when he dies on the cross (15:37).

The witnesses are dazed. They do not wonder at what the unclean spirit proclaims about Jesus. Do they even hear it? Are they stupefied because it is simply too overwhelming for them to comprehend? They remain in the dark

---

6. The cry, "What do you want with us?" (lit., "What between you and me?" 1:24) is the same cry used by the widow of Zarephath in 1 Kings 17:18 and the king of the Ammonites in Judg. 11:12 as a defensive maneuver. Similarly, in the *Books of Adam and Eve* 11:2, Eve says to the devil, "What have you to do with us? What have we done to you, that you should pursue us with deceit? Why does your malice fall on us?" Names frequently appear as incantations in the ancient magical papyri because it was believed that knowing the name of a power or enemy gave one a tactical advantage in defeating it.

7. Gundry, *Mark*, 76.

8. Guelich, *Mark*, 56–57.

9. Achtemeier, "Mark," 4:553.

about the source of Jesus' power or his mission, and no shrieking demon will reveal it to them. The full truth can only be revealed by the one who cries out in pain on the cross.

Healing Fever (1:29–31)

JESUS IMMEDIATELY EXITS the synagogue and enters the house of Simon and Andrew. These disciples just as immediately speak to him of Simon's mother-in-law, who is in bed with a fever. In the time of Jesus, many considered fever an illness in and of itself and not simply a symptom of a disease.[10] It also had more theological significance since, according to Leviticus 26:16 and Deuteronomy 28:22, it was a punishment sent by God to those who violated the covenant.[11] Because of Deuteronomy 28:22, some considered fever to be a divine chastisement curable only by the intervention of God. In a later rabbinic tradition a rabbi pronounces:

> Greater is the miracle wrought for the sick than for Hananiah, Mishael and Azariah. [For] that of Hananiah, Mishael and Azariah [concerned] a fire kindled by man, which all can extinguish; whilst that of a sick person is [in connection with] a heavenly fire, and who can extinguish that?[12]

The implied answer is that no one can extinguish it except God.

In this incident, Jesus goes to Peter's mother-in-law and raises her up by seizing her hand, and the fever forsakes her. The translation "the fever left her" is too mild. A literal rendering, "the fever forsook her," suggests, as do the other two references to fever in the New Testament, that the cause of the fever was supernatural (either induced by demons or as a divine chastisement). What is significant is Jesus' miraculous ability to extinguish a heavenly fire—something that only God or God's agent could do.

Peter's mother-in-law proves that she has fully recovered by waiting on them (lit., "she was serving them"), a sign of her physical wholeness and her spiritual responsiveness to Jesus. Such menial service does not suggest her

---

10. Julius Preuss, *Biblical and Talmudic Medicine*, trans. F. Rosner (New York: Sanhedrin, 1978), 160. See John 4:52 and Acts 28:7–10 (fever *and* dysentery) for other instances of fever in the New Testament.

11. Philo expanded on this list of divine chastisements in his *On Rewards and Punishments*, 143. Fever heads the list, and Philo regarded it and other diseases as the wages of impiety and disobedience. The rabbis had reputed cures for fever (*b. Git.* 67b; *b. Shabb.* 66b); but because of the influence of the biblical texts, they regarded fever as both demonic (caused, for example, by dancing in the moonlight, *b. Ned.* 41a; *b. Git.* 70a) and as a divine punishment (*b. Ber.* 34b).

12. *b. Ned.* 41a.

insignificance; on the contrary, the angels offered Jesus the same service in the desert (1:13). Serving is also a characteristic of discipleship, which Jesus tries to get across with some difficulty to his disciples (9:35; 10:41–45). Jesus' female followers seem to grasp the need to give themselves in service to others more quickly than the male followers. Mark describes the women who saw his death from afar as those who "had followed him [in Galilee] and served him" (15:41; "cared for his needs," NIV). This miracle reveals that God heals so that one may better serve.

Summary of Healing and Jesus' Affirmation of His Ministry (1:32–39)

THE SABBATH ENDS in the evening, and the next scene pictures the whole city pounding at the doors. The townsfolk bring all the ill and demon-possessed to Jesus, and he heals "many."[13] "He would not let the demons speak because they knew who he was" refers back to 1:24, where the evil spirit named him, but the crowd noises the healing abroad so that his fame spreads throughout Galilee (1:28).

The next morning finds Jesus venturing out to "a solitary place" to pray. The noun is the same word (*eremos*) that appeared in 1:3–4, the voice calling "in the desert," and in 1:12–13, the locale of the testing by Satan. "Desert" is an inappropriate word to describe any geographical area around Capernaum, but in Mark's Gospel it connotes the quarter where the divine and the satanic vie for life. After Jesus' victory in the desert, however, it has become a place where one can seek solitude and prayer[14] and receive divine replenishment and where angels give succor. The desire for secluded prayer makes it plain that Jesus is not a sorcerer working by magic independent of God's help. His authority, strength, and power come from God alone (see 9:29).

Jesus meets temptation again in this lonely place when Simon and those who are with him "hunt him down" (*katadioko*—not "look for him" as in NIV, or "follow him" as in the RSV). The verb suggests they have engaged in an urgent manhunt for Jesus. They interrupt his moments of private meditation to inform him that everyone in Capernaum is "looking for" him[15] and to

---

13. The "many" is a Semitism for the "all" (see 10:45; cf. Matt 8:16; Luke 4:40).

14. Jesus prays in Mark three times—here at the beginning of his ministry, in the middle (6:46), and before the end (14:35–36)—always alone, at night, and at times of tension.

15. The verb "looking for" (*zeteo*) is always used by Mark in a negative sense. Jesus' family is "looking for" him to take him back home because they think he is beside himself (3:32). The Pharisees "ask for" a sign from him, which is what only an evil generation would do (8:11–12). The high priests and elders "began looking for" how to destroy him (11:18; cf. 12:12; 14:1) and later "were looking for" false witnesses against him (14:55). Judas was watching for a good time to betray him (14:11). The women were "looking for" a dead

urge him to return to the scene of so many personal triumphs and to where he has such a tremendous following. When Jesus called these men to follow him, this was not what he had in mind. This episode is the first hint that the disciples (who are not called disciples here, but "Simon and his companions") will create more trouble for Jesus than support. They are looking for him in Capernaum because of the miracles, not because of his words, and the disciples would like to accommodate this surge in popularity: more evening healings with a band concert, perhaps they could even develop a Capernaum healing theme park. Jesus is not interested in the fleeting adulation of crowds and refuses to go back to Capernaum because he is to go to preach to all Israel. He came out of the village to find seclusion to prepare himself through prayer to go out on his mission to preach the kingdom.

The good news cannot be static. Throughout the Gospel, Jesus keeps his bags packed, traveling hither and yon. He will not be distracted from his divine purpose, even by success, and will not remain as a localized guru or healer. Consequently, Mark tells us in verse 39 that it is no longer rumors about Jesus that are flying about Galilee (1:28) but Jesus himself.

Healing the Leper (1:39–42)

MARK RECORDS JESUS as barnstorming through Galilee, preaching in the synagogues and casting out demons (1:39), but he zeroes in on one miracle as particularly significant. A leper comes to him and begs him on his knees, "If you are willing, you can make me clean!" We should not automatically equate his leprosy with Hansen's disease, since the term applied to several skin diseases[16] and even to garments and houses (Lev. 14:33–57). Anyone who had suspected signs of leprosy was brought to a priest for examination, who alone could pronounce that he or she had the disease or had been cleansed from it. The priests of Israel differed from those of other religions, who purportedly knew curative secrets, in that they had no power and could offer no ritual to heal disease. Israel believed that healing was entirely in the hands of God. Priests, therefore, simply declared what was clean and unclean (13:59; 14:57). That is why Leviticus 13–14 goes into such detail describing the cases so that the priest could identify the presence or absence of particular

---

body at the tomb (16:6). The seekers are always wrong. Kelber (*Mark's Story*, 22) notes the subtle disagreement. The disciples want to repeat the glory of the previous day, while Jesus is oriented toward new places and the future and plans to move elsewhere.

16. Jacob Milgrom (*Leviticus 1–16* [AB; New York: Doubleday, 1991], 816–20) translates the Hebrew as "scale disease." See also J. Baumgarten, "The 4Q Zadokite Fragments on Skin Disease," *JJS* 41 (1990): 159, 162; Kenneth V. Mull and Carolyn Sandquist Mull, "Biblical Leprosy: Is It Really?" *BibRev* 8 (April 1992): 32–39, 62.

physical signs, such as skin color change, hair color, infiltration, extension, or ulceration of the skin.

If the priest declared a particular skin problem to be leprosy, the sufferer was excluded from the community by divine decree (Lev. 13:45–52; Num. 5:2–4). This banishment was not rooted in any fear of spreading the disease but of spreading religious impurity. Leprosy was considered a primary source of uncleanness. Like a corpse, the leper could impart impurity to objects found within the same enclosure. As a result, he or she was viewed as a living corpse, and a cure was likened to raising the dead.[17] The leper was confined by a strict set of rules that governed his contact and relations with other people.[18] The leper in Mark 1:40, however, does not keep a safe distance but breaks through the religious barricade to confront Jesus. He is willing to chance that Jesus has both the power and the grace to heal him.

A curious textual variant in 1:41 reads that Jesus "is angry" instead of "filled with compassion" for the man. This may be the original reading since Jesus is also said to rage at him (*embrimesamenos*, cf. 14:5) and then immediately casts him out (*exebalen*, 1:43). If Jesus' first response is anger, he is not annoyed at the man for breaching the ritual barriers that bar him from any contact with others.[19] He may be expressing the anger of God toward the ravages of the disease (cf. John 11:33–38).[20] His compassion for the man is expressed in his touch, probably the first time another "clean" human has touched this social derelict in a long time. He also commands him to "be clean." At Jesus' word, the leprosy leaves the man immediately. Jesus just as immediately sends him away.[21]

This healing is the only one that requires some kind of witness from others, for the leper cannot be restored to full functioning in Jewish society until a priest examines him and declares him clean (see Luke 17:14).[22] Jesus' words, "Be clean!" are not in the indicative mood, which would mean that he

---

17. *b. Sanh.* 47ab.

18. A later rabbinic tradition sentences lepers to forty lashes for entering precincts forbidden to them (*b. Pesah.* 67a; *t. B. Qam.* 1:8).

19. According to a tradition in *Lev. Rab.* 16:3, a rabbi, "when he saw a leper, would throw stones at him and shout: 'Go to your place and do not defile other people.'"

20. The snorting could be connected to Jesus' warfare with Satan and might reflect the strain of the struggle. Possibly, the man's flattery implied that if Jesus did not help, he was less powerful than others judged him to be.

21. Literally, he "cast him out," but the verb need not entail force or displeasure. In James 2:25, this word has the meaning "speed on one's way" (see also Matt. 7:4–5; 12:35; 13:52).

22. According to *m. Meg.* 3:1; 4:7–10, only a priest may declare lepers clean or unclean (see Lev. 13:3; *t. Meg.* 1:1). Even if the priest is ignorant of what to say, he is the one who must say it and must therefore be instructed what to say (CD 13:5–6).

is simply declaring that the leper is clean. Rather, the verb is an imperative. Jesus causes the cleansing of the disease, just as the charge to demons to come out effected an exorcism. The leper, however, may not go merrily on his way, even though he has been healed. Every cure had to be consecrated by a religious ceremony, and the one for lepers was long and involved (see Lev. 14:1–32). Until it was completed, the leper remained in social limbo. For this reason, one should not take the phrase "as a testimony to them" in a negative sense. Lane comments that if the priests establish that the man is clean and "fail to recognize the person and power through whom the healing has come, they will stand condemned by the very evidence which they have supplied."[23] But how can the priests know who is behind this healing since Jesus commands the leper to be silent? One should interpret this command positively (Hos. 2:14, LXX), as a witness to the people that he has been cured and that they can associate with him after the procedures prescribed in the law have been followed.

The Commands to Keep Silent (1:43–45; cf. 1:25, 34)

MARK 1 RECORDS the first of Jesus' frequent commands to demons and to those whom he healed to keep silent (vv. 25, 34, 44). He commands the leper to tell no one about the miracle and hastily speeds him on his way. These commands have nothing to do with any so-called messianic secret, as suggested by Wrede.[24] The reasons for the command to silence lie elsewhere.

(1) The command makes clear that as a miracle worker Jesus wants to remain hidden; this is what sets him apart from other miracle workers in the ancient world.[25] Jesus does not work miracles to amaze people as false prophets would do. Many in his age assumed that itinerant religious/philosophical teachers were in the business of building their own reputations and

---

23. Lane, *Mark*, 88.

24. William Wrede, *The Messianic Secret* (London: James Clarke, 1971) argued that the "messianic secret" did not go back to Jesus but was a theological invention of the Evangelist that was read back into the story of Jesus to cover up the fact that the historical Jesus never made any messianic claims for himself and was not recognized as the Messiah by his disciples until after his resurrection. It explained why Jesus was neither acclaimed nor recognized as the Messiah during his earthly ministry. See further the introduction and essays in C. M. Tuckett (ed.), *The Messianic Secret* (Philadelphia: Fortress, 1983), and James L. Blevins, *The Messianic Secret in Markan Research 1901–1976* (Washington, D.C.: Univ. Press of America, 1981).

25. Hengel, *Mark*, 43. Tolbert (*Sowing*, 227–28) contends that "the author's intention in fashioning the secrecy passages is *not* to propose that Jesus remained unknown and did not attract crowds but rather to verify that Jesus did not seek for himself renown or glory, although the spread of fame and the growth of multitudes around him was inescapable, given who he was and what he did. It was not his desire but his fate."

sought out fame for the financial bonanza that came with it. Jesus has no interest in taking on the role of a celebrity healer.

(2) Jesus does not trust a faith based on spectacles, and he knows that the clamor of the moment will not last. He also knows that God's power is not revealed solely through miracles. It becomes clearest in the crucifixion, but those who want only miracles can see nothing.

(3) Jesus prefers to keep the news of his miracles quiet so that it will give him more time to put off his inevitable destruction by the powers that be and to sow the word. Some cannot be trusted with the information because they will only use it to try to destroy him. Others will give him no peace, prying into his life, limiting his free movement, and giving him no time to instruct his disciples in private. Despite the pains he takes to try to squelch the fervor created by his healing powers, however, the news spreads like wild fire. The upshot is that the unwanted publicity that comes from the disobedience to his command to silence hinders important facets of his mission with his disciples. Whenever someone disobeys this command, the next scene begins by mentioning the crush of the crowds. The hubbub restricts Jesus' free movement as he is harried by the increasing numbers of supplicants and autograph hounds (3:9). He is no longer able to enter a town openly, and people from miles around seek him out (1:45). The leper's disobedience forces Jesus to avoid the cities and to retreat to deserted places, but even they are no longer deserted. Throngs who come from all over mob him (see also 6:32–33; 7:24).[26] When he returns to Capernaum, the crowd is so thick that they are hanging from the rafters (2:2, 4). Ironically, Jesus' attempts to cloak himself in secrecy only serve to magnify his reputation.

(4) As far as Mark is concerned, the command to secrecy makes it clear that any charges of insurrection made against Jesus are false. Jesus does not arrogate titles for himself, unlike the false christs who acclaim themselves (13:6); he repeatedly tries to escape and restrain the crowds that gather around him. Consequently, Rome has no reason to fear him as king of the Jews (15:2–5), intent on fomenting an uprising of the people.

(5) The failure to hush those who are healed reveals that the news of his power to heal is not something that can be kept hidden. One cannot keep silent, and the good news will spread to the end of the earth. Ultimately, however, God reveals secrets and mysteries and will unlock the secret in due time (4:21–23).

---

26. Williams (*Other Followers of Jesus*, 134–35) notes that after the disobedience of the deaf man (7:36–37) the next scene also begins with a large hungry mob in the desert (8:1). John J. Pilch ("Secrecy in the Mediterranean World: An Anthropological Perspective, *BTB* 24 [1994]: 155) points out that "an existence that allows little or no privacy is very exhausting."

Bridging Contexts

THE POWER OF Jesus' call. Jesus preaches to the crowds, but the call to follow comes to individuals. Mark does not tell us why Jesus singled out Simon and Andrew and James and John as disciples or why they decided to respond instantly. The accounts of the calling of the first disciples in John and Luke make more sense to the modern reader, who typically wants some rational explanation for their behavior. In the Fourth Gospel, John the Baptist tips off the first disciples (John 1:35–37). In Luke, Jesus gives them a remarkable preview miracle (Luke 5:1–11). Nothing in Mark's narrative, however, has prepared the reader to expect these fishermen to drop their nets and leave everything to follow Jesus. How do they even know who he is?

Modern readers may be tempted to supply some psychological basis for their rapid response. Perhaps they were having bad times in the fishing business and were ready to make a career change. They had been longing for some time for the Messiah to come to relieve foreign oppression and to bring the new Jerusalem or whatever restoration they might have imagined. They had an itch for some kind of action and jumped at the chance to take the plunge and follow him. They had made a decision during one of his sermons to rededicate their lives. But Mark provides no such explanations, and one is not allowed such psychological speculation when preaching from Mark's text. These men have witnessed nothing of Jesus' powers and have no idea what his battle plans might be. They do not take a few days to mull over their decision, to ask their families' permission, or to seek counsel from a panel of religious experts. To us it may seem an incredibly hasty decision to take off after someone who happens to pass by and abruptly beckons people to follow him. We know that something more must have happened—and we learn such details from Luke and John. They must have heard and believed his preaching that the kingdom of God had come. But Mark's text presents us with a sudden call and a response that is just as sudden.

The only explanation for the sudden response of disciples is that Mark wants to underscore the force of Jesus' call. It alone propels them to follow him.[27] He chooses whom he wills, and his call comes like "a sharp military command" that produces obedience. His call, however, is much more than a dramatic summons. Lohmeyer concludes, "He commands as God com-

---

27. Hooker (*Mark*, 59) comments that the scene "conveys vividly the power and authority which he exercises." Gundry (*Mark*, 67) also notes "how great must be the power of Jesus to induce that kind of conduct."

mands. ... He makes of the fisherman something new, that which he wills."[28] Psalm 33:9 exalts the mighty creative word of God, "For he spoke, and it came to be; he commanded, and it stood firm," and provides the backdrop for understanding the response of these disciples. Like God, Jesus speaks, and it happens.

Jesus speaks, "Come, follow me!" and it creates obedience that compels people to follow and join his band. They are willing for their identity and support to come from being his disciples, not simply from being a member of this or that family, this or that profession, or this or that village. Jesus speaks, "Be quiet! ... Come out of him!" and unclean spirits are routed (1:25). Jesus speaks, "Quiet! Be still!" and the wind stops, and there is a great calm (4:39). Jesus speaks, "'*Talitha koum!*' (which means 'Little girl, I say to you, get up!')" and the dead are raised (5:41). Jesus speaks, "'*Ephphatha!*' (which means, 'Be opened!')" and ears are opened (7:34). Jesus speaks, "May no one ever eat fruit from you again," and a fig tree is withered to its roots (11:14, 20). Jesus cries a great cry, and the temple veil splits from top to bottom (15:38–39).

The power of the one who sees persons long before they see him and calls as God calls is the only explanation why these disciples respond immediately as they do, and it may escape the notice of modern readers. This unit has a Christological dimension, and this first incident immediately raises the question: Who is this who can create such immediate obedience? The miracles that Mark records in this unit prompt a similar question: Who is this who can do these things? When interpreted from a biblical perspective, they reveal that Jesus, the bringer of the kingdom, has unique power as God's Son and can overmaster demons, offer forgiveness of sins, and effect healing of disease. The powerful call of this one can still transform lives today.

Casting out unclean spirits: Jesus the exorcist. The New Testament takes the existence of demons for granted but offers no explanation of their origin or descriptions of their appearance. Many are not comfortable with the idea of demons, although we still use phrases like, "What's gotten into him?" or "What's come over you?" The world of demons is exotic and bizarre to most moderns. They either reduce them to cartoonlike gremlins or deny their existence completely. Modern scientific attitudes heavily influence us; and since demons do not show up on scientific radar screens, many dismiss such cases as some primitive misdiagnosis that is now made obsolete by modern medical advances. It would make many happier if Mark had given some medical name to the maladies of these sufferers. If he told us, for example, that the man in the synagogue suffered from Tourette's Syndrome, some psychosis, or had

---

28. Ernst Lohmeyer, *Das Evangelium des Markus* (MeyerK; 2 Aufl.; Göttingen: Vandenhoeck & Ruprecht, 1963), 32.

a bad reaction to drugs, it would not give us pause because these terms are more a part of our worldview. At the opposite pole, however, are those who brand everything that they do not comprehend as demonic. Both views trivialize the problem of an evil that wages mortal combat with God.

To bridge the contexts, one must first recognize that Mark is not giving a medical diagnosis when he identifies a person as demonized or possessed by an unclean spirit. In 1:32, Mark makes a distinction between those who are sick and those who have demons.[29] Those afflicted with demons are never said to be "healed"; instead, the demons go out from them. "Unclean spirit," Mark's favorite expression, is a religious term and a spiritual diagnosis. What is unclean in the Old Testament has "evaded the control of the divine holiness"[30] and banishes humans from God's presence. By attributing the malady to an unclean spirit (or demon), Mark asserts that one should attribute it to an enemy that seeks to estrange one from God. Some spiritual force has taken control in a human being and attempts to thwart God's purposes by twisting and maiming human life and alienating that person from God and from others.

Second, Best notes that the possession is treated as evil but not as sinful. The victim is not offered forgiveness.[31] The unclean spirits require expulsion, and that can only come from divine intervention. What once could invade human personalities and evade God's control can do so no longer. It must submit to the greater power of Jesus.

This raises a third point. Just as the unclean spirit controls the man in the synagogue, the Holy Spirit has taken control of Jesus (1:10, 12). The one who preaches the gospel of God is the Holy One of God, and when the Holy and the unclean meet, it is no contest. The one John predicted would unleash the Spirit of God immediately disarms the unclean spirit. The ousting of the unclean spirits affirms that we are not in the battle with evil alone nor do we need to be helpless victims. Mark's account of an ordinary exorcism shows

---

29. Unlike those who are sick, those identified as controlled by demons in Mark have extraordinary strength (5:4) and suffer violently (5:5; 9:22). They are agitated by Jesus' presence, usually howl their alarm (1:24; 5:7), and cause some kind of damage, harm, or noise when they leave. See Graham Twelftree, *Christ Triumphant: Exorcism Then and Now* (London: Hodder and Stoughton, 1985), 71.

30. G. B. Caird and L. D. Hurst, *New Testament Theology* (Oxford: Clarendon, 1994), 109. Paul identifies his thorn in the flesh as from Satan (2 Cor. 12:4). See *1 Enoch* 7:3–4 for an explication of Gen. 6:1–4; 15:9–11: "The spirits of the giants afflict, oppress, destroy, attack, do battle and work destruction on the earth and cause trouble."

31. Ernest Best, "Exorcism in the New Testament and Today," *Biblical Theology* 27 (1977): 3. We distinguish between the evil of what we call a natural disaster, earthquake, monsoon, tornado and the evil that lies in personal sin.

that something extraordinary is happening: Satan is being restrained until his final defeat. The advent of the kingdom of God is the beginning of the end for the thralldom of Satan, and one need not fear the molesting unclean spirits if God is acting on one's behalf. We should be careful to stress this point. The New Testament contains a dramatic drop in the fear of demons when compared with other literature from this era. It results from the faith that God has won a decisive victory over Satan in the cross and that the more powerful one who baptizes with the Holy Spirit protects his followers.

Twelftree argues that the contemporary church "would do well to follow the example of the early Church—not to ignore the demonic, but to focus attention on Jesus the healer who defeats the demonic." He cites the warning of Karl Barth:

> the theologian ... must not linger or become too deeply engrossed [in the demonic, as] ... there is the imminent danger that in so doing we ourselves might become just a little or more than a little demonic.[32]

In Mark, Jesus' casting out of demons is an undeniable sign that the kingdom of God has come and Satan's realm is being routed. They are not routine miracles; they represent the inevitable submission of this world and its powers to the reign of God. Theissen points out that other miracle workers existed in the ancient world and in Israel before Jesus. But Jesus alone combined "the apocalyptic expectation of universal salvation in the future and the episodic realisation of salvation in the present through miracles." Theissen asserts, "Nowhere do we find miracles performed by an earthly charismatic which purport to be the end of the old world and the beginning of a new one."[33] Mark shows that Jesus does not simply announce the coming reign of God and the end of the reign of Satan; he actualizes it in the lives of individuals with his miracles.

One last point should be noted. Mark makes clear that Jesus' first mighty act is closely tied to his teaching. That means that while we do not have the same access to the one who displayed such great power as did those who met him in the towns and synagogues of Galilee, we still have access to that power in Jesus' teaching. It did not disappear when he died. Jesus' teaching continues to produce mighty acts.[34]

Healing disease: Jesus as the Great Physician. The Old Testament and the later rabbinic literature regard God as the author, controller, and healer

---

32. Twelftree, *Christ Triumphant*, 175, citing CD III/3. 519.
33. Gerd Theissen, *The Miracle Stories of the Early Christian Tradition* (Philadelphia: Fortress, 1983), 278–79.
34. Achtemeier, "Mark," 5:555.

of disease.[35] Most attributed the onset of a disease to divine retribution for some grave sin or to the onslaught of some demonic power. This perspective of disease is also found in the New Testament. Paul tells the Corinthians that some of them are sick and dying because of their sinful abuse of the Lord's Supper (1 Cor. 11:30; see Acts 5:1–11; 12:20–23; 2 Cor. 12:7). James counsels, "Therefore confess your sins to each other and pray for each other so that you may be healed" (James 5:16), because he believed that illness and sin were related. In the time of Jesus, leprosy was viewed as the classic punishment for sin.[36] It was the telltale sign that the sufferer was a culprit who had committed sins unknown to his neighbors. The suffering indicated that while sin might be hidden from others, it could not be hidden from God, and it served as forewarning of the ultimate fate of the sinner.

Almost everyone would have classified the leper as a sinner, who must appeal for mercy to be healed. To understand the full significance of this miracle in a first-century context, one needs to be aware of the widespread belief in Judaism that only God could heal leprosy. One might compare the desperate response of the king of Israel to the request that he heal the Syrian general Naaman of his leprosy, "Am I God? Can I kill and bring back to life? Why does this fellow send someone to me to be cured of his leprosy?" (2 Kings 5:7).

The leper in Mark 1 is bold because everyone believed that he was in that condition as a result of some sin. He is even more bold in thinking that Jesus had the power to cleanse him of the disease. The leper's petition, "If you are willing" (*not* "If you ask"!), assumes that Jesus is like God, who can do as he wills (Wisd. Sol. 12:18). Jesus could have responded to this request in many ways. He could have said as the king of Israel did, "Am I God, to forgive your sin and to cure you of your leprosy?" Or, he could have interceded on his behalf as Moses cried to the Lord for Miriam to be healed of her leprosy (Num. 12:13). Or, he could have told him to go wash seven times in the Jordan, with the hope that God would forgive his sin and heal his leprosy. Instead, Jesus stretches out his hand like God,[37] touches him, announces, "I am willing," and commands, "Be clean!" Modern readers might miss the Christological impact of this healing, which leads into the next incident (2:1–12), set in a crowded house in Capernaum, which emphasizes Jesus' authority to

---

35. David E. Garland, "'I Am the Lord Your Healer': Mark 1:21–2:12," *RevExp* 85 (1985): 327–43.

36. See Lev. 14:34; 26:21; Num. 12:1–15; Deut. 24:8–9; 28:27; 2 Kings 5:20–27; 15:5; 2 Chron. 26:20; in a fragment of CD 4Q270, lepers are listed in a category of transgressors; see also the later tradition in *b. 'Arak.* 15b–16a; *Lev. Rab.* 17:3. The tattered clothing prescribed for the leper in Lev. 13:45 was interpreted in *Targum Onkelos* as a sign of mourning, presumably for the leper's godless life for which he was now suffering punishment.

37. God worked by stretching out his hand (Ex. 4:4; 7:19; 8:1; 9:22; 14:16, 21, 26).

forgive sin. Jesus can heal the man of his leprosy, understood as a smiting by God because of sin, by virtue of his authorization to forgive sins.

Jesus' concern to avoid publicity should give us pause. Unlike modern politicians and pop stars, whose survival depends on their remaining in the public eye, Jesus does not hustle to increase his name recognition. In our day, the miracles might make the headlines for a few weeks, but then interest would probably flag as people hanker after something new and more sensational. Jesus' mission is not to provide sound bites and fresh sensations for the eleven o'clock news each night. He is not after personal glory that will deflect credit from God (see 2:12; 5:19; 10:18). He wants to avoid the adoration of a crowd that is without understanding and personal commitment. The miracles are of "news value," and it is good news to those who are on the receiving end. But it is not the sum total of *the* good news, which also involves suffering and death.[38] At this stage, the crowds can only marvel. They are like those who witnessed the explosion of the first atomic bomb. The great explosion of power fills them with awe, but they do not fully realize that the explosion will change everything for the world—in this case, for good. Its fallout brings life, not death.

DISCIPLESHIP. THE KINGDOM of God is something that only God creates; it is not something built by valiant human effort. But that fact does not mean that one needs only to sit by passively and to wait for God. God has already acted. The kingdom of God invading history in the ministry of Jesus requires submission in discipleship to him and demands all of one's heart, soul, mind, and strength (12:33)—one's whole being. The calling of the first disciples shows that one must not only repent and believe the gospel (1:15) but must also be ready to leave and follow.

Unlike John the Baptizer, Jesus does not wait for people to come to him at some chosen site. He takes the initiative by seeking out followers with the command, "You! Come, follow me!" He does not put up a sign-up sheet (like church softball) asking for volunteers ("Messiah: Interested in a few good men and women") or post office hours when he will be available to discuss the kingdom of God with those who might be curious. The disciples also do not join him as a pupil might select a rabbi to learn the law[39] and absorb his religious wisdom. Jesus selects his disciples, not vice versa (1:16–20; 2:14; 3:13–14, "those he wanted"). One can conclude from this that becoming a

---

38. See Anderson, *Mark*, 204.

39. See *m. 'Abot* 1:6, which advises one to choose a teacher.

disciple of Jesus is more of a gift than an achievement.[40] Jesus models what he calls them to do as fishers of men. They have been caught in the nets of God's grace, and it will transform their lives.

A second noteworthy element in the calling of disciples is that those who are drafted apparently have no special preparation. Jesus does not choose the most socially prominent, the best trained, or even the most religiously devout. He does not find them in some hallowed religious setting, such as the synagogue, but he is just passing by (1:16; see also 2:13; 3:7; 4:1) and finds them in the midst of everyday life, going about their daily routines.[41] His command, however, shatters that comfortable everyday world.

The call and the instant response of these fishermen reveal something of what discipleship to Jesus entails and should shatter our comfortable world of middle-class discipleship. Disciples are not those who simply fill pews at worship, fill out pledge cards, attend an occasional Bible study, and offer to help out in the work of the church now and then. They are not merely eavesdroppers and onlookers. When one is hooked by Jesus, one's whole life and purpose in life are transformed.

(1) To be a disciple means accepting Jesus' demands unconditionally. Jesus requires absolute obedience and sacrifice. Discipleship in Mark is not part-time volunteer work on one's own terms and convenience. One must be prepared to leave everything to follow him. Simon and Andrew turn from their nets; James and John turn from their father and their boat (not just their nets). Theirs was a sacrifice that Peter apparently felt he needed to remind the Lord about now and then: "We have left everything to follow you!" (10:28). They had to leave the securities, even their livelihoods, no matter how meager or substantial they were, for something new and unpredictable. The call to discipleship comes as an unreasonable, scandalous demand. It seems too risky, and for those who respond, too reckless. These first disciples are not given time even to transfer whatever equity they have or to put it in trust. Few would make the radical commitment these first disciples made, and most would hope that Jesus might offer a less rigorous category of auxiliary discipleship, which would promise the same rewards while allowing one to continue the pursuit of money and success.

My maternal grandparents felt a call to India in the early 1900s. My grandfather did not qualify for support by the Methodist Mission Society but decided to go anyway as an independent faith missionary. They were recruited by a man who claimed that if they collected enough money, they could run a wonderful boarding school while learning the language. They

---

40. Marshall, *Faith As a Theme*, 136.
41. Schweizer, *Mark*, 48.

gathered enough money from friends to pay their passage to India and to support them for a year; but when they arrived, they found that the boarding school did not exist and that the man had absconded with all the money. They were stuck in India with no money, no place to live, and no work. They begged a ride on a train to Calcutta, where some other missionaries took them in. For some reason, they did not despair and started an independent work in Bihar that became so successful the Methodist Mission Board requested that they work under their auspices. And they did—for thirty-six years! They made enormous sacrifices—three of their six children died from disease—but they reaped enormous spiritual rewards. Others might offer many explanations as to why they made such sacrifices, but they attributed it to the power of Jesus' call to go and serve.

The problem with trying to balance friendship with the world and service to God is that one becomes religiously a split personality, looking both to God and to the world for standards and assurance. In the imagery of the Bible, one winds up with two hearts (two wills) and tries in vain to walk along two separate ways. When one tries to accommodate God and Mammon, one cannot be totally committed to God. Mammon crowds God out. The advantage of leaving all sources of human security is that the disciples are now totally dependent on Jesus. People take a big chance in putting their lives entirely in God's hands. It is the kind of risk that the rich man refused to take, and it disqualified him from discipleship and the eternal life he so coveted (10:17—22). Most humans spend their lives consumed with anxiety for their earthly destiny; but disciples look beyond this world to their eternal destiny, which, they are convinced, is best left in the hands of God.

What keeps us from this full commitment is a fatal illusion that our real needs are physical, and it results in our self-centered concern for material security. But Jesus is not only able to deliver people from the bondage of unclean spirits and disease, he can deliver us from bondage to material concerns (such as the desire to preserve our standard of living at all costs). He gives us a vision that there is more to life than catching a string of fish. The center of life is to revolve around God. The authority of his call dispels our hesitancy and awakens total confidence in God. Disciples are the ones who throw caution to the winds. Like the field hand who finds a treasure and a pearl merchant who discovers a valuable pearl, the disciples are confronted with a chance of a lifetime. They are fortunate to have the chance, but it requires decisiveness to capitalize on it. One cannot possess the treasure or the pearl without making a commitment. The price is high: One must sell everything to acquire it. One does not get something for nothing; one gets something for everything. What formerly had supreme value, however, now pales beside the supreme worth of the kingdom.

(2) Jesus is going somewhere and requires his disciples to come along with him (1:18; 2:14; 10:21). He does not call them to attend endless seminars on discipleship training with lively discussions on the theological fine points of the law. Discipleship in Mark is not about mastering theoretical ideas; it is about mission, a common mission with Jesus (6:7, 30). The disciples in Mark learn on the way with Jesus what discipleship entails. It is on the way that they encounter the power of his miracles and that they learn about suffering (8:27; 9:33–34; 10:32). They are going to be fishers of people, who will be sent out on mission (6:7–13). Just as they cannot drop a sign into the lake announcing "Fish wanted! Please enter net!" and expect much success, so it is with humans. They may not retreat to the safety of the harbor but must go on a voyage into the deep and turbulent waters and cast their nets widely.

These observations do not mean that study, prayer, and training are not important. The disciples are rebuked more than once for failing to understand, as are Jesus' opponents for failing to know Scripture (12:24). The problem for Christians today is twofold. Some are tempted to lock themselves in the study and never apply their theological and biblical knowledge to life. A study at Princeton Seminary gathered students together and read the parable of the Good Samaritan to them. They were then instructed to go to a building across the quadrangle one at a time to give a brief talk on the parable. They were urged to be punctual and not to keep the researchers waiting. Along the way they planted a shabbily dressed man slumped along the side of the path. Only 40 percent of the students responded to the man.[42]

On the other hand, some Christians rush into action without any theological or biblical reflection. In 1:35–37, the disciples appear more interested in action than prayer. Here Jesus is shown praying *before* going into action. Busy ministers probably can easily identify with Jesus here. The demands of ministry and church members frequently interrupt study and prayer, and they are tempted to spring into action before preparing their hearts and minds before God. The worst thing that can happen is for them to be temporarily successful because they can delude themselves into thinking that prayer and study are dispensable extras in ministry. The same can be said for the busy parent desperately trying to keep up with hectic family schedules.

(3) One final point about what discipleship means: It will become clear later in the story that disciples are not called to a program of self-development but to service. Jesus will require them to deny themselves, to endure suffering, to take up a cross.

---

42. Walter Wink, "The Parable of the Compassionate Samaritan: A Communal Exegesis Approach," *RevExp* 76 (1979): 203.

Jesus' authority and ours. In the first scene where Jesus displays his miraculous power, the bystanders are dazed by his authoritative teaching. Jesus' authority is a key theme for Mark. Not only does he have authority as a teacher (1:21–22); he also has authority over the Sabbath (2:27–28), over forgiveness of sins (2:5–12), over unclean spirits (3:19–27), over nature (4:35–41; 6:45–52), over the law (7:1–13, 14–20), over the temple (11:12–33; 12:1–12), and over the mystery of the kingdom of God, which he gives to others (4:10–11). The next scenes—the healing of Peter's mother-in-law, the leper, and the paralyzed man—make it clear that Jesus is not an inaccessible authority figure but a compassionate healer.

Many today in Christian leadership crave for the same thing to be said of them as was said about Jesus—he or she speaks with authority. They aspire to winning a pliant crowd of devoted followers who bow to their every word. Recent history reminds us how religious leaders can stake a claim to authority and hoodwink the credulous, distraught, and disenfranchised. It is easy for all but a handful to recognize the crackpots who tragically brainwash their followers with their authoritarian ranting and raving, arm them to the teeth, and engage in sexual promiscuity. But what about those who would speak authoritatively within more traditional churches and denominations? They announce: "This is my unanimous decision. I know this is the will of God. Is there any discussion?"

To evaluate religious leaders today, we must judge them by the standard of Jesus. Do they share his aversion to publicity and acclaim? Do they want to receive credit for all that happens? Are they primarily interested in a power grab, in building empires for themselves, and in serving their own needs? Do they truly speak in the name of the Lord from sincere motives? Are they accessible to those in need, not just the wealthy and influential but those from the margins of society?

Healing and our ministry. Humans are psychosomatic beings, and healing involves mind, body, emotions, and spirit. These first miracles reveal that Jesus embodies God's mercy and purpose to take away the diseases, infirmities, and sins of the people. The leper pleads: "If you are willing, you can make me clean" (1:40). Reaching out to touch one who was branded untouchable by religion and society dispels any doubts about Jesus' willingness. The leper does not have to convince him that he is even worth the effort. This man with his disease does not horrify Jesus. His "power to cleanse is thus demonstrably greater than the power of the leprosy to contaminate."[43]

But touching, hands-on contact, makes us vulnerable. In Jesus' day, the concern was impurity; in our day, the concern is contagion. Few would make

---

43. Hooker, *Mark*, 79.

the sacrifice of Father Damien, who, in 1870, went to serve the lepers banished to the island of Molokai. He lived with the corrupted bodies, the stench, the rats and flies, and no running water to fulfill what he said was his priestly duty—to let them know that God has not forsaken them. He himself died a leper, having contracted the disease of those he served.

The miracles in this section also reveal that Jesus is not someone who is aloof, inaccessible, or detached. Our culture does not touch, and many people live in isolation from others. We seal ourselves off from one another with our privacy fences and retreat to the inner sanctum of the family room. The church is sometimes in danger of doing the same by retreating to its members-only, fully equipped Family Life Center, which becomes a safe cocoon from contact with the harsh realities of a disease-ridden, sin-sick world. We want others quarantined from us so that they will not infect us. But those who bear the name of Christ need to minister in the name of their Lord to those who are the untouchables in our society.

The church needs to minister in a nonjudgmental way. The attitude toward leprosy in biblical times is no different from our attitude toward certain diseases today. Some people are afflicted from illnesses that we assume they have contracted because of some sin. Many pronounce them guilty for supposedly having committed worse sins than their own and treat their disease as a curse that sets them adrift from the community and from God's grace. What does it accomplish to declare piously that they are receiving in their bodies the just penalty of their sin (Rom. 1:27) and to stigmatize and ostracize those who already despair? It can only drive people further into despair.

Obviously, our behavior has consequences for our health. We cannot defy the laws of science and health or the laws of God without repercussions. Abuse of alcohol can lead to cirrhosis of the liver; smoking can lead to emphysema. The same people who would hardly assess the suffering from these diseases as divinely appointed judgment for sin, however, will declare that those infected with the AIDS virus because of sexual promiscuity are suffering God's punishment. There is more than one account of those suffering from AIDS, however they contacted the disease, who are turned away from church after church.[44] We do not want the one with the unclean spirit disturbing our worship, or the leper with his hidden sin and thus a public disease defiling our company. Even when we do minister to the suffering, a

---

44. Jimmy Allen, a pastor and former president of his denomination's convention, tells the tragic story of how AIDS infected four members of his family (*Burden of a Secret: A Story of Truth and Mercy* [Nashville: Moorings, 1995]). His daughter-in-law was infected by the virus through a transfusion, which she passed on to two of her children. When his son, also a minister, turned to his church for support, they asked him to resign. They met with similar rebuffs from other churches they later tried to attend.

self-righteous attitude can erode our compassion. A doctor who treated AIDS patients confessed that when he began his treatment of a patient, he had the attitude that this disease was different from other diseases; like the Pharisee in Jesus' parable (Luke 18:9–14), he thanked God he was not like him. He writes:

> I did not consider that this stigmatized man had repented and had been forgiven while I was yet in my sins. In my heart, I approved of his suffering and inevitable death.[45]

If Jesus is the model for the church's ministry, we see that he never condemns the afflicted. He never tells people that they are sinners or that they are possessed by unclean spirits. We see, instead, one who is confident in the power of God, who touches the unclean and restores the banished to his community and the sick to a meaningful role of service. The touch is a sign of acceptance. He does not treat people as outcasts or as some kind of a pollutant. He is able to heal all fever, especially the fevers of the soul: the burnings within from anger, resentment, envy, and feverish lives.

What about healing today? Many people today do not believe that miraculous healing is possible. Morton T. Kelsey has outlined the historical roots of the church's present negative attitude toward healing.[46] First, there are those who believe that only scientific medical means can affect significant healing. Medicine is for the body, it is assumed; religion is for the soul. To try to mix the two only breeds superstition and fraud.

An attitude prevails among others that God controls all sickness and sends it as a chastisement for sin. Sick persons are therefore meant to learn from their wretchedness. The minister has no healing role and can only exhort confession or help the individual to grow in faith through the suffering.

A third view cherishes the historical value of the New Testament but believes that such things as healing miracles do not exist today. The two most influential Reformers, Luther and Calvin, adopted a cessationist approach to miracles, and their influence continues. Deere claims that they were prompted to make cessationist arguments because their Catholic enemies pointed to miracles as proof that God approved of their doctrine and practices, whereas the Reformers could appeal to none. They did not judge the dearth of miracles in their experience to be attributable to any theological error or spiritual deficiency; consequently, they concluded that the gift

---

45. David L. Schiedemayer, "Choices in Plague Time," *Christianity Today* 31 (Aug. 7, 1987): 22.

46. Morton T. Kelsey, *Psychology, Medicine & Christian Healing: A Revised and Expanded Edition of Healing & Christianity* (San Francisco: Harper & Row, 1988).

of healing evident in the New Testament served only a temporary purpose.[47] To many today, God granted to the early church a special ability to demonstrate his power to scoffers, to help the church get started, and to authenticate the apostles. Clearly a large portion of the Gospels and Acts describe a variety of miracles performed by Jesus and his apostles. Today, miracles are not only less prominent, they have virtually disappeared in many churches. Few if any seminary curricula treat this subject. The cessationist's explanation for this miracle shortage is that God has withdrawn this gift.[48]

A fourth view rejects entirely the biblical worldview, which assumes that supernatural beings can intervene in the natural world order as something totally foreign to a modern, educated people now "come of age." It regards healing miracles to be impossible because they violate the laws of nature, and therefore it dismisses the New Testament miracle accounts as legends aimed at magnifying Jesus. Kelsey summarizes the influence of the four views:

> Certainly most Christian thinking, both Catholic and Protestant, has been swept clean of any idea of Christian healing. On the one hand the successes of medicine have made it unnecessary, and on the other, modern theology has made any belief in it untenable. First of all, the church had accepted the necessity of dealing with the natural world on its own natural, material terms. Then there has been an acceptance of sickness as a part of the world, put there by God. Dispensationalism [*sic*] has found a way to divide this world so that healing, once seen as one of the greatest divine gifts, no longer seems needed or even wholesome. Finally, most modern theology has made it clear in ample reasoning why it did not happen at all.[49]

The problem with the cessationist's approach is that it can be interpreted negatively as a kind of bait-and-switch tactic on God's part. The church got started through the power of miracles, but it was withdrawn later. If one does believe that God wills our physical and spiritual wholeness and that God's power remains available to us and can intervene directly in our lives, then one must allow for Christian healing today. Christians and Christian communities can be instruments of that power and love. It does not necessarily follow that because many persons today have not witnessed New Testament qual-

---

47. Jack Deere, *Surprised by the Power of the Spirit* (Grand Rapids: Zondervan, 1993), 99–100.

48. For a thorough interactive discussion on this issue, see *Are Miraculous Gifts for Today? Four Views*, ed. Wayne A. Grudem (Grand Rapids: Zondervan, 1996). This book discusses four different views on this subject advocated by Christians today, each one written by a strong proponent of his particular view.

49. Kelsey, *Psychology, Medicine & Christian Healing*, 24.

ity miracles, they therefore are no longer possible. We do not understand the vast world of microorganisms, let alone how God works in our world. It is best, therefore, not to place limits on God regarding healing.

At the same time, we are required to discern the spirits and must guard against shamanism and religious quackery. We should suspect automatically any promise of an instant cure by a self-appointed miracle worker who couples it with an appeal for money.[50] We should distrust anyone who performs miracles in a showlike atmosphere, exalts his or her own power to heal anyone, anywhere, and at anytime, or makes outrageous claims. We should reject all those who blame the victim's lack of faith for any failure to heal. We should be leery of those who would have us ignore medical treatment entirely or longstanding remedies (see 1 Tim. 5:23). We should also exercise caution, since a community may become divided over the exercise of the gift of healing. Most do not possess this gift, and therefore we should take intercessory prayer more seriously than we perhaps do.

---

50. See Ted Schwarz, *Faith or Fraud? Healing in the Name of God* (Grand Rapids: Zondervan, 1993).

Mark 2:1–12

AFEW DAYS later, when Jesus again entered Capernaum, the people heard that he had come home. ²So many gathered that there was no room left, not even outside the door, and he preached the word to them. ³Some men came, bringing to him a paralytic, carried by four of them. ⁴Since they could not get him to Jesus because of the crowd, they made an opening in the roof above Jesus and, after digging through it, lowered the mat the paralyzed man was lying on. ⁵When Jesus saw their faith, he said to the paralytic, "Son, your sins are forgiven."

⁶Now some teachers of the law were sitting there, thinking to themselves, ⁷"Why does this fellow talk like that? He's blaspheming! Who can forgive sins but God alone?"

⁸Immediately Jesus knew in his spirit that this was what they were thinking in their hearts, and he said to them, "Why are you thinking these things? ⁹Which is easier: to say to the paralytic, 'Your sins are forgiven,' or to say, 'Get up, take your mat and walk'? ¹⁰But that you may know that the Son of Man has authority on earth to forgive sins . . . ." He said to the paralytic, ¹¹"I tell you, get up, take your mat and go home." ¹²He got up, took his mat and walked out in full view of them all. This amazed everyone and they praised God, saying, "We have never seen anything like this!"

Original Meaning THE NEXT SCENE finds Jesus at "home" in Capernaum (2:1). It is not clear whose home it is, but clearly it is now impossible for Jesus to retire from the crush of the crowds after the leper disobeyed Jesus' command and noised abroad his healing. This scene recalls the exorcism of an unclean spirit in the synagogue (1:21–28), which also occurred in Capernaum (1:21; 2:2). In both passages, Jesus is interrupted while he is teaching (1:21; 2:2). A group questions what Jesus says or does among themselves (1:27; 2:6), and the issue of authority comes to the fore. The teachers of the law figure in both scenes. The crowd applauds Jesus as one who teaches with authority and not as their Jewish teachers (1:22), and he responds in 2:10 to the questioning of these teachers by announcing that the Son of Man has authority to forgive sins. Both passages conclude with the crowd's respond-ing with amazement (1:22, 27; 2:12). In the former they recognize the new-ness of his authoritative teaching: "He commands even the unclean spirits, and they obey him." The crowd's amazement in 2:12 leads to their glorify-ing God because they have never seen anything like this. The parallels remind the reader that a new, Spirit-empowered reality has burst forth from heaven and that Jesus works with God's authority.

Healing and Forgiveness

THE IMPENETRABLE THICKET of people surrounding the house Jesus is speak-ing in presents a roadblock for friends of a paralytic man, who want to bring him to Jesus so that he can also be healed. They are undaunted by the human barrier before them, and resourcefully they dig through the roof to lower the man into the middle of the crowd.

This gripping, technicolor detail, so characteristic of Mark's accounts of the miracles, may startle those who worry about property damage. Some might imagine that the owner of the house is as horrified by this destructive invasion of his property by these men as the teachers of the law are later hor-rified by the invasion of the prerogatives of God by Jesus. Archaeological dis-coveries in Capernaum, however, reveal that the houses were made of rough basalt without mortar, and they could not support more than a thatch roof. The sloping roof consisted of wooden cross beams overlaid with a matting of reeds, branches, and dried mud. It had to be replenished and rolled every fall before the onset of the winter rains. It did not take a jackhammer for the men to break through the roof, and it could be easily repaired.[1]

The crowd is only one of the obstacles that needs to be overcome for the paralyzed man to be healed. As the story progresses, the reader learns of two other impediments: the suspicious skepticism of the teachers of the law and the potential hesitancy of the man to act on Jesus' command.

Digging through a roof and dropping their friend before Jesus is a silent but dramatic plea for healing, and Jesus recognizes that only a tenacious faith would have led these men to go to so much trouble.[2] The merciful granting of their request comes when Jesus announces to the paralytic, "Your sins are forgiven." Mark does not report the reaction of the friends or the man to these words, only the silent misgivings of the teachers of the law, whose

---

1. G. H. Dalman, *Sacred Sites and Ways* (New York: Macmillan, 1935), 69.
2. Jesus sees faith in action. The determined friends must have believed that Jesus has the power to heal, if only they could just reach him. Faith in Mark means more than sim-ple belief; it shows itself in actions. It is not thwarted by the obstructions of crowds (see also 10:46–52), ritual taboos (1:40–45; 5:25–34), or social rebuffs (7:24–30).

"sitting" contrasts with the active demonstration of faith of the men on the roof. They question in their hearts, "Why does this fellow talk like that? He's blaspheming! Who can forgive sins but God alone?" (2:6–7). They are asking themselves, "What possible redemptive authority can this man have?"

Jesus' authority has been contrasted previously with that of these teachers by the crowds (1:22), but this is their first appearance in the story.[3] As the experts in law and the custodians of the sacred tradition, they see their task as establishing clear-cut guidelines and boundaries. They decide what is acceptable and unacceptable to God in all spheres of life so that the people might live in accord with God's will. They appear here as disdainful observers, but they are authorities whose observations are right: God alone forgives sins.[4] To presume to forgive sins is an arrogant affront to the majesty of God, which appropriately can be labeled blasphemy.

A priest could pronounce the forgiveness of sins on the basis of repentance, restitution, and sacrifice (Lev. 4; 5; 16; 17:11); but Jesus seems to be claiming that he is be able to remit sins as if he were God. To the theologically trained mind there can be only two possible inferences. The presence of the kingdom of God, which Jesus has been speaking about (2:2; cf. 1:14–15), must usher in the forgiveness of sins. It is the fulfillment of Isaiah 33:22, 24: "For the LORD is our judge, the LORD is our lawgiver, the LORD is our king; it is he who will save us. . . . No one living in Zion will say, 'I am ill'; and the sins of those who dwell there will be forgiven" (see also Jer. 31:34; Mic. 7:18). Or they can conclude that this is "a conceited act of blasphemy"— something worthy of death (Lev. 24:16).[5] The commentary of the scribal authorities serves to notify the reader how incredibly outrageous or how incredibly wonderful Jesus' words are.

Proof that Jesus speaks for God comes in his response to these teachers' unexpressed censure. He knows in his spirit that they question thus in their hearts. Knowing their hearts does not mean that he only reads the concern on their faces. God is the one who knows hearts,[6] and Jesus does as well (see

---

3. P. von der Osten-Saken, "Streitgespräch und Parabel als Formen markinischer Christologie," in *Jesus Christus in Historie und Geschichte*, ed. G. Strecker (Tübingen: J. C. B. Mohr [Paul Siebeck], 1975), 376–81. Scribes appear alone as opponents in 1:22; 2:6; 3:22; 9:11, 14; 12:28, 38. They appear with the Pharisees in 2:16 and 7:15, and with the elders and chief priests in 8:31; 11:27; 14:43, 53; 15:1.

4. See Ex. 34:7; 2 Sam. 12:13; Pss. 32:1–5; 51:1–4; 103:2–3; 130:4; Isa. 6:7; 43:25; 44:22; Dan. 9:9; Zech. 3:4.

5. Marshall, *Faith As a Theme*, 185. The question of blasphemy is unspoken now, but it will reappear publicly at Jesus' interrogation before the high priest and will accelerate his condemnation to death.

6. 1 Sam. 16:7; 1 Chron. 28:9; Ps. 139:1–2; Jer. 17:9–10; Sir. 42:18–20; Luke 16:15; Acts 1:24; 15:8; Rom. 8:27; 1 Thess. 2:4; Rev. 2:23.

8:16; 12:15). He skirts the issue of blasphemy with a riddling question of his own, in effect saying, "Which is easier, to make a theological pronouncement about the forgiveness of sins or to provide empirical proof that the man's sins have indeed been forgiven by virtue of his ability to get up and walk away?"

This response accords with the scriptural guideline for verifying a true prophet and pinpointing a false prophet who presumes to utter in God's name what the Lord has not commanded him to speak. "If what a prophet proclaims in the name of the LORD does not take place or come true, that is a message the LORD has not spoken. That prophet has spoken presumptuously. Do not be afraid of him" (Deut. 18:22). To show the teachers of the law that his pronouncement of forgiveness is not just idle theological prattle, Jesus commands the paralytic to get up and walk so they may know that the Son of Man has authority to forgive sins on earth (2:10–11). The word confirms that their alarm is not misplaced. Jesus does presume to forgive sins on the basis of grace—something that a priest in the temple could not do, that even the law could not do. How is it that Jesus can usurp the prerogatives of God and proclaim forgiveness of sins, willy-nilly? How is he able to speak for God in such startling and untraditional ways? Can sin be dismissed so effortlessly? No! The crucifixion will clarify this matter.

The third obstacle to the man's healing is his own skepticism. Will someone who has to be carried in on a pallet by others believe Jesus' word about the forgiveness of his sins to act on his directive to get up and carry it out? Or, will he accept the judgment of the teachers of the law and say to himself: "This man cannot forgive my sins?" Will he convince himself that this is a hopeless command: "I cannot get up and carry anything because I am paralyzed?" This final obstacle to healing is overcome when the man displays the same faith as his friends by obeying Jesus' command and goes out before all, his mat tucked under his arm. Presumably the crowds now make way, and the roof is raised once more in an explosion of glory to God.[7] Their praise confirms that what Jesus has done is no great impiety but reason to glorify God.

The Son of Man

JESUS' CLIMACTIC ANNOUNCEMENT refers to himself as "the Son of Man." No consensus exists about what this title, if it can be considered a title, was

---

7. Those who glorify God are not identified as "the crowd," but as "all." Is the "all" meant to include the skeptical teachers of the law? If so, then this incident is a controversy story of a quite different stripe. Those who have questioned Jesus secretly in their hearts are persuaded that what he says is valid because of what he has done. The proof is in the pudding. Later, after a series of controversies, "teachers of the law who came down from Jerusalem" will reach a quite different conclusion about the source of his success (3:22).

intended to conjure up in the minds of Jews in the first century (see Dan. 7:13; 1 Enoch 46–53).[8] In Mark, no one else calls Jesus the Son of Man. When Jesus asked his disciples, "Who do people say I am?" "the Son of Man" is not one of the choices (8:27–30). Jesus is also not charged with claiming to be the Son of Man in the trial. The obscurity of the term made it nearly free of any preconceived notions that Jesus' generation may have entertained. Consequently, it is a title that Jesus can fill with his own meaning.

It is clear, however, that in Mark it most adequately expresses who Jesus is. Although the term *Son of Man* is undefined, we do learn what he does. He has authority to forgive sins (2:10). He is Lord of the Sabbath (2:28). He will be betrayed (14:21, 41), suffer ignominy and death, and be raised on the third day (8:31, 38; 9:9, 12; 10:33). He comes not to be served but to give his life as a ransom for many (10:45). He will be seated at the right hand of power, return on the clouds, and gather his elect (13:26–27; 14:62).

WHAT MAY STARTLE the modern reader in this scene is Jesus' initial response to the sudden interruption of his speaking the word. When the man is dropped down through the roof, his first words are: "Son,[9] your sins are forgiven." One commentator voices our modern perplexity by noting that the four men did not bring the paralyzed man to Jesus to have his sins forgiven but to have him healed.[10] Most of us would be put off by any doctor who made this announcement to us when we came for some medical treatment. We are accustomed to view disease as something caused by a virus, bacterium, or other pathogen and best remedied by medicine, not the forgiveness of sins. We are convinced that health results from eating right—high fiber, low cholesterol—exercising right, taking the right medicine that three out of four doctors recommend, and having disease-resistant genes.

The scientific approach to medicine that looks for a single cause for disease overlooks environmental, social, and spiritual contexts. We assume that

---

8. See, most recently, Delbert Burkett, "The Nontitular Son of Man: A History and Critique," *NTS* 40 (1994): 514–21. See also I. Howard Marshall, "Son of Man," in *Dictionary of Jesus and the Gospels*, eds. Joel B. Green, Scot McKnight, and I. Howard Marshall (Downers Grove, Ill.: InterVarsity, 1992), 775–81.

9. "Son" may be a term of endearment like "daughter" (5:34, 41). He addresses the disciples with this term (10:24), and it is a term used for the childlike reception of the kingdom (9:36–37, 42; 10:13–16).

10. Ernst Haenchen, *Der Weg Jesu* (Berlin: Töpelmann, 1966), 101. Pesch (*Das Markusevangelium*, 1:156) suggests that the friends are responding to Jesus' preaching of a merciful God who forgives sins and for this reason bring their friend.

there are fixed boundaries between mind, body, and soul. Therefore, God or our relationship to God has little or nothing to do with our health or sickness. We prefer rational, that is, medical, explanations, as demonstrated by the varied attempts of commentators to diagnose the paralytic's problem as anything from a hysterical nervous condition to an overactive guilty conscience that caused psychosomatic paralysis. Or some suggest that Jesus is merely trying to encourage him or win his confidence with a cheery word. Any other view strikes many today as irrational or as primitive superstition. We therefore are uncomfortable with the worldview of the Bible that presupposes a direct connection between sin and sickness.[11]

But the paralysis is treated as a result of sin in this account. To forgive the sin is to remove its consequences—the paralysis. Healing, therefore, comes as the result of the forgiveness of sins. We are no longer scandalized by Jesus' announcement of forgiveness, which we take for granted; it is the hint that our sin brings physical consequences that causes us to stumble. Relating sickness to sin in any way is thus a modern pitfall we would like to avoid. We do not want to become like Job's friends, blaming the victim by attributing every instance of sickness and suffering to a penal consequence of sin and equating health with holiness.

We must remember, however, that Mark is not interested in explaining why bad things happen to good people or bad people. Jesus' miracles of healing yield three insights that should be emphasized. (1) The first, again, is the Christological point. If God alone forgives sins and God alone heals diseases, as most Jews believed, then Jesus is the incarnation of the words of Exodus 15:26: "I am the LORD, who heals you." The miracles of healing confirm Jesus' divine origin and power. They also prepare the reader to understand the crucifixion in its proper perspective. Jesus always uses his miraculous power for others, never for himself. One can then see that the crucifixion is not a failure of that power but an act of voluntary humiliation in divine love for others.

(2) Jesus has been sent to bring forgiveness to a sinful world. Juel comments: "There is something mysteriously evil about illness that links it to the power of sin. The coming of the kingdom spells the end of both."[12] If one

---

11. The Scripture treats sickness as something caused by God as a chastisement for sin or by some evil power (see Ex. 15:26; Deut. 7:15; 28:22–28; 32:39; Job 2:5–6; Pss. 41:3–4; 103:3; 107:17; Isa. 19:22; 38:16–17; 57:17–19; John 5:14; 9:2–3; Acts 5:1–11; 12:20–23; 1 Cor. 11:30; James 5:16). The assumption is that God is in total control of illness. According to a later rabbinic tradition (*b. Ned.* 41a), "R. Alexandri said in the name of R. Chiyya b. Abba: A sick man does not recover from his sickness until all his sins are forgiven him, as it is written, 'Who forgiveth all thine iniquities, who healeth all thy diseases' (Ps. 103:3)."

12. Juel, *Mark*, 46.

views disease as God's chastening rod, as they did in Jesus' time, then God offers forgiveness through Jesus. Jesus vanquishes those things that in the Old Testament prevented one from coming into the presence of God—whether it be unclean spirits that have taken control of one's life, an unclean disease (Lev. 13:45–46), paralysis (21:17–23), or sin—and thus opens up the way for God's reign to enter into all spheres of life.

Modern society tends to take a mechanistic approach to the problem of illness. When a machine malfunctions, the mechanic diagnoses what is wrong and removes or fixes the faulty part. When our physical bodies break down, we expect the doctor to diagnose what is wrong and remove or correct the faulty part. After this has been done, the body is supposed to function normally again. Humans are not machines, however, and a number of factors contribute to health. Young writes: "The Gospel declares that healing involves relationships with God, with other people, with ourselves and with our environment."[13] One of the things that can destroy our health is the paralyzing weight of sin. It does not show up on any of the blood tests or X-rays, but it is as virulent as any physical disease. In this scene, Jesus is able to restore persons to health by lifting the load of sin that cripples and immobilizes.

The opening scenes in Mark reveal that Jesus has been sent to bring healing to a broken world. Mark singles out these miracles to signify what the advent of the dominion of God promises for this fallen world, as well as what the power of the one who acts in God's name on behalf of humanity entails. It is not the case that Jesus saw the paralyzed man, for example, as particularly sinful, nor did he buy into the deuteronomic orthodoxy that one's suffering comes in proportion to one's sin. Anderson helpfully comments, "The insight is that there is indeed a close and age-old connexion between man's fallen estate and everything that afflicts him, with the further implication that God's will is for man's wholeness, or completeness in every aspect of his being."[14] Sickness belongs to the old aeon, whose prince is being ousted from power.

The healing Jesus works changes the questions that are normally asked when suffering or misfortune strikes. Instead of asking, "Who did this to me?" or "Why did this happen?" one needs to ask, "Who is this who offers forgiveness, healing, and salvation?" and "What does his presence in our lives mean?" One can then see that these miracles "announce and inaugurate what the future will offer; they are the *presence* in history of what will be the *promise* of history, a world restored to wholeness and open to God's pres-

---

13. John Young, "Health, Healing and Modern Medicine," in *The Gospel in Contemporary Culture*, ed. Hugh Montefiore (London: Mowbray, 1992), 157.
14. Anderson, *Mark*, 100.

ence."[15] The universe need no longer be regarded as a hostile place, under siege from invading malevolent forces. God's love and grace reign supreme.

(3) Finally, we should point out that we may exploit the wizardry of medical science but must remember that scientific solutions do not solve all the problems of sickness, suffering, and death. No meaningful healing can take place without reconciliation with God. We should also remember that physical well-being is not the essence of the Christian faith. Paul's thorn in the flesh makes this clear. One might expect that one so divinely connected might receive healing when he prayed to God for it to be removed. No miracle occurred, and Paul received instead the answer that he must accept the thorn because it taught him that God's grace is sufficient and all that one needs for life. It also testified to how God's power is brought to completion in human weakness (2 Cor. 12:7–9).

Another way that we can bridge the contexts and draw out contemporary significance from this section is to read ourselves into the characters in the story and to ask questions. Walter Wink has helpfully outlined this method of studying the Bible.[16] We may thus ask ourselves: What is it about others that makes us feel that they are lepers? What is it that we fear about them? What is it about us that makes us feel like lepers, untouchable? What makes us helpers, who would struggle up a roof and dig our way through it to bring another to the source of healing? What in us makes us give up in the face of the crowds? What in us is like the teacher of the law, the cool intellectual, the skeptical observer, the judgmental specialist? The scribe in us certainly does not want Jesus reminding us that we have sins that need forgiving as well. What in us is like the paralyzed man, who needs to hear the word of forgiveness? What in us makes us feel helpless and enslaved by an alien power, like the man with the unclean spirit? The answers to these questions may lead us to see ourselves and others more clearly.

IF JESUS IS the model for our ministry to others, we see one who announces the forgiveness of sin and the chance of reconciliation with God, which brings in its wake healing. The church needs to proclaim in its words and deeds this offer of forgiveness, which can cleanse all sin. There are many whose souls are strangled by a snarled undergrowth of oppressive guilt. The word of Jesus can tear away the tangles and release

15. John R. Donahue, "Miracles, Mystery and Parable," *Way* 18 (1978): 253.

16. Walter Wink, *The Bible in Human Transformation: Toward a New Paradigm for Biblical Study* (Philadelphia: Fortress, 1973), 49–65.

fresh forces of renewal and energy in people's lives. During the Middles Ages, when sick people came to the church for help, French historian Jules Michelet says they got blamed for their ills. "On Sundays, after Mass, the sick came in scores crying for help—and words were all they got: 'You have sinned and God is afflicting you. Thank Him, you will suffer so much the less torment in the life to come.'"[17] When the sick came to Jesus, he did not spurn them but announced God's forgiveness and manifested God's love. He drove away the handmaidens of illness: hopelessness, guilt, and despair.

Many today are skeptical of miraculous healing that does not use medical means. Thomas Jefferson pruned all the miraculous elements from the Gospels to make them more palatable to the "enlightened" mind in his book, *The Life and Morals of Jesus of Nazareth*. Leonard Sweet contends in his study on medicine and health in the evangelical tradition that medical science has disengaged itself from religion and its moral concerns in the healing enterprise in the modern era, and that the church has acquiesced by maintaining a "safe, respectful distance from medical and healing matters." Our regard for the miracles of modern science often makes the church and the clergy seem superfluous. Many physicians, therefore, do not want the clergy interfering in the sickroom, especially worrying patients about the issues of sin, until the medical fight is over. Sweet writes, "When medicine has done all it can do, which is everything humanly possible, religion is supposed to take over."[18]

The healings of Jesus reveal that God is for healing and therefore can work through medicine and surgery as much as faith and prayer, but faith and prayer may not be neglected. As mind and spirit can effect the onset of a disease, they can also effect healing. Healing involves far more than the physical dimension; it involves mental, social, and spiritual dimensions as well. Faith, prayer, and a deep sense of the forgiveness of sins are therefore not simply "religious placebos." Sweet argues:

> The healing forces of faith, hope, and love are not incidental to health and medicine. Like an antibiotic, faith, hope, and love enter the system quickly and do their work slowly. Curing, or the removal of disease, may take place with medical means alone. But healing, or the triumphal reentry into one's total environment, only takes place in partnership with faith. Medical healing is the knowledge of God manifested through science. Spiritual healing is the knowledge of God manifested through faith. It is the same knowledge. It is the same God.[19]

---

17. Cited by Kat Duff, *The Alchemy of Illness* (New York: Bell Tower, 1993), 50.

18. Leonard I. Sweet, *Health and Medicine in the Evangelical Tradition* (Valley Forge, Pa.: Trinity Press International, 1994), 142.

19. Ibid., 142.

Mark 2:13–3:6

❦

ONCE AGAIN JESUS went out beside the lake. A large crowd came to him, and he began to teach them. ¹⁴As he walked along, he saw Levi son of Alphaeus sitting at the tax collector's booth. "Follow me," Jesus told him, and Levi got up and followed him.

¹⁵While Jesus was having dinner at Levi's house, many tax collectors and "sinners" were eating with him and his disciples, for there were many who followed him. ¹⁶When the teachers of the law who were Pharisees saw him eating with the "sinners" and tax collectors, they asked his disciples: "Why does he eat with tax collectors and 'sinners'?"

¹⁷On hearing this, Jesus said to them, "It is not the healthy who need a doctor, but the sick. I have not come to call the righteous, but sinners."

¹⁸Now John's disciples and the Pharisees were fasting. Some people came and asked Jesus, "How is it that John's disciples and the disciples of the Pharisees are fasting, but yours are not?"

¹⁹Jesus answered, "How can the guests of the bridegroom fast while he is with them? They cannot, so long as they have him with them. ²⁰But the time will come when the bridegroom will be taken from them, and on that day they will fast.

²¹"No one sews a patch of unshrunk cloth on an old garment. If he does, the new piece will pull away from the old, making the tear worse. ²²And no one pours new wine into old wineskins. If he does, the wine will burst the skins, and both the wine and the wineskins will be ruined. No, he pours new wine into new wineskins."

²³One Sabbath Jesus was going through the grainfields, and as his disciples walked along, they began to pick some heads of grain. ²⁴The Pharisees said to him, "Look, why are they doing what is unlawful on the Sabbath?"

²⁵He answered, "Have you never read what David did when he and his companions were hungry and in need? ²⁶In the days of Abiathar the high priest, he entered the house of God and ate the consecrated bread, which is lawful only for priests to eat. And he also gave some to his companions."

²⁷Then he said to them, "The Sabbath was made for man, not man for the Sabbath. ²⁸So the Son of Man is Lord even of the Sabbath."

³:¹Another time he went into the synagogue, and a man with a shriveled hand was there. ²Some of them were looking for a reason to accuse Jesus, so they watched him closely to see if he would heal him on the Sabbath. ³Jesus said to the man with the shriveled hand, "Stand up in front of everyone."

⁴Then Jesus asked them, "Which is lawful on the Sabbath: to do good or to do evil, to save life or to kill?" But they remained silent.

⁵He looked around at them in anger and, deeply distressed at their stubborn hearts, said to the man, "Stretch out your hand." He stretched it out, and his hand was completely restored. ⁶Then the Pharisees went out and began to plot with the Herodians how they might kill Jesus.

IN THE PREVIOUS section, peppered with the phrase "and immediately" (1:21, 23, 28, 29, 31, 42, cf. NASB), Mark has shown Jesus' fame and popularity spreading like wildfire. In this next unit (2:13–3:6), he shows opposition to Jesus from religious competitors rising just as rapidly. This section comprises a cycle of four disputes regarding Jewish ritual laws and customs. Each controversy except the last contains a question posed by objectors, which Jesus answers with a declaration or a proverbial saying. (1) The question, "Why does he eat with tax collectors and 'sinners'?" (2:16) is answered with a truism: "It is not the healthy who need a doctor, but the sick. I have not come to call the righteous, but sinners" (2:17). (2) The question, "How is it that John's disciples and the disciples of the Pharisees are fasting, but yours are not?" (2:18), is answered with proverbial sayings about not patching old cloth with new or putting new wine into old wineskins (2:19, 21–22). (3) The question about why the disciples do what is unlawful on the Sabbath (2:24) is answered with the proclamation, "The Sabbath was made for man, not man for the Sabbath," and, "The Son of Man is Lord even of the Sabbath" (2:27–28).¹ (4) In the last controversy, Jesus turns the tables on his inquisitors and provokes an engagement. He asks those who have gathered to monitor his activity a question about the Sabbath:

---

1. In 2:18–22 and 2:23–28, we find parallel patterns of question (2:18, 24), argumentation (2:19–20, 25–26), and double answer: first answer (2:21, 27), second answer (2:22, 28).

"Which is lawful on the Sabbath: to do good or to do evil, to save life or to kill?" (3:4). The Pharisees have no answer. When Jesus restores a man to a healthy life, their only response is to conspire with the Herodians to kill him (3:6).

The Call of Levi the Tax Collector and Dinner in His House (2:13–17)

JESUS RETURNS TO the sea. As he passes along the shore (see 1:16), he once again singles out a person and challenges him to follow him. This time it is a tax official, Levi son of Alphaeus, busy with his duties at the tax office, just as the fishermen had been with their nets. Levi is no tax baron but one who is stationed at an intersection of trade routes to collect tolls, tariffs, imposts, and customs, probably for Herod Antipas. Toll collectors were renowned for their dishonesty and extortion. They habitually collected more than they were due, did not always post up the regulations, and made false valuations and accusations (see Luke 3:12–13).[2] Tax officials were hardly choice candidates for discipleship since most Jews in Jesus' day would dismiss them as those who craved money more than respectability or righteousness.[3]

Although Levi is called in the same way as the four fisherman were, his name does not appear in the list of disciples in 3:17–18. In Matthew 9:9, one called Matthew is summoned from his toll booth, and that name does appear in all four lists of the Twelve (Matt. 10:2–4; Mark 3:18; Luke 6:13–16; Acts 1:13). A James also appears in all four lists who is identified as the son of Alphaeus, presumably to distinguish him from James son of Zebedee (3:18). Is Levi son of Alphaeus to be identified as one of the Twelve? The puzzle does not offer an easy solution. One explanation is that this toll collector may have been known by two names, Levi and Matthew, in the same way that Simon Peter is identified as Simon or Peter (Cephas). The Gospel of Mark uses the name Levi while the Gospel of Matthew uses the name Matthew. Another solution is that James and Levi may have been brothers or two names for the same person. Some ancient texts solve the discrepancy by reading the name of James here instead of Levi.[4]

The concern to clarify Levi's relationship to the listing of the disciples, however, may cause us to miss something that Mark's text discloses. If Levi is not to be affiliated with the Twelve, as he is not in Mark, the call to follow Jesus is not limited to the Twelve. That Jesus summons a tax gatherer in

---

2. See, further, John R. Donahue, "Tax Collectors and Sinners: An Attempt at Identification," *CBQ* 33 (1971): 39–61.

3. Minear, *Mark*, 60.

4. D, Θ, 565, *f*¹³ (except 346), Tatian.

the same way as he called Peter, Andrew, James, and John reminds the reader that following Jesus is open to "all-comers."[5] One's position or caste, even one's shady reputation, is not a liability when it comes to receiving and responding to Jesus' call. This interpretation is reinforced by the statement in 2:15: "for there were many who followed him."

Levi responds to Jesus' call as promptly as the fishermen did and gets up and follows Jesus, but his obedience marks an even more radical break with his past. The other disciples can always go back to fishing (John 21:3), but not so a toll collector who abandons his post. The next scene finds Levi along with many other toll collectors and sinners who follow Jesus and eat at "his house" (2:15, lit.). The "house" in Mark is connected to Jesus (Levi follows *him* and sits at table in *his* house; see 2:1; 3:19; 7:17, 24; 9:33; 10:10). Jesus then serves as the host of a ragtag assemblage of social pariahs.

In other words, Jesus does more than preach repentance to sinners; he befriends them. On the one hand, the scene suggests that Jesus possesses "a magnetic power" to draw "people who ordinarily would have little or nothing to do with religion."[6] On the other hand, people who have something to do with religion usually would not want to draw this kind of people. This display of open acceptance of sinners appalls the Pharisees. Their dismay precipitates Jesus' comment about the sick needing a physician. No physician waits for the ill to recover fully before consulting with them. As their physician, Jesus offers the remedy that vanquishes the illness of these so-called sinners.

One should not picture Jesus as simply partying with notorious sinners. For one, they may have been labeled "sinners" by pietist groups, such as the Pharisees, out of disdain for their refusal to heed their guidance on proper holiness, their consorting with Gentiles, or their employment in a blacklisted trade, such as a tanner or tax collector. For another, to follow Jesus in the full sense of the word requires repentance and obedience. His goal in reaching out to the sick is to bring about healing and transformation in their lives, not to gather them together for a fun time. Instead of sorting people into classifications, holy and unholy, clean and unclean, righteous and sinner, Jesus gathers them under the wings of God's grace and love.

The Question of Fasting (2:18–22)

NOT ONLY DOES Jesus befriend tax collectors and sinners, Jesus eats and drinks with them (Matt. 11:19). The disciples of John and the Pharisees do not question Jesus' behavior, however. They ask why *his disciples* do not fast.

---

5. Anderson, *Mark*, 103.
6. Gundry, *Mark*, 125.

These two groups have set themselves apart from others by their ascetic practices. The Pharisee in Jesus' parable, for example, gives thanks that he is not like the rest of men and boasts to God that he fasts twice a week (Luke 18:12).

The query about fasting prompts three parabolic answers. The first response assumes that the kingdom of God, which has drawn near in Jesus' preaching and merciful activity, is not a funeral wake but a wedding party. No one wants grim-visaged fasters casting a pall on the joyous celebration. In the presence of such joy, it is not only inappropriate to fast, it is impossible. Jesus does allude, however, to a time when mourning will be more fitting, when the bridegroom is "taken from them," an oblique reference to his passion and death. But even that is not to be a permanent state. The joy of the resurrection will transform all grief and sorrow.

The second and third responses draw on metaphors from everyday life to illustrate the significance of Jesus' ministry. The images of patching cloth and pouring new wine into wineskins do not provide advice for the happy homemaker. No tips are given on how to prepare the patch by prewashing it or the wineskins by moistening them. The garment will tear when it is washed and the patch of new, stronger fabric shrinks. Old wineskins already stretched to their limits and now inflexible will burst when the new wine expands. The point is clear. The new that Jesus brings is incompatible with the old.[7] He has not come to patch up an old system that does not match the revolutionary rule of God. He is not simply a reformer of the old, but one who will transform it. There can be no concessions, no accommodations, and no compromises with the old. The old is not just represented by the Judaism of the Pharisees because the disciples of John and their Judaism are also mentioned. The old, exemplified by the condemnation and exclusion of sinners in the previous controversy and the practice of fasting in this debate, cannot contain the new. Both will be ruined if they are combined.

In the incident that follows, Jesus argues that such things as the Sabbath laws are made for the benefit of humans and not vice versa (2:27). Food laws are superfluous; it is only purity of the heart that matters (7:19–23). Love of neighbor is greater than sacrifice (12:23). The temple will even be destroyed, and a new one not made with hands will be raised in its place. The sound of ripping is discernible throughout the Gospel. The heavens rip open at the baptism (1:10). Caiaphas, the high priest, tears his garment when confronted

---

7. Gundry (Mark, 134) argues that it is the irresistible force of Jesus' new teaching with authority that creates the split. "The point is solely in the power of the new. Mark means the sayings to indicate again that Jesus' authoritative pronouncements end all discussions. They brook no contradiction. They slam the door against all doubt. The story ends without debate."

with Jesus' claim to be the Christ, the Son of the Blessed One (14:63). The temple veil is ripped from top to bottom when Jesus dies on the cross (15:38). The rips signify "the end of the old and the birth of the new."[8]

Two Sabbath Controversies (2:23–3:6)

THIS SECTION CONCLUDES with two Sabbath controversies. The first (2:23–28) is provoked when the Pharisees, who seem to function here as a kind of religious police, spot the disciples plucking grain as they saunter through a field.[9] The law permitted anyone (particularly the needy) to pluck ears in a neighbor's field of standing grain as long as one did not use a sickle (Deut. 23:25), but the Pharisees would have classified this as harvesting, a violation of the Sabbath (*m. Sabb.* 7:2). The negligence of the disciples in such matters, whether because of ignorance or laxity, reflects negatively on Jesus as their teacher. Consequently, the Pharisees direct their challenge to him.

Jesus' first response recalls a Davidic precedent, when David took it upon himself to violate the law by eating the bread of the Presence,[10] the most holy portion of the offering that was to be eaten only by the priests in a holy place (Lev. 24:5–9; see *Lev. Rab.* 32:3). The Scripture tacitly sanctions his actions by not condemning him. David was not just a hungry man, however. He was to become the king of Israel, the ancestor of the Messiah, and a type of the King-Messiah. His personal authority legitimated his actions. If the

---

8. Hooker, *Mark*, 101.

9. To make a path through someone's grainfield was illegal for all but the king. If this action is an open proclamation of kingship, it is suppressed to focus on the issues of the interpretation of the Sabbath laws and the authority of Jesus.

10. Jesus' answer refers to Abiathar instead of Ahimelech, who was the priest involved in this incident (according to 1 Sam. 21:1–6). Abiathar was Ahimelech's son, who barely escaped the massacre of the priests ordered by King Saul when he discovered what had happened. While one might point to the confusion between these two priests in the Old Testament (1 Sam. 22:20; 30:7; 2 Sam. 8:17; 1 Chron. 18:16; 24:6) or suggest a scribal mistake, the explanation for the mention of Abiathar lies elsewhere. The text does not say that David came to Abiathar but that this event happened when Abiathar was high priest. Abiathar is specifically identified as the high priest and was more than just a priest, as Ahimelech was. The term reflects the convention of eponymous dating (see Luke 3:2), and Abiathar was the high priest during David's reign and especially linked to him. Another alternative is to interpret the Greek phrase *epi Abiathar* as a reference to the general section in the book of Samuel, as the phrase in 12:26, *epi tou batou*, "at the bush," refers to the passage in Exodus (so J. W. Wenham, "Mark 2, 26," *JTS* 1 [1950]: 156). Still another explanation attributes the discrepancy to dual traditions embedded in the Old Testament accounts in 1–2 Samuel, 1 Kings, and 1 Chronicles. The minor tradition reversed the roles Abiathar and Ahimelech, and Jesus and/or Mark drew upon it (M. K. Mulholland, "Abiathar," in *Dictionary of Jesus and the Gospels*, eds. Joel B. Green, Scot McKnight, and I. Howard Marshall [Downers Grove, Ill.: InterVarsity, 1992], 1.)

strict regulations regarding the bread of the Presence could be set aside for David, who was fleeing for his life, how much more can holy regulations be set aside for Jesus (and his companions), whom Mark presents as David's Lord (Mark 1:2–3; 12: 35–37) and who is in a situation of far greater urgency in proclaiming the coming of the kingdom of God.[11]

The second part of the argument moves in a different direction, with the premise that God created the idea of the Sabbath for the well-being of humans, not the other way around. God intended the Sabbath to be a "gracious gift, a release from the necessity of seven-day toil, so that anyone who interprets the Law as to make the Sabbath a burden, or to inhibit the free course of God's mercy, merely reveals his own ignorance of God and His purposes."[12] The priority of human need always outweighs the need for humans to conform to ritual formalities. The Pharisees would argue that if the disciples did not have any food prepared for the Sabbath, they should go without.[13] Jesus argues that it does not transgress God's will for hungry people to have something to eat on the Sabbath, even if it infringes on the Pharisees' narrow interpretation of what is permitted.

The third part of the argument consists of the climactic announcement that the Son of Man is Lord of the Sabbath. This segment begins with the statement, "The Pharisees said ..." (2:24). At the conclusion it is clear that it makes no difference what they say. The narrative to this point has demonstrated that the authority of Jesus far outstrips that of the teachers of the law. This statement boldly affirms that as Lord the Son of Man is the one who decrees what is lawful and unlawful, permissible and impermissible, and any customs ordained by the Pharisees or their traditions are thereby rendered null and void. It is Jesus who makes plain the humanitarian purpose of the Sabbath, and his word is final.[14] The Pharisees with their rules and regulations, quibbles and fusses, misrepresent the will of God.

The second controversy over the Sabbath (3:1–6) augments the humanitarian purpose of the law by revealing how easily rules can get in the way of restoring people to health.[15] It also exposes the true nature of

---

11. The incident assumes that the implied listeners already embrace Jesus as an authoritative interpreter of the law and are interested in his argumentation and directives. It is unlikely that this argument would convince the unconverted, but it would reinforce the convictions and practice of Christians. Legalists are more at home with rules and propositions and always seem to have trouble with narrative. What are they to do with a case like David?

12. G. B. Caird and L. D. Hurst, *New Testament Theology* (Oxford: Clarendon, 1994), 47.

13. The disciples choose not to go hungry, but one is not supposed to fast on the Sabbath (see Judith 8:6; *Jub.* 50:12; *m.Sabb.* 16:2; *m.Ta'an.* 1:6; *b. Sabb.* 118–19).

14. Gundry, *Mark,* 142.

15. Jesus has healed on the Sabbath before (1:21–28, 29–31), and no one raised any objections.

Jesus' opponents. It begins with the notice that they are "looking for a reason to accuse Jesus," treacherously inspecting his every move (3:2). They do not question his power to heal—that is presumed by now; they want to see if he will heal *on the Sabbath* and violate their interpretation of the law. A Sabbath violation, just like blasphemy, was worthy of death (Ex. 31:14). The segment ends with the Pharisees joining forces with the Herodians to plot his death. Of what is he guilty? Bringing healing on the Sabbath! This reveals more about the opponents than it does about Jesus or what is permissible on the Sabbath.

Jesus does not flinch in the face of the scrutiny of his actions. Instead, it is his turn to become righteously indignant over the hardness of heart that besets his antagonists. Hardheartedness does not mean that these enemies are cold-hearted, as it does in our idiom. The heart was the place where one made decisions. Hardness of heart thus had a moral and religious meaning and referred to a lack of understanding—a hardness of mind that made one calloused to any spiritual truth—as well as scornful disobedience to God's will.[16] It seems that nothing Jesus can say or do will pierce the thick armor of moral insensitivity that encases the Pharisees' minds. The withered hand of the man is nothing compared to the withered souls of these religious examiners. But Jesus deliberately provokes them in one last bid to get through, the only healing miracle that he initiates without prompting.

He calls a man with a withered hand to stand in their midst.[17] No worry about secrecy here. When he commands him to stretch out his immobile limb, he could also have said, "Your sins are forgiven," as he said to the paralytic, but that is assumed when the man has faith enough to obey his command. The implied forgiveness of sins and Jesus' power to heal underlies what Jesus does but is not stressed in this episode. The focus is on what Jesus' presence means for the observance of holy days. Clearly the Messiah has not come to commemorate the Sabbath but to save life.[18]

With his defiant question in 3:4, Jesus frames the issue around doing good or doing evil, saving life or destroying it. The question contains its own

---

16. In the biblical idiom it is synonymous with a fat heart, a stiff neck, blind eyes, and deaf ears.

17. J. D. M. Derrett, "Christ and the Power of Choice (Mark 3,1–6)," *Bib* 65 (1984): 172, contends that this man would have stood out when the congregation stood for prayer and raised both hands to shoulder height, palms outward, in prayer. A withered hand is frequently the punishment for stretching out one's hand to reach for something sinful (see Ps. 137:5; Zech. 11:17). Jeroboam's hand "dried up" when he tried to take action against the rebellious prophets (1 Kings 13:4–6). His condition would have been regarded as proof of unconfessed sin that had not escaped God's notice (see Ps. 32:1–5).

18. Minear, *Mark*, 63.

answer: Doing good is not to be limited to certain days. The way Jesus phrases the question recalls Deuteronomy 30:15–19: "See, I set before you today life and prosperity, death and destruction. . . . I have set before you life and death, blessings and curses. Now choose life, so that you and your children may live." Even on the Sabbath one must make the right choice. Suffering may be alleviated at any time, and to refrain from doing good is to abet evil and to pick death over life.

The sharp reaction to what Jesus does in this incident is completely unwarranted. Healing by speaking is not a breach of the Sabbath. He prepares no ointments or potions and lifts nothing. Jesus only violates the Pharisees' finespun interpretation of the law—an interpretation that fosters death because these self-appointed guardians of the Sabbath would insist that the man return the next day if he wants healing, so as to avoid any hint of desecrating the sacred day.[19] What does it matter that he suffer through another day? They are hostile to Jesus *and* the handicapped. In their stubborn resistance, it does not dawn on them that if his words are not in accord with God's will, the man would not have been healed, since it is God who forgives sins and effects healing. These critics are so blindly cynical that they are incensed when Jesus does good and saves a life on a holy day, but they have no qualms about doing harm and plotting death on that very same day ("immediately " in 3:6, NASB) with the secular powers that be. The way light creates shadows, Jesus' presence sometimes brings out the worst in people.

The Herodians were the supporters of Herod Antipas,[20] who had arrested John and eventually beheaded him. They were anxious to maintain the social and political status quo, which was nicely propped up by religion. The common enemy causes the unholy Herodians to collude with the pious, religious extremists in the pursuit of self-interest, not truth. Unlike Jesus, who works in the open, they plot in secret. Their pact to destroy him will culminate in 15:1, when another group of power brokers take council to destroy him and are successful—or so they think.[21] Jesus' remark that the bridegroom will be taken from them (2:20) now takes on a more ominous cast.

---

19. Since the man is not in any mortal danger but suffers from a chronic disease, his affliction can wait. All of the rabbis agreed that saving a life overrides the Sabbath (see *m. Yoma* 8:6). They disagreed on the scriptural basis for this conclusion (see *Mekilta Shabbata* 1 on Ex. 31:12).

20. Josephus, *J.W.* 1.16.6 § 319; *Ant.* 14.15.10 § 450.

21. See Ps. 37:31–33; Isa. 29:20–21; Jer. 20:10–11.

Bridging Contexts

THIS SECTION OF the Gospel reveals how Jesus defied the traditional expectations of the religious pundits over what behavior God expects from the devout. He sparks controversy by associating with known sinners, by the failure of his disciples to fast and observe rules of the Sabbath, and by healing on the Sabbath. Many today take it for granted that Jesus rebelled against what we regard as the stuffy piety of the Pharisees, but to understand this passage, we need to examine the underlying issues. What was behind the criticism directed at Jesus? What was Jesus' motivation? Was he simply thumbing his nose at religious conventions, like washing his car or mowing his grass on Sunday? Or was something more going on? It is most certainly the latter. Jesus does not dismiss the law in a cavalier fashion. These incidents present for the reader two incompatible religious outlooks, two ways of doing religion that are in inexorable conflict. One leads to death; the other to life.

Each incident unfolds the contrast. The call of Levi and Jesus' feasting with sinners discloses the contrast between a religious attitude that keeps sinners and the unhallowed at arm's length and one, the good news of God, that welcomes all comers. The query about fasting reveals the difference between religious exercises that weigh down the soul like a ball and chain and a religious experience that allows it to soar with joy. The controversies over the Sabbath reveal the clash between a religious outlook that withers mercy with pitiless rules and one that places human need above the statute book.

Associating with sinners. Hobnobbing with sinners and tax collectors evoked vociferous complaints from the Pharisees. Occasionally Mark explains for the reader the reasons behind their protest, as he does when they object to the disciples' failure to wash their hands (7:3–4). He does not provide an explanation here as to why the Pharisees protest Jesus' camaraderie with sinners because it would have been widely understood across cultures that to associate with the iniquitous was, to say the least, chancy. Many feared that their iniquity might rub off. Companionship with sinners would also sully one's reputation because people have believed throughout the ages that birds of a feather flock together and a person is known by the company he keeps (but see 9:4). But it is helpful to examine why the Pharisees were scandalized by Jesus' action to spot the parallels with our situation.

The term "pharisaic" has come over into English to refer to hypocrites who fake morality or to legalistic nitpickers. The word is considered to be synonymous with "holier than thou," "preachy," "sanctimonious," and "self-righteous." This assumption is an inaccurate caricature of Pharisaism and can perpetuate the notion that God extends grace to all sinners except those of the Pharisaic variety. One may not dismiss the Pharisees as a bunch of hypocrites. In the Gospel of Mark, they are guilty instead of being hypercritical.

The Pharisees (meaning "the separated ones") were a collection of factions consisting mostly of Torah-concerned laymen who sincerely sought to extend into the lives of ordinary Jews the concerns of ritual purity usually associated in the law with only the priests and the temple.[22] Their driving motivation was to fulfill God's command: "Be holy because I, the LORD your God, am holy" (Lev. 19:2). They especially fastened on the purity rules that classified things, times, and persons according to different degrees of holiness and unholiness. It was essential to their sense of identity as Jews, a holy and separate people, to be able to know and determine what was permissible or proscribed, clean or unclean. Their purity concerns magnified the agricultural rules and specified not only what might be eaten, but out of which vessel one might eat and with whom one might eat.

The Pharisees were also attentive to tithing foodstuffs, for this indicated what foods might be eaten in ritual cleanness. They shunned the unobservant and the wicked because they feared, with some justification, that their food had not been properly tithed or prepared. The upshot of their concern for holiness was their conviction that the sinner should be kept at arm's length until disinfected by concrete repentance and the proper ceremonial rites.

Jesus' bold outreach to sinners was something new and different. It was easy for the pious to construe this behavior as a violation of the instructions laid down throughout Scripture not to associate with evildoers. Did not the psalmist say: "Blessed is the man who does not walk in the counsel of the wicked or stand in the way of sinners or sit in the seat of mockers" (Ps 1:1)? A later rabbinic tradition takes this attitude to the extreme: The wise say, "Let not a man associate with sinners even to bring them near to the Torah" (*Mekilta Amalek* 3 to Ex. 18:1).

In other words, the Pharisees represented an attitude that approached sin from the preventive side. They wanted to make and enforce rules that would safeguard people from becoming impure and immoral. Jesus represented an attitude that approached sin from the creative side, seeking to reclaim the impure and immoral. One could argue that the Pharisees' attitude

---

22. For the various views of the Pharisees in contemporary debate, compare Jacob Neusner, *From Politics to Piety* (Englewood Cliffs, N.J.: Prentice-Hall, 1973); Elias Rivkin, *The Hidden Revolution: The Pharisees' Search for the Kingdom Within* (Nashville: Abingdon, 1978); Anthony J. Saldarini, *Pharisees, Scribes and Sadducees in Palestinian Society* (Wilmington, Del.: Michael Glazier, 1988); E. P. Sanders, *Jewish Law From Jerusalem to the Mishnah* (Philadelphia: Trinity Press International, 1990); idem, *Judaism: Practice and Belief 63 BCE—66 CE* (Philadelphia: Trinity Press International, 1992); and Günter Stemberger, *Jewish Contemporaries of Jesus* (Minneapolis: Fortress, 1995).

toward the people was defined by Ezekiel 44, which lays down rules about who may enter the sanctuary and priestly service, consisting of closed gates and signs saying "No admission." Jesus' attitude was defined by Ezekiel 34, which describes the shepherd who seeks out the weak, the sick, and the lost sheep and feeds them in good pasture (34:4, 12, 16). Pharisaic piety required concrete evidence of repentance before it would permit contact with the flagrant sinner; Jesus did not. While the Pharisees may have looked down on sinners (Luke 18:18), Jesus looked for them (19:10). Meals defined social boundaries in terms of who was approvable and who was not. By eating with sinners Jesus gave them a concrete sign of God's loving acceptance and conveyed that repentance comes by means of grace.

This episode reveals four things that are applicable today. (1) Sinners do not need to do something first to become worthy recipients of God's love. They do not have to strive to become worthy and then apply with a glowing résumé to follow Jesus. One becomes worthy by responding to the call.

(2) By eating with sinners, Jesus does not condone sinful lifestyles but attests that these persons and their lifestyles can be transformed. Celsus, a vigorous pagan critic of Christianity in the late second century, was astounded that Christians deliberately appealed to sinners because he believed that it was impossible for people to undergo any radical moral transformation.[23] These Christians were but following the pattern of their Lord, who conveyed God's grace to sinners in ways that changed their lives. They were not to be snubbed or ignored no matter how vile or irredeemable they might seem. A self-righteous contempt for "sinners" does little to help them and may only compound their alienation and self-hatred.

(3) Jesus makes no distinction between persons and spurns the whole system of ranking and classifying people—to the disadvantage of the Pharisees, who worked so hard to attain their status of sanctity (see Phil. 3:5–6). Jesus does not set up a table open to full members only (as at Qumran) but one open to all possible guests, wherever they may be gathered: in his house (or a toll collectors' house), in the desert on both sides of the lake, at the home of a leper, and in an upper room.

(4) Jesus does not fear being contaminated by lepers or sinners but instead contaminates them with God's grace and power. He is not corrupted by sinners but transmits blessing on them. If the object of religious life is believed to be the preservation of purity, whether ritual or doctrinal, one tends to look at all others as potential polluters who will make one impure. Jesus rejects this perspective. He does not regard his holiness as something that

---

23. See Origen, *Against Celsus*, 3.59–65.

needs to be safeguarded but as "God's numinous transforming power,"[24] which can turn tax collectors into disciples.

The first incident, therefore, depicts two contrary religious outlooks: one that draws strict boundaries, pigeonholes people, and excludes them from God's grace and power, which is to be rejected; the other that throws open the doors to one and all. Unfortunately, it is the religious outlook of the Pharisees and not that of Jesus that has more often than not governed the attitudes of churches and church members throughout the ages. People are still scandalized by Jesus' welcome of all sinners. To bridge the context one should let people see how much more they share the judgmental and growling attitudes of Jesus' foes toward others than the loving and welcoming spirit of Jesus.

Fasting. The inquiry about fasting does not contain a mandate to fast nor does it forbid it. What Jesus taught about fasting was completely misunderstood in the *Didache*. It changed the days when fasting was required but retained the legalistic outlook: "Let not your fast be with the hypocrites, for they fast on Monday and Thursday, but do you fast on Wednesday and Friday" (*Did.* 8:1). The question about fasting in this scene of Mark allows Jesus to confirm obliquely that the new age had dawned with his arrival. He is the bridegroom who has come in fulfillment of the hopes of Israel. If that is the case, then it is clear that Jesus did not come simply to teach or reinforce standard rules of religious deportment. The rulebook was being overhauled.

The practice of voluntary fasting was associated with several ideas in Judaism,[25] which, from Jesus' perspective, were incompatible with the coming of the kingdom of God. Fasting was related to the fear of demons, and some thought that they could ward off demons by fasting. The binding of Satan by Jesus and his power to exorcise demons with a word made this unnecessary. Some used fasting as a meritorious act of self-renunciation, which ultimately was intended to impress or sway God in some way. That is, one fasted to try to get God to bestow some good that he might otherwise withhold. But how can one fast in the presence of God's greatest gift to humankind? The ministry of Jesus makes it clear that one does not need to perform acts of self-mortification to gain favor with God or to manipulate God to do one's bidding.[26]

Some fasted to atone for sins or to avert further calamity from falling on

---

24. Walter Wink, *Engaging the Powers: Discernment and Resistance in a World of Domination* (Minneapolis: Fortress, 1992), 117.

25. See Johannes Behm, "νῆστις κτλ.," *TDNT* 4:929–31.

26. See the discussion of 9:29, below.

the nation.[27] If fasting was used as means to prompt mercy (2 Sam. 12:22–23) or to attain forgiveness for sin, it was unnecessary. Jesus has released people from sin, healed diseases, and cast out demons without requiring any prior acts of devotion. Fasting that was done to humiliate oneself before God could also easily be perverted so that it exalted oneself before humans. Jesus rejects any religious behavior that is turned into a show to win the applause and admiration of others (Matt. 6:1–6, 16–18). If fasting is used as a badge of one's piety (Luke 18:11–12), it is inappropriate at a feast filled with sinners.

Jesus does not exclude fasting altogether. Fasting was also connected to sorrow for the loss of a loved one,[28] and the advent of the kingdom of God does not bring an end to mourning. Jesus' own death will be a cause of sorrow, but his death and resurrection change the meaning of death. We are not to grieve like those without hope (1 Thess. 4:13). Consequently, the disciples of Jesus as a whole are not to be characterized by their mourning but by their joy, not only during his earthly ministry but today as well.

Christians are not to be weighed down by sadness, the burden of sin, or the dread of death. They are not to be killjoys, who frown on the convivial fellowship with tax collectors and sinners and who cannot lift their arms in praise. Christian spirituality is not a ball and chain that keeps the spirit from soaring. The exultation over the coming of the one who forgives sins and feasts with sinners and the glad expectation of the glory to come is to affect our mood and outlook on life. One need only check the references to joy in the New Testament to see how it pervades the experience of Christians, even in the direst of circumstances.

Keeping the Sabbath. The Sabbath controversies show how God's purposes for humankind are frustrated when circumscribed by a bunch of rules from pettifogging religionists. God commands that the Sabbath be kept holy, so what is one to do? The negative framing of the answer, "You do not work," raised another question, What precisely is to be classified as work? The Pharisees represented those who tended to amplify ways one could violate this command.

The *Mishnah* contains two tractates that address complex Sabbath regulations: *Shabbat*, which seeks to define what constitutes a burden, and *Erubin*, which seeks to define what constitutes a Sabbath resting place and how to expand it. In *Mishnah Hagiga* 1:8, it is admitted: "The rules about the sabbath,

---

27. According to the *Psalms of Solomon* 3:6–8, the righteous one can atone "for [sins of] ignorance by fasting and humbling his soul, and the Lord will cleanse every devout person and his house." In the *Apocalypse of Elijah* 1:21–22, fasting is said to release sin, heal diseases, and cast out demons, and is effective even up to the throne of God.

28. See 1 Sam. 31:13; 2 Sam. 1:12; 3:35; 12:21; 1 Kings 21:27; Est. 4:3; Pss. 35:13–14, 69:10; Isa. 58:5.

festal offerings and sacrilege are as mountains hanging by a hair, for Scripture is scanty and the rules many." A midrash to Psalm 50:3 assumes that the closer one gets to God, the more exacting one needs to be in observing restrictions. The fondness for negatives and casuistry (for example, one could help someone in need only if he were in mortal danger or tie a knot only if it could be untied with one hand) is easily caricatured. One should also be aware that rabbinic literature is sprinkled with beautiful homilies about the joys and splendor of the Sabbath, which share a spiritual kinship with Jesus' view.[29] Church history reveals that the Pharisees did not have a corner on the market of harsh legalism.

For Jews in the time of Jesus, the Sabbath was more than just a matter of obedience to rules. Sabbath observance was regarded as a way to honor the holiness of Yahweh (Ex. 20:8–11; Deut. 5:12–15). It also marked the joyful entry into sacred time, the time of the beginning before human work. The Sabbath "was a sanctuary in time."[30] It was also regarded as a sign of Israel's sanctification among all the nations. Its observance made Israel distinct as a nation, bolstered Jewish identity over against others, and served as a bulwark against assimilation to pagan culture.[31] For Jews in the Diaspora, keeping the Sabbath was a profession of faith,[32] a national identity marker. In Justin Martyr's *Dialogue with Trypho the Jew* (sec. 10), Rabbi Trypho is amazed at the Christians' way of life in the world. He says:

> But this is what we are most at a loss about: that you professing to be pious, and supposing yourselves better than others, are not in any particular separated from them, and do not alter your mode of living from the nations, in that you observe no festivals or sabbaths, and do not have the rite of circumcision.

The Pharisees are inflamed here by Jesus' disciples' violation of Sabbath regulations; Jesus is grieved by their hardened hearts. To make his point with his religious critics, he is deliberately provocative in the second episode. He

---

29. *Mekilta Shabbata* 1 to Ex. 31:13.

30. Abraham Joshua Heschel, *The Sabbath: Its Meaning for Modern Man* (New York: Farrar, Straus and Giroux, 1951), 29.

31. George B. Caird and L. D. Hurst (*New Testament Theology* [Oxford: Clarendon, 1994], 386–87) comment, "The Sabbath was therefore the chief, almost the sole, safeguard against the lapse of Jews into beliefs and practices of their pagan neighbours, and to take away this safeguard meant the end of Judaism. The Pharisees believed they were fighting for the very existence of Israel."

32. The strict observance of the Sabbath by Jews was so proverbial that the emperor Augustus said that not even a Jew fasts on the Sabbath as diligently as he did on a certain day (Suetonius, *Augustus* 76.2).

could just as easily have healed the man with the withered arm in privacy after the synagogue crowd had gone home. The aim is not to goad his opponents further but to confront them with two clashing views of how to be properly religious. He forces them to confront the real issue that is at stake: Is God for health or for death? If God is for health, how can he deplore the working of good in people's lives even on a holy day? Which is more important, rules or people? Jesus stresses the universal aspect of the Sabbath ("the sabbath is made for humankind," 2:27 NRSV) and ignores any other significance it might have.

The Pharisees' approach treats ritual and institution as key. If the law contains any ambiguities, it must be made specific so that one may know precisely what must be done at all times and who is guilty of an infraction. Such an approach easily veers into a kind of slavery (Gal. 4:10; Col. 2:16)—religion for religion's sake. And the pietist can become like an ill-taught piano student who plays all the right notes but fails to make music, like an actor in a B movie who woodenly recites a memorized script but who does not carry any conviction, or like a dancer who carefully counts the steps but never cuts loose to dance. A fondness for negatives and a long checklist of rules, particularly for other people,[33] can make religious life a burdensome ordeal that never sings nor exults, and religious duties an obstacle course that weeds out weakling sinners.

The real danger of a rigid legalism is that it can delude one into thinking that God is satisfied when one is a stickler for religious details, even if one is merciless to others. It can turn the devout into Reverend Thwackums, the preacher whose name reveals his character in Henry Fielding's novel, *Tom Jones*. Devotion to principle can outweigh concern for individuals and can become deadly in more ways than one, as the ensuing plot against Jesus reveals. Pascal said, "Men never do evil so completely and cheerfully as when they do it from religious conviction" (*Pensées*, 894). Christians have been known to be no less devoted to what they believe is the truth and have been just as willing to bludgeon anyone who violates it.

Jesus' approach gives the personal aspect priority. He does not first ask, "What are the rules and what do people think I should do?" but "Who needs to be helped?" He presumes that religion and its institutions are not ends in themselves. God gave the law for the benefit of humankind. Its intention is summed up in love for the neighbor, which is worth more than all the burnt

---

33. In "The Devil's Dictionary," Ambrose Bierce defines the Christian as "one who believes that the New Testament is a divinely inspired book admirably suited to the spiritual need of his neighbor," and the Christian version of the fourth commandment is, "Remember the seventh day to make thy neighbor keep it wholly."

sacrifices heaped together (see 12:32–33). One cannot interpret the law correctly unless one refers back to God's intention in giving the law. Jesus' teaching makes clear that Sabbath observance does not require that one be loveless or merciless simply to sustain its ceremonial provisions. He is not being cavalier with the law. As Willimon states it: "The clash with authority is not over the rules but over *who* rules."[34] On the contrary, Jesus consistently carries out the law when it conforms to God's intentions (1:44; 3:4; 7:8–13; 10:3–9; 12:29–31). He asserts that his followers need not concern themselves about appearances of being irreligious or fear condemnation of the slightest transgression when they are carrying out their greater tasks for God, doing God's will.

One should be cautious in using this passage to define what is permissible or impermissible for Christians on a Sunday. That is not its purpose. One needs to look elsewhere for such guidance. The controversies over the Sabbath are intended to affirm that Jesus is the Lord of the law and to expose the sinister wickedness of his opponents. The early Christians possibly used this teaching to attest that Jesus sets us free from the tyranny of the requirement to observe "special days and months and seasons and years" (Gal. 4:10), and many felt no obligation to keep the Sabbath.

As the Jews expanded the significance of the Sabbath day from its association with the mystery of creation and connected it to an event in history, God's deliverance of Israel from Egypt, Christians changed the day to celebrate Christ's resurrection (Rev. 1:10).[35] They venerated an event[36] and observed it not with rest but with worship. Paul acknowledges that differences existed among the Christians, however. "One man considers one day more sacred than another; another man considers every day alike" (Rom. 14:5). He insists that one not judge another in how one lives out one's commitment to God. God loves and blesses both. One is without guilt if that person has thought through what he or she does ("each one should be fully convinced in his own mind," 14:5), is not simply complying to external pressures, and intends to honor or give thanks to the Lord in what is done.

It is no wonder that Jesus' attitude toward sinners, fasting, and the Sabbath was threatening to the pietists. It seems to leave little room for outward religious performance—their specialty. In taking these passages into our

---

34. William H. Willimon, "Lord of the Sabbath," *Christian Century* 108 (1991): 515.

35. For the debate on Sabbath and Sunday, see Donald A. Carson, ed., *From Sabbath to Lord's Day: A Biblical, Historical, and Theological Investigation* (Grand Rapids: Zondervan, 1982); and Tamara C. Eskenazi, Daniel J. Harrington, and William H. Shea, eds., *The Sabbath in Jewish and Christian Traditions* (New York: Crossroad, 1991).

36. Compare Ex. 20:11, which recalls God's rest on the seventh day of creation, and Deut. 5:15, which connects the Sabbath to the exodus from Egypt.

contemporary setting, we will find that the opposition has not changed. Many today will be no less upset if their sanctified prejudices and cherished customs are challenged.

WHEN ONE LOOKS again at the scenes in this unit, one can ask the question: What does not belong in this picture? The answer becomes clear: categorizing and excluding sinners, fasting and gloom, and religious customs that obstruct doing good for others. What does belong is reaching out to sinners, joy, and helping others

Reaching out to sinners. Other religions are the result of a human search for God; Christianity presents itself as God's search for humans—even those the world deems the most unworthy. The toll collectors and sinners are in as much need of healing and forgiveness as the leper and the paralytic. The surprise of the suddenness of Jesus' call of Levi to follow him is magnified by the shock that he would call such a one as this.

This incident exposes a persistent tendency among God's people throughout history to exclude and to write off others we classify as irredeemable. We are predisposed to believe that those chosen by God are those who are most like us, and we tend to forget that Jesus went to those who were despised and unclean to win them for God's rule. William Carey met a similar resistance when he raised the question at the Minister's Fraternal of the Northhampton Association in 1787 of whether the commission given to the disciples to go and make disciples of the nations was still binding. The infamous response of John Ryland Sr. was no: "Sit down, young man. You are an enthusiast! When God pleases to convert the heathen, He will do it without consulting you or me." I have known many a young minister anxious to reach out to their community who were crushed by the stone wall of resistance to "these kind of people" by their church members.

Many Christians today do not recognize that they harbor the very same attitude as these first-century Pharisees. We sing "Amazing grace ... that saved a wretch like me," but we have in mind only our kind of wretches. It is too amazing for us that the same grace is extended to save those whom we believe truly deserve punishment. Outsiders, however, are quick to discern it. Ambrose Bierce, in his *Devil's Dictionary*, defined an "evangelist" as "a bearer of good tidings, particularly (in a religious sense) such as assure us of our own salvation and the damnation of our neighbors." Many still believe that everyone has his or her place and expect them to stay within accepted boundaries.

I am aware of a student in seminary who worked as a mission pastor in a rent-by-the-week trailer park. Bringing the thirty or more children who participated in the Sunday school to functions at the sponsoring church met with jaundiced eye and a quick plan to make sure that the kids were segregated from the children of "regular" members. In another case, the outreach program of one church consisted of a community clambake, charging $30.00 per person. The get-together ensured, perhaps unconsciously, that only the right kind of people, who could afford a such a high-priced ticket, would show up and maybe join the congregation. The church wanted to reach out to others, but they only wanted to reach out to "good" prospects.

Modern parishioners would probably be no less agitated than the Pharisees if their pastor violated their unwritten social conventions. They might tolerate their pastor hanging out with the wrong crowd in honky-tonks if they were convinced that this was a fleeting bid to witness to them. It would be something else, however, if the pastor made a regular habit of it, or worse, invited the madam of the local brothel or the folks who gather every night at the tavern for Sunday dinner in the parsonage. It is one thing to go to them to witness to them; it is quite another to treat them as if they were in some way respectable and acceptable, persons whom God loves as much as the righteous (healthy) who need no repentance. It creates religious confusion so that one cannot distinguish the righteous from the unrighteous. It scares those who are convinced that society will crumble if these barriers are not maintained.

Yet this is precisely what Jesus did, and by so doing he makes it clear that one cannot win people with whom one is not willing to eat. Jesus' preaching creates a new playing field. The old categories by which sinners are classified are breaking down with the advent of the kingdom of God in the ministry of Jesus. No longer are the righteous those who scrupulously obey traditions derived from their interpretation of the law. They have made out the test, graded it themselves, given themselves an A+, and flunked everybody else. The test is flunked by God and discarded. The issue now is whether one accepts or spurns the good news, follows or rejects Jesus. Jesus says that he has "not come to call the righteous, but sinners" (2:17). By the end of the Gospel it becomes plain that there were no righteous to call. All, including the inner circle of disciples, have fallen short of the glory of God.

The religiosity of the Pharisees is therefore something we must guard against. It is inward and upward and results in a narcissistic selfishness— God is only interested in us and not the likes of them. This stuffy attitude is captured in Dean Jonathan Swift's ditty:

We are God's chosen few
All others will be damned
There's room enough in hell for you
We can't have heaven crammed.

The direction of Jesus' ministry is downward and outward and implies that the church must bring Jesus to people, not simply people to Jesus. This spirit was captured in the motto of John Wesley, who said, "The whole world is my parish." Leonard observes that Wesley

> moved out or was thrown out of the sedate and aristocratic Anglican churches of his day and "consented to be more vile," proclaiming the gospel in highways and hedges. "Field preaching," it was called, standing in English meadows and markets, on hillsides and in city squares with a gospel to and for the disenfranchised whom the "decent people" had written off as incapable of moral transformation or spiritual experience. Many from the poor and working classes believed and were changed and Wesley scandalized Anglicans by recruiting his first lay preachers from the lower classes.[37]

It is the spirit captured in a story told by Tony Campolo. He had flown into Honolulu and was unable to sleep, so he ventured into an all-night diner, where he overheard a group of prostitutes talking. One mentioned to her friends that the next day was her thirty-ninth birthday. Another replied scornfully, "What do you want? A birthday party?" She retreated into her defensive shell: "I've never had one in my whole life. Why should I expect one now?" It struck Campolo that it would be a good idea to conspire with the owner of the diner to throw her a surprise party the next night. A cake was baked, and all was prepared. The cries of "Happy Birthday!" from her small group of friends and this stranger left her stunned. She was shocked that anyone would go to this much trouble just for her. She asked if she could take the cake home and then left with her prize. When she left, Campolo offered to pray and prayed for her salvation, for her life to change, and for God to be good to her.

The prayer startled the owner, who asked antagonistically, "You never told me you were a preacher. What kind of church do you belong to?" He responded that he belonged to a church that threw birthday parties for prostitutes at 3:30 in the morning.[38] The answer may meet with skepticism from outsiders: There is no church like that. It may meet with disdain from insiders: We would never do anything like that. But it parallels the kind of thing that Jesus did in reaching out to those who were lost and despised. "While we look for him among priests, he is among sinners. While we look for him

---

37. Bill. J. Leonard, *Way of God Across the Ages: Using Christian History in Preaching* (Greenville, N.C.: Smith and Helwys, 1991), 51–53.

38. Tony Campolo, *The Kingdom of God Is a Party* (Dallas: Word, 1990), 3–9.

among the free, he is a prisoner. While we look for him in glory, he is bleeding on the cross."[39]

Thomas Long tells of staying in a motel in a large city and finding a notice posted on the elevator door: "Party tonight! Room 210. 8:00 P.M. Everyone invited!" He imagined the odd assortment of people who might show up—tired salesmen, bored vacationers, weary travelers, and the curious, all looking for a break in their individual tedium and a little festivity and not wanting to be left out of something exciting. But the sign was a hoax, a practical joke. He thought it was too bad.

> For a brief moment, those of us staying at the motel were tantalized by the possibility that there just might be a party going on somewhere to which we were all invited—a party where it didn't make much difference who we were when we walked in the door, or what motivated us to come; a party we could come to out of boredom, loneliness, curiosity, responsibility, eagerness to be in fellowship, or simply out of a desire to come and see what was happening; a party where it didn't matter nearly as much what got us in the door, as what would happen to us after we arrived.[40]

This text announces that Jesus is willing to throw such a party, and it is not a hoax. Those who belong to his church should therefore be willing to do the same thing. Too often, however, the church is the one taking down the sign that invites one and all.

Joy versus gloom. Jesus' ministry is associated more with table fellowship, even feeding huge crowds in the desert, than with ascetic fasting. The question about fasting forces us to question the purposes of our religious rites and observances. Fasting or any other religious discipline does not elicit God's grace, forgiveness of sins, or acceptance. Any renunciation of the pleasures of earthly life as an attempt to gain favor with God or to achieve eternal life is to be rejected (see Col 2:16–23). Any observance that we do simply to conform to external rules imposed upon us—fasting because it is a certain season—is to be rejected. The calendar is not to rule our religious devotion. Fasting is only meaningful when it arises from concerns so deep that food does not matter, not when it is dictated by some rule book. All spiritual exertion that aims only at setting ourselves apart from and above others is to be rejected.

---

39. Gerald O'Collins, *Interpreting Jesus* (London: Geoffrey Chapman, 1983), 74, citing Carlos Alberto Libanto Christo.

40. Thomas G. Long, *Shepherd and Bathrobes* (Lima, Ohio: C. S. S. Publishing, 1987), 68–69.

If we fast to give to others (to put money into the Rice Bowl program to help hungry people, for example) or to try to free ourselves from our own self-centeredness, it is fine. In fact, fasting may help purge our souls of our consuming efforts to gratify ourselves all the time. One needs to remember, however, that one does not become a saint by fasting or by giving alms more than others or by any other activity that is associated with the Christian way of life. Only when these things are done with a heart filled with thankfulness for God's goodness can we offer real praise to God.

We should be mindful that the incident recorded in Mark occurs in a context of a joyous celebration and feasting together with others. One can fast alone, but one cannot celebrate alone! One goal of our religious observances should be to make commitment to God attractive to others.

Keeping the Lord's Day. Throughout the history of the church, Jesus' criterion of compassion has been less influential in the observance of the Lord's Day than the stern and rigid code that characterized the Pharisees' opposition to Jesus. The dour religiosity that marked the observance of the Lord's Day of a bygone era is depicted in Robert Graves' poem "The Boy Out of Church":

> I do not love the Sabbath,
> The soapsuds and the starch
> The troops of solemn people
> Who to salvation march.

Mr. Arthur Clennam, in Charles Dickens's novel *Little Dorrit*, bitterly recalls how as a child he hated Sunday as the day when he was threatened with perdition. "He was marched to chapel by a picquet of teachers three times a day morally handcuffed to another boy, and when he would willingly have bartered two meals of indigestible sermon for another ounce or two of inferior mutton at his scanty dinner. . . . There was a legion of Sundays, all days of unserviceable bitterness and mortification . . . ."

That austerity is in little evidence today as Sunday blue laws are repealed throughout the nation. Advertisers tell us that weekends are made for different brands of beer or sports events, and many take advantage of a wide variety of diversions during the weekend. What they miss is a time of spiritual renewal. We live in a world that knows only itself and the scores of our modern-day circus games but that does not know God. While some have connected a neglect of the Sabbath or the Lord's Day to the collapse of vibrant Christianity in some nations, the church experienced remarkable growth in the first centuries when there was no legal day of rest; Christians had to worship before or after work. We do not need to reestablish a rigorous observance like Nehemiah, who stationed soldiers over the city gates to enforce obedience (Neh. 13:15–22). We do not need to impose a slavish obedience to Sabbath laws on a world that does not honor God even though it would be beneficial, cutting down on pollution, restoring a sense of rhythm to life, and giving people a chance to catch their breath. We do need, however, to recapture Jesus' liberating vision of the Sabbath (Lord's Day) as a gift (2:27) and as a time for doing good (3:4).

The Christian Sunday began as a day of worship, celebrating the historical event of the resurrection of Jesus, the foundation of our faith (1 Cor. 15:17). It became, like the Sabbath, a day of rest. A day of rest is a gift. Philo, a prominent and learned member of the Jewish community in Alexandria in the first century, defended the Jews' custom of not working on the Sabbath. He argued that it was not because of any indolence on their part. The object was

> to give man relaxation from continuous and unending toil and by refreshing their bodies with a regularly calculated system of remissions to send them out renewed to their old activities. For a breathing spell enables not merely ordinary people but athletes also to collect their strength with a stronger force behind them to undertake promptly and patiently each of the tasks set before them.[41]

In this century, Abraham Heschel profoundly expresses this value of the Sabbath for our technological age. It is a day when we can celebrate "time rather than space." Our modern technological society can boast of our conquest of space, but we have not conquered the "essential ingredient of existence": time. It is the realm of existence where "the goal is not to have but to be, not to own but to give, not to control but to share, not to subdue but to be in accord."[42] Many spend all their lives acquiring material possessions but shrink from sacred moments. Everyone needs a time to be able to lay aside the feverish pursuit of success, trying to "wring profit from the earth" or to amass more goods. Heschel concludes:

> Six days a week we live under the tyranny of things of space; on the Sabbath we try to become attuned to *holiness in time*. It is a day on which we are called upon to share in what is eternal in time, to turn from the results of creation to the mystery of creation; from the world of creation to the creation of the world.[43]

---

41. Philo, *On the Special Laws* 2.60.
42. Heschel, *The Sabbath*, 1.
43. Ibid., 10.

In our culture we have lost this gift of a day when we can reconnect with the holy and recharge our spiritual batteries. Our daily struggles may produce economic triumphs but can make our lives a spiritual wasteland. Lily Tomlin said the trouble with the rat race is that even if you win, you are still a rat. We need time for ennobling our souls and must enjoy this gift. One must be cautious, however. The incident recorded in Mark reveals how a gift can be nullified by rules that saddle others with additional burdens rather than unchaining them from their load.

The strict observance of the Sabbath served to distinguish Jews from Gentiles in their world. Christians are also not to be conformed to the world around them, and observing a day of worship and rest is one way they distinguish themselves from others and give witness to their faith. Instead of heeding the calls to bow down to the gods of materialism or to play with their pile of recreational toys, Christians set aside time to worship their God and celebrate their faith.[44]

The observance of days and seasons is not to be the sole element that distinguishes Christians from others. What Jesus affirms is that the Sabbath is for doing good. Jesus never criticizes the law that requires the Sabbath to be treated as holy. He simply affirms that the Sabbath can become an occasion to do good rather than simply a time to refrain from work. The criterion is mercy, not ritual. The question then is not whether something is or is not allowed, but whether or not what we do helps or hinders those who are in need. To do evil is always prohibited, regardless of the day of the week. To do good is always required, regardless of the day of the week.[45] Christians should be distinguished by their doing good. As one outsider observed about the early church: "See how these Christians love each other!"

---

44. David T. Williams, "The Sabbath: Mark of Distinction," *Themelios* 14 (1989): 98.
45. Lohmeyer, *Markusevangelium*, 68.

Mark 3:7–35

❧

J ESUS WITHDREW WITH his disciples to the lake, and a large
crowd from Galilee followed. ⁸When they heard all he was
doing, many people came to him from Judea, Jerusalem,
Idumea, and the regions across the Jordan and around Tyre
and Sidon. ⁹Because of the crowd he told his disciples to have
a small boat ready for him, to keep the people from crowding
him. ¹⁰For he had healed many, so that those with diseases
were pushing forward to touch him. ¹¹Whenever the evil spirits saw him, they fell down before him and cried out, "You are
the Son of God." ¹²But he gave them strict orders not to tell
who he was.

¹³Jesus went up on a mountainside and called to him those
he wanted, and they came to him. ¹⁴He appointed twelve—
designating them apostles—that they might be with him and
that he might send them out to preach ¹⁵and to have authority
to drive out demons. ¹⁶These are the twelve he appointed:
Simon (to whom he gave the name Peter); ¹⁷James son of
Zebedee and his brother John (to them he gave the name
Boanerges, which means Sons of Thunder); ¹⁸Andrew, Philip,
Bartholomew, Matthew, Thomas, James son of Alphaeus,
Thaddaeus, Simon the Zealot ¹⁹and Judas Iscariot, who
betrayed him.

²⁰Then Jesus entered a house, and again a crowd gathered,
so that he and his disciples were not even able to eat. ²¹When
his family heard about this, they went to take charge of him,
for they said, "He is out of his mind."

²²And the teachers of the law who came down from
Jerusalem said, "He is possessed by Beelzebub! By the prince
of demons he is driving out demons."

²³So Jesus called them and spoke to them in parables:
"How can Satan drive out Satan? ²⁴If a kingdom is divided
against itself, that kingdom cannot stand. ²⁵If a house is
divided against itself, that house cannot stand. ²⁶And if Satan
opposes himself and is divided, he cannot stand; his end has
come. ²⁷In fact, no one can enter a strong man's house and
carry off his possessions unless he first ties up the strong man.
Then he can rob his house. ²⁸I tell you the truth, all the sins

and blasphemies of men will be forgiven them. ²⁹But whoever blasphemes against the Holy Spirit will never be forgiven; he is guilty of an eternal sin."

³⁰He said this because they were saying, "He has an evil spirit."

³¹Then Jesus' mother and brothers arrived. Standing outside, they sent someone in to call him. ³²A crowd was sitting around him, and they told him, "Your mother and brothers are outside looking for you."

³³"Who are my mother and my brothers?" he asked.

³⁴Then he looked at those seated in a circle around him and said, "Here are my mother and my brothers! ³⁵Whoever does God's will is my brother and sister and mother."

IN THIS SECTION, Jesus' demanding pace of ministry continues as the crowds still flock to him in droves to be healed and as the demons still cringe in alarm (3:7–12). He creates the Twelve, who will help extend his ministry of preaching and exorcisms and who will be prepared to supplant the current leadership of Israel (3:13–19). Members of Jesus' family try to curtail his ministry, and teachers of the law from Jerusalem engage in a smear campaign in an attempt to check his surging popularity. Jesus' response to them insinuates that they are guilty of committing the unpardonable sin of blaspheming against the Spirit of God, who is working in and through him (3:20–35). Those who have assumed jurisdiction over teaching and wisdom in Israel demonstrate themselves to be spiritually unfit.

The official challenge of the teachers of the law to Jesus compels the reader to decide who the true leaders of Israel are. Jesus' announcement in 3:35 also raises the question of who are the true people of God, the members of the family of the Messiah.

Summary of Jesus' Ministry (3:7–12)

JESUS RETREATS FROM the threat posed by the Pharisees and Herodians (3:6) and returns to the sea with his disciples (3:7, 9).[1] Mark's brief summary of Jesus' mission reiterates themes from the previous sections: his extraordinary magnetism, his amazing power to heal, and the demons' nervous recognition of him.

---

1. Swete (*Mark*, 54) contends that the open beach was safer than the narrow streets of a village.

Jesus may withdraw to elude the conspirators, but he cannot escape his immense popularity.[2] Throngs flocked to John the Baptist from all Judea and Jerusalem (1:5), but they come to Jesus from even more far-flung regions: Galilee, Judea, Jerusalem, Idumea, across the Jordan, and Tyre and Sidon (3:8)—a geographical area that matches that of the Israel of old (see Isa. 43:5–6). The sick and downcast no longer wait for his touch but now throw themselves upon him. This exuberant crush of people stands in stark contrast to the grim verdict of the teachers of the law from Jerusalem and also explains why they are so worried about Jesus. His surging popularity threatens to undermine their leverage with the crowds.

The great crowds (emphasized twice, 3:7, 8) converge on him because of what they have heard, but it is fair to suggest that Mark believes that they are more interested in what "he does" (3:8) than what he says. Crowds by their very nature are seldom able to grasp truth. Only the demons and the reader have access to the secret information of who Jesus really is and by what power he is working. Nevertheless, the crowds *are hearing* (3:8). People respond by hearing, which makes the sending out of disciples to preach so crucial (3:14). The word about Jesus will be broadcast by authorized representatives and will reach even wider audiences. The question of how they hear is to be taken up in 4:1–34.

The unclean spirits continue to know him immediately, fall before him in surrender,[3] and blurt out his identity. Unlike the demon who hailed him as the "Holy One of God" (1:24), their cry of recognition acknowledges him as "the Son of God" and more closely echoes the heavenly voice at the baptism (1:11). The voices of demons are always off key. The demons utter orthodox confession but are by no means "well pleased" by the presence of the Son of God. Mark does not narrate what effect, if any, their cries have on the crowds or the disciples in the story. He is more interested in the secrecy motif, as Jesus continues to prevent them from making him known.

More is at stake than an attempt to avert a premature disclosure of his identity.[4] The ravings of demons can never be an agent of revelation. And his rebuke of the demons shows his power over them. In the first-century context, it would have been considered ominous for demons to shout out a name in recognition. The original readers would not necessarily assume that the demons were paying him homage, but instead might imagine that they were attempting to control him by pronouncing his divine name, thereby hoping

---

2. Jesus must make take precautions to escape in a boat in case they mob him (3:9). They swarm around his house so that he is unable even to eat (3:20), and he is almost trapped in his own home.

3. The crowds "fall upon him" (*epipipto*) and the demons "fall before him" (*prospipto*).

4. See, for example, Swete, *Mark*, 57.

to impede his deliverance of the persons in their clutches. The translation, "he gave them strict orders not to tell who he was," is too mild. Jesus is not merely putting them under a gag order. The verb *epitimao* is frequently translated "rebuke," but even this does not adequately capture its meaning.[5] He also "rebukes" the wind and sea to "be still" (4:39), and the muzzling of the demons, like the quelling of the storm, is a sign that Jesus has overmastered them. He therefore both expels and silences the demons with a word.

Creating the Twelve (3:13–19)

THE SCENE SHIFTS from the sea to a mountain. The huge multitude is thinned as Jesus invites "those he wanted" to come with him. This call creates a distinction between those who follow after him desperately seeking healing, those who are only caught up in the spectacle of these strange events, and those who are summoned to follow after him as disciples with a particular task. Jesus "appointed twelve" out of this group who came to him. The verb *poieo* means "to make" or "to create" and recalls biblical themes. The Lord "appointed" Moses and Aaron to lead Israel (1 Sam. 12:6), and Moses "appointed" able men as heads over the people (Ex. 18:25). The initiative in creating and naming the Twelve belongs to Jesus, as it belongs to God in creating, naming, and choosing humans (Isa. 43:1, the Lord "created" and "summoned by name").[6] The Twelve have symbolic significance, pointing to the restoration of the twelve tribes of Israel, and Jesus stands over them as leader.[7] Implicit in the choice of the Twelve is a renunciation of the powers that be in Jerusalem.

The list of the names of the Twelve gives us scant clues as to their status, background, or religious training, but Jesus gives the first three striking nicknames. Simon is given the name Peter (*petros*, meaning "rock"), and James

---

5. See Howard Clark Kee, "The Terminology of Mark's Exorcism Stories," *NTS* 14 (1968): 232–46; J. Kilgallen, "The Messianic Secret and Mark's Purposes," *BTB* 7 (1977): 60. This view is challenged by Guelich (*Mark*, 148–49), who contends that the demons are not in a power struggle with Jesus and that the problem stated by Mark is that they knew Jesus to be the Son of God (1:34; 3:11) and that he did not want them to make it known. The dramatic of revelation demons, no matter how doctrinally correct their confession might be, does not divulge who Jesus is. His self-giving death on a cross reveals him to be the Son of God (15:39).

6. See John 15:16; cf. Isa. 49:1; Jer. 1:5; Amos 7:15; Gal. 1:15.

7. See Num. 1:1–19, 44, where God commands Moses to take a man from each tribe "to help [him]" (1:4) as representatives of the "heads of the clans of Israel" (1:16). The men were registered according to their clans (1:18) to represent their ancestral house (1:44) in military service. The importance of the symbolic significance of twelve can be seen in the church's felt need to replace Judas (Acts 1:15–26).

On the symbolism of the Twelve, see E. P. Sanders, *Jesus and Judaism* (Philadelphia: Fortress, 1985), 106.

and John, formerly introduced as the sons of Zebedee, are called the "Sons of Thunder." One can only speculate what occasioned these names or what they reveal about these men—their character, their faith, or their future roles?[8] Judas comes last in the list and is identified as the betrayer, a name the church, not Jesus, bestowed on him.

The mission of the Twelve is twofold. The Gospel of Matthew ends with Jesus' promise to be with his disciples until the end of the age (Matt. 28:20). By contrast, Mark stresses the disciples' task of being "with [Jesus]" (Mark 3:14; see Acts 1:21–22). What does that mean? Most important, it denotes the Twelve as the witnesses to his ministry, who have learned from him and are qualified to pass on and authenticate the traditions about him (see Luke 1:2). Peter, James, and John, who comprise an inner circle, are with Jesus at momentous points in the Gospel: when he raises Jairus's daughter to life (5:37), when he is transfigured on the mountain (9:2–13), and when he prays in Gethsemane (14:33). The task of being with Jesus is one that is harder than it might first appear. The Twelve will have to learn that there is a difference between hanging around with Jesus and truly being *with* him. The latter means that they must follow wherever he leads and share the toil of the ministry, the harassment of the crowds (3:20; 6:31–33), and the same bitter draught of suffering (10:39).

The Twelve are also created because God requires human cooperation to touch, enlighten, and heal others. Their second task is to fulfill the commission of extending Jesus' work by preaching and casting out demons. Their companionship with him is to lead to service that benefits others. They are not merely on the receiving end of this outbreak of power but are to become channels by which it touches others. One should note, however, that the task of preaching and exorcising demons is not limited to the Twelve in Mark. The cured Gerasene demoniac is told to preach to his family in the Decapolis what the Lord has done for him (5:19–20; see 7:36). Others—one is identified only as "a man" who does not follow the disciples—are reported to be successful in casting out demons in Jesus' name (9:38–39). The unique function of the Twelve that is not granted to others (see 5:18–19) is to be with Jesus.

The Reaction of Jesus' Family and the Pharisees (3:20–35)

MARK REPORTS TWO other groups besides the awestruck crowds who have heard of Jesus' deeds and who come to him (3:8, 21), but they come with

---

8. It was assumed in this culture that "as a man is named, so is he" (Hans Bietenhard, "ὄνομα," *TDNT* 5:254). Boanerges means nothing in Greek and is probably a transliteration from Aramaic. It could mean "sons of feeling," which implies that they are excitable, or "sons of anger," which implies that they are angry young men (see Luke 9:54).

quite different designs. Jesus' family intrudes to round him up, not to rally around him. They are intent on silencing him, presumably to squelch any further unwanted attention from the populace or the authorities. They may be spurred by the noble but misguided desire to protect him from danger or, less nobly, to salvage the family reputation. The scribal authorities from Jerusalem come with the ignoble intention of defaming Jesus and sabotaging his movement. Both groups receive a stunning reproof.

This segment is the first example of the Markan technique of bracketing (intercalation or "sandwiching"), where the narration begins with one story but is interrupted by another before it is concluded. In 3:20–21, Jesus' family goes out to seize him because they say "he is out of his mind." Their action breaks off with the description in 3:22–30 of teachers of the law who come down from Jerusalem, claiming that Jesus is possessed by Beelzebub,[9] and of Jesus' rebuttal of the charge. In 3:31–35, the camera returns to Jesus' mother and brothers, who arrive and call for him; and Jesus reinterprets what family means. This bracketing fills in time in the narrative, in this case between the family's departure and arrival; but, more importantly, the technique allows the two separate stories to make a similar point.[10] Both Jesus' closest relations and the theological specialists from Jerusalem offer mistaken speculation about Jesus (cf. "they said," 3:21–22); ironically, neither has any inkling of the truth. The insertion of the Beelzebub accusation between the bid to curb Jesus' ministry makes the point that any attempt to derail or redirect his mission is as serious a sin of defaming him as Satan might do. "To avert Jesus from his mission is satanic," as Peter will abruptly discover later in the narrative (8:33).[11]

Jesus' mother and his brothers are not making a friendly visit but want to "take charge of him." The same verb (*krateo*) means "to seize forcibly" elsewhere in Mark (6:17; 12:12; 14:1, 44, 46, 49, 51). They are left to cool their heels outside as Jesus dissociates himself from their authority. Jesus' circle of intimates consists of those whose first allegiance is to do the will of God, and he adopts them as his brothers, sisters, and mothers. His biological family,

---

9. The origin of the term *Beelzebub* is vague, but Mark clearly understands him to be "the prince of demons."

10. Other examples occur in 5:21–43; 6:7–31; 11:12–25; 14:1–11; 14:53–72. Paul J. Achtemeier ("Mark As Interpreter of the Jesus Tradition," *Int* 32 [1978]: 346) writes: "By bracketing one tradition within another, he tells us he thinks that they share some point, clearer, usually, in one of them than the other." It clarifies their message more sharply or has a rhetorical effect, such as heightening the dramatic tension, creating irony, or adding emphasis. See also James R. Edwards, "Markan Sandwiches: The Significance of Interpolations in Markan Narratives," *NovT* 31 (1989): 193–216.

11. Edwards, "Markan Sandwiches," 210.

who "call" and "are looking for" him, oppose the will of God without realizing it and become outsiders.

Jesus' response to the visit from his family would have been a shocker because it runs counter to the received wisdom of the age. The family was the basis of social and economic life and the source of one's identity. In the first-century Mediterranean world, an individual's identity was basically that of a member of a group (dyadic personal identity). The genealogies and laws relating to family life in the Scriptures show the importance of membership in a family or clan (and village). In the Old Testament, "life" is used almost interchangeably with "family." One's family was one's life, and to reject family or to be cast out of the family was to lose one's life (see Luke 14:26).

But Jesus affirms that life under God is not defined by relationships in a biological family, which was primarily geared for the preservation of the family line, its wealth, and its honor (see Sir. 26:19–21). One's ultimate devotion is owed to God, who is head of a new divine family, and becoming a member of this family is open to all persons regardless of race, class, or gender. The only requirement is that they share Jesus' commitment to God. When Jesus asks, "Who are my mother and my brothers?" it strikes us as a rude disregard of the feelings of his family (see also Luke 11:27–28), but it would have been a comfort to those first Christians who lost their families because of their loyalty to Christ (see Matt. 10:35–39; Luke 12:51–53). They can be cheered that they are not without family but have become a part of a greater family of faith (see Mark 10:28–30). The setting in which grave charges are leveled against Jesus indicates, however, that becoming a member of this new family has its costs. Devotion to him is likely to bring abuse and persecution.

The scene shifts to irate teachers of the law from Jerusalem. Those in power in the holy city must have thought that the rumors regarding this popular teacher, preacher, and healer warranted sending deputies to investigate and to debunk any aura of holiness surrounding Jesus' ministry. He comes from outside the system, which can only create alarm and resentment for those inside, and these critics do not plot in hushed secrecy but go publicly on the attack. They take for granted that Jesus is able to cast out demons successfully,[12] but they insist that his success results from a special relationship to Satan, not God. He has Beelzebub (3:22); he has an evil spirit (3:30).

On the one hand, people frequently attribute to Satan what they fear or do not understand. The teachers of the law may have concluded that one who flouts hallowed traditions and who does not kowtow to their authority could

---

12. Mark implies that they are quite unable to drive out unclean spirits (1:27).

only be an undercover agent for Satan. On the other hand, they may be venomously attempting to undermine Jesus by branding him as the devil's spawn.[13] The latter seems to be the case since Jesus warns them against blaspheming the Spirit. The religious experts do not allow as a possibility what the demons themselves avow and experience: This one is the Son of God, empowered by the Spirit. They are partially correct that Jesus' ministry has to do with the kingdom of Satan, but they balk at admitting the obvious, that it has to do with its collapse, not its advance.

Jesus no longer responds to opponents with direct statements (2:10, 28) but speaks to them in parables (3:28), which draw out the absurdity of their accusation and open the way to the truth. Since exorcisms bring healing and not harm, Jesus asks if they really think that a malignant power would cooperate in widespread deeds of mercy and grant authority to another to decimate its minions. If their accusation is correct, the demonic empire is either crumbling from a conflict between warring factions engaged in some takeover plot, or Satan is irrationally trying to do in himself. If Jesus does not work by Satan's power, however, another explanation is at hand: that a stronger one has bound the strong man and is pillaging his house.[14] What is happening is not the result of a civil war within Satan's ranks but a direct onslaught from outside.

This parable is an allegory. The strong one is Satan. His house is his domain, the present world, which he seeks to hold secure. His vessels are those hapless victims whom he has taken captive. The stronger one is Jesus, who has come from God, invaded Satan's stronghold, and bound him.[15] The allegory prompts us to remember the prologue, where John announced that one who was more powerful than he would come. It turns out that he is also stronger than Satan. Mark did not describe in full detail the temptation in the desert, but clearly Jesus must have bound the strong man for him to be able to plunder his house now. The parable prompts one schooled in Scripture to remember the promise in Isaiah 49:24–25, that God himself will overcome the mighty one:

> Can plunder be taken from warriors,
>> or captives rescued from the fierce?
> But this is what the LORD says:

---

13. The same thing was said about John the Baptist (Matt. 11:18; Luke 7:33). The charge is ominous. According to later rabbinic tradition, Jesus was condemned to death for practicing sorcery and misleading the people (*b. Sanh.* 43a; 107b; *b. Sota* 47a; *t. Sabb.* 11:15; see also Justin, *Dial.* 69:7).

14. The emphasis is not on the strong man's ability to plunder but on the certainty that he will plunder.

15. The verb "to tie up" recurs in 5:3, where Mark narrates the inability of the townspeople "to bind" the so-called Gerasene demoniac even with chains.

"Yes, captives will be taken from warriors,
　　and plunder retrieved from the fierce;
I will contend with those who contend with you,
　　and your children I will save."

With the advent of the kingdom of God, the battle is being waged not just against the petty tyrants and their domains but against the kingdom of Satan, which has enslaved all humanity.

This encounter with the teachers of the law from Jerusalem marks a shift in Jesus' approach to his religious antagonists. The previous section reveals "that objective displays of the miraculous and public explanations were ineffective in persuading the Jewish religious-political leadership to side with Jesus."[16] The demonstrations of power and authority have only convinced them that he needs to be liquidated. Consequently, Jesus no longer offers them evidence to substantiate his claims, nor does he try to persuade them with argument from Scripture. He withdraws from the Pharisees' sphere of influence and does not enter a synagogue again until he returns to his home town of Nazareth in 6:2.[17]

Although he withdraws, from now on he will give no quarter to his opponents whenever they confront him. Geddert compares Jesus' response to questions raised by the Pharisees in 2:23—28 and in 7:5—13 about the deportment of his disciples to point up the contrast in his tactics. The inquiries are similar: "Why are [your disciples] doing what is unlawful on the Sabbath?" (2:24); "Why don't your disciples live according to the tradition of the elders instead of eating their food with 'unclean' hands?"(7:5). In the first incident, Jesus gives an explanation from Scripture (2:25—26). In the second, he ignores their question and instead uses Scripture to lambaste them as hypocrites and lampoons their whole tradition as perverting God's commands (7:6—13). He gives an explanation only to the crowds and the disciples, who come when he calls them (7:14—23).

For their part, the Pharisees have become allies with the secular Herodians in hatching plots against Jesus and have relinquished any "right to be treated as honest inquirers."[18] Their hardened hearts also cause them to align with Satan. Jesus will no longer attempt to coax these leaders to faith. Instead, he will invest his energies with those who have demonstrated a willingness to follow him. But his approach to those who are not overtly hostile also changes. Jesus modifies the approach of providing "objective proofs" and

---

16. Geddert, *Watchwords*, 42.

17. Ibid., 44.

18. Ibid., 43. In 11:27—12:44, Jesus no longer even defends himself against charges by his opponents but goes on the offensive against them.

instead begins to plant "seeds in receptive hearts that will germinate and, if the soil is right, eventually come to fruition."[19]

THIS UNIT, WHICH describes the excited response of vast crowds, the frightened response of demons, the frightening response of Jerusalem leaders, and the worried response of his own family, again brings to the fore the question of who Jesus is. Is he working by God's Spirit or by Satan's cunning, and how does one tell the difference? It also raises sober questions about those who would oppose and resist him. How one responds to this one in whom God's Spirit works so mightily is not a matter of indifference. The issue of who can and will follow him and what Jesus expects of them also arises.

The section begins with a large crowd, which is reduced to a limited group of twelve who are called to be with him. It ends with Jesus' naming all those who have gathered around him and who submit to God's will as his closest family. To bridge the contexts, one should pay attention to three major issues: the opposition to the Spirit (labeled as the unpardonable sin), the task of the disciples and how it relates to ours, and the redefinition of the family.

Opposing Jesus. The reader of Mark is continually confronted with the Christological question, "Who is Jesus?" In the first half of this unit (3:7–19), people flock to Jesus from all over Israel, the demons acknowledge him as the Son of God and fall down before him, and he heals many who are possessed. In the second half (3:20–35), the resistance to Jesus grows in proportion to his popularity with the crowds. Jesus' family comes from their home, and teachers of the law come from Jerusalem. The latter allege that Jesus is an agent of the devil (3:22), and his family thinks he is "out of his mind," something frequently attributed to demon possession. The teachers of the law declare that indeed Jesus has an unclean spirit (3:30). The stark contrast between the reactions to Jesus forces the reader to decide who is right.[20] Either Jesus is the Son of God who liberates the possessed, or he is himself possessed and an agent of Satan. Which is it? Either he is guilty of blasphemy (2:7), or the theological authorities from Jerusalem are.

In bringing this passage into our culture we would do well to ask ourselves what it takes to convince people that Jesus is the Son of God. What are the best tactics? There may be times when it is expedient to retreat in the face of deadly antagonism (3:7; see 13:14), to keep the boat ready to get away

---

19. Ibid., 43–44.
20. Lane, *Mark*, 28.

from the persecutors as well as the crowds that would swallow us up (see 4:36). There may be other times when a frontal assault will be effective. Most of the time, we refute more effectively the claims of hardened enemies with enigmatic parables, which tease the mind into discovering the truth for itself, than with abstract arguments or shouting matches designed more to win over the opponents than to win them over. Jesus' use of parables with his opponents is the way of true love. He does not simply want to rout them in debate but to entice them to think together with him. His use of arresting imagery provides a common ground that they can understand and that can enlighten them with the truth if they are willing to open up their minds to God.[21]

Many readers of this passage, however, get sidetracked by the issue of the unpardonable sin. Jesus suggests (note the indefinite, "whoever," 3:29) that his opponents are guilty of blasphemy against the Spirit, which he labels as unforgivable.[22] Such a harsh statement has gripped the attention of many over the years and does need special attention, since many despairing church members have tortured themselves with fears that they have committed it. First, they do not recognize that what is condemned is the spiteful denial of the activity of God's Spirit in the ministry of Jesus—to label the Holy Spirit an unclean spirit and to deny that the Holy Spirit works directly in our fallen world through humans to subdue the evil powers and to free persons and institutions from the bondage of Satan. Jesus makes the fierce assertion that this sin is unforgivable. Second, they do not allow for Jesus' use of hyperbole to underscore that rejecting or obstructing the work of Holy Spirit is a terrible sin. They take his words literally and assume that some actions are unforgivable. McNeile explains that serious (or defiant) sin was often spoken of as "unpardonable" in the Old Testament (Num. 15:30–31; 1 Sam. 3:14; Isa. 22:14) and comments:

> If the Lord spoke as a Jew to Jews and used the type of expression current in His day, and derived from the Old Testament, He meant, and would be understood to mean, no more than that blasphemy against the Holy Spirit, by whose power He worked, was a terrible sin,—more terrible than blasphemy against man.[23]

---

21. Ernst Fuchs, *Studies of the Historical Jesus* (London: SCM), 129.

22. Contrast *Jub.* 15:34, where the unpardonable sin is the failure to circumcise one's sons.

23. Alan Hugh McNeile, *The Gospel According to St. Matthew* (London: Macmillan, 1915), 179. Matthew Black (in *An Aramaic Approach to the Gospels and Acts* [3d ed.; Oxford: Clarendon, 1967], 140 n.3) contends that the word "sin" derives from a mistranslation of the underlying Aramaic word, which means "condemnation." See the critique of this view in Gundry, *Mark*, 183.

The problem is that Christians frequently seize on the negative aspect of this saying—one is "guilty of an eternal sin"—and neglect the positive statement—"all the sins and blasphemies of men will be forgiven them." The KJV translation, "is in danger of eternal damnation" (3:29), certainly grabs one's attention. Since this passage has caused so many such unnecessary anguish, one wisely stresses that the love, grace, and patience of God are never exhausted by our abundant sinfulness: "Whoever comes to me I will never drive away" (John 6:37).[24] The gospel proclaims that God forgives what may seem to us to be unforgivable.

Clarifying from the context in which this saying appears what makes the blasphemy against the Holy Spirit unpardonable should help. People need to learn that rejecting Jesus out of ignorance is one thing, but attacking the power by which he works is something far more serious. If one is weak, one can be encouraged. If one is ignorant, one can be informed. If one is willfully blind and deaf and rejects help, what can be done? One has cut oneself off from what might lead to repentance. The sworn enemies of Jesus have shut their eyes to the truth. They say good is evil in order to turn others away from Jesus, to preserve their own authority, and to resist becoming disciples. God is willing to forgive even this sin, but they have willfully shut themselves off from God's forgiveness. It is not a single action but a continual state of spurning the Spirit's work.

If one understands the so-called unforgivable sin as deliberately scorning the power and forgiveness of God, one can perhaps help those in the church who become worried, or even terror-stricken, that they have committed some sin that is unpardonable. That they even worry about it provides proof that they have not committed such a sin. Jesus affirms that blasphemy is forgivable (3:28), and the testimony of Paul confirms it. He identifies himself as a former blasphemer (1 Tim. 1:13), one who was no different from these teachers of the law in rejecting Jesus and maligning Christians as a satanic cancer destroying the fabric of Judaism (Gal. 1:13–14). He came to a new understanding through the direct intervention of God. It would have been unforgivable had he continued to spurn the Lord, not because he had squandered his one opportunity to respond, but because his heart would have grown more calcified and harder to penetrate and his ways more settled in iniquity.

If one errs on this issue, the Gospels indicate it is safer to err on the side of emphasizing God's forgiveness; but there may be occasions when the dreadful nature of this sin needs to be emphasized as a warning. The paral-

---

24. E. M. Blaiklock, *The Young Man Mark: Studies in Some Aspects of Mark and His Gospel* (Exeter: Paternoster, 1965), 31.

lel phrases, "whoever blasphemes against the Holy Spirit" (3:28) and "whoever does God's will" (3:35), suggest that one can move from one behavior to another. That teachers of the law from Jerusalem are guilty of blasphemy against the Spirit and that Paul, a former Pharisee, who excelled in the tradition of the fathers (Gal. 1:13–14; Phil. 3:5–6), confesses himself to have been a blasphemer in the past is suggestive. In this account, those who know Jesus best and those who should know the most about God are the ones who oppose him.[25] Those who are probably most in danger of this sin today are the theologians, biblical experts, and leaders in the churches. They are also the most likely to level charges of blasphemy against others.

Mark's use of the bracketing technique links to the charge of blasphemy an attempt by Jesus' bosom family to obstruct his mission. Blasphemy against the Spirit is not just slandering the Spirit of God, which is easy to recognize; it also includes attempts to subvert the work of the Spirit of God, which is not so easy to recognize. The reason it is harder to detect is because those who may be guilty of it are those closest to Jesus and those who have convinced themselves that they are acting with the best of intentions. Few who have read this text have seen the connection created by Mark's bracketing technique between the slander of the scribes and the attempted subversion of Jesus' mission by his family. The latter sin is no less a blasphemy against the Spirit and is no less serious. Those who regard themselves as the intimates of Jesus, who seek and call for him, should guard themselves against their own attempts to undermine the Spirit's working that runs counter to their wishes or expectations. Even those in Jesus' family can unknowingly ally themselves with his enemies, and a divided house cannot stand.[26]

Continuing the disciples' task. The original disciples were picked to be with Jesus to witness his deeds and words. To be with Jesus means that they learn to be as their Lord so that they can extend his ministry of power. At this point our task and theirs intersect. Mark believes that his readers can learn from their failures. The Twelve are not called to sainthood or to sit on thrones, nor are they presented as ideal disciples, who serve as models for the readers. The performance of the these twelve men in Mark makes it clear that humans, being what they are, are free to make their own choices

---

25. Achtemeier, "Mark," 4:549.

26. Obviously, Jesus' family came to a new understanding after the resurrection (see Act 1:14), and his brothers became leaders in the Jesus movement (see Acts 15; 21:17–26; 1 Cor. 9:5; and the letters of James and Jude). We therefore should not use this text to castigate Jesus' immediate family but should read ourselves, as the latest additions to his family, into the story. If those closest to Jesus could have misunderstood him and tried to impede his mission, then we are no less vulnerable to the same failing, even after the cross and resurrection. We therefore should take care to guard against it.

and frequently fail in their partnership with God. Jesus chose Judas, for example, to be one of the Twelve, not to be a betrayer; but Judas made his own choice to desert him and to deliver him to the enemy. The story of Peter in this Gospel reveals one who is anything but rocklike. He is more rockheaded when he wrangles with Jesus about his messianic role (8:32–33) and more like the rocky soil whose sprouting seed withers under the feeble floodlight of hostile scrutiny (4:5–6, 16–18) when he denies his Lord three times (14:66–72). The Sons of Thunder are shown hankering after glory and riches that they think should abound when Jesus ascends his throne. They want the best seats in the house, to sit on the king's left and right.

In spite of the failures of the Twelve, God's purposes in calling them will not be thwarted, and God's power can still work through them to multiply Jesus' ministry. Disciples come with all their ignorance, weakness, and frailty and must learn to follow the pattern of their Lord for God to work through them to extend his ministry. Jesus alone is our model. Being with him means learning from his positive example.

To be with Jesus is therefore far more difficult than it sounds, and we should be careful, in bridging the contexts, not to soft sell the task of discipleship. The many hymns that exult in being with Jesus, such as "In the Garden," may mislead us into thinking only in terms of the joys we share with him as we tarry in some idyllic setting. For the Twelve in the Gospel of Mark there was little time for tarrying as they rushed hither and yon with Jesus. It was not all luminous joy, prestigious authority, and triumphant exorcisms. To be with Jesus in Gethsemane (14:33) was certainly no picnic.

Because being with Jesus calls for sharing his travail, the disciples, like us, will be tempted instead to withdraw from him. Judas deserts Jesus and comes to Gethsemane with "a crowd," brandishing swords and clubs (14:43). He would rather side with those who rule by brute force than suffer with one who looks so powerless and rules by love. When the posse comes to arrest Jesus, all of the disciples abandon him to face his fate alone. In the courtyard of the high priest, a suddenly shy Peter is recognized as one who was "with that Nazarene" (14:67), but he vehemently denies it. He would rather melt into the crowd and sit with the squad of Jesus' captors, warming himself by a cozy fire (14:54). It should be made plain to those who might be attracted only by the exciting prospect of having authority over demons that to be with Jesus means to share his toil and adversity. Paul fully understood what it meant to be with Jesus and for Jesus to be with us when he wrote to the Corinthians: "We always carry around in our body the death of Jesus, so that the life of Jesus may also be revealed in our body. For we who are alive are always being given over to death for Jesus' sake, so that his life may be revealed in our mortal body" (2 Cor. 4:10–11).

The disciples' task is also to proclaim God's victory over evil and to liberate others. The fight against Satan continues. Jesus' image of the strong man bound and his house plundered might lead us to conclude that he has been totally defeated. But the twisted bodies and minds and the moral and institutional vileness that we see all around us and even in ourselves belies this conclusion. The image does intimate that establishing the kingdom of God will not be effortless but requires struggle and conflict.

A tension therefore exists between the presumed shackling of Satan and Satan's continued potency. Satan is defeated in one skirmish after another in the Gospel (the temptation, the exorcisms) but still has considerable battlefield strength that can inflict damage, and he will continue to resist. The slanderous attack on Jesus by the teachers of the law from Jerusalem is living proof of that. It might be compared to the Battle of the Bulge, when Hitler made one last desperate gamble and threw all of his forces into battle to try to halt the Allies' advance after the successful invasion of Europe. The arrival of the kingdom of God in the ministry of Jesus is only the beginning of the end for evil powers. Satan is able to consume the seed that falls on the hardened path (4:15), but that is more to the blame of the faulty hearer than Satan. The plundered house is like a building that has been primed for demolition with dynamite. When the dynamite detonates, the building remains standing for an instant before it crumples in a heap of rubble and dust. The disciples are promised spiritual power to engage and defeat the enemy; they need spiritual discernment to recognize who the enemy truly is.

Redefining the family. Jesus did not teach much about the family, nor did he give us a model for family living, and many have found what he does say about family relationships to be disturbing. Most would not find this text to be ideal for Mother's Day or for a family enrichment theme. In an age when the fabric holding nuclear families together is so threadbare, we might wish that Jesus had given us ten tips on how we ought to relate to family members instead of giving his own family the brush-off. Jesus is alienated from his family, who apparently regard him as a lunatic, foolishly throwing his life away. How can we use Jesus' exceptional view of the family espoused in this passage to strengthen the lives of families today?

Ernest Renan concluded in his life of Christ, written in the nineteenth century, that Jesus "cared little for the relations of kinship." He described Jesus' attitude as a "bold revolt against nature," which trampled "under foot everything that is human, blood, love, and country."[27] Jesus' curt response to his mother and brothers and his seemingly heartless response to a man who

---

27. Ernest Renan, *The Life of Jesus* (A. L. Burt, 1897), 97–98.

begged off following him immediately so that he might bury his father ("Let the dead bury their own dead," Matt. 8:22) lends credence to the opinion that Jesus sought to undermine rather than strengthen family commitments.

But Jesus' fierce condemnation of those who dodged their responsibilities to their parents through legal casuistry (Mark 7:6–13), his dispatch of the healed Gerasene demoniac back to his family (5:18–19), and his condemnation of divorce (10:1–12) reveals that Renan's conclusion is exaggerated. Jesus' radical image is not without precedent. It can be found in the strict monotheistic religious traditions of Judaism, which required a proselyte to forsake former relations, and in the diverse philosophical traditions of the Greco-Roman world. Followers could make sense of the demand to subordinate family ties for the sake of a higher good. All other allegiances must take a backseat.[28]

To bridge the contexts one needs to confront head-on Jesus' reevaluation of the significance of biological family ties. If we are selfishly looking for how to make our nuclear families happier and more secure, we will not find much here. If we are looking for God's grander purpose for the family, we will find good news, particularly for those who, for whatever reasons, are alone and without family. Jesus demonstrates absolute allegiance to God's purposes and requires it of his disciples as well. He rejects the exclusiveness and selfishness that is often whipped up by biological kinship and claims that the anonymous crowds can become family to him and to one another.[29] They become part of an even greater family, whose bonds, created by their commitment to God, are stronger even than the ties of blood (see 10:28–30; Rom. 16:13; Phil. 2:19–22; Philem. 10).

At the beginning of the section Jesus invited those whom he wanted (3:13). One might mistakenly take this to mean that those who may have desired to follow Jesus are turned away because he did not want them. The end of the section, however, throws the doors wide open. Anyone who does the will of God becomes a member of his family, and he redefines family beyond the biological kinship of the nuclear family and the clan. Biological family relationships are not based on choice, but becoming a member of the

---

28. Stephen G. Barton, *Discipleship and Family Ties in Mark and Matthew* (SNTSMS 80; Cambridge: Cambridge Univ. Press, 1994), 23–56, 220–21.

29. Louis Feldman (*Jew and Gentile in the Ancient World* [Princeton: Princeton Univ. Press, 1993], 196–99) observes that Christianity differs from Judaism "in its very essence." "Jews historically have defined themselves as a people, a nation, a family, whence we can understand the Talmudic formulation [*b. Qidd.* 68b] defining the born Jew as one who has a Jewish mother (a biological rather than a credal definition); religion is an accoutrement of the nation." Christianity, on the other hand, was the "first religion devoid of nationalistic connection" and was attacked for it by ancient critics.

family of God is. The only membership requirement in this new messianic family is obeying God, whose commands are defined by what Jesus taught and did.

BLASPHEMY AGAINST THE **Spirit**. The accusation that the enemies raise against Jesus challenges those who try to make Jesus over into a failed Jewish revolutionary, a peasant teacher who spoke timeless ethical truths, or a wandering Cynic preacher. The only reasonable explanation for the deep hostility of Jesus' challengers is that Jesus must have claimed that what he did was the manifestation of God's Spirit working in and through him. C. S. Lewis recognized that when one is faced with the claims of Jesus there are only two options:

> A man who was merely a man and said the sort of things Jesus said would not be a great moral teacher. He would be either be a lunatic— on a level with the man who says he is a poached egg—or else he would be the Devil of Hell. You must make your choice. Either this man was, and is, the Son of God: or else a madman or something worse. You can shut Him up for a fool, you can spit at Him and kill Him as a demon; or you can fall at His feet and call Him Lord and God. But let us not come with any patronising nonsense about His being a great human teacher. He has not left that open to us. He did not intend to.[30]

The church does not openly revile the Spirit as these bitter opponents of Jesus did, but her blasphemy against the Spirit may take more subtle forms. Tied to this serious charge is the attempt by his family members to divert Jesus from his purposes. The church has been guilty of the very same thing more than once in its history. A classic example is the Grand Inquisitor in Dostoevsky's *The Brothers Karamazov*. The Grand Inquisitor openly regards Jesus as a failure and boasts that he and his church "have corrected Thy work and have founded it upon miracle, mystery and authority. . . . We took from him what Thou didst reject with scorn, that last gift he offered Thee, showing Thee all the kingdoms of the earth."[31]

The danger is that we will see this serious sin only in others—our deadly opponents—and not in ourselves. Slandering those who belong to Jesus

---

30. C. S. Lewis, *Mere Christianity* (London: Fontana: 1960), 52–53.

31. Fyodor Dostoevsky, *The Brothers Karamazov*, trans. Constance Garrett (New York: Random House, 1929), 305.

poses as much danger as confusing Jesus with Satan. Church history is riddled with those who labeled their theological disputants as blasphemers and proceeded to excoriate, excommunicate, or execute them. If one describes one's enemies as inherently evil or subhuman in some way, it makes it easier to justify doing away with them. When one characterizes an enemy as demonic, one can rationalize doing whatever one wants to eliminate that devil, no matter how devilish it might be.

The slander of Jesus by the teachers of the law reveals the extreme danger of labeling him. They may have been sincere in their denunciation of him and the power by which he worked. They may have been frightened by the new wine that was bursting their old wineskins. Someone has said that hell hath no fury like a coreligionist who feels betrayed. Vicious criticism of others in religious circles stems from a variety of motives: sincere distress over something radically new, genuine alarm over what is perceived to be heresy, a desire to reassure that we belong to the good guys by branding others as the bad guys, or a craven dread of losing power. The teachers of the law were seeking to protect the law, their tradition, and their stake in it. They may have firmly believed that God and Scripture were on their side. They were dead wrong, however, and their view was deadly to themselves and others.

Such people are still with us and still as deadly. At the end of the day, will they discover that they have obstructed the working of God's Spirit? Anyone who deals with this text should be wary of pointing condemning fingers at others and should ask whether he or she may be guilty of obstructing the Spirit who is working in persons in ways that may be foreign and even frightening to them. One must pray for the discernment of the Spirit so that our pride, self-interest, and inflexibility do not cloud our judgment of what the Spirit can do.

Authority over evil. The apostles are not simply given authority, but authority to do good—to drive out demons. This does not mean that we need to have exorcism services in our churches or to train ministers for this task (although I have many missionary acquaintances who have said that it would have been useful for them to have been better prepared to meet this phenomenon on the mission field). What it does mean is that the church should do more than just talk about the power of God; it should be a community that exhibits some evidence of the power.

In other words, the church should be a community that does more than just confess his name, which is no more than what the demons do. The church is not to sit on the sidelines, watching the world go by and doing nothing more than offering people a different religious option for salvation. The church has the task of standing up and confronting evil in the arena of life. Jesus sends his disciples out to tackle evil that is larger than personal evil and to deliver people from whatever enslaves them. One may ask: Where is the evidence in the church of this power to change lives? Thomas Aquinas is reported to have had an audience with Pope Innocent II and came upon him counting a large sum of money. The Pope boasted: "See, Thomas, the church can no longer say, 'Silver and gold have I none'" (Acts 3:1–10). Aquinas responded, "True, holy father, but neither can she now say, 'Arise and walk.'"[32] One may ask whether the church confronts the powers of evil today.

Some have placed an undue emphasis on miracles, however, by magnifying the significance of healing and exorcisms. It certainly brings excitement and drama to the worship service but opens the door to fraud and exploitation by the entrepreneurs of emotional stimulation. The shenanigans of ministerial con men have given the media plenty of fodder to parody. The church should always be wary of hucksters who manipulate crowds to their advantage and generally turn their ministry into stunts designed more to bring in dollars than to drive out evil. What is frequently ignored in the show is the internal evil that grips individuals, institutions, and whole societies. The church frequently can peg the charlatans who specialize in healing people with minor physical maladies but who are silent and helpless before the evils that corrode the souls of people.

Many prefer to retreat into a shell of comfortable Christianity. David Gushee's sobering account of those few righteous Gentiles who risked their lives to save Jews during the holocaust is disturbing because it documents how few Christians confronted the evil that swept Europe. What Hitler did could not have been accomplished without the complicity of a nation that was predominantly Christian. Gushee documents that of the three hundred million under Nazi domination, 90 percent were Christian and 60 percent would have described themselves as "very" or "somewhat" religious before the war. But the number of those who acted to save Jews was less than 1 percent. One of his conclusions is particularly disturbing: "The irrelevance of Christian faith for many self-identified Christian rescuers in so-called Christian Europe is an extraordinary finding." Some of the rescuers took action "despite some of the teaching they received at church." Lech Sarna, a devout Polish Catholic, was tormented after his attendance at church. He lamented, "I am sure to lose in both worlds. They will kill me for keeping Jews and then I will lose heaven for helping Jews."[33] The church is responsible for the moral formation of its members so that they can recognize evil and be willing to challenge it regardless of the cost.

---

32. F. F. Bruce, *The Book of Acts* (NICNT, rev. ed.; Grand Rapids: Eerdmans, 1988), 77–78.

33. David P. Gushee, *The Righteous Gentiles of the Holocaust: A Christian Interpretation* (Minneapolis: Fortress, 1994), 165.

The movie *Schindler's List* drove home the violence and horror that went on every day in the Kraków-Plaszów concentration camp, led by *Unter-sturmführer* Amon Göth. The survivors report that the full obscenity of the violence could not be depicted in a film to be shown to the general public. Many of those who survived could not bring themselves to talk to Thomas Keneally, the author of the book that was the basis for the movie. The movie did embolden some to tell their story to Elinor J. Brecher, who followed up on the lives of the *Schindlerjüden*. One she wrote about was Helena Sternlicht Rosenzweig, who served as the housemaid of Amon Göth and tells of having arranged some flowers in the home. The commandant commented to his live-in lover how beautiful they were. She pointed to the housemaid Helena and said she put them there. He turned and looked at Helena and said: "So even if she does things well, I have to hate her; she's a Jew."[34] One does not know who was the worse prisoner—the tortured Jew who could still arrange flowers for her tormentor, or the tormentor. The church must exorcise the demons of bigotry, intolerance, parochialism, chauvinism, racism, and sexism—all the isms that imprison humankind and impel them to devote themselves to inflicting pain on others.

The temptation is for us to retreat from the world or to overlook the evil in our midst. The last option is exemplified by the Reverend Tooker, pastor of St. Paul's in Grenada, in Tennessee Williams's *Cat on a Hot Tin Roof*. He mixes with a family in his church that is overrun by hatred, distrust, lust, avarice, and abuse. He is oblivious to it all. He only talks about building up the church, which means for him improving the looks of the church building. The former option is represented in Luther's bitter comments about monks:

> For when one flees and becomes a monk, it sounds as though he were saying, "Pfui! How the people stink! How damnable is their state! I will be saved, and let them go to the devil!" If Christ had fled thus and become such a holy monk, who would have died for us or rendered satisfaction for us poor sinners? Would it be the monks, with their strict lives of flight?[35]

We have been sent by Christ into the midst of an evil world to confront evil head-on with the power of God.

Jesus and the family. Jesus' statement about the family has enormous repercussions for the way we live out our family commitments and the way we should minister to families. In Forrest Carter's account of depression-era

---

34. Elinor J. Brecher, *"Schindler's Legacy: True Stories of the List Survivors* (New York: Plume/Penguin, 1994), 64.

35. Martin Luther, "On the Councils and the Churches," *Works of Martin Luther* (Philadelphia: Muhlenberg, 1931), 5:161.

life in the 1930s, the grandfather explains to his grandson his use of the phrase, "I kin you." It meant to love and to understand.

> Granpa said back before his time "kinfolks" meant any folks that you understood and had an understanding with, so it meant "loved folks." But people got selfish, and brought it down to mean just blood relatives; but that actually it was never meant to mean that.[36]

Jesus' teaching reflects a similar understanding. His stance is radically different from what we might want to hear. A reporter's interview of two gang members living in a large American city reflects a similar but perverted understanding of family bonds. They were first cousins, who had been raised together in the same home by their grandmother but somehow wound up as members of rival gangs. They confessed that they would not hesitate to do harm to the other if the situation or the orders of the gang required it. The dedication to the gang family would override the commitment to blood relatives. They defined family according to their common purpose rather than according to blood relationships. Jesus' definition of family is similar: Our shared commitments to God tie us more closely together than biological kinship. The key difference between the gang family and the family of God is the commitment to live out the will of the Father, to bring good rather than evil to others.

As our world is drawn closer together by instant communication and supersonic travel, we seem to be growing further apart. Jesus' definition of family embraces those outside one's kith and kin as brother and sister. His understanding counters the ruinous tribalism and the ethnic strife that rears its ugly head in our cities and in nations around the world. If Christians would take to heart Jesus' words about the family, the tragic slaughter of Christians by other Christians would not occur as frequently as it does. General Colin Powell tells the story of a young African-American soldier who was asked if he was afraid on the eve of going into battle. He said, "I am not afraid. And the reason I am not afraid is that I'm with my family." He nodded over his shoulder to the rest of his unit, composed of white, black, and yellow young adults. "That's my family. We take care of one another." The members of the Christ's church should be able to say the same thing as they take the gospel to a hostile world and as they face the struggles that come with everyday life.

On the other hand, Jesus' definition of the family may create problems for many individuals instead of providing answers. The commitment to do

---

36. Forrest Carter, *The Education of Little Tree* (Albuquerque: Univ. of New Mexico Press, 1976), 38.

the will of God may force some to make a wrenching choice between their biological family and God. The memoirs of Perpetua in *The Martyrdom of St. Perpetua and Felicitas*, which are said by the compiler to be written by her own hand, vividly present the divided loyalties that early Christians experienced. She was imprisoned for refusing to sacrifice for "the welfare of the emperors" during the African persecution. Her father pleaded with her to recant, but she responded that she could be nothing other than what she was, a Christian. Her father "was so angered by the word 'Christian,' that he moved towards me as though he would pluck my eyes out" (3.3). Later, he begged:

> Daughter have pity on my grey head—have pity on me your father, if I deserve to be called your father, if I have favoured you above all your brothers, if I have raised you to reach this prime of your life. Do not abandon me to the reproach of men, think of your brothers, think of your mother and your aunt, think of your child, who will not be able to live while you are gone. Give up your pride! You will destroy all of us! None of us will ever be able to speak freely again if anything happens to you. (5.2–4)

She rejected his plea, and her final response was that she had found a new family, in which she had become a sister to her former slave, Felicitas (18.2).[37] They died for their faith in each other's arms. Bonhoeffer knew that one's faith might lead one into situations where one had to make wrenching decisions when he wrote: "Neither father nor mother, neither wife nor child, neither nationality nor tradition, can protect a man at the moment of his call. It is Christ's will that he should be thus isolated, and that he should fix his eyes solely upon him."[38]

While some may be forced to disengage themselves from close family relationships that would strangle their commitment to God, we as Christians still need special people in our lives, a family of folks who support us, who are committed to us and we to them. We were not created to live alone, but to live in families. Augustine believed that the particular love of special persons in our lives schools us for the universal love of all others as neighbors.[39] When Lyndon Johnson left Washington to retire to his Texas ranch, he was asked why he would want to leave the city. He responded: "Out there they ask about you when you are sick and they cry when you die." People need community and want somebody to care for them.

---

37. Herbert Musurillo, *The Acts of the Christian Martyrs* (Oxford: Clarendon, 1972), 106–31.

38. Dietrich Bonhoeffer, *The Cost of Discipleship* (New York: Macmillan, 1963), 105.

39. As cited by Gilbert Meilaender, *Friendship: A Study in Theological Ethics* (London: Univ. of Notre Dame Press, 1981), 16–24.

The social sciences corroborate what God says in Genesis 2:18: "It is not good for the man to be alone." Studies have shown that isolation of individuals, and even of the nuclear family, is correlated with a whole array of problems such as physical illness, suicide, psychiatric hospitalization, alcoholism, difficult pregnancies, depression, anxiety, child abuse, family violence, and proneness to accidents.[40] Sometimes people can be surrounded by others and still feel alone because they do not feel that they belong to anybody or that anybody belongs to them. Researchers have found, for example, that if you put a mouse with a group of strange mice in a situation where they have to share an insufficient source of food, the outsider develops high blood pressure. But if you put the same mouse with its brothers and sisters in a group the same size and with the same inadequate amount of food, its blood pressure does not rise.[41] Mice can handle stress if they have their family around them but not when they are alone among strangers. Other research shows that people are no different. People need to have families to help bear the stresses that life brings; and when they do not have one, the church needs to get busy and help make one or straighten out the feeling of isolation in a family gone sour.

In our culture, where so many feel alone, cut off from family for various reasons and surrounded by strangers, we should stress the positive aspects of this passage. The French novelist André Gide, in *Les nouvelles nourritures*, bitterly expressed a forlorn attitude shared by many: "Families! I hate you! Shut-in homes, closed doors, jealous possessors of happiness." To those who feel shut out, Jesus' word can be good news. Jesus knits his followers into a family that transcends kinship boundaries.[42]

---

40. See, for example, Sidney Cobb, "Social Support As a Moderator of Life Stress," *Psychosomatic Medicine* 38 (1976): 300–14; N. D. Colletta and C. H. Gregg, "Adolescent Mothers' Vulnerability to Stress," *Journal of Nervous and Mental Disease* 169 (1981): 50–54; James Garbarino, "Using Natural-Helping Networks to Meet the Problem of Child Maltreatment," in *Schools and the Problem of Child Abuse*, eds. R. Volpe, M. Breton, and J. Mitton (Toronto: Univ. of Toronto Press, 1979); B. H. Gottlieb, "Social Networks and Social Support in Community Mental Health," in *Social Networks and Social Support*, ed. B. H. Gottlieb (Beverly Hills, Calif.: Sage, 1981); Marc Pilisuk, "Delivery of Social Support: The Social Inoculation," *American Journal of Orthopsychiatry* 52 (1982): 20–31; Marc Pilisuk and Susan Parks, "Social Support and Family Stress," *Marriage and Family Review* 6 (1983): 137–56; D. Scheinfeld, D. Bowles, S. Tuck, and R. Gold, "Parents' Values, Family Networks and Family Development: Working with Disadvantaged Families," *American Journal of Orthopsychiatry* 40 (1970): 413–25.

41. J. Henry and J. Cassel, "Psychosocial Factors in Essential Hypertension: Recent Epidemiological and Animal Experimental Evidence," *American Journal of Epidemiology* 104 (1976): 1–8.

42. As he did on the cross with the beloved disciple and his mother (John 19:26–27).

We need to create special family relationships within the community of God that cut across the boundaries of blood and marriage. A congregation of a thousand people, or even two hundred people, cannot really be family to one another except in the extended family sense. Within that large family there need to be intimate family relationships. Thomas Helwys recognized this back in 1612, when he published his *Declaration of Faith of English People*. Article 16 maintains that the size of a church should be small "so that they may performe all the duties of love one towards another both to soul and bodie." But even in a large church there can be small cells that function as family to one another. The church needs to seek out the lonely and not only help them mend their families but create new family relationships in the bonds of faith. Family ministry programs should not focus on ministering only to the nuclear family and meeting its needs but should use the family to minister to and to include others who are without family. The families in our churches can become means of ministry to those beyond the bounds of our nuclear families.

Jesus' words about the family can therefore become good news for everyone. It strengthens the nuclear family by helping it to establish bonds beyond the cloistered walls of the family room by giving it a sense of purpose and ministry. Those who are family-less may find comfort from this word—the special-needs child waiting for adoption, the homeless mentally ill young adult, the teenage mother on her own at age sixteen, the aging adult who has outlived his children, the businesswoman trying to survive emotionally in an ugly divorce, the struggling single mother who needs a temporary foster home for her child. The goal of Christians in marriage is not to make a house an island of intimacy, shut off from others in the world, but to make a home for humankind. Through families, the church is to extend the kind of accepting love that transforms a runaway slave like Onesimus into one whom Paul claimed as his own child and as a brother to his former master (Philem. 10, 16), the kind of embracing love that transforms the runaway and throwaway children in our culture into "our children."

The president of Asbury College, David Gyertson, testifies how this kind of grace transformed his life. His father abandoned his family when he was ten, and his mother forced him to leave home three years later. His life was turned around when he was taken in by a humble pastor and his wife, who shared with him the good news in Psalm 27:10: "Though my father and mother forsake me, the LORD will receive me." This family did not simply share Scripture with him but shared their lives and home with him, taking him in as a son and modeling God's love for him. If the church takes seriously Jesus' ideal of what the family is, one of its tasks is to create and nurture families that make a place for all those who want a relationship with God as

Father and with one another. This requires more than sharing a pew on Sunday morning and a fellowship doughnut afterward. Instead, we are to allow these persons to become our parents, our children, our siblings. We are to adopt one another, accepting responsibility for and commitment to one another.[43] The church is to take those who know the hurt of the world and bring them into the healing of community acceptance.

43. For other work on the implications of this passage, see David E. Garland and Diana R. Garland, "The Family: Biblical and Theological Perspectives," in *Incarnational Ministry: The Presence of Christ in Church, Society, and Family: Essays in Honor of Ray Anderson*, ed. Christian D. Kettler and Todd H. Speidell (Colorado Springs: Helmers and Howard, 1990), 226–40.; Diana S. Richmond Garland, "An Ecosystemic Perspective for Family Ministry," *RevExp* 86 (1989): 195–207; idem, *Church Agencies: Caring for Children and Families in Crisis* (Washington, D.C.: Child Welfare League of America, 1994); Rodney Clapp, *Families at the Crossroads: Beyond Traditional and Modern Options* (Downers Grove, Ill.: InterVarsity, 1993).

Mark 4:1–20

A GAIN JESUS BEGAN to teach by the lake. The crowd that gathered around him was so large that he got into a boat and sat in it out on the lake, while all the people were along the shore at the water's edge. ²He taught them many things by parables, and in his teaching said: ³"Listen! A farmer went out to sow his seed. ⁴As he was scattering the seed, some fell along the path, and the birds came and ate it up. ⁵Some fell on rocky places, where it did not have much soil. It sprang up quickly, because the soil was shallow. ⁶But when the sun came up, the plants were scorched, and they withered because they had no root. ⁷Other seed fell among thorns, which grew up and choked the plants, so that they did not bear grain. ⁸Still other seed fell on good soil. It came up, grew and produced a crop, multiplying thirty, sixty, or even a hundred times."

⁹Then Jesus said, "He who has ears to hear, let him hear."

¹⁰When he was alone, the Twelve and the others around him asked him about the parables. ¹¹He told them, "The secret of the kingdom of God has been given to you. But to those on the outside everything is said in parables ¹²so that,

> "'they may be ever seeing but never perceiving,
>   and ever hearing but never understanding;
>   otherwise they might turn and be forgiven!'"

¹³Then Jesus said to them, "Don't you understand this parable? How then will you understand any parable? ¹⁴The farmer sows the word. ¹⁵Some people are like seed along the path, where the word is sown. As soon as they hear it, Satan comes and takes away the word that was sown in them. ¹⁶Others, like seed sown on rocky places, hear the word and at once receive it with joy. ¹⁷But since they have no root, they last only a short time. When trouble or persecution comes because of the word, they quickly fall away. ¹⁸Still others, like seed sown among thorns, hear the word; ¹⁹but the worries of this life, the deceitfulness of wealth and the desires for other things come in and choke the word, making it unfruitful. ²⁰Others, like seed sown on good soil, hear the word, accept it, and produce a crop—thirty, sixty or even a hundred times what was sown."

JESUS' PARABLES BY the sea form a large section (4:1–34) that is set off as a unit by the phrase "many parables": "He taught them many things by parables" (4:2); "With many similar parables Jesus spoke the word to them" (4:33). Key terms appear throughout this section,[1] but the most important is the verb "to hear" (*akouo*), which occurs thirteen times (vv. 3, 9 [2x], 12 [2x], 15, 16, 18, 20, 23 [2x], 24, 33). It brackets the parable of the sower: "Listen!" (v. 3); "He who has ears to hear, let him hear" (v. 9). The command "to hear" is the first word in the *Shema* (Deut. 6:4; see Mark 12:29), the confession of faith that faithful Jews recited daily. For that same command to preface Jesus' parables may suggest that his words stand "in continuity with the words of God to Israel in the past."[2] The verb "to hear" appears twice in the quotation from Isaiah 6:9, explaining why everything comes in parables: (lit.) "so that . . . hearing they might hear and not understand" (4:12).

The idea of hearing is the key word in the interpretation of the parable of the sower (or soils). Each type of soil hears the word but reacts differently (4:15, 16, 18, 20). For the good soil, the participle "hearing" is in the present tense (v. 20), suggesting that it needs to continue. The command to hear concludes the parable of the lamp, "If anyone has ears to hear, let him hear" (v. 23), and precedes the parable of the measure, "Consider carefully what you hear" (v. 24). This leitmotif ringing through the discourse is a summons "to look beneath the surface," to "discern the inner meaning of what they hear and see."[3] Everyone may listen, but not everyone can catch what Jesus says.

For too many, Jesus' words go in one ear and out the other. In the opening scene, Jesus teaches all the crowd (4:1–2), but in the closing scene a split has occurred among the hearers (4:33–34). He "spoke the word" to them in many parables "as much as they could understand [hear]," and privately he explained all things to his disciples. This discourse explains how and why that division occurred, and it serves as a warning to the readers. Mark's concern is that his readers be attentive and reflective so that the nature of the kingdom of God and how it advances in the world will not whiz by

---

1. "Sowing" appears in 4:3, 4, 14, 15 [2x], 16, 18, 20, 31, 32 and is defined as "sowing the word" (v. 14). The noun "seed" appears in vv. 26, 27 and is referred to in vv. 4, 5, 7, 8, 15, 16, 18, 20, 31. "Word" appears in vv. 14, 15 [2x], 16, 17, 18, 19, 20, 33 (see 2:2; 5:36), and "soil" ("earth") in 4:2, 5, 8, 20, 26, 31.

2. Hooker, *Mark*, 125, drawing on the arguments of Birger Gerhardsson, "The Parable of the Sower and Its Interpretation," *NTS* 14 (1968): 165–93.

3. Geddert, *Watchwords*, 82. The verb recurs in 6:11, 14, 20, 29; 7:25, 37; 8:18; 9:7; 12:29; 13:7.

them, leaving them in a stupefied daze as if they were outsiders.

This section forms a chiasm.[4]

    A. Narrative introduction (4:1–2)
      B. Seed parable (4:3–9)
        C. General statement about hiddenness (4:10–12)
          D. Interpretation of the first parable (4:13–20)
        C'. Parables about hiddenness (4:21–25)
      B'. Seed parables (4:26–32)
    A'. Narrative conclusion (4:33–34)[5]

We will divide our treatment of the parables into two units: the parable of the sower (4:1–20), and the hiddenness of the kingdom (4:21–34).

The Parable of the Sower (4:1–9)

THE SCENE OPENS with another notice of Jesus' magnetic attraction on the crowds. They are now so large he must use the boat that was previously prepared for his emergency getaway (3:9) to face all of them massed on the shore (4:1). The word translated "shore" (*ge*) literally means "soil" (or "earth") and is the same word used for the soil that did not have much depth of earth (4:5) and for the "good soil" where the seed is sown (4:8, 20; see also 4:26, 28, 31). The crowds on "the soil" may thus be understood as the recipients of Jesus' sowing of the word.

Mark has told us that Jesus has taught (1:21, 27; 2:13), but this is the first time in the Gospel that he gives us a lengthy report of that teaching. Jesus is teaching them "by parables" (4:2),[6] and the first parable happens to be a parable about his teaching. His question to the disciples in 4:13 implies that understanding this parable somehow helps one unlock the meaning of all of Jesus' teaching. His commentary on why he teaches in parables in 4:10–12 suggests, however, that sowing the word brings to light the disparity that exists in the hearers' capacity to respond. In the previous story (3:31–35), Jesus' person and mission created a distinction between insiders and out-

---

4. An inverted parallelism or crossover of parallel ideas that are repeated in reverse order.

5. See Greg Fay, "Introduction to Incomprehension: The Literary Structure of Mark 4:1–34," CBQ 51 (1989): 65–81.

6. Of the "many similar parables" (4:33) we get only five and only one interpretation. The term *parable* (*parabole*) is related to the Hebrew word *mashal* in the Old Testament, which could be used for short popular sayings, ethical maxims, oracles, wisdom discourses or short utterances, scornful, satirical sayings, allegories, riddles, and fables. See further, K. R. Snodgrass, "Parable," in *Dictionary of Jesus and the Gospels*, eds. Joel B. Green, Scot McKnight, and I. Howard Marshall (Downers Grove, Ill.: InterVarsity, 1992), 591–601.

siders—those who committed themselves to be with him and to do God's will and those who misunderstood him and sought to undermine or interfere with his work. In this section, Jesus' teaching creates a split between insiders and outsiders (4:11)—those who gather around him to learn the mysteries of the kingdom (4:10, 34) and those who do not.

The parable of the sower and the parable of the tenants of the vineyard are the two major parables in Mark. Both come after challenges from religious authorities from Jerusalem (3:20–35; 11:27–33). Both are allegories that provide vital clues for interpreting what is happening in Jesus' ministry. The parable of the tenants of the vineyard allegorizes the rejection of Jesus, the son who has come to collect the fruit of the harvest, and portends his death. The parable of the sower evaluates the various responses to his sowing of the word and portends the misunderstanding that accompanies his word and deeds as well as the harvest that will occur among those who do understand and respond.

A first reading of the parable of the sower tempts one to ask: What kind of careless farmer is this, who casts good seed on a pathway, on rocky terrain, and among thorn bushes? One influential interpretation paints the scene as a realistic portrayal of a farmer's frustration in trying to grow a crop in Palestine.[7] Sowing, it is argued, precedes plowing. The seeds fall on the path, the rocky ground, and among the thorns because of the broadcast method of sowing; the field would be plowed under after it had been sown with seed. The parable is said to depict a contrast between a discouraging beginning and a triumphant end. The manifold obstacles that frustrate the sower's labor are only recounted to bring out the contrast between the impediments and the spectacular harvest (assuming that the harvest total of thirty, sixty, and a hundredfold is the bulk yield, the proportion of seed sown to harvest reaped) that will come in the end. Jeremias concludes:

> To human eyes much of the labor seems to be futile and fruitless, resulting apparently in repeated failure, but Jesus is full of joyful confidence: he knows that God has made a beginning, bringing with it a harvest of reward beyond all asking or conceiving. In spite of every failure and opposition, from hopeless beginnings, God brings forth the triumphal end which he had promised.[8]

The information that Jeremias uses to reconstruct the realistic Palestinian setting and the point of the parable does not derive from the parable itself but from vague rabbinic texts that stem from a much later time. His

---

7. Joachim Jeremias, *The Parables of Jesus* (rev. ed.; New York: Charles Scribner's Sons, 1963), 11–12.

8. Ibid., 150.

reconstruction is an unnecessary attempt to make the parables realistic, which is based on a misleading canon that parables must be realistic. Otherwise, they are allegories, and many scholars assume that Jesus did not employ allegories.[9] In response to Jeremias, (1) note that sowing did not necessarily precede plowing. In normal farming practice, the field would have been prepared before the seed was sown and would have been continually worked. (2) The harvest yield of thirty, sixty, and one hundred hardly represents the bulk yield of a single field. The yield represents the fruit produced by the individual plants.[10] (3) These numbers do not represent a spectacular harvest. In Genesis 26:12 the hundredfold yield given to Isaac is the normal blessing that comes to those who are righteous.[11]

If one should not talk about a sensational harvest, what is the point? A parallel in 4 Ezra 8:41 may shed some light on the matter when compared to Jesus' parable:

> For just as the farmer sows many seeds upon the ground and plants a multitude of seedlings, and yet not all that have been sown will come up in due season, and not all that were planted will take root; so also those who have been sown in the world will not all be saved.

The point of the parable of the farmer in 4 Ezra is that all seed that is sown will not prosper; not everyone will be saved. This point is stated concisely (see 4 Ezra 3:20; 8:6; 9:17, 31, 34). By contrast, Jesus' parable gives remarkable attention to describing the failure of the seed and the reasons for it (68 out of 97 words in the Greek). The harvest is therefore not the sole focus of

---

9. On the history of parable interpretation that challenges these assumptions, see Craig L. Blomberg, *Interpreting the Parables* (Downers Grove, Ill.: InterVarsity, 1990). The parable is realistic in recounting Palestinian methods of sowing but is less than realistic in not mentioning any plowing of the field, the fact that some yield comes from even bad soil, or the fact that the good soil faces no hazards from the birds or thorns.

10. A textual variant occurs in 4:8, 20. The best reading is *hen* (one), which refers to each plant: One yields thirty grains, another sixty, and another one hundred. Pliny mentioned that wheat with branching ears yielded one hundred grains (*Natural History* 18.21.94–95; see also 18.40.162; Theophrastus, *Enquiry into Plants* 8.7.4; Varro, *On Agriculture* 1.44.1–3; Strabo, *Geography* 10.3.11; Columella, *On Agriculture* 2.9.5–6). John H. Martin, Warren H. Leonard, and David L. Stamp (*Principles of Field Crop Production* [New York: Macmillan, 1976], 436) write that wheat "normally produce two or three tillers under typical crowded field conditions, but individual plants on fertile soil with ample space may produce as many as 30 to 100 tillers. The average spike (head) of common wheat contains 25 to 30 grains in 14 to 17 spikelets. Large spikes may contain 50 to 75 grains."

11. Sib. Oracles 3:261–64: "For the Heavenly One gave the earth in common to all and fidelity, and excellent reason in their breasts. For these alone the fertile soil yields fruit from one- to a hundredfold, and the measures of God are produced" (cited by Marcus, *Mystery*, 42–43).

the parable, because the parable places more emphasis on the utter waste of seed in most places than on the plentiful success in one.[12]

The one constant throughout the parable is the reference to the seed and the soil that receives the seed. The details of the parable indicate that a good crop depends entirely on the soil, and this configuration suggests that the parable is not simply describing the miraculous harvest of the kingdom, something pious Jews took for granted, but the kind of reception the kingdom receives.[13] The sowing of the seed reveals the nature of the soil, whether it will produce a harvest or not. The harvest also is not miraculous but average to good. If so, then the parable compares the reception of Jesus' ministry to what happens to the average farmer when he sows.

In sum, the parable portrays a sower who sows with abandon—casting seed upon a pathway, rocks, and thorns as well as on good ground. He is cultivating marginal ground and laboring against formidable odds, so the rate of failure is not surprising nor is the report of an average to good yield from the seed in good soil. Given the nature of the land, the average farmer meets with frustration and failure, but in the end he does receive a reward for his labors—a harvest where the seed has prospered in good soil and borne fruit. Jesus implies in the parable that he fully expects to meet with failure and success, but he fastens more attention on the reasons for the failure than the reasons for success.

Just as the field has different yields, the parable yields a number of points.[14] Sider argues that Jesus' story parables and many of his similitudes were too complex to be restricted to one simple idea. Jesus did not develop elaborate analogies simply to convey a single point but used them because they could argue "several things at once."[15] One must be careful not to assign to every detail absurd allegorical meanings that are foreign to a first-century Palestinian background and to the context of the Gospel of Mark. One must not rule out, however, that parables were designed to evoke a constellation of images that would give rise to various trains of thought. The following ideas may legitimately be gleaned from the parable.

---

12. Some might argue that the losses help build tension before the mention of the climactic harvest.

13. Matthew Black, "The Parables as Allegory," *BJRL* 42 (1959–60): 278.

14. Blomberg (*Interpreting the Parables*, 68–69) comments: "The parables of Jesus are sufficiently similar to other demonstrably allegorical works that many of them too must probably be recognized as allegories. The Gospel parables . . . are allegories, and they probably teach several lessons apiece. This does not mean that every detail must stand for something."

15. John W. Sider, "Proportional Analogy in the Gospel Parables," *NTS* 31 (1985): 18–19; see also his recently published book, *Interpreting the Parables: A Literary Analysis of Their Meaning* (Grand Rapids: Zondervan, 1995).

(1) It makes all the difference in the world who tells this parable and what one's stance is toward that person for how one understands this parable. The parable by itself has no meaning at all: A farmer goes out to sow and meets with failure and a good yield. So what? It could represent the effect that any teacher might have with an audience. But sowing in the Old Testament is a metaphor for God's work. God promises to sow Israel to begin her renewal (Jer. 31:27–28; Ezek. 36:9; Hos. 2:21–23; 4 Ezra 8:6; 9:31).[16] If one has a faith commitment to the teller of the parable, one can make the connection between God's promise to replant Israel and Jesus' ministry. The astounding implication, which only a few will see, is that Jesus comes as the end-time sower of God. Mark has framed his mission as one who goes out to sow the word: "Let us go somewhere else—to the nearby villages—so I can preach there also. That is why I have come [out]" (1:38). "I have not come to call the righteous, but sinners" (2:17). The metaphor of sowing takes on the greatest significance in that it implies that Jesus comes to renew Israel, and how one responds to his teaching decides whether one will be included or excluded.

(2) The sower sows liberally even in unfruitful ground in hope of a harvest. Someone could ask him, "Why sow there? Why not diminish the prospect of loss and be more choosy where the precious seed is sown?" No farmer, however, refuses to sow his seed because some might be wasted. The sower is not afraid to risk scattering his seeds wherever they may fall. Although speaking to some people is like trying to grow wheat in the passing lane of the local expressway; to others, like trying to grow wheat in a two-inch flower pot; and to still others, like trying to grow wheat in Brer Rabbit's briar patch, the seed will be sown—and generously. Only sowing will lead to a harvest. Just as God sends rain on the just and the unjust, Jesus sows his word on good and bad soil. The parable therefore depicts a prodigal sower who excludes no one on principle. From what we learn of the Pharisees in Mark, we might imagine that if they controlled the sowing process, they would try to cut the losses by drastically limiting the terrain where the seed is sown. Clearly they would exclude lepers, sinners, and tax collectors as barren soil not worth the waste of seed. As it turns out, the Pharisees will be soil least receptive to the seed; but Jesus still sows lavishly.

(3) The parable affirms that despite the reversals caused by voracious birds, the scorching heat of the sun on skimpy soil, and a profusion of thorns, the farmer will have a harvest from good soil. The farmer does not go out to waste seed but to gain a harvest. The word of God will not fail (Isa. 55:10–11), and therefore one should not despair over the apparent failures, the

---

16. See also 2 Apoc. Bar. 70:2; 1 Enoch 62:8; Ignatius, *To the Ephesians* 9.1.

blindness of unfaith, the defections, or the pernicious opposition. One can be assured the harvest will come from the response of the good soil.

(4) The parable reveals that the kingdom of God's appearance in the ministry of Jesus does not come in one dramatic fell swoop, which instantly upends the old age. Evil does not vanish straightaway with the coming of the Christ, and people do not universally respond. Failure is not unexpected because the seed is susceptible to being devoured, withered, and choked. This issue is prominent in the explanation of why Jesus teaches in parables, a section inserted between the parable and its interpretation (4:10–12). Some will reject the truth no matter how it comes. They will see and see nothing; they will hear and understand nothing.

(5) The parable makes clear that fruit bearing (translated, "produced a crop" in 4:8) is an essential mark of the kingdom of God. The text mentions fruit bearing before the growth. Jesus' teaching is a summons to obey the commands of God, and those who bear fruit heed his call and do his will (3:35). God expects to harvest this fruit (see 12:2).[17]

The Explanation for Teaching in Parables (4:10–12)

WHEN THOSE AROUND Jesus with the Twelve ask him about the parables, his response sets them apart from outsiders: To them has been given the mystery of the kingdom, while to outsiders everything comes in riddles (see also 3:31–32, 34). Isaiah 6:9–10 is then cited to justify his enigmatic teaching. We will examine first the meaning of the term *mystery of the kingdom* and then turn to the hard word that seems to suggest that Jesus deliberately clouds the truth to keep outsiders on the outside. Finally, we will identify what qualifies one as an insider.

The mystery of the kingdom. The term *mystery* may convey to us something that cannot be explained or understood, but it has a different coloring in its biblical roots. It does not refer to something unknowable or esoteric but to something that can only be communicated by divine revelation.[18] In Mark, it refers to a heavenly truth that is concealed from human understanding but is made known by God. It is "not a mystery in the sense that it is incomprehensible, but it is a 'secret' in that not everyone yet knows it."[19]

---

17. Bearing fruit is a rich image in Scripture; see Isa. 27:6; Ezek. 17:23; John 15:8, 16; Rom. 7:4; Phil. 1:11, 22; Col. 1:6, 10; Titus 3:14; Heb. 6:7; 12:11; 2 Peter 1:8.

18. Marcus, *Mystery*, 46. Behind this concept (and also here) is the Old Testament idea of God's secret (Job 15:8; Ps. 25:14; Prov. 3:32; Amos 3:7). Cranfield (*Mark*, 152) writes: 'The idea that God's thoughts and ways are not men's, but that they are his secret, which is not obvious to human wisdom but which he may reveal to those whom he chooses, was familiar to everyone who listened attentively in the synagogue."

19. R. T. France, *Divine Government*, 36–37.

Mark does not tell us specifically what the nature of this mystery of the kingdom is. A careful reading of the context suggests that the secret has to do with the kingdom of God coming in a veiled way in the person, words, and works of Jesus.[20] A distinction exists between the secret of Jesus' identity and the mystery of the kingdom. The secret of Jesus' identity as the Messiah and the Son of God has been revealed to the reader in the prologue. The secret of the kingdom is that people cannot see that his sowing the word, which will lead to his crucifixion and resurrection, is God's decisive eschatological action. Those who "think the things of men" do not perceive that defeats turn into victories, that the rejected one is indeed the cornerstone, that the risen one is Jesus, "who was crucified" (16:6).[21] Those who possess the secret of the kingdom, however, will eventually be able to see what others cannot: The kingdom of God is advancing not just through miracles but also through suffering and persecution. Only in its final stage will it be publicly manifest for all to see (4:22).

Because Jesus characterizes the parables as mystery, everyone needs his interpretation to understand them.[22] But Jesus says (lit.) that "all things *come*," not "*are told*," "in parables" to those outside (4:11). The parables are not the only things that are opaque and require special insight; rather, everything, including the miracles, require interpretation (see 3:22–30; 6:51–52; 8:14–21). Geddert observes that "virtually all of the events of 4:35–8:26 are parabolic events, pointing beyond themselves to the kingdom in process of coming."[23]

The phrase "in parables" in 4:11 takes on a different meaning from its use in 4:2. It now means bewildering puzzles. Revelation becomes riddles and stumpers to the hardened, shallow, and indifferent mind; and the end result is befuddlement. God's mysterious revelation consequently reveals the blindness of the world, and that blindness is manifest in surprising groups: the religious authorities, the Pharisees and the teachers of the law (2:1–3:6; 3:22–30), Jesus' nearest relatives (3:31–35), and even his disciples (8:14–21). They are wedded to old ways of perceiving and evaluate things only from human perspectives and potentialities. They see but see nothing special. These persons do not suffer from a thick skull but a hardened heart. The parables are therefore a "two-edged sword" that reveal the mystery of the kingdom to dis-

---

20. Cranfield, *Mark*, 153.

21. Geddert, *Watchwords*, 154.

22. The passive voice refers to God, who gives the secret. It "is not something which men discover by their own insight: it can only be known by God's revelation" (Cranfield, *Mark*, 154).

23. Geddert, *Watchwords*, 76; see also Marshall, *Faith As a Theme*, 62.

ciples who understand but create blindness in others.[24] Edwards comments that they are

> like the cloud which separated the fleeing Israelites from the pursuing Egyptians. It brought "darkness to the one side and light to the other" (Exod 14:20). The same cloud which condemned the Egyptians to their hardness of heart also protected Israel and made a way for her through the sea. That which was blindness to Egypt was revelation to Israel.[25]

Outsiders see no revelation of the kingdom of God in Jesus' miracles, his teaching, or his death. Only insiders, even if they are sometimes confused by its enigmatic concealment, can see the truth.

The secret is therefore revealed to those who respond to Jesus by hearing and following. Jesus' charge to hear only occurs in the public parables and not in the private explanations because insiders have already heard and have responded by coming to Jesus to hear more. Disciples are not quicker than others, nor are they able to unravel mysteries for themselves. The mystery is something that is "given" to them. The understanding comes by grace as Jesus' interpretation unlocks the mystery for them.

The quotation from Isaiah 6:9–10. The citation from Isaiah has long troubled commentators because it suggests that Jesus deliberately excludes people by making things hard to understand with dark sayings that cloak the truth. The context in Isaiah is helpful for interpreting what is meant. God tells the prophet to preach in spite of warning him in advance that it will only harden the hearts of the hearers until God carries out the punishment.[26] That command brims over with irony and scorn. God calls a faithful prophet to preach to faithless people. Jesus' explanation for the parables has the same ironic tenor and can be translated: "So that they may indeed see but not perceive, and may indeed hear but not understand; because the last thing they want is to turn and have their sins forgiven."[27] In Isaiah's time the people could not understand the

---

24. Joel Marcus, "Mark 4:10–12 and Marcan Epistemology," *JBL* 103 (1984): 566.

25. James R. Edwards, "Markan Sandwiches: The Significance of Interpolations in Markan Narratives," *NovT* 31 (1989): 215.

26. C. F. D. Moule ("Mark 4:1–20 Yet Once More," *Neotestamentica et Semitica*, eds. E. E. Ellis and M. Wilcox [Edinburgh: T. & T. Clark, 1969], 99–100) argues that Isa. 6:9–10, in spite of the purpose clause, was not God's instruction to the prophet to make his message unintelligible. "It is only reasonable to take the final clauses as, at most, a vigorous way of stating the inevitable, as those by a very forceful indicative clause." Hooker (*Mark*, 128) comments: "Jewish thought tended to blur the distinction between purpose and result; if God was sovereign, then of course what happened must be his will, however strange this appeared."

27. B. Hollenbach, "Lest They Should Turn Again and Be Forgiven: Irony," *BibTrans* 34 (1983): 320.

message until the land and Jerusalem were decimated (Isa. 6:11–13). What was true for the days of Isaiah holds true for the time of Jesus. The present time is one of concealment and suffering, and understanding may have to wait destruction—the death of the Son of God and the desolation of Jerusalem.[28]

Insiders and outsiders. What is it that makes one an insider over against an outsider? Kermode objects that the outsider seems to be kept "outside, dismayed and frustrated in a seemingly arbitrary manner."[29] But this misreads the text, because the key element that distinguishes one from the other is that the insider *gathers around* Jesus as an honest inquirer (Mark 4:10). Disciples are no different from anyone in needing explanations for the parables, but they are different from outsiders in that they choose to come to Jesus for explanations. They also have to puzzle out the parables, but they ask questions sincerely.[30] The decisive difference is that insiders are not indifferent. At the conclusion of this section of parables, Mark tells us that Jesus explains the parables to his disciples privately because they come to him and ask for an explanation (4:34). The fact that Jesus does this in private does not mean that he intends to exclude the others. Outsiders simply do not regard what he says to be critical enough to bother joining the disciples around Jesus in order to receive illumination.

Being an insider, however, does not mean that one knows everything. Insiders are elite only in the sense that they have knowledge that will save their lives. But insiders can be baffled and deceived and must watch how they listen. Malbon observes, "The resounding pattern is this: Hear. Understand? Listen again! See. Understand? Look again!"[31] Insiders and outsiders are not separated by an unbridgeable chasm, such as the one that divided Lazarus from the rich man. So-called outsiders can become insiders, otherwise "the whole mission of preaching the good news of God's kingship is a cruel hoax."[32] "The Twelve and the others around him" (4:10) must not be considered a closed group. So-called insiders can become outsiders; other-

---

28. The prophet Ezekiel also had to endure a people who had eyes to see but did not see, and ears to hear but did not hear (Ezek. 12:2–3). They did not listen to his announcement of judgment because they believed that it only applied to distant times (12:27). He laments that the people think his preaching is unclear, only riddles and allegories (17:2; 20:49).

29. Frank Kermode, *The Genesis of Secrecy* (Cambridge: Harvard Univ. Press, 1979), 27–29.

30. At Qumran a similar idea is expressed. According to 1QS 5:11–12, the wicked ones who are outside the covenant are those who have not "sought nor examined his decrees in order to know the hidden things in which they err by their own fault and because they treated revealed matters with disrespect."

31. Elizabeth Struthers Malbon, "Echoes and Foreshadowings in Mark 4–8: Reading and Rereading," *JBL* 112 (1993): 225.

32. France, *Divine Government*, 40.

wise there would be no reason to caution them to pay heed to how they listen so that they can discern what lies hidden beneath the surface.

As the story progresses, the disciples' dazed incomprehension (7:17–18; 8:14–21, 27–33; 9:9–13, 30–32; 10:23–31, 32–45; 11:20–25) and blindness (4:35–41; 6:45–52; 9:2–8; 14:17–25, 32–43) reveals that even they are at risk of becoming outsiders. They particularly fail to grasp fully the secret of the cross and resurrection. At the end, one becomes a traitor and betrays him; another denies him. All flee, leaving him to die alone. On the other hand, apparent outsiders often show the faith of insiders: the woman with the flow of blood (5:34), the Syrophoenician woman (7:29), the father of an epileptic (9:24), the exorcists who do not follow the disciples (9:38–41), the mothers of children (10:13–16), blind Bartimaeus (10:46–52), the woman who anointed Jesus (14:3–9), and the Roman centurion (15:39).

Blind Bartimaeus is even located "by the roadside" (10:46), the place where Satan is supposed to carry away the seeds before they have a chance even to take root (4:4, 15). One might not regard it as a promising spot for a disciple to be, but he acclaims Jesus and follows him (see 8:27; 9:33–34; 10:32). There is good news in the misunderstanding of the disciples. If we fail to comprehend perfectly all of the mystery, neither do these first disciples,[33] and Jesus does not discard them for a more insightful lot. But there is also a stern admonition for us to be earnest listeners lest we fail to bear fruit.

The Interpretation of the Parable of the Sower (4:13–20)

THE CONTEXT IN Mark assumes that there can be no understanding without interpretation,[34] and Jesus provides one for those who ask. In Hellenistic

---

33. James G. Williams, *Gospel Against Parable: Mark's Language of Mystery* (Sheffield: Almond, 1985), 63.

34. For some time scholars have argued that Jesus did not use allegory and that parables do not need interpretation. Therefore, they have assumed that when a parable includes an interpretation, the early church added the interpretation. One can make a case that the interpretation of the parable of the sower does go back to Jesus.

(1) The version of the parable in the *Gospel of Thomas* does not include an interpretation, and some scholars assume that it is an independent witness to early tradition. This assumption is doubtful, and the interpretation could have been omitted because this work intentionally deletes explanations to keep Jesus' teaching arcane. (2) Some argue that the allegorical interpretation of the parable misses the supposed eschatological point, which has to do with the miraculous harvest at the end of time. This argument begs the question if that is not the key point of the parable. The interpretation is not out of balance with the parable. If the emphasis is on the abundant harvest, the interpretation gives it the same amount of attention that it receives in the parable. It also gives the same amount of attention to the losses that they receive in the parable. (3) The interpretation supposedly contains the vocabulary of the early church, which has applied the parable to its own setting to

literature, the sower is a stock image for a teacher; sowing, for teaching; and soils, for students. Readers would have easily grasped the connections, but there are crucial differences. Since the sowing of the seed was a fixed metaphor in Jewish tradition for something God would do, Jesus' parable is not about the cultivation of minds through education but the renewal of Israel. The interpretation of the parable shows that the things that cause the seed to come to grief are not the limited mental aptitude of the student (the reasons given in Hellenistic comparisons); they are caused by a cosmic struggle between God and Satan, by persecution, and by ethical (not intellectual) impoverishment.

In Mark, the challenge to "listen" or "hear" begins and ends the parable (4:3, 9). The interpretation stresses that all of the soils have heard the word (4:15, 16, 18, 20). The sower has been successful in getting the seed sown; what happens next depends on the soil. The verb "to sow" is used in two senses: to sow in the sense of scattering seed, and to be sown in the sense of the ground being implanted with seed. The interpretation raises the question of whether the listener is going to produce any harvest, thus turning the parable of the sower into the parable of the soils. The parable shows that the productivity of the seed depends entirely on whether it lands in good or bad soil. Moving from the world of farming to spiritual realities, the parable suggests that the reception of the word (the seed) is directly related to the pre-existing spiritual state of the hearers' hearts, and the interpretation draws out the special differences among them.

The soil along the path (hodos) serves as a warning that Satan, though bound, is still a danger to those who hear indifferently. Two kingdoms are in deadly combat for the souls of humans, and Satan feasts off the types represented in the story by the teachers of the law from Jerusalem, the Herodians, and the chief priests.[35] They hear Jesus and immediately want to

---

describe what typically happens in mission situations. This judgment is based on a limited statistical basis and assumes that Jesus did not reflect on the response of the people to his mission; that was something that only the later church did. It is conceivable that Jesus' parable affected church terminology or that the language in the interpretation was influenced by terms in use at the time it was translated from Aramaic into the Greek. (4) Finally, the interpretation of the fates of the seed is not inconsistent with Jesus' teaching elsewhere in the Gospels, and a parallel in m.'Abot 5:10–15 contains six paragraphs, each analyzing four different types of people, including four different types of hearers (5:12). W. D. Davies and Dale C. Allison, Jr. (The Gospel According to Saint Matthew [ICC; Edinburgh: T. & T. Clark, 1991], 2:376) conclude from this parallel: "It is not inconceivable that already in Jesus' time it was conventional to make a point by referring to four different classes of people (see 'Abot R. Nat. A 40), and this might be part of the background of the parable of the sower."

35. Jewish literature also identifies Satan with a bird or birds; see Jub. 11:5–24; 1 Enoch 29:5; T. Ben. 3:4; Apoc Abr. 13; b. Sanh. 107a.

destroy him (3:22; 11:18). For some listeners it will be of no avail, no matter what Jesus says or does. They observe his deeds, such as his healing the sick and casting out demons, and conclude that he works by black magic or Beelzebub, or that he is crazy. The explanation for their failure to hear is that Satan has caused them to oppose the kingdom. Satan controls them, not Jesus (3:22). Significantly, Mark tells us that the disciples were on the road (*hodos*) when they demonstrated their failure to understand the mystery that Jesus revealed to them about his death and resurrection by quarreling about who was the greatest (9:33–34) and who would get to sit on his right and left in his glory (10:32–41).

The seed in the rocky ground springs up immediately and receives the word joyfully. But the impenetrable stratum of rock does not allow the root of the plant to sink deep into nourishing soil. When the good times of joy are over and the time of tribulation and persecution arrives, the plant shrivels. The faith of such people is "like the morning mist, like the early dew that disappears" (Hos. 6:4). These listeners fall away (lit., "are scandalized") when threatened by the slightest challenge to their faith.

In the story, we find crowds who are like flares, glowing with astonishment at Jesus' teaching and miracles and rejoicing at his arrival in Jerusalem (12:37); but they do not have a deeply rooted faith, and when suffering looms on the horizon, they quickly fizzle out. Even the disciples, who have been so quick to respond, will also be quick to fall away when the pressure mounts. Jesus warns them about this danger at the Last Supper (14:27, 29), and his prediction is fulfilled when they run for their lives after his arrest. They are obsessed with their own safety and the preservation of life as they know it. Peter (Rock) discredits himself further. He follows Jesus from a safe distance into the courtyard of the high priest but withers in the face of a gentle accusation from a slave girl. He cannot withstand the heat of opposition and denies his Lord three times. The rocky ground serves as a warning that one's faith must run deep if one hopes to endure the coming trials and tribulations.

The third soil is not infertile but so weed-ridden that the good seed is ultimately suffocated. Jesus frequently warns in his teaching against the things identified with the choking thorns: the cares of the world, the delight in riches, and the desire for other things. Herod's story provides an example of one who hears the word gladly (6:20), but whose greater concern to preserve his honor and power extinguishes any chance that his hearing will bear fruit for God (6:21–29). The rich ruler is the most obvious example of how concern for material wealth blocks one from responding to Jesus' call to discipleship (10:17–22). Judas's story offers another warning of how money, not even riches, can entice even one of the Twelve to make the wrong choice. He sells out his master for the promise of some silver (14:10–11).

Jesus' preaching reveals the good earth as well as the bad. One knows something is good earth simply because it bears fruit. In contrast to the bad soil, good soil hears rightly. Gundry draws out the vital differences. The good hearer welcomes the word immediately so that it cannot be snatched away by Satan. The good hearer welcomes it deeply so that it is not withered by persecution. The good hearer welcomes it exclusively so that other concerns do not strangle it.[36] As the seed fails in three different ways in the bad soils, it succeeds in three different ways in good soil; but the parable and interpretation do not expand on the reasons for this varying success.

Bridging Contexts

IN BRINGING THE message of this parable into our age, we will first focus on the parabolic method of making the kingdom known and will then turn to the scandal that the explanation for the parables rouses. The disciples and those around Jesus asked about the parables; we want to know why he spoke in riddles that seem designed to conceal his message from outsiders. How could Jesus intentionally devise barriers to exclude people from coming into a saving relationship with God? Finally, we will discuss the parable's capacity to have multiple meanings.

Making the kingdom known. In bridging the contexts one cannot avoid the parables' purpose to hide the truth from those who are spiritually calcified. Parables are not homely stories for sluggish minds or visual aids designed to illustrate a simple point. As a didactic method, they are "the opposite of prosaic, propositional teaching." The teaching is indirect and requires an investment of imagination and thought to seek their meaning for us.[37] If one refuses to make that investment, then one will find no meaning in Jesus' parables.

But parables are more than simply a didactic method. Jesus did not come merely to unveil fresh ideas about God or to confirm what everyone already believed but to call people to repent and to revolutionize their entire perspective about God and life. In Mark, parables are the form of God's revelation that both reveal the mystery and hide it at the same time. The mystery is so great that prosaic propositions cannot fully express it. Claud-Adrian Helvétius in *De l'Esprit* wrote: "Almost all philosophers agree, that the most sublime truths once reduced to their plainest terms, may be converted into facts, and in that case present nothing more to the mind than this proposition, *white is white, and black is black.*" Parables are the means of making the kingdom authentically known. They require a flexible mind and an open

---

36. Gundry, *Mark*, 206.
37. France, *Divine Government*, 30.

heart to stretch around such an enormous concept as the kingdom of God, which comes with no objective proofs.

The only way parables can be understood at the deepest level is for one to dare to become involved in their world, to be willing to risk seeing God with new eyes, and to allow that vision to transform one's being. Parables do not always make something obscure clearer by using vivid picture language. On the contrary, they may only befuddle. If one is blasé and takes no interest in what they might mean or in the one who speaks them, or if one refuses to make any decision until all the facts are in, one will remain in a fog.

If one is not indifferent but seeks to understand, however, then one mulls them over in the mind and comes for an interpretation. Only then does the parable perform its work of transforming our vision of God and the world and of leading us to spiritual insight. We can only learn what the riddle means "in respectful allegiance to the riddler"[38] and by "learning to 'see' and 'hear' that which goes beyond the data available to the senses."[39] Ultimately, one does not grasp the mystery through intellectual capacity. God gives it to those open to the truth.

This indirect means of revealing God's truth may make us uncomfortable. As teachers or preachers we do not want to be accused of being unclear. We may provide careful outlines and offer lengthy explanations to help everyone understand. We may feel that we have somehow failed if people remain confused. How many would have the courage to deliver a deliberately obscure message, as Jesus did, and then wait in the church parlor for worthy inquirers to come for an explanation? This text suggests, however, that we may fail to understand the truth of the gospel and rob it of some of its power if we think that everything must be kept simple and clear. It may lead us to reexamine what we are trying to do and how we are to go about making committed disciples. Jesus did not strive to make things easier for the crowds to comprehend or to make them feel more comfortable. His enigmatic teaching served to separate those who were curious from those who were serious, those who were seeking only a religious sideshow from those who were truly seeking after God. He was intent on eliciting genuine faith, and Mark's Gospel insists that faith is born of the tension between the revealing and the veiling of the truth.

Geddert offers the stimulating thesis that Mark himself adopted this enigmatic method in composing his Gospel. He argues that the subtle mystery, the deliberate ambiguity, and the veiled clues that have so intrigued

---

38. F. C. Synge, "A Plea for the Outsiders: Commentary on Mark 4:10–12," *Journal of Theology of South Africa* 30 (1980): 55.

39. Geddert, *Watchwords*, 255.

scholars about this Gospel were the deliberate means chosen by the Evangelist to communicate his profound theology and to challenge would-be disciples. He is "modelling himself after the Markan Jesus who also speaks ambiguously, calls for hearers to grasp points not made explicitly, and firmly believes that divine illumination will bring hearers to the understanding they need."[40]

This passage forces us to reflect on our goals and methods in proclaiming the kingdom of God. Are we trying to lead people to a deeper understanding of the truth of God and to deepen their commitment, or are we trying to pad our statistics? Many churches that have used mass-marketing strategies and have tailored their worship services to attract customers are successful at least in beating Satan from devouring the seed before it even has a chance to germinate. People come to hear who otherwise would never darken the door of a church. But these churches may find that they, like churches following more traditional patterns, have assembled persons who run for the exits the first time there is the slightest cost for their faith. Their growth in discipleship will be stunted by their desire for God to bless their craving for material securities and comforts more than their spiritual lives.

Some research suggests that the boom in Baby Boomers' church attendance has flattened out. Recent reports show that they now show up once in every four to six weeks rather than four times a month, and that they volunteer less and give less. Seekers must move beyond the seeker stage! How do we make disciples who can focus what they see into clear images of God? How do we make disciples who can separate what they hear into the clear commands of God, which they will then heed? This is the church's crucial task and one that Mark's Gospel seeks to address.

The scandal of the gospel. One thing that must be done is to allow the scandal of the gospel to have its full force. McCracken argues that parables "are not modes of instruction but rather forms of offense" designed to obstruct the truth.[41] This in itself is a scandal to us. Elements that are odd, fantastic, extravagant, and offensive are crucial to parables that aim at shattering the comfortable world where everything is in its place. McCracken contends that the parables were not invented to convey points or to express propositions but to precipitate internal action, forcing the hearer or reader to a crisis or collision that requires movement. In New Testament terms, that crisis is an either/or proposition: either stumbling or changing-and-becoming, either enacting a lie that we want or being transformed. The danger is that we will

---

40. Ibid., 256.

41. David McCracken, *The Scandal of the Gospels: Jesus, Story and Offense* (New York/ Oxford: Oxford Univ. Press, 1994).

try to minimize and domesticate the offense, making it barely recognizable and conveniently dodging any bothersome collision with the truth.[42]

Scandal is a necessary part of encountering the divine and having faith, even though it presents an obstacle that may block the way to truth and alienate one from God. It creates a crisis that reveals the hidden desires of the heart. Being offended reveals one's sin, and it can lead one further away from God or back toward the God who always resists human aspirations. If one yearns for God, one can work through the offense and come closer to God. If the heart's desires reign supreme, one will be alienated. We might ask ourselves what we find offensive about these parables and Jesus' explanation for them and then try to examine why we are offended. Does our offense stem from the discovery that God's ways are not our ways?

Sower and soils. We would argue that the parables of Jesus are open to a variety of meanings, and one need not feel constrained to limit a parable to a single point. The one-point dogma places the interpreter in a straightjacket and can limit the effectiveness of the parables.[43] The parable of the sower can be explored from several perspectives. One can reflect on the parable from the perspective of the task of sowing, proclaiming the word. The sower is not interpreted allegorically. Jesus does not say, "I am the sower"; and this indefiniteness allows the parable to apply to those besides Jesus who sow the word (see 3:14). For Mark's church and for ours the task of sowing continues, and the varieties of response and the reasons for them have little changed.

One can also apply the parable to help clarify the mission of the church in times of discouragement. It helps downcast sowers begin to understand that sowers can only sow and can do nothing about the nature of the soil. The parable mentions nothing about plowing, manuring, weeding the field, or even putting up a scarecrow to scare off the birds. The sower in this parable is not responsible for the soil on which he sows.

One can also look at the parable from the perspective of the soils and the responsibility to hear rightly. Individuals can take responsibility for what kind of soil they are, fruitful or unfruitful. It has been impossible to conceal the miracles that Jesus has done. The word has reached everywhere, including Jerusalem, and experts are sent to check things out. Jesus has taught

---

42. One can see an example of this in all the attempts to explain away the *hina,* "in order that," in 4:12.

43. J. Dominic Crossan (in "Parable," *ABD,* 5:152) goes so far as to say, "It is a parable's destiny to be interpreted and those interpretations will be diverse. When the diversity ceases, the parable is dead and the parabler is silent." Walter Wink (*Transforming Bible Study* [Nashville: Abingdon, 1980], 161) says: "The fallacy of the one-point theory should have become manifest the moment it became clear that scholars themselves could not agree on what the one point was—though each was certain that *he* knew!"

openly. But not everyone can make the connection between what Jesus says and does and the advent of the kingdom of God. The obscurity of the parables does not cause the listeners' unbelief so much as their unwillingness to repent. This recalcitrance makes them unable to grasp the mystery of the kingdom. What is hard to see is that Jesus the Nazarene who was crucified (16:6) is Lord of the world. We become blind because we would rather give our allegiance to other lords who oblige our selfish desires.

WE CAN APPLY the parable to our role as sowers of God's word. Many churches are making adjustments in the worship to make it more user-friendly for those labeled "seekers." Jesus' method of proclaiming the kingdom of God should cause us to ask, however, to what end are we doing this? Three observations can be made related to issues of church growth.

(1) The sower in the parable does not prejudge soil. He casts the seeds with abandon and does not decide in advance whether the soil has potential or not, whether it is a waste of time or not. The message is not test-marketed first to see what the response is likely to be and then to adjust the message to ensure the best reception of the product. There is no concern to hit target groups only, to visit only certain kinds of people who are like us. There is no fear of sowing outside the boundaries.

In his proposals for church growth, Wagner has contended that resources of time, personnel, and money should be focused where there is the greatest receptivity to the gospel.[44] Although he insists that we not bypass those who are resistant but must establish a friendly presence and quietly sow the seed,[45] this parable should make us cautious that we not preempt the sovereignty of God or the role of the Holy Spirit. Any farmer knows that sowing is risky business, but that does not keep the farmer from risking his seed. The danger is that we might hide behind principles of church growth to justify our neglect of those whom we prejudge to be resistant and to assuage our conscience when we decide to abandon ministry in the hardscrabble soil of the inner cities and flee to the "more fruitful" suburbs.

The parable makes the point that some seed falling in the right place yields fruit. One should not infer from this that Jesus advises sowers to sow seed only in the right place, where the conditions promise a good crop.

---

44. C. Peter Wagner, *Church Growth and the Whole Gospel: A Biblical Mandate* (San Francisco: Harper and Row, 1981), 77–78.

45. C. Peter Wagner, *Strategies for Church Growth* (Ventura, Calif.: Regal 1987), 88–89.

When one is sowing something like the word in the hearts of people, how does one know that the conditions are right until the sowing occurs? When dealing with human hearts, how long does one wait before giving up hope for a harvest? Adoniram Judson went seven years before he made a convert. The parable invites us to become prodigal sowers, scattering the seed far and wide.

(2) The explanation for the parable indicates that success comes from God. Jesus affirms that insight into the mystery of the kingdom is something given by God. As sowers we can take no credit for any success that comes from our sowing, nor need we beat ourselves down for any failure. Paul's argument to the Corinthians about the unity of the work is apropos (1 Cor. 3:5–9):

> What, after all, is Apollos? And what is Paul? Only servants, through whom you came to believe—as the Lord has assigned to each his task. I planted the seed, Apollos watered it, but God made it grow. So neither he who plants nor he who waters is anything, but only God, who makes things grow. The man who plants and the man who waters have one purpose, and each will be rewarded according to his own labor. For we are God's fellow workers; you are God's field, God's building.

Some will minister where one type of soil might predominate, but no one can boast over success when laboring in a particularly productive field. Tradition says that the Palestinian plowman began his task with a prayer:

> Lord, my task is the red [referring to the reddish soil]
> the green is Thine
> We plow, but it is Thou that dost give the crop.[46]

(3) Sowers are not called to be successful but to be faithful. As sowers, we are to aim for success, a harvest. But the peril is that we may become so consumed with the outward signs of success that we get converts with no deep root system that will support them over the long haul. We read about or hear others brag about those whose ministry has met with enormous numerical and financial victories. Frequently people judge success by numbers. Americans in particular assume that bigger is better and that the presence of large numbers is a sure sign of the Spirit's presence. The corollary is that failure is also measured by numbers, and a low response is construed as a sign of the Spirit's absence. The danger of these assumptions for the spiritual development of disciples is that we will offer the lowest common

---

46. Henri Daniel-Rops, *Daily Life in the Time of Jesus* (Ann Arbor: Servant, 1980), 233.

denominator spirituality, which caters to mass appeal and fails to challenge the hearers' sins and worldviews.

A newspaper interview recently reported that the creator of a long-running, irreverent TV show was "born again." He claimed, however, that his conversion did not lead to any new moral standards at the network: "All it does is give me peace of mind in my personal life, and I enjoy the pastor who holds my attention with his good natured sermons full of jokes and anecdotes." One is reminded of Dante's chiding of recreant preachers in *The Divine Comedy*.

> Now they go with jests and buffoonery
> to preach and, provided people laugh loudly,
> the cowl puff up [pleased] and no more is required.[47]

Marsha Witten writes about receiving a slick direct-mail solicitation from a new church in her neighborhood. It trumpeted itself as a "new church designed to meet your needs," with "positive, practical messages which uplift you each week." The topics were about how to feel good about yourself, how to overcome depression, how to have a full and successful life, how to handle money, how to handle stress, and so on. She noted that it offered a "cheerful, practical list of the social and psychological pleasures one might receive from affiliation within its church, with no mention whatsoever of faith or God, let alone of suffering or spiritual striving."[48] To be faithful sowers of the word, one needs to preach the whole gospel—including the discomforting parts that hack away at our selfish concerns to be at ease and uplifted—and let whatever happens happen.

The opposing kingdom puts up a fight, and the world is not uniformly productive. The word will meet with adversity and opposition. Not everyone is going to receive God's word with open arms; many will spurn it. The same sun that melts ice also bakes clay as hard as a brick. It was Paul's experience. He writes in 2 Corinthians 2:15–16: "We are to God the aroma of Christ among those who are being saved and those who are perishing. To the one we are the smell of death; to the other, the fragrance of life." We need a deep sense of God's call not to be overcome by discouragement when our faithful labors meet with little response. Isaiah was not allowed to use the failure of the people to respond to his message as an excuse to quit preaching.

Sometimes people respond to the word as airline passengers respond to the stewardess's instructions before the takeoff on what to do in case of an

---

47. *The Divine Comedy*, "Paradise" 29.115–17, trans. H. R. Hulse (New York: Holt, Rinehart and Winston, 1954), 462.

48. Marsha G. Witten, *All Is Forgiven: The Secular Message in American Protestantism* (Princeton: Princeton Univ. Press, 1994), 3–4.

emergency. She invites passengers to watch and listen and follow along with the card in the seat pocket in front of them, but most blithely ignore the instructions. They are preoccupied in conversations, absorbed in their reading, staring out the window, or dozing off. The stewardess looks bored with it all herself as she goes through the motions for the umpteenth time, but she is dealing with life-and-death matters. No airline would allow the stewardess to skip those preflight instructions simply because no one seems to bother to listen. Since the power of the seed to bring forth fruit in good soil does not belong to the sower, one should not despair over the apparent failures, the blindness of unfaith, or the pernicious opposition. Minear astutely observes: "If some prove to be blind, that is God's business, not yours. If they do not have hearing ears, you will never know it except by speaking to them."[49]

The preaching of the word may not be received, but it remains powerful. Sometimes we find it difficult to believe that God's word does not fail when we are in the midst of decline. We may fall victim to despair when we cannot point to great successes to confirm that our faith is not just whistling in the dark, that there is substance to it. Opinion polls and a triumphant response, however, do not determine the truth of what we believe.

We can also apply the parable to our responsibility to receive the word as good soil. Soil is unable to change its character, but humans can. The parable serves as a warning to listeners, that they need to do a soil test on themselves. Insiders can easily become outsiders and become like the unproductive soil. One must constantly heed the dangers that plagued what makes bad soil bad and be mindful that in the parable the failure comes in different stages. Some seed is lost immediately and does not even get into the ground. Some is lost eventually; it gets into the ground but withers at the root. Some gets down deep enough into the ground to grow but ultimately is choked out by the thorns.[50]

Sometimes we can be like the hardened soil on the path. Nothing sinks in. We remain untouched by the word in the center of gravity in our lives. We do not understand and do not care to invest what it takes to come to any understanding. Louis Armstrong once was asked to define jazz. He responded, "Man, when you got to ask what it is, you'll never get to know." Many do not care about jazz and so do not bother to find out what it is. Many do not care about the good news of God, but the difference is that what Jesus is talking about affects all of life and one's eternal relationship with God.

---

49. Minear, *Mark*, 70.

50. J. Dominic Crossan, *Cliffs of Fall: Paradox and Polyvalence in the Parables of Jesus* (New York: Seabury, 1980), 47.

Sometimes we are in danger of becoming like the shallow-rooted soil. Any hint of persecution or tribulation shrivels any faith we might have. How many would pack the pews if they knew that their license plate numbers were being written down by Gestapo-like police, and that their lives, property, and children were threatened because of their faith? Someone has said that it takes courage to stand up and be counted but even more courage to keep standing up after you have been counted. Jesus' discourse in Mark 13 reveals that tribulation is not some tedious detour, it is the main highway for Christian disciples (see also 9:49, "everyone will be salted with fire"; 10:30, "with ... persecutions"; 1 Thess. 3:1–3). Jesus does not promise freedom from oppression but plenty of it. Mark's Gospel contends that the courage to withstand the oppression derives from a deeply rooted faith. If we must enter the kingdom of God by way of many afflictions (Acts 14:22), then one must be prepared when they come. Many rejoice during the days of miracles, but the days of suffering test their faith (see James 1:2–3, 12; 1 Peter 1:6–7; 4:12). The deepest walk with God comes when we are under pressure, yet can see beyond the immediate suffering. It transforms pain into privilege (see Acts 5:41–42; Phil. 1:6, 29).

The third danger is that of materialism, which cramps faith. Many in the church would like to have it both ways—to have wealth (or at least a comfortable nest egg) and to be faithful to God—and they try to pursue both equally. Jesus likened this to trying to serve two different masters (Matt. 6:24)—as futile as trying to follow a road that forks. Jesus knew that such things always crowd in and strangle any commitment to God.

Peter de Vries, in his novel *The Mackeral Plaza*, describes people who live "a kind of hand to mouth luxury, never knowing where their next quarterly installment of taxes or the payment on the third car is coming from." Most know firsthand the well-known axiom that our yearnings always exceed our earnings, and in our consumer-oriented society, a faith that calls for sacrifice and service for others soon takes a back seat. Those who are satisfied with their level of devotion to God but never satisfied with the abundance of what they already have will never bear a harvest worth taking away. The glut of how-to books flooding the market, which promise to teach the buyers how to relax their way to success, to be energetic and beautiful, to win big money, unlimited power, and control over others, reveals that we live in a narcissistic age. Many Christians travel so heavily laden with concerns for such things in their own walk with God that they soon drop back and then drop out. They are unwilling to take the risks required by any deeply rooted commitment to God for fear of sacrificing their standard of living.

Ministers are not immune to these temptations. A retired pastor advised a young seminary student puzzling about what to do when he graduated:

"Son, go where the money is. God is everywhere." This attitude only prepares the soil for thistles to flourish and creates followers who do not seek first the kingdom of God. Instead, they believe that they must first get a good education, first get a good job, first marry, first find a nice house in a nice locality surrounded by nice people, first have some nice children, first furnish their home with nice things ... and on and on.[51] After all these other firsts, God comes in a distant last.

The parable identifies what makes bad soil bad: the beaten-down path represents those who do not want to repent; the rocky soil, the dropouts who want only life without tribulation; the thorn-infested ground, those whose life is wrapped up in making money and having the best things in life. But the parable does not identify what makes good soil good so that it produces a good yield. What is a thirtyfolder, a sixtyfolder, a hundredfolder? Jesus tells us the reasons for the failures but not the precise modes of success. The parable does not tell us how to become good earth—only to be careful how we hear.[52] One can only know that after reading the whole of the Gospel of Mark and learning from the example of Jesus.

---

51. Compare Søren Kierkegaard, "The Instant, No. 7," *Kierkegaard's Attack Upon "Christendom" 1854–1855*, ed. W. Lowrie (Princeton: Princeton Univ. Press, 1944), 208–11.

52. Note Deut. 11:13–17, which commands single-minded obedience to God if the land is to produce a physical harvest. The same is required for a spiritual harvest.

Mark 4:21–34

HE SAID TO them, "Do you bring in a lamp to put it under a bowl or a bed? Instead, don't you put it on its stand? ²²For whatever is hidden is meant to be disclosed, and whatever is concealed is meant to be brought out into the open. ²³If anyone has ears to hear, let him hear."

²⁴"Consider carefully what you hear," he continued. "With the measure you use, it will be measured to you—and even more. ²⁵Whoever has will be given more; whoever does not have, even what he has will be taken from him."

²⁶He also said, "This is what the kingdom of God is like. A man scatters seed on the ground. ²⁷Night and day, whether he sleeps or gets up, the seed sprouts and grows, though he does not know how. ²⁸All by itself the soil produces grain—first the stalk, then the head, then the full kernel in the head. ²⁹As soon as the grain is ripe, he puts the sickle to it, because the harvest has come."

³⁰Again he said, "What shall we say the kingdom of God is like, or what parable shall we use to describe it? ³¹It is like a mustard seed, which is the smallest seed you plant in the ground. ³²Yet when planted, it grows and becomes the largest of all garden plants, with such big branches that the birds of the air can perch in its shade."

³³With many similar parables Jesus spoke the word to them, as much as they could understand. ³⁴He did not say anything to them without using a parable. But when he was alone with his own disciples, he explained everything.

Original Meaning

THE CONCENTRIC PATTERN of this discourse[1] helps us see that the first two parables about the lamp and the measure in 4:21–25 complement the explanation about the parables in 4:10–12. They express in parable what Jesus spoke plainly to the Twelve and to those around him when they asked him privately about the parables. The second pair of parables, the seed cast on the earth (4:26–29) and the mustard seed sown on

---

1. See above, p. 152.

the earth (4:30–32), are counterparts to the parable of the sower of the seed (4:3–9) and complement each other in developing the theme of the hiddenness of the kingdom.

The Parable of the Lamp (4:21–23)

GOD'S MEANS OF making the kingdom manifest through hiding it may mystify those who prefer that God do things in ways that match human methods and expectations. The parable of the lamp affirms that God's purpose is not to shroud the light in darkness but to make it manifest to all. The Greek text reads literally, "Does the lamp come?" and may allude to Jesus as the lamp who "comes" (compare John 9:5).[2] For the present, secrecy abounds, not because there is anything wrong with the lamp, but because God intends it (*hina*, "in order that," occurs four times in 4:21–22). Paradoxically, what is hidden becomes plain by the process of concealing it.[3]

In other words, God's glory is revealed indirectly in disarming ways through riddling parables, weakness, suffering, and death. The mystery of the relationship of Jesus to God's reign will become clearer after his death on the cross and his resurrection—after his earthly ministry—but even then it will go unrecognized by those who grope in their own darkness. Many will remain clueless until the end because their eyes have been blinded by the dazzle of this world's fond hopes and because their ears have been deafened by the din of this present evil age.

The Parable of the Measure (4:24–25)

THE PARABLE OF the measure refers to the ways people respond to the light.[4] The economic axiom that the poor get poorer and the rich get richer also holds true for the spiritual life. Those who do not hear well will become the have-nots who lose everything they might have as they become mired deeper in a slough of indifference and ignorance. Those who hear well will get more explanation of God's purposes and will have a superabundance of understanding. The parable contains both a warning and a promise and exhorts the readers to take care how they listen and respond to the word and the light.

---

2. Lane, *Mark*, 165; Hooker, *Mark*, 133. See the statements about the coming of Jesus in 1:7, 24, 38; 2:17; 10:45.

3. See Job 12:22, "He reveals the deep things of darkness and brings deep shadows into the light."

4. In Jesus' day, items were not purchased in prepackaged amounts but were measured out in standard-sized vessels. The merchant could be generous or could try to short customers. The saying reflects the consumer's wish that God (using a divine passive) would reward the generous and punish the chiseler.

One has access to the truth and must be careful not to turn a deaf ear to it. The one who snubs it has everything to lose; the one who risks faith in what now lies hidden has everything to gain.

The Parable of the Seed Cast on the Earth (4:26–29)

IN THE PARABLE of the seed sown on the earth Jesus again compares the things of God to the everyday world of a farmer.[5] The farmer casts his seed and then goes about his everyday routine of life: He sleeps; he rises, night and day.[6] Meanwhile, the seed sprouts and grows long—"he does not know how" (lit., "while he is unknowing," 4:27b). That the farmer has no idea how it grows implies that he is not the cause of the growth and is ignorant of the process.[7] The seed holds within itself the secret of its growth, and the earth is said to produce "all by itself" (*automate*, 4:28a). This word would be better rendered "without visible cause," "incomprehensibly," or even "effected by God," because pious Jews considered the growth of plants to be the wondrous work of God, not simply the result of a law of nature.[8]

The growth of the seed into a blade, a head, and then the full grain (4:28b) suggests an appointed order of development that may not be hurried or skipped over, nor can it be delayed. This sequence also assumes that whatever has transpired under the ground will become visible. When the seed is full grown, immediately the farmer reacts by putting his sickle to the grain, for the harvest has come. Curiously, the usual Greek word for ripen is not used.[9] Instead, the fruit is said literally "to deliver itself," "to hand itself over" (*paradidomi*). The conclusion may be a quotation from Joel 3:13: "Swing the sickle, for the harvest is ripe. Come, trample the grapes, for the winepress is full and the vats overflow—so great is their wickedness!" (see Jer. 51:33; Rev. 14:15). The context in Joel is one of judgment on the inordinate wickedness

---

5. This is the only parable peculiar to Mark, but parallels can be found in 1 Clem. 23:4; *Gos. Thom.* 21; *Ap. Jas.* 12:22–31.

6. This order reflects a Palestinian perspective of time where the day begins in the evening, not in the morning. In 14:30, Mark recognizes his audience does not tell time this way. He clarifies Jesus' announcement that Peter would deny him three times "today," by adding, "yes, tonight."

7. He can hardly cause what he does not know, and this detail makes difficult any interpretation that allegorizes the farmer to represent Christ or God. Consequently, these options will be eliminated in the discussion.

8. Beasley-Murray, *Jesus and the Last Days*, 439. Nils Dahl ("The Parables of Growth," in *Jesus in the Memory of the Early Church* [Minneapolis: Augsburg, 1976], 147) writes: "To Jews and Christians organic growth was but the other side of the creative work of God who alone gives growth."

9. The two main Greek words are *akmazo* (Rev. 14:8) or *pepeiros* (Gen. 40:10).

of the Gentiles who are about to be judged. They stand in the valley of decision, and the Day of the Lord is near.

What this parable illustrates about the kingdom of God is open to several interpretations. The variety of titles given to it testifies to its ambiguity: The Growth of the Seed, The Seed Growing Secretly, The Seed Growing by Itself, The Seed Growing Gradually, The Patient Husbandmen, The Confident Sower, The Unbelieving Farmer, The Grain Is Ripe, and The Automatic Action of the Soil.[10] The parable is an example of what Sider calls proportional analogy: Humans are to the advent of the kingdom of God as a farmer is to the harvest. The listener must infer, however, with respect to what?[11] Should the interpreter focus on what happens to the seed? If so, should it be on the seed's growth or the harvest at the end? Should the interpreter focus on what the farmer does? If so, should it be on his inactivity while the seed grows of itself or on his sudden activity at the time of the harvest?

Various interpretations have been offered, depending on what is identified as the key element of the parable. One interpretation stresses the farmer's apparent confidence in the inevitability of the growth of the seed while waiting for the harvest. The parable begins with the sowing and ends with the harvest. This contrast might convey the idea that the kingdom of God follows as certainly as harvest follows the sowing of seed. A farmer is confident that there will be a harvest simply because the seed has been sown and will germinate in the soil and find the sun. Jeremias applies this confidence to Jesus in the context of his ministry:

> This unwavering assurance that God's hour approaches is an essential element in the preaching of Jesus. God's hour is coming: nay more, it has already begun. In his beginning the end is already implicit. No doubts with regard to his mission, no scorn, no lack of faith, no impatience, can make Jesus waver in his certainty that out of nothing, ignoring all failure, God is carrying on his beginnings to completion. All that is necessary is to take God seriously, to take him into account in spite of all outward appearance.[12]

The seed planted in the earth carries its own future in its bosom, and its growth to maturity is irresistible and certain. This certitude could encourage

---

10. See Claude N. Pavur, "The Grain Is Ripe: Parabolic Meaning in Mark 4:26–29," *BTB* 18 (1987): 21.

11. John W. Sider, "Proportional Analogy in the Gospel Parables," *NTS* 31 (1985): 18–19.

12. Joachim Jeremias, *The Parables of Jesus* (rev. ed.; New York: Charles Scribner's Sons, 1963), 153. The problem with this interpretation is that in Mark's Gospel, Jesus has met with astounding success with the crowds. Things look quite promising.

downcast disciples who may have been dismayed by apparent rejections and failures.

A second interpretation construes the detail of the farmer's rising and sleeping as an evidence of his patience while the seed bears fruit and the blade pushes through the earth, forms a stalk, and then the ear full of grain. The parable encourages those who excitedly await the kingdom of God to have the same unhurried patience as the farmer. As the harvest is God-given—the earth produces of itself, the farmer does not know how—so it is with the kingdom of God. The growth of plants cannot be forced. All the farmer can do is leave everything to God while continuing his daily routine, waiting patiently until the grain is ready to be harvested. The seed has been sown by God's agent, and now listeners can only wait for God to do what God is sure to do (see Lam. 3:26). A similar idea is expressed in prose in James 5:7–8:

> Be patient, then, brothers, until the Lord's coming. See how the farmer waits for the land to yield its valuable crop and how patient he is for the autumn and spring rains. You too, be patient and stand firm, because the Lord's coming is near.

A third interpretation construes differently the meaning of the farmer's inactivity while the seed sprouts. It may suggest that the farmer is unable to affect the process. The parable underlines the fact that the earth reproduces of itself, and the germination of the seed and its transforming growth is unrelated to the farmer's ability, activity, or wisdom. The growth leading to the harvest comes from God and takes place because of the seed's inherent power, independent of human resources, aid, or force. It may convey that the kingdom of God is "unstoppable by human unbelief and unhelped by human effort."[13] Humans can only respond when it invades their life.

A fourth interpretation emphasizes the hiddenness of the process. The parable may teach that it does not matter that the kingdom is hidden to so many; something is taking place underground that will become fully visible in due course. The kingdom has begun to work even though its significance is yet to be appreciated by all because the growth is so imperceptible. Something is occurring underground with the seed that may be overlooked. When it is in its blade stage, only the practiced eye can see what it will become. When the field is fully ripe, however, it cannot be overlooked.

Still another interpretation seizes on the sudden conclusion of the process. The inactivity of the farmer while the wheat was growing contrasts with the sudden rush of activity at harvest time when the wheat is ripe. Some suggest that Jesus intended to announce that the eschatological harvest has begun:

---

13. Geddert, *Watchwords*, 76.

"The time has come" (1:15). The long history of God's dealings with Israel has reached its climax. The routine of life must be broken by the urgency of the hour, which will not wait. Others interpret it as a call to action at harvest time. The farmer might not know how the seed grows, but he does know how to reap, and he needs to spring into action when the critical harvest time arrives. If the disciples plan to join in the harvest work, they must first recognize that the kingdom is being realized in Jesus' ministry.

In deciding the meaning of the parable, one should allow the context in Mark to be a key factor. This parable is linked closely to the parable of the mustard seed, and like the preceding parables of the lamp and measure, they help interpret one another. In both parables there is a sowing. The seed is scattered "on the ground" (4:26); the mustard, the smallest of seeds on the earth, is planted "in the ground" (4:31). The result of the growth of the seed in both parables has eschatological overtones: the sickle sent to gather the harvest (4:29; Joel 3:13), and the birds of heaven nesting in the greatest of all bushes (Mark 4:32).[14] Both parables indicate that the seed will produce the results inherent within it, although the farmer cannot begin to fathom how the change takes place and though the smallest of seeds looks so unpromising.

The parable of the mustard seed does not mention the process of growth, nor does it refer to any sudden conclusion to the process or intense activity at the end. It does not issue a call to join in the harvest. It also does not hint of patience, waiting for the small seed to grow into a bush. Instead, the parable points to a smallness that dissuades one from anticipating the dramatic transformation that will take place when it is sown in the earth. The ideas of hiddenness and of confidence in the inevitability of the harvest that can be found in the parable of the seed sown in the earth best fit with the companion parable of the mustard seed.

Both parables address the deceptive insignificance of the coming of the kingdom before its final manifestation. God's purposes will be fulfilled in God's way, and God entrusts the secrets of those purposes only to those who are willing to trust him despite unpromising appearances. Can one believe that the kingdom of God advances through ignominy, through defeat, through crucifixion? Can one believe that Jesus of Nazareth, who was hanged on a tree, is indeed the judge of the living and the dead (see Acts 10:38–43)?

---

14. The nesting of the birds in its branches is an eschatological image that symbolizes the incorporation of the Gentiles in the people of God in *Joseph and Asenath* 15:6: "And no more will you be called Asenath, but your name will be 'City of Refuge,' for in you many nations will take refuge and will lodge [same verb as in Mark 4:32, which means "nest"] under your wings, and many nations will find shelter through you." See also Ps. 104:12, 16–17; Ezek. 31:3, 6; Dan. 4:9–12, 21–22.

The Parable of the Mustard Seed (4:30–32)

THE NEXT PARABLE uses the imagery of the annual mustard bush that was cultivated in the field and grown for its leaves as well as its grains. The smallness of its seeds was proverbial (see Matt. 17:20), but Jesus does not compare the kingdom of God to a mustard seed but to *what happens* to a mustard seed.[15] As God transforms a tiny speck of mustard seed into a six-to-ten-foot-high shrub (Mark 4:32; in Matthew and Luke it becomes a tree), what God will accomplish through the death and resurrection of Jesus will be just as extraordinary. The tiniest of seeds grows into the greatest of shrubs, and how this happens is veiled in mystery.[16] Even a modern scientific knowledge of the DNA structure of the mustard seed does not dispel the mystery of its growth. The seed holds within itself the power to transform itself dramatically into something else. One cannot make a judgment about its potential based on empirical evidence when it is in the seed stage. One could dismiss the microscopic seed as something inconsequential, but it has a power within itself to evolve into something that one cannot ignore and that eventually attracts the birds of heaven.[17]

The same thing, Jesus implies, is true of the kingdom of God. During the sowing stage, the beginning of the gospel (1:1), one must make a leap of faith that what Jesus says about himself and God's kingdom is true. The kingdom of God is already present in the work of Jesus but remains concealed and modest. Many would never guess that this inconspicuous presence manifests God's power and dominion that will reach out to all the nations. Religious professionals misjudged it. Even Jesus' own family missed it. The final stage will reveal a dramatic change from the beginning, but by then it will be too late for those who were unable to see what God was doing all along.

Conclusion (4:33–34)

THE NARRATIVE SUMMARY concludes the unit of parables as it began—with Jesus teaching the word to them in many parables (4:2)—but it adds the

---

15. Lane, *Mark*, 171.

16. Pliny commends mustard as something "extremely beneficial for the health," but notes that it grows entirely wild. "Though it is improved by being transplanted: but on the other hand when it has once been sown it is scarcely possible to get the place free of it, as the seed when it falls germinates at once" (*Natural History* 19:170–71). One could ask if Jesus might also be likening the kingdom to a weed that tends to take over where it is not wanted. Is he saying that it is like kudzu? The image should not be interpreted negatively, however. Mark understands it to refer to the great success of the church's worldwide mission.

17. Because the mustard bush is mostly hollow, it hardly provides a suitable place for the nesting of birds, and many translations choose to translate the verb *kataskenoo* as "perch" or "roost." The verb, however, means "to nest," "dwell," "lodge," or "live." The noun form, *kataskenosis*, is used in Matt. 8:30 and Luke 9:58 for nests.

phrase "as much as they could understand [lit., hear]." How can one hear? The comment that he explained everything to his disciples privately clarifies that one must come to Jesus as a disciple and listen carefully to receive explanations and a deeper understanding. Parables are not Zen koans that defy rational understanding, but they are the only form of language that can capture appropriately the astounding mystery that God's reign is effected in and through Jesus, who as the Son of God goes unrecognized by most and will die rejected on a cross.

The description of the word of God in Hebrews 4:12 applies also to the parables; they discern the thoughts and intentions of the hearts of the listeners. To understand them requires more than intellectual comprehension; it requires submitting to the word in one's heart. Jesus uses parables to plumb the spiritual perception of the audience, because he knows that a Messiah who dies can only be perceived through a rare spiritual discernment. The message that Christ crucified conquers the world remains a scandalous and foolish riddle to those who are unable to hear the word with understanding and refuse to gather around Jesus as a disciple.

SINCE JESUS SPENDS so much time in the Gospels explaining in parable what the kingdom of God is like, one may infer that he believed that his vision of God's reign was quite different from the usual one. He used vivid, thought-provoking imagery to awaken that vision in others. When Jesus begins with the statement "the kingdom of God is like," he assumes divine authority to explain what God's rule is. He seeks to dispel the myths about how God's reign manifests itself and works in the world, which the majority accept with little question. Wright observes that Jesus' announcement of the kingdom of God was doubly revolutionary. To say that God was becoming king was to hoist the flag of revolt. To undermine cherished national institutions, hopes, and agendas at the same time was to court harassment from those in Israel who held them dear. He writes that Jesus

> managed *both* to claim that he was fulfilling the old prophecies, the old hopes, of Israel *and* to do so in a way which radically subverted them. The Kingdom of God is here, he seemed to be saying, *but it's not like you thought it was going to be*.[18]

---

18. N. T. Wright, *Who Was Jesus?* (London: SPCK, 1992), 98–99. He goes on to say that it is no wonder that Jesus employed parables to convey his views of the kingdom: "If too many people realized the doubly revolutionary implications, he would not have lasted five minutes."

In bridging the contexts, one should reflect on our received tradition about how God supposedly acts in our world that Jesus' teaching needs to correct. Is there anything revolutionary about our teaching? Do we force the parables to fit our preconceived theological pigeonholes and not allow them to do their work—to explode our myths and illusions about God?

One should also be mindful of two pitfalls in interpreting these parables. First, we should guard against interpreting them from a triumphalist perspective. As some understand the parable of the mustard seed, Jesus is comparing its smallness to the small beginnings of his own ministry, which will eventually burst forth into something spectacular. The church, looking backward, may be tempted to think that we are now that grand stage that Jesus had in mind. We may be tempted to say to ourselves, "If those first disciples only knew what we know now"—how the movement of Jesus of Nazareth has swept the world and now manifests itself gloriously in whatever movement we might belong to. From just a ragtag crew of disciples wandering around Galilee,[19] the church has steadily grown into a grand organization with multibillion-dollar budgets, grand edifices, and great denominations with missionaries marching across the globe.

We too quickly identify the kingdom of God with our own human aspirations and institutions that "reach unto heaven" and "make us a name." We tend to be overly impressed with mass movements and high-powered organizations, and these parables that stress the ambiguity of the presence of the kingdom of God in the midst of this current evil age should caution against this mistake. In the nineteenth century the parable of the seed cast upon the earth was interpreted in terms of the conception of the steady evolution of the kingdom, which would transform society on earth until it eventually would yield entirely to God's will. A. B. Bruce interpreted the parable as pointing to "progress according to natural law, and by stages which must be passed through in succession."[20] The Great War quickly wrecked this myth about humankind's inevitable progress toward conformity to God's will.

The imagery of the parable of the mustard seed should check any triumphalist interpretation. Jesus' picture suggests that the kingdom of God may continue to look like a failure. The tiniest of seeds becomes the greatest of all shrubs, but a shrub is still a shrub. The parable may be a rebuke to those expecting something grandiose from God, like the mighty cedar of Lebanon (Ezek. 17:22–24; see Ps. 104:12, 16–17; Sir. 24:13; 1QH 6:14–17;

---

19. Mark has not pictured Jesus' movement as small. Everywhere Jesus goes he is surrounded by huge crowds that come from all over and are so large that Jesus cannot eat and is in danger of being crushed.

20. A. B. Bruce, *The Parabolic Teaching of Christ* (London: Hodder & Stoughton, 1882), 120.

8:4–8). In America, a three-thousand-year-old giant redwood, three hundred feet high and thirty feet in diameter and still growing, would be the proud tree we would be more likely to choose as the best comparison to our image of what the kingdom is like.

But the kingdom will not fit our expectations or specifications. For those who want to be the top cedar in the world and want something more show-stopping and messianic, the kingdom of God as it is manifest in our world will be mostly disappointing. It comes incognito; and up to the very end, one can only trust that Jesus' movement is God's work when all things will finally be revealed. The kingdom of God was present with the coming of Jesus. It was hidden but not invisible. Most did not see it. They were looking in all the wrong places for all the wrong things. Times have not changed, because people continue to fix their attention on all the wrong things in their search for God and meaning in their lives.

A second caution for interpreting these parables concerns their subject matter. Jesus is talking about God's reign. Some have combined Jesus' statement about having faith as small as a grain of mustard seed (Matt. 17:20; Luke 17:6) with the parable of the mustard seed to make it refer to the spiritual faith of individuals.[21] Small faith will grow from small beginnings into something large. The parable of Jesus is concerned about broader matters, however. It has to do with the kingdom of God, which we should not constrict to personal spiritual growth.

We are perhaps disinclined to think of these parables as describing what happens to the kingdom of God because the imagery is so disconcerting. We associate the kingdom of God with Spirit and fire, with a mighty fortress, not with seeds growing quietly and being transformed into shrubs. The imagery used in the parables is so ordinary: a lamp giving light, a measuring cup, seed being scattered. Some may be moved by the ordinary and see something extraordinary in it. Others may dismiss it as merely ordinary. The ordinary imagery of the parables in Mark 4 is significant, however. Bilezikian notes that the imagery Jesus employs is

> not that of marching armies, heroic deeds, and valorous exploits, but the humble, homely imagery of sowing, tilling, and harvest. The seed is scattered, falls, and lies on the ground, and meets a variety of fates. Instead of striking out, defiant and aggressive, the Kingdom of God appears lowly and vulnerable. The seed is subject to adversity, rejection, delays, and loss. The parables contain no promise of instant and universal triumph.[22]

---

21. A popular interpretation deriving from Bruce, *Parabolic Teaching*, 125–43.
22. Bilezikian, *The Liberated Gospel*, 74.

The spectacular exercise of power is not always a sign of real strength. God's reign, as Jesus pictures it, is not some massive juggernaut that mows down everything in its path. The signs pointing to God's reign appear to be incredibly humble even when it grows large into a shrub and attracts the birds of the air. That is why so many will overlook its presence, underestimate its power, and shrug off its claim on their lives.

To allow these parables to speak to us in our setting, we should emphasize two themes that emerge from them: the hiddenness of God's kingdom, and the confidence that even though the kingdom lies hidden, it is working to produce the harvest that God intends. The beginning predetermines the end. We live in the in-between time, between the beginning when the seed is sown and the end time when the final stage becomes manifest and all God's purposes are accomplished. One may succumb to discouragement during this time, be tempted to look for something that appears more secure, or follow someone else who seems more promising (Matt. 11:3; Luke 7:19). Those who are confidently faithful to end will be saved (Mark 13:13). They will see the significance of the seed growing and the fig tree putting forth its leaves (13:28–29).

These parables are appropriate to apply to those times in our ministry when we might feel that the Spirit has gone on holiday. They convey the truth that God's kingdom works powerfully, independently of the skill or power of its herald, and sometimes invisibly. We need to look at our world from the way Jesus sees it, with seeds sown everywhere preparing for the harvest.

 THE WORKING OF the reign of God in the world rarely if ever makes headlines. It will seem inconsequential to outsiders and even to insiders because God so often works silently and in ways human eyes are prone to overlook. The parables in this section emphasize the hiddenness of the kingdom. It requires spiritual discernment, given only by God, before one can begin to recognize that God's purposes are being fulfilled when there is little or no certifiable or quantifiable proof. As H. L. Mencken stated it, the problem is that "the public, with its mob yearning to be instructed, edified, pulled by the nose, demands certainties; it must be told definitely and a bit raucously that this is true and that is false."[23]

Mencken goes on to say that there are no certainties, but Jesus' parables dispute that conclusion. We can be certain that God's kingdom is at work in

---

23. H. L. Mencken, "Arnold Bennett," in *Prejudices: First Series* (New York: Alfred A. Knopf, 1919), 46.

the world in ways we do not know and in a manner that is not subject to empirical verification or mathematical formulation. From our finite perspective, we are ignorant of God's grand schemes even when we are living in the midst of them. Paul wrote to reassure the Philippians that his recent imprisonment was not a great setback to the gospel as they had believed. Instead, it served to advance the gospel: The whole palace guard had heard about the gospel, and his Christian brothers dared to preach the gospel even more boldly (Phil. 1:12–14). It was more evidence that God draws straight with what looks to us to be crooked lines.

The mystery of how God accomplishes his purposes in the world—so often silently and mysteriously—also applies to our situation. One finds life by giving one's life, power by humbling oneself, and victory by being subject to defeats (see Isa. 52:13–53:12). The world operates from different standards by taking life, exerting power over others, and going out to conquer in order to conquer (Rev. 6:2). No wonder the world is blind to God's presence and rule.

The hiddenness that characterized Jesus' ministry applied also to the early church's situation, surrounded as it was by scoffing and deadly hostility. What could they point to that would convincingly reveal to others the truth about God? They could only point to the cross and the news that God had raised Jesus from the dead. Many laughed, such as one in the second century who drew a graffito picturing a figure on a cross with a donkey's head and captioned it: "Alexamenous worships his god." The Markan community found itself "driven to the uttermost state of powerlessness, suffering, and death," but discovered "that in the midst of its weakness God's glory is revealed."[24]

Our situation is no different. God's purposes are revealed in the cross and resurrection of Jesus, but many remain blind. Those who prize worldly wisdom and who seek fully certified proof still regard the cross as foolishness. But for those who can see, the foolishness of God plus the weakness of God add up to the power of God that will inevitably bring a future triumph and the final culmination of God's reign. One needs a special faith to risk trusting one's whole life to something that lies hidden—when it is in the seed stage or the blade stage. Grant helps us understand what this faith is like:

> Faith means believing beyond the range of the evidence—not in spite of the evidence—but beyond it. Faith means the discovery of further evidence higher in kind and of subtler validity than mere outward proofs. As virtue is its own reward, so faith supplies, in a

---

24. Marcus, *The Mystery of the Kingdom*, 151.

similar way, its own verification. This does not mean that it supplies outward and visible proofs, the evidence is still spiritual things which are spiritually apprehended. A faith which rests upon tangible demonstration is a contradiction in terms, and is really "unfaith clamoring to be coined to faith by proof," as the poet said. Faith means trust, adventure, self-committal; and its evidences are still the "things not seen."[25]

It takes faith to see how God exalts the lowly tree of the cross so that persons from every nation can find protection and an everlasting home under the outstretched arms of the one hanged upon it.

(1) These parables should instill confidence that overcomes despair. When we cannot see what transpires under the ground as the seed winters in the earth, we can become discouraged. Observers can easily write off this movement, particularly in our hurried, pragmatic age that wants immediate gratification and results. The slightest failure may drive us to a sense of hopelessness. Nearly every missionary has a "darkest chapter" story to tell when they were disheartened by setbacks that seemed insurmountable; a feeling of inadequacy, a feeling of complete defeat, overcame them. In the 1800s, for example, Robert and Mary Moffat labored for many years as missionaries in Kuruman (South Africa) among the Bechuanas without great success. Robert compared it to "a husbandman labouring to transform the surface of granite rock into arable land. . . ." His wife lamented: "Could we but see the smallest fruit, we could rejoice midst the privations and toil which we bear; but as it is, our hands do often hang down."[26]

The same despair descended on Clarence W. Jones. He felt God's call to begin pioneer work in radio evangelism in South America in the late 1920s. He asked and expected God to do great and mighty things. In the early going it seemed that every door of opportunity closed and his zeal flagged. He was discouraged, broken, "unable to shake off the feeling of total inadequacy and failure, and chagrined that his obsession with South America had made him look like a fool." He decided to scuttle his ministry and to enlist in the Navy but was rejected—ironically, for imperfect vision.[27]

Many a discouraged minister suffers from myopic spiritual vision that makes one unable to see what God is doing in the soil and unable to envision triumph in what looks like utter failure. We cannot see into next week, let alone eternity, and we can become impatient waiting for God's purposes

25. F. C. Grant, *The Earliest Gospel* (Nashville: Abingdon, 1943), 85–86.

26. Ruth A. Tucker, *From Jerusalem to Irian Jaya: A Biography of Christian Missions* (Grand Rapids: Zondervan, 1983), 144–45.

27. Ibid., 373–74.

to come to fruition. The proverb "A man reaps what he sows" (Gal. 6:7) is usually applied negatively. One cannot sow wild oats during the week and pray for a crop failure on Sunday. Behavior has consequences. But the principle of reaping what you sow also holds true in a positive sense. The parables assure us that when we sow God's seed, it will accomplish its purpose. We may not be the ones who harvest the bounty, but it is not our harvest (1 Cor. 3:6–9). It belongs to God.

(2) These parables make the case that the seed's success does not depend on our feeble efforts. In spite of the assurance of the harvest—and no mention is made of its size—we are still left with a mystery of how it comes about. Success does not depend on the one who preaches but on God. Even Jesus did not have complete control over the harvest—who would be in it or what would be its size. One therefore need only bear witness and not worry about creating a response. That does not mean that one is to be indifferent to how people respond, but we do not need to try to manufacture a response.

The seed grows without our assistance, yet Jesus does not intend to encourage inertia or sloth. Nor does awareness of this principle spare us the sleepless nights that Paul, for example, said he spent worrying about his churches (2 Cor. 11:27–28). Jesus' parable does caution us from thinking that the kingdom is furthered by our grand schemes or our latest programs. Church growth experts try to figure things out to help us map out strategies. Their work is helpful, but the harvest remains under the sovereignty of God. We do not make the seed grow; we do not know how it grows— even in our own lives. Sometimes our frenetic activity may be a smoke screen that hides our lack of trust in God. We feel we need to take control before God's will can be done. The parable allows us to stop concentrating on what we need to accomplish or have accomplished and to reflect on what God is accomplishing. It encourages us to trust the seed to do what seeds do in the soil.

(3) The parables encourage patient faith. In an age of instantaneous communication and a time when children may ask their parents, "Why do microwave ovens take so long?" waiting can be intolerable. We are always in a hurry. Some may expect to plow the field, plant the seed, reap the harvest, thresh the grain, and bake the cake all in one worship service. The parables do not promise instantaneous growth. God gives the growth, and it follows an appointed order that cannot be hurried or bypassed. One must learn to allow the seed to do its work, to allow the word to persuade and to convert. All anxiety is therefore superfluous since events are out of human control. One needs to cultivate patience so that one can wait for God to bring about the culmination in its appointed time.

In a time of frenetic end time speculation, patience becomes essential. Dahl writes,

> To the growth which God gives in the sphere of organic life, in accordance with his own established order, corresponds the series of events by which God leads history toward the end of the world and the beginning of the new aeon, in accordance with his plan of salvation.[28]

Elijah must come first; the Son of Man must suffer, the gospel must be preached to all nations, the disciples must face suffering, judgment will fall upon Jerusalem. Then we await our Lord's coming, who comes in God's time.

---

28. Dahl, "The Parables of Growth," 154.

Mark 4:35–41

W

THAT DAY WHEN evening came, he said to his disciples, "Let us go over to the other side." ³⁶Leaving the crowd behind, they took him along, just as he was, in the boat. There were also other boats with him. ³⁷A furious squall came up, and the waves broke over the boat, so that it was nearly swamped. ³⁸Jesus was in the stern, sleeping on a cushion. The disciples woke him and said to him, "Teacher, don't you care if we drown?"

³⁹He got up, rebuked the wind and said to the waves, "Quiet! Be still!" Then the wind died down and it was completely calm.

⁴⁰He said to his disciples, "Why are you so afraid? Do you still have no faith?"

⁴¹They were terrified and asked each other, "Who is this? Even the wind and the waves obey him!"

IN A LARGE unit beginning in 4:35 and ending in 6:6a, Jesus continues to spend much of his time by the Sea of Galilee and even ventures across the lake. In the first episode, panicked disciples rouse Jesus from sleep; in the next-to-last episode, he rouses a girl from the sleep of death (5:39). Jesus is shown to possess power to still outward storms that threaten life and to still the inward storms of torment and grief that threaten our souls. We learn in these scenes that Jesus is not only sovereign over the demonic forces and debilitating and defiling illnesses, but he is also sovereign over the potent forces of nature and of death. Despite the mighty works that Jesus performs, this second section (3:7–6:6a) concludes with the report of his rejection in his hometown (6:1–6a), just as the first section (1:14–3:6) concluded with his rejection by the Pharisees and Herodians (3:6). As the parable of the sower made clear, many are unable to hear and bear fruit.

Overview of 4:35–6:6a

SEVERAL THEMES EMERGE in this unit (4:35–6:6a). The motif of death runs through most of the incidents. Jesus does not still an average storm but a "furious squall" that threatens to swamp the boat (4:37). He delivers the disciples from the peril of death at sea, the place where Jews believed that evil and God clash. In the Gerasene territory across the lake Jesus does not exorcise one who is marginally possessed but one who is victimized by a legion of demons (5:1–20). No one has been able to subdue this ugly customer, so he has been ousted from society and forced to live in the tombs, the realm of death. Back home in more welcoming territory, Jesus "saves" a woman who has had a devitalizing ailment that has stymied physicians for twelve years (5:24–34). She is walking death. He then does not simply cure a child of sickness but raises her from death (5:35–43). The message is clear: Jesus is equal to any threat that may shatter human life.

Compared to the previous miracles, Mark now gives us much more information about the people who are healed by Jesus. Each of the characters is driven by a sense of *desperation*. The disciples find themselves in dire straits, whirled about by a sudden tempest while Jesus slumbers. The demon-possessed man has been beaten and chained by others and now lashes himself with stones in a desperate attempt to purge himself of his inner turmoil. The legion of unclean spirits causes the possessed man to race toward Jesus and prostrate himself before him (5:6) in a desperate bid to ward off an exorcism. The townsfolk from the Gerasene region are desperate to get Jesus to leave their territory before he destroys any more businesses. The father whose daughter lies at death's door is desperate that she be restored to health and falls before Jesus' feet in a frantic plea for help (5:22). He is no less desperate than the woman who has wasted her living on fruitless remedies for an affliction that cuts her off from normal social functioning. She touches Jesus' garment in the desperate hope of a miracle. Those most open to receiving Jesus' power in their lives are those who recognize their own desperate need of it. Those who are not open to his power are no less desperate but have convinced themselves that they do not need it.

A third common feature that appears in these accounts is the contrast between fear and faith. One might expect that someone with such power would arouse overwhelming joy. Instead, many respond to Jesus with fear. The disciples fail to have faith and panic when threatened by the sea squall. Jesus chides them for their lack of faith, which here means confidence in Jesus' power; but they are dumbfounded by his power to quiet the sea and are "terrified" (4:41). The townsfolk of Gerasa become afraid when they observe the demonized man, whom they have been powerless to control, now in his right mind and sitting at Jesus' feet (5:15). The woman with the flow of blood is petrified when Jesus looks around to see who touched him and when she realizes what has happened to her. She musters enough courage to confess to him (5:33), and Jesus commends her faith, which has saved her (5:34). Jesus tells the ruler of the synagogue not to fear at the news of his daughter's death, only to continue to have faith (5:36). Finally, the disrespect Jesus receives in Nazareth leads him to marvel because of their lack of faith (6:6a). Faith flings wide the gates to receive his power, and that casts out all fear.

The Storm at Sea (4:35–41)

THE UNIT OPENS with Jesus urging his disciples to set sail for the other side of the lake. Obedience to this command requires leaving the crowd and joining Jesus in the boat (4:36a). The "other boats" with him suggests that the group is not limited only to the Twelve (4:36b). The boat in this section becomes an "image of those who travel in intimate fellowship with Jesus, separated from other followers and the masses who stand on the security of the shore."[1] The disciples take him with them in the boat because the fishermen in the group are presumably the expert mariners. Ironically, they are the ones terrified by the unexpected storm, while Jesus, the carpenter (6:3), sleeps serenely on a sandbag used for ballast (translated "cushion") in the stern. One can imagine that at the close of a hard, full day, preaching to hardened hearts, Jesus is physically exhausted. Those attuned to Scripture, however, catch a deeper significance behind his peaceful repose. Jesus' sleep in the midst a raging storm churning the sea around him and filling the boat with water is a sign of his trust in God (Job 11:18–19; Pss. 3:5; 4:8; 121:3–4; Prov. 3:23–26) and contrasts with the terror of the disciples.

The disciples, however, do not interpret his untroubled sleep as evidence of his trust in God, which will also ensure their welfare. They regard it as a token of his indifference to their safety in their hour of danger.[2] They awaken Jesus with an indignant wail of complaint, as if he were in some way responsible for their plight. Their question expects the answer yes: "You do care that we are perishing, don't you?" (4:38), but it suggests that they are peeved with his apparent lack of concern. There is bitter irony that these same disciples will go to sleep on him in his hour of terror in Gethsemane, unmoved by his pleas for them to watch and pray with him (14.37, 40–41). They do not doze off then because of their trust in God but, as Mark tells us, because of a bad case of heavy eyes (14:40). Jesus reproaches them, "Are you still sleeping?" in a far more critical hour. Their sleep reveals that they do not care that he is about to perish. The early symptoms of heavy eyes that cannot see appear in this scene as their fear in the face of the storm overwhelms them. It shows that they are like the ones the psalmist

---

1. James G. Williams, *Gospel Against Parable: Mark's Language of Mystery* (Sheffield: Almond, 1985), 100.

2. Marshall, *Faith As a Theme*, 216–17.

describes in Psalm 107:23–32 as witnesses of the works of the Lord but whose courage melts away, and they reel like drunken men at their wit's end:

> Then they cried out to the LORD in their trouble,
> and he brought them out of their distress.
> He stilled the storm to a whisper;
> the waves of the sea were hushed.
> They were glad when it grew calm,
> and he guided them to their desired haven.
> Let them give thanks to the LORD for his unfailing love
> and his wonderful deeds for men (vv. 28–32).[3]

Having to rouse Jesus from his sleep evokes another biblical theme of sleep as a divine prerogative and a symbol of divine rule.[4] Isaiah 51:9–10 may shed more light on Jesus' sleep.

> Awake, awake! Clothe yourself with strength,
> O arm of the LORD;
> awake, as in days gone by,
> as in generations of old.
> Was it not you who cut Rahab to pieces,
> who pierced that monster through?
> Was it not you who dried up the sea,
> the waters of the great deep,
> who made a road in the depths of the sea
> so that the redeemed might cross over?[5]

Jesus' rest is another token of his divine sovereignty that the disciples do not yet recognize, and the formidable power of the tempest is promptly overcome when he arises and speaks. He answers their anxious cries by rebuking the wind with a word.[6] That he is able to transform a great storm (4:37) into a great calm (4:39) with just a word reveals he has power to do what only the God who created the sea can do (see Gen. 8:1; Job 26:12; Pss. 65:7; 74:13–14; 89:9; 93:3–4; 104:5–9; 106:9; 114:3; Isa. 50:2; Nah. 1:4; 2 Macc. 9:8). Jesus has mastery over the sea, the place of chaos and evil, as God does. If the disciples only understood that they had set to sea with one who has

---

3. See also Ps. 69:1–2.

4. B. F. Batto, "The Sleeping God: An Ancient Near Eastern Motif of Divine Sovereignty," *Bib* 68 (1987): 153–77.

5. See also Ps. 44:23–24.

6. The translation in the KJV, "Peace, be still," hardly captures the forcefulness of Jesus' word. Jesus uses the same rebuke when he tells the demons to shut up (Mark 1:25; 3:12; 9:25). See 2 Enoch 40:9; 43:1–3; 69:22; 4 Ezra 6:41–42; Jub. 2:2.

such power, they would confess that all their fears were groundless. The disciples' faith must continue to grow and become tempered as hardened steel by life's hard circumstances.

After calming the sea, Jesus rebukes the disciples for their hysteria, "Why are you so afraid? Do you still have no faith?" Faith here refers to faith in the divine power present in Jesus' person. The incident reveals their utter dependence on Jesus; he is their refuge and strength, an ever-present help in trouble, their comforter, who can still the fury of the oppressors though they roar like the waves of the sea. Consequently, they should not fear (Ps. 46:1–3; Isa. 51:12–16). Faith is clearly not something that is inborn; it can ebb and flow, depending on circumstances, and is most likely to fizzle in situations of danger. Despite the disciples' fear and lack of faith, Jesus muzzles the storm and preserves their lives. What can he do when people show faith?

The fear of the disciples, however, does not alleviate after the storm quiets down. Instead, their fear intensifies as it shifts to the person with them in the boat, who has just shown his divine control over the sea. Jesus' explanation of his parables did not prepare them for anything as portentous as this miracle. In the Jonah story, which has some parallels with this incident, the sailors become frightened because this prophet serves the God who made the sea and the dry land (Jonah 1:5–6). The disciples' fear stems from Jesus' God-like control of the sea (see Ps. 89:9).[7] Although they have had the greatest opportunity to see and hear Jesus and have been given the mysteries of the kingdom, they are still haunted by doubt and fear. Now they are eyewitnesses of his divine power that can still both the whirlwind and the sea.

The disciples' awe before the numinous is appropriate, but they still have only the vaguest inkling of who this man is in their midst, who wields such power. The light may be too bright for their eyes to take it all in. One might compare the disciples who have been delivered at sea with the Israelites who were rescued from Egypt. After God saved Israel from their captors through mighty works, "the people feared the LORD and put their trust in him and in Moses his servant" (Ex. 14:31). The question in Mark's

---

7. Hooker, *Mark*, 140. Gundry (*Mark*, 245–46) argues that "Mark uses the OT by way of analogy" and points out significant differences between the accounts in Mark and Jonah. Jesus is not fleeing the presence of the Lord, and there is no hint that the Lord sends the storm as some warning (Jonah 1:3–4, 10). Jesus is asleep in the stern, not in the hold (1:5). The disciples do not battle the storm as the sailors did or cast lots to see who caused the calamity (1:5, 7). The calm comes when Jonah is thrown overboard, not when he speaks (1:15). Jesus does not pray to God but addresses the sea directly, and his word creates the great calm. The differences in the stories, when read together, make it clear that something greater than Jonah is here (see Matt. 12:41; Luke 11:32).

Gospel will be whether the fear of the disciples will turn to absolute trust in this new and greater deliverer.

THE CALMING OF the storm is the first so-called nature miracle in the Gospel of Mark. Anderson notes that our modern scientific skepticism makes moderns "less shy of healings and exorcisms," for which "some scientific analogies can be produced" or some psychological explanation can be given, than they are of nature miracles, which are likely to be dismissed as impossible.[8] There is no shortage of modern scholars who treat these stories as legendary accretions or as exaggerated expansions of normal events. The approach of the nineteenth century still lives today. Scholars at that time assumed that God created immutable laws of nature and, having set them in motion, left them to operate mechanically like the movement of a clock. David Hume, in his *Enquiry Concerning Human Understanding*, defined a miracle as a violation of natural laws and assumed that it was impossible.

This doctrine of natural laws governing the universe forced interpreters to look for more rational explanations of what really happened in miracles since the suspension of natural physical laws could not happen. H. E. G. Paulus, for example, explained away the miracle by claiming that Jesus did not speak to the sea but only cried out, "What a dreadful storm! It must be over soon." The disciples misunderstood his words as the cause of the sudden calm. One is no less credulous if one believes this kind of natural explanation than if one believes that Jesus calmed the sea with his word, as Mark reports. One should also think twice about the authoritative pronouncements of scholars who say that moderns can no longer believe in the notion of miracles and the supernatural. There are so many exceptions to this imagined "modern person" who does not believe in miracles that it is useless. The assertion may be true of the "Cultured Despisers of Religion" but not of ordinary people, many of whom are no less educated and intelligent.

Most today would concede that in dealing with the miracles of Jesus one should not decide in advance what is or is not possible. We ought never prejudge that something certainly cannot happen. We miss the point if we swap the miraculous elements with some natural explanation that supposedly will make more sense to the well-educated modern mind. But the modern scientific worldview, which insists on verification through repeated measurements, blinds many to the miraculous and spiritual dimensions of life. For example,

---

8. Anderson, *Mark*, 142.

one scholar states regarding the issue of unclean spirits: "A conclusive answer has to wait for further scientific developments in order that scientists can arrive at true findings in this field."[9] Science is useful in debunking fraudulent claims, but it is not the final appeal for the truth of miracles because its basic assumption is that something is not real if it is not replicable and not measurable.

Bonhoeffer has an interesting discussion of those who complain that they find it hard to believe. He argues that they may not simply be wrestling with intellectual issues. Instead, it may be a sign of "deliberate or unconscious disobedience." He imagines a pastor properly responding to the crisis of faith in this way:

> "You are disobedient, you are trying to keep some part of your life under your own control. That is what is preventing you from listening to Christ and believing his grace. You cannot hear Christ because you are wilfully disobedient. Somewhere in your heart you are refusing to listen to his call. Your difficulty is your sins. . . . Only those who obey can believe and only those who believe can obey."[10]

The modern embarrassment over the miracles because they are contrary to what we know about nature assumes that we know everything about nature even when we know so little about God.

At the same time, one can also miss the point by trying to muster conclusive evidence to prove that the miracles happened as reported in the Gospels. Endless reams of attempted scientific proof can kill the miracle as well. A miracle is a miracle only if God speaks to us through it. Buechner defines a miracle as "an event that strengthens faith."[11] Miracles may speak louder than words but not always as clearly, and the miracles in Mark are frequently ambiguous. To the eyes of faith, one thing is seen; to the eyes of the blind, the healing or the exorcism simply proves that Jesus works as the devil's sorcerer (3:22, 28–29).[12]

In Mark's Gospel, the nature miracles offer more profound clues for the disciples to learn Jesus' full identity as the Son of God. Their willingness to be at Jesus' beck and call, to join the little flotilla of boats and go across to the other side at his command, shows their openness to new revelation.

---

9. Raoul Syx, "Jesus and the Unclean Spirits: The Literary Relation Between Mark and Q in the Beelzebul Controversy (Mark 3:20–30 par)," *Louvain Studies* 17 (1992): 180.

10. Dietrich Bonhoeffer, *The Cost of Discipleship* (New York: Macmillan, 1963), 76.

11. Frederick Buechner, *Listening to Your Life* (San Francisco: Harper & Row, 1992), 304.

12. To Jews, the Exodus was a great miracle of deliverance, but Josephus describes one Egyptian explanation of it as "the expulsion of rebellious lepers and criminals who had been expelled and pursued to the frontiers of Syria" (*Ag. Ap.* 1:26–27).

The parables and their explanations do not clarify everything. The miracle on the sea points the disciples further along the way to the truth. Divine power is at work through Jesus. Again, Buechner is on target when he writes: "Faith in God is less apt to proceed from miracles than miracles from faith in God."[13]

Even when they are confronted with a miracle of this magnitude, the disciples are still in a fog and cannot immediately put two and two together. The rescue at sea displays who Jesus is and what he can do for those whose lives are threatened. Jesus has power over the forces of chaos and can rescue them from whatever storms may rampage through their lives, including the storms of persecution. This miracle is not against nature so much as it is against Satan, who would destroy Jesus' followers and their faith. Jesus' dominion over the wind and the sea points to what it will be like when "the rule of Satan is no more."[14] In John's vision of the new heaven and earth, the sea is no more (Rev. 21:1; see 4:6; 15:2; 20:13).

In bridging the contexts in Gospel narratives, we may ask three questions: What does it reveal about Jesus? What does it reveal about the human predicament? What solution does it present for that predicament? The awestruck disciples raise the key issue in this story when they ask, "Who is this? Even the wind and the waves obey him!" (4:41). Achtemeier gets to the essence when he comments: "The subduing of the sea and wind was not merely a demonstration of power; it was an epiphany, through which Jesus was unveiled to his disciples as the Savior in the midst of intense peril." The answer to the first question is that Jesus has the power of God to "conquer the powers of darkness arrayed against him."[15]

Comparing Isaiah 43:1–10 with the story in Mark illuminates the high Christology of Mark. Jesus is doing in Mark's story what Isaiah proclaims that God promises to do.

Isaiah 43	Mark
[1]But now, this is what the LORD says— he who *created* you, O Jacob, he who formed you, O Israel: "Fear not, for I have redeemed you; I have *summoned you by name;* you are mine.	Jesus has created the Twelve (3:12) and summoned disciples by name (1:16, 20; 2:14; 3:16–18).

13. Buechner, *Listening to Your Life,* 305.

14. James Kallas, *The Significance of the Synoptic Miracles* (London: SPCK, 1961), 78.

15. Paul J. Achtemeier, "Person and Deed: Jesus and the Storm-Tossed Sea," *Int* 16 (1962): 176.

Isaiah 43	Mark
[2]When you pass through the waters, 　I will be with you; and when you pass through the rivers 　they will not sweep over you. When you walk through the fire, 　you will not be burned; 　the flames will not set you ablaze. [3]For I am the LORD, your God, 　the Holy One of Israel, your Savior; I give Egypt for your *ransom*, 　Cush and Seba in your stead. [4]Since you are precious and honored 　　in my sight, 　and because I love you, I will give men in exchange for you and people in exchange for your life. [5]*Do not be afraid*, for I am with you; 　I will bring your children from the 　　east 　and gather you from the west. [8]Lead out those who have eyes but are 　　blind, 　who have ears but are deaf. [10]"You are my witnesses," declares 　the LORD, 　"and my servant whom I have 　　chosen, 　so that you know and believe me 　and understand that *I am he*. Before me no god was formed 　nor will there be one after me.	Jesus is with them when they pass through the waters (4:36) and saves them from peril at sea. The assurance that they not be harmed by fire is echoed in 9:49: "Everyone will be salted with fire." Jesus announces to the disciples that he gives his life as a ransom for many (10:45). Jesus rebukes the cowardice of the disciples and tells a synagogue ruler (5:36) and his disciples not to be afraid (6:50). See 4:12; 8:18; Jesus heals two blind men (8:22–26; 10:46–52) and heals a deaf man (7:31–37). When Jesus comes to the disciples walking on the waves, he announces , "It is I [or, I am he]!" (6:50).

The conclusion in Isaiah 43:11–12 proclaims,

> "I, even I, am the LORD,
> 　and apart from me there is no savior.
> I have revealed and saved and proclaimed—
> 　I, and not some foreign god among you.
> You are my witnesses," declares the LORD, "that I am God."

Mark would have the readers draw the same conclusion about Jesus. Jesus is the one who delivers his people, and in his hands they are safe.

The text also reveals something about the human predicament. We live in a fallen world beset by powers of chaos that are out to destroy us. Our faith is weak, and we do not know in what or in whom we can trust. Jesus' power to calm the storm presents the solution to this human plight. Trusting that he has God's power and cares for the community of faith is particularly reassuring in times when the powers of darkness seem to swallow it. Christ's first appearance in Revelation 1:9–20 presents a similar picture. John describes the exalted Son of Man with imagery that characterizes the Ancient of Days in Scripture. The Son of Man announces that he shares the divine title, "the First and the Last," and holds in his hands the keys of death and of Hades. With God's awesome power he is standing in the midst of his churches.

WE CAN EASILY claim to be courageous when everything is calm. We can have faith in God's deliverance when we do not sense any urgent need to be delivered. When we come under extreme pressure, however, the courage and assurance that Jesus even cares for his own, let alone preserves them from ultimate danger, can fade fast. Mark wrote his Gospel for communities facing intense stress and a raging storm of persecution. Marcus correctly argues that the Evangelist intended to lift the community's "eyes from the surging chaos that seems to engulf it and to fix them instead on the vision of the one enthroned in heaven, the monarch omnipotent in every storm." He continues:

> In the light of this vision, the wild opposition of demons and human beings is seen not to be the deadly serious thing that it first appears to be, but rather a phenomenon that is worthy only of a disbelieving shake of the head. How do the "rulers" dare to set themselves against the living God? Do they not know who it is they oppose? ... Mark's depiction of the invincible power of Jesus as he spearheads the battle against the demonized world enables his community not only to conquer its fear of the enemies but even to join in the divine laughter that sounds forth in the psalm [Ps. 2]. Let the enemy forces do their worst, striking even—as they think—unto the death. The joke will be on them .... [16]

Throughout church history, believers have seized on this account of the disciples assaulted by waves in the boat and applied the image to the church. Tertullian commented in the second century "that little ship is presented as

---

16. Marcus, *The Way of the Lord*, 76.

a figure of the church, in that she is disquieted in the sea, that is, in the world, by the waves, that is, by persecutions and temptations" (*On Baptism* 12). To apply this to our contemporary situation we need only to name the storms that threaten the community of faith and paralyze it with fear. We must then lift our eyes above the tumult to the one who rules all things so that we may have the same assurance as Paul, who endured literal storms at sea that resulted in at least four shipwrecks (2 Cor. 11:25; also Acts 27:39–44). Faced with persecution's deadly peril, he knew what it was like to feel unbearably crushed and despairing of life itself (2 Cor. 1:8–10). He confesses: "We are hard pressed on every side, but not crushed; perplexed, but not in despair; persecuted, but not abandoned; struck down, but not destroyed" (4:8–9).

This account in Mark touches on the plight of the human situation in a world still under Satan's sway. There will be many times when it looks like the foes are winning and the church is losing. As e. e. cummings expressed this anxiety: "King Christ, this world is all aleak, and life preservers there are none." But Jesus has already saved us, not from the perils of this mortal life, but from ultimate destruction. Confidence in this fact allows us to face all threats with courage and trust. How will we react when our ship feels tossed about and swamped by waves of opposition? Will we need to be rebuked like the disciples for losing our nerve and our faith? What will it take for us to know that Jesus is God and will protect us even through death?

The calming of the storm has to do with Jesus' announcement that God reigns, "that the hostile forces of Satan, wherever they might be; inside man, outside man; are being overthrown by Jesus, the Holy One of God."[17] He restores God's dominion over a chaotic world invaded by forces that wreak havoc. Most people, however, are worried about their own little worlds and the storms that roar in to destroy them. In these personal situations many feel swamped by waves of a quite different sort. Like the disciples, they may feel that their cries for help meet with only a stony silence from heaven. Life is filled with hazards—and not just from the sea.

The desperation of the disciples while Jesus serenely sleeps may seem to parallel the church's sense of Jesus' absence in times of trial or an individual's sense of abandonment. There come times when we feel more acutely that the bridegroom has been taken away (2:20) or that he is not here (16:7). When the hurricanes sweep through our lives, Jesus may seem indifferent to our plight, asleep at the helm, or even absent. Many who lose their jobs, their health, and their friends may feel that Jesus deliberately ignores their fate and shows no concern for them. Fear leads to despair that God does not care. Adoniram Judson, America's first foreign missionary, fell into deep

---

17. Kallas, *The Significance of the Synoptic Miracles*, 91.

despondency after the death of his baby, Maria, which followed his wife's death by only months. His grief was compounded because he was not with his wife during her illness. Swamped by waves of spiritual despair, he lamented: "God is to me the great Unknown. I believe in him but I find him not."[18]

The miracle of the storm does not teach us how to endure adversity patiently because Jesus immediately eliminates the problem. The emphasis in this story is on who Jesus is, not on how he rescues fretful disciples from danger whenever they cry out to him. One cannot expect a miraculous intervention that will calm all the storms in life. Storms are a part of life from which no one escapes. There are no stormless seas, and all sailors must learn to expect the unexpected. Chaos hits our lives, and it can all happen so quickly. One moment all is well; then, in a flash, all is hell. The disciples who were fishermen knew that the sudden squalls were a threat on the lake, but that did not make it any easier to cope when they appeared. C. S. Lewis lectured others about suffering, but it did not make it any easier to endure when it became a reality in his own life. The death of a cherished loved one, the loss of a job, the betrayal of a friend, the onslaught of those bent on destroying everything dear to us churn our lives as if we were a tiny cockleshell facing a hurricane.

Euripides wrote, "Happy is he who has escaped a storm at sea, who has come to harbor. Happy is he who has come up from under his troubles" (*Bacchae* 2.901–2). Euripides did not know the merciful God who saves people from squalls that roar through their lives. He did not know what true happiness (blessedness) is in following this one who can calm any storm in life. Reading Mark helps one learn to trust in a Savior who does not deliver us *from* storms but *through* the storms. Christianity is not a refuge from the uncertainties and insecurities of the world. Some may be too cowardly to get into the boat in the first place. Others may wish they never had embarked and want to retreat to the safety of the shore. But then they meet raging demons (5:2). There are no safe places in life, and one can only find security with Jesus and a serenity that this world does not know and cannot give. Christians know that Jesus has done battle with the strong man and has won. He has beaten down the savage storms, and one has no reason to fear anything from nature or the supernatural, from life or death (see Rom. 8:31–39).

---

18. Courtney Anderson, *To the Golden Shore: The Life of Adoniram Judson* (Grand Rapids: Zondervan, 1972), 391.

Mark 5:1–20

THEY WENT ACROSS the lake to the region of the Gerasenes. ²When Jesus got out of the boat, a man with an evil spirit came from the tombs to meet him. ³This man lived in the tombs, and no one could bind him any more, not even with a chain. ⁴For he had often been chained hand and foot, but he tore the chains apart and broke the irons on his feet. No one was strong enough to subdue him. ⁵Night and day among the tombs and in the hills he would cry out and cut himself with stones.

⁶When he saw Jesus from a distance, he ran and fell on his knees in front of him. ⁷He shouted at the top of his voice, "What do you want with me, Jesus, Son of the Most High God? Swear to God that you won't torture me!" ⁸For Jesus had said to him, "Come out of this man, you evil spirit!"

⁹Then Jesus asked him, "What is your name?"

"My name is Legion," he replied, "for we are many." ¹⁰And he begged Jesus again and again not to send them out of the area.

¹¹A large herd of pigs was feeding on the nearby hillside. ¹²The demons begged Jesus, "Send us among the pigs; allow us to go into them." ¹³He gave them permission, and the evil spirits came out and went into the pigs. The herd, about two thousand in number, rushed down the steep bank into the lake and were drowned.

¹⁴Those tending the pigs ran off and reported this in the town and countryside, and the people went out to see what had happened. ¹⁵When they came to Jesus, they saw the man who had been possessed by the legion of demons, sitting there, dressed and in his right mind; and they were afraid. ¹⁶Those who had seen it told the people what had happened to the demon-possessed man—and told about the pigs as well. ¹⁷Then the people began to plead with Jesus to leave their region.

¹⁸As Jesus was getting into the boat, the man who had been demon-possessed begged to go with him. ¹⁹Jesus did not let him, but said, "Go home to your family and tell them how much the Lord has done for you, and how he has had mercy

on you." ²⁰So the man went away and began to tell in the Decapolis how much Jesus had done for him. And all the people were amazed.

JESUS DOES NOT limit his miracles to one side of the lake. He declares God's rule and sows God's grace far and wide, including the region of the Gerasenes.[1] Crossing the lake to an area where swine are kept is more than a sportive outing. Jesus embarks on a daring invasion to claim alien turf under enemy occupation and reveals that there is no place in the world into which God's reign does not intend to extend itself. The confrontation that ensues reveals that every square inch, at sea and on the land, will be contested by Satan.

The Encounter with a Demon-Possessed Man (5:1–5)

AS JESUS DISEMBARKS from the boat, he immediately locks horns with another person in the grip of demons. Wherever Jesus goes, his holy presence, like some chemical catalyst, triggers an immediate reaction from the unholy. These demons do not cower in fear but cause the man to rush at Jesus. Mark alone gives us a vivid account of this man's condition and how he had been treated. This description reveals that he is "as storm-tossed by the demons as the disciples' boat had been."[2] The man's home is the unclean place of the dead,[3] and he himself is home to unclean (evil) spirits.[4] He may have survived in the tombs by feeding off food that had been left for the dead. The tattered remnants of his clothing symbolized the wreckage of his life. His harum-scarum behavior apparently had spooked the community in which he lived. They tried unsuccessfully to bind him, but he was powerful enough to snap the fetters and chains like string (5:3).

The fierce strength of this demon-possessed man is reiterated in 5:5: No one had the strength to "subdue" him. The Greek word used here (*damazo*) is used for taming a wild animal and is better translated, "no one was able to

1. Gerasa, modern Jerash, was thirty miles from the lake. The text allows it to be a reference to territory controlled by Gerasa. Possibly the original reference was to a town on the eastern shore that is now called Kersa or Koursi, which was later mistaken for the better-known Gerasa, a member of the Decapolis. The distance of Gerasa from the sea may have prompted the textual variants, locating the incident at Gadara or Gergesa.

2. Minear, *Mark*, 73.

3. Tombs were frequently located in caves and were known as haunts for demons, and the mountains were considered to be places of danger.

4. Waetjen, *Reordering of Power*, 114.

tame him." Obviously this demoniac roams free because all attempts to constrain him have failed. He is one tough customer, and only a power more potent than iron bars and chains will bridle him. Translating the verb "tame" also opens up another dimension to the text. It strikes us immediately that something is wrong. One does not normally "tame" human beings; one tames wild animals (or the tongue, James 3:8). People treat him like a wild animal, and he acts like one.

He is banished as an outcast from society and must dwell with those whose sleep will not be disturbed by his shrieks echoing through the night as he lacerates his body with stones.[5] He is a microcosm of the whole of creation, inarticulately groaning for redemption (Rom. 8:22). He is condemned to live out his days alone amid the decaying bones of the dead, with no one who loves him and no one to love. Malignant spirits always deface humanity and destroy life.

The Encounter with Unclean Spirits (5:6–13)

MARK PRESENTS A suspenseful confrontation between Jesus and the evil spirit(s) that control this ravaged man. The puzzling shifts in number from the singular (5:7, 9, 10) to the plural (5:9, 12, 13) suggest that the evil spirits are using him as a mouthpiece and that he is a miniature Pandemonium, the abode of all demons. Apparently, Jesus was telling the evil spirit to come out of the man (5:8), which meets with evasive tactics. Unlike humans, who cannot quite fathom the reality of the divine breaking into human history (4:41), evil spirits always recognize Jesus' divine origin (1:24; 3:11; see James 2:19) and quake in his presence. They know that they are pitted against vastly superior firepower.

These demons, however, are feisty. In their desperate attempt to resist any exorcism, they are momentarily successful in creating a standoff with gambits from an exorcist's bag of tricks. This is no ordinary demon that can be dismissed with only a word to shut up and leave. They try to wheel and deal as equals, and the struggle not only makes for an entertaining account but makes Jesus' ultimate victory all the more significant.[6] Nevertheless, the exorcism requires a struggle.

The evasive tactics consist of the demonized man prostrating himself before Jesus. Whether this action is counterfeit worship or conniving submission,

---

5. He is clearly one who would have been regarded as a demented soul screaming in his tortured isolation. The imbecile was one who went out alone at night, slept in burial places, ripped his clothes, and lost what he was given (t. *Ter.* 1:3; y. *Ter.* 1:1, 40b; b. *Hag.* 3b); but if these things were done in an insane manner, such a person was considered deranged.

6. Gundry, *Mark*, 251.

the evil spirits employ subterfuge to persuade Jesus to leave them alone. The man in their clutches cries out with a loud voice, "What do you want with me?" (cf. 1:24), and attempts to control Jesus by pronouncing his name, "Jesus, Son of the Most High God." As noted earlier, it was assumed that one had power over others when one knew their name. When they pronounce Jesus' name, they are basically saying, "We've got your number." They also abjure Jesus by the name of God not to torment them (presumably to destroy them, 1:24), although they themselves had tormented this poor man past endurance. They invoke the name of God to keep the Son of God off their back—to protect themselves.

Jesus seems to parry these diversionary tactics by asking for the demon's name. The evil spirits evade the question, however, by giving a number instead of a name: "My name is Legion" (5:9), the number in a Roman regiment (consisting of 6,000 foot soldiers and 120 horsemen). This man is captive to a legion of demons (cf. 5:15, "the man who had been possessed by the legion of demons"), at least enough "to drive 2,000 swine crazy."[7] This explains the switch to third-person plural verbs in 5:12–13 and the plural "evil spirits" (5:13). An engrossing battle of wits between Jesus and the demons unfolds as the evil spirits worry about being forced to leave their familiar surroundings. It would make sense from a Jewish perspective for demons to be most at home in this pagan setting. They perceive it to be their territory, but the kingdom of God manifest in Jesus' ministry is laying claim to all the earth. There is no protectorate of Satan that is safe.

It was popular belief in the first century that evil spirits were not content to wander aimlessly about. They abhor a vacuum and want to inhabit something. A human host is best; wanting that, a bunch of pigs will do. Anything is better than wandering in dry places (Matt. 12:43; Luke 11:24) or being consigned to the sea if you are a land demon.[8] The evil spirits therefore request to be sent into an enormously large herd of pigs feeding on the hillside.

Jesus seems all too gracious in granting the request, but it leads to the surprise ending. Christians are warned to watch because "your enemy the devil prowls around like a roaring lion looking for someone to devour" (1 Peter 5:8). He is even ready to devour a herd of pigs. These demons create fits of frenzy in whatever they inhabit, and the very thing they want to avert happens. The united legionary force is broken up as the pigs, an animal without a herd instinct, begin to stampede, lemminglike, down the bank and into the waters, where both they and the evil spirits are

---

7. Minear, *Mark*, 74.
8. *T. Sol.* 5:11 pleads: "Do not condemn me to water."

destroyed.[9] The destructive power of the sea that almost sank the disciples' boat now swallows up the pigs.[10] Jesus, who has just demonstrated his dominion over the sea (4:39, 41; compare Pss. 65:7; 88:9; 106:9; 107:23–32), does not need to know the names of the evil spirits in order to drive them out. The kamikaze demons "fall victim to their own designs and tumble headlong into chaos."[11] "The joke is on them."[12] From a Jewish perspective, the scene is a joke: unclean spirits and unclean animals are both wiped out in one fell swoop, and a human being is cleansed.

The Encounter with the Townspeople (5:14–17)

THE TOWNSPEOPLE'S RESPONSE to the man's restoration (5:15–17) is startling. When the community arrives, they are not frightened by what has happened to the pigs but by seeing this man now clothed and in his right mind! They do not rejoice at his recovery but are afraid. What is so scary about seeing a person sitting at the feet of Jesus? The community had desperately tried to tame him with chains and fetters, all to no avail. Now Jesus frees him from the chains of demons with a word. The disciples have also expressed fear at

---

9. Some commentators provide a rationalistic explanation for the stampede by claiming it was caused when the demoniac began to scream and run frantically among the pigs, causing them to scatter. But in Mark, demons never leave quietly (1:26); and they bring about self-destruction to whatever they inhabit. Lane comments (*Mark*, 186): "It is their purpose to destroy the creation of God, and halted in their destruction of a man, they fulfilled their purpose with the swine." Some commentators also argue that the demons destroyed the pigs in a vengeful bid to turn the town against Jesus. If that is the case, they were successful.

10. Some have tried to make the account into a revolutionary moral tale about the Romans. Paul Winter (*On the Trial of Jesus* [Berlin/New York: Walter de Gruyter, 1974], 180–81) pointed out that the standards of the tenth Roman legion, which destroyed Jerusalem in A.D. 70, bore the image of a wild boar. He suggested that the story derived from some Roman legionnaires taking a swim in the lake and drowning. J. Dominic Crossan (*Jesus: A Revolutionary Biography* [San Francisco: Harper, 1994], 89–91) broadens this theory by arguing that the story derives from the colonial oppression of the Romans, which was incarnated individually as demonic possession. True, many felt keenly the shackles of the Roman army and would have liked nothing better than to see the Roman legions driven into the sea. It is unlikely, however, that this story was invented to convey such a point. If the striking parallel to this account in the *Testament of Solomon* 11:1–6 is influenced by the account in the Gospels, then the encoded political message was missed. If that parallel is independent of the Gospels, then it provides evidence for the concept of a legion of demons without any hint of reference to Rome. For Mark, the evil that God's people face is far more serious than the oppression of Roman legions.

11. Robert G. Hamerton-Kelly, *The Gospel and the Sacred: Poetics of Violence in Mark* (Minneapolis: Fortress, 1994), 93.

12. Minear, *Mark*, 74.

Jesus' manifestation of great power (4:41) and wondered who this one with them is.

These townspeople do not seem to care that Jesus has such power; they just want him gone. Instead of giving him the key to the city, they give him a cold shoulder. The demons had begged Jesus to let them stay in the region (5:10); the townspeople now beg Jesus to leave the region. They are more comfortable with the malevolent forces that take captive human beings and destroy animals than they are with the one who can expel them. They can cope with the odd demon-possessed wild man who terrorizes the neighborhood with random acts of violence. But they want to keep someone with Jesus' power at lake's length—on the other side of the sea. They must consider Jesus more dangerous and worrisome than the demons.

Demons tend to keep to their own turf, but who can control someone with such power as Jesus possesses? As Jesus had granted the request of the demons, he now also grants the request of the community to leave them. This benighted community becomes another example of the outsiders who see but do not see, who hear what happens but who do not hear (4:10–12). They do not recognize the help that Jesus offers and do not invite him to stay or bring their sick and demonized to him (8:16; 9:32). They chase off the source of their deliverance and salvation. People can tolerate religion as long as it does not affect business profits (Acts 16:19; 19:24–27).

Jesus' Instructions to the Restored Man (5:18–20)

THE SPOTLIGHT SHIFTS back to the man, whose fear of Jesus is vanquished with the expulsion of the demons. He is seated, the position of the disciple (Luke 10:39; Acts 22:3), and requests to "to be with Jesus, " the role of the disciple (3:14). The community has begged Jesus to leave them (5:17); this man begs to be with Jesus (5:18). Another surprising twist in the account comes when Jesus declines his petition—the only request that he does not grant in this story. Mark does not give us any explanation for this refusal.[13] While Jesus' dismissal of this man may seem like bad news, it can only be good news for one who yearned for the warmth of family, for a sense of place and identity, and for a sense of purpose.[14] Jesus sends him to his own house so that he can be restored to his family.

Jesus also reverses his usual demand of silence by telling the man to spread the news how God has mercied him. Why? Is it because he does not fear a

---

13. Perhaps Mark would have us assume that the man is a Gentile, living in the tombs and surrounded by pigs. As a Gentile he does not yet fit into Jesus' plans for his mission to Israel, just as Jesus, the Jew, does not fit well in Gentile territory and is asked to leave.

14. In Mark, Jesus never asks anyone he heals to follow him as a disciple.

messianic upsurge in the midst of Gentiles or because this place needs some witness to begin sowing the word? Jesus may grant the community's wishes for him to leave, but he leaves this disturbing evidence of his presence. The infamous man with the legion remains to proclaim how he has been delivered by God's mercy. The upshot is that the preaching of the gospel about Jesus expands into the Decapolis.[15] The splash created by the testimony of the man is more effective in divulging who Jesus is than the splash created by the demons in the pigs.

A Christological subtlety in 5:19–20 should not be overlooked. Jesus tells the man, "Go home to your family and tell them how much the Lord has done for you, and how he has had mercy on you." (5:19). The man is not simply to tell people about the miracle that happened to him but what that miracle signifies: The Lord has been at work. Yet Jesus is the one who healed him, and the man announces the things that Jesus has done for him (5:20). For Jesus, all that he does is designed to bring glory to God. For Mark, Jesus is synonymous with the Lord (1:3; 12:36–7). Where Jesus acts, God acts.[16]

THIS ACCOUNT RAISES two interesting issues for our attempts to bring this story into our age. (1) It serves as an example of prevenient grace. (2) This brush with demonic slavery requires careful analysis before we can communicate its message successfully to our contemporary culture. The encounter has multifaceted dimensions, each of which can speak to different modern situations.

An Example of Prevenient Grace

ISAIAH 65:1–5A FORMS an interesting backdrop for this story:

"I revealed myself to those who did not ask for me;
  I was found by those who did not seek me.
To a nation that did not call on my name,
  I said, 'Here am I, here am I.'

---

15. The list of cities in the Decapolis is inexact but most include Damascus, Raphana, Dius, Canata, Scythopolis, Gadara, Hippos, Pella, Gerasa, and Philadelphia. They were under the administrative control of the Roman governor of Syria and were distinguished from their surrounding environment by their Greek way of life, in culture and religion. Passages in Josephus suggest that their relations with Jews was one of hostility (*Life* 65 §§ 341–42; 74 § 410).

16. Marcus, *The Way of the Lord*, 40.

> All day long I have held out my hands
> > to an obstinate people,
> who walk in ways not good,
> > pursuing their own imaginations—
> a people who continually provoke me
> > to my very face,
> offering sacrifices in gardens
> > and burning incense on altars of brick;
> who sit among the graves
> > and spend their nights keeping secret vigil;
> who eat the flesh of pigs,
> > and whose pots hold broth of unclean meat;
> who say, 'Keep away; don't come near me,
> > for I am too sacred for you!'"[17]

One can immediately spot the parallels with the story in Mark: the mention of demons (5:2; Isa. 65:3), dwelling in the tombs (5:3, 5; Isa. 65:4a), the warning to keep away (5:7; Isa. 65:5a), and the reference to the pigs (5:11; Isa. 65:4b). This Isaian backdrop helps clarify that Jesus lands at a place awash in pagan practices and one that has not called on God's name (Isa. 65:1). For the early Christian community, this story may have provided proof that the gospel was to extend beyond the holy confines of Israel to a heathenish world.

This case hardly needs to be made to churches today, but reading this incident alongside the Isaiah narrative brings out the theological principle of prevenient grace that governs the spread of the kingdom of God. God takes the initiative in turning to human beings—even those across the lake in an unholy land filled with swine and demons. God searches out those who have never searched for or thought about turning to God. The psalmist says, "I call on the LORD in my distress, and he answers me" (Ps. 120:1). The demoniac's incoherent cries are directed into the air to no god in particular. Not surprisingly, they receive no answer. He is not seeking God or even seeking healing. Caught in the web of demonic powers, he even resists healing when it comes. The region where he resides also resists it. Yet we see the power of God's mercy and love that captures and transforms those who do not even know that it exists and may initially resist it when it invades their lives.

A Multifaceted Account

TO BUILD A bridge to our world, it helps to recognize that what happens in this story is multifaceted. Jesus encounters three different characters in the

---

17. See Franz Annen, *Heil für die Heiden* (Frankfurt: Joseph Knecht, 1976), 182–84.

story: the evil spirits, whom he outfoxes; the man, whom he heals; and the community, whom he frightens. Each of these makes a request. The demons beg him to allow them to stay in the same country and to send them into the nearby swine. The community begs him to leave their country. The man begs to be with him. Jesus grants every request except the man's.

Engaging the demonic. Jesus' victory over wily and death-dealing spirits returns to one of Mark's themes: Jesus' power over the demonic, the dark side of reality, which enslaves and dehumanizes human beings. Jesus crosses to the opposite side of the lake and has the strength to rout even the most severe cases of evil spirits with sensational effects. The story emphasizes the drastic nature of the man's possession, and the large number of demons who try to fend off being expelled underscores the difficulty of the exorcism. The man is under the control of a demonic force that appears to use him as a personal gymnasium. When one compares the accounts of Jesus' exorcisms to stories of exorcisms from the contemporary Greco-Roman world, one thing stands out: Jesus does not resort to any special techniques employed by other exorcists to purge the demons—such as odd recipes, secret prayers, bizarre formulae, or knowledge of the names of the demons or their thwarting angel. The power of his person alone drives the demons out.

Many today, however, including conservative Christians, are put off by stories of demons, particularly one that records what seems to be a wanton destruction of two thousand innocent animals. This story is also likely to disturb anyone who sympathizes with the aims of the Society for the Prevention of Cruelty to Animals. Some ask, Why were these innocent pigs destroyed? Consequently, preachers are tempted to shy away from this passage.

Indeed, one might wonder, if God knows every sparrow that falls, does he also know when pigs drown? But Jesus' point about the sparrows is that God knows and cares about birds that are not worth two cents to humans. How much more will God care about humans who are of more value than a sparrow (Matt. 10:29–31)? From Jesus' perspective, the deranged man in this incident is of more value than two thousand pigs. Modern hearers frequently miss this point because they are more sensitive to the problem of the destruction of innocent animals and the loss of someone's property. One therefore needs to make clear that Jesus did not consign the animals to destruction in the sea. The demonic spirits ignited the rampage that led to their destruction, not Jesus.

Characters such as Piglet, Porky Pig, Miss Piggy, and Babe have won our hearts, and we feel no aversion to pigs. Consequently, some background on the Jewish aversion to pigs helps explain why their violent demise would have evoked cheers instead of tears. The deep antipathy toward these animals has nothing to do with the biblical injunction against eating pork

(Lev. 11:7–8). In first-century Palestine, swine's flesh was associated with the brutal persecution of Jews by pagans, who wanted to eradicate peculiar Jewish practices. An account in 1 Maccabees 6:18–31 and 7:1–42 poignantly describes the gallantry of those who endured extreme torture and refused to compromise their faith when forced to eat swine's flesh, a symbolic rejection of the religion of their fathers. Swine were therefore indelible reminders of paganism and persecution. On hearing this account, Jews would have hailed the swine's destruction as a token of God's ultimate vindication over the powers of oppression. There is no similar phenomenon associated with animals in our culture, although modern readers would probably not think twice if the animals destroyed by demons run amok were a pack of bubonic plague-carrying rats or a nest of venomous snakes.

Even if one can resolve the destruction of the animals, one may still be uncomfortable with the demons in this incident. Judging from the media, moderns are becoming interested in angels, perhaps because they are so benign and seem nondenominational. But they are not sure what to make of demons, and many choose to neglect this biblical subject altogether. Some modern hearers will therefore miss the point of this story because they are put off by the idea of exorcisms. By contrast, C. Peter Wagner writes confidently about real battles in various parts of the world with powers experienced as personal beings.[18] He reflects the views of many Christians today, who do not question that demons are real, created, personal beings. Since the Bible takes for granted that such beings exist, so do they; and they assume that Jesus' confrontation with demons reflects a reality that our modern scientific approaches cannot measure or grasp. They recognize that evil is attributable to Satan, who violently resists God's good purposes for creation.

But how does one communicate with those many others who dismiss any idea that supernatural evil beings can take control of a person's life as a relic of ancient superstition? Such persons would probably feel more comfortable with a polysyllabic medical term to describe this man's condition, and psychiatrists might propose several possible psychoses. Others might blame the man's condition on a chemical imbalance, a history of being abused as a child, or some genetic propensity to violence. By giving this condition a scientific name, perhaps we believe that we can understand it and have some control over it. Such diagnoses might make the account more attractive to those who are unsympathetic to supernatural phenomena, but they do not solve the problem of evil. We may change the names of the demons, but they are not thereby conquered and they do not lose their malice. As Leenhardt

---

18. C. Peter Wagner, *Warfare Prayer: Strategies for Combatting the Rulers of Darkness* (Ventura, Calif.: Regal, 1992).

perceptively observes, "We have renamed the demons of the past, but we have not exorcised them."[19]

One need not try to recreate in a congregation a first-century worldview about the demonic. That is not our task. But we do need to make people aware that we are up against supernatural powers that oppose God, destroy life, deface it, defeat it, and deform it. Daniel Day Williams wrote that the belief that evil issues from a "power from beyond the self may be more realistic than humanism, which expects its overcoming through human effort alone." That belief is not only more realistic, it is, from the New Testament perspective, essential. It will prevent us from naively putting our trust in some wistful idea of inevitable human progress and will keep us from ever fooling ourselves into thinking that we can get along fine without God. Sometimes tragic events force us to admit that an evil exists beyond that which lurks in the hearts of individuals. Williams quotes Alfred Weber's description of his experience in Europe between the two world wars:

> It was as if certain forces sprang up out of the ground; giants of action, crafty, hungry for power, which nobody had noticed before, seemed to shoot up like a crop of dragon's teeth.[20]

One newspaper columnist wrote in response to a terrorist bombing that slaughtered many innocent people, including a day-care center: "From what universe beyond this one that most of us inhabit does this kind of evil arise?" A belief in supernatural evil powers keeps us from whittling down the source of evil to our size and prevents us from deceiving ourselves that we can defeat it alone. People need to recognize that creation is fallen and needs redeeming, for then they will look to the One who has the power to redeem it. The incident with the Gerasene demoniac therefore has relevance even for skeptics. It shows that through Christ God is eradicating what Rosa Coldfield, in William Faulkner's novel *Absalom, Absalom,* called "the sickness at the heart of things."

One should also make a careful distinction between the demonized person and the satanic. In the New Testament, the demonized individual is a victim to be pitied and to be liberated from oppression. Such people are never rebuked, never told to repent, and never told that their sins are forgiven. The demoniacs are never aggressive unless one interferes with them or darkens the door of the places where they have withdrawn.

---

19. F. Leenhardt, "An Exegetical Essay: Mark 5:1–20," in *Structural Analysis and Biblical Exegesis* (Pittsburgh: Pickwick, 1974), 91.

20. Daniel Day Williams, *The Demonic and the Divine,* ed. Stacy A. Evans (Minneapolis: Fortress, 1990), 9.

The satanic is another matter, however. There is a difference between being possessed by Satan's minions and playing the role of Satan. The satanic is aggressive, responsible, and guilty. The satanic is a victimizer. It does not need to be liberated; it needs to be judged. A direct relationship exists between the sin and the predicament. The satanic needs repentance so that it will become submissive to the will of God. For example, we recognize that there is a difference between the drug abuser who has turned to drugs because he or she sees no other hope in a dreary and despairing life, and the drug kingpin who sells drugs simply to make profit and to live well off the suffering of others. This analogy breaks down, however, because in the New Testament no direct causal connection exists between the predicament of the demoniac and any sin he or she may have committed. There is no hint that the demoniac invited the demons to take control of his life. Therefore, those who are possessed are not told to repent. What they desperately need is a new, benevolent power to come into their lives and take control. This is what Christ offers the wreck of a man in this story.

Engaging a deranged human. The destructive power of the demonic that can take over a human life is an important ingredient in the story. One can also approach the story from the perspective of Jesus' engagement with a human being whom everyone regards as a madman. This man has been written off by others as a hopeless, terrifying, rogue elephant. Others have so brutalized him that when he sees Jesus, he sees only another who comes to torment him—like a dog that has been mercilessly beaten or a child who has been outrageously abused. Evil has so completely taken over his life that it assumes a personality of its own. It distorts his perception of reality. The man has no sense of self-identity; he does not know who he is.

But when he meets with Jesus' powerful mercy, he is restored to wholeness. His encounter with Jesus makes him fully human again, with a family, a home, and a mission in life. He no longer is a beast whom people thought needed to be tamed, but a human being called to proclaim the explosion of God's mercy in his life. How is it that Jesus can transform this berserk derelict into a sane and well-balanced human with just a word? The incident is a perfect illustration of what happens in conversion. C. S. Lewis recalls the imagery of this story in describing his life before his conversion as "a zoo of lusts, a bedlam of ambitions, a nursery of fears, a harem of fondled hatreds. My name was legion."[21]

Engaging a possessed community. Mark goes into detail about how others tried to overpower this man (5:3–4) and then describes how those who converged

---

21. C. S. Lewis, *Surprised by Joy* (New York/London: Harcourt Brace Jovanovich, 1955), 226.

on the scene begged Jesus to leave their neighborhood. These details do not simply add color to the narrative but indicate that this incident also has to do with Jesus' encounter with the community. It is a community that beats, chains, and dehumanizes other human beings. It knows only how to use force, how to crack down on madmen, and how to protect its property. But this community fears someone like Jesus, who wields a different kind of power. It expresses total indifference to the restoration of a human being to wholeness, particularly if they deem the cost too high. It prefers pigs to the healing of individual demoniacs.

The passage also reveals something about the societal nature of evil. Societies are no less possessed in their angry punishment of poor wretches who are discarded on the waste heap of humanity for interfering with normal society. This community opts for violent solutions to problems that solve nothing and only compound the agony. They ignore Jesus' way of compassion and mercy. This facet of the account, which reveals a society possessed by violence and money, should not be ignored. Wink raises the issue:

> What troubles me ... is that by attempting to fight the demons "in the air," evangelicals and charismatics will continue largely to ignore the institutional sources of the demonic. By so doing, they will fail to do the hard political and economic analysis necessary to name, unmask, and engage these Powers transformatively.[22]

In bringing the contexts to our lives, we may try to deal with all three different vantage points in presenting this story or we may focus on one or two. We cannot neglect, however, the focus on Jesus' power to drive out evil, which is beyond any human power to control.

 MOST PEOPLE IN Western societies today do not fear the influence of demons. If modern movies and novels are any indication, however, people today do have a sense of foreboding that some supernatural, malicious evil is out there that haunts and assaults human beings in a seemingly arbitrary way.

Movie producers and novelists capitalize on this modern uneasiness in their science fiction thrillers and horror tales. In these plots, an insidious alien power bursts on the scene. It usually takes the form of some virtually indestructible being who can metamorphose into any shape and is bent on

---

22. Walter Wink, *Engaging the Powers: Discernment and Resistance in a World of Domination* (Minneapolis: Fortress, 1992), 314.

destroying individuals and eventually the whole world. Other movies have to do with an outbreak of some deadly, incurable disease that strikes fear throughout a region and threatens to devastate it. Still others center on a murderous human monster who has nine lives and comes back in sequel after sequel to savage his victims. The villains are usually dispatched by some violent means or scientific wizardry, which ends the movie but never completely solves the problem. These cinematic battles that pit the forces of light (so-called) against the forces of darkness show no knowledge of God's purposes or power to overcome evil and have no awareness of how God works to defeat it. They assume that humans have the power and ingenuity to expel the evil from our midst.

Mark presents a quite different picture of the source of evil and how it is overcome. Evil comes from a demonic power that seizes human beings. It is not something that we can defeat on our own. It takes a greater supernatural power to vanquish it—the power of God. Martin Luther's words are apropos:

Did we in our own strength confide
Our striving would be losing.

Only in Christ can we find "a shelter from the stormy blast" and the power to overcome demonic forces, which can swamp not only individuals but whole nations and continents. Only in Christ are we delivered from the dominion of evil powers. In Mark's account we also see that this evil is dispatched when Jesus calmly speaks a word. All of the violence is caused by the evil spirits, not by Jesus. Mark emphasizes Jesus' mercy (5:19), not his blustering power, that vanquishes evil. In Christ we see God destroying evil through love.

The exorcisms are visible aspects of God's rule. Jesus routs the demonic forces; those who are in Christ may take their power seriously but need not fear them today.[23] They also need not bemoan the sad state of affairs in our fallen world. One can confidently join in the battle against these powers that take others captive, knowing that God is on our side.

Sydney H. T. Page argues that we have much to gain from revitalizing a belief in the supernatural world and from renewing the biblical emphasis on conflict and victory. He offers several important cautions, however.[24] (1) Such beliefs, if they become exaggerated, breed fear and paranoia. We should not see demons behind every rock and tree, ready to ambush unsus-

---

23. See Everett Ferguson, *Demonology of the Early Christian World* (New York/Toronto: Edwin Mellen, 1984), 170–71.

24. The following five points are taken from his book *Powers of Evil: A Biblical Study of Satan and Demons* (Grand Rapids: Baker, 1995), 269–70.

pecting, innocent bystanders. The exorcisms in Mark convey exactly the opposite mood. Jesus is always victorious. The enemy powers are being vanquished—usually with just one little word. (2) One may be tempted to blame demons for everything and thereby evade any personal responsibility. Some things that people call demons are simply the displays of human vices. (3) Some present-day expressions of belief in demons border on the superstitious and sub-Christian. One should exercise discernment and not accept every claim about the demonic at face value. (4) Scripture shuns any attempt to name and rank demons, and one should avoid any such speculation. We do not conquer demons by knowing their names. (5) Demon possession is a rare phenomenon. We should not explain every strange behavior as demonic or label every human opponent as demonic. Those who focus their efforts on a sensational warfare with demons and the rescuing of their victims may neglect the more mundane spiritual warfare that each Christian must wage in his or her own heart. People today are more likely to be controlled by a legion of cravings, captivations, and destructive impulses than by a legion of demons.

The story can also be looked at from the vantage point of the demoniac, who meets Jesus and is restored to wholeness. Those uncomfortable with the story about demons should not skip over it in embarrassment. The text also allows one to look at it as a struggle with a demented mind. This man is a rent soul, raw and infected with fear and fury. He inflicts wounds on himself in a vain attempt to relieve his inner torment. When the man sees Jesus, he sees only another tormentor because something has penetrated his being that prevents his liberation. The bonds of Satan are far stronger than the human chains. He is much like Benjy, the gelded man with the mental capacity of a two-year-old in William Faulkner's novel *The Sound and the Fury*, a tale told by an idiot. Benjy would wail for long periods of time, and his brother Jason would beat him quiet. "Then Ben wailed again, hopeless and prolonged. It was nothing. Just sound. It might have been all time and injustice and sorrow become vocal for an instant by a conjunction of planets."[25] Like Benjy, the man in Mark 5 experiences a misery that does not know how to voice its pain except in loud groans. The pain is deep, whether it is from the torment within, from the times people trying to beat him quiet, or from the times he lacerated himself with stones.

We may see a mirror of ourselves in this disturbed man—beaten down by others, divided against ourselves, a civil war raging within, living among

---

25. Noted by Gail R. O'Day, "Hope Beyond Brokenness: A Markan Reflection on the Gift of Life," *Currents in Theology and Mission* 15 (1988): 250. The citation comes from p. 359 in Faulkner.

the gloomy tombs of life, and feeling all alone. Lowry has paraphrased this man's response to Jesus:

> I feel like 6,000 soldiers inside me ... sometimes they all march left, sometimes right ... sometimes in all different directions. I'm pulled one way, then another. There's an army inside me, and I think I'm losing the war.[26]

If we can recognize ourselves in this tortured man, we can also see that deliverance is not something that someone else needs—derelicts and foaming lunatics. The power of the gospel is also for us. We are just as battered, though we may do a better job of hiding it behind our coherent words, our well-kept homes, and our smart attire. But deliverance can also come to us when Jesus lands on the shores of our lives. The great calm that came over the sea (4:39) matches the great calm that now governs this man, who now sits fully clothed and quietly at Jesus' feet (5:15).

The problem is that those who need deliverance most sometimes offer the greatest resistance. The tormented man begged Jesus not to send his demons too far away, which reveals that he does not want to be delivered. He wants "Legion" to stay close by. Sigmund Freud said that there is something within the patient, "a force which defends itself with all its means against healing and definitely wants to cling to the illness and to the suffering."[27] Many counselors have experienced this resistance in their clients. Persons come for therapy, saying that they want to change, and then fight for all their worth against changing themselves. Some people find security in the demons they know and are afraid to be delivered from them. One can derive comfort from Jesus' persistence in this account. He will not be put off by evasive tactics and does not give up the fight to deliver this one from his personal demons.

This incident also has to do with a community that resists supernatural power. They are callously indifferent to the restoration of a man. It is one thing to encounter the impersonal forces of evil in nature run amok in an individual; it is quite another to encounter them in a whole community. Whole societies and institutions can be caught in the grips of evil and never recognize it.

We might ask whether our society treats people like this demonized man in the same way. Do we beat and chain persons and drive them from our midst so that they must fend for themselves in the contemporary equivalent of the

---

26. Eugene L. Lowry, "Cries From the Graveyard: A Sermon," in *The Daemonic Imagination: Biblical Text and Secular Story*, eds. Robert Detweiler and William G. Doty (Atlanta: Scholars: 1990), 30–31.

27. Cited by Leenhardt, "An Exegetical Essay: Mark 5:1–20," 95.

tombs? They are usually the kind of broken persons we label as dangerous. More often than not, we deny bearing any responsibility for their condition and shift all the blame for their problems onto them. We exonerate ourselves by making them the scapegoats for society's ills. It is their problem, not ours. We allow them to hole up by themselves with their raging anguish in the graveyards of their lives. We may put blind trust in the use of force, stone walls, iron bars, and police crackdowns to keep them away.

The solutions to such problems are not more government programs, better housing, or prison reform, though these may alleviate some pain. People who live in such lonely despair need to meet Jesus Christ and allow that encounter to transform their lives. Churches, however, have fled the places where these troubled human beings usually gather to settle in more comfortable locations. Who will bring Christ to them? And when they meet Jesus Christ and there are no jobs, decent housing, or good schools and covert discrimination still prevails, major problems remain. Evangelism must go hand in hand with social concern.

The solution is a power that comes from without, but some may be too afraid to let that power loose in their own lives, let alone to unleash it on society. Healing, compassion, and evangelism have their costs, and many do not want to pay. Perhaps people fear that they will be healed at the expense of losing more pigs. Concern for the bottom line may outweigh concern for those caught in the grips of suffering. Calvin Stowe, for example, a professor of biblical studies, lived in the shadow of his more internationally famous wife, Harriet Beecher Stowe, the author of the poignant denunciation of slavery, *Uncle Tom's Cabin*. When she toured England, he preached before a large crowd gathered to observe Anti-Slavery Day. He told the listeners in no uncertain terms that they were hypocrites. They were proud that slavery had long since disappeared in England, but 80 percent of the cotton picked by slaves in the southern states was bought by England. He said slavery would die in America if England would boycott its cotton and went on to ask, "Are you willing to sacrifice one penny of your profits to do way with slavery?" The crowd booed.[28]

---

28. C. Douglas Weaver, *A Cloud of Witnesses* (Macon, Ga.: Smyth & Helwys, 1993), 139–40.

Mark 5:21–43

W HEN JESUS HAD again crossed over by boat to the other side of the lake, a large crowd gathered around him while he was by the lake. ²²Then one of the synagogue rulers, named Jairus, came there. Seeing Jesus, he fell at his feet ²³and pleaded earnestly with him, "My little daughter is dying. Please come and put your hands on her so that she will be healed and live." ²⁴So Jesus went with him.

A large crowd followed and pressed around him. ²⁵And a woman was there who had been subject to bleeding for twelve years. ²⁶She had suffered a great deal under the care of many doctors and had spent all she had, yet instead of getting better she grew worse. ²⁷When she heard about Jesus, she came up behind him in the crowd and touched his cloak, ²⁸because she thought, "If I just touch his clothes, I will be healed." ²⁹Immediately her bleeding stopped and she felt in her body that she was freed from her suffering.

³⁰At once Jesus realized that power had gone out from him. He turned around in the crowd and asked, "Who touched my clothes?"

³¹"You see the people crowding against you," his disciples answered, "and yet you can ask, 'Who touched me?'"

³²But Jesus kept looking around to see who had done it. ³³Then the woman, knowing what had happened to her, came and fell at his feet and, trembling with fear, told him the whole truth. ³⁴He said to her, "Daughter, your faith has healed you. Go in peace and be freed from your suffering."

³⁵While Jesus was still speaking, some men came from the house of Jairus, the synagogue ruler. "Your daughter is dead," they said. "Why bother the teacher any more?"

³⁶Ignoring what they said, Jesus told the synagogue ruler, "Don't be afraid; just believe."

³⁷He did not let anyone follow him except Peter, James and John the brother of James. ³⁸When they came to the home of the synagogue ruler, Jesus saw a commotion, with people crying and wailing loudly. ³⁹He went in and said to them, "Why all this commotion and wailing? The child is not dead but asleep." ⁴⁰But they laughed at him.

After he put them all out, he took the child's father and mother and the disciples who were with him, and went in where the child was. ⁴¹He took her by the hand and said to her, "Talitha koum!" (which means, "Little girl, I say to you, get up!"). ⁴²Immediately the girl stood up and walked around (she was twelve years old). At this they were completely astonished. ⁴³He gave strict orders not to let anyone know about this, and told them to give her something to eat.

AFTER JESUS RETURNS from across the lake, an official of a synagogue immediately waylays him. Except for the disciples, he is one of the few characters in this Gospel who is given a name—Jairus. He falls before Jesus' feet and desperately begs him to come to his home to lay hands on his daughter that she might be healed and live (5:22–23), just as the Gerasenes had begged him to leave their shores. Jesus agrees, but the rush to the girl's side is interrupted by an anonymous woman. She is so desperate to be healed from her hemorrhaging that she sneaks up to touch Jesus' garments in hopes that it will restore her to health.

The suffering of the woman for twelve years stresses her great need and why she is so compelled to seek Jesus' help (see 9:21; Luke 13:11; Acts 3:2, 9:33; 14:8). The text does not specify the nature of her loss of blood, but one can presume it was related to uterine bleeding, which would make her ritually unclean (see Lev. 15:25–33).[1] One should not confuse her problem with the regular menstrual cycle, a normal part of life. Her perpetual bleeding is abnormal, which makes it far more serious for her. The woman's impurity is transmissible to others until the problem is cured. Anyone who has contact with her by lying in her bed, sitting in her chair, or touching her becomes unclean and is required to bathe and to launder clothing.[2] Her discharge of blood causes her to be discharged from society because it makes her a major

---

1. Blood was the only detergent for the altar in the temple and cleansed from sin, but it was also a major pollutant for people (Lev. 12:7; 15:19–24; 20:18). Ezekiel 36:17 describes the sinfulness of the people, "Their conduct was like a woman's monthly uncleanness in my sight." In the Greco-Roman world, the touch of a menstruating woman was considered harmful (see Pliny, *Natural History* 7.64). On purity issues in Judaism, see Hannah Harrington, *The Impurity Systems of Qumran and the Rabbis: Biblical Foundations* (SBLDS 143; Atlanta: Scholars, 1993).

2. The question is often asked how others would know about her condition. In a small village society, word would have leaked out from friends and family, from the doctors, or even from divorce proceedings.

bearer of impurity as a person with a flux.[3] She is therefore similar to the leper as one suffering from cultic uncleanness and is excluded from normal social relations.[4]

This woman suffers physically, living every day with the signs of our decaying mortality as the blood essential for life drains from her body.[5] She suffers socially and psychologically, knowing that she is a contaminant. Her plight is compounded because she has become impoverished after wasting her living on the fruitless cure of physicians.[6] Their failure underscores that Jesus can succeed when others sources of healing have failed, and it costs nothing except a bold faith. Jesus has just exorcised a demon from a man that no one could control; now he heals a woman that no physician can cure and restores to life a girl when all hope is gone.

The woman refuses to accept this disease as her lot in life and boldly takes matters into her own hands by touching Jesus' garment (mentioned four times in 5:27, 28, 30, 31). She is not the first to do so. Earlier Mark tells us that many who suffered diseases pushed forward to touch him (3:10); and in 6:56, he reports that people beg him to let them touch the hem of his cloak, and all who touch him are healed.[7] The difference is that this woman slinks up from behind so that she will not be observed and hopes that she can slink back into the anonymity of the large crowd without anyone knowing of her unlawful contact. When she touches Jesus, immediately her fountain of blood stops. But just as immediately Jesus knows that power has gone forth from him, and he mystifies the disciples by asking who in the throng pushing around him has touched him.[8] The disciples respond as the straight men, say-

---

3. See Jacob Milgrom, *Leviticus 1–16* (AB; New York: Doubleday, 1991), 745.

4. The Mishnaic tractate on the menstruant is entitled *Nidda*, which means "banished." Josephus, *J. W.* 5:5.6 § 227, reports that the temple was closed to women during their menstruation (see also *Ag. Ap.* 2:103–4; *Ant.* 3.11.1 § 261).

5. Milgrom (in *Leviticus 1–16*, 1002) points out that the laws on bodily impurities focus on four phenomena: death, blood, semen, and scale disease. "Their common denominator is death. Vaginal blood and semen represent the forces of life; their loss—death." "The wasting of the body, the common characteristic of all biblically impure skin diseases, symbolizes the death process as much as the loss of blood and semen."

6. One can see a listing of physician's remedies for the women's condition in *b. Sabb.* 110a.

7. The belief that the power of a person is transferred to what one wears or touches can be seen also in Acts 5:15 and 19:12. M. Hutter ("Ein altorientalischer Bittgestus in Mt 9:20–22," *ZNW* 75 [1984]: 133–35) claims that this woman's gesture does not reflect a belief in magic but means to pray fervently (1 Sam. 15:24–27).

8. This detail suggests that the power is something beyond his control; God controls it. Cranfield's comments (*Mark*, 185) are helpful:

The power residing in, and issuing from, Jesus is the power of the personal God. Though Jesus himself does not himself make a decision (at least so it seems) in this

ing in effect, "How are we supposed to know? Everybody is touching you."
But only one was healed, and she is seized by fear.

A number of things could have caused her alarm. She may have felt guilt
for violating Jewish purity regulations as one who, with cultic uncleanness,
has dared to touch Jesus. Readers know, however, that Jesus has never shied
away from ceremonial uncleanness and that his power can overcome it and
reverse it. The woman may have been concerned that she has illegitimately
stolen power from Jesus and fears that her plague might have passed on to
him in some way. She may have expected a scolding instead of a blessing—
but Mark connects her fear to knowing what has happened to her (5:33).
Because she has experienced healing from Jesus' amazing power, she is conscious of his power and fears, much as the disciples feared earlier on the lake
when they witnessed his power over the storm (4:41). Like the ruler of the
synagogue, she now prostrates herself before him.

Why does Jesus call attention to what she has done? Has she not suffered
enough public embarrassment? Could he not let her go in peace with a silent
wink? The public embarrassment caused by singling her out signifies his
individual care for her. He will not allow her to slip away and remain anonymous. He forces the issue so that when she leaves healed, she will leave
knowing that the one who healed her knows her and cares for her. She is a
person who is worth taking time with and addressing.

It turns out that the healing does not come free. Jesus forces her to step
out on faith and be identified. It will not bankrupt her as the physicians had
done, but she must publicly acknowledge her debt to Jesus, that he is the
source of her healing. When she does, he blesses her and announces that her
faith has made her well. Faith, then—not any magical properties in Jesus'
clothing—accomplishes her healing and saving.[9] He restores her as a daughter of Israel and tells her to go in peace (Judg. 18:6; 1 Sam. 1:17; 2 Sam. 15:9;
Acts 16:36).[10] This is not simply a word of dismissal. The Hebrew term for

---

case, nevertheless God does. God controls his own power. He knows about the
woman and wills to honour her faith in the efficacy of his power active in Jesus,
even though her faith is no doubt very imperfect and indeed dangerously near to ideas
of magic. The cure does not happen automatically, but by God's free and personal
decision.
See also Gundry, *Mark*, 270.

9. Robert G. Hamerton-Kelly (*The Gospel and the Sacred: Poetics of Violence in Mark* [Min-
neapolis: Fortress, 1994], 94) puts it well: "The act of faith was to reach out from the crowd
and touch Jesus, and then at his behest to stand forth and be identified."

10. A woman who suffered her affliction was supposed to bring a sacrifice in the temple when she was healed (Lev. 15:29–30), but Jesus makes no mention of this as he did for
the leper (Mark 1:44). Someone with a hemorrhage did not have to go through the same
public procedure before he or she could be reintegrated into society.

peace that forms the background for the New Testament concept of peace is *shalom*. It covers wholeness, well-being, prosperity, security, friendship, and salvation.[11] Jesus bestows this peace on her (see Matt. 10:13; Acts 10:36).

Meanwhile, the distraught father has been left to cool his heels. One can only guess what he must be thinking about this delay. One usually finds it difficult to rejoice with those who receive good news (salvation and health) when one is worried to death over one's own bad news. Was Jairus chafing as Jesus took time for this woman: "Why is he dawdling? I was in line first; take care of my problem first." Jairus is no more needy than this nameless woman, and he can learn something from this woman's faith and be better prepared for the raising of his daughter.[12]

He too must publicly demonstrate his trust in Jesus as the worst possible news comes. The bearers of the bad tidings do not mince words: "Your daughter is dead. . . . Why bother the teacher any more?" Meier comments: "The subliminal message here is that Jesus is only a teacher, and death marks the limit of whatever power he may have."[13] Just as the woman overcame her fear with her faith, so Jairus is told, "Don't be afraid; just believe [i.e., keep on believing]." He had shown faith in coming to Jesus in the first place, now he must continue. But how can faith endure in the face of death, particularly when it hovers over one's cherished child? Both the woman and Jairus reveal that faith is something that trusts in the midst of hopelessness.

Jairus obeys because he leads Jesus to his house, but his faith is again challenged by the grievous chorus of those already assembled to mourn the little girl's death. They do not have the faith of the woman and would undermine the faith of the father. Jesus' announcement that the girl is not dead but only sleeping meets with laughter and jeering. They are not crazy; they know when someone has died. Of course she is dead. Jesus, however, can transform a deadly storm into a great calm, a ferocious brute into a calm and gentle man, death into a calm sleep, and the laughter of scorn into the laughter of joy. Their skepticism puts them outside. There will be no miracles for the scornful throng.

In private, with only the parents and Peter, James, and John, Jesus grasps the little girl's hand to raise her up, saying *"Talitha koum."* The translation from this bit of Aramaic, "Little girl . . . get up!" makes it clear for the listener that

---

11. See T. J. Geddert, "Peace," in *Dictionary of Jesus and the Gospels*, eds. Joel B. Green, Scot McKnight, and I. Howard Marshall (Downers Grove, Ill.: InterVarsity, 1992), 604; P. B. Yoder, *Shalom: The Bible's Word for Salvation, Justice and Peace* (Newton, Kans.: Faith and Life, 1982).

12. Camery-Hoggatt, *Irony*, 138–39.

13. John P. Meier, *A Marginal Jew: Rethinking the Historical Jesus. Volume Two: Mentor, Message, and Miracles* (New York: Doubleday, 1991), 2:786.

Jesus does not utter some mysterious mumbo jumbo but an ordinary phrase.[14] Perhaps the tradition retained it as the word of Jesus that raised the girl from death. The offer of food shows that the child is really alive and not a disembodied spirit (Luke 24:39–43). The command to secrecy reveals that Jesus is not interested in turning jeers into cheers. He has consistently avoided publicity and now responds only to those with faith. One cannot fully understand the life-giving power of God until after the resurrection of Jesus.

Hooker notes the irony in Jesus' order. He tells the parents not to let anyone know about what has happened, yet he insisted that the woman come forward out of the crowd. She had endeavored to be healed in complete secrecy, but Jesus did not allow her to keep her recovery to herself. The difference is that proof that the woman's affliction had been cured "could not be openly demonstrated or cause wonder." The crowd may not know her case history and can only take her word for it that she is healed. The revival of the child is another matter. A funeral interrupted by the sudden appearance of the corpse frisking about alive and well would make headlines, but witnesses of the cure are told to keep the news secret.[15] This incident starkly contrasts with the raising of Lazarus in the Gospel of John. Jesus deliberately dallies when news comes that his friend is ill and allows time for him to die, be buried, and the body to begin to decompose (John 11:1–46). The delay makes the miracle all the more marvelous.[16]

It is unlikely that "Jesus wants to delay the discovery so as to get away from the large crowd that have been crushing him (5:24, 31)," as some contend.[17] He did not say to the gathered mourners that he would raise her from the dead but that she was not dead, only sleeping. He does not want it broadcast that he has raised her from death. The reasons are twofold. (1) The timing is not right for belief in the miracle of resurrection. It must wait until Jesus is himself raised from the dead (9:9). One must see the whole picture of Jesus' ministry and death. Now, he only keeps death at bay, and the parents and their daughter receive a temporary reprieve. Jesus will bring complete release from the jaws of death through his own death and resurrection. (2) There is a danger that he will be known only as a miracle worker, a magician-healer who can do wonders. People will lose sight of the big picture and how all that he does is tied to the proclamation of the kingdom of God.

---

14. Possibly Jesus addresses her by name, "Talitha, stand up!" See Max Wilcox, "Talitha Cumi," *ABD* 6:309–10.

15. Hooker, *Mark,* 151.

16. F. Watson, "Ambiguity in the Marcan Narrative," *Kings Theological Review* 10 (1987): 11.

17. Gundry, *Mark,* 277.

IN BRIDGING THE contexts, one should take careful note of three issues. (1) For the second time Mark uses his "sandwiching" technique,[18] and we must see the message that the two stories reveal when viewed in stereo. (2) We should note the purity issues that surface in each healing. (3) Jesus has great success in these two cases, but we know that illness and death are a normal part of life. Jesus' power does not make us immune to them. The interpreter must stress that raising the little girl from death points forward to the time when God will finally loosen the vise grip of death on all who are in Christ.

(1) The episode of the raising of a synagogue leader's twelve-year-old daughter wraps around the healing of the woman suffering from a hemorrhage for twelve years. While the second episode allows time to pass for the death of the girl to occur, the two accounts are thematically parallel. Their point is more compelling and clear when they are interpreted in association with each other, as Mark intended. One must therefore resist the temptation to detach these accounts from one another and to read them separately.

The two main characters interacting with Jesus here occupy opposite ends of the economic, social, and religious spectrum. Jairus is a male, a leader of the synagogue. As a man of distinction, he has a name. Jairus has honor and can openly approach Jesus with a direct request, though he shows the greatest deference. By contrast, the woman is nameless, and her complaint renders her ritually unclean. She is walking pollution. Her malady therefore separates her from the community and makes her unfit to enter the synagogue, let alone the temple. She has no honor and must slink about and approach Jesus from behind, thinking that she must purloin her healing.

Moreover, Jairus has a large household and is thus a man of means. The careworn woman has become destitute because of her medical bills. Her complaint makes childbearing hopeless and marriage next to impossible.[19] The only thing that these two persons share in common is that they both have heard about Jesus, they desperately desire healing, and they have run out of options.

Jairus gains Jesus' attention first by prostrating himself before him and begging him to come with him to touch his "little daughter." Though he is a respected religious leader, he is no different from the leper who came to Jesus kneeling and beseeching Jesus (1:40). The woman is no different from the leper as a source of uncleanness and takes matters into her own hands by

---

18. See comments on 3:20–35, where this stylistic feature of Mark was first observed.
19. Marshall, *Faith As a Theme*, 104.

stealthily touching Jesus' cloak from behind without asking his leave. Both Jairus and the woman believe that contact with Jesus is sufficient for healing (5:23, "Put your hands on her"; 5:28; "If I just touch his clothes").

Dovetailing the stories of two such dissimilar individuals reveals that being male, being ritually pure, holding a high religious office, or being a man of means provide no advantage in approaching Jesus. Being female, impure, dishonored, and destitute are no barrier to receiving help. God always takes the side of those who have been denied rights and privileges, the oppressed and poor. In God's kingdom the nobodies become somebody. In other words, the only thing that avails with God and Jesus is one's faith. Health, wholeness, and salvation are not extended to just the lucky few who already have so much of everything else. But neither does Jesus set the lowly over against the lofty. Faith enables all, honored and dishonored, clean and unclean, to tap into the merciful power of Jesus that brings both healing and salvation. All are equals before Jesus. One should also note that Jairus is a member of the Jewish establishment that seems on the whole to be hostile to Jesus. His rank as a leader in a hostile institution does not disqualify him from Jesus' care because he is willing to lay aside whatever social status he has by humbling himself before Jesus in a desperate plea for help.

(2) In both of these stories, Jesus has the power to overcome the defilement of ceremonial uncleanness (bleeding and death) and to reverse it. The Jewish laws concerning impurity sought to prevent it from infringing on the realm of God's holiness. Jesus' ministry shows that God's holiness is unaffected by human impurity when it comes in contact with it. Throughout the Gospel of Mark, Jesus' connection with what is unclean does not render him unclean. Quite the reverse, Jesus purges the impurity. He touches a leper and cleanses him. He ventures into tomb areas and drives out a legion of demons into a herd of pigs. He is touched by one with a hemorrhage, and she is made whole. He touches a dead girl and brings her to life. Jesus does not need to purify himself from the pollution of a person with a flux or from contact with a dead body (Hag. 2:13); he overcomes it.

True, we may have difficulty in conveying this important idea in our culture, which does not make such distinctions between clean and unclean. We do, however, treat some diseases as respectable and some as not respectable. For example, we attach no blame to someone who suffers a heart attack. But we may regard someone who has contacted a venereal disease quite differently. We perhaps can recapture the original impact of this account if we try to think of equivalent characters with whom we are more familiar. The synagogue ruler would be someone well-bred, well-groomed, well-respected, and well-heeled. The woman would be just the opposite, one who would cause others to wrinkle their noses and curl their lips. She is someone who is at the mercy of those who make the rules and the money. She suffers from a disease that others judge to be degrading and that makes her life a misery. Attempting to translate these characters into their modern counterparts allows one to raise telling questions. Should Jesus bother stopping for a woman like this when he may endanger the life of one who is more worthy? Can the love and power of Jesus overcome anything, no matter how contemptible?

(3) These accounts raise a third issue: Jesus' triumph over death. The good news that is proclaimed in this section is that in Jesus' presence storms subside, demons beat a retreat, infirmities are put right, and death loses its hold. In 5:39, Jesus declares the girl's death to be merely sleep. This is not some cagey medical diagnosis, a comforting euphemism, or a general eschatological hope. He calls it sleep because he "wills in this particular case to make death as impermanent as sleep by raising the girl to life."[20] At the same time, however, one must also be sensitive to the reality that no matter how genuine or desperate the faith, all are not healed or saved from death. One must look beyond the moment of suffering to the eternal significance of Jesus' power. That power is related to the kingdom of God, which is present but which is yet to be fully manifest. In the meantime we will suffer from maladies and death. Our faith is in God's power to conquer death, not simply to restore things as they were. We can face the tragedies of everyday existence with confident faith that God is not through with us.

VANSTONE DESCRIBES THE effects of Jesus' ministry well:

As He moves about He leaves behind him a trail of transformed scenes and changed situations—fishermen no longer at their nets, sick people restored to health, critics confounded, a storm stilled, hunger assuaged, a dead girl raised to life. Jesus' presence is an active and instantly transforming presence: He is never the mere observer of the scene or the one who waits upon events but always the transformer of the scene and the initiator of events.[21]

The healings in these two scenes show that one appropriates Jesus' power through faith. An act of faith can make a person well. The synagogue official and the woman do not come to faith *after* they are healed; they had a *prior*

---

20. Meier, *A Marginal Jew*, 2:844, n. 26.

21. W. H. Vanstone, *The Stature of Waiting* (New York: Seabury, 1983), 17–18.

faith that led to their healing.[22] One gets further insight into what faith entails by examining these two models of faith.

(1) Faith opens the door to the power of God. Faith transfers divine power to those who are utterly powerless. It saves: "Your faith has healed [lit., saved] you" (5:34). Faith can be imperfect; it can be bold; it can be halting; it can be brave; it can be laced with fear and trepidation. What counts for it to be effective is for it to be directed rightly to Jesus and God (11:22). What saved this father's daughter and this woman was that their faith was directed toward Jesus.

(2) Faith shows persistence in overcoming any obstacles. The woman works her way through the crowd and overcomes any sense of shame she might have had or fear that she might somehow contaminate Jesus or others by reaching out to touch him. The synagogue official must disregard the sad announcement of his daughter's death and ignore the laughter of the mourners. He must trust Jesus' verdict that she is only sleeping, against all evidence to the contrary. Faith then steps forward in the midst of an intimidating crowd despite fear and trembling and acknowledges Jesus' power to heal. Faith goes forward in the face of mocking laughter and refuses to give in to fear and scorn.

(3) Faith is embodied in action. Faith is something that can be seen, like the men digging through a roof to bring their friend to Jesus. It kneels, begs, and reaches out to touch. Belief about Jesus does not bring healing, but faith in Jesus that takes action does. Neither the man nor the woman identify Jesus as the Messiah or even as a prophet. They are unclear precisely who he is, but they believe that he has the power to heal and are willing to put their faith to the test. A rabbinic tradition interprets Exodus 14:22 to mean that only after the Israelites had gone into the sea up to their nostrils did the waters divide and expose dry ground (*Exod. Rab.* 21:10). This interpretation accurately captures what faith is all about. It does not wait to see if the waters will divide and then step out. It steps out, trusting God to do what is needed.

We should note a major problem in applying this text today. The woman's faith that she would be cured if she could just touch Jesus' garment smacks of magic. Aune writes: "The ideas expressed in the story of the woman's healing do not border on magic, they are of the essence of Greco-Roman magical notions."[23] Such an imperfect faith may make us uncomfortable. It may

---

22. As Tolbert (*Sowing*, 169) puts it well, "One does not have faith *because* one was healed; one has faith *so that* one can be healed. The miracles in Mark are not intended as signs to induce belief; they are, instead, the visible tangible fruits of faith."

23. David Aune, "Magic in Early Christianity," in *ANRW*, vol. 2, pt. 23 (Berlin: Walter de Gruyter, 1980), 1536.

remind us of modern-day miracle mongers who invite supporters to put their hands on the TV set or to send them money for strips of healing cloth or vials of holy oil. What may strike us as superstition, however, Jesus calls faith. He interprets her action as something based on trust. This means that one does not need sophisticated intellectual and theological clarity before one can access Jesus' transforming power.

The personal encounter is vital, however, for anything really significant to happen—for faith to become real faith. In the Hellenistic world, the power to heal was viewed as impersonal, and magic ventured to manipulate these forces for personal advantage. When Jesus forces the woman to shed her anonymity in the crowd and publicly acknowledge her cure, it becomes a transforming personal encounter, not just a get-healed-quick scheme. One cannot secretly hold to faith. Faith requires public testing. The woman's faith is directed toward God who is manifested in a person, Jesus, who speaks with gentle affection to her and cares for her as an individual. One needs to be tolerant of faith that we may judge to be primitive, but one also needs to lead it to direct meeting with Jesus and to a deeper level.

(4) Faith is impelled by desperation that Jesus is sufficient to meet whatever need one has. The ruler and the woman did not take their plight stoically but desperately sought healing from Jesus. The woman refused to grin and bear it. One student of this text draws a strange conclusion: She applauds that Jesus broke through purity barriers and social barriers but comments that Jesus should have accepted "the woman as she was, even if she was bleeding. If that had happened, I would call it a true miracle."[24] One wonders how the woman in the account would have reacted to this comment. The problem for her was not simply a patriarchal system that treated those with a flow of blood as impure.[25] She was physically ill and needed healing. She forces her way to Jesus, confident that he will provide a cure for her disease. She serves as a model for people who are shy, ashamed, or afraid to come boldly to Jesus for healing. Desperation drives one to him. Martin Luther once remarked that his insight into God's grace came to him while he was "on the toilet" (*auff diser cloaca*). George points out that the phrase was a common metaphor for being in a state of utter helplessness and dependence on God.

Where else are we more vulnerable, more easily embarrassed. . . ? Yet is it precisely in a state of such vulnerability—when we are reduced

---

24. Hisako Kinukawa, "The Story of the Hemorrhaging Woman (Mark 5:25–34) Read From a Japanese Feminist Context," *Biblical Interpretation* 2 (1994): 292.

25. Tal Ilan (*Jewish Women in Greco-Roman Palestine: An Inquiry into Image and Status* [Texte und Studien zum antiken Judentum 44; Tübingen: J. C. B. Mohr (Paul Siebeck), 1995], 102) notes that menstruation was viewed by the rabbis as punishment meted out to Eve for her sin in Eden.

to humility, when, like beggars, we can only cast ourselves on the mercy of another—that the yearning for grace is answered in the assurance of God's inescapable nearness.[26]

Evil, sickness, and the death of little children continue to exist in our world. Not every touch heals, and those with faith still hear the dreaded word from the doctor, "Your little girl is dead." This passage does not offer any explanation for why a loving God allows evil to continue to exist or why the inexplicable still occurs. It does affirm that God is on the side of those who suffer and are stricken by grief. A miracle does not occur in every disastrous situation, but it does not lessen God's power to save. The miracle of the healing of emotional pain is no less miraculous. If God intervened in every situation, we would never have to exercise faith. Shadrach, Meshach, and Abednego expressed the only kind of faith that carries us through any and all tragedy when they declared to their tormentor (Dan. 3:17–18):

> "If we are thrown into the blazing furnace, the God we serve is able to save us from it, and he will rescue us from your hand, O king. But even if he does not, we want you to know, O king, that we will not serve your gods or worship the image of gold you have set up."

The little girl is spared death for now but has not been given a total reprieve. The woman has been healed for now, but she will face new ailments as she grows older. Faith, however, is able to hold on in the face of death, knowing that God has conquered death in the resurrection of Christ. George recalls one of the lowest points of Luther's life: His beloved daughter Magdalena, barely fourteen years of age, was stricken with the plague.

> Brokenhearted he knelt beside her bed and begged God to release her from the pain. When she had died and the carpenters were nailing down the lid of her coffin, Luther screamed out, "Hammer away! On doomsday she'll rise again."[27]

---

26. Timothy George, *Theology of the Reformers* (Nashville: Broadman, 1988), 105.
27. Ibid.

Mark 6:1–6a

JESUS LEFT THERE and went to his hometown, accompanied by his disciples. ²When the Sabbath came, he began to teach in the synagogue, and many who heard him were amazed.

"Where did this man get these things?" they asked. "What's this wisdom that has been given him, that he even does miracles! ³Isn't this the carpenter? Isn't this Mary's son and the brother of James, Joseph, Judas and Simon? Aren't his sisters here with us?" And they took offense at him.

⁴Jesus said to them, "Only in his hometown, among his relatives and in his own house is a prophet without honor." ⁵He could not do any miracles there, except lay his hands on a few sick people and heal them. ⁶And he was amazed at their lack of faith.

Original Meaning

JESUS MOVES ON from the area where his extraordinary works would seem to guarantee astounding success and travels to his own country. Mark never explains the rationale behind Jesus' movements to and fro. We only know that Jesus intends to proclaim the message throughout Galilee (1:38–39), that he will not be confined to any one town, and that he frequently seeks to escape the press of the crowds (3:9; 4:36; 6:31, 45–46). Jesus' home turf would seem to have good potential for success except that we know his family has already tried to collar him and bring him back there because they were convinced he was unbalanced if not insane (3:21, 31). Again Jesus teaches in the synagogue on the Sabbath (6:2a; see 1:21, 39; 3:1), and again "many who heard him were amazed." The reader should not be surprised that Jesus rouses astonishment in others (1:22; 2:12; 5:20), but in this town it swiftly becomes suspicion.

Blindness to the truth takes many forms, and those closest to Jesus do not have an advantage in understanding who he is. They are perplexed about the source of Jesus' wisdom and deeds and ask themselves (6:2b), "What's this wisdom that has been given him...?" Mark does not tell us the content of Jesus' teaching or what mighty works he performed that stimulate the curiosity of his fellow townsmen, but the miracles are integrally related to his teaching and wisdom (1:27). The question assumes that wisdom has been given to

Jesus and that miracles have been done by his hands. What they cannot ascertain is where one so familiar to them could get all this power. Their preoccupation with this issue means that they never get around to asking the crucial question: What does it all mean? The answer to that question will ultimately lead them to the answer of its source (see 3:27). They are not driven so much by a desire to know what is behind Jesus' miracles as by an itch to confirm their private prejudice that he cannot be all that remarkable.

Their query about Jesus is the third in a series of questions raised by those who have been bowled over by his teaching and his deeds. First, a synagogue gathering asked, "What is this?" (1:27); next some teachers of the law and then Jesus' disciples asked themselves, "Who is this?" (2:7; 4:41). Now, the question has to do with the origin or source of his deeds and teaching, "From where is this?" The hometown crowd does not go as far as the teachers of the law from Jerusalem and ascribe it to Beelzebub (3:22), an unpardonable sin. They simply think it unlikely that God can work so dramatically in this fellow who comes from their midst. They cannot get beyond the infinitesimal size of the mustard seed and can see nothing else.

Jesus is in his old stamping ground, and his townsfolk believe they know all there is to know about him and his family background. Nothing about it leads them to suspect anything portentous about him. The circumstances of Jesus' birth and his life before his baptism and ministry were unimportant to Mark. He has only told us that Jesus came from Nazareth in Galilee (1:9). The reader belatedly learns more about Jesus' background from the incidental question, "Isn't this the carpenter? Isn't this Mary's son and the brother of James, Joseph, Judas and Simon?" These details are not crucial to the gospel about Jesus, but they stir our curiosity.

A *tekton* (traditionally translated "carpenter") is someone who could work with wood, metal, or stone. He could be a builder, a mason, or a carpenter. In Jesus' Palestinian context, it probably denoted a woodworking handyman. He would have the skill to do almost anything—from crafting plows and yokes, to making pieces of furniture, cupboards, stools, and benches, to erecting small buildings, particularly making the beams, window lattices, doors, and bolts. Jesus must have been technically skilled and physically strong. Meier asserts: "The airy weakling often presented to us in pious paintings and Hollywood movies would hardly have survived the rigors of being Nazareth's *tekton* from his youth to his early thirties."[1] The names of his brothers—James (lit., Jacob), Joseph, Judah, and Simon—are those of the patriarchs and two of the famous Maccabee brothers, and they suggest a family

---

1. John P. Meier, *A Marginal Jew: Rethinking the Historical Jesus* (New York: Doubleday, 1991), 1:281.

that observed the law strictly and hoped for the redemption of Israel. His sisters are unnamed and unnumbered, reflecting the ancient bias that females are embedded in males and do not merit much attention.

The people of Nazareth identify Jesus as "Mary's son." Normally, a man is identified as the son of his father.[2] Some have suggested that by identifying him only as the son of his mother they are maligning him (see Judg. 11:1–2) and perhaps are harking back to rumors that the circumstances of Jesus' birth were suspicious.[3] Others have argued that they refer to him as Mary's son to distinguish him from Joseph's children by his first wife.[4] Still others suggest they refer to him in this way because his father is no longer alive and they are expressing their familiarity with his mother, who resides there. The first option has little to support it. The second is possible, but the last seems to be the most likely because the references to his brothers and sisters emphasize that he is simply "a local boy." He is well known as a carpenter. Everyone knows his brothers and his sisters, living right there among them. They think they have Jesus pegged. This one is just Mary's boy, who used to be one of us.

Their ruminations about Jesus imply some annoyance: Who does he think he is, going around preaching and healing? Is this not the brother of those we know so well? Are not his sisters living here with us? Their questions are phrased in such a way in the Greek to expect the answer "yes." The attentive reader knows, however, that on another level the answer to their questions is more complicated: "No, they are not." For Mark, Jesus is the Son of God (1:1, 11; 9:7; 15:39), which answers the question about the source of his wisdom and mighty works; and Jesus has already made it clear that only those who do the will of his Father are his mother, brothers, and sisters (3:34–35).

The upshot of their analysis of Jesus' origins is that they are scandalized by him. They do not seem to be put off by what he taught. Their questions have to do with his origin, and they think they know who this one is and where he comes from.[5] The scandal of the gospel turns up again. There is

---

2. Other texts read "son of the carpenter and of Mary" or "son of the carpenter." It is likely that these readings issued from an assimilation to Matt. 13:55 (see also Luke 4:22; John 6:42).

3. Meier (*A Marginal Jew*, 1:222–27) provides strong arguments against any interpretation that this "flip comment" suggests any moral scandal associated with Jesus' birth. It only conveys a sense of familiarity.

4. Richard Bauckham ("The Brothers and Sisters of Jesus: An Epiphanian Response to John P. Meier, *CBQ* 56 [1994]: 698–700) argues that the brothers and sisters listed were the children of Joseph's first wife. The locals would have made a distinction between a man's children from two different wives. Outside of Nazareth, where the family was unknown, Jesus would have been identified simply as the son of Joseph.

5. Marshall (*Faith*, 192) writes: "Their unbelief lies not in a failure to perceive the quality of Jesus' words or the reality of his miracles; it lies rather in a refusal to admit the true

nothing phenomenal or rare about Jesus' family or trade, and his humble origin makes him implausible as some great figure of wisdom. How can someone so ordinary do marvels and speak wisdom? How can this one so familiar to us be God's anointed? It is almost as if they themselves admit that nothing this good can come out of Nazareth (John 1:46).

Perhaps familiarity breeds contempt. The expert at a conference is usually the one who has come from farthest away. The people in Nazareth know Jesus "from a worldly point of view" (2 Cor. 5:16), and their "very familiarity with him is a hindrance to knowing him truly, for it makes it all the more hard for them to see through the veil of his ordinariness."[6] They see him as only a local yokel like themselves.

Perhaps others are put off because he is a craftsman. Jews had a high regard for manual labor, but some drew a sharp distinction between the scribe, who devotes himself to study, and the laborer, who must work with his hands. According to Sirach 38:24–34, the wisdom of the scribe depends on the opportunity of leisure to study while the artisan is too much engaged in business to become wise. The artisan labors night and day and talks only of his work. Consequently, "they do not sit in the judges' seat, nor do they understand the decisions of the courts; they cannot expound discipline or judgment, and they are not found among the rulers" (Sir. 38:33, NRSV). The passage concludes by underscoring how different the one is who devotes himself entirely to the study of the law, and it goes on in 39:1–11 to glorify the scribe.

Jesus responds to the skepticism of his townsfolk by recalling the old saw that a prophet is without honor among his own (6:4). It provides an explanation for their unbelief, but not an excuse. His response marks the first time in this Gospel that the term *prophet* is applied to Jesus, and it evokes images associated with the prophets in the Scripture. Jesus has come like a prophet and is rejected like a prophet. The saying intimates that he will suffer the inevitable fate of a prophet, and the martyrdom of the prophet John the Baptizer will soon be described (6:17–29). Jesus' rejection in his own hometown foreshadows his rejection by his own people whom he came to deliver—a rejection that will culminate in Jerusalem.

Mark concludes this incident with a notice that Jesus can do no miracles in Nazareth except heal a few people and that he marvels over their unbelief (6:5–6a). His fellow citizens do not think that he even comes up to the level of prophet; how can they begin to comprehend the full truth about

---

source of this wisdom and power (v 2) and to accept the unique *identity* of the one who manifests them (v 3)."

6. Cranfield, *Mark*, 193.

Jesus? Both he and his countrymen are dumbfounded by each other. The reader may also marvel that they will not believe. The negative reaction to Jesus in Nazareth makes them little different from the land where the pigs and pagans dwell, and one can better appreciate the difficulty faced by the one who is known formerly as the Gerasene demoniac and must give witness in his hometown. Jesus will not enter the synagogue again but moves to open places, where crowds can come from all over (cf. 6:6b).[7]

A POINT, COUNTERPOINT pattern develops in Mark's account as the demons cry out Jesus' identity and humans question it.[8] The people gathered in the Nazareth synagogue are the last in a series of persons to raise the question about who Jesus is.

Demonic Cry	Human Question
1:24: "I know who you are—the Holy One of God!"	1:27: "What is this? A new teaching—and with authority!"
1:34: "He would not let the demons speak because they knew who he was."	2:7: "Why does this fellow talk like that? He's blaspheming! Who can forgive sins but God alone?"
3:11: "You are the Son of God."	4:41: "Who is this? Even the wind and the waves obey him!"
5:7: "What do you want with me, Jesus, Son of the Most High God?"	6:3: "Isn't this the carpenter? Isn't this Mary's son and the brother of James, Joseph, Judas and Simon? Aren't his sisters here with us?"

This alternating pattern of declaration and question forces the reader to ask why the human characters cannot see and to wonder if they ever will see. What will it take for humans to recognize, as the demons immediately do, that this is the Son of God? Since Jesus still goes unrecognized, we should ask the same question of our contemporaries.

In his magisterial commentary, Gundry claims that Mark wrote his Gospel "to rescue people" from falling into the trap of being offended by Jesus, "by identifying the true origin of Jesus' wisdom and power, which may counter-

---

7. The word "synagogue" is only mentioned again in Mark as the location where scribes hanker after the status of having the first seats (12:39) and where his disciples will be flogged (13:9).

8. Kingsbury, *Christology*, 86–87.

act the scandal of the Crucifixion (cf. Matt. 11:6 par. Luke 7:23)."[9] The truth is that one must pass through the scandal before one can see with the eyes of faith. The people in Nazareth had plenty of evidence of Jesus' authority but rejected him because they could not get past their evaluation of what they took to be his modest credentials. In bridging the contexts, we should point out the scandal and allow it to stand.

The American bias expects to hear that a famous industrialist, politician, or celebrity came from servile roots, pulled himself or herself up by the bootstraps, and escaped from a web of poverty to rise up the ladder of success. Many wear their humble background as a badge of honor. In the time of Jesus the world was ordered by rigidly defined class lines. Social mobility was limited, and one could expect to remain within the confines of the class in which one was born. A noble parentage, being "well-born," was considered essential if one hoped to be considered great.[10]

Compare, for example, Josephus's introduction of his qualifications to the readers of his *Life*. He gives a brief rundown of his genealogy to identify himself as descending from a noble family (*Life* 2 § 7; *J. W.* 5.9.4 § 419). He comes from priestly descent, those considered to be of the highest rank (*Life* 1 § 1; see *J. W.* 1.1.1 § 3; 3.8.3 § 352; 5.9.4 § 419; *Ag. Ap.* 1 § 54). He also claims royal stock, the Hasmoneans, on his mother's side (*Life* 1 §§ 2–4). He boasts that he excelled all his compatriots in his exact knowledge of law and that he is uniquely capable of interpreting the Scriptures for a Greek audience (*Ant.* 20.12.1 § § 262–65). Regarding Jesus, therefore, it would have been a shock in the ancient world that the supreme God would come to us in one from such a humble town, from such a humble family, and from such a humble trade. We would ask what the Nazareth hometown folk asked: How does this Jesus dare rise above his roots?

Mark does not ease the problem of Jesus' humble origins but accentuates it. He tells us nothing of Jesus' noble genealogical pedigree that would augur his rise to stardom, only that his fellow citizens recognize nothing remarkable about his background. No one apparently notices him as a prodigy or says to him: "I always knew that you would grow up to be the Messiah." No one notices the halo that adorns most of our portraits of the young Jesus. Not even his family members, according to Mark, recognize his divine vocation. His fellow townsmen deem themselves to be his equal and regard him simply as the neighbor's boy, a local artisan.

The Greeks and Romans viewed labor as demeaning. Secundus, an Athenian orator, was mocked as a "wooden nail" because he was the son of a

---

9. Gundry, *Mark*, 292.
10. Steve Mason, *Josephus and the New Testament* (Peabody, Mass.: Hendrickson, 1992), 36.

carpenter. Celsus (in the late second century) derided Jesus for having been simply a carpenter, sarcastically connecting his work to his crucifixion. Origen countered that the Gospels never describe Jesus as working with his hands (*Contra Celsum*, 6.36). The elite in the Greco-Roman world assumed that a person in such a craft was uneducated and uncouth, and the contemporary readers of Mark's Gospel had to overcome whatever bias they might have had about such things to believe that a humble carpenter could be the mighty Son of God.[11] Many could not see how God could speak and act through such a one who seemed so commonplace.

WE HAVE TENDED over the years to remove the original offense associated with Jesus' background and to romanticize his trade as a carpenter. Some today imagine him as a master builder of grand edifices in the surrounding cities rather than a journeyman carpenter crafting simple yokes and beams or a rough construction worker working in stone. The apocryphal infancy Gospels invented all kinds of fantastic stories about Jesus, attempting to glorify his youth as a Wunderkind. Modern preachers have suggested that Jesus would have been the star of their favorite sport at his high school as well as the class valedictorian. This attempt to inject more grandeur into Jesus' background reveals that we are still influenced by the world's standards of judgment and its concern for prestige. That standard always fails to appraise correctly God's messengers and ways.[12] As Anderson puts it, the people from Nazareth want "an altogether glorious, supernatural Jesus whose credentials will be obvious to all, and refuse to believe that God discloses himself in the humanity of this one who is a member of a humble family and whose way, according to Mark's testimony is the way of the cross."[13]

We today may be no different. If Jesus were issued identity papers, his profession would list him as a carpenter, not Messiah. He is blue collar. To paraphrase a popular song from many years ago, he might ask us today, "If I were a carpenter, would you believe in me anyway?" His dress, style, and background might be off-putting to those who want a Savior more at home in high society. One preacher describes the once-over he regularly got when he was a guest speaker in affluent churches in a large American city. He writes:

---

11. See Cicero's comments that there is nothing genteel about the vulgar work of a craftsman (*An Essay About Duties* 1.42; 2.225).

12. Juel, *Mark*, 91.

13. Anderson, *Mark*, 161.

... the greeters and other members did not even try to hide a head-to-toe scan of coiffure, shave, tie, shirt, suit, and shoes. I do not mean your usual, casual glance. They x-ray you. All of this is done in two seconds, but a very obvious two seconds.[14]

One can only imagine the reception that Jesus might receive if he showed up in his tradesman's attire.

One might also compare an advertisement for a highly successful evangelistic team with Paul's description about how others regarded him (1 Cor. 4:9–12). The team billed themselves as "the world's greatest exhibition of power, strength, speed, inspiration and motivation" and noted that they had been featured in national magazines and television. By contrast, Paul was viewed as "a spectacle," like one sentenced to death in the arena. He was judged a fool, weak, dishonored, ill-clad, buffeted, homeless, an exhausted laborer, and the dregs of all things.

All is not as it seems, however. When one evaluates people according to human criteria, Paul says that one will come up with the wrong answer (see 2 Cor. 5:16). When one looks at the messengers of the gospel from God's perspective, one can see divine treasure in earthen vessels. They may look like cracked pots, but the cracks allow the divine light within to shine through. Then one can see that the power belongs to God (2 Cor. 4:6–12). The lesson in the story of the Ugly Duckling applies. When we judge others by appearances, we may be dead wrong. Those who evaluate Jesus by outward appearances will miss the truth about him. They are also likely to misjudge his commissioned messengers.

We should also notice that Jesus' teaching and miracles do not automatically produce faith. The miracles are not unambiguous signs that allow for no uncertainty. "They do not convey a clear, unobstructed view of Jesus' mission and authority."[15] In this instance, they only lead to incredulity and doubt. The lack of faith in Jesus' home country forms a marked contrast with the faith exhibited by those in the previous scenes (5:23, 28, 34, 36). Faith preceded the miracles for the synagogue leader, Jairus, and the woman with the hemorrhage—though faith is not always a necessary prerequisite for miracles, for some occur despite unbelief (3:1–6; 4:35–41; 6:35–44).

Jesus does not demand honor and recognition. He has come to sow the word, not reap accolades. The qualms raised about Jesus' credentials for wisdom, however, block the people in Nazareth from receiving God's blessings

---

14. Joel Gregory, *Too Great A Temptation: The Seductive Power of America's Super Church* (Fort Worth: The Summit Group, 1994), 38.

15. L. W. Countryman, "How Many Baskets Full? Mark 8:14–21 and the Value of Miracles in Mark," *CBQ* 47 (1985): 652.

through him. The text shows that doubt and suspicion can affect a whole community. It can cut off God's power for others. In Nazareth many blind, lame, and deaf continued in their affliction because they continued in their unbelief.

Their reservations about Jesus and his failure to do any "miracles there, except lay his hands on a few sick people and heal them" suggest that Jesus is powerless to work miracles apart from people's faith. The text prompts us to ask why. The people of Nazareth already knew of Jesus' miracles (6:2) but refused to believe. Their cynicism prevented most from bringing their sick to him for healing. Only a handful did so, and he healed them. Doubt has trouble believing; unbelief obstinately refuses to believe. Mark portrays Jesus' hometown as mired in an obstinate unbelief that deprived them of the gracious benefits of God's reign. Those who have ever worked with suspicious and cynical people may recognize that getting such to believe comprises a miracle more marvelous than even healing those who are physically sick.

Mark tells us that his disciples accompanied him to Nazareth (6:1). Part of their task is to be with Jesus, but being with Jesus also provides opportunities for learning. They can learn from this indifferent response to Jesus' teaching and miracles that rejection will come sometimes when and where it is least expected. Rejection is not the end of the world, however. Failure is common to the experience of anyone who sows the seeds of the gospel. Jesus is perplexed but not paralyzed by it and goes on to other villages and towns. This lesson will serve the disciples well when they are sent out on a mission on their own and meet with resistance, scorn, and doubt (6:7–13). Christian missionaries perhaps can take comfort from this episode from Jesus' life when they too meet with skepticism.

This passage can also apply to the contemporary phenomenon where persons raised as Christians search for the answers to life's questions by turning to other religions. One can only wonder why many Christians turn to something other than the faith of their youth for help in their lives or for meaning. Does familiarity with the stories about Jesus breed contempt? Has his story become humdrum? Have we lost our sense of awe? Does our fascination with the unfamiliar and exotic lead us to look for truth in what is new or different? We must guard against the attitude that beset the synagogue of Nazareth: "I already know him from the Bible stories of my youth. What can he teach me now?"

Mark 6:6b–30

THEN JESUS WENT around teaching from village to village. ⁷Calling the Twelve to him, he sent them out two by two and gave them authority over evil spirits.

⁸These were his instructions: "Take nothing for the journey except a staff—no bread, no bag, no money in your belts. ⁹Wear sandals but not an extra tunic. ¹⁰Whenever you enter a house, stay there until you leave that town. ¹¹And if any place will not welcome you or listen to you, shake the dust off your feet when you leave, as a testimony against them."

¹²They went out and preached that people should repent. ¹³They drove out many demons and anointed many sick people with oil and healed them.

¹⁴King Herod heard about this, for Jesus' name had become well known. Some were saying, "John the Baptist has been raised from the dead, and that is why miraculous powers are at work in him."

¹⁵Others said, "He is Elijah."

And still others claimed, "He is a prophet, like one of the prophets of long ago."

¹⁶But when Herod heard this, he said, "John, the man I beheaded, has been raised from the dead!"

¹⁷For Herod himself had given orders to have John arrested, and he had him bound and put in prison. He did this because of Herodias, his brother Philip's wife, whom he had married. ¹⁸For John had been saying to Herod, "It is not lawful for you to have your brother's wife." ¹⁹So Herodias nursed a grudge against John and wanted to kill him. But she was not able to, ²⁰because Herod feared John and protected him, knowing him to be a righteous and holy man. When Herod heard John, he was greatly puzzled; yet he liked to listen to him.

²¹Finally the opportune time came. On his birthday Herod gave a banquet for his high officials and military commanders and the leading men of Galilee. ²²When the daughter of Herodias came in and danced, she pleased Herod and his dinner guests.

The king said to the girl, "Ask me for anything you want, and I'll give it to you." ²³And he promised her with an oath, "Whatever you ask I will give you, up to half my kingdom."

²⁴She went out and said to her mother, "What shall I ask for?"

"The head of John the Baptist," she answered.

²⁵At once the girl hurried in to the king with the request: "I want you to give me right now the head of John the Baptist on a platter."

²⁶The king was greatly distressed, but because of his oaths and his dinner guests, he did not want to refuse her. ²⁷So he immediately sent an executioner with orders to bring John's head. The man went, beheaded John in the prison, ²⁸and brought back his head on a platter. He presented it to the girl, and she gave it to her mother. ²⁹On hearing of this, John's disciples came and took his body and laid it in a tomb.

³⁰The apostles gathered around Jesus and reported to him all they had done and taught.

THE DEPUTATION OF the disciples to preach repentance (6:6b–13) and their reporting back to Jesus (6:30–32) sandwiches the account of the death of John the Baptizer (6:14–29). These two events seem to be totally unrelated to each other, but Mark deliberately links them together.

The Mission of the Disciples

JESUS LAUNCHED HIS public ministry by calling Israel to repentance (1:14–15); now he expands that mission by sending the Twelve to their unbelieving countrymen to preach repentance, to cast out demons, and to anoint the sick. Jesus invests them with his authority over unclean spirits (see 3:15) and appoints them to travel two by two, satisfying the requirement of two or three witnesses (Num. 35:30; Deut. 17:6; 19:15; 2 Cor. 13:1; 1 Tim. 5:19) and providing them with some measure of protection. When Jesus gives them their marching orders, we might expect him to give detailed advice on what to do when they encounter unclean spirits, for example; but instead he instructs them on what not to pack for the trip. He allows them to take a staff and to wear sandals, but they are to take no provisions, no beggar's bag, no money in the belt, and no change of clothing.

Why must they travel so lightly without standard gear, and why are only a staff and sandals allowed? Some connect this command to the urgency of the impending doom of the temple and Jerusalem. Caird argues, for example, that Jesus believed that Israel "was at the cross-roads; it must choose between two conceptions of its national destiny, and the time for choice was terrifyingly short."[1] A pressing sense of urgency did have an impact on Jesus' ministry, but how will the disciples travel faster without provisions? The list reflects something about the character of their mission. To go on mission entirely dependent on the generosity of others for food and lodging is an expression of extreme poverty.[2] They do not travel first class. They do not come like an invading army living off the land. The Twelve come more humbly and must be totally dependent on God for their support.[3] They are to go out as the poor to those who are also poor and hungry. As Minear puts it, "Weakness and poverty are effective means of proclaiming that men should repent (1 Cor. 2:3–5)."[4]

Since God instructed Isaiah to walk naked and barefoot, like a prisoner of war, as a sign of coming judgment (Isa. 20:2–4), the poverty of the disciples may be intended as a prophetic warning of judgment that will come upon Israel.[5] The staff Jesus allows them to take may simply be a reference to a traveler's stick, but it has a rich imagery in the history of God's dealings with Israel, beginning with Moses' staff (Ex. 4:2–5, 20). It may be connected to the staffs of the twelve tribes (Num. 17) and a symbol of a tribal leader's authority or a prophet's authority (2 Kings 4:29). It may have some symbolic connection to the covenant renewal of Israel (see also Ezek. 20:37; 37:15–28). They are to call Israel back to God.

Jesus instructs the Twelve to accept the first accommodations offered to them and not to move if they chance to find something better. This demonstration of commitment is a testimony of their devotion to their mission and not to themselves. It also reduces the chance that they will create jealousy by moving to better quarters, which will interfere with their mission. Jesus seems to expect either mass reception or mass rejection, and he instructs them to do as he did when the Gerasenes rejected him. If a place neither receives nor hears them, they are to shake the dust from their feet and leave. There is no time to waste arguing.[6] This gesture within the land of Israel

---

1. G. B. Caird and L. D. Hurst, *New Testament Theology* (Oxford: Clarendon, 1994), 361.

2. Luke 15:22; *b. Besa* 32b; *b. Shabb.* 152a.

3. The command parallels the one given Israel before they set out into the desert (Ex. 12:11). The Israelites were commanded to eat the Passover "with your cloak tucked into your belt, your sandals on your feet, and your staff in your hand. Eat it in haste." As Israel was sustained in the desert by God's provision, so the disciples will be.

4. Minear, *Mark*, 80.

5. Ulrich Luz, *Das Evangelium nach Matthäus (Mt 8–17)* (Evangelisch-katholischer Kommentar zum Neuen Testament; Zurich: Benziger/Neukirchener, 1990), 2:97.

6. Jews shook the dust from their feet when they returned to Israel from Gentile territory (see *m. Ohol.* 2:3; *m. Tohar.* 4:5).

serves as a prophetic, if enigmatic, warning that this is a pagan place and will be cut off from the kingdom of God if they fail to respond.

The mission of the Twelve communicates in dramatic and harrowing fashion the seriousness of the need for Israel to repent *now*. The message of repentance is that God reigns. The messengers do not invite Israel to accept God's reign if it suits them; they confront people with a yes or no decision, so that there can be no middle ground. If they reject the message, they will deprive themselves of the opportunity to receive healing and deliverance. If they continue in their dogged defiance, they will face the judgment of God.[7]

Mark tells us the disciples obey Jesus' commission. They preach repentance, cast out demons, and anoint the sick with oil.[8] But Mark tells us nothing more about the results of their mission, whether it is successful or not. Why? The best answer is that Mark sees it as preparatory for the later mission of the disciples after Jesus' death and resurrection. It introduces them to the requirement of total self-sacrifice in commitment to their mission. It also acquaints them with the reality of rejection—sowing the word means they can expect to find that some ground will be unproductive. It therefore prepares them for Jesus' teaching about his destiny, which will follow.

The Death of John the Baptizer (6:14–29)

MARK INTERRUPTS HIS report of the disciples' mission with a flashback, recounting the execution of John the Baptizer. It begins with the ominous news that Jesus' growing reputation has been causing ripples of concern in the highest circles.[9] The review relating the lurid details behind the slaying of John the Baptizer explains why Herod guesses that Jesus may be John raised from the dead. The account divides into two parts: the reason behind John's arrest and imprisonment (6:17–20), and the sordid account of his beheading (6:21–29).

The question raised by Jesus' disciples, "Who is this?" (4:41), is now rousing the interest of the political gentry as Herod's court is abuzz with the news of him. Perhaps the mission of the Twelve has expanded Jesus' reputation, for Herod has heard about his "name" (6:14; see 9:37–41; 13:6, 13). We almost get the impression that a worried Herod is hearing theories concerning this new menacing prophet bandied about in emergency cabinet meetings. They are asking the same basic question as was posed in Jesus'

---

7. So Pesch, *Das Markusevangelium*, 1:329; Gnilka, *Das Evangelium nach Markus*, 1:240.

8. Oil had medicinal value (see Isa. 1:6; Luke 10:34; James 5:14–15).

9. Herod Antipas, identified only as Herod by Mark, was the son of Herod the Great and Malthace, a Samaritan, and was tetrarch of Galilee and Perea from 4 B.C. to A.D. 39. "Tetrarch" literally means "ruler of a quarter of the country."

hometown: "Where does this guy get the power to do what he is doing?"

Herod comes closer to the truth than the synagogue in Nazareth. The estimation that Jesus is "John the Baptist ... raised from the dead" (6:14), and Herod's opinion that he is "John, the man I beheaded, ... raised from the dead!" (6:16), brackets the best guesses of others who think he might be Elijah or a prophet like one of the prophets of old. Herod believes that Jesus' power must derive from some divine action—resurrection. If prophets like the prophets of old are abroad, or if one recently executed has been raised, then the new age of God's dealing with humanity has been ushered in; but Herod makes no move to go to find out more about him. Like the skeptics of Nazareth, he has no ambition to become his follower in spite of the reports of his wondrous deeds.[10] Herod's fear is not a fear of God. What he heard may cause him some consternation and a sleepless night or two, but it has no other effect on him. He may be thinking, "You no sooner kill one preacher of repentance than another pops up to stir up the masses."

One of the things that must have troubled someone like *"King* Herod" (6:14) is that Jesus and his disciples were proclaiming the kingdom of God. It boils down to the simple message: God is king, and Herod (and anybody else) is not. Matthew 14:1 and Luke 3:19; 9:7 refer to Herod's title correctly as tetrarch. Mark's designation of him as a king may reflect a less technical, popular usage, or it may be intentionally ironic. The emperor Augustus specifically refused Herod that royal title when his father, Herod the Great, died, and his former kingdom was sliced up and parceled out to the surviving sons.[11] Allegedly, his wife, Herodias, was so jealous when his nephew, Herod Agrippa, received the title king from the emperor Gaius Caligula in A.D. 37 that she egged on her husband to request the title for himself. His petition ultimately led to his dismissal and exile when opponents reported that he had stashed away a stockpile of weapons.[12] Mark may be scornfully mocking Herod's royal pretensions by giving him the title he coveted and that led to his ruin.[13]

Herod's dealing with his prophetic nemesis, John, provides a classic example of how official Israel treats its prophets. He is a swollen peacock pitted against a humble and holy prophet (6:20) and is too timid to do anything

---

10. Perhaps Herod was manifesting a guilty conscience working overtime, combined with a superstitious nature (Cranfield, *Mark*, 207; cf. Macbeth, "Out, damned spot!"). His conclusion reinforces the fact that Herod Antipas witnessed John's actual head being delivered on a platter, and though he may be terrified to think that he is alive again, he does nothing.

11. Josephus, *Ant.* 17.18.1 § 188; 17.9.4 §§ 224–271; 17.11.4 § 318; *J. W.* 2.2.3 §§ 20–22; 2.6.3 §§ 93–95.

12. Josephus, *Ant.* 18.7.1–2 §§ 240–56; *J. W.* 2.9.6 §§ 181–83.

13. Lane, *Mark*, 211.

about him. It recalls the conflict between king and prophet that runs through the Old Testament. As a true prophet, John has no fear of the great and powerful and boldly confronts them with their sin. Strangely, Herod wants to protect John from the wrath of his wife, Herodias, a Jezebel-like figure, and places him in custody.[14]

The account of John's imprisonment and execution underscores the great impiety of Herod.[15] First, John reproachs him publicly for marrying Herodias, his niece, who is already the wife of his half brother.[16] According to Josephus, when Herod Antipas stayed with them on his way to Rome, he fell in love with her and brazenly proposed marriage. Herodias may have perceived this arrangement as a move up the social ladder and agreed upon the condition that he divorce his wife, the daughter of Aretas IV, the ruler of neighboring Nabatea. The divorce may have touched off a border war with the outraged Aretas years later, which resulted in serious military losses for Herod.[17] His new marriage ignited religious protests at home because it was classified as incestuous (Lev. 18:16; 20:21).

Ironically, Herod's young stepdaughter captivates him with her presumably erotic dancing, which also hints of incestuous lust. John condemns Herod for the lust that led to the first incest; his inflamed passion for his stepdaughter results in John's execution. Herod is therefore presented as one who knows no taboos. The lascivious behavior at Herod's court would also have been considered disgraceful to a pious Jew, and Jews viewed birthdays

---

14. Mark does not say where John was imprisoned and beheaded. Josephus says that it was in Machaerus—the fortress-palace that served as the military headquarters in southeastern Perea, east of the Dead Sea, thirteen miles southeast of Herodium. Josephus described the citadel as luxurious (*J. W.* 7.6.2 §§ 171–77). Archaeologists have uncovered a large triclinium (dining room) that would have been suitable for a banquet and a small one where the women would have eaten during the banquet (Gundry, *Mark*, 313–14).

15. Chapman (*The Orphan Gospel*, 186) summarizes well Herod Antipas's unpopularity as a monarch:

> The Jews hated his father. Antipas had close ties with Rome, and the Jews hated Rome. His mother was a Samaritan, and the Jews hated Samaritans. He built or rebuilt towns or cities naming them after *Roman* royalty. To populate Tiberias, he forcibly relocated his subjects (today's Palestinian controversy should cast light on how popular that move must have been). In Tiberias, he built a royal palace and adorned it with a frieze of animal figures, in violation of the Second Commandment.

16. Herodias was the daughter of Herod Aristobulus, one of the sons of Herod the Great (half brother of Antipas), and Mariamne, and is therefore the half niece of Herod Antipas. On the issue of the confusion with Herod Philip, see Harold W. Hoehner, *Herod Antipas* (SNTSMS 17; Cambridge: Cambridge Univ. Press, 1972), 131–36.

17. Josephus *Ant.* 18.5.1 §§ 109–15.

as pagan celebrations.[18] The party is rife with paganism: the presence of dancing girls at a stag party (Herodias is not present), a drunken king doing the bidding of a woman, and the beheading of a prophet on a whim.

Herodias understandably holds a grudge against someone who has called for her removal from the seat of power. Either Herodias seizes the moment to sacrifice her daughter's dignity by sending her in to dance to win Herod's favor or takes advantage of an opportunity to do away with her prophetic nemesis when her daughter comes to consult with her. The delighted king impulsively or drunkenly offers the girl half of his kingdom, a proverbial expression for generosity (1 Kings 13:8; Est. 5:3, 6; 7:2). As a puppet of Rome, Herod does not have the right to give half of his kingdom away.[19] By contrast, Jesus bestows the gift of the power of the kingdom of God on his disciples, which brings healing to others. Herod Antipas offers up half of his pitiful little kingdom, which brings death to one of God's prophets.[20] Herod, whom Jesus calls a shaking reed (Matt. 11:7) and a fox (Luke 13:32), is himself outfoxed by his wife, who is engaged in court intrigue. He values his honor in keeping his rash oath more than John's life and winds up killing the one he fears and has gladly heard. It will not be the last time that a ruler submits to the will of others to have an innocent man executed.

The grisly detail of John's head brought to Herod and the other partyers on a platter caps off a banquet already polluted by excess. John dies according to the caprice of an evil woman and the weakness of her impotent and debauched husband. Even beheaded, John is more powerful than this so-called king. Herod's ghastly crime will live on in infamy while John's message of moral outrage and call for repentance still rings in the corridors of power.

The Return of the "Apostles" (6:30)

IN 6:30 THE Twelve are called "apostles" for the first and only time in this Gospel. The title has in view their function as those sent out rather than some permanent office or status. They have fulfilled the particular commission Jesus gave them to do and now report to him. The mission of the apostles therefore brackets the account of the death of John. As we have seen before (3:20–35; 5:21–43), recognizing this sandwich technique is crucial for unfolding Mark's theological purpose. The insertion does more than provide an interlude between the sending out and return of the disciples; it

---

18. *m. 'Abod. Zar.* 1:3.

19. Anyone aware that Herod Antipas lost all of his kingdom when he was sent into exile and that it was given to Agrippa would find this rash promise ironic.

20. Minear, *Mark*, 80.

interprets the flanking halves.[21] It foreshadows the suffering that comes to God's messengers. What happens to John will happen to Jesus in his mission and to the disciples in theirs.

By identifying himself as a prophet in Nazareth (6:4), Jesus links himself to the fate of prophets. The report of the execution of John then follows. Mark has only spoken of John as a forerunner who came preaching a baptism of repentance, in order to prepare the way for the one who will baptize in the Holy Spirit. He does not mention the circumstances of his birth (cf. Luke 1:5–25) or of his lingering doubts about what Jesus was doing (cf. Matt. 11:2–6). Nor does John serve in Mark as a prominent a witness to Jesus, as he does in the Gospel of John (1:15, 19–35; 3:22–30; 5:33; 10:41).

What is pivotal about John's role for this Gospel is what happens to him when he goes out to preach (Mark 1:4). It foreshadows what will happen *to Jesus* when he goes out to preach (1:14). Just as John was "handed over" (1:14; "put in prison," NIV), so Jesus will be "handed over" (3:19; 9:31; 10:33; "betrayed," NIV). Just as John is executed by a reluctant political ruler at the instigation of a conniving individual who plotted his death behind the scenes (6:14–29), so Jesus will be sentenced to death by a reluctant political ruler at the instigation of hostile leaders who engineer his death behind the scenes (14:1–2; 15:1–2, 11). Just as Herodias seized an "opportune time" to carry out her evil designs (6:21), so Judas will seek an "opportunity" to betray Jesus to the high priests (14:11). Just as Herod was caught off guard by the response to his reckless offer (6:23–26); so Pilate will be surprised by the response to his offer of releasing a prisoner (15:6–15). The violent and shameful death of John augurs the violent and shameful death of Jesus.

When Jesus is dying on the cross, those who taunt him in his last moments think that he calls for Elijah and wait to see if the prophet will come in dramatic fashion to rescue him. Jesus has already identified John the Baptizer as Elijah who has come: "But I tell you, Elijah has come, and they have done to him everything they wished, just as it is written about him" (9:13). The message is clear. If they did this to the messenger of the Lord who preached repentance (1:4), they will do it also to the Lord himself, who also preaches repentance (1:15).

John's death foreshadows the suffering of the Son of Man, but the sending out of the Twelve and their return "sandwiches" the account of his death. John's beheading, therefore, casts the shadow of death over the disciples' mission. The bracketing suggests that what happened to John the Baptizer presages what will also happen to any who preach the same message of

---

21. James R. Edwards, "Markan Sandwiches: The Significance of Interpolations in Markan Narratives," *NovT* 31 (1989): 196.

repentance in a hostile world (6:12). They too will be handed over (13:9, 11–12). They too will have to stand before kings (13:9). While Jesus' ministry began after John's imprisonment (1:14), the disciples' preaching begins after John's death.

In spite of the disciples' success in casting out demons and healing the sick, death and evil loom on the horizon because humankind is evil and resists the message that God is king. All would-be kings will consider this message subversive and will do all in their power to stamp it out. The power to do miracles does not grant them immunity from suffering and death. The world is filled with villainous people in high and low places, who will try to rub out the messengers of God and their disturbing message. But it will not work. When the princes of this world have done their stamping, God is not through. The world will not easily be rid of prophets like John because of the God who raises the dead and enables disciples to remain faithful. The kingdom advances in spite of the murderous evil in the world.

THE REVIEW OF the circumstances of John's execution inserted into the account of the disciples' mission informs the meaning of the disciples' mission. The gruesome account of John's undoing by a wicked queen and a feckless so-called king should not be interpreted simply as an engaging digression. Mark's use of the bracketing technique elsewhere suggests that he wrapped the sending of the disciples off on their mission around the death of John so that the two accounts would help interpret one another. The account of Herod's weakness, Herodias' scheming, and John's death has something do with the mission of the disciples. Recognizing this helps us in our attempt to bring this passage into contemporary society. This passage is not about how to do mission but about the character of the disciples' mission.

(1) Jesus' strange instructions reveal that the mission is to be carried out with the utmost urgency. All that the disciples do in their mission—their proclamation, their healing, their provisions, their housing—reveal to others that they go with Jesus' authority and that the call to repentance is not routine preaching that can be casually ignored. To scorn their message has dire consequences.

(2) The account of John's death reveals that mission to a world under the domination of the powers is filled with danger. Not only may disciples face rejection and be forced to abandon an area, they may actually face execution. Secular rulers do not want to hear preaching about another king, even if that king is God. They do not want to be confronted with their sins, and they do

not fear the power of those who work wonders or even the power of the One who is able to raise the dead. The prospect of death when one ventures on mission for Christ into a world ruled by such kings is not some remote possibility. It is real.

WHILE WE MUST always trust God to supply all our needs, Jesus' charge dispatching his disciples on their mission without preparations or provisions hardly applies today. Few churches or mission agencies send off missionaries to fend for themselves without any support. Some missionaries may be required to line up their own financial support before they go; others receive generous support from the cooperative giving of their denomination or home church. Hardly any missionaries from wealthy countries go out expecting to depend entirely on the goodwill of those to whom they preach. Other than the judicious advice to go two by two, which provides some measure of protection from the twin dangers of attack and temptation, this passage informs us more about the character of mission for Christ than the specifics of mission. From a close reading of the text we can draw the following principles about their mission that apply today.

(1) The disciples' mission is an extension of Christ's work in the world. They go as the voice and action of Christ. Jesus will not do it all. He sends out disciples to help make ministry happen. They go in his name, preach what he taught, and work by his power. He does not send them out hat-in-hand to beg for a positive response but with divine authority to call others to repentance.

(2) They are to be so dedicated to the task of their mission that personal comforts become inconsequential. When Jesus sends out his disciples, he expects them to concentrate more on getting the message out than getting the finest accommodations. They are not sent out on a vacation excursion but are charged with a matter of life and death for others. They not only need to win their attention but also their confidence. No one will take seriously messengers who claim to bring an urgent message of life and death when it becomes evident that their first concern is to secure their own ease. Interest in luxurious living can only undermine the message's gravity. If disciples must from time to time shake the dust from their feet, they must be free from any worldly entanglements. The more they become entrenched in power structures of society with its values and pleasures, the harder it will be to disengage themselves and point to God's judgment.

Devotion to the task rather than devotion to oneself is therefore an absolute requirement for those who serve God. Some students leave seminary with their hearts set on gaining some great church where they will be well paid and applauded for their great successes; the less affluent churches go begging for someone to serve them. Few graduates want to go to places where no established churches exist and start from scratch. How can we pray for the evangelization of the world when we are unwilling to make sacrifices ourselves to help in that task? How can we expect to reach others when we seek shelter behind a stained-glass curtain? When Jesus calls us, he sends us out. He does not promise a successful career or protection from sickness, ordeals, or tyrants. We do not always get to choose where we will go. It may be next door; it may be to death's door. In order to be of service to Christ and others we must die to ourselves, something Jesus will expand upon later in the Gospel (8:34–37). Answering the call to serve others is risky business, but ignoring it or scorning it is even riskier.

(3) The disciples' mission is not just a matter of preaching the good news but of bringing into effect in people's lives the good news of healing and deliverance. They do not offer people something new to believe in but something that tangibly changes their lives. The good news is not just about saving souls but is also connected to physical healing. If people ask, as they frequently do, "What's in it for me?" the answer is clear: healing and restoration.

(4) Jesus does not commission his disciples to bestow blessings on people if they first believe and are willing to pay them for their ministry. They are to touch any who are in need, without any conditions. They are not sent to places that promise to be the most lucrative but to places where there is the greatest need.

(5) We should note the hint of triumph in the midst of suffering. Geddert maintains that Mark is not intent on giving only "ominous warnings of doom" in 1:14 and 6:14–29 but tries to help the discerning reader "trace the silver lining" in the dark cloud. The powers of evil seem to deal a dismal defeat with the arrest and death of John, but John's beheading does not silence God's message. Twelve messengers take his place, who, like Jesus, go about preaching, healing, and exorcising demons. Geddert comments: "One is rejected, but the work goes on and expands. The kingdom cannot be stopped by human opposition."[22] Ironically, even John's executioner suspected that he might ultimately triumph (6:16); and he was right. Death to God's messengers will not defeat God's cause. Justin Martyr's famous dictum, "the blood of the martyrs is the seed of the church," applies, as does Søren Kierkegaard's: "The tyrant dies and his rule ends, the martyr dies and his rule begins." God raises the dead and raises up new witnesses to take their place here in this life.

---

22. Geddert, *Watchwords*, 157.

Two final notes: On Jesus' instruction to shake dust from the feet and the theme of "hearing." The instructions to shake the dust from their feet indicates that the disciples' mission is to have a dramatic flair. It does not eternally condemn those who reject the rule of God, but it does convey how serious it is to do so. It also frees the messenger to move on. One cannot coerce, entice, or threaten people into the kingdom of God. Each person must make his or her own decision. Jesus recognizes that people can and will reject the gospel, but the gesture of shaking dust drives home the gravity of their rejection.

Today, this instruction may create a dilemma. When does one decide that it is time to "shake the dust from one's feet" in an unproductive area and when to stick it out and continue to try to find the lost? During his earthly ministry, Jesus and his disciples had only a short time to call Israel to repentance. The urgent time constraints of his ministry, therefore, make this command less applicable for us today. We have the luxury of staying in one place longer, even if results are not immediately apparent or people are overtly hostile. We should not use this phrase as an excuse to move on when the going gets hard, though there are times when it is necessary to close the book and relocate. But how do we express the grave danger of spurning the message of the kingdom without allowing a vindictive spirit to creep in? How many times have we heard someone say, "I showed them—I shook the dust of that place from my feet"? Mission work is a never-ending task, and one must be careful before writing a place off as a failure or chalking another one up as a success.

The account of John's death throws cold water on the rush of excitement that being able to cast out demons and heal illnesses might bring. It makes plain that Jesus sends disciples into a dangerous world. They may encounter something far more perilous than indifference. Herod is said to have listened to John the Baptizer with fascination. John elicited both gladness and perplexity in the ruler (see Paul and Felix in Acts). How often God's message exerts a strange power that makes people want to listen to things that disturb them greatly. Apparently, Herod could listen to sermons all day long; but like so many, he had a rock-hard resistance to repentance and was too weak to obey. The cost would have been enormous for him. He would have had to give up his wife, his dancing parties, and his abuse of power.

Hearing John's message and acknowledging that he was a righteous man, however, only served to compound the enormity of Herod's guilt. The theme of hearing reemerges in 6:14 and 20, which brackets the first section 6:14–20. According to the criteria of Jesus' parable of the sower, Herod qualifies as bad ground. He hears gladly, but does nothing. He reveres John as a prophet but cannot muster enough courage to admit he made a rash oath and should not submit to his wife's wicked request. A fearless prophet is undone by a cowardly king, who saved his face but lost his soul.

On her part, Herodias refuses even to listen to John and is perhaps worried over her husband's fascination with this troublesome prophet. She is a social climber, who is willing to sacrifice even her daughter to secure her hold on her husband and power. She is hardly a shining parental example. What does her daughter learn from being encouraged to dance lasciviously before her father and his guests? What does she learn from the joy of her mother when she presents her with the head of John? Surely Herodias would probably not have openly taught her daughter to be conniving, heartless, and cruel. But she taught her through her actions. More than one parent has communicated to their children more through action than through words: I'm willing to sacrifice you, your integrity, your self-esteem, to get what I want. Children are resilient and can overcome bad parenting, but, more often than not, the result is a shattered life.

Mark 6:31–44

THEN, BECAUSE SO many people were coming and going that they did not even have a chance to eat, he said to them, "Come with me by yourselves to a quiet place and get some rest."

32So they went away by themselves in a boat to a solitary place. 33But many who saw them leaving recognized them and ran on foot from all the towns and got there ahead of them. 34When Jesus landed and saw a large crowd, he had compassion on them, because they were like sheep without a shepherd. So he began teaching them many things.

35By this time it was late in the day, so his disciples came to him. "This is a remote place," they said, "and it's already very late. 36Send the people away so they can go to the surrounding countryside and villages and buy themselves something to eat."

37But he answered, "You give them something to eat."

They said to him, "That would take eight months of a man's wages! Are we to go and spend that much on bread and give it to them to eat?"

38"How many loaves do you have?" he asked. "Go and see."

When they found out, they said, "Five—and two fish."

39Then Jesus directed them to have all the people sit down in groups on the green grass. 40So they sat down in groups of hundreds and fifties. 41Taking the five loaves and the two fish and looking up to heaven, he gave thanks and broke the loaves. Then he gave them to his disciples to set before the people. He also divided the two fish among them all. 42They all ate and were satisfied, 43and the disciples picked up twelve basketfuls of broken pieces of bread and fish. 44The number of the men who had eaten was five thousand.

Original Meaning

A SWARM OF excited fans continue to besiege Jesus, making it impossible for him and his disciples even to take time to eat. He seeks to gain some respite by retreating with his disciples in a boat (see 3:9) and going ashore at a deserted place. The crowd foils this attempted escape by racing around the lake and beating the boat to its destination. This relentless pursuit of Jesus is further proof of his immense, super-star popularity. Jesus does not show any irritation with the crowds for chasing him down. Instead, he has compassion on them because they are "like a sheep without a shepherd." His first response to their need is to teach them.[1]

Mark refrains from giving a full account of Jesus' teaching to the crowd, as is his tendency throughout the Gospel, but he describes instead a miraculous feeding of the crowd in the desert. After long hours of teaching, the disciples express concern that it is late and they are stuck in a solitary place, where food is hard to get. They urge Jesus to send the crowds off to buy food for themselves. The disciples may be motivated by an altruistic concern that the crowd get something to eat or by a selfish desire for privacy so that they can at last eat in peace (3:20; 6:31). Jesus staggers them by ordering them to feed the crowd from their own scanty supply of food. He told them earlier when they went out on their mission to take no bread with them but to live off the hospitality of others (6:8); now they are to return the favor for this crowd.

The disciples again function as straight men whose alarm accentuates the magnitude of the miracle (see 4:41; 5:31). They stress that they are in a deserted place (cf. 1:3–4, 12–13), and they ask incredulously how they can possibly feed such a number. It would require at least two-hundred denarii, the equivalent of two hundred days' pay for a day laborer (Matt. 20:2). Jesus had also instructed them earlier to take no money with them (6:8), so where can they suddenly come up with the cash to feed all these people? They have neither the money nor enough food even for themselves with their meager ration of five loaves and two fish. Their squawking also reveals that they still have no inkling that Jesus has divine power to supply whatever they need.

Their outcry is a familiar one in Scripture. Moses objected when God told him to feed the people (six hundred thousand soldiers) for a month: "Would they have enough if flocks and herds were slaughtered for them? Would they have enough if all the fish in the sea were caught for them?" (Num. 11:22). When Elisha asks his servant to feed the company of prophets, he balked, "How can I set this before a hundred men?" (2 Kings 4:43a).

The feeding in the desert evokes several biblical themes. (1) It recalls God's miraculous provision of food. The disciples begin with hardly anything and end up with enough to satisfy five thousand. The fragments collected into twelve baskets reveal both the great abundance and the magnitude

---

1. Hooker (*Mark*, 165) comments: "Jesus has compassion on the crowd and cares for the leaderless people of Israel by giving them first an abundance of teaching, then an abundance of food." One can translate 6:34 that Jesus taught them "at length" instead of "many things" (see the use of *polla* in 5:23, 43; 6:20; 9:26).

of the miracle; they end with far more than they began. The miracle recalls God's answer to Moses: "Is the LORD's arm too short? You will now see whether or not what I say will come true for you" (Num. 11:23), and Elisha's response to his servant, 'The LORD says: 'They will eat and have some left over'" (2 Kings 4:43b). The feeding also echoes Isaiah's call for Israel to come now to God's banquet, celebrating the salvation about to be realized:

"Come, all you who are thirsty,
   come to the waters;
and you who have no money,
   come, buy and eat!
Come, buy wine and milk
   without money and without cost.
Why spend money on what is not bread,
   and your labor on what does not satisfy?
Listen, listen to me, and eat what is good,
   and your soul will delight in the richest of fare. (Isa. 55:1–2)

Jesus' banquet for the rabble of Galilee foreshadows the messianic banquet and contrasts with the drunken debauchery of Herod's feast for the high officials, captains, and the leading men of Galilee (6:22).[2] Herod's feast, with its exotic fanfare and dancing girls, cannot ultimately satisfy human hunger. Herod serves up only death, with the head of John the Baptizer brought to him on a platter (6:28). His lackeys bind (6:17) and behead (6:27) others. Only the spread offered by Jesus in the desert can satisfy human needs. Jesus brings life-giving bread with an abundance of leftovers. His disciples feed and serve others.

(2) The feeding recalls the exodus of the Israelites from Egypt and their being fed in the desert. The wilderness motifs suggest that Jesus is a new and greater Moses, leading a new and greater exodus.[3] Like Moses, Jesus feeds the people with teaching and with miraculous food. The image of sheep without a shepherd recalls Moses' supplication to God to appoint a successor when he is informed that he cannot lead the people into the Promised Land:

Moses said to the LORD, "May the LORD, the God of the spirits of all mankind, appoint a man over this community to go out and come in

---

2. John Bowman, *The Gospel of Mark: The New Jewish Christian Passover Haggadah* (Studia postbiblica 8; Leiden: Brill, 1965), 155.

3. A later rabbinic tradition describes a current belief in the time of Jesus: "As the former redeemer [Moses] caused manna to descend, as it is stated, Behold I will cause to rain bread from heaven for you [Exod 16:4], so will the latter redeemer cause manna to descend ..." (*Eccl. Rab.* 1:9).

before them, one who will lead them out and bring them in, so the LORD's people will not be like sheep without a shepherd." (Num. 27:15–17)

Jesus quickly organizes the shepherdless throng and makes them sit in groups (6:39) in rectangular sections (6:40), which makes it easier to feed them in an orderly fashion. More suggestively, it reflects the encampment of Israel (see Ex. 18:21, 25; cf. 1QS 2:21–22; 1QSa 1:14–15, 27–2:1; CD 13:1–2). The bread and fish parallel the manna and quail (Ex. 16; Num. 11:6; Wis. 19:12). The few small fish may relate to the bitter grumbling of the people in Numbers 11:4–6:

> The rabble with them began to crave other food, and again the Israelites started wailing and said, "If only we had meat to eat! We remember the fish we ate in Egypt at no cost—also the cucumbers, melons, leeks, onions and garlic. But now we have lost our appetite; we never see anything but this manna!"

Jesus is therefore able to provide the people in the desert what Moses could not. Moses had to contend with disgruntled people teetering on the edge of starvation. Those gathered around Jesus are all satisfied. In contrast to the manna that could not be gathered up and held over until the next day, Jesus' bread can be collected.

(3) Jesus has brought the disciples across the sea to this place to give them rest (6:31), and God's provision of rest in the desert is a recurring theme in Scripture (Ps. 95:7–11; Isa. 63:14; Jer. 31:2; Heb. 3:7–4:13).

(4) Psalm 23 also reverberates in the account of the feeding of the five thousand. Jesus has compassion on the people because they were like sheep without a shepherd, and his actions reflect the first line of the psalm, "The LORD is my shepherd" (see Isa. 40:10–11). The principal task of a shepherd is to bring sheep to food and water. Jesus is not like worthless shepherds who do not care that the people are perishing (Jer. 23:1–2; Ezek. 34:1–10; Zech. 11:15–17). He is the true shepherd (Ps. 95:7; Isa. 40:10–1; Jer. 23:3–4; Ezek. 34:11–31; Pss. Sol. 17:40), who feeds his sheep so that they may "not be in want." They do not get a cracker crumb or two but a full serving, which completely satiates their hunger.[4] Jesus makes them lie down in green pastures (Mark 6:39; cf. Ps. 23:2). Readers might be startled to read that the crowd reclines on a carpet of green when twice Mark tells us that this is a desert (6:31–32, 35). The barren desert has suddenly become green as the shepherd finds good pasture for his flock beside the waters of the sea

---

4. Jesus does not provide the elaborate feast anticipated in Isa. 25:6 but simple nourishment.

(Mark 6:32–33, 45; cf. Ps 23:2). Most importantly, however, Jesus restores their soul and guides them in right paths by teaching them (Mark 6:34; cf. Ps. 23:3).

(5) A fifth biblical echo comes from the Elijah/Elisha cycle. Some observers have already guessed that Jesus might be Elijah (6:15) or one of the prophets because he speaks with authority and performs wonders. Like Elijah and Elisha, Jesus works in northern Israel, speaks rather than writes, and gathers disciples. Elijah provided miraculously for the widow of Zarephath (1 Kings 17:8–16) and mediated divine power by raising her son from the dead (17:24). Elisha fed the guild of a hundred prophets with twenty barley loaves, over his servant's objections (2 Kings 4:42–44); Jesus feeds five thousand people with five loaves. If we are meant to recall the works of these sainted prophets of old, we see that in Jesus one greater than Elijah and Elisha is here.

(6) Finally, the feeding account is a foretoken of the Last Supper in Mark. The action of taking bread, giving thanks,[5] breaking it, and giving it to the disciples (6:41) matches his action at the Last Supper (14:22). While this gesture is not out of the ordinary, the reader familiar with Jesus' action on his last night (see 1 Cor. 11:23–24) could not help but make the connection. The abundance of food left over after feeding five thousand means that there is more to go around and much more where it came from. Those who come to hear the teaching of Jesus and to share in the broken bread will receive the same abundant blessing.[6]

Mark does not refer to the astonishment of the crowd, which normally accompanies his miracles. Do they even know that a miracle has occurred? Could it be that they have eaten a miracle in a deceptively simple meal and did not realize it (see John 2:9–10; cf. 2 Kings 4:42–44)? Do they just accept this bounty without reflecting on the gracious gift offered to them? Are they like dumb sheep who eat the grass without a thought for the one who made the grass? The disciples, who distribute the bread from their meager supply, must know that a miracle is occurring, but the next episode in the boat makes it clear that they do not comprehend its significance and what it says about the one who did it.

---

5. Jews did not bless their food but instead gave thanks to God as the provider of food.

6. In 2 Chron. 31:10, the prosperity and the great supply left over are attributed to the people's great generosity in giving to the temple. In the desert feeding, the people have contributed nothing to earn God's gracious bounty.

Bridging Contexts

MANY MODERN SCHOLARS have tried to rationalize the feeding miracles away. Some resort to desperate measures. They claim that Jesus had a secret stash of food hidden in the desert. He stood at the secret entrance to a cave where the bread was hidden, and the crowd was fooled into thinking that something miraculous was happening. This ludicrous explanation ignores the text, which does not mention the crowd's reaction to the feeding. Another contends that "rich and pious ladies used to inquire of Him where he thought of preaching to the people on a given day, and sent baskets of bread and dried fish to the spot which He indicated, that the multitude might not suffer hunger."[7]

Others have argued more reasonably that Jesus got his disciples to share their own provisions they had selfishly tucked away for themselves. The crowd, observing their generosity, followed suit and shared what they had with others. Barclay claimed, "This is a miracle of the birth of love in men's souls; it is a miracle of the awakening of fellowship in men's souls; it is the eternal miracle of Christianity, whereby a miscellaneous crowd of men and women becomes a family in Christ."[8] Still others have explained the miracle away by contending that the numbers for the crowd were greatly exaggerated in the oral tradition. Schweitzer claimed that it was a sacramental meal—each receiving a tiny fragment as a token of the eschatological feast to come.[9]

All these rationalizations approach the text with an a priori dismissal of the miraculous. It may reconcile our scientific skepticism that asks, Can something like this really happen? but it causes us to miss the Christological point that Mark wants to underscore: Here is one who is like Moses but greater than Moses, who is like Elijah and Elisha but greater than these prophets. When the Israelites complained to Moses and Aaron about the lousy provisions in the desert, they responded, "Who are we? You are not grumbling against us, but against the LORD" (Ex. 16:8). This statement is a confession that only God can bring food in the desert. In feeding the five thousand, Mark shows that Jesus exercises God's power and uses it for the good of his flock (Ps. 78:52–55). He is the true shepherd of his people, who provides the necessities of their spiritual and physical life.

---

7. Albert Schweitzer, *The Quest for the Historical Jesus: A Critical Study of Its Progress from Reimarus to Wrede* (New York: Macmillan, 1968), 328–29, citing Pierre Nahor (Emilie Lerou), *Jesus*.

8. William Barclay, *And He Had Compassion on Them* (Edinburgh: The Church of Scotland, 1955), 163.

9. Albert Schweitzer, *The Mystery of the Kingdom of God* (New York: Macmillan, 1950), 103–6.

This incident also emphasizes the need to combine teaching with social concern. As God did not neglect the physical and spiritual needs of the people of Israel in the desert, so the church cannot neglect either need. Jesus provides the bread of life. He offers the people bread that feeds the soul and bread that satisfies the needs of the body. On the one hand, giving Bible lessons to large crowds and sending them away hungry does too little. Starving people rarely make good religious followers because they are intent on physical survival. On the other hand, simply filling their bellies without also filling their hearts with a spiritual challenge does too little. The two go hand in hand.

THE IMAGE OF Jesus as the good shepherd of the flock is prominent in this feeding episode. Bonhoeffer eloquently describes the plight of the people without a shepherd. "There were questions but no answers, distress but no relief, anguish of conscience but no deliverance, tears but no consolation, sin but no forgiveness." They were waiting for good news, and all they got was good advice. Bonhoeffer asks, "What is the use of scribes, devotees of the law, preachers and the rest, when there are no shepherds for the flock?"[10]

To say that the people were like sheep without a shepherd seriously challenged Israel's religious leadership (see Zech. 11:5, 15–17). It was not that they did not have enough priests to go around. They had so many that they had to use a platoon system (see Luke 1:8–9). The problem was that the religious leaders were not doing what they were meant to do. Jesus did not seem to care how big the temple stones were, how big its budget was, or how many showed up for prayers and sacrifices. All he cared about were the results of all this religiosity. What he saw were spiritually and physically hungry people, wrapped up in all sorts of religious red tape. They were spiritually starved as well as materially impoverished, and nobody seemed to care. He would see the same things today. Jesus recognizes both needs and moves to correct them.

Most contemporary listeners are unfamiliar with the job description of a shepherd. Lena Woltering has pointed out that a shepherd "is needed only when there are no fences. He is someone who stays with his sheep at all cost, guiding, protecting, and walking with them through the fields. He's not just a person who raises sheep." They lead sheep to food and water and are ever mindful of the sheep's condition (Gen. 33:13). They gather lambs

---

10. Dietrich Bonhoeffer, *The Cost of Discipleship* (New York: Macmillan, 1963), 224.

that cannot keep up in their arms (Isa. 40:11). They seek out lost sheep; and when they find them, they carry them back to the fold on their shoulders (Luke 15:5). They guard against predators and thieves. It is a dirty and hard job. Woltering castigates those bishops who regard themselves as "tenders of the flock" and brands them as little more than "mutton farmers." "They build fence after fence after fence, keeping the flock within sight so they don't have to dirty their feet plodding along the open fields."[11] They turn the difficult role of shepherd into a position of rank and superiority and sequester themselves from the sheep. Ezekiel's castigation of the self-indulgent and irresponsible shepherds in his day (Ezek. 34) is no less applicable today to those who want to dominate and crush others rather than feed them.

This incident also reveals that Jesus recognizes his disciples' need for rest. One cannot serve others twenty-four hours a day. Ministers need to take time for themselves, and Jesus' word, "Come with me by yourselves to a quiet place and get some rest," is an important one for weary laborers. But this incident also reveals that when we do try to get away, we often find more hungry people—both spiritually and physically. The need can be overwhelming, and we are tempted to send the suffering and needy away empty-handed. We may have heard or even voiced the same protest the disciples made: It will cost too much for us to do anything about their need. Let them take care of themselves. They are not our responsibility. What we may really be saying is that we will not have enough money for ourselves if we have to take care of "them" as well.

Disciples of Jesus need to do more than lament the crowd's hunger and the lack of food while sending them away with nothing. We have not done our duty if all we have done is point out the problems in society and lament them. Some make a career out of itemizing the world's ills. The church, however, has been called out into the world to do something about these problems. We must minister to the spiritual needs at the root of many social problems and extend material aid to those who are in need. Everywhere we turn, we find the need of a hungry crowd and little or no food. Jesus instructs us to feed them.

James makes the point: "Suppose a brother or sister is without clothes and daily food. If one of you says to him, 'Go, I wish you well; keep warm and well fed,' but does nothing about his physical needs, what good is it?" (James 2:15–16). And John the elder argues in 1 John 3:17–19:

> If anyone has material possessions and sees his brother in need but has
> no pity on him, how can the love of God be in him? Dear children,

---

11. Cited in *Salt of the Earth* 15 (July/August, 1995): 34.

let us not love with words or tongue but with actions and in truth. This then is how we know that we belong to the truth, and how we set our hearts at rest in his presence.

Sending the hungry and needy away to fend for themselves does not solve the problem. Jesus works the miracle when his disciples share what they have with others. The church cannot neglect either spiritual or physical hunger. In this account, the disciples are stymied when they think that the task is impossible or the cost too great. Only when they have faith to tap into the divine provision do they accomplish the job and provide everyone with enough. Jesus insists that the disciples share in his ministry to the world and take responsibility for the crowd. We may be exhausted and need a well-deserved rest when Jesus says to us, "You give them something." Disciples are always servants of others—called to feed the sheep and not just themselves. The lesson from this account is clear: They will always have enough to feed the church.[12]

Modern disciples are no different from Jesus' first disciples, however, and frequently cannot see that even when they are drained physically and financially, they have the resources to help others. They are challenged to tackle impossible problems with limited resources and to discover the possibilities of God. Before we can say, "There is nothing that we can do; send them away," we should first "go and see" how many loaves we have.

> How many loaves have ye?
> Jesus thy Savior still asks of thee,
> For the multitudes hunger in deserts drear,
> And the cry of their need has reached his ear.[13]

Before we say, "We have counted, and we do not have enough," we need to venture out in faith to help others. When Christians on average give about 3 percent of their income to the church and even less of their time in direct ministry, we know that we do have enough but we are keeping it for ourselves. Perhaps a miracle will occur (as Barclay interprets it): that human hearts and pocketbooks will be opened when we begin ministering to others. The passage confirms that compassion combined with God's bounty and power can meet both the spiritual and physical needs of people.

---

12. Bruce Chilton, *Feast of Meanings: Eucharistic Theologies from Jesus Through Johannine Circles* (NovTSup 72; Leiden: Brill, 1994), 128.

13. Marian E. Doyle, "Loaves and Fishes," cited by Hillyer Hawthorne Straton, *Preaching the Miracles* (New York/Nashville: Abingdon, 1950), 53.

Mark 6:45–56

IMMEDIATELY JESUS MADE his disciples get into the boat and go on ahead of him to Bethsaida, while he dismissed the crowd. ⁴⁶After leaving them, he went up on a mountainside to pray.

⁴⁷When evening came, the boat was in the middle of the lake, and he was alone on land. ⁴⁸He saw the disciples straining at the oars, because the wind was against them. About the fourth watch of the night he went out to them, walking on the lake. He was about to pass by them, ⁴⁹but when they saw him walking on the lake, they thought he was a ghost. They cried out, ⁵⁰because they all saw him and were terrified.

Immediately he spoke to them and said, "Take courage! It is I. Don't be afraid." ⁵¹Then he climbed into the boat with them, and the wind died down. They were completely amazed, ⁵²for they had not understood about the loaves; their hearts were hardened.

⁵³When they had crossed over, they landed at Gennesaret and anchored there. ⁵⁴As soon as they got out of the boat, people recognized Jesus. ⁵⁵They ran throughout that whole region and carried the sick on mats to wherever they heard he was. ⁵⁶And wherever he went—into villages, towns or countryside—they placed the sick in the marketplaces. They begged him to let them touch even the edge of his cloak, and all who touched him were healed.

Original Meaning

JESUS COMPELS HIS disciples to get into the boat to set sail for Bethsaida before dispersing the crowds, who have eaten their fill. Mark gives us no explanation why he needs to force the disciples to weigh anchor and leave (contrast John 6:15), but he dispatches them along with the crowd and goes up the mountain to pray alone (see 1:35).

Separated from their Master, the disciples undergo an ordeal, fighting against the waves. A storm does not endanger their lives as earlier (4:35–41), but they find themselves stuck in the middle of the lake, fighting against the wind after hours of strenuous rowing. Jesus can see their struggle (one must assume supernaturally in the darkness) and rejoins them during the fourth watch of the night (3:00 A.M.–6:00 A.M.) by walking on the sea. Just as Jesus did not first feed the hungry multitudes but taught them (6:34), so he does not first rescue the disciples from their predicament but tries to teach them something by passing by them. Their eyes and ears are not up to it, however; they see only a phantasm, a ghost. The waves and the wind have not thrown them into a panic, but the sight of Jesus passing by on the water does.

The wind poses no obstacle to Jesus and the waves provide firm footing as he marches across the sea. Treading the waves, however, is something that only God can do (Job 9:8; Isa. 43:16; 51:10; Sir. 24:5–6). When Jesus comes strolling across the waters, he shares in the unlimited power of the Creator. In Habakkuk 3:15, the image of God trampling the sea conveys his power to control the chaos of the seas to save his people Israel (see Ps. 77:19–20; Isa. 51:9–10).

Mark's explanation that Jesus "wanted to pass by them" (6:48, lit. tr.) has caused confusion and prompted numerous interpretations:

- Jesus intends to overtake the disciples and playfully surprise them on them other side. But it seems rather pitiless on his part to whisk by and leave them floundering and frightened, all in the interest of fun.
- Jesus wants to pass by but does not do so when he sees the disciple's distress. The problem with this view is that he has already seen them in distress before he sets out on the sea. Why would he want to pass by?
- Jesus is trying to test their faith. But what does such a test comprise?
- The NIV adopts the view that the verb *thelo* ("to wish, will") functions as an auxiliary verb like *mello* ("to be about to"): "he was about to pass by them." The evidence for this use of the verb is too slim to make this interpretation likely.
- The phrase refers to the disciples' mistaken impression of Jesus' intentions—they think he intends to pass by them. The text does not say this, however.
- Some try to relieve the problem by suggesting that he intends simply to go beside them.
- Jesus wants to be seen walking on the sea but wishes to remain unrecognized—something that supposedly fits the author's theology of the messianic secret. There is no good reason for Jesus to want to frighten hapless disciples and then disappear into the mist.
- Another view takes its cue from Amos 7:1–8:3 and interprets the phrase metaphorically: Jesus wanted to help the disciples in their difficulty.[1]

---

1. Harry Fleddermann, "'And He Wanted to Pass by Them" (Mark 6:48c)," *CBQ* 45 (1983): 389–95. Fledderman interprets the verb "to pass by" (NIV, "spare") in Amos 7:8 and 8:2 to express God's intention to avert catastrophe and argues here for Mark: "A free, but accurate, translation would be: 'And he wanted to save them.'"

None of these explanations adequately explains or explains away the phrase, but the last has the virtue of interpreting Jesus' action from the background of the Old Testament. This account is not about a rescue of the disciples on the sea. They are frustrated but not in peril. Since walking on the sea is something no ordinary mortal can do, Jesus' desire to pass by the disciples is not related to some mundane purpose. The verb *parerchomai* ("to pass by"), when connected to a divinity, refers to an epiphany. The Old Testament records that God made "striking and temporary appearances in the earthly realm to a select individual or group for the purpose of communicating a message."[2]

This verb occurs in two key passages in the Old Testament. In Exodus 33:19–34:7, Moses asks God to show him his glory, and God responds by passing before him and proclaiming his identity.

> And the LORD said, "I will cause all my goodness to pass in front of you, and I will proclaim my name, the LORD, in your presence. I will have mercy on whom I will have mercy, and I will have compassion on whom I will have compassion. But," he said, "you cannot see my face, for no one may see me and live."
>
> Then the LORD said, "There is a place near me where you may stand on a rock. When my glory passes by, I will put you in a cleft in the rock and cover you with my hand until I have passed by. Then I will remove my hand and you will see my back; but my face must not be seen."
>
> ... Then the LORD came down in the cloud and stood there with him and proclaimed his name, the LORD. And he passed in front of Moses, proclaiming, "The LORD, the LORD, the compassionate and gracious God, slow to anger, abounding in love and faithfulness, maintaining love to thousands, and forgiving wickedness, rebellion and sin. ..."

And in 1 Kings 19:11–12, the Lord tells Elijah to stand on the mountain, "for the LORD is about to pass by."[3] One can conclude from these passages that when Jesus wants to pass by his disciples, he wills for them to see his transcendent majesty as a divine being and to give them reassurance.[4]

---

2. John P. Meier, *A Marginal Jew: Rethinking the Historical Jesus;* vol. 2: *Mentor, Message, and Miracle* (New York: Doubleday, 1994), 2:996, n. 118.

3. In the Septuagint, the verb *parerchomai* is used to refer to an epiphany. In Gen. 32:31–33, the face of God "passed by" Jacob when he was wrestling with the angel (see 2 Sam. 23:3–4). Job 9:8, 11 reads, "He ... treads on the waves of the sea. ... When he passes me, I cannot see him; when he goes by, I cannot perceive him." See also Dan. 12:1, which refers to the glory of the Lord passing by; Amos 7:8; 8:2.

4. The fourth watch becomes significant when one remembers that God delivers his people early in the morning. Barry Blackburn (*Theios Aner and the Markan Miracle Traditions* [WUNT

God cannot be fully seen, but Jesus can. The one who comes to them on the sea is not simply a successor to Moses, who fills baskets with bread in the desert. Only God can walk on the sea, and Jesus' greeting is not simply a cheery hello to assuage the disciples' fears. He greets them with the divine formula of self-revelation, "I am."[5] Isaiah 43:1–13 is significant as a backdrop for interpreting this passage. The disciples have been summoned by Jesus to pass through the waters, and Jesus is with them (Isa. 43:2).

> "You are my witnesses," declares the LORD,
>> "and my servant whom I have chosen,
> so that you may know and believe me
>> and understand that I am he.
> Before me no god was formed,
>> nor will there be one after me.
> [It is] I, even I, am the LORD,
>> and apart from me there is no savior." (43:10–11)

Here is the answer to the disciples' question in 4:41, "Who is this? Even the wind and the waves obey him!" This person is the God who needs only say, "I am." But that answer sails by the disciples.

Jesus displays his divine power further when he gets into the boat. His mere presence causes the wind to cease howling and enables the disciples to continue their journey. It does not calm their apprehension, however. Mark offers a surprising explanation for the disciples' terror and amazement: "For they had not understood about the loaves; their hearts were hardened" (6:52). The two incidents are somehow connected. What is it that they do not understand about the loaves? What does it have to do with walking on the water? Minear is on target when he comments that the disciples are "blind to the presence of God and his care for men . . . to the full glory of the revelation of God 'in the face of Christ.'"[6] They do not recognize that the blessing pronounced at the meal, "Praise be Thou, O Lord our God, King of the Universe, who causes bread to come forth from the

---

2/40: Tübingen: J. C. B. Mohr (Paul Siebeck) 1991], 146) writes: "Thus Jesus, like Yahweh in the O.T. (and the New), manifests his saving power *proi* [early]" (see also Ex. 14:24; Ps. 46:5; Isa. 17:14).

5. See Ex. 3:14; Deut. 32:39; Pss. 115:9; 128:5–6; Isa. 41:2–14; 43:1–13 [v. 2: "When you pass through the waters, I will be with you"]; 44:1–5; 46:4; 48:12; 51:9–16; 52:6; John 8:58.

6. Minear, *Mark*, 84. Lane (*Mark*, 238) comments that they failed "to grasp that this event pointed beyond itself to the secret of Jesus' person. Because they were not truly open to the action of God in Jesus they had missed the significance of the miracle of the loaves for them, and saw only 'a marvel.'"

earth," applies also to Jesus. The condition of hardened hearts refers to disobedience, dullness, and obstinacy and is the predicament of Jesus' opponents (3:5; see Eph. 4:18). Mark repeats this description in Mark 8:17. The disciples are drawing closer to Jesus' opponents than to Jesus in their life stance. The difference between them and the opponents is significant, however. The disciples may be confused and blind, but they are not hostile to Jesus.

Jesus sends the disciples off to Bethsaida (6:45), but they land in Gennesaret.[7] Perhaps they have been blown off course by the wind, although it was calmed when Jesus entered the boat.[8] Perhaps Mark wants the reader to see some significance in their going off course. They are unable to go to Bethsaida, just as they have been unable to understand about the loaves (6:52), and do not reach this destination until later (8:22). Meanwhile, the activities of Jesus comprise a second series of mighty works, intended to help the disciples to see.[9] Jesus never gives up on the disciples in spite of their failures, but takes them through the whole process again so that they may understand. He does not require disciples to grasp things immediately. They are not to be condemned for their natural bent to human hardheartedness or for their inability to grasp the mind-boggling reality that God is in their midst in the very person of Jesus. He veils his self-disclosure, and full understanding will not come until after his death and resurrection.

When the people recognize Jesus, they rush about, lug their sick on mattresses, beg to touch the tassels of his garments, and are healed. Some claim that this pursuing of Jesus is only an indication of "the blindness of those whose only interest is in the miraculous."[10] If so, then Jesus meets their misunderstanding with grace by healing them. It is more likely that the pursuit reveals Jesus' immense popularity. The disciples do not know who he is, but the people of Gennesaret are convinced that he has power to heal. They may not fully understand who heals them either, but their great faith in Jesus' power contrasts with the little faith of the disciples.

---

7. Bethsaida was a town on the northeast side of the Sea of Galilee; Gennesaret was a densely populated plain on the northwest side of the sea, between Tiberias and Capernaum.

8. Gundry (*Mark*, 346) argues that before Jesus joins the disciples, they have been blown off course too far to make landing in Bethsaida practicable or desirable.

9. See Elizabeth Struthers Malbon, "The Jesus of Mark and the Sea of Galilee," *JBL* 103 (1984): 363–77; "Echoes and Foreshadowings in Mark 4–8: Reading and Rereading," *JBL* 112 (1993): 226–37.

10. So Schweizer, *Mark*, 143.

TO UNDERSTAND THE full significance of Jesus' walking on the water, one must appreciate the web of Old Testament motifs behind the text. This Old Testament background makes it harder to bridge the contexts. Our unfamiliarity with these traditions, compounded by a tendency to interpret details literally, causes us to miss their symbolic significance. The incident is thus trivialized. Jesus did not walk across the water as an amusing gimmick to astound his friends. His action conveys to the disciples and to the reader schooled in Scripture who he is. He comes as a divine figure to rescue his floundering disciples.

The alternative interpretations that try to make sense of why Jesus wanted to pass by his disciples require much less work to express its meaning. They may therefore be more attractive, because one need not explain Old Testament imagery so foreign to many modern listeners. But these interpretations paint a rather mundane scene that misses the enormous significance of what Mark describes. This is an epiphany, a surprise self-disclosure of Jesus' deity to bewildered disciples.

This epiphany does not occur on a mountain, the traditional locale for encountering the divine presence, where one's vision seems unlimited, but on the deep waters, traditionally viewed by Israel as a place of dangerous storms and sinister power, where one's vision is blinded by fear. The sea, however, was the scene of Israel's greatest deliverance, when God parted the waters of the Red Sea and revealed his divine power over both the deadly forces of nature and humans. The Old Testament motifs in Mark's account of Jesus' walking on the water recall God's mastery over the waters of chaos as Creator and Savior. Jesus walks on the waves like God and speaks like the one true God, "It is I. Don't be afraid." Jesus wants to show his disciples a glimpse of his divinity in order to help them unravel the clues to his identity. They do not follow a great prophet or superhero but the very Son of God. He does what no human can do and will do what no human can do—redeem humankind from the bondage of Satan and sin.

Miracles do not always evoke faith, however; nor do they always communicate. One can make this particular miracle look trite, as in the musical drama *Jesus Christ Superstar* Herod taunts Jesus to "walk across my swimming pool." Many may fail to appreciate the Christological implications of this miracle and, in that sense, are like the disciples who do not understand about the loaves. Jesus is not pulling off a staggering visual stunt to amaze his friends. Rather, the miracle attests that God himself has visited us in the flesh. This spine-tingling, knee-buckling reality cannot be captured by a jaded Hollywood and may be overlooked by modern Christians who have lost their sense of awe before the holy. Even those disposed to believe that God meets us in Jesus Christ may find it hard to believe that Jesus walked on the water and may dismiss it as pious legend or look for some rational explanation. Such attempts eviscerate this text of its imagery and power. Christians believe they know God through Jesus Christ. In this account, Mark presents Jesus' revelation of himself to his disciples as God incarnate. But he comes as "an elusive presence they cannot control."[11]

We not only meet God in Jesus Christ, we also learn about ourselves through him. The disciples' fear and lack of comprehension in response to this miracle says something about the human condition when it comes in contact with the divine. The disciples thought they were seeing a ghost. They did not understand the loaves, and their hearts were hardened. We rarely see God walking past or recognize his blessing, bounty, or presence in our lives. In bridging the contexts we ought to reflect on similar experiences from our past where God met us but we were too dense to see it at the time. Like the disciples on the road to Emmaus, we only recognize in retrospect who it was who appeared in our lives (Luke 24:13–35).

One thing no one can miss in this miracle: Jesus clearly cares for his disciples. He sees their distress and comes to them during the darkest part of the night, when they are having trouble in the deepest part of the lake. He shows patience when they fail to see what it all means but recoil in fear. There is no rebuke, only calm assurance. He then delivers them safely to the shore. The disciples see more than God's back, as Moses did; they saw the face of God in the face of his Son. He is the Savior, who brings calm and deliverance. One can imagine the early Christians who heard this story taking great comfort in it as they applied it to their own distressed situation. As Rawlinson imagines it:

> ... faint hearts may even have begun to wonder whether the Lord Himself had not abandoned them to their fate, or to doubt the reality of Christ. They are to learn from this story that they are not "forsaken," that the Lord watches over them unseen, and that He Himself—no phantom, but the Living One, Master of wind and waves—will surely come quickly for their salvation, even though it be in the "fourth watch of the night."[12]

11. Fleddermann, "'And He Wanted to Pass by Them,'" 395.
12. A. E. J. Rawlinson, *St. Mark* (Westminster Commentaries; London: Methuen, 1925), 88.

Contemporary
Significance

JESUS' RETREAT FROM the throngs and his disciples shows that all humans need solitude, rest, and prayer (1:35; 6:31). In such moments we can meet ourselves face to face and hear God speaking most clearly. Unfortunately, many parishioners do not value that experience enough to ensure that their ministry staff gets it, and many ministers try to get by without it. The pastor's study is more frequently known as the church office. We value busyness, and by it we measure our effectiveness. Few schedule time for solitude and meditation in the church calendar, usually chock full of activities. Many feel besieged by persons constantly pulling at their sleeves and hearts strings and never take time to recharge their batteries with study, prayer, and rest. The whirlwind of activity spins them like tops, and they end up becoming bone weary physically and bone dry spiritually. They may feel like the disciples—rowing furiously against the wind but getting nowhere, and blind to the God who calls out and says, "I am."

We can also look at this passage from the perspective of the disciples, who face adversity, feel separated from Jesus, and are distressed in the rowing. Many people may feel that way as they serve in the church. They keep rowing but seem to make no progress. Discouragement sets in when one always seems headed into a gale. They feel cast adrift and may ask why they ever left the shore in the first place; they long to go back. Rowers grow tired and then slack. Or they become so involved in the task that they cannot see the revelation of Jesus' power and the care that he also gives them.

Some may find comfort in knowing that even when they do not see Jesus, Jesus sees them and comes in the hour of need. He is like Aslan, the lion/Christ figure in C. S. Lewis's *Narnia Chronicles*, who appears from over the sea without warning but exactly when he is needed: "'Aslan was among them though no one had seen him coming.'"[13]

Jesus does not rescue his disciples out of the sea but enables them to continue the voyage.[14] His coming is like the letters to the churches in the Apocalypse. The churches receive the word that the Lord knows what they have endured and are encouraged to continue to endure. The Lord knows the works, toil, and endurance of Ephesus (Rev. 2:2), the affliction and poverty of Smyrna (2:9), the faithful witness of Pergamum in the midst of Satan's throne (2:13), the patient endurance of Thyatira (2:18), and the little power of Philadelphia (3:8). He does not relieve them of their struggle but promises victory if they are faithful. They must keep rowing, but the power to cross

---

13. C. S. Lewis, *The Horse and His Boy* (London: Penguin, 1965), 182; cited by Richard A Burridge, *Four Gospels: One Jesus?* (Grand Rapids: Eerdmans, 1994), 35.

14. See Best, *Following Jesus*, 232.

over the sea of life and reach the final destination is not theirs. It belongs to God. The congregation of which I am a member has a church hymn composed by two gifted friends. The last stanza captures the significance of this passage in Mark:

Not our choice the wind's direction,
unforeseen the calm or gale.
The great ocean swells before us,
and our ship seems small and frail.

Fierce and gleaming is Thy mystery
drawing us to shores unknown:
plunge us on with hope and courage
'till Thy harbor is our home.[15]

A disturbing element of this miracle is the response of the disciples to Jesus' sudden appearance. They do not recognize him and are more frightened by his presence than his absence. He comes with all the power of God who controls the mighty forces of the wind and the sea. He tries to reassure them by making himself known in his glory and power. It fails to calm their hearts. Instead, they are stupefied, frightened, and confused. Often Christ may pass by our lives in ways that we fail to see and that might frighten us. How do we see him while we struggle in the dim hours of the night in this present age, besieged by windy opposition? It may only become clear in retrospect, as it did for those first disciples. We realize that in that horrible hour we were in the very presence of God and that Christ revealed his glory to us. We were too blind, too petrified to see it. One should then be alert that in the times of discouragement and greatest fears Christ is passing by, showing his love and power and leading us across troubled waters.

We must admit that we do not live in an age where we witness theophanies. Some may claim today to have been abducted by aliens and whisked away into their spacecraft, but few profess that they have been caught up to the third heaven and seen visions. Most would not believe either one and dismiss both as delusional. God may not encounter us in this way anymore because the cross and resurrection are the clearest revelation of God. It may also be that our vision is weak and dim and we are not attuned to God's presence. Maybe there are different intensities of the human vision of God at different times in history.

---

15. From "We, O God, Unite Our Voices" (*The Crescent Hill Hymn*), by Grady Nutt and Paul Duke, used with permission.

Mark 7:1–23

THE PHARISEES AND some of the teachers of the law who had come from Jerusalem gathered around Jesus and ²saw some of his disciples eating food with hands that were "unclean," that is, unwashed. ³(The Pharisees and all the Jews do not eat unless they give their hands a ceremonial washing, holding to the tradition of the elders. ⁴When they come from the marketplace they do not eat unless they wash. And they observe many other traditions, such as the washing of cups, pitchers and kettles.)

⁵So the Pharisees and teachers of the law asked Jesus, "Why don't your disciples live according to the tradition of the elders instead of eating their food with 'unclean' hands?"

⁶He replied, "Isaiah was right when he prophesied about you hypocrites; as it is written:

"'These people honor me with their lips,
    but their hearts are far from me.
⁷ They worship me in vain;
    their teachings are but rules taught by men.'

⁸You have let go of the commands of God and are holding on to the traditions of men."

⁹And he said to them: "You have a fine way of setting aside the commands of God in order to observe your own traditions! ¹⁰For Moses said, 'Honor your father and your mother,' and, 'Anyone who curses his father or mother must be put to death.' ¹¹But you say that if a man says to his father or mother: 'Whatever help you might otherwise have received from me is Corban' (that is, a gift devoted to God), ¹²then you no longer let him do anything for his father or mother. ¹³Thus you nullify the word of God by your tradition that you have handed down. And you do many things like that."

¹⁴Again Jesus called the crowd to him and said, "Listen to me, everyone, and understand this. ¹⁵Nothing outside a man can make him 'unclean' by going into him. Rather, it is what comes out of a man that makes him 'unclean.'"

¹⁷After he had left the crowd and entered the house, his disciples asked him about this parable. ¹⁸"Are you so dull?" he

asked. "Don't you see that nothing that enters a man from the outside can make him 'unclean'? ¹⁹For it doesn't go into his heart but into his stomach, and then out of his body." (In saying this, Jesus declared all foods "clean.")

²⁰He went on: "What comes out of a man is what makes him 'unclean.' ²¹For from within, out of men's hearts, come evil thoughts, sexual immorality, theft, murder, adultery, ²²greed, malice, deceit, lewdness, envy, slander, arrogance and folly. ²³All these evils come from inside and make a man 'unclean.'"

THE POLEMICS OVER washing hands and food laws divide into two parts. The first (7:1–13) reports Jesus' confrontation with the Pharisees and teachers of the law over the issue of eating with unwashed hands. These religious directors are completely oblivious to the miracles that God is working through Jesus and only notice inconsequential matters. Jesus has miraculously fed the crowds in the desert with an abundance of bread, but they only dither about eating bread with unclean hands. Jesus turns their niggling complaint about his disciples' conduct into a caustic condemnation of their whole tradition. The second part (7:14–23) consists of Jesus' stunning announcement to the crowd that defilement only comes from within, from an individual's heart, and not from contact with anything external. He follows up this radical declaration with a private explanation to his disciples about the nature of purity and impurity.

Confrontation Over the Tradition of the Elders (7:1–13)

ANNOYED PHARISEES AND teachers of the law, who regard themselves as the keepers of the tradition, clash with Jesus by publicly protesting the glaring failure of his disciples to observe the rules about unclean hands. This marks the second time that teachers of the law have come "from Jerusalem," chafing over Jesus' influence as a rule-breaker (see 3:22), and it foreshadows Jerusalem's hostility to Jesus that will ultimately lead to his death. In this confrontation, they appear with Pharisees (see 2:16).[1]

To understand the controversy we must digress and discuss briefly the program of the Pharisees. They were not the power brokers in Jewish society, as many imagine, but were struggling to impose their vision of morality and obedience to the law on Israel. Maintaining purity was a key item in their

---

1. These huffy inspectors "from Jerusalem" probably inspired the same contempt that bureaucrats who come from Washington, D. C., do in some quarters today.

agenda. The disagreement over washing hands had nothing to do with hygiene but was a matter of purity.[2] These Pharisees obviously expected Jesus and his followers to conform to their standards of piety. They tried to promote obedience among the people and must have been galled when a popular prophetic figure like Jesus appeared to subvert it. To them, Jesus was religiously incorrect, and his cavalier attitude toward such things threatened their vision of a smoothly running, holy community.[3] His immense popularity also threatened to reduce their sphere of influence since he called into question the authority and validity of their traditions. "The tradition of the elders" was unscriptural law, and they may have been particularly defensive about the washing of hands since it had no explicit biblical basis.[4]

The conflict in Mark 7 revolves around the issue of defilement. The Pharisees accuse the disciples of eating with hands that are "unclean" ("common," the opposite of "holy," "devoted to God"). Mark explains that "unclean hands" refers to "unwashed hands" (7:2) and inserts a parenthetic explanation about Jewish ritual washings for readers unfamiliar with these customs (7:3–4).[5] The levitical system regarded uncleanness as something transferable to persons, vessels, clothes, and even houses by touch, lying, sitting, or by an overhang. Layers of impurity could be removed by ablutions.

The brief explanation of Jewish washings clarifies the seriousness of the charges.[6] The statement "the Pharisees and *all* the Jews" implies that to be Jew-

---

2. A similar complaint about Jesus' own failure to wash hands is raised when he eats in the home of a Pharisee (Luke 11:37).

3. The feelings about this issue could be strong. As one rabbi expressed it according to a later tradition in *b. Sota* 4b, "Whoever eats bread without previously washing the hands is as though he had intercourse with a harlot.'"

4. Later rabbinic tradition insisted that it did have a biblical basis. According to *b. Ber.* 60b, "When he washes his hands he should say, 'Blessed is He who has sanctified us with his commandments and commanded us concerning the washing of hands.'"

5. The explanation, "the Pharisees and all the Jews . . . ," drops a hint about the implied audience of the Gospel. Referring to them as "all the Jews" suggests that Mark envisions a Gentile audience only vaguely familiar with Jewish traditions. One does not explain for Jews what every Jew does.

6. Rabbinic traditions, codified in the *Mishnah* in the second and third centuries and expanded in the Palestinian and Babylonian Talmuds in the fourth and fifth centuries, cover regulations concerning valid and invalid ways of washing the hands, the quantity of water, the position of the hands, and the type of vessel to be used.

The explanation in 7:3 that the Pharisees and all the Jews do not eat unless they wash, literally, "with a fist" (*pugme*) is a difficult phrase. Its obscurity caused some texts to omit it, and some modern translations (such as the NIV) leave it untranslated. A number of textual variants arose in apparent attempts to interpret its meaning: "often," "thoroughly, " "in a moment," "first." Some interpreters understand it to refer to the manner of washing, "to the wrist," "with a fist" (rubbing the fist into the other hand), or with "a cupped hand" (in a fist-

ish, one washes hands, cups, and vessels. If Jesus undermines this tradition, he is redefining what being a Jew means. Moreover, the disregard of purity is serious because it was assumed that uncleanness belongs to the realm of death and demons and breaks fellowship with God.[7] To disregard such concerns means that Jesus redefines what it is that inhibits fellowship with God.

Jesus does not try to justify or explain his disciples' behavior but vilifies his challengers instead. He scornfully pronounces that Isaiah beautifully prophesied concerning them that they are nothing but hypocrites, who cleverly swap their own words for God's commands. Hand washing from the Pharisees' perspective was a sign of piety that allowed one to come close to God. Jesus insists, however, that they have drifted away from God, who cares nothing about their ablutions or their lip service. He will explain privately to his disciples that God cares only about morality, which comes from a pure heart.

The charge of hypocrisy causes surprise.[8] The Pharisees have asked about a matter of pressing concern to them, and nothing seems inherently hypocritical about giving thoughtful attention to matters of purity and the traditions of the elders. But they have challenged Jesus in public and thereby have sought to shame him as an incompetent teacher. If his disciples have violated purity rules, then he must be held responsible as their teacher. The situation would be similar to guests from denominational headquarters interrupting a worship service and asking the pastor, "Why does your congregation not close their eyes and bow their heads and refrain from talking during the prayers? Is it because you are so poorly trained and have not taught them?" Understanding that the Pharisees are trying to shame him publicly in a culture where a good reputation is the highest authority helps us see that Jesus does not simply evade the issue but regains command of the situation. He exposes their rigid and superficial religiosity as something that permits one to transgress the direct commands of God.

---

like fashion with fingers held slightly apart). Others interpret is as referring to the amount of water as well as the means: "with a handful (or fistful) of water." The later rabbinic traditions that define the valid amount of water (*m. Yad.* 1:1–2, 2:3; *b. Hull.* 106ab) and the method of pouring (*m. Yad.* 2:1; *b. Sabb.* 62b) would suggest that this word refers both to the amount of water and the means of washing.

7. The issue is clearly expressed by Barnabas Lindars ("All Foods Clean: Thoughts on Jesus and the Law," *Law and Religion*, ed. B. Lindars [Cambridge: James Clarke & Co., 1988], 65): "Transgression of the taboo not only constitutes a formal disqualification for worship, requiring the proper procedure to restore the situation, but also stains the inner conscience, creating a barrier in personal relationship with God."

8. Similar charges went against the Pharisees in the Dead Sea Scrolls. The hymnist excoriates the teachers of lies and seers of falsehood, who have exchanged the law for smooth things (1QH 4:14–15).

Jesus' counterattack cites an extreme example to show how the tradition of the elders sanctions the subversion of God's will. God commands children to honor their parents, and in Jewish tradition that entails more than showing them respect. It also requires providing them with physical necessities.[9] In the case example, the Pharisees would allow a son to duck that responsibility by informing his parents that what support they might expect from him is "Corban," dedicated to God, and therefore it cannot be touched to help them.

"Corban" was a dedicatory formula used in setting aside property for God and barred one from gaining profit from it. It only expressed an intention to give property and not its actual disposal. From Jesus' point of view, the command from the Decalogue to honor parents soars above the command to honor vows. The Pharisees' tradition turned the law on its head by insisting that the sanctity of the vow superseded the parents' right to support.[10] The son can say to his parents that he cannot offer them any help because he has dedicated to God everything that could help them. He could claim that doing so would be a sin against God.

Jesus assumes that such a vow, whether made spitefully or not, is automatically invalid because it violates God's command to honor parents. One cannot elude God's commands by resorting to shrewd legal loopholes. Jesus exposes these sticklers for the law as more interested in legal niceties than the requirement of love, more devoted to unwritten traditions than the written law, and more concerned with property than care of one's parents. Because they set aside God's will with their tradition (7:8, 13), Jesus annuls their tradition. In this controversy Jesus comes out as the champion of God's law over scribal law.

A Public and Private Explanation of Purity (7:14–23)

JESUS GIVES THE Pharisees no answer to their question about why his disciples eat with unclean hands. The explanation comes only in a general announcement to the crowds (7:14–15) and in private instruction in the house for the perplexed disciples, who request it.

The general announcement goes beyond the issue raised by the Pharisees, for they did not ask about unclean foods, only about unclean hands!

---

9. *b. Qidd.* 31b.

10. From the time the vow is made, the property is set aside as sacred. See the explanation in Josephus *Ant.* 4.4.4 §§ 72–73; *Ag. Ap.* 1.166–167. It is assumed that the Pharisees would defend the position that fulfilling the vow, no matter how rash or unworthy, was a greater obligation than fulfilling the duty to parents. To the credit of the later rabbis, they allowed for leniency in annulling such a vow (see *m. Ned.* 8:1–9:1). But Z. W. Falk (in "On Talmudic Vows," *HTR* 59 [1966]: 311) noted: "While Jesus considered the vow to be illegal and void, the Rabbis held it to be merely voidable."

One can only infer from Jesus' vigorous response that he rejects the Pharisees' opinion that unclean hands defile food. He now goes much further by explicitly rejecting the proposition that contact with anything profane defiles a person. Not only does he challenge the validity of the traditions of the elders but the very legitimacy of the food laws.[11] Jesus does not differ with the Pharisees only over details such as washing hands; he rejects their whole approach to God's law. They are concerned about surface impurity and piety; Jesus is concerned about internal impurity that one cannot wash away by washing the hands. They do not understand that true holiness that imitates God and opens one up to God is something internal.

Jesus' straightforward announcement to the crowds puzzles the disciples, and they ask him about "the parable" when they enter the privacy of the house (7:17). This word recalls Jesus' remark in 4:11 that everything comes "in parables" to those outside. Are the disciples moving closer to the outsiders? Jesus expresses his dismay when he responds: "Are you so dull?" His response takes for granted that the crowd has not grasped the implication of his pronouncement but assumes the disciples possess some token of knowledge. "Don't you see that nothing that enters a man from the outside can make him 'unclean'?" This question expects the answer "Yes." They do know something, but they cannot carry this knowledge through to its logical conclusion, which requires a radical change in their whole outlook as Jews.

Jesus does not disown his dense disciples but follows his pattern of providing them with a further explanation when they do not understand. He illustrates his point by reminding them of what happens to food when it is consumed. It passes through the digestive tract and winds up in the latrine.

Many take 7:19b as the narrator's aside that crowns the argument. The NIV reflects this interpretation: "In saying this, Jesus declared all foods 'clean.'" The phrase "In saying this, Jesus declared," however, is not to be found in the text. Literally the words used here translate, "cleansing all foods." The masculine nominative participle, "cleansing" (*katharizon*, with an omega), would modify the verb "he says" in 7:18. A well-attested variant reading, however, has a nominative neuter participle (*katharizon*, with an omicron).[12] It is the hardest reading and may be the best.[13] It would affirm that the food has somehow become clean in the process of its elimination. This reading

---

11. See Lev. 11; Deut. 14:3–20.

12. The distinction in the pronunciation of the long o and short o has disappeared in modern Greek, and it is likely that the two words would have been pronounced the same when texts of the Bible were being copied. Scribes could have easily made an accidental mistake if they were copying texts as someone read aloud from the master copy.

13. So Bruce J. Malina, "A Conflict Approach to Mark 7," *Forum* 4 (1988): 22–24.

has two things to commend it. It would help explain why such a dramatic pronouncement from Jesus that declared all foods to be clean was not cited to settle the later debate over this issue in the churches.[14] Jesus' explanation does not explicitly declare that all foods are clean, only that they somehow come out clean.

Furthermore, the statement fits the rabbinic perspective on defecated food. According to the *Mishnah*, excrement is not ritually impure though it may be offensive.[15] This surprising judgment may be the key to Jesus' argument. With a droll twist Jesus argues that if food defiles a person, why is it not regarded as impure when it winds up in the latrine—at least according to the tradition of the Pharisees? Defilement must come from some other source than food. Jesus' logic derives from the Pharisees' own rules regarding clean and unclean, which sets up his concluding words on the real source of defilement. The only defilement that the disciples need worry about has to do with the heart, not the hands, with evil thoughts that leak out from within a person, not food that ends up in the latrine. What does not enter the heart does not make a person unclean. The heart is the core of motivation, deliberation, and intention. How one handles food, therefore, does not make the heart clean or unclean. It has nothing to do with the internal purity (what is "inside," 7:21, 23) that matters to God.

The list of vices that come from the heart deals with behavior that harms others. After the general "evil thoughts," the list in Greek contains six nouns in the plural that refer to acts and six nouns in the singular that refer to characteristics. The first six divide into three parallel actions:

fornications	adulteries
thefts	covetings
murders	malicious acts

---

14. An appeal to Jesus' authoritative word would have been a knock-down argument in Acts 15; Gal. 2:11–14; and Rom. 14–15. Heikki Räisänen, "Jesus and the Food Laws: Reflections on Mark 7:15," *JSNT* 16 (1982): 79–100, argues from the absence of the "effective history" of Jesus' remarks on food that he never uttered them. He claims that these words were added to the tradition to provide "a theological justification for the practical step taken in the Gentile mission long before" (89). This supposed silence, however, may have been attributable to the ambiguity and arcane nature of Jesus' argument.

15. *m. Maksh.* 6:7; *t. Miqw.* 7:8. R. Jose is said to ask: "Is excrement impure? Is it not for purposes of cleanliness?" (*y. Pesah.* 7:11). Even the excrement of the *zab* (a person suffering a flux) is not impure according to *Sifra Mes. Zab.* § 1:12–13. By contrast the Qumran sectarians, under the influence of Deut. 23:12–14 and Ezek. 4:12–15, considered it to be impure (see Josephus, *J. W.* 2.8.9 §§ 148–49; 1QM 7:3–7; 11QT 46:15–16). See further the discussion in Hannah K. Harrington, *The Impurity Systems of Qumran and the Rabbis: Biblical Foundations* (SBLDS 143; Atlanta: Scholars, 1993), 100–103.

The second six—deceit (treachery), licentiousness, evil eye (stinginess), slandering (blasphemy), insolence, foolishness (moral senselessness)—reflect the kind of spiritual defilement that is the most difficult to detect and to remedy. One needs more than a little water poured over cupped hands to cleanse this impurity.[16]

EVERY COMMUNITY HAS to apply the word of God to situations in real life, and traditions inevitably develop from this undertaking. One should note that Jesus does not reject tradition as such. Societies need traditions to function. Stern points out a significant fact:

> A state cannot be run by a constitution without legislation. Likewise the Jewish nation could not be run by the Written *Torah* alone, without the orderly application of it and in addition to it implied the concept of tradition. But just as a country's legislation cannot contradict or supplant its constitution, so too tradition . . . cannot violate or alter God's word.[17]

Jesus recognized that we need wineskins—forms and traditions—to hold the wine; otherwise, we will be standing in a puddle of juice. He warned only about wineskins that become old and brittle and no longer serve their intended purpose. Traditions become evil when they run counter to God's purposes expressed in the ethical commands of how to relate to others. Traditions become dangerous when persons are blind to how they undermine God's commands. Traditions become corrupt when people become more devoted to upholding them than obeying God's direct commands. As Pelikan astutely puts it: "Tradition is the living faith of the dead, traditionalism is the dead faith of the living."[18] One may compare tradition to the shell of the blue crab. To live and grow it must shed its shell from time to time. Until it creates a new shell, the crab is extremely vulnerable. But if the shell becomes so strong and rigid that the crab cannot escape, that is the shell in which it dies. Losing traditions that make one feel safe and comfortable can cause great anxiety. But hanging on to traditions so that one becomes "hard-shelled" is fatal.

---

16. Lane (*Mark*, 254, n. 40) cites Jer. 17:9–10: "The heart is deceitful above all things and beyond cure. Who can understand it? 'I the LORD search the heart and examine the mind, to reward a man according to his conduct, according to what his deeds deserve.'"

17. David H. Stern, *Jewish New Testament Commentary* (Clarksville, Md.: Jewish New Testament Publications, 1992), 92.

18. Jaroslav Pelikan, *The Vindication of Tradition* (New Haven: Yale Univ. Press, 1984), 65.

With our 20/20 spiritual hindsight we can readily see how the Pharisees' tradition thwarted God's will and strangled faith. We quickly dismiss their traditions about purity of hands, pots, and pans as a silly fixation on matters of no consequence. To bridge the context to our own situation, however, we must understand the honest concerns behind these traditions. We should not disdain their issues before asking why they were important to them so that we can relate it to our own religiosity. We will thus first look at the custom of washing hands, which precipitated the controversy, and then analyze the purposes behind the tradition of the elders. We can then see how they resemble our traditions so that we can spot parallel dangers.

Legislation in Exodus 30:19—21 (see 40:12) required only priests engaged in the tabernacle service to wash their hands. The law also required the priests to regard as holy the portion of the sacrifices that they were allowed to eat. They and everyone in their household could share in this food only when ceremonially clean (Num. 18:8—13). The Pharisees' tradition extended these laws to everyone in the land, not just to priests serving in the temple, and to all food, not just to holy offerings. The Pharisees were striving for holiness above and beyond what the law prescribed. In a variation of the aphorism that a man's home is his castle, the Pharisees believed that a man's home was his temple.[19] This statement is an exaggeration, but it conveys how important purity issues were to them. God demanded for the people to "be holy because I ... am holy" (Lev. 19:2). To the Pharisees, holiness was not restricted to the sacred temple area but extended to the entire land in descending degrees from the temple (see *m. Kelim* 1:6—9).[20]

---

19. Stern, *Jewish New Testament Commentary*, 92.

20. Recent discussion of the Pharisees has centered around the debate between Jacob Neusner and E. P. Sanders, two influential scholars on Judaism. Neusner argues that the Pharisees insisted that food should be treated as though offered in the temple (in *From Politics to Piety: The Emergence of Pharisaic Judaism* [Englewood Cliffs, 1973]). Sanders counters his definition of the Pharisees as a "pure-food club." He contends that "they did not for one moment believe that their own food was kept as pure as priests' *in* the temple, and not even as pure as the food eaten by priests and their families outside the temple (heave offering)" (in *Judaism: Practice & Belief 63 BCE—66 CE* [Philadelphia: Trinity Press International, 1992], 437). He contends that they only made "minor gestures that partially imitated priestly purity" (438; see further his *Jewish Law From Jesus to the Mishnah: Five Studies* [Philadelphia: Trinity Press International, 1990], 184—236). Martin Hengel and Roland Deines (in "E. P. Sanders' 'Common Judaism,' Jesus, and the Pharisees," *JTS* 46 [1995]: 1—70) offer a middle way. They agree that "the Pharisees did not want to 'imitate' the various states of purity required of cultic personnel inside or outside the temple in the sense of being put on the *same level* with the priests." Nevertheless, they argue: " ... since the basic *obligation to be holy* applied to the *entire people*, the Pharisees wanted to deduce what was involved from scripture and tradition, and then live this out as an example for the rest" (47). See also the critique of Sanders by Bruce Chilton, *Feast of Meanings: Eucharistic Theologies From Jesus Through Johannine Circles* (NovTSup 72; Leiden: Brill, 1994), 159—68.

The Pharisees identified the washing of hands as belonging to "the tradition of the elders" (Mark 7:5; see Gal. 1:14), but Jesus labels it pejoratively as "the traditions of men" (7:8). The Pharisees and their spiritual heirs, however, believed that their tradition had been delivered to Moses by God (*m. 'Abot* 1:1–2). This tradition consisted of unwritten law that tried to fill the gaps and silences in the purity laws in Leviticus and Numbers. Because they based their decisions on the logical analysis of the explicit and implicit data in Scripture, the Pharisees considered them rooted in Scripture and equal in authority.

We can identify three purposes behind the development of this tradition that have affinities with the development of traditions in Christian circles. (1) The tradition of the elders tried to make the basic requirement that Israel be holy to the Lord (Lev. 19:2) something that was attainable in everyday life. The Pharisees were quite liberal in reducing the biblical requirement of bathing the whole body (Lev. 15; 16:26, 28; 17:15–16; 22:1–7) to the simple act of washing hands. They did not attempt to skirt the demands of the law. These pious interpreters had a genuine desire to provide precise guidance for laypeople on what one must do to be holy. They did not think they were voiding the commands of God but making them applicable. The tradition was designed to give laypeople a map that charted what was permissible or proscribed, clean or unclean, so that they could live the life of godliness.

(2) The tradition of the elders was intended to deter pagan influences that surrounded the nation from making inroads into Judaism (see Lev. 20:1–7). This attitude is expressed in the *Letter of Aristeas* 139, which exults in the law that "surrounds us with unbroken palisades and iron walls, to prevent our mixing with any of the other peoples in any matter being thus kept pure in body and soul, preserved from false beliefs, and worshiping the only God omnipotent over all creation." It encouraged people to make a conscious effort to set themselves apart from the unwashed hordes who were destined for destruction. Actions such as immersion and washing hands were tangible, positive gestures that displayed who God's elect were who would be vindicated at the end of the age.

The Pharisees acted like Daniels by trying to preserve and proclaim their distinctive holiness, not like Mordecais, who counseled Esther to keep her national identity a secret (Est. 2:10, 20). The concern for ritual cleanliness was motivated by a desire to insulate Israel from the onslaught of Hellenism (the secular humanism of the day). Harrington writes: "The purity laws were emphasized because they plainly distinguished Israel from non-Israel and defined Israel as physical and dependent on history and genealogy not on a universal, spiritual idea."[21] The laws created the illusion of an ordered cosmos,

---

21. Harrington, *Impurity Systems*, 164.

with carefully erected boundaries that kept every person and thing in its proper place. All these distinctions became important for conserving the distinctive nature of Judaism and to prevent it from being mongrelized.[22] By making such things critical, they could reinforce group identity and increase devotion to the law.

(3) The tradition assumes that God ordered the details, and one must study and enact them to meet God. The later oral law specifies, for example, not only how to wash your hands, but where to lay your napkin during the meal so as not to defile it, when to say the prayers, when and how to sweep up. These may seem like trifling things to concern a religion. But Neusner counters that the claims of the law were important precisely because they could be extended to the humble things that one can actually control in life. If one were to ask, "How do I approach almighty God?" the psalmist says, with "clean hands and a pure heart" (Ps. 24:4). But what precisely is a person supposed to do? The rabbis would say that when one eats, one approaches the throne of the almighty God, and one must wash one's hands and hold the wine in the right hand and the oil in the left. That is something that one can do! "And in doing it," Neusner says, "one shall know that there are rules for guidance, and these rules stand for reverence and awe, for mindfulness and thoughtfulness, in God's presence."[23]

This tradition gives everyday acts of life holy significance and reminds one of God and how one can concretely show one's devotion to God. The Pharisees affirmed that God created order and that human affairs prosper only when things are ordered. Consequently, they preferred strict rules, orderly programs, and careful debates about the application of texts, lest they lose control. From their perspective Jesus was completely out of control because he disregarded their rules and crossed their boundaries.

What are the Christian affinities with the Pharisees' traditions of the elders? (1) Christian communities also have an oral tradition that fills the gaps and directs them on what precisely they should and should not do. For example, someone may ask, Should we tithe gross income or net income? Do we need to tithe the produce from the garden? Should a church accept a tithe from lottery winnings? The answers to these questions usually do not come from explicit passages in the Scripture but from a tradition that tries to honor God's requirements and make things definite so that we know what we are to do and when we have done it. But we court danger when we treat decisions on such matters as sacrosanct and apply them rigidly.

---

22. See Jub. 22:16: "Separate yourselves from the nations . . ."; and Acts 10:28, "You are well aware that it is against our law for a Jew to associate with a Gentile or visit him."

23. Jacob Neusner, *Invitation to the Talmud* (San Francisco: Harper & Row, 1984), 81.

(2) Christian communities will also stress one thing or another to reinforce their identity over against others. Sometimes the stress will be on a particular practice; sometimes, a distinctive doctrine. In holding to this tradition, they want to make clear that they are this kind of people and not like "them" (whoever "them" may be). The danger lurks that we may turn our distinctiveness and purity into an idol that supersedes the word of God. Many years ago a professor who taught at my seminary was challenged on his teaching concerning a particular belief. He overwhelmed his critic with passage after passage from the Scripture to support his point. The critic refused to yield, however. In frustration the critic exclaimed, "That may be Bible, but it's not Baptist!"

Maintaining our heritage can be valuable as we seek to be faithful to our vision of the truth. Insisting on doctrinal purity to fend off corruption from outside is not ignoble. Yet we must guard against the pitfall of the Pharisees, who drew the circle so narrowly that they excluded 99 percent of the human race. Christian communities may erect barriers so high and so thick to preserve their theological virtue that they cannot reach others. The outward signs of obedience in Jesus' day—keeping the Sabbath, observing food laws and circumcision, washing hands—became the badges that marked out the elect as those who are "in." These same badges were used to bar others from the circle of God's grace and acceptance.

Mark shows Jesus' whole ministry challenging the categorization of persons and things into pure and impure. The law of clean and unclean establishes boundaries, and the Pharisees set themselves up as the border guards. Keep lepers, sinners, and those with a flux out; follow Sabbath rules and wash hands before eating clean food. They defended a certain kind of community and order. Jesus overstepped the boundaries by attacking their purity regulations and by claiming that true uncleanness is a moral, not a ritual, deficiency. One need not protect holiness with a fence of rules. On the contrary, God's holiness bursts all bounds. It does not suffer contamination but transforms everything it touches. As Augustine said, "Light, even though it passes through pollution, is not polluted." Jesus displays this power when he touches a leper, is touched by a woman with a flow of blood, and touches a corpse. He is not made unclean but instead cleanses and restores to life. Jesus' conflict with the Pharisees reveals that religious observance should not clash with common sense and common decency.

(3) Christian traditions also have parallels with the elders' concern for details. Things are to be done in a certain way. All sorts of disputes have broken out in church history and local churches over what are perceived to be violations of those ways. Baptism is to be done in a certain way. Celebration of the Eucharist is to follow certain patterns. We must guard against

the danger that we become so focused on the details that we develop tunnel vision and miss the grand design. We can easily become enmeshed in technicalities and in minutia while ignoring the weightier commands of the law—the broad and inexhaustible principles, such as the exercise of justice, mercy, and faith (Matt. 23:23–28).

For years preachers have ridiculed the petty concerns of pharisaic tradition without bothering to understand what evoked them. Many do not realize that their own traditions will be just as easily ridiculed by those who may live centuries later in a different culture. In bridging the contexts we should reflect on our own pious concerns that may contravene God's will expressed in the love for parents and neighbor. Such reflection poses hazards. One who questions sacred cows will usually meet with the same fate as Jesus.

The purity system of the Pharisees was based on the assumption that God lives in the temple and that the biblical laws provided guidelines for how the priests were to approach the holy God and perform their duties. Their application of these laws to life in general made it possible even for those who were not priests to have access to God outside the sacred temple precincts. Obeying their requirements was not easy but was possible. But Jesus made God accessible to everyone, even those who did not practice pharisaic purity. One did not have to be a priest or pretend to be a priest. Being inside the temple has nothing to do with access to God. What matters is what comes from inside of you.

IN INTERPRETING THIS passage we should be careful not to belittle first-century Judaism as a dead letter, awash in legalism, when our own Christianity can be just as dead and just as legalistic.[24] Christians also add traditions to the essentials of the faith, apply them legalistically, and treat them as if they have been ordained forever by God. They feel no less troubled or angry than the Pharisees did in Jesus' day when anyone challenges or undermines them. We will look at the contemporary significance of the concern for purity, the problem of establishing boundaries, and the danger of hypocrisy.

(1) Most Christians today do not believe that food is subject to religious defilement. Many eat pork sausage and cheeseburgers (a forbidden mixture of meat and dairy foods) without any moral qualms and may only worry about high cholesterol, chemical additives, and the destruction of rain forests

---

24. We should recognize that what we derisively call legalism today was to the Pharisee a sincere effort to apply God's will to everyday life. All law requires interpretation.

to raise cattle to stock fast-food restaurants. Yet the issue of impurity, so vital to the Pharisees, is not irrelevant to contemporary life. Purity has to do with the way one orders and classifies persons, things, and times. Purity regulations label persons, objects, and places as pure or polluted, fit or unfit, as susceptible to impurity or as a cause of impurity.[25]

While many today may not think that they worry about such notions, the basic idea behind purity laws is one with which everyone is familiar: "A place for everything and everything in its place."[26] We judge something "impure" when it seems out of place. Impurity arises when "the wrong *thing* appears in the wrong *place* at the wrong *time*."[27] For example, many enjoy firecrackers exploding on the Fourth of July. These same people, however, would regard setting off firecrackers during the Lord's Supper as reprehensible. We therefore have clear ideas about what is pure and impure, whether we are fully conscious of them or not. The universal aversion to dirt, disease, and death governs these concerns. What one regards as "dirt" can take many forms. The danger lurks that one can develop a defensive religious posture, as the Pharisees of Jesus' day did, and become all-consumed in keeping out the dirt.

Many engage in heated religious arguments over what they regard to be life and death issues that to the outside world and to the average Christian are much ado about nothing. The root issue has to do with what one considers proper or pure (which becomes one's sacred tradition) and improper or impure. Jonathan Swift satirized this pettiness in the Lilliputians' war over whether an egg should be cracked at the big end or at the little end.[28] Garrison Keillor does the same when he describes his religious heritage. He says in his *Lake Wobegon Days* that he came from an "exclusive" group that believed in keeping itself pure of false doctrine by avoiding association with the impure: "We made sure that any who fellowshipped with us were straight on all the details of the Faith." Unfortunately, he writes, the firebrand founders "turned their guns on each other."

> 'Scholarly to the core and perfect literalists every one, they set to arguing over points that, to any outsider, would have seemed very minor indeed but which to them were crucial to the Faith, including the question: if Believer A is associated with Believer B who has somehow associated himself with C who holds a False Doctrine, must D break off association with A, even though A does not hold the Doctrine, to avoid the taint?

---

25. Jerome H. Neyrey, "The Idea of Purity in Mark's Gospel," *Semeia* 35 (1986): 92.
26. Ibid., 93.
27. Ibid., 92.
28. Cited by Luccock, "The Gospel According to St. Mark: Exposition," 7:750.

The correct answer is: Yes. Some . . ., however, felt that D should only speak with A and urge him to breakoff with B. The [ones] who felt otherwise promptly broke off with them.[29]

Many may recognize this caricature in their own religious traditions. It results in a church devoted to turning Christianity into an unassailable fortress by building impregnable walls to keep the pure in and the impure out. The concern for purity directly affects evangelism. This closed system, more often than not, shuts one off from fellow human beings and from real fellowship with God. Roy Pearson comments that God meant for the church to get mixed up in messes and with people who have messed up their lives.

> It is a fact too long neglected that the church has in common with the chimney sweep that it cannot do its job in comfortable surroundings or with clean hands. In this sense, cleanliness is not next to godliness: dirt is. Dirt, pain, sorrow, prejudice, injustice, and treachery.[30]

Jesus is like those who want to run the church for those who do not yet attend. How do we include them into the family rather than exclude them? His teaching had a direct impact on Christian missionary practice when Paul advised the Corinthians to eat whatever was set before them (1 Cor. 10:27) and told the Romans "that no food is unclean in itself" (Rom. 14:14). Quit judging others (14:4, 10, 13). Quit putting stumbling blocks in their way (14:13). Learn to live in harmony (15:5) and build up one another (14:19) rather than walls of separation. We can imagine how we would respond if guests turn up their noses at the food we offered them because it somehow did not meet their religious standards. What if their rejection of our food also implied that we were somehow impure, somehow untouchable? It would hardly dispose us to hear their message. In applying this passage, we should ask ourselves, "Are there subtle and not so subtle ways in which we communicate to others that they are 'dirty' and unfit for contact with us? How does it hinder our ability to evangelize them?"

The issues at stake in this passage also have to do with question of religious identity. It raises the question: What is appropriate to mark us off as the people of God from others who are not, and what is inappropriate? A danger lurks in drawing no boundaries at all so that we have no identity over against pagan culture. Purity concerns are boundary markers. One can see from Jesus' reproach of the Pharisees' tradition, however, that boundaries drawn too tightly choke out love. Worldliness excludes God from our lives,

---

29. Garrison Keillor, *Lake Wobegon Days* (New York: Viking, 1985), 105.

30. Roy Pearson, "The Unangelic Mission of the Church," *Congregations* 21 (July/August 1995): 25.

but we must be careful not to exclude the worldly from the love of God. One writer confesses:

> God does not always respect the boundaries we create and carefully protect. Drawing lines in the theological sand may serve our purposes; separating good guys from bad guys and can be helpful, because it is hard to know that you're on the inside unless you know who is on the outside. But God has a studied disregard for anxieties of this sort. Prodigal grace keeps spilling over into alien territory.[31]

Jesus continues to cross boundaries in the very next episode in Mark, where he extends grace to a pagan, Syrophoenician woman.

The Pharisees believed that others would know they were God's people by their purity: washing hands, cups, pots, eating kosher, keeping the Sabbath. Paul understood the tenor of Jesus' teaching when he asserted: "For the kingdom of God is not a matter of eating and drinking, but of righteousness, peace and joy in the Holy Spirit" (Rom. 14:17). Christians today sing, "They will know we are Christians by our love." Christians do not always live that way, but the inner purity of heart that radiates love and morality should make them stand out amid a wicked and perverse generation.

Jesus accused the Pharisees of being hypocrites in this passage. The Pharisees did not corner the market on hypocrisy, and hypocrites continue to plague the church. Jesus was not against the overt act of doing God's will, but he refused to cotton to any attempt to reckon something as moral and pleasing to God that was not a true expression of character—either make the tree good and the fruit good, or make the tree bad and the fruit bad (Matt. 12:33).

The most infamous hypocrites are those who try to cloak the evil within them with a show of external piety. Judas best fits that category of hypocrite in the Gospel. He comes to Gethsemane with a show of affection and honor, but it is all a sordid ploy to capture his Master. Other hypocrites deceive themselves as much as others. The scrupulous Pharisees best fit this category. When Jesus calls them hypocrites, he reveals how easily sincerity and a desire to do precisely what God commands can go astray and ignore what God requires. The Pharisees' lip service and religious gestures fool others and themselves into thinking that they are pious.

It is so easy for religious people to obey all the regulations and believe all the correct doctrines in a perfunctory way, but their heart is not in it. They may also concentrate on executing religious actions that certify their external purity while totally neglecting issues of inner purity. Hypocrites may

---

31. Donald W. McCullough, "Serving a Wild Free God," *Christianity Today* 39 (Apr. 3, 1995): 17.

fool themselves that they have done all that God requires by doing this or that with the greatest of care. They play by the rules but allow them to run roughshod over others. How many times do Christians ignore the vices in the list and concentrate on minor pieties? They wind up with a religion that affects only the hands but that never touches the heart. The church needs reminding again that it can be correct in outward form and theology but not have the spirit of Christ. Goodness comes from inner purity, a life transformed within, rather than from the pure observance of rules and doctrine.

Mark 7:24–30

JESUS LEFT THAT place and went to the vicinity of Tyre. He entered a house and did not want anyone to know it; yet he could not keep his presence secret. ²⁵In fact, as soon as she heard about him, a woman whose little daughter was possessed by an evil spirit came and fell at his feet. ²⁶The woman was a Greek, born in Syrian Phoenicia. She begged Jesus to drive the demon out of her daughter.

²⁷"First let the children eat all they want," he told her, "for it is not right to take the children's bread and toss it to their dogs."

²⁸ "Yes, Lord," she replied, "but even the dogs under the table eat the children's crumbs."

²⁹Then he told her, "For such a reply, you may go; the demon has left your daughter."

³⁰She went home and found her child lying on the bed, and the demon gone.

<p>

Original Meaning

JESUS TRAVELS TO the regions of Tyre, which extended into upper Galilee, and seeks to sequester himself in a house. Mark does not tell us why he decides to venture into this area or why he wishes to remain incognito. Perhaps he wants to teach his disciples in private (see 9:30–31), but they do not appear in this scene. Perhaps he wants to retreat from irate opponents, or he simply wants to get away to rest (6:31). One thing is sure. Jesus' presence can never remain secret for long because his fame has preceded him everywhere, even into this predominantly Gentile region. Earlier, folks streamed to him from this area when he began his ministry in Galilee (3:8). Now when word leaks out that he is in the vicinity, a woman whose daughter is a victim of an unclean spirit immediately begins to hunt for him to ask his help. We see a token of her faith in seeking him out and her resourceful determination when she detects his whereabouts.

Mark describes the woman as a Greek and a Syrophoenician (7:26). This repetition is a two-step progression that Mark uses to get the reader to notice something. The first step expresses a generality, while the second gives more specific detail and usually contains a crucial element.[1] She is a Gentile pagan, which introduces a new wrinkle in the story. She hails from a city that the Old Testament deemed to be a wealthy and godless oppressor of Israel (see Isa. 23; Jer. 47:4; Ezek. 26–28; Joel 3:4; Amos 1:9; Zech. 9:2). Most Jews in the first century (John 18:28; Acts 10:28) shared without question the prejudice that Gentiles defiled by touch, just like a person with a flux. They regarded their uncleanness as something innate, not caused by the list of impurities in Leviticus 11–15.[2] Gentiles were impure simply because they were Gentiles. The humble request of this Gentile woman, therefore, creates dramatic tension. Will Jesus be as gracious to this lady from Tyre as he was to the unclean outcasts within Israel?

The resulting dialogue between Jesus and his Gentile petitioner offers many surprises. First, Jesus is not the affable fellow we imagine him always to be. He dismisses her appeal out of hand with a sharp insult: "First let the children eat all they want ... for it is not right to take the children's bread and to toss it to their dogs" (7:27).[3] The word "first" implies that Gentiles have some ray of hope, but for the time being this woman must wait patiently for her turn. Jesus asserts the same priority of Israel that Paul affirms: "first for the Jew, then for the Gentile" (Rom. 1:16; 2:9–10). Jesus comes as the Messiah of Israel, and she has no right as a Gentile to jump the queue to receive benefits from him.

The second surprise unfolds in the woman's unwillingness to be put off by this less-than-genial response to her request. She accepts Jesus' premise that the children are to be fed first before the dogs get anything. She reacts with a quick wit and expands on his parable: "Yes, Lord ... but even the dogs under the table eat the children's crumbs" (7:28). This clever woman catches the meaning of Jesus' riddle immediately, which comprises the third surprise. Most of Jesus' listeners in Mark's Gospel do not comprehend his riddles without some explanation. The riddle about what really pollutes a person, for example, zooms right by the disciples (7:14–18). By contrast, this woman recognizes, without any prompting, that "the children" in the parable represent Israel and "the dogs" represent the Gentiles. Israel understood itself to be the children of God.[4] Some expressed scorn for unclean, idolatrous Gen-

---

1. David Rhoads, "Jesus and the Syrophoenician Woman in Mark: A Narrative-Critical Study," *JAAR* 62 (1994): 352–53.

2. *t. Zab.* 2:1; *m. Pesah.* 8:8: "The school of Hillel says: One who separates from the circumcision is as one who separates from the grave." See *b. 'Abod. Zar.* 36b.

3. The verb "all they want" describes the results of the feeding of five thousand (6:42) and of the four thousand (8:8).

4. Deut. 32:6; Isa. 1:2; Jer. 31:9; Hos. 11:1; Rom. 9:4; Jub. 1:28; *m. 'Abot.* 3:15: "Beloved are Israel, for they were called children of God; still greater was the love in that it was

tiles by denigrating them as "dogs."[5] She understands and accepts the riddle's implications: Israel has precedence over Gentiles, and the time for Gentiles has not yet come.

But the implied insult does not embitter her. Instead, she becomes the first person in the narrative to engage Jesus in a constructive exchange about his mission. She does not selfishly worry that others have an advantage over her, and her cheerful acknowledgment of Israel's preeminence leads to the fourth surprise. She refuses to accept his dismissal and will not take no for an answer.

The mother may have taken heart that Jesus has alluded to the pet dogs scampering around the house, not to the mongrels prowling the streets. One cannot be sure. She clearly accepts the role of dog and comes begging for food. She disputes, however, the stress placed on "first" in the riddle. She logically reasons that the dogs' master does not snatch food from the children's mouths to throw them scraps. The "little crumbs" (a diminutive, matching "little dogs") fall from the table while the children messily eat their meal. The dogs under the table feed when the children drop a morsel or two. She is not asking for a catered, full-course meal, just a little crumb of Jesus' power for a little dog.

The woman's response reveals that she comprehends more about the bread that Jesus offers than even his disciples do. They have witnessed the feeding of the five thousand (6:31–44, 52) and will witness the feeding of four thousand (8:1–10) but still do not understand the bread that Jesus offers (8:14–21). This woman, who did not partake in either feeding, begs to receive only the bread crumbs falling from the diners' laps. She knows that she cannot insist on God's mercy and does not take offense when Jesus tells her so. She will gladly accept the rank of household dog if it means getting fed.

Jesus relents and grants her request: "For such a reply, you may go; the demon has left your daughter" (7:29). The little dog is now accepted as a little girl. Many commentators suggest that Jesus relents because of the woman's cleverness. But she has no interest in engaging in a game of wits while her child is in the grips of a demon. Like any parent, she desperately wants healing for her daughter and will go to any lengths to get it. Her witty comeback expresses sincere humility. She concedes the differences between children and dogs. She accepts Jewish priority—the bread rightly belongs to the children, Israel. She is willing to humble herself, to become as a dog, to save her little child with just a crumb.

---

made known to them that they were called children of God, as it is written: Ye are the children of the Lord your God [Deut. 14:1]."

5. *Pirqe R. El.* 29: "Whoever eats together with an idol worshiper is like one who eats together with a dog; as the dog is uncircumcised, so also is the idol worshiper uncircumcised."

This willingness to humble oneself is a key requirement for discipleship and something the disciples of Jesus have difficulty learning (9:35–37; 10:44). They have trouble receiving the kingdom as "little children" (10:15); she has no qualms about receiving the kingdom as a little dog. Like a dog, she will gobble down whatever is granted. The woman does not get a crumb, but precisely what she has begged from Jesus. When Jesus says that the demon has left her daughter, she does not insist that he go home with her to make doubly sure. She goes in faith as she came in faith. Mark concludes the scene by reporting that she goes home and finds the child lying in bed and the demon gone (7:30).

Chapter 7 opened with the Pharisees' rebuking Jesus' disciples for eating with unwashed hands—these seemingly impious disciples were too unclean to eat at a Pharisee's table. It concludes with bread crumbs now being offered to dogs, who are at the bottom rung of the ladder when it comes to clean/unclean. The reader should grasp the implication that God will heal Gentiles, no matter how unclean or how far away from God they may seem. Others might dismiss someone as the wrong race, nationality, or social class, or as from the wrong religious background, but none of these things prevents one from receiving God's merciful healing. Those who exercise humble faith will receive bread.

Bridging Contexts

JESUS' GRUFF REACTION to this desperate mother has confounded readers for many years. Why does he seem so to be so surly when she pleads for her demonized daughter? She comes asking, seeking, and knocking. Why does he speak about throwing bread to dogs? She does not ask about bread; she asks for help for her little child. How can Jesus compare a sick child to a dog? He seems to say that the only legitimate diners are members of the people of Israel. Others, no matter how deserving or needy, can expect nothing from him. He will not give what is holy to dogs (Matt. 7:6).

The scene upsets our sense of justice. We also cannot understand why Jesus does not respond more sensitively to this Gentile's cry for help. She cannot help that she was born a Gentile, lives in the region of Tyre, and is culturally Greek. We do not mind Jesus being rude to Pharisees and Sadducees, whom we believe deserve it, but it is not like him to be rude to a forlorn mother. He seems to be acting much like the Cynic philosophers, who were distinguished by their impudent style. Consequently, those abashed by Jesus' harsh response have offered many explanations to sugarcoat his use of the epithet "dogs."

Some contend that Jesus spoke in a gentle tone of voice. McNeile comments, "But if the words were audible to her, we may be sure that a half-humorous tenderness of manner would deprive them of their sting."[6] France writes: "Written words cannot convey a twinkle in the eye, and it may be that Jesus was jocularly presenting her with the sort of language she might expect from a Jew in order to see how she would react."[7] Others argue that the use of the diminutive form of the word "dog" takes the bite out of what he says. These are the pets of children that frisk around the table, not the feral packs that prowl the outskirts of towns (Luke 16:21). But a dog is a dog, whether it is a pampered household pet or a street cur. Most would not understand the epithet as a term of endearment whether Jesus spoke kindly or not.

Others have speculated that this incident reflects Jesus' own struggle with the scope of his mission, which he believed was limited to Israel. The Gentiles would be brought into the fold only when God's purposes with Israel were consummated (see Isa. 19:19–25; 66:19–20; Mic. 4:1–2; Zech. 8:20–22). Some assume that Jesus is wrestling here with the question, What is God's will in this situation? Should he be diverted from his single-minded attention to his mission to Israel? Taylor imagines that there is "a tension in the mind of Jesus concerning the scope of His ministry, and . . . in a sense He is speaking to Himself as well as to the woman. Her reply shows that she is quick to perceive this."[8] The woman's answer supposedly allays his doubts and opens his eyes to a wider extension of his mission to include Gentiles. Presumably, Mark includes this story so that the original readers, who may share these same doubts about Gentiles, will reach the same conclusion. The problem with this interpretation, which tries to read the mind of Jesus, is that it has no basis in the text. Jesus has previously crossed the border into Gentile lands in Gerasa and apparently had no trepidation about reaching out to Gentiles. He did not reject them; they rejected him and asked him to leave the region (5:1–20).

Another interpretation contends that Jesus temporarily withholds his help to test the woman's faith. He does not tell her outright that fulfilling her request is completely out of the question. Cranfield cites Calvin's comments on the passage. Jesus wanted "to whet her zeal and inflame her ardour." She intuits "that the door is shut against her, not for the purpose of excluding her altogether, but that, by a more strenuous effort of faith, she may force her way, as it were, through the chinks."[9] If this were a test of faith, Jesus does

6. Alan Hugh McNeile, *The Gospel According to Matthew* (London: Macmillan, 1915), 231.

7. Richard T. France, *Matthew* (TNTC; Grand Rapids: Eerdmans, 1985), 247.

8. Taylor, *Mark*, 350; see also Cranfield, *Mark*, 247.

9. Cranfield, *Mark*, 248–49.

not commend her for passing the test. One can assume she acts from faith; but unlike the healing of the hemorrhaging woman (5:34), Mark does not specifically mention it.[10] What would have happened had she failed the test? What if she had weak faith, like the father of the epileptic (9:24)? Why did Jesus not encourage her faith as he did with the leader of the synagogue (5:36)? This interpretation summons as many questions as solutions.

Others try to exonerate Jesus from any breach of courtesy by maintaining that the story is entirely the invention of the church, which was then read back into the life of Jesus. They claim that the church's struggle over the mission to Gentiles stamps this incident, and the hostility toward Gentiles reflects the attitude of the discredited right-wing segment of the church.[11] Without doubt, the abandonment of legalistic distinctions of clean and unclean opened the door to the Gentile mission, and this story has implications for the inclusion of Gentiles. But to dismiss what is troublesome to us as a vestige of the early church's primitive understanding is a cavalier reading of the text.

Nevertheless, we can draw insight from this view when we place this text alongside those that reflect the tension in the early church over the acceptance of Gentiles (see Acts 10:1–11:18). This incident occurs after Jesus has fed five thousand Jews in the Jewish desert and after the controversy with the Pharisees over eating food with defiled hands and his explanation that only what comes from within a person pollutes.[12] The Pharisees' concern about clean and unclean is bogus. He then retreats to Gentile territory, where this Gentile woman locates him. After this encounter, Jesus next ventures into Gentile territory in the Decapolis, where he heals a deaf and tongue-tied man and feeds four thousand in a Gentile desert. As Rhoads recognizes, "This episode is fundamentally about crossing boundaries."[13] It challenges the reader "not to set limits on the universality of the good news of the kingdom of God."[14] The power of the kingdom cannot be limited to a narrow domain of Israel but will encompass all people. Today, this text may have implications for those who would regard women in the same way that the Jews regarded

---

10. Lane (*Mark*, 262) contends that Jesus did not respond because, as a Gentile, she approached him from a belief in superstition and magic, which is not an appropriate context to release the power of God. Is this to say that the woman with the hemorrhage, who thought that healing would come from touching Jesus' garment, does not reflect a magical view?

11. Anderson, *Mark*, 191.

12. Hooker (*Mark*, 182) astutely comments, "If 'cleanness' only depends on men's attitudes, then the distinction between Jew and Gentile will also fall: Jews may produce evil thoughts and Gentiles good ones (cf. Rom. 2:13f.)."

13. Rhoads, "The Syrophoenician Woman," 363.

14. Ibid., 370.

Gentiles in the first century. This woman understands Jesus (something most rare in Mark's story) and engages him creatively in debate.

Another explanation for Jesus' harsh reaction attributes it to the socio-economic relations between Tyre and Galilee. The city of Tyre was well stocked with produce from the hinterland of Galilee (see Acts 12:20), while those who grew the food frequently went hungry. Economically, Tyre took bread away from Galilee. Galileans perceived Tyre politically as posing a permanent threat with expansionist policies since there were no natural boundaries to mark off the two regions. The hostility between Tyrians and Jews is reflected in Josephus's statement that the people from Tyre are "our bitterest enemies" (*Ag. Ap.* 1 § 70). At the outbreak of the Jewish revolt against Rome, he reports that Tyrians killed and imprisoned many Jews (*J. W.* 2.18.5 § 478). This woman is, therefore, not just a Gentile but a member of a resented class of privileged foes.[15] She has a lot of Gentile chutzpa to ask a Galilean Jewish healer for help. It would be analogous to a rich Brahmin pulling up in a fancy limousine to a shelter run by Mother Teresa and insisting that she leave her untouchable charges to pray over her sick child. Would we be surprised if she were treated less than kindly? If this woman does come from the domineering high society, her acceptance of such a term as little dog for herself and for her daughter would be "all the more remarkable."[16]

Mark is apparently oblivious to the problems in the story that so jar our sensitivities. We assume that Jesus is obligated to respond to every request and to heal everyone. Our prejudice is that Gentiles are just as important as Jews, if not more so, because we know that most of the latter will reject the Messiah while many Gentiles will respond gladly. We are prone to dejudaize Jesus and are offended by the particularity of God's election. We can expose our own biases by imagining a similarly despised foe from our context as the petitioner.

In bridging the contexts we should not try to relieve Jesus' supposed want of chivalry. Jesus is deliberately scandalous—throwing stumbling blocks in people's way. He affronts the Pharisees by calling them hypocrites to their face and scoffing at their beloved tradition, and he insults this Gentile woman by hinting she is a dog. One should allow the scandal to stand and emphasize that one must overcome the scandal before one can open the door for Jesus to help.

We can ask ourselves, What in the story would have offended us, and how would we have responded? Our answers should reveal much about ourselves. We might say, "If that is the way he feels, I will never come to him for help."

---

15. See Gerd Theissen, *The Gospels in Context: Social and Political History in the Synoptic Tradition* (Minneapolis: Fortress 1991), 72–80.

16. Gundry, *Mark*, 378.

No one likes being called hypocrites, an evil generation, brood of vipers, whitewashed tombs, foxes, or dogs. Our pride kicks in and keeps us from ever asking for help again. We will turn to gods of our own making who will not offend us, because we convince ourselves that we are special and truly worthy of God's grace and help. Only when we are truly desperate are we willing to do anything it takes, including humbling ourselves, to find God's help.

The woman's attitude in the face of refusal is the key to this passage. She comes empty-handed and can make no claim. She has no merit, no priority standing, nothing to commend her. Her manner is the opposite of the snippy "you-owe-me" attitude that prevails among so many today. She does not argue that her case is an exception or lobby for special treatment. She does not point out that Jesus is not even in the land of Israel; how could he deprive Jews of bread by helping her? On the other hand, she does not cut herself off from the miraculous power of Jesus by thinking that she is too unworthy to receive anything at all. She accepts his judgment and bows down as a beggar for grace.

In bridging the contexts, we need to be mindful of how this text offends modern readers, but we should not try to remove its sting. We should let it stand, imagine Jesus speaking these words to us, and visualize our response. What causes us to respond the way we do? Can we then picture Jesus saying these words to a bitter enemy or a privileged rival? What would be our response to the rebuff of others? The honest answers to these questions ought to shed light on what prevents us from receiving God's help and from reaching out to others.

Like so many other persons in Mark, this woman comes to Jesus because of his enormous magnetism that transcends nationalities, borders, and social classes. She comes because she wants something from him. She knows that he offers bread—life free from the heartache of the oppression of unclean spirits. She does not yet know that Jesus as Savior offers bread of even greater significance—eternal life and permanent freedom from the powers of evil. To receive this bread requires that we be willing to give our lives completely to him. This woman serves as a model of what it means to become last of all (9:35) and to get down low (10:43), which is required of all disciples, both Jew and Greek.

JESUS' RESPONSE TO this mother's appeal assumes the special election of Israel. Israel has a central place in the history of salvation. Nevertheless, this incident strikes at the heart of the ancient prejudice of Jews against Gentiles. It also blunts Gentile umbrage over the priority of Jews. In the previous controversy (7:1–23), Jesus swept away the traditional distinction between clean and unclean. In this encounter with a desperate mother, he sweeps aside the distinctions between Jews and Gentiles. Just as many of Jesus' closest disciples could not easily disregard the deeply ingrained reverence for food laws (Acts 10:1–33), so many disciples could not rid themselves of the ancient prejudice against Gentiles.

There is a ditty that goes:

How odd
of God
To choose
the Jews.

To which Leo Rosten responded

Not odd
of God.
Goyim
Annoy 'im.[17]

Prejudice toward others, nurtured by religious teaching and encouraged by societal divisions, does not relinquish its hold on the heart without difficulty. The ancient world was rife with prejudice. The issues and groups have changed, but the same bent toward prejudice grips a modern world. It strangles hopes for peace and even stifles interest among Christians to reach with the gospel those who are loathed and resented. Morgan Godwyn, a graduate of Oxford University, came to Virginia around 1665 and served parishes there and on the island of Barbados. He met resistance from slave owners when he tried to encourage the conversion of the slaves. He wrote that they commonly protested: "What, such as they? What, those black Dogs be made Christians? What, shall they be like us?"[18]

Prejudice derives from distrust of an alien group and causes us to swallow lies about their beliefs and conduct. It derives from resentment over their social and economic success, fear of their competition in these areas, or simply because they choose to be different. Demagogues seize on this fear to blame misery on a scapegoat. One can use this passage in an oblique assault on prejudice by substituting a contemporary object of bias for the

---

17. *The Penguin Dictionary of Modern Humorous Quotations*, ed. Fred Metcalf (London: Penguin, 1986), 139.

18. H. Shelton Smith, *In His Image, But . . .: Racism in Southern Religion, 1780–1910* (Durham, N.C.: Duke Univ. Press, 1972), 11, citing *The Negro's and Indian's Advocate, Suing for their Admission into the Church: Or a Persuasive to the Instructing and Baptizing of the Negro's and Indians in our Plantations . . . To which is added, A Brief Account of Religion in Virginia* (London, 1680), 61.

Syrophoenician woman. The listener may be outraged that Jesus would speak to someone in such a tone and would even consider withholding the help she so desperately wants. Then the listener may realize that this sympathetic figure belongs to a group that excites our hatred or disdain. It may allow the listener to see the prejudice in a new light. The passage may allow one to recognize that all humans share the same desperation when demonic powers and sickness batter us about. All yearn for help—high and low, rich and poor, urban and rural, Jew and Gentile. Jesus turns no one away who comes with humble faith.

Prejudice against others is a form of egoism. The woman shows the greatest humility that expels her prejudice when she begs for a few crumbs from the bread sent to the Jews. She does not become caustic or bitter about the privilege of others. She does not resent their share of God's blessing. She accepts her place and comes, as everyone must, as a sinner, poor and needy. Dwight Moody is reported to have said that Jesus sent no one away empty except those who were full of themselves. She may have been a Gentile idolater, but she did not suffer from I-dolatry. She did not come expecting praise for her faith but wanting healing for her sick daughter. She accepts that she is unacceptable. Jesus' ministry reveals that God has not sent him to reward the deserving but to serve the needy, whoever they are and wherever they may be found. God helps those who confess that they are needy and deserve nothing.

Bernard of Clairvaux said:

> It is only when humility warrants it that great graces can be obtained. ... And so when you perceive that you are being humiliated, look on it as the sign of a sure guarantee that grace is on the way. Just as the heart is puffed up with pride before its destruction, so it is humiliated before being honored.[19]

He concluded, "It is the possession of a joyful and genuine humility that alone enables us to receive grace."[20] The humble woman in this story does not abase herself so that she becomes a doormat. She aggressively seeks help and will not turn away. She is like the men who dig through the roof to lower their friend to Jesus. She is like the woman who relentlessly pushes her way through the crowd to touch his garment. She is like the widow who knew no shame and screamed out daily in the court of the wicked judge for justice. She will not be put off. She shows a dogged determination to get help

---

19. Sermon 34:1, in *The Works of Bernard of Clairvaux. Volume Three. On the Song of Songs II*, trans. Kilian Walsh (Cistercian Fathers 7; Kalamazoo, Mich.: Cistercian Publications, 1976), 160–61.

20. Ibid., 34:3 (p. 162).

for her daughter. She knows that she is unworthy, but that does not keep her from believing that she and her daughter are worth healing.

Many would be sorely tempted to walk away or to thumb their nose at anyone who treated them with disrespect. Who wants to be likened to a dog? Who wants others to regard them as a spectacle of weakness? We walk away when we do not feel so desperate for ourselves or our children. We may convince ourselves that we can handle the problem on our own or find another means. Pride changed angels into devils, Augustine said, and Satan uses pride as a favorite device for separating us from God and from God's help. Pride stiffens the knees so that they will not bow down and muzzles our voice so that we do not call out in humble supplication.

Mark 7:31-37

THEN JESUS LEFT the vicinity of Tyre and went through Sidon, down to the Sea of Galilee and into the region of the Decapolis. ³²There some people brought to him a man who was deaf and could hardly talk, and they begged him to place his hand on the man.

³³After he took him aside, away from the crowd, Jesus put his fingers into the man's ears. Then he spit and touched the man's tongue. ³⁴He looked up to heaven and with a deep sigh said to him, "Ephphatha!" (which means, "Be opened!"). ³⁵At this, the man's ears were opened, his tongue was loosened and he began to speak plainly.

³⁶Jesus commanded them not to tell anyone. But the more he did so, the more they kept talking about it. ³⁷People were overwhelmed with amazement. "He has done everything well," they said. "He even makes the deaf hear and the mute speak."

Original Meaning

JESUS' TRAVEL ITINERARY takes him to the sea of Galilee by way of a circuitous route that passes through Sidon and then back through the district of the Decapolis. The curious detour may be part of Jesus' attempt to maintain secrecy (7:24), or his encounter with the Gentile woman has caused him to zigzag his way through the middle of the territory of the Decapolis.

The mention of Tyre, Sidon, and the Decapolis emphasizes that Jesus passes into Gentile territory.[1] Just as the Jewish crowds in Galilee brought their sick to Jesus (1:22; 8:22; 9:20), so a Gentile crowd brings a deaf and speechless man to him and begs him to place his hand on him (see 5:23; 6:5; 8:22, 25). Jesus does not intend for his healing activity to become a spectator event and ushers the man away from the crowd.[2] He shuns self-promotion and has no interest in turning his ministry into a three-ring circus.

---

1. Chapman (*Orphan*, 171–72) observes that Mark lived in a "pre-map culture" and may be intending to locate Jesus "culturally rather than coordinately." He is culturally "in the midst of a foreign ethos even while on the shore" of the sea of Galilee.

2. A dead child is raised in private (5:37, 40), and another blind man is cured in private (8:23).

In healing this deaf man Jesus uses a sequence of actions, not just a spoken word. The vivid account creates an atmosphere of mystery and drama. He begins by putting his fingers in the man's ears, symbolic of opening them. Next, he spits and touches his tongue, symbolic of loosening his tongue. Then he looks up to heaven, the source of his power (as he did when he uttered a blessing before the feeding of the five thousand, 6:41), and sighs deeply, a gesture of prayer. Cranfield comments that the sigh "indicates the strong emotion of Jesus as he wages war against the power of Satan, and has to seek divine aid in urgent prayer."[3] Mark gives us Jesus' healing words, "*Ephphatha*," which he translates, "Be opened!" so that the reader will not mistake it for some hocus-pocus incantation. Immediately, the man's ears are opened and his tongue loosened. He now speaks plainly, but Jesus orders "them" (Mark does not identify the onlookers) to say nothing. To ask a man who has just been given his voice to keep quiet may only strike us as strange (see 1:44; 5:43; 8:26; 9:9).

Jesus can command storms, demons, and illnesses, but his orders for people to keep silent fall on deaf ears. The failures to obey his command for silence reveal that what Jesus does is so sensational that it is hopeless to try to hush it up. But the command to keep silent also underscores for the reader what needs special attention. As Hooker states it, these miracles

> symbolize the Christian faith—sight, hearing, resurrection—which become full realities only after the death and resurrection of Jesus; these physical cures cannot really be spoken of with understanding at this stage, because they point forward to events and spiritual changes which still lie in the future.[4]

While onlookers may jabber excitedly about what Jesus has done, the magnitude of what it signifies escapes them. They do not have all the pieces of the puzzle to see a completed picture. Hooker continues, "The secrecy motif underlines the fact that it is only those who believe in the risen Lord who can understand the full significance of what was taking place in Jesus' ministry."[5] The command to go and tell comes after the resurrection (16:7).

The chorus of Jesus' admirers nevertheless proclaims the truth even if they do not fully understand it. When one interprets Jesus' miracles from the contours of the biblical landscape, one sees again that Jesus does what only God can do. The Lord had responded to Moses' excuses, for example, with these words: "Who gave man his mouth? Who makes him deaf or mute?

---

3. Cranfield, *Mark*, 252.
4. Hooker, *Mark*, 185.
5. Ibid.

Who gives him sight or makes him blind? Is it not I, the LORD?" (Ex. 4:11). Jesus' actions here show that he has that same divine power.

When the people are struck out of their senses and exult over Jesus (see Isa. 29:14) with "he has done everything well" and "he even makes the deaf hear and the mute speak" (Mark 7:37), their words echo Scripture. The first echo comes from Genesis 1:31: "God saw all that he had made, and it was very good." The second one comes from the prophet Isaiah, who promises that God will remedy the physical and spiritual disabilities of the people: "Then will the eyes of the blind be opened and the ears of the deaf unstopped. Then will the lame leap like a deer, and the mute tongue shout for joy" (Isa. 35:5–6a).[6] These echoes from Scripture recall God's promise to restore creation, and they hint that the promised renewal begins with Jesus. The surprise is that this restoration occurs in Gentile territory. Gentiles will be included in God's renewal plan.

Bridging Contexts

MODERN READERS MAY regard the details of Jesus' sticking his fingers in a man's ears and spitting and touching his tongue as bizarre and hard to explain. Healing in the ancient world, however, was a "hands-on" activity. The crowd had asked Jesus to lay his hand on the deaf and mute man (7:32), and he fulfilled their expectations. In our culture we anticipate that medical doctors will follow certain procedures and use certain devices. When doctors deviate from our expectations, we become suspicious and question whether our visit was worth the time and money. People in the ancient world expected a healer to do some purposeful action to bring about restoration. Malina notes that this "same external activity in Western culture is viewed predominantly from a technological perspective. ..."[7] We would not be so put off if Jesus had used an otoscope and a tongue depressor, things we are accustomed to seeing doctors use. Lane suggests that Jesus intended to show the deaf man that he could expect healing.[8] He cannot speak to the man because he cannot hear, so he acts out what he intends to do for him. Perhaps these gestures also indicate the difficulty of the healing. His is a complicated case.

---

6. The Greek word *mogilalos*, translated "could hardly talk" in 7:32, is a rare word that appears only here in the New Testament and in the LXX version of Isa. 35:6. It was chosen deliberately to echo that passage.

7. B. J. Malina, *Biblical and Social Values and Their Meanings: A Handbook* (Peabody, Mass.: Hendrickson, 1993), 95.

8. Lane, *Mark*, 266.

The healing of the deaf and mute man parallels the healing of the blind man in 8:22–26. In both instances, others bring the individuals in question to Jesus, and they want him to lay his hand on or touch the men (7:32; 8:22). Jesus does both miracles apart from the crowds and uses his spittle (7:33; 8:23). Both miracles occur in stages: first the ears, then the tongue (7:33); first partial sight, then full vision (8:23, 25). Both times Jesus discourages publicity (7:36; 8:26). Isaiah 35:5–6 (see also 29:18; Wis. 10:21) rings clearly in both healings. The allusion suggests that Jesus unleashes the creative power of God.

The crowd is excited about the physical healing, but spiritual healing is more important and more difficult. Isaiah uses blindness and deafness as metaphors for the people's spiritual disabilities (Isa. 6:9–10; 29:18; 32:3; 35:5–6; 42:18–20; 43:18; 50:5).[9] Both miracles serve as a paradigm for how the disciples, who are unable to hear, speak, and see on a spiritual level (8:17–18), will gain their hearing, voice, and sight.

Like the mute man here, the tongues of the disciples are also tied through fear (16:8), or when they do open their mouths, they say all the wrong things (9:5–6; 14:66–72). Jesus has taught the crowds "many things" (6:34) and constantly exhorts them to "hear" (7:14). The disciples, however, have failed to hear with any understanding (6:52; 7:18), even when Jesus has taken them aside privately to instruct them. In 8:18, Jesus laments that the disciples have eyes but do not see and ears but do not hear. To open their ears and eyes and to loosen their tongues will take no less of a miracle. It will occur in private, apart from the clamor of the crowd. Jesus heals the deaf and tongue-tied man by first opening his ears and then healing his tongue. He will do the same with the disciples. First he will open their ears so that they can hear what God is saying. Then he will loosen their tongues so that they can speak what God would have them say.

If the biblical echoes are deliberate and help interpret this miracle, and if Mark has woven this episode into the fabric of his narrative strategy as a paradigm for what needs to happen spiritually to the disciples, then this miracle has as much to do with spiritual as it does with physical healing. One can therefore apply this miracle to the spiritual situation of many Christians today, to the continuing human plight of spiritual deafness. The transformation from one who is spiritually deaf and mute into one who hears God's voice and speaks God's word to others is a difficult one. For some, it may be quick and dramatic; for many, it takes time. But Jesus does give new hearing so that one can hear what was never heard before and new sight so that one can see what was never seen before. When one allows the Lord to open the

---

9. See also Jer. 5:21; 6:10; Ezek. 12:2; Zech. 7:11; Acts 7:51; Rom. 11:8.

ears, one is steeled to follow the suffering servant in the face of persecution (see Isa. 50:4–11).

WE HAVE ARGUED that this narrative can be applied to the human plight of spiritual deafness. The man's physical hearing is impaired, but the biblical background that associates deafness with spiritual disability and Mark's reference to the disciples' having ears but not hearing (8:18) have allowed us to make this application. St. Ambrose said: "Everything that we believe comes either through sight or through hearing. Sight is often deceived, hearing serves as guaranty."[10] Opening up a person's ears is vital since Jesus places so much emphasis on hearing his words (4:3, 9, 12, 15, 18, 20, 23, 24, 33; 7:14; 8:18; 9:7). Beethoven died with the words, "I shall hear in heaven." He hoped for the restoration of his physical hearing. Unless one hears spiritually God's words on earth, one will never hear them in heaven.

Spiritual deafness in the Scriptures applies to the people of God. Today God's people still do not always open their ears to God. They may only hear muffled vibrations and speak in inarticulate grunts. Perhaps in our culture we are deafened to God's voice by the ceaseless droning of televisions and the blaring of radios. Perhaps the hurry and bustle of modern life drowns out God's voice for us. Christians need to hear more clearly and to remedy their slurred speech. Mark's narrative shows that Jesus seeks to cure his disciples' blindness and deafness by taking them away from the madding crowd and teaching them. Modern Christians may need to have times when they retreat and allow the miracle of Jesus' power to penetrate plugged-up ears so that we may hear God's word afresh and speak it to others more clearly.

Spiritual deafness is also the condition of the world. How does one break through to tell the gospel? Mark's account—which describes Jesus looking up to heaven, groaning, and shouting out in Aramaic—emphasizes the difficulty of the miracle. I was a faculty member on call at a seminary and was summoned to the emergency room where a new student had been admitted with severe stomach pains. He was Japanese and deaf and had only recently come to this country to study in a deaf ministry program. He was in pain and looked frightened because he was unable to hear or understand what the doctors gathered about him were asking and saying. It was painful not to be able to talk with him. I sighed with great relief when someone who knew sign language arrived. But our student had not yet learned American Sign

---

10. *Commentary on St. Luke*, 4.5.

Language. We had to resort to a kind of primitive sign language to act out what was wrong and what the doctors were planning to do. The situation was not ideal but communication occurred. Perhaps the church needs to act out the message of good news for those who cannot understand in a language universally understood—deeds of loving-kindness. The church needs to love as Christ loved, to touch those who need assurance, to pray visibly for healing.

The way Jesus healed this man might also offer a helpful touchstone for comparison with those caught up in miracles today. Jesus intentionally took the man away from the crowd. One can only guess why he did so—did he need privacy for a particularly difficult miracle?—but the effect is clear. In private, he could concentrate entirely on the sufferer's needs and desires. The focus was on the man and his needs, not on Jesus. Presumably Jesus did not want the man to become part of some miracle show, and he had no desire to add to his own personal glory or revenue. He wanted to make a sufferer hear and speak. The contrast with modern faith healers who intentionally assemble a crowd to watch them heal others is striking. It leads one to ask whether they want to be in the spotlight at the expense of the individual needs of the sufferer. We should always ask whether we do ministry to win publicity for ourselves or to do good for others.

URING THOSE DAYS another large crowd gathered. Since they had nothing to eat, Jesus called his disciples to him and said, ²"I have compassion for these people; they have already been with me three days and have nothing to eat. ³If I send them home hungry, they will collapse on the way, because some of them have come a long distance."

⁴His disciples answered, "But where in this remote place can anyone get enough bread to feed them?"

⁵"How many loaves do you have?" Jesus asked.

"Seven," they replied.

⁶He told the crowd to sit down on the ground. When he had taken the seven loaves and given thanks, he broke them and gave them to his disciples to set before the people, and they did so. ⁷They had a few small fish as well; he gave thanks for them also and told the disciples to distribute them. ⁸The people ate and were satisfied. Afterward the disciples picked up seven basketfuls of broken pieces that were left over. ⁹About four thousand men were present. And having sent them away, ¹⁰he got into the boat with his disciples and went to the region of Dalmanutha.

¹¹The Pharisees came and began to question Jesus. To test him, they asked him for a sign from heaven. ¹²He sighed deeply and said, "Why does this generation ask for a miraculous sign? I tell you the truth, no sign will be given to it." ¹³Then he left them, got back into the boat and crossed to the other side.

¹⁴The disciples had forgotten to bring bread, except for one loaf they had with them in the boat. ¹⁵"Be careful," Jesus warned them. "Watch out for the yeast of the Pharisees and that of Herod."

¹⁶They discussed this with one another and said, "It is because we have no bread."

¹⁷Aware of their discussion, Jesus asked them: "Why are you talking about having no bread? Do you still not see or understand? Are your hearts hardened? ¹⁸Do you have eyes but fail to see, and ears but fail to hear? And don't you remember? ¹⁹When I broke the five loaves for the five thousand, how many basketfuls of pieces did you pick up?"

"Twelve," they replied.

20"And when I broke the seven loaves for the four thousand, how many basketfuls of pieces did you pick up?"

They answered, "Seven."

21He said to them, "Do you still not understand?"

22They came to Bethsaida, and some people brought a blind man and begged Jesus to touch him. 23He took the blind man by the hand and led him outside the village. When he had spit on the man's eyes and put his hands on him, Jesus asked, "Do you see anything?"

24He looked up and said, "I see people; they look like trees walking around."

25Once more Jesus put his hands on the man's eyes. Then his eyes were opened, his sight was restored, and he saw everything clearly. 26Jesus sent him home, saying, "Don't go into the village. "

THE PHRASE "DURING those days" loosely connects the miracle of the feeding of the four thousand with the preceding events (7:24–37) and places it in the same Gentile setting (7:31). Jesus is once again in a teaching situation, though, as is typical in Mark, no record of the content of Jesus' words is given.

The Feeding of Four Thousand (8:1–10)

JESUS' COMPASSION FOR the crowd prompts him a second time to feed a large crowd (8:2; see 6:34), which has been with him for three days without anything to eat. The "three days" emphasizes their great need, which is compounded by their traveling a long distance to hear Jesus. They are in a desolate area far from home, and Jesus fears that they might faint if he sends them away without some nourishment. This detail underscores the great attraction of Jesus. People flock to him to a desert place and are willing to go hungry for three days without a single complaint.[1]

This second feeding miracle invites comparison with the first. Both occur in a desert place (6:35; 8:4), and Mark notes that the plight of each crowd spurs Jesus' compassion. Both feedings feature an exchange between Jesus and

---

1. Reading this Gospel after the cross and resurrection, we might connect these three days to another three-day wait, to relieve the hunger of humanity after Jesus' crucifixion.

the disciples about the logistics of feeding such a large crowd. In the first incident, the disciples worry over the great expense of buying bread for such a
huge throng (6:37); in the second, they fret that there is no place nearby for
the crowd to buy bread for themselves (8:4). These remarks emphasize both
the extent of the miracle that Jesus works and the extent of their misgivings
that he can do anything to solve the problem. Jesus asks the disciples how
much they have (6:38; 8:5), and their meager supplies only convince the
disciples that the task is impossible. In both incidents, Jesus blesses what
they scrounge together and has them distribute it to the crowds (6:41; 8:6).
Miraculously the crowd eats its fill, and the disciples collect an abundance
of leftovers (6:42; 8:8). In the second feeding, the number fed drops from five
thousand to four thousand, while the loaves and fishes increase from five
loaves and two fish (6:41) to seven loaves and a few small fish (8:5, 7). The
number of baskets of fragments leftover diminishes from twelve (6:43) to
seven (8:8).

Many have read some allegorical significance into the numbers in the
two feedings[2] or press the significance of the different terms for the baskets
used to collect the fragments to support the argument that Jesus offers himself to Jews in the first feeding and to Gentiles in the second.[3] The allegorical explanations for the numbers are unconvincing, but setting the second
feeding in Gentile territory suggests that Mark understands the recipients to
be Gentiles.[4] Note how this feeding occurs immediately after Mark has
recorded how Jesus crossed purity boundaries and social barriers. Jewish
purificatory customs comprised the chief hindrance to associations between
Jews and Gentiles, and Jesus has dismissed these concerns as peripheral (7:1–
23). The healing of a Syrophoenician woman's daughter opened the door to

---

2. Some argue that the five loaves in the first feeding represent the five books of the law
and the twelve baskets, the twelve tribes of Israel. The seven loaves in the second feeding
refer to the seven Hellenist deacons (Acts 6:1–6) or may represent the seven Noachian commandments (justice, idolatry, blasphemy, immorality, murder, stealing, eating live animals)
enjoined on all. These numbers may be related to 1 Sam. 21:1–7 (see Mark 2:25–26),
which recounts David's finding twelve loaves, five of which he took to feed his men in the
desert and left seven (see Tolbert, *Sowing*, 183). Some also interpret the number 4,000 as a
multiple of the four points of the compass.

3. The word *kophinoi* ("basketfuls," 6:43; 8:19) is associated with Jews by Juvenal (3.14;
6.542), but that does not make the common word *spurides* ("basketfuls," 8:8, 20) into a Gentile basket.

4. The word used to describe the desert area differs. In 6:35, Mark uses the phrase *eremos . . . topos*, a common phrase in the LXX; in 8:4, he describes the area as an *eremia*, which
occurs only five times in the LXX. Chapman (*Orphan*, 62–65) contends that it refers to Gentile territory, a place that has become a desolation (Isa. 60:12; Ezek. 35:4, 9; Wis. 17:17;
Bar. 4:33).

the possibility that Gentiles might also be fed without filching bread from the children (7:24–30).

The context, therefore, suggests that Jesus is now offering a predominantly Gentile crowd the same opportunity to be fed by his teaching and by his miraculous power that he offered to the Jewish crowd. We may think that it is only fair that Gentiles get a share in Christ's benefits, but from Mark's Jewish perspective the inclusion of Gentiles is a token of the end-time reign of God. The miracle signifies that Jesus is not simply "*a* redeemer, *a* messiah like Moses and David";[5] he is *the* Redeemer, offering redemption to more than just the people of Israel.

In 6:34, Jesus characterizes the crowd as sheep without a shepherd, a classic description of a woeful Israel (Num. 21:17; 1 Kings 22:17; Ezek. 34:5). The disciples are the ones who raise a concern about the needs of the crowd when they ask Jesus what is to be done with them (6:35). In the second feeding, Jesus raises the concern about the hunger of the crowd, noting that many have come from a great distance (8:2–3). If Mark intends for Gentile readers to see themselves represented in this feeding, they may take comfort that Jesus recognizes their great need and prods the disciples to feed them.

The present account brings into bold relief the arrested development of the disciples. They were in on the first miracle feeding of five thousand in a deserted place, but this does not stop them from asking Jesus, "But where in this remote place can anyone get enough bread to feed them?" (8:4). The answer to their question is obvious: from Jesus. The disciples are slow on the uptake and grope for answers in the dark, expecting nothing miraculous from Jesus. Again, Jesus patiently has the disciples go through their inventory of provisions. They do not yet realize that even with their scanty supplies, they have in Jesus enough to feed the entire world.

Seeking a Sign (8:10–12)

AFTER THE FEEDING, Jesus sets sail with his disciples to Dalmanutha, a destination never mentioned by anybody in extant ancient literature. The best guess is that it refers to the anchorage of the district of Magdala.[6] What appears to be an ad hoc committee of Pharisees immediately accosts him when he disembarks and presses him to give them some sign from heaven. The phrase "he sighed deeply" (see 7:34) reflects Jesus' dismay at being tempted again. The Pharisees challenge his faithfulness and provoke his irritation.[7]

---

5. Chapman, *Orphan*, 66.

6. James F. Strange "Dalmanutha," *ABD* 2:4.

7. Jeffrey B. Gibson, "Mark 8:12a: Why Does Jesus 'Sigh Deeply'?" *BibTrans* 38 (1987): 122–25.

The English translation of the second part of Jesus' response misses his sharp denial. The text reads literally, "If a sign will be given to this generation." This comment is part of an oath formula, though it omits the threat of evil on oneself that normally accompanies such a comment: "May God strike me down," or, "May I be accursed of God," if a sign is to be given to this generation. This oath fragment does more than say that no sign will be given this generation; it conveys with some vehemence that he will prevent it from happening at all costs.

Why does Jesus oppose giving the Pharisees a sign from heaven? In the Old Testament a sign was a public event that certified or confirmed a distrusted prophecy or a disputed claim. One sought a sign when a claimant did or said something that was strange, surprising, unconventional, or contrary to the Mosaic law.[8] The sign did not happen by chance but had been predicted and thereby proved the legitimacy of a suspected utterance or claim. It did not have to comprise anything spectacular or miraculous but had to correspond to the prediction of what would occur.[9] Some incorrectly argue that Jesus resolutely refuses to give any signs in Mark's Gospel. For example, when the teachers of the law muttered under their breath that Jesus verged on blasphemy by announcing that the sins of the paralytic were forgiven, he proved his claim by making something happen (2:1–10). The reason Jesus balks at giving a sign here in 8:11–12 revolves around two issues: the meaning of the expression "a sign from heaven," and the defiant disposition of these opponents.

(1) "A sign from heaven" does not refer to the author of the sign—a sign from God. Signs by their very nature came from God, so that the phrase "a sign from God" is redundant. The Pharisees specifically ask for a sign *"from heaven."* They have in mind a peculiar type of sign distinct from another sign they may have requested. Gibson argues that "a sign from heaven" refers to "apocalyptic phenomena which embody or signal the onset of aid and comfort for God's elect and/or the wrath that God was expected to let loose against his enemies and those who threaten his people."[10] This generation, represented by the Pharisees, asks Jesus to do something that will signal Israel's deliverance from her enemies and their crushing defeat. A sign from heaven is something that "is apocalyptic in tone, triumphalistic in character, and the embodiment of one of the 'mighty deeds of deliverance' that God had worked on Israel's behalf in rescuing it from slavery."[11]

---

8. See 2 Kings 20:1–10; Isa. 7:10–11, 18–25; 38:1–20; John 2:13–18; 6:26–31.

9. Jeffrey B. Gibson, "Jesus' Refusal to Produce a 'Sign' (Mark 8.11–13)," *JSNT* 38 (1990): 38–40.

10. Ibid., 45–47.

11. Ibid., 53.

Ironically, this request comes after the miraculous feeding, a miracle that pointed to the blessing, not the destruction, of Gentiles. Jesus refuses to give the Pharisees a sign from heaven because God has sent him to give his life on the cross for all humanity, not to smash the enemies of Israel or to give the nation political mastery of the world. He will not give in to pressure to take a course of action different from God's purposes.

(2) The Pharisees have already received plenty of proof in Mark 1–2 of the source of Jesus' power, and they come now only as detractors who wish to tempt him. When Jesus addresses them as "this generation," this phrase recalls the stubborn, disobedient generation of the desert (Deut. 32:5, 20; Ps. 95:10–11). Those who claim to know God and to teach God's law to others do not recognize the signs that God has already displayed through Jesus because they are spiritually blind.

What is it that blinds them? Is it Jesus' unconventional behavior? Their concern to preserve their own power and status? Their constipated faith? Their skepticism that God would work in such an enigmatic fashion? Their desire that God destroy Gentiles and not feed them? Their wish to embarrass Jesus when he fails to produce such a sign? Plenty of others will come pandering to the desires of the people to see concrete signs of the nation's military triumph. Jesus says that false prophets and false christs will give signs and wonders to deceive (13:6, 22). But Jesus will offer this generation no noisy sign from heaven, only the wind whistling through an empty tomb after his crucifixion.

The Disciples' Incomprehension (8:13–21)

THE DISCIPLES HAVE also failed to discern the signs Jesus has shown them. Mark records a third sea incident, where the disciples' failure to grasp the significance of what Jesus has done in their midst becomes disturbingly obvious. Their dim-sightedness shows how much they still have to learn about their Master.

In the first boat scene (4:35–41), Jesus calmed the sea and rebuked his disciples for their lack of faith. Their terror over the storm shifted to wonderment about Jesus: Who is this one who can still storms? In the second boat scene, they are again terrified, this time when Jesus comes to them walking on the waves. Mark explains their fear with the notice that "they had not understood about the loaves; their hearts were hardened" (6:52). Now in this third boat scene, Jesus rebukes them for their quarrel over not having any bread and accuses them of having hardened hearts, blind eyes, and dull hearing (8:17–18). The feedings of the multitudes and the sea adventures have given the disciples a unique opportunity "to learn who Jesus is, to understand the nature and source of the power that comes through him."[12] But the disciples have moved no closer to comprehension and remain bamboozled by it all.

This last scene in the boat opens with an awkwardly phrased notice that the disciples forgot to bring loaves, "except for one loaf they had with them in the boat" (8:14). Why the contradiction between no loaves and one loaf? Have they forgotten that they have the one loaf (for they immediately begin to argue that they do not have loaves, 8:16)? Do they not even know that they have one loaf? Or do they think that one loaf is insufficient for their needs? Most likely, Mark teases the reader by allusively referring to Jesus as that one loaf. Without any clear antecedent, the next verse continues, "Jesus warned them, 'Watch our for the yeast of the Pharisees'" (8:15). Mark wants the reader to recognize Jesus as that one loaf who can multiply one into an abundance of loaves to feed thousands (see John 6:48–51; 1 Cor. 10:16–17).

Jesus' sudden warning about "leaven of the Pharisees and the leaven of Herod" (RSV) seems to intrude on the context. Some argue that 8:16 makes more sense if it followed 8:14. But the warning clarifies the danger of the disciples' worry about a bread shortage. In the Old Testament, leaven symbolized corruption and the infectious power of evil. The translation of the word *zyme* as "yeast" assumes that "yeast" and "leaven" are the same thing and obscures the negative connotation that leaven had for the first-century Jew. Yeast connotes to us that fresh and wholesome ingredient that makes dough rise and gives bread a pleasing, light texture. The ancient world used the more dangerous leaven. It was produced by keeping back a piece of the previous week's dough, storing it in suitable conditions, and adding juices to promote the process of fermentation. But this homemade rising agent was fraught with health hazards because it could easily become tainted; it would then spread poison when baked with the rest of the dough. It, in turn, would infect the next batch.[13] That is the idea Jesus uses to refer to his enemies.

The Pharisees and Herod seem to have little in common—the one steeped in religious duties, the other sunk in iniquity. But they do share one poisonous fault that can infect others. Jesus does not explicitly identify what that toxic flaw is, but the context points to their obstinate refusal to believe in spite of the evidence. They will not admit the truth, let alone embrace it, even when it stares them in the face. Herod and his confidants failed to believe when they heard of Jesus' mighty works (6:14–16). The Pharisees are

---

12. Elizabeth Struthers Malbon, "The Jesus of Mark and the Sea of Galilee," *JBL* 103 (1984): 364.

13. Plutarch (*Roman Questions* 289F) wrote that leaven "is itself also the product of corruption, and produces corruption in the dough with which it is mixed ... and altogether the process of leavening seems to be one of putrefaction; at any rate if it goes too far, it completely sours and spoils the dough"; see also Pliny, *Natural History* 18.26.

---

insisting that Jesus provide a sign conforming to their own goals and aspirations before they will commit themselves to believe.

Jesus thus warns the disciples not to fall victim to this same insidious unbelief. Their worry about where their next meal is coming from makes them deaf to the warning about not hearing and blind to the warning against blindness. Mundane concerns distract them too much, and they do not catch the subtle connection. They consistently fret about insufficient resources—it will take too much money to feed the crowd; there is no way the crowd can get bread in a deserted place; they have no bread. Their anxiety over such things keeps them from looking up and seeing what Jesus has done in their midst. It is as if they have tuned into Jesus with a primitive crystal radio set, and all they hear is a faint scratchy voice overwhelmed by background hiss.

Jesus asks his disciples why all the squabbling about the loaves and then gives a quick recap of recent events to jog their memories (and the reader's). He prods them to recall how much was left over when he fed the five thousand and the four thousand. They can recall the numbers easily enough, but they cannot see past them to recognize that they have a bread maker with them in the boat. The scene is almost comical. Jesus has fed nine thousand people with next to nothing. The disciples themselves helped distribute the food and helped gather up the leftovers, twelve mat basketfuls and seven large basketfuls. Though they had a ringside seat at both events, it has apparently slipped their minds, and they come off as dunderheads worrying about not having enough to fix lunch for thirteen. Even when Jesus refreshes their memories, they still do not fully comprehend because they have hardened hearts.

Jesus apparently believes that the feedings in the desert are the key events that should explain everything for the disciples. They did not generate the rush of excitement that his other miracles did, however. Mark does not report that anybody marveled. The disciples were only amazed *before* the miracle—that Jesus would even entertain notions of feeding such a huge mass of people. When they collected the leftovers, they appear to take it all in stride and do not ask, "Who is this who can feed thousands on such a small amount?" The meaning of the event clearly escapes them, but Jesus implies that it should point them on the way to recognizing Jesus as the Messiah, who works by the power of God. They are mired in their own little world, with its petty alarms, and cannot see God's reign breaking into their midst.

Jesus never gives up on the disciples and still holds out hope for them even when he expresses his exasperation: "Do you *still* not understand?" Jesus defines outsiders in 4:12 as those who see but do not perceive and those who hear but do not understand. The disciples therefore react to his miracles like outsiders (8:17–18). They are not going to forfeit their position as insiders, however, as some interpreters maintain. The "not yet" implies that eventually they will see and understand, though it will not come easily. Unlike the Pharisees, their problem is not that they refuse to see but that they *cannot* see until after the Jesus' death and resurrection. Geddert correctly describes the disciples' situation in Mark:

> Followers, however dull and unfaithful, are patiently instructed. If they follow all along the way Jesus leads, they will eventually be transformed from mere 'data-collectors' into 'meaning-discerners.' It all hinges on the decision for or against Jesus."[14]

If they succumb to the unbelieving leaven of the Pharisees and of Herod, however, they will never see. If they continue to follow him along the way, Jesus will multiply the meager resources of their understanding.

Healing a Blind Man (8:22–26)

THE NEXT INCIDENT records unidentified persons in Bethsaida bringing Jesus a blind man for him to touch. With vivid detail Mark describes Jesus' whisking the blind man away from the village, spitting into his eyes to heal them, and meeting with only partial success. For the first time Jesus asks an afflicted person about the success of his healing attempt, the way a physician would do.

Mark describes the initial moment when the blind man receives rudimentary sight but things are out of focus.[15] He can see people, but they look like walking trees. Jesus then repeats the procedure by placing his hands on the man's eyes, which brings complete healing. Three verbs describe the man's progressive restoration of sight. He opens his eyes wide (*diablepo*), his sight is restored (*apokathistemi*), and he can see all things clearly (*emblepo*). Jesus then sends him to his house and orders him not to go into the village. He continues to shy away from unnecessary publicity for his healing and steers clear of the towns and villages until he enters Jerusalem. His contact with crowds tapers off as he focuses his attention on instructing the disciples.

Since the man does not recover his sight immediately, the reader gets the impression that his blindness is stubborn and hard to cure. The miracle shows Jesus' power to heal even the most difficult cases. The Markan context, which portrays Jesus' struggle to get his disciples to see anything, gives this unusual

---

14. Geddert, *Watchwords*, 69.

15. The Greek verb *anablepo* (8:24) can mean "to look up" (see 6:41; 7:34; 16:4), as it is translated in the NIV, but when used to refer to blindness it means "to regain sight" (see 10:51, 52). See E. S. Johnson, "Mark viii.22–26: The Blind Man from Bethsaida," *NTS* 25 (1979): 376–77.

two-stage healing added significance. The blind man's healing occurs between two examples of the disciples' blindness (8:14–21; 8:31–33). This physical healing of blindness serves as a paradigm for the spiritual healing of the disciples' sight, which also comes gradually and with difficulty.[16]

As we near the midway point of this Gospel, the first half has drawn attention to the disciples' inability to recognize that Jesus is the Messiah empowered by God. When it finally dawns on Peter, the spokesman for the group, that Jesus is the Christ, the disciples encounter a new hurdle to their understanding. The second half of the book will reveal their inability to understand that this Messiah must suffer and die and be vindicated in his resurrection.

As Jesus asked the blind man, "Do you see anything?" so he will ask the disciples, "Who do you say I am?" Peter does see something. After all of Jesus' mighty works and deeds, he has a flash of insight: "You are the Christ" (8:29). The first stage of healing is complete. But he only has partial sight, as Jesus' stern rebuke in the next sentence makes clear (8:33). Peter sees, but he sees the equivalent of walking trees. Both Peter and the disciples require a second touch before they will see all things clearly—that the Messiah must suffer and die.[17]

The next major section, 8:27–10:52, shows Jesus concentrating his efforts on curing the disciples' deafness and blindness, which need more than one course of treatment.[18] Only after the crucifixion and resurrection will anyone begin to unravel the baffling mystery that the reign of God comes in the person of Jesus, who suffers and dies a humiliating death. The resurrection will reveal God's power to restore both sight and life.

PROBING THE REASONS for Jesus' refusal to give a sign from heaven to the Pharisees will help build a bridge to our present situation. Geddert's discussion on this passage is valuable.[19] He first points out that the clamor for the sign from heaven came from the wrong peo-

---

16. Ibid., 370–83; Frank J. Matera, "The Incomprehension of the Disciples and Peter's Confession," *Bib* 70 (1989): 153–72. Elizabeth Struthers Malbon argues that it alludes "backward to 4:1–8:21, where Jesus repeatedly works in two stages so that the disciples may see and see clearly" ("Echoes and Foreshadowings in Mark 4–8: Reading and Rereading," *JBL* 112 [1993]: 225–26).

17. Peter suffers a serious relapse of blindness in his denials (14:66–71). Twice he says that he does not know Jesus and once that he does not understand. He exhibits a stubborn case of blurred spiritual vision, but one Jesus can also remedy.

18. Guelich, *Mark*, 420.

19. Geddert, *Watchwords*, 32.

ple. They represent "this generation" (8:12), which continually defies Jesus, tempts disciples to be ashamed of him (8:38), and is faithless (9:19). These people only want to engage in disputes and to test others so that they can embarrass them. They think that they can dictate to God the conditions under which they will or will not believe. They will not accept any ambiguity or paradox. These opponents want an irrefutable, unequivocal, visible proof that removes any doubt from the decision of faith. What they want from Jesus, therefore, eliminates the need for faith. As Geddert puts it, "They imagined that they could demand whatever sort of signs they wanted, and then maintain critical distance and draw whatever conclusions from the data that happened to suit their inclinations."[20] Jesus recognizes that he has little chance of convincing these hard-core opponents no matter what he does.

Second, the request for a sign comes too late. Jesus had dealt with his skeptical opponents patiently until they began to plot his death (3:6). Before this, Jesus "carefully defends his actions when they accuse him and he demonstrates his authority when they challenge it."[21] He sent the healed leper as a witness to them (1:44). He confirmed his authority to announce the forgiveness of sins by commanding the paralytic to walk, something that everyone there could witness (2:10). When challenged, he explained why he ate with sinners (2:17) and why his disciples did not fast (2:19–22). He justified the so-called breaking of the Sabbath by appealing to an Old Testament precedent (2:25–28). But they rejected this evidence and his explanations, then plotted his death, and attempted to discredit him. As a result, Jesus now shifts his approach to them. He refuses to give them any more evidence since they refuse to believe no matter what he says or does. Hence, the brusque response when they have the temerity to demand a sign from heaven.

Third, Jesus refuses to submit to their demand because they are trying to tempt him, just as Satan had. Temptation presents one with the choice of obedience or disobedience to God. They try to preempt the Spirit by lobbying for a sign that conforms to their own longing and aims, not to God's. According to Gibson, "the sign from heaven" has to do with the deliverance of Israel coupled with the destruction of Israel's enemies. They want him "to advocate, initiate, and engage in triumphalism—a type of activity that according to Mark, was forbidden to Jesus if he wished to remain faithful to the exigencies of his divine commission."[22]

Bilezikian clearly pinpoints the problem: "The kind of messiah they want will never come. They are determined to find a compliant superman who is

---

20. Ibid., 68.
21. Ibid., 41.
22. Gibson, "Jesus' Refusal," 55.

endowed with heavenly powers and will fulfill their own earthly program. The messiah of their dreams. ..."[23] Theirs is a messiah of empty dreams, who will throw out the tyrants of the world and install them as the new tyrants. They want Jesus to give them proof of what they want to be true. Jesus refuses to yield to their false hopes, knowing that they will reject him as a fake and worse. Outsiders and insiders can exert enormous pressure on ministers and churches to conform to their false expectations and to coddle their self-indulgent fantasies. To resist this pressure and remain obedient to God requires a clear vision of God's will, unwavering dedication, and constant prayer.

A fourth reason why Jesus refuses to give the Pharisees the sign of their choosing has to do with the nature of the kingdom of God and faith. The kingdom of God requires individuals to exercise faith and discernment. The sign the Pharisees request removes any need to risk faith or to discern what God is doing in the present when the evidence is ambiguous. Jesus' warning about sign prophets in Mark 13 identifies those who provide convincing signs (which may deceive even the elect) as frauds (13:21–22).

That is what people want—convincing signs (see 1 Cor. 1:22). Their foolish hopes make them all the more gullible to the cries, "Look here!" "Look there!" The bystanders gathered around Jesus' cross demand that he come down in a dramatic show of force so that they might believe that he is indeed the Christ (15:28–32). Jesus refuses to do anything to get scoffers to believe. They must discern the truth from the way he gives his life on this cross and from the reports of his resurrection. No angelic host will descend from heaven with trumpets blaring to herald the news that Jesus is king until it is too late, when they arrive at the end of the age to gather the elect who have risked trusting in Jesus (13:27).

Sign seekers and scoffers appear in every generation. They continue to make their demands, ask for proofs, and ridicule a faith that trusts God's faithfulness against all evidence. William Blake wrote against the mockers:

> Mock on Mock on, Voltaire Rousseau
> Mock on Mock on! 'tis all in vain!
> You throw the sand against the wind,
> And the wind blows it back again.
> And every sand becomes a Gem
> Reflected in the beams divine
> Blown back they blind the mocking Eye
> But still in Israel's paths they shine.[24]

---

23. Bilezikian, *The Liberated Gospel*, 66.

24. *The Complete Poetry and Prose of William Blake*, ed. David V. Erdman; rev. ed. (Berkeley/Los Angeles: Univ. of California Press, 1982), 477.

Each era can fill in new names for Voltaire and Rousseau. Every generation of Christians must resist the temptation to satisfy their demands and to try to provide confirmation that fits the world's standards of evidence. The world wants visible, temporal, triumphant realities. According to Mark's Gospel, spiritual truth does not lend itself to such demands. One should learn from Jesus' example. He rebuffed all antagonistic demands to provide evidence to convince others. Rather than entangle ourselves in fruitless debates with agnostics, whose taunts usually reflect their personal fury with God, we should follow Jesus' example and turn away. Jesus proved his faith by his commitment to obey God and by giving his life as a sacrifice for others.

The disciples do not do well in this scene, and things will only get worse. In Mark's Gospel, they seem to have wool in their ears. Jesus' hints, warnings, and even his miraculous deeds do not get through. It is like winking at the blind or whispering to the deaf. The disciples function like the clever detective's dull-witted associate in crime novels—Holmes's Watson or Poirot's Hastings. They never catch on to the truth immediately and go off chasing red herrings.

The failure of the disciples, however, does not mean that they are incorrigibly ignorant. They do not represent the heretical positions of Mark's opponents (as some scholars have insisted). Mark presents the disciples as those who understand (4:11–12) and as those who do not understand (6:51–52; 7:19; 8:17–21). Their failure to grasp everything reflects the condition of those governed by the spirit of human wisdom before the resurrection, who have not received God's Spirit to reveal God's ways. As Paul writes: "No eye has seen, no ear has heard, no mind has conceived what God has prepared for those who love him" (1 Cor. 2:9). "No one knows the thoughts of God except the Spirit of God" (2:11). As the Corinthian situation reveals, however, even those who have received the Spirit can be badly mistaken and self-willed. The disciples, therefore, are the mirror images of disciples in Mark's church and of modern-day disciples, who are no less obtuse or subject to confusion, but gifted with occasional insight. The disciples' major problem is not simply their blindness, but the failure to recognize that they are blind.

The text does its work when readers can see their own blindness in the disciples' blindness. If we ask, "How could the disciples be so dense?" we need immediately ask the same question of ourselves. The disciples saw dimly in a glass coated with the dust of traditional ways of viewing things and warped by the curvature of their own dreams and ambitions. The glass we look through is no different. We are no less in need of healing before we can see what God is doing, and it may not take on the first try. Many get frustrated with others in their own church or denomination who seem to suffer from a terminal case of spiritual insensibility. We can learn from the example of Jesus' patience with his own dull disciples. He does not give up on them, even after their disastrous failures during his trial and death. The same one who could transform a few loaves into a banquet for thousands can transform the stony hearts and hardened minds of palsied disciples, who will then go into the world preaching the gospel.

Jesus admits that disciples are susceptible to the decay of unbelief. Mark 8:14–21 reveals that unbelief begins to rise like leaven when one becomes preoccupied with mundane matters—cares for the things of this world. When the disciples become consumed with worry that they do not have enough bread, the reader rightly asks, Why should they feel so insecure? They travel with one who already has shown his care for them and his power to satisfy all their needs as well as others. They worry about all the wrong things. In bridging the contexts, one needs to show that the petty worries of modern disciples look just as silly and unnecessary.

Several dangers arise when we become, like the disciples, focused on concerns for material well-being. (1) We begin to doubt the power of Jesus to provide enough and may be tempted to look to other sources. (2) We begin to vent anxiety by quarreling with others, which undermines community. (3) The never-ending pursuit for daily bread distracts us from obeying God's will. If the disciples lift their eyes from their searching for bread, they will see that God provides them with all the food they need in Jesus.

Jesus analyzes the disciples' condition and diagnoses it as hardness of heart, blind eyes, and stopped-up ears. They are little different from the outsiders who cannot understand anything (4:11–12) and from Jesus' bitter opponents (3:5). Hengel helpfully comments: "It is this *universal* disobedience which necessitates Jesus' course towards a representative expiatory death."[25] The disciples' failure illustrates Paul's affirmation, "There is no difference, for all have sinned and fall short of the glory of God (Rom. 3:22b–23).

THESE INCIDENTS DEPICT opponents and disciples as blind to what God is working through Jesus. The blindness stems from many causes. Being able to see what God is doing and where it will all lead is like being able to visualize the building of a church. The architect goes over the landscape and has a vision of what the building will look like. This spot is where the sanctuary will be; this is where the pulpit will be; this

---

25. Hengel, *Studies in the Gospel of Mark*, 35.

is where the choir loft will be; and so on. The one tagging along beside the architect may see nothing but bushes, knolls, and rocks.

Jesus has a vision of what the kingdom of God looks like. The disciples see nothing, no matter how hard they strain their eyes. Everything looks to them like a barren landscape. They may remain in the dark, but Jesus calls them to trust his vision. They may doubt because the resources seem so pitiful, and they do not remember God's bounteous provision they enjoyed in the past even when they can count their blessings. They may hold back their commitment until they get more proof. They may faint along the way, give out, and lose heart because they think they have no bread. They may try to fill empty pews with eye-popping programs inspired by the latest cultural craze. They wind up distributing spiritual junk food that can never satisfy.

Marshall outlines the differences between rational belief and trust. He points out that rational belief is "involuntary" because the evidence compels belief. Trust, on the other hand, is a voluntary act of the will. One trusts even when there is no objective evidence. Schweizer compares it to the trust that a spouse has that his or her mate is faithful. One can hire a private investigator to gather indisputable proof that the spouse is faithful. Doing anything like this would shatter a relationship that is supposed to be based on love and trust.[26]

Belief can exist and not affect one's conduct. One can believe statistical evidence that flying in an airplane is far safer than traveling the highways in a car, but fear of flying may prevent one from ever booking a trip on a plane. Trust, on the other hand, results in certain actions. Both belief and trust intertwine. As Marshall states it:

> All belief involves at least a modicum of trust (e.g., trust in one's cognitive powers), while an act of trust would be absurd without some minimum convictions about the character of the one being trusted or the benefits inherent in the act of trusting itself. Every human judgment, in other words, has a complex character involving both rational and non-rational elements, in varying proportions depending on the circumstances.[27]

It is both belief that and belief in. Christians believe that Jesus is the Christ, the Son of God, that he is sufficient for all their needs, and then they live their belief. Schoonhoven offers the following illustration.

A certain tight rope walker publicized that he was going to walk across Niagara Falls. A large crowd gathered. He dusted his hands

---

26. Schweizer, *Mark*, 159.

27. Marshall, *Faith As a Theme*, 55.

and feet with powdered chalk, grasped with both hands the pole he used for balance, and proceeded confidently across the rope. He not only went across but also made a return trip. The crowd stood amazed and responded with cheers. The man proclaimed he would do it again without his pole. Again he successfully went over and back. As he stepped off the rope, he turned to the crowd and asked how many thought he could make a third trip, this time with a wheelbarrow. Some responded with confidence while others with skepticism. He set off on his task and completed it with the greatest of ease. He then inquired of the crowd as to whether they believed he could do the same thing with the wheelbarrow full of cement. This time the crowd responded with great confidence. Again, he performed his feat with unbelievable ease. Having completed these four trips successfully, he asked the spectators if they believed that he could wheel a human being across the dangerous expanse. The response was unanimous. He could do it. Upon their reply he turned to a gentleman and said, "All right, my friend, let's go."[28]

---

28. Calvin R. Schoonhoven, "The 'Analogy of Faith' and the Intent of Hebrews," in *Scripture, Tradition, and Interpretation*, ed. W. Ward Gasque and William Sanford LaSor (Grand Rapids: Eerdmans, 1978), 110, n. 14.

Mark 8:27–9:1

JESUS AND HIS disciples went on to the villages around Caesarea Philippi. On the way he asked them, "Who do people say I am?"

²⁸They replied, "Some say John the Baptist; others say Elijah; and still others, one of the prophets."

²⁹"But what about you?" he asked. "Who do you say I am?" Peter answered, "You are the Christ."

³⁰Jesus warned them not to tell anyone about him.

³¹He then began to teach them that the Son of Man must suffer many things and be rejected by the elders, chief priests and teachers of the law, and that he must be killed and after three days rise again. ³²He spoke plainly about this, and Peter took him aside and began to rebuke him.

³³But when Jesus turned and looked at his disciples, he rebuked Peter. "Get behind me, Satan!" he said. "You do not have in mind the things of God, but the things of men."

³⁴Then he called the crowd to him along with his disciples and said: "If anyone would come after me, he must deny himself and take up his cross and follow me. ³⁵For whoever wants to save his life will lose it, but whoever loses his life for me and for the gospel will save it. ³⁶What good is it for a man to gain the whole world, yet forfeit his soul? ³⁷Or what can a man give in exchange for his soul? ³⁸If anyone is ashamed of me and my words in this adulterous and sinful generation, the Son of Man will be ashamed of him when he comes in his Father's glory with the holy angels."

⁹:¹And he said to them, "I tell you the truth, some who are standing here will not taste death before they see the kingdom of God come with power."

THE RAPID PACE of the Gospel slows down to a deliberate march in this large unit (8:22–10:52).[1] Jesus is no longer simply on the go, moving from town to town and back and forth across the lake. He now leads his disciples "on the way." The journey now replaces the boat as the classroom for the disciples' lessons. Several themes emerge in this unit.

(1) Jesus unveils the secret of his vocation as Messiah by giving his disciples explicit teaching about his impending suffering, death, and resurrection. The scales are beginning to fall from their eyes as they start to recognize him as the Messiah. At the beginning of this unit Peter proclaims Jesus as the Christ (8:29). At the end, Bartimaeus hails him as the Son of David (10:47). They are correct, but only partially. The question shifts from "Who is Jesus?" to "What has God sent him to do?" Three times Jesus tries to bring his disciples to a new definition of what being the Messiah means by explaining the necessity of his suffering (8:31–38; 9:30–37; 10:32–45). Significantly, he speaks about this suffering *"plainly"* (8:32), not in parables (4:33). The gist of his teaching is that the messianic king will reign from a splintery cross. Traditionally, scholars have called these passages passion predictions, but that term neglects that Jesus also prophesies his vindication and resurrection.

(2) Jesus spells out the fine print of the requirements of discipleship. The cross is not his to bear alone. It is necessary not only as a means of redemption but as a way of life that disciples must bear if they want to be his disciples. They too will face suffering and will be tempted to take an easier path that sidesteps any call for sacrifice. Anyone who faithfully follows a suffering leader will become a sitting duck and the object of hate crimes.

(3) The "way" (*hodos*) plays a crucial role throughout this unit. Jesus does not point the disciples to the way but walks it himself and takes them there. Mark records the milestones along the route (8:27; 9:33–34; 10:17, 32, 46, 52):

- Jesus is "on the way" to the town of Caesarea Philippi when he asks the disciples who they think he is; he makes his first announcement of his impending fate (8:27).
- In 9:33–34, he asks his disciples what they were arguing about "on the road."
- As Jesus starts out "on his way" (10:17), a man urgently interrupts him, asking what he must do to inherit eternal life. The answer comes back: Sell everything you have, give it to the poor, and join the procession.

---

1. The word "immediately" has appeared thirty-two times in 1:1–8:26 but appears only four times in this unit (8:27–10:52), three in the healing of the boy with the demon (9:15, 20, 24).

- Mark does not tell us where Jesus is leading his disciples until 10:32, just before the third and final announcement of his suffering and resurrection: He is leading them "on their way" to Jerusalem. Those following in his train have a vague sense of foreboding, because they are astonished and afraid. The "festive circuit through Galilee" now becomes a "somber cortege" to Jerusalem.[2]
- In the section's last scene, Jesus cures blind Bartimaeus, who was sitting "by the roadside" (10:46); he then follows Jesus "along the road" (10:52).

In retrospect, the reader realizes how the shadow of the cross looms over the entire journey and understands that Jesus leads his disciples along a way where all the signs point to Golgotha.

(4) This section reveals how Jesus' power blends with weakness. There is no power shortage in the events that Mark records. Only select disciples witness Jesus' transfigured glory (9:2–8), and he continues to cast out demons (9:14–29) and heal illness (10:46–52). Even those who do not follow the disciples find the power of his name effective in casting out demons (9:38–41). But Jesus gives up all claims to earthly power and expresses the willingness to submit to maltreatment. He will be handed over, mocked, and put to death. He will submit to God's plan. God's power will be revealed in weakness. Mark emphasizes that earthly authorities who employ the power tactics of the beast will be conquered ultimately by a lamb who renounces all show of power.

(5) The disciples' shortcomings become even more prominent in this section. In scene after scene, their blindness becomes distressingly evident. Each time Jesus instructs the disciples about his coming suffering and resurrection, they manifest in some way their complete lack of understanding. In the first instance, Peter openly rebukes Jesus for thinking that he will suffer (8:32–33). In the second, all the disciples begin to bicker privately about who is the greatest (9:33–34). In the last, James and John bid for places of power and glory in the kingdom, which rankles the other disciples. They resent this bid to gain a competitive edge, for they want to be the ones who rule the roost (10:35–41). The disciples' tenacious thickheadedness gives Jesus an opening in each instance to make a statement about the true nature of discipleship (8:34–38; 9:35–37; 10:42–45). Many have noted that the healing of two blind men form a pair of bookends around this section (8:22–26; 10:46–52). While on the way, Jesus applies a second and third touch to help the disciples see that he is truly God's Messiah by dying, not in spite of dying.

---

2. Bilezikian, *The Liberated Gospel*, 102.

Jesus As the Messiah (8:27–33)

THE FIRST COURSE of instruction takes place in the unlikely location of Cae-sarea Philippi, which lay on the border between the Holy Land and Gentile territory and was famed for its cultic associations with the nature god, Pan. Herod the Great built a grand marble temple here to revere the Roman emperor; and his son Herod Philip enlarged the city and renamed it in honor of Caesar. A Roman governor exercising Caesar's power will execute this Christ, but the resurrection will begin to topple the very foundations of the empire and reveal the power of God. Peter's recognition that Jesus is the Christ occurs in a pagan outpost—as far away from Jerusalem as one can get and still be in Israel. Jesus will push from here to Jerusalem, the Holy City, where they will only mock him as the Christ as he suffers on a cross (15:32).

Jesus teaches his disciples by asking them probing questions. The first one is (8:27): "Who do people say I am?" The disciples report his favorable rat-ings in the polls. The man in the street holds a good opinion of Jesus. Their views offset the slander of his bitter opponents, who regard him as a pawn of Beelzebub; the worries of his kinsmen, who think that he is out of his mind; and the bias of his fellow citizens in Nazareth, who dismiss him as just one of them. Most put Jesus in the pigeonhole of prophet figure, maybe even John the Baptizer or Elijah. These opinions remind the reader of Herod's top-level speculation about Jesus—that he was John the Baptizer, Elijah, or one of the prophets (6:14–15). Whether the people believed that God sent him to announce doom and gloom or doom and dawn, they at least believe God sent him.

These people have not hit on the truth, however. Jesus is more than just another in a long line of messengers God has dispatched to the people. Thus, Jesus probes further, "Who do you say I am?" So far, the disciples have only called him "Teacher" (4:38), but they have asked themselves the same question, "Who is this?" (4:41). Peter moves to the head of the class by giving the answer that makes sense of all that they have witnessed: "You are the Christ" (8:29). His confession occurs in the very center of the Gospel. This passage serves as a hinge between the first half of the Gospel, where Jesus' power is so prominent, and the second half, where his weakness becomes predominant.

This confession represents a significant leap of faith, given the current expectations associated with the Messiah. It was by no means obvious that Jesus was the Messiah. A few people were healed, many were fed, but Israel was not yet free from pagan domination. In the first century most Jews believed the Messiah would be a royal figure, the offspring of David, whom God would empower to deliver Israel from her foes. This kinglike figure would be as triumphant as David and as wise as Solomon. This hope is expressed in the Psalms of Solomon 17:21–25:

> See, Lord, and raise up for them their king,
> > the son of David, to rule over your servant Israel
> > in the time known to you, O God.
> Undergird him with the strength to destroy the unrighteous rulers,
> > to purge Jerusalem from gentiles
> > who trample her to destruction;
> > in wisdom and in righteousness to drive out
> > the sinners from the inheritance;
> to smash the arrogance of sinners
> > like a potter's jar;
> To shatter all their substance with an iron rod;
> to destroy the unlawful nations with the word of his mouth;
> At his warning the nations will flee from his presence;
> > and he will condemn sinners by the thoughts of their hearts.[3]

Moreover, the author of 4 Ezra pictures the Messiah as a lion from the posterity of David, who will triumph over the eagle (4 Ezra 12:34). He will judge the world and then deliver the faithful remnant of Israel. Jesus has not yet delivered on any of these hopes, but Peter brims with confidence nonetheless. Jesus has been preaching the kingdom of God, and Peter is now convinced that he has learned the name of the king. He and the rest of the disciples, however, do not have a clue how he will be enthroned or how he will prevail over the enemies. Jesus endeavors to open their eyes so that they can see that God will accomplish these purposes in an unexpected way. As Matera puts it: "Jesus is the expected Messiah in the most unexpected manner."[4]

The reader knows that Peter's answer is correct from the title of the Gospel (1:1). It seems a major breakthrough. He has finally caught on, and the reader might expect that the disciples have finally begun to shake off their persistent stupor. The secret will soon be out. But Jesus does not confirm Peter's confession or praise him for his insight. Instead, he rebukes him to tell no one (8:30). The verb (*epitimao*) should be translated "rebuke" rather than "warn" or "charge." Mark uses the same verb to describe Jesus' rebuking the demons to be silent (1:24–25; 3:11–12), and it appears in 8:32–33, where it is translated "rebuke" in the NIV. Either Jesus wants Peter to keep a lid on things a while longer so that he can remain incognito, or he rebukes Peter to remain silent

---

3. Trans. by R. B. Wright, "Psalms of Solomon," in *The Old Testament Pseudepigrapha*, ed. James H. Charlesworth (Garden City, N.Y.: Doubleday, 1985), 667.

4. Matera, *The Kingship of Jesus*, 145.

because his understanding of what "Christ" means is wrong and needs correction. Jesus does not want Peter's faulty opinions proliferating among the crowds, whose ability to grasp Jesus' identity is even more limited than the disciples.

The latter option is supported from what follows. After rebuking Peter, Jesus explains that it is necessary for the Son of Man to suffer (8:31); and this announcement, spoken to them "plainly" (8:32), plunges them back into an uncomprehending daze. Jesus undermines Peter's new-found faith to lead him to a higher level of faith. The Son of Man's suffering, rejection, and death all have to do with God's hidden way of salvation. The secret is not that Jesus is the Christ but has to do with what he will do as Messiah—or, rather, what will be done to him. Only after the power brokers of the Jewish nation—the elders, the chief priests, and the teachers of the law—put Jesus to death will vindication follow.[5]

Jesus does not explain his mission to his disciples simply to predict future events but to verify for his disciples that what is about to happen fulfills God's plan.[6] The disciples can understand it only after the fact because this plan runs counter to everything they were conditioned to expect. Lofty visions of majesty fill up their eyes and the noise of cheering crowds plugs up their hearing so that Jesus' teaching about suffering and death flies in one ear and out the other. It is all a muddle to them.

Peter displays astonishing nerve by trying to set Jesus straight on what is and what is not necessary. He calls Jesus aside and "rebukes" him for being so mistaken as to think that the Messiah will ever have to suffer. His counter-rebuke reveals his ignorance about the nature of Jesus' messiahship and his deep offense at Jesus' teaching. Paul said that the cross was foolishness to Greeks and a stumbling block to Jews (1 Cor. 1:23), and Peter is the first to stumble over the offense of a suffering Messiah. Like the blind man from Bethsaida, the scales have partially, and only partially, fallen from his eyes. Preconceived notions about the Messiah blur his vision, and he only appraises things from a human perspective. He has begun to understand that Jesus' great manifestation of power means that he must be the Messiah, but he does not have any understanding how Jesus' passion ties into his identity.

Peter's concept of the "Christ" is too narrow, too laden with selfish, human fantasies. He thinks that the Christ will establish a reign of peace and righteousness by overthrowing the powers who hold God's people Israel in a vise

---

5. "After three days" is a standard phrase for the time when God intervenes (see Gen. 22:4; 42:17; Ex. 15:22; 2 Kings 20:5; Hos. 6:2; Jonah 2:1).

6. Lane, *Mark*, 296. The verb "it is necessary" (*dei*) expresses that God aims to establish the kingdom through Jesus' suffering, death, and resurrection (see also 9:12; 14:21).

of oppression. The Christ is, by definition, a winner, destined for honor and glory. Anyone with Jesus' amazing powers to silence the sea and unclean spirits, to heal the sick with a word or a touch, and to feed thousands from a few scraps is headed for glory and universal veneration. Anyone who has heavenly authority to forgive sins on earth (2:10) and to determine what is permissible on the Sabbath (2:28) need not suffer on earth. How can such a Messiah be rejected and become a victim of violence? For Peter, a suffering Messiah is impossible. The Messiah will come as a triumphant hero, dishing out punishment to those who oppose him.[7] He may have shared the hopes expressed in the *Targum Yerushalmi* on Genesis 49:11:

> How fine is the King, the Messiah, who will arise from those of the house of Judah! He girds his loins and goes forth and sets up the ranks of battle against his enemies and kills the kings together with their commanders and no king and commander can stand before him. He reddens the mountains with the blood of their slain and his garments are dipped in blood. . . . [8]

Peter, therefore, shows himself at cross-purposes with Jesus; and, along with the other disciples, he wants to impose his own private agenda on how Jesus will live out his vocation as Messiah and how they will benefit as his followers. He looks for a human reign while Jesus tries to prepare them for the reign of God. He thinks in human terms, while Jesus seeks the divine will. This conflict leads the reader to wonder how he and the other disciples can ever overcome the scandal of the cross and see a transformed vision of God's power. It also reveals that the quest to uncover Jesus' identity does not end with the confession that he is the Christ. The disciples cannot know who Jesus really is without accepting the necessity of his suffering and death, and they cannot be his disciples unless they accept that fate for themselves.

Jesus' second touch to heal this blindness begins with a second "rebuke" (8:33). He turns around, looks at the disciples, and calls Peter "Satan." The archenemy has surfaced in Jesus' most prominent disciple. Peter has set

---

7. Francis Watson ("Ambiguity in the Marcan Narrative," *Kings Theological Review* 10 [1987]: 13) states it well:

> What Peter expresses is not simply a conclusion from what has preceded, but a hope for the future: that Jesus will now begin to exercise his power in order to inaugurate the glorious new age in all its fullness. He must act not simply to free individuals from the power of Satan, but to remove the entire dominion of Satan from the face of the earth. In this way, the secrecy, misunderstanding and rejection which have so far characterized Jesus' ministry will be removed. There is no room for any ambiguity in the bringer of the new age.

8. Cited by Martin Hengel, *The Zealots* (Edinburgh: T. & T. Clark, 1989), 277.

himself over against the plan of God and therefore, without knowing it, has lined himself up behind Satan, who earlier attempted to usurp the Spirit in steering Jesus' course (1:13).[9] Satan cunningly uses one disciple, Peter, to try to turn Jesus away from death, and another disciple, Judas, to lead him into death.

Why does Mark tell us that Jesus turns around (8:33)? Must he halt his progress "on the way" to deal with Peter's misunderstanding (see 5:30)? That Jesus looks at the disciples when he rebukes Peter may suggest that he is not alone in his opinion about Jesus' suffering, just more daring in voicing it.[10] On the other hand, the other disciples may have been following properly behind their Master, while Peter had moved out in front of Jesus or alongside him.[11] Whichever is the case, Jesus chides him publicly for trying to block the way. This will not be the last time that Peter is openly confronted for getting things wrong (see Gal. 2:11–14). Peter is supposed to follow on the way with Jesus, but his human yearnings cause him to get in the way as he wants Jesus to do things his way. Jesus did not choose him to be the drum major, and Peter cannot follow if he is out in front. He needs to get back in line behind his Master and follow after him—which is what Jesus first called him to do (1:17). Mark's message is clear: A disciple must do more than get Jesus' title right. That is only the first step in following Jesus on the way. The next sayings lay out plainly what following Jesus requires (8:34–38).

The Demands of Discipleship (8:34–9:1)

WHEN JESUS LAYS out the demands and expectations of discipleship, he calls the crowd along with the Twelve and therefore opens it to anyone willing to accept his conditions. He presents them with three demands (8:34), a rationale for accepting these demands (8:35–37), a solemn warning (8:38), and a confident promise (9:1).

Three demands. (1) Jesus insists that if the disciples want to follow him, they must deny themselves. He does not ask disciples to deny something to themselves but to deny the self and all self-promoting ambitions. Discipleship is not part-time volunteer work that one does as an extracurricular activity. God refuses to accept a minor role in one's life; he requires a controlling place. Those who deny themselves have learned to say, "Not my will but thine be done."

---

9. We learn later that just as Satan speaks here through Peter, so Jesus will speak through him. He tells the disciples that when they are handed over for trial, they need not worry what to say, because the Holy Spirit will speak through them (13:11).

10. Best, *Following Jesus*, 24–25.

11. Gundry, *Mark*, 451.

(2) Jesus demands that his disciples take up a cross. This vivid imagery must have sounded strange before Jesus' crucifixion and resurrection but would have communicated danger and sacrifice. Public executions were a prominent feature of life. Cicero described crucifixion as a cruel, disgusting penalty, the worst of extreme tortures inflicted on slaves and something to be dreaded.[12] The Romans made the condemned carry the transverse beam of the cross to the place of execution, where they affixed it to the execution stake. By requiring disciples to carry their cross, Jesus expects them to be willing to join the ranks of the despised and doomed. They must be ready to deny themselves even to the point of giving their lives.

(3) Jesus tells his disciples to follow the way *he* has chosen, not the way they would choose for themselves. Jesus does not want a convoy of followers who marvel at his deeds but fail to follow his example. The procession he envisages is a rare sight: disciples following after their Master, each carrying a cross. The imagery means that disciples must obey his teaching, including what he says about giving their lives.

The rationale. Jesus appeals to the basic human desire to secure one's life as the rationale for making such a sacrifice. Humans seek to guarantee their lives but usually choose ways destined to fail. Jesus offers a paradoxical principle for successfully saving one's soul: To save one's life, one has to lose it. Human beings make futile attempts to safeguard their lives by storing up goods in bigger barns, but nothing that one acquires in this life can ransom one's soul from God. If we give up our lives for his sake and the gospel, we will be given the only life that counts, life from God.

A solemn warning. Jesus next warns his disciples about the judgment, when each one will have to give an account before the Judge. The warning implies that when the Son of Man comes in the glory of his Father, he will come as the Judge (see Matt. 25:31–32). He warns disciples not to retreat from his present shame in the eyes of this world as the crucified Messiah. They must side with him now in his suffering and humiliation, or they will not be at his side in the glorious age to come. The individual's stance toward Jesus will determine the final verdict.

Jesus uses the threat of judgment to induce his followers to be faithful. To be put to shame is the opposite of divine vindication (Pss. 25:3; 119:6; Isa. 41:10–11; Jer. 17:18). Those who may be frightened by the edicts of earthly courts (represented in this Gospel by Herod Antipas, the high priest's Sanhedrin, and the Roman governor, Pilate) should fear even more the decision

---

12. Cicero, *Against Verres* 2.5.64, 165; 5.66, 169; *Pro Rabiro* 5.16. Tacitus (*Histories* 4.11) described it as "a slave's punishment," and Josephus (*J. W.* 7.6.4 § 203) called it "the most pitiable of deaths."

of the heavenly tribunal, which determines their eternal destiny. The petty tyrants, who for a fleeting moment hold the whip hand, can inflict fearful punishment. But one cannot appease them or straddle the fence. To win the favor of the world and its despots means to lose the favor of heaven. To win the favor of heaven means to lose the favor of the world.

In the judgment, the utter powerlessness of God's hostile adversaries will be manifest as they are brought to the bar to answer to God. Those who have thrown in their lot with them will find that they have made a fatal choice. They have bartered a few more years of life on earth with this wicked and adulterous generation for an eternity with them in hell. Giving one's life in service to God may mean losing a few years on earth, but the result will be spending eternity with the glorified Son of Man. Jesus does not say that confessing him will make us happier but that it will save us from God's judgment. The better part of wisdom is to follow Jesus' way, even if it leads to earthly humiliation; the only other choice leads to divine condemnation. This warning hits home when Peter cannot make the same bold confession in a hate-filled courtyard (14:66–72; see also 13:9).

A confident promise. Jesus concludes this first lesson on discipleship requirements with a solemn promise that some of them will not taste death before they see the kingdom of God coming in power (9:1). The suffering will not go on forever. The resurrection of the Son of Man (8:31) and his coming in glory with the holy angels (8:38) removes the sting from the humiliation of a cross.

Interpreters do not agree on what event corresponds to "the kingdom of God com[ing] in power." It may refer to the end time since the previous verse mentions the Son of Man's coming in the glory of his Father with the holy angels (8:38; see 13:26–27).[13] It may refer to the Transfiguration, which Mark narrates in the next verses (9:2–8). The two passages are linked in time ("after six days," 9:2); and three selected disciples "see" Jesus' glistening appearance with Elijah and Moses, which foreshadows his impending appearance in glory with the "holy angels."

But why such a dramatic prediction, "some ... will not taste death," when the Transfiguration occurs only a week later? Why not say "within a week"? The Transfiguration makes more sense as pointing to the fulfillment of this promise rather than being its actual fulfillment. The phrase may refer to the final outcome of Jesus' suffering and death—his resurrection.[14] This verse concludes the unit that began in 8:31, when Jesus first announces his suffering, death, and resurrection. It promises a reversal. Some will be able to see his powerless death transformed into glorious vindication and give evidence of God's powerful

---

13. So E. Nardoni, "A Redactional Interpretation of Mark 9:1," *CBQ* 43 (1981): 373–74.

14. J. J. Kilgallen, "Mark 9:1—The Conclusion of a Pericope," *Bib* 63 (1982): 81–83.

reign in Jesus. France argues that Jesus may not be referring to a single event but to a series of events—Jesus' transfiguration, death, resurrection, and ascension, Pentecost, and the destruction of the temple. As one sees the seed develop into a stalk, head, and full kernel, some of Jesus' disciples will see the fulfillment of his prediction in stages. The kingdom's power will be undeniably visible.[15]

The problem continues to perplex interpreters. If Jesus refers to the Parousia, then he expresses a mistaken confidence that it will occur during the lifetime of the disciples—a belief that Mark, writing in the first century, may have shared. As the commentary on chapter 13 will show, however, Mark underscores that no one can know with any precision timing the day of the Lord. Jesus gives no assurance that it will be soon. The best option assumes that the promise in 9:1 is somehow fulfilled within the story and in the events that take place after the resurrection.

This conclusion raises further questions. What does it mean to "see"? It may refer to physical perception, intellectual perception, or both. When Jesus dies on his cross, bystanders taunt him to come down from the cross so that they might "see and believe" (15:32). They want to "see" Jesus rescued miraculously by Elijah (15:36). The centurion, however, "sees" how he dies and proclaims him to be the Son of God (15:39). After his resurrection, the disciples are promised that when they go to Galilee, they will "see" him. Seeing the kingdom of God coming with power refers to Jesus' death and resurrection. The Greek participle in 9:1, "having come" (*elelythuian*), is in the perfect tense and indicates a coming that takes place before the action of the verb "see." The visible manifestation of God's mighty rule does not appear in a form that people will expect. It comes as a hidden mystery. The cross and resurrection transform the meaning of power and glory and the way God will establish his reign on earth.

One therefore may no longer think of power and glory in the ways that humans usually think. Many imprisoned under the powers will see nothing of what God is doing in the world and will be judged. Others will see in the darkness at noon, the splitting of the temple veil, the empty tomb, and the reunion with the risen Lord the kingdom of God coming in power.

THIS SCENE SHOWS that one can be simultaneously right yet so wrong. Peter makes a stunning confession, and Jesus just as stunningly rebukes him to keep quiet. Peter does not yet understand that this Messiah is destined to die at the hands of God's enemies. When Jesus

---

15. France, *Divine Government*, 66–76.

breaks the news, it throws Peter for a loop. One can hardly blame him for being incredulous. Nothing in his religious background prepared him to foresee anything that Jesus predicts. The message of a suffering Messiah was nonsensical. Justin Martyr describes how the majority of his contemporaries in the second century regarded Christian faith: "They say that our madness consists in the fact that we put a crucified man in second place after the unchangeable and eternal God, the Creator of the world" (*First Apology* 13.4).

Jesus not only has to contend with the false expectations of his bitter rivals who challenge him but also with the wishful fantasies of his closest supporters, who want to redirect his mission. Satan takes many guises. He appears when the Pharisees tempt Jesus to verify the truth of his implicit claim to be the Messiah by doing something decidedly messianic. They want him to provide clear signs that he will overthrow the enemies of Israel. Otherwise, they will refute him as another failed messianic figure (see Acts 5:36–37), a deceiver. Jesus resists their pressure. Next, Satan incites the blusterous interference of Peter. Peter quickly plummets from the brightest student with his A+ answer, "You are the Christ," to class dunce, when he insists that Jesus must conform to his expectations of what the Messiah should and should not do.

Jesus, therefore, must counter both the Pharisees' blind enmity and his disciples' blind enthusiasm. For the moment, the former are a lost cause. Nothing short of a blinding flash of light on the Damascus road will convince one of them that Jesus is God's Messiah. Jesus concentrates his energies, instead, on patiently instructing his disciples to unlearn everything they have been taught or have believed about the role of the Messiah. They will learn the lesson with difficulty. Nothing happens as they expect or wish. Everyone has trouble learning that victory comes through giving one's life, not by taking others' lives.

Wink traces the disciples' blindness to "an interest-conditioned and experience-conditioned manner of seeing and hearing and reacting." He compares it to experiments where the subjects wore stereopticons, allowing them to see two different pictures simultaneously, one for each eye. The subjects described seeing only the picture familiar to their cultural conditioning. He reports:

> When a picture of a baseball player was flashed to one eye and a bullfighter to the other, Mexicans reported seeing the bullfighter and North Americans saw the baseball player. Subjects shown an anomalous red six of spades will experience vague physical discomfort but identify it as a six of spades. We tend to see what we are trained to see, not what is there.[16]

---

16. Walter Wink, "The Education of the Apostles: Mark's View of Human Transformation," *Religious Education* 83 (1988): 287.

The same thing happens to Peter. The word "Christ" and Jesus' words about his suffering and death flash on the screen. Peter feels more than a vague sense of discomfort; he feels profound abhorrence. This cannot be. Our predispositions cause us to see what we want to see, to hear what we want to hear. Preachers may experience congregations responding this way on a weekly basis. One may preach a sermon on God's prodigal grace, for example, and someone inevitably congratulates him or her on getting tough on sinners and coming down hard on the need to obey the Ten Commandments.

In bridging the contexts we must be sensitive to how much we, like Peter, project our aspirations on Jesus. We fail to see what is actually on the screen. This text, therefore, should force us to examine honestly the many ways we want to correct Jesus' teaching to suit our own prejudices, particularly when it comes to the theme of suffering and sacrifice. If Jesus' reaction is any indication, the adulteration of his stark demand should meet with stinging rebuke.

Jesus' sharp rebuke may give the listener a jolt. While some churches might proudly inscribe on their building Jesus' praise from Matthew's Gospel, "Upon this rock I will build my church," few would choose to have his words, "Get behind me, Satan," etched in a place of prominence. The church probably needs to hear that rebuke more than any praise. The problem is that we do not like to hear criticism, especially when it is so public. Many take a rebuke as rejection. Jesus' rebuke of Peter, however, does not mean that he rejects him. Rebuking was an important pedagogical method. In Qumran literature, chastisement by God was regarded as almost mandatory for membership in the community and for spiritual growth. It was something for which one was grateful to God. The rebuke comes as a challenge to understand and leads to repentance. No one wants to hear it, but soothing words of assurance do not help those who imperil their souls and others' by setting their minds on human things.

This passage will help acquaint people with the rigors of discipleship. Jesus calls for disciples to deny themselves, take up their cross, lose their lives to save them, and be intrepid in giving their testimony. One cannot live as a disciple the way many people watch television—sitting in a lounge chair with remote control in hand, ready to switch channels whenever anything unpleasant, tedious, or demanding appears on the screen. In his exposé of the influence of television on our culture, Postman writes:

> I believe I am not mistaken in saying that Christianity is a demanding and serious religion. When it is delivered as easy and amusing, it is another kind of religion altogether."[17]

---

17. Neil Postman, *Amusing Ourselves to Death* (New York: Viking, 1985), 121.

An actor remarking on the popularity of his science-fiction TV show said that it tapped into the search for spirituality of this age: "People are hungry for transcendence, they're looking for that feeling of mystery, that tingle you get when you feel God." Jesus has given the disciples plenty of opportunities to feel tingles, but discipleship and true spirituality involves much more than that. One must guard against turning God into a commodity for self-gratification.

(1) *Self-denial.* We must be careful not to confuse the call for self-denial with some kind of asceticism—denying things to oneself that delight one—or with self-discipline. Asceticism and self-discipline need not be Christian. Best aptly comments:

> It is not the denial of something to the self but the denial of the self itself. It is the opposite of self-affirmation, of putting value on one's being, one's life, one's position before man or God, of claiming rights and privileges peculiar to one's special position in life or even of those normally believed to belong to the human being as such.[18]

One therefore cannot limit self-denial to a season of the year, such as Lent, because it is an attitude that generates daily submission of one's own will to another's. Those who deny themselves say "no" to the "I" that would enslave them and say "yes" to God, who leads them to life. Bonhoeffer defines self-denial in this way:

> To deny oneself is to be aware only of Christ and no more of self, to see only him who goes before and no more the road which is too hard for us. Once more, all that self-denial can say is: "He leads the way, keep close to him."[19]

Every day we must open ourselves up to God's initiatives and control. Self-denial takes shape in many ways. For some, it may mean leaving job and family as the disciples have done. For the proud, it means renouncing the desire for status and honor. For the greedy, it means renouncing an appetite for wealth. The complacent will have to renounce the love of ease. The fainthearted will have to abandon the craving for security. The violent will have to repudiate the desire for revenge. On it goes. Individuals know best what hinders them from giving their lives over to God. Entire churches too may need to learn to deny themselves—to tithe their offerings to help other struggling congregations rather than build a new recreation center with a

---

18. Best, *Following Jesus,* 37.

19. Dietrich Bonhoeffer, *The Cost of Discipleship* (New York: Macmillan, 1963), 97.

bowling alley and basketball court, to go without new choir robes so that the money can go instead to missions.

(2) *Bearing a cross.* The cross is the heart of the gospel, and bearing a cross is a central requirement of discipleship. Making the confession that Jesus is the Christ is not enough. If he is the Christ, then he expects to be followed and obeyed. He does not ask for modest adjustments in our lives but a complete overhaul of our behavior. He calls us to bear a cross.

Cross-bearing refers to self-sacrifice, even to the point of giving one's life. The call for self-sacrifice, however, is given the soft sell in too many congregations and television ministries today. Unlike some contemporary peddlers of the gospel, Jesus does not offer his disciples varieties of self-ful-fillment, intoxicating spiritual experiences, or intellectual stimulation. He presents them with a cross. He does not invite them try the cross on for size to see if they like it. He does not ask for volunteers to carry one for extra credit. This particular demand separates the disciples from the admirers. Disciples must do more than survey the wondrous cross, glory in the cross of Christ, and love the old rugged cross, as beloved hymns have it. They must become like Jesus in obedience and live the cross.

To take up your cross means that you have to matriculate in the school of suffering. As Gundry comments, it means "subjecting yourself to shame, to the 'howling, hostile mob.'"[20] Disciples stake their lives on their confession that he is the Messiah and follow him on the way to suffering. Admirers may acknowledge him as the Messiah and even as the Son of God, but they dig in their heels when he calls them to follow him down the particular path that may lead to martyrdom. In Albert Camus's novel *The Stranger*, a priest tries to convince an unbeliever about the faith and pulls open a drawer, taking out a silver crucifix. He then brandishes it at him to reinforce his argument. Yet Jesus does not call us to wave the cross but to carry it.

In bridging the contexts one should challenge false ideas of what the cross means. For many, the cross has become a fashion accessory, a piece of jewelry, often worn but seldom borne. For others, it is a decoration for military heroism: the Victoria Cross, the Iron Cross. Still others regard the cross they bear as some bodily affliction, some problem in their family, or some catastrophe that strikes. Because Jesus delivers people from demonic possession, from illness, and from the destructive forces of nature, the cross is not something that comes from "non-human oppression."[21] The cross represents the oppression caused by humans who oppose the faith and witness

---

20. Gundry, *Mark*, 436.

21. David Rhoads, "Losing Life for Others in the Face of Death: Mark's Standards of Judgment," *Int* 47 (1993): 363.

of Christians. It does not refer to bearing patiently the aches and pains of life.[22] We have only found Christ when we are more concerned about others' suffering than our own.

We must also come to terms with the sad fact that for a significant portion of humankind the cross evokes the twisted ideology of Nazism represented by the swastika (*Hakenkreuz*). David H. Stern writes of the painful association the cross has for him.

> To many Christians the cross represents all they hold dear; I do not object to their use of it to symbolize their faith. But for centuries Jews were done to death under the sign of the cross by persons claiming to be followers of the Jewish Messiah. Therefore to me the cross symbolizes the persecution of the Jews. As a Messianic Jew, still feeling pain on behalf of my people I do not have it in me to represent my New Testament faith by a cross.[23]

Stern prefers to translate the word for cross as "execution stake." When one translates it this way, it will eliminate the trivial ways we apply this saying. Dietrich Bonhoeffer, who was eventually hanged by the Nazis, wrote: "The cross is laid on every Christian. ... When Christ calls a man he bids him come and die."[24] Following Jesus to Golgotha is not some tedious detour; it is the main road. We can only hope to be ready when he leads us along paths that we would never have chosen for ourselves.

(3) *The cross as a stumbling block.* This episode lays bare how the cross becomes a stumbling block, particularly for those who assume they know what a Messiah is supposed to do. Worldly wisdom will always dismiss it. Love that serves others no matter how much it costs clashes head to head with worldly wisdom that believes that we should seek our own advantage no matter how much it hurts others. Jesus turns conventional wisdom on its head. His self-giving love remains a permanent mystery even to Christ's most devout followers.

Jesus offers paradoxical advice on how to save one's soul: One has to lose one's life to save it. Disciples must grasp the cross, the very thing that will put them to death. This truth challenges the way most people go about living their lives. A saying attributed to football coach Knute Rockne—"Show me a good loser and I will show you a loser"—reflects a pervasive attitude: One must win at all costs. A local sports figure was quoted as saying:

---

22. Eduard Schweizer, "The Portrayal of the Life of Faith in the Gospel of Mark," in *Interpreting the Gospels*, ed. James Luther Mays (Philadelphia: Fortress, 1981), 173.

23. David H. Stern, *Jewish New Testament Commentary* (Clarksville, Md.: Jewish New Testament Publications, 1992), 41.

24. Bonhoeffer, *The Cost of Discipleship*, 99.

People think if you're a Christian, you're wimpy and you don't care. Well if you know God, you know that's wrong. That's way wrong. God is a winner. God never loses. That's why he's God.

But how does God win? As we bring this passage into our age, we will profit from reflecting how often our thinking reflects the ways of humans instead of God's ways.

JESUS WAS "TOO new and unique, too big and oddly shaped" to fit into his contemporaries' traditional pigeonholes.[25] The same holds true today. Modern scholars tend to make Jesus over into their own image and, in the process, eliminate any eternal claim he might exert on their lives. Some present him as a revolutionary who gathered a band of desperadoes to bring about a social liberation of the oppressed peasants. Others present him as an itinerant, nonviolent teacher spouting pithy maxims; still others as a charismatic healer trying to reform Judaism. These speculations, all dressed in the garb of academic expertise, are no closer to the truth than the best guesses of Jesus' contemporaries, but the media will often seize on these opinions. Brown sagely points out that this kind of media hype "can be presented with enthusiasm and does not require radio, newspaper, or TV presenters to take a stance about Jesus' religious claims that might offend viewers."[26]

Many respect Jesus as an ethical, if impractical, teacher, whose memorable sayings about turning the other cheek, not casting the first stone, and loving your neighbor make for absorbing reading. The Jesus Mark presents and the church confesses, however, is not simply a Galilean holy man, a nice teacher, a fervent prophet, a peasant leader, a wandering Cynic calling people to live according to common sense and natural law—all options proposed by recent scholars on the historical Jesus. *He is the Son of God.* We cannot put him into nonreligious categories that allow us to evade the claim that God makes on our lives. He is the Messiah whom God sent to suffer and save his people through his death and resurrection.

Jesus must resist the pressure to conform to the expectations of his opponents, who challenge him to prove his claims with a decisive messianic sign. He must also fend off the wishful thinking of his closest followers, who are influenced by popular expectations of what the Messiah is supposed to do. They expected one who will be Solomon-like in performing exorcisms,

25. Luccock, "The Gospel According to St. Mark: Exposition," 7:733.
26. Brown, *The Death of the Messiah*, 1:677–78.

Moses-like in providing bread in the desert, Joshua-like in leading a conquest that will recapture the Promised Land from the pagans, and David-like in establishing a triumphant kingdom with all Israel's enemies serving as footstools. The temptation for Jesus to meet the expectations of his little band of followers must have been enormous lest they desert him in disappointment. But Jesus pledges to do only God's will, even if he must die all alone. His commitment to obey God and not to pour syrup on everybody's waffle, as one has phrased it, serves as the model for present-day ministers who face the same kind of pressures to conform to the expectations of what others think a minister ought to be and do.

Many church members treat their ministers as coolies whom they have hired to take them to the top of a spiritual Pike's Peak—and watch the bumps. They act like stockholders who have retained a CEO to shape up the bottom line. Expectations are diverse. Some expect the minister to bring instant success to the church so that people overflow into the aisles. As Buttrick trenchantly states it, many expect that their ministers will be "sage counselors, wise as Freud . . . , able to unshackle troubled minds," and that they will be activists matching the politically correct or incorrect prejudices of their parishioners regarding every hot-potato political issue from social issues to foreign policy. He observes how easily ministers can get trapped by social expectations since most humans "crave social approval." Consequently, ministers may find it difficult "to ignore all social expectations and allow God to define our ministry in every new situation." They may find it much easier "to succumb to inauthenticity." "If enough people speak and act favorably toward us, maybe we will be able to enjoy our own company and can manage a modicum of self-esteem." "Social justification" is easier to attain than justification by faith since the latter is "a matter of hard relentless, trusting faith in God." It is often a lonely business when one must leave the pack and head off in a direction demanded by God.[27]

To preach Christ crucified and to live it means that one will court rejection and ridicule. Paul understood this well (1 Cor. 4:9–11):

> For it seems to me that God has put us apostles on display at the end of the procession, like men condemned to die in the arena. We have been made a spectacle to the whole universe, to angels as well as to men. We are fools for Christ, but you are so wise in Christ! We are weak, but you are strong! You are honored, we are dishonored! To this very hour we go hungry and thirsty, we are in rags, we are brutally treated, we are homeless.

---

27. David Buttrick, *The Mystery and the Passion: A Homiletic Reading of the Gospel Traditions* (Minneapolis: Fortress, 1992), 115–16.

Those who follow this solitary path will know, if only a little, the pain that Jesus felt in dealing with willful and dull disciples, not to mention the cold-hearted opposition that was bent on his total destruction. Present-day Christians can learn from the example of their Lord, who knows their travail and calls them to be faithful.

Thomas à Kempis wrote:

> Jesus today has many who love his heavenly kingdom, but few who carry his cross; many who yearn for comfort, few who long for distress. Plenty of people he finds to share his banquet, few to share his fast. Everyone desires to take part in his rejoicing, but few are willing to suffer anything for his sake. There are many that follow Jesus as far as the breaking of bread, few as far as drinking the cup of suffering; many that revere his morality, few that follow him in the indignity of his cross; many that love Jesus as long as nothing runs counter to them; many that praise and bless him, as long as they receive comfort from him; but should Jesus hide from them and leave them for a while, they fall to complaining or become deeply depressed.
>
> Those who love Jesus for his own sake, not for the sake of their own comfort, bless him in time of trouble and heartache as much as when they are full of consolation.[28]

Jesus had no intention to fill the ranks of his army with volunteers who professed allegiance to him and talked grandly of victory but were unwilling to make sacrifices.

Mark's first readers literally faced the prospect of death for being Christians, and the Evangelist wanted to encourage them to face it with courage and to resist the temptation to retreat. Most Christians today do not live with such physical danger. Yet many of us are tempted to retreat from dying with embarrassment when we stand up for our faith. Stephen L. Carter has argued that to prevent religion from dominating politics in the United States, we have "created a political and legal culture that presses the religiously faithful to be other than themselves, to act publicly, and sometimes privately as well, as though their faith does not matter to them."[29] Many find it difficult to go against the crowd and to stand up for Christ. Jesus does not offer an option for secret discipleship; he requires bold confession. As Minear puts it: "Their coming confession of faith, like his, would

---

28. Thomas à Kempis, *The Imitation of Christ*, trans. Ronald Knox and Michael Oakley (New York: Sheed and Ward, 1959), 2.9 (pp. 76–77).

29. Stephen L. Carter, *The Culture of Disbelief: How American Law and Politics Trivializes Religious Devotion* (New York: Basic Books, 1993), 3.

be given not in a church but in a courtroom."[30] If we are not faithful to bear witness under little pressure, we will hardly prove true if our very lives are on the line.

We face the temptation to seek worldly security rather than risk our lives for Christ. Those whose sole aim is material well-being lose the one life that is worth living; those who sacrifice for others, gain it. Many devote themselves to gaining the security that this world provides, but there is a difference between feeling secure and being secure. Those who surround themselves with material goods, insure them to the hilt, and accumulate a comfortable nest egg may feel secure. They are like the rich fool who says to himself, "You have plenty of good things laid up for many years. Take life easy; eat, drink and be merry" (Luke 12:19). In God's reality, they are like children in a thunderstorm who close their eyes and hide under the covers. Those who risk their lives even to the point of death rest in the complete security of God. Those who devote themselves to gaining the whole world—busily grinding axes, climbing ladders of worldly success, achieving prestige, acquiring luxuries—do not find fulfillment. They may find themselves asking the question, "I have reached the top, become number one—so what?"

Both ancients and moderns have experienced this empty feeling. Lucius Septimus Severus (146–211) died with these words, "I have been everything and everything is nothing. A little urn will contain all that remains of one for whom the whole world was too little." In David Lodge's novel *Therapy*, the main character's therapist asks him to make a list of all the good things about his life in one column and all the bad things in another. Under the good column he wrote: "professionally successful, well off, good health, stable marriage, kids successfully launched in adult life, nice house, great car, as many holidays as I want." Under the bad column he wrote just one thing: "feel unhappy most of the time."[31]

Trying to ensure one's advancement in this life leads only to the irreparable loss of something far more valuable to oneself. Who wants someone to say at their funeral, "He was the richest man I know—a hard hitter"? Many people today, if they do a little serious soul-searching, will find themselves coming up empty-handed. They have sold their souls for what will prove to be utterly worthless. Christians who give their lives to God get self-fulfillment by not seeking self-fulfillment. Nancy Mannigoe, in William Faulkner's *Requiem for a Nun*, says in her simple way that Jesus "dont tell you not to sin, He just asks you not to. And he dont tell you to suffer. But He gives you the

---

30. Minear, *Mark*, 95.
31. David Lodge, *Therapy* (New York: Viking, 1995), 23.

chance. He gives you the best He can think of, that you are capable of doing. And He will save you."[32]

We also face the temptation to evade Jesus' stern demands by substituting a more congenial, less rigorous variant of Christianity. Many today appear to want choices, not eternal imperatives. We live in a consumerist society, and many approach religious life no differently from any other aspect of their life. They come to churches as consumers, wanting to know, "What am I going to get from this?" They want a full-service church with pleasing worship, a good youth program, excellent child care, nice facilities, pastoral care when they need it, and at least passable preaching. They want the best but are not always willing to pay for it. They prefer religion à la carte and opt for the salads and desserts, but not the main course with its hard demands of obedience. They may shy away from anything that calls for heroism or sacrifice. Roof offers some hope, however. He writes that many "are hungry to find ways to commit themselves, if they can find personal enhancement, or extension of their own selves, in whatever they do or in however they give of themselves."[33] The church should tap into this hunger by presenting the clear demands of the gospel instead of trying to attract seekers by offering a self-indulgent escapism.

Jesus promises that the Son of Man will be vindicated by God by being raised from death and promises that he will come in the glory of the Father. Even though Paul proclaims, "Now is the day of salvation" (2 Cor. 6:2), one must guard against an overheated, spiritualistic illusion that we are already living in the kingdom, as if the Day of the Lord has already come (2 Thess. 2:2). Heaven is not yet, and neither is our glory. Paul challenged those "spiritually wise" Corinthians who believed that they already were filled, had become rich, and reigned as kings. In his catalogue of sufferings he argued that the present age is not the time to be filled or rich, for strength or honor. It is instead the time for hunger, for homelessness, for persecution, and for being reviled (1 Cor. 4:8–13). The Christian's transformation into the glory of Christ will not take place until the resurrection and the new creation. The Spirit received in this life is only the first installment of this future transformation, not the actual transformation (2 Cor. 1:22; 5:5; Eph. 1:14). In his suffering Paul argues that he gives testimony both to Christ's death and his resurrection (2 Cor. 4:10–11).

---

32. William Faulkner, *Requiem For a Nun* (New York: Random House, 1951), 278.
33. Wade Clark Roof, *A Generation of Seekers* (San Francisco: Harper, 1992), 247.

Mark 9:2–13

A FTER SIX DAYS Jesus took Peter, James and John with him and led them up a high mountain, where they were all alone. There he was transfigured before them. ³His clothes became dazzling white, whiter than anyone in the world could bleach them. ⁴And there appeared before them Elijah and Moses, who were talking with Jesus.

⁵Peter said to Jesus, "Rabbi, it is good for us to be here. Let us put up three shelters—one for you, one for Moses and one for Elijah." ⁶(He did not know what to say, they were so frightened.)

⁷Then a cloud appeared and enveloped them, and a voice came from the cloud: "This is my Son, whom I love. Listen to him!"

⁸Suddenly, when they looked around, they no longer saw anyone with them except Jesus.

⁹As they were coming down the mountain, Jesus gave them orders not to tell anyone what they had seen until the Son of Man had risen from the dead. ¹⁰They kept the matter to themselves, discussing what "rising from the dead" meant.

¹¹And they asked him, "Why do the teachers of the law say that Elijah must come first?"

¹²Jesus replied, "To be sure, Elijah does come first, and restores all things. Why then is it written that the Son of Man must suffer much and be rejected? ¹³But I tell you, Elijah has come, and they have done to him everything they wished, just as it is written about him."

Original Meaning

JESUS TAKES PETER, James, and John to a high mountain, the traditional place for special revelation in Scripture. In Mark's Gospel, the greater the revelation, the smaller the number of people who witness it: three male disciples behold Jesus' transfiguration, and three women followers discover the empty tomb and first learn of Jesus' resurrection (16:1–8).

The three disciples mentioned here figure prominently in this Gospel. They were the first called (1:16–20), and their names head the list of the Twelve (3:16–17). Jesus also chose them to come with him when he raised Jairus's daughter from the dead (5:37–43). Peter is the first to confess Jesus as the Christ (8:27–30); and James and John will be the first to try to exploit their close ties to Jesus to get seats of power in his kingdom (10:35–45). During the dark hours in Gethsemane, Jesus will take these three with him when he separates himself from the other disciples to pray (14:33). Then they will witness his great distress and agitation; now they witness his glory as he is "altered to a purer and brighter essence."[1] They also hear the same divine voice that spoke at Jesus' baptism and identified him as God's unique Son. These select disciples are therefore the first persons in the Gospel to receive information about Jesus that only the readers of the prologue and the malevolent demons know.

The Transfiguration (9:2–8)

MARK HAS MADE no attempt to fix times or dates for the reader in his narrative. He introduces most events with "immediately" or "and," but the Transfiguration account begins with a chronological note, "after six days." This specific logging of the time recalls Moses' six-day preparation before God appeared to him on the mountain (Ex. 24:15–16). The Transfiguration has other parallels with Moses' ascent and descent of Mount Sinai (Ex. 24; 34:29–35).

Jesus	Moses
Jesus takes three disciples up the mountain (Mark 9:2).	Moses goes with three named persons plus seventy of the elders up the mountain (Ex. 24:1, 9).
Jesus is transfigured and his clothes become radiantly white (Mark 9:2–3).	Moses' skin shines when he descends from the mountain after talking with God (Ex. 34:29).
God appears in veiled form in an overshadowing cloud (Mark 9:7).	God appears in veiled form in an overshadowing cloud (Ex. 24:15–16, 18).
A voice speaks from the cloud (Mark 9:7).	A voice speaks from the cloud (Ex. 24:16).
The people are astonished when they see Jesus after he descends from the mountain (Mark 9:15).	The people are afraid to come near Moses after he descends from the mountain (Ex. 35:30).

---

1. Tolbert, *Sowing*, 204.

These echoes of Exodus 24 and 34 suggest that a Moses typology under-girds Mark's shaping of the Transfiguration.[2] Typology assumes that God's prior redemptive acts recorded in Scripture prefigure later events. These prior events then become the paradigm for describing and understanding later events, and Mark expects the biblically literate reader to see the linkage between the two events. What happened to Moses on Sinai sheds light on the meaning of Jesus' transfiguration. Since Jewish traditions interpreted Moses' ascent of Sinai as an enthronement, the parallels with the Transfiguration cast Jesus as a king. Marcus concludes, "Like the Moses of Jewish legend, Jesus is a king—indeed a king who participates in God's own rule."[3]

The chronological note, "after six days," also expressly connects the Transfiguration to the previous incident. Peter confesses Jesus to be the Christ, and Jesus divulges his future suffering, warns of the coming judgment when the Son of Man comes in the glory of his Father with the holy angels, and promises that some present will see the kingdom coming in power before they die (8:27–9:1). The Transfiguration occurs on the seventh day after this incident and connects Jesus' announcement of suffering with the foretaste of his promised resurrection glory that occurs at the end of the Passion week.[4] The unearthly white glow emanating from Jesus' clothes alludes to resurrection since white garments characterize the righteous in the resurrection.[5] Jesus specifically mentions the resurrection of the Son of Man as he descends the mountain with his disciples (9:9).

The Transfiguration, therefore, serves to confirm that the suffering Jesus will endure is not incompatible with his glory. The scene functions like a hologram. For a brief moment, the disciples glimpse the truth as divine glory shines through the veil of suffering. It foreshadows the time when God will

---

2. Marcus, *The Way of the Lord*, 82, citing Joachim Jeremias, "Μωυσῆς," *TDNT* 4:867–73, n. 228. In *Bib. Ant.* 11:15–12:1, the biblical story is retold so that Moses' descent from the mountain with a transfigured appearance (Ex. 34:29–35) follows immediately after his ascent. See also Dale C. Allison Jr., *The New Moses: A Matthean Typology* (Minneapolis: Fortress, 1993), 243–48.

3. Marcus, *The Way of the Lord*, 92. The reference to the Transfiguration in 2 Peter 1:16–18 pictures it as an enthronement.

4. The only other precise reference to time in Mark's narrative appears in 14:1. When his enemies plot his death, the high priests note that the Passover would arrive "after two days," that is, on the third day. See E. L. Schnellbächer, *KAI META HEMERAS HEX* (Markus 9:2)," *ZNW* 71 (1980): 252–57.

5. Acts 1:10; Rev. 3:4; 4:4; 7:9, 13–14; see also 1 Enoch, 62:15–16; 2 Enoch 22:8. Compare the vision of a "man dressed in linen" in Dan. 10:4–11:1 and the Ancient of Days, whose clothing was "white as snow" (7:9). In 16:5, the young man at the tomb is dressed in a white robe. See also Dan. 12:3; 4 Ezra 7:97; 2 Apoc. Bar. 51:3, 5, 10, 12; 1 Enoch 38:4; 39:7; 104:2; Matt. 13:43.

gloriously enthrone Jesus after the degradation on the cross. This white flash of the splendor to come brightens the dark cloud of tribulation that presently hangs over Mark's first readers and confirms Jesus' promise that those who follow and suffer for him will not have done so in vain.

A third theme relates to the presence of Elijah and Moses conversing with Jesus. Since Mark reports nothing of the conversation, the significant element is their appearance with Jesus. Their precise role in this scene, however, is puzzling.[6] Possibly, Moses represents the Law and Elijah the Prophets. If this is the case, this "salvation-history summit conference" adds authority to Jesus' teaching. His predicted suffering accords with, and is anticipated by, the Law and the Prophets.[7] Since the two do not speak but later fade from view when the voice from the cloud commands obedience to the Son, one can also interpret the scene to mean that Jesus completes their work and surpasses them. As Lane puts it, "His word and deed transcend all past revelation."[8]

This interpretation is inconvenienced by two problems: Elijah was not a writing prophet and seems an unusual choice to represent the prophets, and Mark lists Elijah before Moses. Since Moses was considered the first and greatest of the prophets, why does he come second? The discussion on the way down the mountain (9:11–13) provides the answer. The disciples recite the scribal expectations about the end, and they maintain that Elijah must play a key role before the restoration of all things. Elijah and Moses are both eschatological figures. Moses was Israel's first deliverer, and people expected a prophet like Moses (Deut. 18:15) to appear and liberate Israel. Elijah was supposed to appear at the dawning of the end time and God's ultimate redemption of Israel.[9] Both are mentioned in Malachi 4:4–6:

> "Remember the law of my servant Moses, the decrees and laws I gave him at Horeb for all Israel.
>
> "See, I will send you the prophet Elijah before that great and dreadful day of the LORD comes. He will turn the hearts of the fathers to

---

6. Both Elijah and Moses witnessed theophanies on mountains. Both were faithful servants who suffered because of their obedience, were rejected by the people of God, and were vindicated by God. Jewish tradition claimed that both did not die: Elijah was caught up to heaven in a fiery chariot (2 Kings 2:11), and later Jewish interpreters combined Deut. 34:6, "no one knows where his grave is," with Exod. 34:28, "Moses was there with the LORD," to conclude that Moses did not experience death (so Philo, *Questions and Answers on Genesis* 1.86).

7. Myers, *Binding*, 250.

8. Lane, *Mark*, 321.

9. In *Deut. Rab.* 3:17 (on 10:1), God tells Moses: "When I will send Elijah, the prophet, you are to come both of you together." 4 Ezra lists seeing "the men who were taken up, who from their birth have not tasted death" as a sign of the end of the age (4 Ezra 6:25–26).

their children, and the hearts of the children to their fathers; or else I will come and strike the land with a curse."

Their presence with Jesus on the high mountain, therefore, rouses Jewish hopes about the final redemption of Israel and suggests that the time has been fulfilled. The kingdom of God has drawn near (1:15).

A fourth theme emerges in Peter's unthinking response to these sights. He chatters on about building shelters: "Rabbi, it is good for us to be here. Let us put up three shelters—one for you, one for Moses and one for Elijah." Surprisingly, he calls Jesus "Rabbi" when he has just confessed him to be the Christ and has just witnessed his Transfiguration.[10] His desire to build shelters (booths, tents, or tabernacles) is also a perplexing feature. The reader needs some explanation for them as we have for the Jewish customs in 7:3–4, and one can only guess what Peter intended. Are the shelters meant to recall the Exodus and an elusive reference to the Feast of Tabernacles (Lev. 23:39–43)? Are they intended to recall the ancient battle cry, "Every man to his tent, O Israel!" in anticipation of a military uprising (2 Sam. 20:1; 1 Kings 12:16; 2 Chron. 10:16)? Does Peter want to set up the messianic headquarters here on the mountain? Maybe he only wants to prolong the blessed moment and offers the three figures hospitality since tents were regarded as the habitations of divine beings (Ex. 25:1–9; Acts 7:43; Rev. 21:3). Does he mistakenly believe "that the eschatological rest in which God and his heavenly retinue would dwell upon earth had already begun"?[11] If he does, then he fails to realize that before this final rest occurs, Jesus must go through suffering.

Mark clarifies only one thing: Peter does not know what to say because he is afraid (9:6). This comment makes it plain that whatever Peter has in mind, his remarks are ill-advised. He continues to see and react to things from a human perspective, and fear continues to cloud his mind. If the offer to build three shelters suggests some desire to venerate the trio, he mistakenly puts Jesus on a par with Elijah and Moses and fails to recognize his true rank. Elijah and Moses, great as they were, do not share God's glory with Jesus. Moses could not correct human hardness of heart (10:5), and Elijah succumbed to vindictiveness (2 Kings 1:9–12; see Luke 9:51–56). Only the Son offers the solution to the human predicament, and only he will fulfill God's purposes for Israel and humankind. Thus Elijah and Moses vanish, and Jesus alone stands before the disciples. God then intervenes to make things clearer for addled and fearful minds.

---

10. See 11:21; 14:45.

11. Schweizer, *Mark*, 182.

Jesus has spoken plainly of his suffering and death (8:31); now God speaks plainly about the Son: "This is my Son, whom I love. Listen to him!" (see Ps. 2:7; 2 Sam. 7:14).[12] The voice from the cloud represents a higher authority than either Elijah or Moses, who do not speak, and confirms that Peter's earlier confession was on target. Tolbert notes the irony in that this scene places so much emphasis on the sights—Jesus robed in glistening white, Elijah and Moses appearing with him, the overshadowing cloud—yet the voice does not command them "to look upon him" but to listen to him.[13]

Yet Jesus says nothing. What then are they to hear? Peter and the rest of the disciples must keep quiet and bend their minds around what Jesus says about his suffering—seven days before this event and immediately after it as they descend the mountain. In the first instance, Jesus announces that the Son of Man "must" suffer greatly (8:31). In the second, he declares that "it is written" that the Son of Man will go through many sufferings and be scorned (9:12). Elijah has already come and they did violence to him; the Son of Man can expect the same treatment (9:12–13). Announcements that God's reign advances through the death of the Messiah therefore surround the Transfiguration. Jesus' appearance, bathed in divine glory, attended by the great saints of old, and heralded by the voice of God, may take away the sting of these announcements about suffering by offering assurance of ultimate vindication, but it does not remove the necessity of travail for him and for all those who follow him.

The Question About Elijah (9:9–13)

AS THEY DESCEND, Jesus commands the three disciples to keep mum about what they saw and heard until the Son of Man should rise from the dead (9:9). God has given them another piece of the puzzle, and the picture is rapidly taking shape, but the secret is not for public proclamation until all the pieces fall into place. They have not reached the end of the road, and Jesus' task as Messiah lies before him.

For once, someone obeys Jesus' injunction to silence. Mark reports that the disciples hold fast to the word but are confused about the reference to the resurrection from the dead. Some interpreters claim that the disciples had no understanding about what resurrection meant. The disciples, however, are not like the Athenian gadflies who are ignorant of basic Jewish convictions (Acts 17:19, 32). Most Jews in the first century believed in the resurrection

---

12. The overshadowing cloud represents the presence of the Lord. See Ex. 16:10; 19:9; 24:15–18; 33:7–11; 34:5; 40:34–35; Deut. 31:15; 1 Kings 8:10–11; 2 Chron. 5:13–14; Ps. 97:2; Ezek. 1:28; 10:3–4; 2 Macc. 2:8.

13. Tolbert, *Sowing*, 206.

(Mark 12:18–27); even Herod knows it (6:14, 16). The phrase "the rising from the dead," therefore, does not refer to resurrection in general but specifically to the Son of Man's rising from the dead (9:9).

The disciples are stumped because Jesus' teaching that he must suffer has not yet sunk in, which explains why Jesus orders them to keep quiet. They are still listening to the teachers of the law and their opinions, not to Jesus. The disciples appeal to the authority of scribal opinion (based on Mal. 4:5–6) that Elijah was to appear first, before the great and terrible Day of the Lord that they hope will launch an earthly kingdom of messianic splendor. They are confused how the Son of Man's rising from the dead fits into this timetable. If Elijah comes before the Day of the Lord, when the Messiah is to be made manifest, how can the Messiah be dead and need to be resurrected? Their bewilderment reveals that Jesus must continue to drill into their heads that God's plan entails that the Son of Man must suffer and die.

It may appear that Jesus agrees with the scribal doctrine about Elijah's coming (9:12), but he gives it a twist by announcing that Elijah has already come. Clearly, he has John the Baptizer in mind, whom Mark has described as coming in the garb of Elijah (1:6). Matthew 17:13 makes the connection explicit, but Mark leaves it ambiguous, allowing readers to reason things out for themselves. Jesus' statement means that, contrary to received opinion, Elijah's return does not herald the approach of messianic happy days. If Elijah has indeed come, the disciples must rethink what it means for him to "restore all things." They can no longer think in terms of eschatological triumphalism.

Elijah's mission, according to Malachi 4:6, was to restore the hearts of the fathers to their children (see also Sir. 48:10). Did John the Baptizer/Elijah successfully execute that purpose when all Judea and Jerusalem came for baptism, confessing their sins (Mark 1:5)? Or did he fail because so many refused to repent (see 11:31)? If he failed, it bodes ill for the land because Malachi's prophecy also threatens destruction: God sends Elijah to transform hearts "or else I will come and strike the land with a curse" (Mal. 4:6). According to Mark 13:12, this transformation has not taken place. Jesus predicts, "Brother will betray brother to death, and a father his child. Children will rebel against their parents and have them put to death," and warns that the holiest site in all the land, the temple, will soon lie in ruins (13:2).

One can punctuate Jesus' answer in 9:12 as a question, which then gives his response a quite different slant. Jesus replies, "Is it true that, when Elijah comes before the Messiah, he will restore all things? How then has it been written of the Son of Man that he should suffer many things and be rejected...?"[14] This response implies that the heart of this generation is too

---

14. See Gnilka, *Markus*, 2:41–42; Marcus, *The Way of the Lord*, 99.

hard; the powers that be, too entrenched; the wiles of Satan, too keen. Besides, God's plan, hidden in the Scriptures, calls for humiliation first, then vindication. John, as Elijah, has been imprisoned because of a grudge and beheaded on a whim, and he lies dead and buried. Eschatological expectations have been fulfilled in totally unanticipated ways. Elijah does come first and has already come, but they did to him whatever they wished. The disciples, however, still question if Jesus has got it right. How can the Messiah be rejected and suffer? Jesus answers that their expectations are all wrong. Elijah goes before the Messiah in the way of suffering and death.

MARK'S FIRST-CENTURY AUDIENCE knew only pain and worldly insecurity. The Transfiguration, set amid announcements of suffering, does three things. (1) It serves to debunk any false hopes of eschatological triumphalism. His readers should not expect to reign as kings anytime soon (see 1 Cor. 4:8). (2) It offers comfort and hope of ultimate vindication. In spite of the terrible suffering, they will be glorified with Jesus (Rom 8:17–18). (3) It reveals Jesus' divinity as God's Son. The Messiah surpasses even the greatest saints of old.

Jesus' teaching about the Son of Man in Mark reveals that he is not just a figure of glory and power as many in Jesus' day might have imagined. The Son of Man has authority to forgive sins (2:10), is Lord of the Sabbath (2:28), will be enthroned at the right hand of Power (14:62), and will come in clouds with great power and glory (13:26). But the Son of Man also will suffer betrayal, ignominy, humiliation, and death (8:31, 38; 9:9, 12; 10:33; 14:21, 41) because he came to give his life as a ransom for many (10:45). To see Jesus in all his glory one must see how his power merges with suffering.

Comparing the Transfiguration with Jesus' crucifixion clarifies this truth. The two events have parallels that show how glory and death intertwine, and one sees Jesus "humiliated and exalted, surrounded by saints and ringed by sinners, clothed with light and yet wrapped in a garment of darkness."[15] Davies and Allison helpfully note the parallels and contrasts:[16]

- The glory revealed on the mountain is a private epiphany while the suffering on the cross is a public spectacle.
- Jesus is surrounded on the mountain by two prophets of old, Moses and Elijah; on Golgotha, by two thieves.

---

15. W. D. Davies and D. C. Allison, Jr., *The Gospel According to Saint Matthew* (ICC; Edinburgh: T. & T. Clark, 1991), 2:706.

16. Ibid., 2:706–7.

- On the mountain, Jesus' garments glisten in his glory; on Golgotha, they take his garments from him, compounding his humiliation.
- Three male disciples view his glory at close range; three female disciples view his suffering from afar.
- A divine voice from the cloud announces that Jesus is the Son of God; one of his executioners, a Roman centurion, acclaims him to be the Son of God after his death.
- In both scenes someone raises the question of Elijah. Coming down the mountain, Jesus informs his disciples that Elijah has already come and they did to him as they pleased. When Jesus hangs from the cross in torment, the bystanders taunt him with one last jibe: "Let's see if Elijah comes to take him down" (15:36). The perceptive reader knows that they have things all wrong. There will be no deliverance until the end of the age and only a few will discern the glory of God manifest on Golgotha.

What the disciples see on the Mount of Transfiguration is the promise of glory in Jesus' shimmering garments. What they need to hear when they come off the mountain and reenter the everyday realm is the requirement of suffering—the way of the cross and death. The biblical heroes vanish from sight. The splendor fades. The voice of God falls silent except as God speaks through the Son. Visions come and go, but his word remains. On the mountain they get a brief glimpse of Jesus' resplendent glory, but they are too dazed by the sights to understand fully.

A pitfall for interpreters is the temptation to get caught up in the glorious vision and forget the desolate suffering. When Peter spoke out of turn, his interjection may illustrate this temptation. Chrysostom commented that Peter "wanted to settle down in the security of this temporary bliss and also thus prevent the going down to Jerusalem to the cross."[17] Mark wants his first readers to see that the suffering of Jesus is not incompatible with his glory. Moses and Elijah may have escaped death according to Jewish tradition; the Messiah will not. Jesus offers no explanation why the Son of Man must suffer except that it is written and that it is necessary. We may surmise that God purposed the Son of Man to suffer and raise him up in glory so that humans could see more clearly God's love, God's strength, and the example of perfect obedience to God.

To convey Mark's message faithfully one must present the glory and suffering of Jesus in stereo and not overemphasize one at the expense of the other. The two go hand in hand. The suffering of the Messiah will be far

---

17. *Homilies in Matthew*, PG 59, 552, cited by Leopold Sabourin, *The Gospel According to St. Matthew* (Bombay: St. Paul, 1983), 2:704, n. 33.

greater than imagined, but so will his glory. The text invites the interpreter to reflect on how weakness and humiliation go with power and glory. As Paul writes, "For to be sure, he was crucified in weakness, yet he lives by God's power" (2 Cor. 13:4). It also should make us ponder how we may fail to listen to Jesus and how our received traditions from our teachers cause us to be confused about how God works in our world.

The first-century Christians lived in a world where leaders such as Herod could do as they wanted to God's messengers. The Transfiguration offers a peek into the future, but only a peek. We still live in that world where earthly powers can wreak vengeance against those who oppose them with God's word. Many Christians will suffer for their faith; others may escape. All must be prepared for wars, famines, arrests, and the siren of false prophets, who lure the elect astray as they carry the gospel to all the nations. Glory awaits them, but they must not begin the celebration too soon. Christians do not live on the mountain but down in the valley, where confusion and mayhem reign and where they must continue to joust with Satan. Yet even in the midst of suffering, God's presence shines through.

 MOST READERS WOULD prefer to be with the disciples basking in the glory on the mountain top than to trudge along with the disciples as they struggle and fail to help an epileptic boy and end up surrounded by hissing opponents and a disgruntled crowd. We spend most of our lives, however, down below in the valley, where the shadow of death hovers over us. John Bunyan, in *Pilgrim's Progress*, said that Christ, in the flesh, had his country house in the valley of humiliation. In moments of failure and opposition one can easily fall prey to despair. Remembering the times when we experienced truth emblazoned before us like a bright gleaming light can carry us through the dark times when faith is challenged from within and without.

The moments when God breaks through and shines in our hearts take many forms for different people, but they take us through the difficulties that lie ahead and sustains us in the face of opposition. One can see an example of this in 2 Peter 1:16–18:

> We did not follow cleverly invented stories when we told you about the power and coming of our Lord Jesus Christ, but we were eyewitnesses of his majesty. For he received honor and glory from God the Father when the voice came to him from the Majestic Glory, saying, "This is my Son, whom I love; with him I am well pleased." We

ourselves heard this voice that came from heaven when we were with him on the sacred mountain.

Another example occurs when the travel companions of John Bunyan's Pilgrim begin to doubt whether the Celestial City ever existed. He encourages them by crying, "Did we not see it from the top of Mount Clear?"[18]

The problem is that we cannot cling to these visions, just as Mary Magdalene could not cling to her Lord in the garden (John 20:17), or the children of Israel could not freeze-dry the manna, or Peter could not memorialize this blessed moment with shelters. Earthly life cannot be all heavenly visions. Sometimes the memory fades, and one may doubt if it was real. Was it all a mirage or a hallucination? The words of our Lord remain constant, however. One must continue to listen to Jesus, whose words are able to sustain us when tingling visionary moments have grown dim.

Christians must be warned against celebrating too soon the glory that awaits them and becoming like the football player who recovered a fumble in the waning moments of the Super Bowl. As he neared the goal line, he began to go into his victory dance, holding the football out in a taunting gesture. Out of nowhere an opposing player raced to knock the ball from his hands on the two-yard line. Instead of crossing the goal line for a touchdown, a glorious moment rarely achieved by an interior lineman, he blew his opportunity by his premature merriment. Mark makes it clear that glory is to come; in the meantime, we live and serve in a hostile world bent on destroying God's messengers and servants.

Scientists have predicted children's success in later life with an interesting experiment conducted when they are four years old. A researcher invites a child into a room and gives the child a marshmallow. The researcher tells the child that he can eat it immediately, but the researcher must leave for a moment to run an errand. If the child waits to eat the marshmallow until the researcher comes back, the child can have two marshmallows. Some children gobble the marshmallow immediately; others hold out for a few minutes. Some wait until the researcher returns in order to get that second marshmallow. They do everything they can to stave off temptation while the researcher is out of the room. The children who resist eating the marshmallow grow up to be better adjusted, more popular, more adventurous, more confident, and more dependable.[19] Those who give in are more likely to be lonely, to buckle under stress, and to shy away from challenges. Christians need to learn this deferred gratification so that they can live well in every

---

18. Luccock, "The Gospel According to St. Mark: Exposition," 7:775.
19. Daniel Goleman, *Emotional Intelligence* (New York: Bantam, 1995), 80–83.

condition, buoyant in the midst of trouble, confident, resilient, and willing to take on challenges.

Many in the church today suffer from a form of Bible amnesia. They remember only the parts that promise wealth, happiness, and glory and forget, or fail to listen, to the calls for self-sacrifice, suffering, and bearing one's cross. They want to skip Suffering 101 and move on to advanced placement in Glory 909. The Gospel of Mark emphasizes that the Messiah must shoulder a cross, embrace humility, and renounce brute force, and his disciples must do the same if they bear Christ's name. The disciples in Mark, however, show reluctance to do so. They want it all now. They want to share his power over unclean spirits (9:28), to be great (9:34), to control others (9:38; 10:13), to get a reward for following him (10:28), and to sit on his left and right in his glory (10:37). They must first learn from him that if they are to share these things with him, they must share his suffering on earth. As Paul says, we are "heirs of God and co-heirs with Christ, if indeed we share in his sufferings in order that we may also share in his glory" (Rom. 8:17).

Mark 9:14–29

WHEN THEY CAME to the other disciples, they saw a large crowd around them and the teachers of the law arguing with them. ¹⁵As soon as all the people saw Jesus, they were overwhelmed with wonder and ran to greet him.

¹⁶"What are you arguing with them about?" he asked.

¹⁷A man in the crowd answered, "Teacher, I brought you my son, who is possessed by a spirit that has robbed him of speech. ¹⁸Whenever it seizes him, it throws him to the ground. He foams at the mouth, gnashes his teeth and becomes rigid. I asked your disciples to drive out the spirit, but they could not."

¹⁹"O unbelieving generation," Jesus replied, "how long shall I stay with you? How long shall I put up with you? Bring the boy to me."

²⁰So they brought him. When the spirit saw Jesus, it immediately threw the boy into a convulsion. He fell to the ground and rolled around, foaming at the mouth.

²¹Jesus asked the boy's father, "How long has he been like this?"

"From childhood," he answered. ²²"It has often thrown him into fire or water to kill him. But if you can do anything, take pity on us and help us."

²³"'If you can'?" said Jesus. "Everything is possible for him who believes."

²⁴Immediately the boy's father exclaimed, "I do believe; help me overcome my unbelief!"

²⁵When Jesus saw that a crowd was running to the scene, he rebuked the evil spirit. "You deaf and mute spirit," he said, "I command you, come out of him and never enter him again."

²⁶The spirit shrieked, convulsed him violently and came out. The boy looked so much like a corpse that many said, "He's dead." ²⁷But Jesus took him by the hand and lifted him to his feet, and he stood up.

²⁸After Jesus had gone indoors, his disciples asked him privately, "Why couldn't we drive it out?"

²⁹He replied, "This kind can come out only by prayer."

Original Meaning

THIS FOURTH AND last of Jesus' exorcisms presents the downhill side of the Transfiguration. It comprises four scenes. The first scene (9:14–19) begins with crowds gathered around the helpless disciples, engaged in a debate, and climaxes in Jesus' lament over this faithless generation. The second scene (9:20–24) brings Jesus face to face with a desperate father and culminates in the man's moving confession of uncertain faith. The third scene (9:25–27) shows faith at work as Jesus drives out a spirit that has tormented the boy and struck him down as dead. The final scene (9:28–29) returns to the disciples' failure to accomplish the exorcism themselves and connects that failure to insufficient prayer.

When Jesus leaves the mountaintop's sublime glory he must reenter the everyday world of human and demonic discord. He finds his disciples embroiled in controversy with the teachers of the law and a large crowd ringing the combatants. The disciples' abortive attempt to exorcise a demon from a lad ignited the squabble. Jesus had deputized them to cast out demons (3:15; 6:7), and they had success (6:13–14), but not with this difficult case. Mark describes the boy's horrific afflictions in graphic detail. He is mute and racked by seizures that dash him to the ground, cause him to foam at the mouth and grind his teeth, and make him as stiff as a board. Attempts to give his affliction a modern medical name do not alleviate the evil behind his suffering. The boy's father complains painfully, "I asked your disciples to drive out the spirit, but they could not [were not strong enough to do so]" (9:18; cf. 5:4; 14:37). Jesus' disciples are found wanting, and the resulting hubbub exposes their inadequacy and brings them public shame. The theological teachers quarreling with them are no less impotent when confronted by the evil spirits.

When Jesus appears from the mountain, the crowds respond with fearful amazement and run to greet him. Is it his sudden arrival, his air of authority, or something about his countenance—some residual effects from the Transfiguration (see Ex. 34:29–30)—that stirs their astonishment? Mark does not tell us. He focuses instead on the spectacle of the disciples' glaring failure.

The noisy dispute causes Jesus to declare: "O unbelieving generation . . . how long shall I stay with you? How long shall I put up with you?" (9:19). This lament expresses his exasperation at an unbelieving, quarrelsome crowd (see Deut. 32:5; 20; Isa. 65:2; Jer. 5:21–23; Phil. 2:15). Jesus could do no mighty works in Nazareth because of their unbelief (Mark 6:6), and now the crowd's and his disciples' lack of faith contribute to failure. Jesus expresses in a complaint "the loneliness and the anguish of the one authentic believer in a world which expresses only unbelief."[1] His lament also expresses urgency. "How long?" does not convey a wish to be rid of inept disciples but refers to how little time he has left to soften their hardheartedness and to acquaint them more fully with the power that can expel evil. Time is short. Will they ever catch on? Faced with his disciples' failure and the crowd's unbelief, Jesus does not throw up his hands in disgust but immediately takes action to rectify the situation.

In the second scene (9:20–24), the people bring the beleaguered boy to Jesus, and the boy's father takes center stage with Jesus. Jesus does not dialogue with the spirit that possesses the boy but instead directs questions to the distraught father. For the first time, Jesus demands faith as a condition for an exorcism, although we have seen it displayed by the equally desperate Syrophoenician mother. At the heart of this exorcism is the struggle for faith, not the struggle with a demon (cf. 5:1–13). Jesus' probing questions reveal the problem's severity and prompt the father's cry for compassion (9:22). For too long the boy has been in the thrall of an evil spirit that would destroy him by throwing him into fire or water. He is also mute and cut off from all human communication. When he comes into Jesus' presence, the evil spirit exerts its power by throwing the lad into frightening spasms so that he falls to the ground and foams at the mouth.

Seeing his son's renewed torment on top of the disciples' miserable failure can only pierce the father's heart even more and drain away his faith that Jesus can do any better than his disciples. He has not lost all hope, however, and woefully entreats him, "If you can do anything." His plea reveals that he does not doubt that Jesus would like to do something if he could, but he is uncertain whether Jesus can prevail in such a pernicious case. His guarded hope contrasts dramatically with the leper who boldly asserted: "If you are willing, you can make me clean" (1:40). The implied skepticism of his plea, "If you can," meets with a sharp comeback from Jesus.[2] His capability is not at issue: "Everything is possible for him who believes" (9:23). This affirmation does not mean that faith can accomplish anything but that those who have faith "will set no limits to the power of God."[3]

---

1. Lane, *Mark*, 332.

2. The Greek reads literally, "The if you can" (9:23a). Jesus repeats the doubt expressed by the father and challenges it. Marshall (*Faith As a Theme*, 116–17) paraphrases it well: "So far as your 'if you can' is concerned, I tell you that all things are possible to the one who believes." Lane (*Mark*, 333) also paraphrases it: "As regards your remark about my ability to help your son, I tell you everything depends upon your ability to believe, not on mine to act." The disciples are therefore not the only ones in this generation who lack faith.

3. A. E. J. Rawlinson, *St. Mark* (Westminster Commentaries; London: Methuen & Co. 1931), 124.

Whom does Jesus have in mind when he singles out "him who believes"? Does he refer to the miracle worker's faith or the faith of those who seek miracles? The answer is both. Unlike the disciples, Jesus as a miracle worker possesses unlimited power because of his potent faith. He therefore chides the father for putting limits on what he can do to help him. But petitioners also need to possess faith in him, and aggressive faith has been a characteristic of all those who beseech him for healing in the Gospel (1:40–45; 2:1–10; 5:21–43; 7:24–30; 10:46–52).

The faith of both the miracle worker and the petitioner leads to success. The father belongs to the unbelieving generation, but we see him straining to have this faith. Unlike the people at Nazareth, who refuse to believe, the father's unbelief is repentant. He is unable to believe but is desperate enough to ask for a miracle and for a faith that expects the impossible. He has not been privy to any vision on the mountain, and his poignant cry, "I do believe; help me overcome my unbelief," has resonated with those fighting the same battle across the centuries. He pleads for help just as he is, a doubter.

The third scene (9:25–27) presents Jesus doing battle with the spirit as he commands it to leave the boy and never to enter him again. Jesus' presence throws demons into fawning submission or into a fury, and this one defiantly flails his young victim about in one last gasp of malice.[4] After thrashing about with convulsions, the boy becomes as dead, so that many think he has died. For a moment, things look as if they have gone from bad to worse and that the old chestnut, "the operation was a success, but the patient died," applies.[5] The boy is "withered" (9:18), but Jesus has handled "withering" before (3:1, 3, 5). The evil spirit cries out, but Jesus has handled that before (1:23–24; 3:11; 5:7–8). The convulsions leave the boy looking as if he is dead, but Jesus has handled death before. Jesus seizes his hand as he did Jairus's dead daughter (5:41; see 1:31) and raises him up. One should not miss that Mark uses resurrection language: "he raised him" (*egeiren*; "he lifted him to his feet"), and "he was raised" (*aneste*; "he stood up"). Jesus drives the evil spirit out and gives the boy new life.

In the final scene (9:28–29), the disciples want to review their failure in the privacy of the house. Mark tells us nothing of the father's or the crowd's reaction to the boy's deliverance. Everything focuses on the lesson for Jesus' followers.[6] While the exchange with the father highlights the importance of faith, the conversation with the disciples emphasizes the necessity of prayer

---

4. Many have noted that the demonic resistance to Jesus increases as the story progresses in Mark.

5. Chapman, *Orphan*, 111.

6. The two miracles that occur during the journey to Jerusalem convey lessons for discipleship.

(9:29). Jesus' response, "This kind can come out only by prayer," implies that they failed because they had not prayed. The disciples were too busy arguing among themselves and with the opponents to pray.

Since Jesus did not offer up a prayer to exorcise the unclean spirit, the prayer that he has in mind is not some magical invocation but a close and enduring relationship with God. Mark hints that Jesus regularly engaged in intense prayer. He went out alone to pray (1:35; 6:45–46), but the disciples interrupted him because they were preoccupied with their own agenda. The one time he specifically asks them to pray with him they sleep instead (14:37–40). The readers therefore can learn from the disciples' negative example what happens to those who neglect prayer and try to operate on their own steam.[7] Jesus' positive example reveals that only a life governed by faith and prayer can repel the threat from the evil spirits.

A textual variant adds "and fasting" to the requirement of prayer in 9:29.[8] This reading does not fit the context for two reasons. (1) Jesus has already dismissed fasting as inappropriate until the bridegroom is taken away (2:18–20). How can he now fault the disciples, as his opponents had done earlier, for not fasting? (2) This reading turns fasting into a work that succeeds in acquiring power from God. The incident stresses the necessity of faith and prayer, which involve complete dependence on God. The power grows out of one's relationship to God in prayer and comes as a gift of grace, not as a prize for self-mortification.[9]

THE PANDEMONIUM THAT greets Jesus and the three disciples after they descend the mountain might give Peter new incentive to return to the place of glory to build those shelters, far removed from the confusion, din, and discord below. But disciples cannot sequester themselves from life's failures or from a faithless generation.

This episode differs from other exorcisms in Mark, and one learns where the central concerns are by looking at the differences. It does not focus so much on Jesus' power over the demonic but turns our attention to the disciples' failure (at the beginning and end of the pericope) and to the father's

---

7. These same disciples ironically have the gall to report to Jesus that they obstructed the successful exorcisms of an outsider "driving out demons in your name." The reason they did this was because "he was not one of us" (9:38).

8. It has weak manuscript support and was added because fasting was an interest of the early church (Acts 13:2; 14:23). "Fasting" was added to "prayer" in some texts of Acts 10:30 and 1 Cor. 7:5.

9. Hooker, *Mark*, 225.

need for faith (in the middle). The key moments are Jesus' pronouncements: "Everything is possible for him who believes" (9:23), and, "This kind can come out only by prayer" (9:29). Our interpretation should therefore focus on the parallels between us and the blundering disciples and the man's cry for help and faith—both of which are easy to carry over into our contemporary world.

This vivid account shows that disciples are just like the rest of us: beset by failure, too ready to engage in arguments, undisciplined in prayer life, and more eager to learn techniques than to take time to walk closely with God. The incident also reveals how feeble the disciples are when they are on their own. We can draw lessons from each of these failures.

To their credit, the disciples do want to learn from their mistakes. Their question to Jesus, "Why couldn't *we* drive it out?" reveals a basic misconception deriving from assumptions about exorcism in their first-century world. The question places an emphasis on "*we*" and betrays the longing to rely on their own professional skill and power. They may have wondered if there was something wrong with their technique that made things go awry. In the ancient world, magicians, sorcerers, and exorcists sought to hit the right combination of words and actions that would invoke the appropriate divine power to achieve the desired effects. They would weave esoteric spells employing potent divine names, perform mysterious actions, and use special instruments. It was all a matter of technique. Any relationship to the deity, such as love or devotion, was not required for success, just as the one who possessed Aladdin's lamp need only rub it to get the three wishes.

Josephus represents this view of exorcism when he exalted Solomon's prowess in demonic exorcism:

> And God granted him knowledge of the art used against demons for the benefit of healing and healing of men. He also composed incantations by which illnesses are relieved, and left behind forms of exorcisms with which those possessed by demons drive them out never to return.[10]

He then describes an exorcism done by one Eleazar before the Roman general Vespasian.

> He put to the nose of the possessed man a ring which had under its seal one of the roots prescribed by Solomon, and then as he smelled it, drew out the demon through his nostrils, and, when the man at

---

10. *Ant.* 8.2.5. § 45.

once fell down, adjured the demon never to come back into him, speaking Solomon's name and reciting the incantations which he had composed. Then, wishing to convince the bystanders and prove to them that he had this power, Eleazar placed a cup or footbasin full of water a little way off and commanded the demon, as it went out of the man, to overturn it and make known to the spectators that he had left the man. [11]

Jesus' answer to his disciples makes clear that his exorcisms have nothing to do with secret lore, techniques, or incantations. The disciples cannot take courses to learn the ins and outs of exorcism or hone their skills in some kind of exorcism lab. Lane comments, "The disciples had been tempted to believe that the gift that they had received from Jesus (6:7) was in their control and could be exercised at their disposal." This attitude springs from a subtle form of unbelief. When one has success, it encourages trust in oneself and one's techniques rather than in God.[12] Marshall points out that the disciples are therefore guilty of an "anxious self-concern" and a "misplaced self-confidence." He comments:

> Presumably they had come to regard their power to heal and exorcise as their own autonomous possession rather than being a commission from Jesus to realize his delegated authority afresh each time through dependent prayer. Mark is suggesting then that self-confident optimism may "feel" like faith, but it is in fact unbelief, because it disregards the prerequisite of human powerlessness and prayerful dependence on God.[13]

Only when the disciples are caught up short do they learn that they do not possess anything. Those who belong to the faithless generation do not cast out evil; God does. The power belongs entirely to him and must be received anew each time from him through a life of prayer. The prayerful attitude of "I do believe; help me overcome my unbelief" is therefore necessary for the healer as well as the sufferer.

The second thrust of this passage turns on Jesus' dialogue with the man who brought his child to the disciples. The forlorn father's struggle for faith helps to clarify the nature of faith as well as to reveal much about our human predicament.

---

11. *Ant.* 8.2.5. § § 47–48.
12. Lane, *Mark,* 335; see also Cranfield, *Mark,* 305.
13. Marshall, *Faith As a Theme,* 223.

Contemporary Significance

IN DRAWING OUT the contemporary significance of this passage we will look at the parallels between the disciples' failure in a ministry situation and ours so that we might spot the causes of those failures. We will also look at the father's desperate need and cry for help and what the exchange between him and Jesus says about faith.

The Disciples' Failure and the Need for Prayer

WE MAY PREFER the disciples' experience of Jesus' inspiring transfiguration to the disciples' disheartening failure, where they are unable to heal a demon-possessed boy. But Jesus calls us to go down where the cries of help are the loudest, because this is where we put faith into practice. Attending a Bible study conference, charged with inspirational talks and singing and girded about by like-minded, devout Christians, has more attraction to us than slogging through the trenches of life where a sense of failure can become an everyday companion.

Failure may seem a bad thing, something to be feared; but, depending on how we react, it can become a positive learning opportunity. It can become a teaching moment, when we become more deeply aware how utterly we must depend on God. It also can help us cope better with the shipwrecks, breakdowns, and disasters that inevitably come in our lives. Young ministers who hear only praise for brilliant sermons and applause for stunning statistical growth can be fooled into thinking that they succeed by their own power and that they are the star attraction. Failure can teach humility, although the disciples' later attempt to restrain other successful exorcists (9:38) suggests that they were slow learners on this point.

But failure can also have negative results. It can lead to arguments. We may try to fix blame on others rather than try to fix the problem. We may engage in feuds with enemies who gloat over our failures. The disciples fell into this trap. They wrangled with their opponents while a father stood by, agonizing over the suffering of his child. Cynics would contend that this reflects the church's normal state of affairs: They spend more time arguing than helping anybody or praying. People come to Christ's followers for help, and they get trivial arguments instead.

Most people in desperate straits do not care about learned disputations over fine points of interpretation or theological controversies over suspected heresies; they want help. Far too many people have turned away from God and the church because they were turned off by the petty bickering of those more interested in winning arguments within the church or with the secular world than in winning the world to faith. While we debate who is right, who is wrong, and who is at fault, the world stands by helplessly in the grips of evil. One side may win a skirmish with others but lose the battle with Satan. We can probably think of immediate examples of this flaw in our own church body and can apply this story to the situation. In our secular age, the church is no longer seen by many as the place to come for help. Why? Is it because the church seems too preoccupied with heavenly concerns or earthly controversies to offer any real aid in emergencies except a few unctuous bromides?

We should also never forget that people come to get help from Jesus, not from us. The father says to Jesus, "I brought *you* my son" (9:17); he did not bring him to the disciples. Jesus responds by saying, "Bring the boy to *me.*" (9:19). The gospel draws people who are in pain, and they place their hope in Jesus, not us. They come with a deep sense of desperation. Lewis B. Smedes confesses that he belatedly came to this insight.

> They came to my church on Sunday, ordinary people did, but I did not recognize them in the early days. I know now why I did not recognize them; I did not want them to be ordinary people. . . . I wanted them to be spiritual athletes, shoulders strong to bear the burdens of global justice that my prophetic words laid on them. But while I was offering them the precious promises and walloping them with the heroic mandates of the Word of God, many of them were secretly praying, "O God, I don't think I can get through this week—HELP ME!" . . . What they have in common is a sense that everything is all wrong where it matters to them most. What they desperately need is a miracle of faith to know that life at the center is all right.[14]

The cause of the disciples' power failure becomes clear in the final scene: They had deficient faith and insufficient prayer. Their prayers were mute. Nouwen argues that this has become a significant problem in the church.

> We have fallen into the temptation of separating ministry from spirituality, service from prayer. Our demons say: "We are too busy to pray, we have too many needs to attend to, too many people to respond to, too many wounds to heal." Prayer is a luxury, something to do during a free hour, a day away from work or on a retreat.[15]

The prayer that Jesus has in mind is "not merely a pious exercise"; rather, it is "the sense of complete dependence on God from which sincere prayer

---

14. Lewis B. Smedes, *How Can It Be All Right When Everything Is All Wrong?* (New York: Harper & Row, 1982), 80–81.

15. Henri J. M. Nouwen, *The Living Reminder: Service and Prayer in Memory of Jesus Christ* (New York: Seabury, 1977), 12.

springs."[16] A life of prayer goes hand in hand with effective ministry. It makes one receptive to the action of God. One cannot get ready for the moment by quickly uttering a special prayer; one has to be ready through a prayerful life when the moment comes. One cannot separate professional ministry to others from one's own spiritual condition. "Ministry is not an eight-to-five job but primarily a way of life."[17] That way of life must be permeated with prayerfulness.

Even when one has prayed, there will be times when we feel utterly helpless as members of our church fellowship face debilitating or terminal illness. All too often we spin our wheels, asking why and trying to come up with answers. Our time will be better spent in prayer and putting prayer into action by assuring these fellow believers that we will help take care of the medical bills, the meals, and the children. Maybe God can speak to us more clearly and use us better in times when we keenly sense our inadequacy for the moment. Nouwen asserts that prayer "is a way of being empty and useless in the presence of God and so of proclaiming our basic belief that all is grace and nothing is simply the result of hard work."[18]

The disciples must have felt quite empty and useless when they failed to make any headway with the demon controlling the young lad. They came to Jesus wanting to learn how to fill themselves so that they would not bungle things in the future and look so absurd. What Jesus teaches them applies to us: They need to learn from their emptiness and their failures that all healing comes from God, and they must depend entirely upon God.

The Father's Desperation and the Need for Faith

THE FATHER'S PAIN has immediacy for our situation. He is like so many parents today who helplessly watch their child suffering from some malignant disease, caught in the grip of some addiction, or living at the mercy of gangs and societal violence. They experience anger, frustration, and anguish in not knowing where to turn for help. They fear in their deepest soul that something has taken control of their children's lives that will kill them unless they can be delivered.

We also witness more and more children in our society who are convulsed by values that roll them around in the dirt. Hopelessness throws them into the fire of drugs and alcohol and drowns them with despair. Teenagers get caught in the grips of anorexia, and parents stand helplessly by, seeking answers and worrying themselves sick. Their best efforts are to no avail.

---

16. Cranfield, *Mark*, 305.

17. Henri J. M. Nouwen, *Creative Ministry* (Garden City: Doubleday, 1978), xxiii.

18. Nouwen, *The Living Reminder*, 52.

What is worse, there are some parents who show no concern for their children or who feel that they can do nothing to help. The answer begins when we prayerfully bring these children into the presence of Christ.

The most severe challenge to faith comes when loved ones suffer or die, particularly when they are very young. When hopes are raised only to be dashed, one finds it hard to dare hope again for God's benevolent intervention. The father in Mark 9 has almost reached the point where he has given up all hope when Jesus encourages him to have faith. Faith unleashes a new power in one's life, but several cautions need to be raised.

(1) People too glibly say to others, "Just have faith," and mouth platitudes about the great power of faith. Living out one's faith is never easy, and it grows harder when tragedies buffet one's life. The father's psychological turmoil reflects how easily the despair of doubt mixes with and thins the fiber of faith to watery gruel. We may get the impression from Mark 4:40 and 6:6 that doubt and faith are mutually exclusive: Either one has faith, or one is stuck in the morass of unbelief. This father's plea, "I do believe; help me overcome my unbelief," and Jesus' commands to have faith (5:36) reveal a paradox about faith that most believers experience. As Marshall states it, "There is within every believer a tension between faith and unfaith, and that faith can only continue to exist by dint of divine aid."[19] Chesterton wrote:

> There is something in man which is always apparently on the eve of disappearing, but never disappears, an assurance which is always apparently saying farewell and yet illimitably lingers, a string which is always stretched to snapping yet never snaps.[20]

Faith is always at a disadvantage and seems so fragile but nevertheless can outlive all its would-be conquerors. This father tethers what little faith he has to Christ and asks for help just as he is. Jesus does not expect him to summon up a mighty faith before anything can be done but only to trust that God can act decisively through him.

(2) Dwight L. Moody said there were three kinds of faith. There is struggling faith, like a man in deep water desperately swimming; clinging faith, like a man hanging to the side of a boat; and resting faith, like a man safely within the boat and able to reach out and help others get in. Many, like this father, have a struggling faith. Faith becomes a struggle because one must believe in the fantastic against all odds. Many experience all three kinds of faith and can move back and forth between them. One may have resting faith until life's storms threaten to swamp the boat and one feels about to

---

19. Marshall, *Faith As a Theme*, 121.
20. G. K. Chesterton, *G. F. Watts* (London: Duckworth, 1904), 98.

drown. The Gospel of Mark intends to lead the reader to a resting faith, but it reveals that it can only come by divine aid.

(3) Faith requires humble trust. The father comes to Jesus hesitantly, not with a bold swagger, and humbly stammers his plea. He does not try to varnish his spiritual poverty or to fake his trust. He does not ask for some sign from heaven to help jump-start his faith but turns his empty hands toward God and asks God to fill them. Like a man desperately treading water in a deep ocean, he pleads for Jesus to throw him a life preserver. The father shows faith in that he "expects everything from God and nothing from [his] own piety or power."[21] Jesus is not put off by the humble honesty of one who says, "I believe, but I am not certain of it." He grants what is asked.

(4) Faith comes as a gift and is sustained by the power of Jesus, the same power that can cast out the evil that held the boy captive. Thus one cannot regard faith as "a secure possession attained once and for all." As the father did not trust his own capacity to believe but asked for Jesus' help, so disciples of every age must rely on Jesus' help to give them faith.[22] God offers help for faith as well as healing.

(5) Faith and prayer make a powerful combination. Faith is not just an inner comfort; it changes human reality. But one must be cautious not to interpret Jesus' statement as a "general principle that limitless divine power is released through human faith."[23] In our culture, the phrase "just have faith" can apply to faith in almost anything and assumes that faith in whatever is a principle that supplies anyone with supreme power. In 10:27 and 14:36, Jesus ascribes this power to God alone. Marshall offers a helpful analysis:

> For Mark, all things are possible to the believer because, actively or passively, the believer sets no limits on God's power to break into his or her concrete situation, for the very existence of faith within the believer is the ground which allows God to act in his or her context. Since faith is God going into action, it is legitimate to ascribe to faith what is in fact a matter for God.[24]

---

21. Eduard Schweizer, "The Portrayal of the Life of Faith in the Gospel of Mark," in *Interpreting the Gospels*, ed. James Luther Mays (Philadelphia: Fortress, 1981), 178.
22. Marshall, *Faith As a Theme*, 121–22.
23. Ibid., 119.
24. Ibid., 120.

Mark 9:30–50

THEY LEFT THAT place and passed through Galilee. Jesus did not want anyone to know where they were, ³¹because he was teaching his disciples. He said to them, "The Son of Man is going to be betrayed into the hands of men. They will kill him, and after three days he will rise." ³²But they did not understand what he meant and were afraid to ask him about it.

³³They came to Capernaum. When he was in the house, he asked them, "What were you arguing about on the road?" ³⁴But they kept quiet because on the way they had argued about who was the greatest.

³⁵Sitting down, Jesus called the Twelve and said, "If anyone wants to be first, he must be the very last, and the servant of all."

³⁶He took a little child and had him stand among them. Taking him in his arms, he said to them, ³⁷"Whoever welcomes one of these little children in my name welcomes me; and whoever welcomes me does not welcome me but the one who sent me."

³⁸"Teacher," said John, "we saw a man driving out demons in your name and we told him to stop, because he was not one of us."

³⁹"Do not stop him," Jesus said. "No one who does a miracle in my name can in the next moment say anything bad about me, ⁴⁰for whoever is not against us is for us. ⁴¹I tell you the truth, anyone who gives you a cup of water in my name because you belong to Christ will certainly not lose his reward.

⁴²"And if anyone causes one of these little ones who believe in me to sin, it would be better for him to be thrown into the sea with a large millstone tied around his neck. ⁴³If your hand causes you to sin, cut it off. It is better for you to enter life maimed than with two hands to go into hell, where the fire never goes out. ⁴⁵And if your foot causes you to sin, cut it off. It is better for you to enter life crippled than to have two feet and be thrown into hell. ⁴⁷And if your eye causes you to sin, pluck it out. It is better for you to enter

the kingdom of God with one eye than to have two eyes and be thrown into hell, ⁴⁸where

> "'their worm does not die,
>   and the fire is not quenched.'

⁴⁹Everyone will be salted with fire.

⁵⁰"Salt is good, but if it loses its saltiness, how can you make it salty again? Have salt in yourselves, and be at peace with each other."

THIS UNIT BEGINS with Jesus' second announcement of his coming suffering and resurrection. Again, the implications sail over the heads of the disciples, and as soon as they continue their journey "on the road" (9:33), they begin to quarrel over who is the greatest. The disciples' hydra-headed dullness allows Jesus (or compels him) to give more teaching on the requirements for discipleship. Catchwords thread the sayings together: "in [the] name" (9:37, 38, 39, 41), "to cause to sin [stumble]" (9:42, 43, 45, 47), "fire" (9:43, 48, 49), and "salt" (9:49, 50).

The Second Prediction of Jesus Suffering and Resurrection (9:30–37)

JESUS PASSES THROUGH Galilee again but does not want anyone to know because his public ministry is coming to an end. He needs privacy to continue teaching his small band of disciples about the suffering and death that God requires of him and about what he requires of them. Success hinges on training these few, who will carry the gospel to the world, not on the ovations from dumbfounded crowds. When he makes his second prediction of his death and resurrection, the disciples keep silent. They do not comprehend what he is talking about, but they are afraid to ask him what it means (9:32). Either they are chary of being rebuked if they say anything, as Peter was earlier (8:33), or they prefer to live in a state of denial. They may not have wanted to understand the unpleasant reality staring Jesus in the face.

Fear, however, will increasingly control their reactions to the events Jesus predicts (14:50–52, 66–72; 16:8). Jesus adds a new detail here to his previous announcement of his suffering (8:31): He is "going to be handed over into the hands of men" (NIV, "betrayed into the hands of men"). The disciples should worry who it is who might betray him, but instead they spar with one another about who ranks the highest (9:33–34).

When they arrived in Capernaum, Jesus exposes their spat and their misunderstanding by asking them what they were discussing on the way. The question meets with an embarrassed silence; he has caught them in another dispute. They had argued among themselves over who forgot the loaves (8:16). They had argued with the teachers of the law when they failed to exorcise an unclean spirit (9:14). They will argue with successful exorcists who do not follow them (9:38). They will snort at a woman who displays extravagant devotion to Jesus and denounce it as a waste (14:4–5). This competitive spirit even taints their last supper with Jesus as Peter boasts that he will outdo all the other disciples in remaining faithful to Jesus (14:29). In this present passage the disciples are jockeying for position to be honored alongside their powerful liberator Messiah. The picture Mark presents has tragic-comic dimensions. Jesus walks ahead in silence on his way to his sacrificial death while his straggling disciples push and shove, trying to establish the order of the procession behind him.

The dispute opens the door for Jesus' teaching on selfless service, and Mark notes its importance by relating that Jesus sits to teach and calls the Twelve. When he first spoke of his suffering, he told them that the one who tries to save his or her life will ultimately lose it, but the one who loses his or her life for his sake will save it (8:35). Now he presents them with another paradox: The one who wants to be first must become last of all and servant of all. The disciples still have visions of grandeur and do not fantasize about becoming servants, who are at everybody's beck and call. They suffer from puffed-up ambition that will never be ready to take up a cross and follow a suffering servant Messiah.

To reinforce the lesson, Jesus places a little child in their midst and announces: "Whoever welcomes one of these little children in my name welcomes me." Jesus does not set up the child as a model to be imitated, for his culture had no romanticized notions about children. They were not regarded as especially obedient, trusting, simple, innocent, pure, unself-conscious, or humble. The point of comparison is the insignificance of the child on the honor scale. The child had no power, no status, and few rights. A child was dependent, vulnerable, entirely subject to the authority of the father; yet Jesus chooses such a one to represent those who are needy and lowly. If one wants to be great, one should shower attention on those who are regarded as insignificant, as Jesus himself has done. Jesus requires his "great" disciples to show humble service for the humble.

Jesus follows this up with another paradox: When his followers serve those without any status, they receive Jesus and the One who sent him. The greatest thing they can do is serve those who are forgotten and regarded as insignificant—those who have no influence, no titles, no priority, and no importance except to God. Mark pictures a community where no one is to be treated either as a kingpin or as a nonentity (see 1 Cor. 12:12–26). Realizing that one is as small and slight as a child before God evokes repentance.

The Unfamiliar Exorcist (9:38–41)

JOHN PROUDLY ANNOUNCES to Jesus that they saw someone casting out demons in his name and they obstructed him.[1] Their reason for intervening? "Because he was not one of us." The complaint drips with irony. The disciples only recently bungled an exorcism, yet they do not hesitate to obstruct someone who is successful but who is not a member of their team. Jesus catches them by surprise when he does not commend them for their vigilance but instead reproves them: "Do not stop him" (9:39).

This response recalls Moses' reply to Joshua. Joshua implored Israel's leader to do something about unauthorized prophets, "Moses, my lord, stop them!" Moses answered, "Are you jealous for my sake? I wish that all the LORD's people were prophets and that the LORD would put his Spirit on them!" (Num. 11:26–29).[2] Are the disciples jealous for Jesus or for themselves? Do they want to corner the exorcism market, which would make them indispensable and revered, whereas Jesus wishes that all were exorcists casting out Satan in his name?

In the ancient world, exorcists used whatever name of deities they thought would work. Jesus' explanation for condoning the exorcist's success in Mark's account is practical, not theological. He argues that they cannot use his name to do mighty works and speak ill of him later. Anyone who recognizes the power of Jesus' name will not accuse him of working by Beelzebub, as the teachers of the law from Jerusalem had done (3:22).

Jesus then opens the doors wide to include on his side all those who are not against him. He knows that both he and his disciples are locked in a life-and-death struggle against evil, and he is prepared to accept any ally willing to join the fight. Jesus concedes the possibility that good can come from circles outside of his own. The forces who call on Jesus' name in the battle against evil (Acts 3:6, 16; 4:7, 10, 30) can only be weakened by cutthroat competition among themselves. This undogmatic openness to others will

---

1. Harry Fledderman, "The Discipleship Discourse (Mark 9:33–50)," *CBQ* 43 (1981): 66, notes that Mark is not interested in any details about the strange exorcist who is simply identified as a "certain one." Mark cares only about the disciples' reaction and Jesus' correction of their attitude. He comments: "Like the dispute about greatness the episode of the strange exorcist reflects an attitude of the disciples that leads to conflict. In both cases Jesus intervenes. The disciples' exclusivism is rejected, as was their self-seeking."

2. Cited by Myers, *Binding*, 261.

trouble anyone more intent on establishing the limits of who is in and who is out than on winning the war against the enemy. The enemy becomes anyone who is "not one of us," instead of Satan.

While John worries about the competition's works of power, Jesus shifts to the humblest act of compassion. He asserts that those who give his followers even a cup of cold water in his name will be rewarded (9:41). The reward is more than the satisfaction of doing someone a kindness but is an eschatological reward. The cup of cold water image suggests that those who bear Christ's name will find themselves in grievous circumstances and desperate for just a drink of water. Later, Jesus will warn them that they will be persecuted and hated by all (13:13). Cups of water will be hard to come by, and then they will appreciate more the neutrality of those who do not join the persecution but extend only the most basic kindness.

Warning About Causing Others to Stumble (9:42–48)

JESUS PROMISES A reward to outsiders who show Christians a bare minimum of goodwill (9:41), but he threatens Christians with dire judgment if they cause a little one who believes in him to slip. He uses hyperbole to make the point: They would be better off to drown at the bottom of the sea with a millstone hung around their necks.[3] Better off than what? Jesus omits the conclusion, but one can easily fill in the blanks. It is better to drown in the sea with no chance of escape than to face the judgment that God will dish out to those who lead others to sin. One can infer that God shows more concern for the little ones' fragile faith than for the great ones' fragile egos, which cause them to lord it over or ignore others.

A string of maxims warns disciples that they need to be more worried about the evil within them than about outsiders. Again, Jesus uses hyperbole. If your hand/eye/foot causes you to stumble, remove them.[4] Judaism prohibited self-mutilation (Deut. 14:1; 1 Kings 18:28; Zech. 13:6), and Jesus did not intend for followers to take this advice literally, any more than one should take literally Paul's reference to the Galatians' willingness to tear out their eyes for him (Gal. 5:15). Maiming sometimes was substituted for capital punishment and was considered more merciful than executing a death sentence. Being deformed or crippled was better than being dead. Jesus applies this principle to the disciples' spiritual life. It is better now to take

---

3. The millstone was a familiar object in the ancient world. The phrase translated "large millstone" literally reads, "the millstone of a donkey." The rotary mill requires a strong beast of burden to pivot the heavy upper stone.

4. The eye is the cause of covetousness, stinginess, jealousy, etc. See *b. Nid.* 13b, which speaks of adultery with the hand (masturbation) and with the foot (euphemism for penis).

every precaution and to cut off everything in our lives that leads us to sin than to be punished later in fiery Gehenna.[5]

Salt (9:49–50)

JESUS CONCLUDES HIS teaching in this section with two enigmatic sayings about salt. The first, "Everyone will be salted with fire," appears only in Mark. An early interpretation of this saying appears in a textual variant: "for every sacrifice will be salted with salt" (Lev. 2:13). Salt was used for purification (Ezek. 16:4; 43:24), and the one who substituted this gloss associated fire with persecution, "which would purify the Christian community in the way that salt purified a sacrifice"[6] This interpretation fits other sayings of Jesus in the Gospel. Jesus has asked the disciples to take up a cross (8:34), promises James and John that they will drink his cup and be baptized with his baptism (10:39), and promises all the disciples that they will have rewards "with . . . persecutions" (10:30). If they endure to the end (13:13), the suffering they undergo will not destroy them but will purify them for God.

The second salt saying divides into two halves. The first half, "salt is good, but if it loses its saltiness, how can you make it salty again" (9:50a), assumes that one recognizes salt by its distinctive tang. If salt fails to salt food, it is not salt and is worthless.[7] The same applies to disciples. If they do not manifest the distinctive characteristics Jesus requires, they are not real disciples and are worthless to him.

The second half of the saying, "Have salt among yourselves [*not* in yourselves] and be at peace with one another" (9:50b), is in synonymous parallelism. To have salt among yourselves means to share salt, a reference to having meals together in the context of fellowship and peace (Ezra 4:14; Acts 1:4). When people share meals together, they are at peace with one another.[8] The discourse began, however, with the disciples disputing among themselves about their status (9:33–37) and objecting to a stranger's right to use Jesus' name. It continued with Jesus' warning about causing other believers

---

5. The term "Gehenna" means the valley of Hinnom, referring to the valley south of Jerusalem that was used in ancient times as a crematorium, where children were sacrificed to the gods of Canaan (2 Kings 23:10; Jer. 32:35). The deep gully later became a refuse dump, where fires were kept continually burning, and the name became associated with the place of fiery punishment. In *b. 'Erub.* 19a, Gehenna has seven names: Netherworld (Sheol; Jonah 2:3); Destruction (Ps. 88:12); Pit (of destruction; Ps. 16:10); Tumultuous Pit (Ps. 16:10); Miry Clay (Ps. 40:3); Shadow of Death (Ps. 17:10); and Underworld.

6. Hooker, *Mark*, 233; see 1 Peter 1:6–7; 4:12–19.

7. Salt could spoil, according to Pliny, *Natural History* 31.44.95.

8. Fledderman, "Discipleship," 73.

to stumble. These concluding sayings present peaceful fellowship as the model for disciples' relations.[9]

Bridging Contexts

THE DISCIPLES CAN hide nothing from their Master even when they try to cover up their quarrels and secret ambitions with silence. Jesus knows that each wants to rule the roost and that they have been arguing about the pecking order. Their quarrel over greatness allows him to redefine how one measures greatness and to formulate norms to govern relationships in the community. This section teaches that the Christian community should exemplify a spirit of lowliness instead of swaggering cockiness, acceptance of others instead of exclusion, humble service instead of haughty insolence, and harmonious relations instead of strife and division. The disciples' behavior again serves as a negative example for readers to learn what not to do.

On being great. The disciples have a mistaken sense of their own self-importance. They want to be great so that others will serve them. A church filled with prima donnas who want to control everything rarely ministers effectively to those inside or outside the fellowship. Everyone is too busy trying to direct others rather than trying to get the job done. This prickly pride spills over into quarrels with outsiders.

The scene here is ironic. Mark has just reported the disciples' disturbing failure to cast out an unclean spirit, but they do not blush to interfere with someone who successfully casts out demons using Jesus' name. The reason for obstructing him is telling: "He was not one of us."[10] Their rationale betrays a selfish desire to be regarded as special. They want to preserve their position in a select circle and do not want to share their power because it might undermine their status. They want exclusive rights to Jesus' name, as if they owned a special copyright to it. Others must apply to them before they can use it. This same attitude emerges in churches today: If we cannot do it, we do not want anyone else to do it either.

The disciples want to establish a hierarchy and to keep all the kingdom power to themselves, as if it is theirs by divine right. This elitist outlook can infect many Christians and leads to pettiness and party politics. Censuring this self-important, self-admiring, and self-glorious spirit within a church becomes tricky because those tainted with it wield their power with determination. Only those who exude a loving and humble spirit themselves and

9. Ibid.
10. Since John alone speaks to Jesus, is this a royal "we" (cf. Myers, *Binding*, 261)?

are willing to take the consequences will be able to challenge and help others who imperiously try to throw their weight around. All followers of Christ must learn how God ranks things. God evaluates persons differently from the way people do in our world. We tend to look at such things as heritage, rank, wealth, and position; God looks for self-giving service. Anyone who wants to be first in God's eyes must become the slave of all. Whoever puts himself or herself first will become last. To become last with God puts one's soul in jeopardy.

Harmony with others. The incident with the unfamiliar exorcist raises other questions. Clearly disciples cannot limit the power of God to themselves, though they may try. They may assume that their way is the only God-blessed way of doing things. Others do not do it right, which may only mean that they do not do it our way or they do not pay homage to us. This intolerance insists that God can only work through those whom we condone and who have first met our standards. We want to be the ones who make things happen—the movers and shakers—and be recognized accordingly.

A deep sense of lowliness understands that God can use anyone and applauds others who are successful for God, even though they may not be on our team. Jesus' reaction implies that disciples who go along with him must get along with others. He not only opens admission to the reign of God to all and accepts any who come in his name, he sanctions anyone using the power of his name. The barrier between insider and outsider in this episode becomes nebulous. Augustine said: "Many whom God has, the Church does not have; and many whom the Church has, God does not have."

But this ambiguity creates problems in trying to apply the text today. What is the qualitative difference between the healing performed by a disciple in the name of Jesus and one by a nondisciple in the name of Jesus? We must recognize that good can come from circles outside ours, but from how far outside? Is one unable to draw limits, and if so, where and how? This openness to others who work independently from our group may make many uncomfortable. It seems too broad-minded and tolerant. Is the church to sanction anyone who works in the name of the Lord? Can this acceptance not lead to doctrinal indifference? The account of the sons of Sceva, who unsuccessfully employed the name of Jesus to cast out evil spirits, reveals a less tolerant attitude toward outsiders who try to pirate Jesus' power (Acts 19:13–16). Do we reject those who are unsuccessful and accept anyone who successfully uses the name of Jesus? Or can even success be demonic?

We may be open to others, but we are not relieved of the responsibility to discern the spirits. Two keys can help us in this task. (1) We must examine our own motives. Do we oppose others because we are jealous of them, because we are anxious to protect our own turf, or because we insist that others follow us? (2) We must recognize who the real enemy is. Our common enemy is the evil that maliciously destroys human lives. Missionaries who struggle in hand-to-hand combat with this evil frequently understand that cooperation with soldiers who come from different armies but who fight the same foe makes more sense than competing with them. Should we not rejoice that others outside our close circle can be our friends in a world where we need all the friends we can get? Those who engage in petty disputes with others may have forgotten who the enemy is and how easily that enemy can infiltrate behind the lines to disrupt the plan of battle with clever distractions. When we become embroiled in disputes with others and within our own ranks, we cannot win the battle with the real enemy.

One final caution. The phrase, "whoever is not against us is for us" (9:40) can easily be misunderstood. It does not mean that all God requires is that others show no hostility to Jesus and his followers. Ministers grasping for straws to ease a family's grief have read this passage at funerals to commend persons who had no overt affiliation with Christ. At least the dearly departed was not brazenly against Christ, and they imply that God will reward this neutrality with eternal bliss. Mark, however, was writing in a context of bitter persecution, where Christians were hated by all (13:13) and could barely hope to receive even a cup of cold water (9:41). This statement is, therefore, only applicable in an openly hostile environment.

Those who know violent persecution for their faith understand better what is meant. We might reflect on the few who risked their lives to protect and to hide Jews from the Nazis. There were others who did not risk as much, but they did little things, like not reporting those whom they knew were sheltering Jewish families. When one is being hunted down and people are ready to betray anyone who offers any aid, one appreciates small kindnesses, even benign neutrality. This was the situation of early Christians and explains Jesus' statement. One may therefore not turn this statement into a principle for salvation.

Radical surgery. The violent images of cutting off hands and feet and tearing out eyes are shocking. Although Jesus is not encouraging masochism, some Christians have taken Jesus' words literally and have mutilated themselves in obedience (such as Origen, who castrated himself). Few modern readers need to be warned against self-mutilation, however. Most will have two quite different reactions to Jesus' saying. Some will be offended that Jesus would use such ghoulish imagery and dismiss him as another cruel, mind-control leader who requires fanatical allegiance from his followers. They may interpret his words as monstrous threats to keep followers in line. Others will recognize that Jesus uses hyperbole, and they will substitute something less offensive for the hand, foot, and eye. They are correct; Jesus does not literally mean what he says.

This latter interpretation, however, conveys that Jesus requires much less. The interpreter must then decide how much less Jesus requires. Instead of hand, foot, and eye, what must we cut off? For some today, turning off the television would be as bad as plucking out an eye. One must be careful about the answer to this question. We may dull the saying's sharp edge so much that no one takes notice—the other extreme of taking them literally. Our culture prefers it that way. We prefer to soften the harshness of guilt, assuage the fear of hell, and live in peaceful compromise with the world. Jesus, however, deliberately chose harsh, scandalous imagery to alert disciples that their lives tremble in the balance. Indifference to others, inducing them to sin, and a lackadaisical disregard for sin in one's own life imperils one's salvation. One should be careful not to mute the imagery and muffle Jesus' alarm.

JESUS HAS CONSISTENTLY avoided self-acclamation, but his disciples are all too ready to exalt themselves over others. If Jesus directed the same question to contemporary followers that he asked his first disciples, "What were you arguing about on the road?" the answer will be no less embarrassing. Christians still jockey for prominence. The unbridled will to power still surfaces in local churches and in denominational politics, destroying fellowship and eviscerating Christian love. Little has changed. Seminary students who begin their studies with high ideals frequently grow disillusioned by the political gamesmanship that infests churches and denominations. Some ministers become so disillusioned by such machinations that they leave the ministry; others quickly learn to play the game; still others correctly recognize that Jesus does not reject ambition, but they sublimate it by aspiring to become the greatest servant in the church rather than the greatest overlord.

Unfortunately, too many leaders use their position in the church to enhance their own status. Billboards and television advertisements for churches give the pastor top billing above God and Jesus, who may not even be mentioned. Church members can likewise be sensitive about receiving full recognition for their service. Forget to mention someone's name in the church bulletin or newsletter, and one usually will hear about it. On the other hand, many serve selflessly in the church. They will do anything asked of them and will not be offended if they are not asked. Preachers need to take to heart Jesus' words and inspire others to outdo one another in selflessness. They will do it most effectively by setting the example.

In seeking leaders for the church, committees and bishops usually consult their references, which are often written by peers or superiors. It might be wise to consult those who have worked under their leadership, such as the secretaries and janitors. One can discover the true spirit of an individual by learning how they treated those under their authority. If people know that is how they will be evaluated, they may treat these persons differently. Jesus seems to imply that God looks for these things in evaluating us.

The disciples are shown in this section shaking a forbidding forefinger in the face of others. They forbid the unfamiliar exorcist to work without their permission; they will soon forbid the parents to bring their children to Jesus. The example of the little child is designed to check haughtiness in the Christian community. Real greatness means caring about people—not the people who are regarded as "important" but simply people, such as the (unimportant) child.[11]

Jesus uses the child as a symbol of the little ones who are little esteemed, who are needy, who are socially invisible and easily ignored, who can be hurt and dominated without anyone knowing or protesting. They are the untutored, the persons on the fringes, the ones whom no one misses when they absent themselves from worship, the ones who are tolerated but not embraced into the fellowship. Leaders might secretly say to themselves and others: "We do not need them, they take up so much time, they are a drain on the budget, we need to focus our energies on more important people or things," and so on. To those dedicated to serving the high and mighty (who in turn reward special attention with generous support), these humble members may easily be written off as only marginal. But these little ones are not insignificant in the eyes of their Lord. As there is no insignificant family member, so there is no insignificant member in a church. These are the ones to whom Jesus ministered and through whom God works.

One can use the text about the unfamiliar exorcist as a helpful corrective for any community that would presume that God can act only through them. The Christian world is becoming increasingly divided. So-called liberals afraid of so-called evangelicals denigrate them, and vice versa. Each regards the other with deep suspicion and as a lesser caste of Christian. We must guard against the attitude of superiority that says, "You are different from me and I despise you for being different." You can uncover this spirit by asking yourself and members of your church how they feel about the other churches in the area. Would they pray that another church in the neighborhood might have success in its ministry even if it would siphon off members from their own church? Would they pray for that success if it were of another denomination?

---

11. Moule, *Mark*, 75.

Bill Leonard takes the title of his book *God's Last and Only Hope* from a convention sermon delivered in 1948. The preacher had no doubt that God could work only through his group: "I am more tremendously convinced than ever before that the last hope, the fairest hope, the only hope for evangelizing the world on New Testament principles is the Southern Baptist people represented in that convention."[12] Those who are not Southern Baptists may demur. Mark's text should cause us to reflect on our role and others' role in God's plan with greater humility. We must recognize that God's mission in the world is bigger than we are. We need to recognize who the real enemy is who must be exorcised from our midst and from others. In 1265–66 the Mongol Empire spanned Asia from the Black Sea to the Pacific Ocean, and Khubilai Khan asked Marco Polo to persuade the Christian church in Rome to send one hundred men to teach Christianity to his court. The Christians were in such disarray fighting among themselves that it was twenty-eight years before a single man—let alone a hundred—reached the great court. Already retired, the emperor said, "It is too late, I have grown old in my idolatry."[13]

In the battle against evil, we must recognize that whatever particular group we belong to is not the only group of Christians in the world. We can then learn from others who worship the same Christ as Lord and Savior but who may use different language and emphasize different parts of the Scripture from what we do. Perhaps when we lay aside our labels, we will recognize that together we are all Christ's servants and will then find ways to cooperate rather than to compete in serving him. Without compromising our convictions we can have fellowship (have salt) with one another. We may not think the same thoughts but we will have the same mind in Christ Jesus (Phil. 2:1–4). Our unity will be a sign of what God's power can do to drive out the evil and chaos infecting our world.

---

12. Bill J. Leonard, *God's Last and Only Hope: The Fragmentation of the Southern Baptist Convention* (Grand Rapids: Eerdmans, 1990).

13. C. Douglas Weaver, *A Cloud of Witnesses* (Macon: Smyth & Helwys, 1993), 52–53.

Mark 10:1–16

❦

JESUS THEN LEFT that place and went into the region of Judea and across the Jordan.¹ Again crowds of people came to him, and as was his custom, he taught them.
²Some Pharisees came and tested him by asking, "Is it lawful for a man to divorce his wife?"

³"What did Moses command you?" he replied.

⁴They said, "Moses permitted a man to write a certificate of divorce and send her away."

⁵"It was because your hearts were hard that Moses wrote you this law," Jesus replied. ⁶"But at the beginning of creation God 'made them male and female.' ⁷For this reason a man will leave his father and mother and be united to his wife, ⁸and the two will become one flesh.' So they are no longer two, but one. ⁹Therefore what God has joined together, let man not separate."

¹⁰When they were in the house again, the disciples asked Jesus about this. ¹¹He answered, "Anyone who divorces his wife and marries another woman commits adultery against her. ¹²And if she divorces her husband and marries another man, she commits adultery."

¹³People were bringing little children to Jesus to have him touch them, but the disciples rebuked them. ¹⁴When Jesus saw

---

1. The phrase "he went into the region of Judea and across the Jordan" reverses the natural geographical order, as many commentators point out. The majority of texts represent a concern to correct it by changing the "and" to "through the far side of the Jordan." Some interpreters attribute the original, harder reading to a vague geographical knowledge on the part of Mark. Others suggest that this reference reflects some knowledge of a longer stay in Judea than Mark narrates. Still others contend that Mark uses a clumsy expression to indicate that Judea was the ultimate goal of the journey (see 7:31; 11:1; so Gundry, *Mark,* 529). Schweizer gives it a theological twist, suggesting that Judea comes first "to show that Jesus goes to his suffering deliberately" (Schweizer, *Mark,* 202). The best solution regards the phrase as an imprecise reference to an area. Chapman warns against "the intrusion of map-reading perspective" in reading the text. He observes that while modern maps contain specific boundary lines outlining a region, the earth does not. Nor were there road signs to greet travelers entering into a different region, so that one did not know exactly when one entered into a new political entity. He contends that the word *orion* (trans. "region") is more correctly translated "area" or "neighborhood" and depicts "Judea and beyond the Jordan" as one culturally cohesive area (Chapman, *Orphan,* 171).

---

this, he was indignant. He said to them, "Let the little children come to me, and do not hinder them, for the kingdom of God belongs to such as these. ¹⁵I tell you the truth, anyone who will not receive the kingdom of God like a little child will never enter it." ¹⁶And he took the children in his arms, put his hands on them and blessed them.

DESPITE JESUS' ATTEMPT to remain incognito (9:30), crowds persist in flocking to him as he travels from Capernaum to Judea. The Pharisees also persist in their futile opposition to him by testing him, which recalls their plot to destroy him (3:6). In this way, they hope, they will be able to derail him.

The Question About Divorce (10:1–12)

THE SPECIFIC QUESTION the Pharisees ask Jesus is about divorce, though they are really interested in something more than Jesus' legal opinion on this issue. Most Jews took for granted that a man had an inalienable right to divorce his wife. The later rabbis only argued about what were the legitimate grounds for divorce, not whether it was lawful. Malachi's lone protest against divorce in the Old Testament—"'I hate divorce,' says the LORD God of Israel" (Mal. 2:16)—was turned on its head in the Aramaic translation in the *Targum Jonathan*, which reads, "If you hate her, divorce her."

Why the Pharisees test him on this specific matter is unclear. They hardly need proof of his different approach to Scripture. Their query may be a tactic designed to expose him as an aberrant teacher who goes against the grain of Scripture and common sense. They may be trying to provoke him to say something about divorce that will arouse the antipathy of the Herodian family. Divorce was a sensitive topic to them, and any disapproving salvos from Jesus could imperil his life as it did John the Baptizer's, whose denunciation of Herod Antipas's divorce and remarriage to Herodias, his brother's wife, led to his arrest and violent death (6:17–29). The Pharisees have allied themselves with the Herodians (3:6; 12:13) and may have tried to compromise Jesus in Herod's jurisdiction of Perea.[2] In the Markan context, however, Jesus' statements about divorce continue a theme begun in 9:33. Jesus sets forth the stringent demands for disciples, and his teaching on divorce dramatizes further the radical claims that God's reign makes on individuals.

---

2. Lane, *Mark*, 354.

Jesus typically fends off his opponents by going on the counterattack. When the Pharisees ask whether divorce is lawful, he asks them, "What did Moses *command you?*" This rejoinder recasts the issue from a hypothetical debate about some unspecified husband to a command directed to *them*. It also exposes a fatal flaw in the Pharisees' whole approach to the law. They come at the law asking, "What does it allow me to do?" or, to put it more bluntly, "What can I get away with?" This preoccupation with legal subtleties ultimately neglects God's will, which is primarily concerned with love for the neighbor (12:31). They are interested in their rights, not their responsibilities, and pursue legal exoneration for a behavior no matter how it might affect another person. They ask only about the husband's right to divorce and pay no attention to the needs of the wife—what it does to her or to children, whether she has any right to object to a divorce. Jesus' question uncovers their sinful hearts hidden behind the mask of legal rectitude.

The Pharisees respond to Jesus' counterquestion by citing the Mosaic regulations covering the divorce process: Moses *permitted* divorce, provided the husband gives his wife a certificate of divorce.[3] The instruction in Deuteronomy 24:1–4 leaves the matter of divorce entirely to the husband's discretion. It does not outline the grounds for divorce, nor does it endorse it. It simply places restrictions on the husband if he should decide to put his wife away. The law impassively dictates that if the wife finds no favor in her husband's eyes because she is guilty of some indecency, or if he simply dislikes her, he must give her a bill of divorce but may never remarry her after she becomes the wife of another man.

Jesus has set up the Pharisees for his counterstroke. He contends that what Moses commanded was only a compromise situation designed to reduce the fallout from men's hardness of heart. The legislation on divorce certificates protected wives from brutal abandonment. It freed a wife from the accusation of adultery when she, out of necessity, remarried; and it prevented the first husband from destroying her new marriage by trying to reclaim her. It deterred anything that might look like wife-swapping. The law was therefore intended to keep the social upheaval associated with divorce to a minimum.

Jesus' line of reasoning becomes clear. If the Mosaic legislation on this issue had its roots in men's hardness of heart—willful defiance against God— then it cannot reflect God's will. Moses may have given laws to regulate divorce, but divorce is not God's will for marriage. One therefore should not construe the stipulations in Deuteronomy 24:1–4 to mean that God condones discarding a wife or that it will not come under God's judgment if

---

3. The word *apostasion* is a legal term in the papyri that contains "the idea of giving up one's right to something" (Cranfield, *Mark*, 319).

one follows the guidelines to the letter. Divorce is sin in God's eyes because it originates in human hardness of heart.

The Pharisees need to discover what God commands, not what Moses has permitted. The Pharisees' approach to the law is wrong; their approach to marriage is also wrong. They begin with the end of the marriage relationship and scrutinize the correct procedures for ending it. The later Mishnaic tractate *Gittin* (*Divorce Certificates*), for example, is devoted to outlining the procedures for giving a wife her marital pink slip. By contrast, Jesus addresses the marriage from the perspective of God's intention at the beginning of creation and also the couple's intention at the beginning of the marriage relationship. One does not find God's true intentions for marriage in Deuteronomy 24:1–4 but earlier, in Genesis 1–2, which is also a "book of Moses."

Jesus' opponents have consequently misunderstood both Scripture and God's will for marriage. God created male and female and joins them into a one-flesh relationship. Since God is the one who joins the two together, he is the Lord of the union. Who are males to make themselves the lords of the marriage by ousting an unwanted wife as they might discard a piece of used goods? God abandons no one; the husband is not to abandon the spouse even if it has legal precedent. The answer to the Pharisees' question is therefore, "No! It is not lawful for a husband to put away a wife," if one understands "lawful" in terms of God's will and not in terms of finding escape clauses in the legal fine print. Jesus directly opposes the view expressed in Sirach 25:26: "If she does not go as you direct, separate her from yourself." His argument gives dignity and value to the wife; she is not an appendage that the husband can jettison at will.

As has been his custom, Jesus gives his disciples additional instruction when they privately ask him for an explanation (see 4:34; 7:17; 9:28, 33). What he says about divorce and remarriage carries things further and is no less revolutionary than his private explanation of food laws after the Pharisees raised the issue of washing hands (7:17–23). One discovers that Jesus allows what the Pharisees prohibited, eating with defiled hands, and prohibits what they allow, divorce. Not only does he maintain that divorce is wrong, he declares that remarriage after divorce is even more wrong and labels it adultery. Deuteronomy 24:3–4 forbids a husband from remarrying his divorced wife, who has since remarried and been divorced again, and labels it an abomination. Jesus brands remarriage to anyone after a divorce as adultery.[4] Divorce stems from hardness of heart, and it can lead to more hardness of heart.

---

4. Jesus' statements about divorce include a prohibition against a wife's divorcing and remarrying. In Judaism, a woman could not divorce her husband except in special circumstances. She could, however, take actions that would entice her husband to divorce her.

Mark does not record the shocked reaction of the disciples to these words as Matthew does (19:10), but Jesus' statement could only have created astonishment. The divorce certificate carried with it the right to remarry—"Behold thou art permitted to any man" (*m. Git.* 9:3)—so that no one could be accused of adultery after divorce. Jesus rejects this provision and insists that the marriage bond must never broken no matter how punctilious one is in following the legal process.[5]

Blessing the Children (10:13–16)

JESUS' CONCERN FOR children follows immediately after his statements about divorce. Both women and children could be mistreated and abused because of their lack of power. Jesus' next words and actions give value to children as he returns to the issue of the little ones (9:42). Both wives and children are to be respected and cherished.

Others have brought the paralyzed and the blind to Jesus; now parents bring children for Jesus to touch (10:13). The disciples act like truculent bouncers. They rebuke these parents and try to block their children's access to Jesus. Again, they want to throw their weight around and exercise control by keeping at bay others who come from outside their circle. These aspiring leaders want to be the gatekeepers, who determine not only who can use Jesus' name (9:38), but also who can have admission to his presence. He must indignantly intercede on behalf of the children and inform his disciples that the kingdom of God belongs to such as these.

The true disciple must become as a child to receive the kingdom rather than act like an overseer, who drives others away. This childlikeness does not refer to any supposedly inherent qualities that children are said to possess, such as humility, trustfulness, transparency, hopefulness, modesty, or willingness to believe (see comments on 9:36–37). Children can also be demanding, short-tempered, sulky, stubborn, thankless, and selfish. We call it childish behavior (see Jesus' parable of the squabbling children, Matt. 11:16–19; Luke 7:31–35).

In the ancient world, children had no status. They were easily ignored and barred access because no one would take the trouble to complain and fight

---

Christians may have adapted Jesus' teaching to a Hellenistic setting, where women did have the right to divorce. Seneca paints a bleak picture of upper-class Roman matrons: "Surely no woman will blush to be divorced now that some distinguished and noble ladies count the years not by the consuls but by their own marriages, and divorce in order to be married, marry in order to be divorced" (*On Benefits* 3.16.2).

5. See further, Craig S. Keener, *"And Marries Another": Divorce and Remarriage in the Teaching of the New Testament* (Peabody, Mass.: Hendrickson, 1991); Andrew Cornes, *Divorce and Remarriage: Biblical Principles and Pastoral Practices* (Grand Rapids: Eerdmans, 1993).

for them. These children, who must be brought to Jesus by others, have nothing to commend an audience with him and cannot defend themselves against bullies. Jesus holds them up again as an example. Their littleness contrasts sharply with the overbearing disciples, who want to assert their power and influence. The disciples need to learn not only to minister to the little ones but also to adopt the attitude of littleness. The little ones are easily pushed aside because they are weak, but God works most powerfully in weakness. When one is appropriately little, like a child, or poor in spirit (Matt 5:3), one is more open to receiving the reign of God. Children are also more open to receiving gifts than adults. Adults want to earn what they get, as the next scene with the rich man reveals.

IN OUR CONTEXT, we think of divorce in terms of a judgment decided by a court of law that legally dissolves a marriage. In biblical times, however, divorce was an independent action taken by a husband to cast off his wife (who was regarded as property, Ex. 20:17; Num. 30:10–14; Sir. 23:22–27). Divorce was so accepted as a regular part of life that Isaiah uses it as an image to describe the broken relationship between Israel and God. Even God divorced: "This is what the LORD says: 'Where is your mother's certificate of divorce with which I sent her away?'" (Isa. 50:1; see Jer. 3:8).

The legal stipulations in Deuteronomy 24:1–4 took for granted the time-honored practice of putting away a wife and tried only to regulate it. Later teachers of the law argued about the grounds for divorce and differed on how to interpret the phrase "a matter of indecency" (Deut. 24:1; "something indecent," NIV). Some emphasized the word "matter"—any matter was grounds for divorce; others stressed the word "indecency"—the wife had to be guilty of some misconduct (see m. Git. 9:10). In Jesus' time, wives had little or no recourse to justice in a law court when their husbands turned them out. A wife could only expect to receive the sum of money (ketuba) the groom pledged before the marriage to give his wife upon his death or if he divorced her.

In the Greco-Roman world in which Mark wrote his Gospel, divorce was even more easy and informal. Either spouse could divorce simply by leaving home with that intention; no justification was needed. The wife might keep her dowry, but the children remained with the father under his authority. The result was that most families were blended with children born from different mothers.

When applying what Jesus says about divorce to our context, there are several things that we need to recognize. (1) Jesus is responding here to hostile questioners, who are bent on trapping him (10:2). We should therefore not expect to find in this passage instructions for the pastoral care of divorced persons. Jesus is not addressing those contemplating divorce and seeking his counsel or those struggling in broken relationships and needing encouragement. He directs his answer to bitter opponents, whom he has already accused of mishandling the Scripture and distorting God's will (7:6–13). His reply presents God's will for marriage, which challenges those who want to impose their own will on the marriage relationship.

(2) Jesus proclaims throughout this Gospel that God's reign is breaking into our world and lives. This has direct implications for how we are to live. We can no longer deal with God based on what Moses may have "permitted" and where the pettifoggers might find loopholes. God's will, as Jesus reveals it, invades all areas of life, including what is culturally accepted and legally allowed. Divorce happens, but Jesus attributes it to a sclerosis of the heart—deliberate disobedience of God. In this section of Mark, Jesus makes radical demands of his disciples. He has called for them to put themselves last in service to others and to be willing to sacrifice for others. These commands apply also to the marriage relationship even when one may think that there are irreconcilable differences. If disciples obey the great commandment to love one's neighbor as oneself (12:31), that neighbor also includes the spouse. Loving a spouse as oneself rules out the possibility of divorce.

(3) Jesus' reaction to the Pharisees' appeal to what Moses allowed in Deuteronomy means that one cannot simply search Scripture and look for proof-text escape clauses. One has to discern the will of God even in Scripture.[6] Jesus always interprets Scripture in terms of a higher claim and a more complete obedience. At least three principles come into play in his interpretation. (a) He argues that Moses made a concession in the law about divorce certificates to rein in human sinfulness and prevent greater evil. (b) Jesus finds God's will in what God intended in creation, an ideal that most couples embarking on marriage for the first time would endorse. (c) Marriage is to be a lifelong union, not a temporary romantic dalliance that a husband (or wife) can undo whenever it becomes inconvenient.

(4) The issue of the legitimate grounds for divorce does not surface in this passage. The Pharisees ask, "Is it lawful for a man to divorce his wife?" (10:2), not, "Is it lawful for a man to divorce his wife *for any cause?*" as in Matthew 19:3. Jesus' answer to their question in essence is, "No, it is not lawful," and Mark's account contains no exception clauses (see Matt. 5:32; 19:9).[7] One therefore

---

6. Dan O. Via Jr., *The Ethics of Mark's Gospel—In the Middle of Time* (Philadelphia: Fortress, 1985), 101.

7. On this see David E. Garland, *Reading Matthew: A Literary and Theological Commentary* (New York: Crossroad, 1993), 67–70.

should eschew any casuistry that tries to argue that what Jesus says about divorce here in Mark does not apply in certain cases. Jesus does not say divorce is permissible if such and such conditions occur. He presents God's ideal for marriage, which is not debatable.

(5) Jesus' opponents treated marriage as a contract that a husband could cancel on a whim. Jesus reckons marriage to be indissoluble because of the one-flesh union. His argument implies that a piece of paper does not affect the permanence of this union. This passage is therefore more about the permanence of marriage than about divorce. The sexual union marks a person indelibly as nothing else does (1 Cor. 6:16–18).[8] Jesus reinforces his argument that marriage is a permanent union by declaring that remarriage is adultery.

This last statement has caused grief and soul-searching for many who have divorced and remarried. They ask, "Am I living in adultery?" or someone may accuse them of living in adultery. One needs special sensitivity to convey Jesus' argument. As noted above, the essential words of a bill of divorce were: "Behold, thou art permitted to any man" (*m. Git.* 9:3). The whole point of the document was to avoid the charge of adultery should anyone ever remarry. The word used in the Greek text for the bill of divorce (*apostasion*) was used as a technical term for relinquishing property. The husband relinquished his rights to the wife with the certificate of divorce, and one would be surprised at being found guilty simply for getting rid of property and replacing it with something else. Malina argues that Jesus' audience must have been as startled as we would be if he said to us, "Anyone who sells his car and buys another is guilty of theft."[9] On his part, Jesus makes this statement to argue the permanence of marriage, not to accuse persons of adultery. Legal actions define the limits of relationships, but human legal definitions do not always reflect God's perspective. The spouse is not a piece of property but bone of one's bone and flesh of one's flesh (cf. Gen. 2:23).

Modern social scientists have come to recognize this truth quite independently of Jesus' teaching. A marriage that can be dissolved in the courts cannot be so easily dissolved in life. Divorce may end the covenant between two partners, but it does not end the relationship. Whitaker writes:

> The craziest thing about marriage is that one cannot get divorced. We just do not seem to make it out of intimate relationships. It is obviously possible to divide up property and to decide not to live together any more, but it is impossible to go back to being single. Marriage is like a stew that has reversible and irrevocable characteristics that the

8. Via, *Ethics*, 102.
9. Bruce J. Malina, *The New Testament World* (Atlanta: John Knox, 1981), 120.

parts cannot be rid of. Divorce is leaving a part of the self behind, like the rabbit who escapes the trap by gnawing one leg off.[10]

Marriage partners are like two plants that have grown together in the same pot for so many years that their roots have become intertwined. It becomes difficult ever to separate the two neatly or completely. Even if one does, the plant has become shaped by the presence of the other that it has lived with. A divorced person might ask, "What do I do with the photo albums for the past twenty years? Do I discard the last twenty years of my life?" Spouses may no longer be spouses but they are kin because they remain the parents of their children. Tannehill comments: "[In] the suffering perhaps more than in the happiness a man and a woman may discover how deeply involved they are. In the poisoning of their marriage a part of them is dying."[11]

"What about the children?" is a question frequently asked in divorce cases. Jesus' concern for the care and acceptance of children immediately follows his statements about marriage and divorce. Helpless children are the ones most affected by divorce, and studies have shown that while they are incredibly resilient, divorce can have a devastating effect on them. They easily get lost in the shuffle as parents seek to work their will on one another.

In bridging the contexts of Jesus' blessing of the children, Barton cautions that we should not read back our modern fascination and sentimentalization of childhood into the Gospels. The discovery of childhood as an important developmental stage is a modern phenomenon, as is the Sunday school for instruction of children.[12] The ancient world did not have a romantic notion of children. Children added nothing to the family's economy or honor and did not count. In the Greco-Roman world one could literally throw children away by exposing unwanted infants at birth.[13] The unscrupulous would collect exposed children and raise them to be gladiators or prostitutes and even disfigure them to enhance their value as beggars. In rabbinic Judaism, one rabbi voices sentiments shared by many: A sage should not

---

10. C. A. Whitaker and D. V. Keith, "Counseling the Divorcing Marriage," *Klemer's Counseling in Marital and Sexual Problems*, eds. R. F. Stahmann and W. J. Hiebert, 2d ed. (Baltimore: Williams and Wilkins, 1977), 71.

11. Robert C. Tannehill, *The Sword of His Mouth* (Philadelphia: Fortress, 1975), 97; cited by Myers, *Binding*, 266.

12. Stephen C. Barton, "Child, Childhood," in *Dictionary of Jesus and the Gospels*, eds. Joel B. Green, Scot McKnight, and I. Howard Marshall (Downers Grove, Ill.: InterVarsity, 1992), 100.

13. See the infamous letter written in 1 B.C. by a poor laborer to his pregnant wife in Alexandria, advising her to keep the child if it is a boy and to cast it out if it is a girl (*POxy* 744).

bother with children: "Morning sleep and mid-day wine and children's talk and sitting in the meeting-houses of the ignorant people put a man of the world" (*m. 'Abot* 3:11).

Jesus goes against the grain and identifies with the powerless, with those who have no rights and whom most regard as insignificant. The new community Jesus founds embraces the powerless little ones rather than dismissing them or banishing them. Since he has special regard for them, so should his disciples. Those who adopt the sense of childlike dependence on God that is captured Charles Wesley's hymn will be the ones who will fulfill this charge more readily:

> Gentle Jesus, meek and mild
> Look upon a little child,
> Pity my simplicity.
> Suffer me to come to thee.

Some interpreters have used Mark 10:13–16 as a proof-text to justify infant baptism. The verb "to hinder" (*koluo*, 10:14) appears in the story of the Ethiopian eunuch: "What hinders me from being baptized?" (Acts 8:36; NIV, "Why shouldn't I be baptized?"). But the use of this verb in baptismal contexts (see also Matt. 3:14; Acts 10:47; 11:17) does not make the context baptismal wherever else the verb appears. Mark certainly does not use it this way (cf. Mark 9:38–39). In the present section, people bring their children to Jesus so that he will touch them and bless them. Mark does not connect what Jesus does to anything related to baptism. The text does not argue that parents are allowed to bring their children for baptism but that disciples must not impede or restrain little ones from coming to Jesus.

MARRIED COUPLES SOON learn that marriage is not a fairy tale lived happily ever after in a castle. Romantic emotion, which may have been the only thing that drew the couple together, quickly wears thin within two years of marriage. Human hardness of heart has not softened since the time of Moses. Given the escalating divorce statistics in our country, the issue of divorce is constantly before us. Committed Christians also get divorced. Many suffer from anger, anguish, and guilt. Others take the shattered relationships with a spouse and the impaired relationships with their children in stride. The extraordinarily high divorce rate in our society reflects most people's belief that marriage is dissoluble at will. As a result, in 1973–74, the number of marriages that ended in divorce exceeded for the first time the number of marriages that were ended by the death of a spouse.[14]

Many factors contribute to the rising tide of divorce. Couples who try to live on islands of intimacy isolated from others are more easily deluged when hit by the typhoons of trouble. Family members may be too distant to offer support, friends too few. The institution of marriage has changed from a predominantly socioeconomic one to something supposed to meet personal and emotional needs. We expect more from marriage than people did in the past. The vow "to have and to hold ... as long as we both shall live" has been updated to "as long as my spouse meets my needs and I feel fulfilled." Beyond the desire for financial security, companionship, and children, we expect unconditional love, emotional support, personal fulfillment, and ardent romance.

We have these high expectations at a time when there are fewer external forces to hold marriages together. Work and home life were not separated in the past. Now husbands and wives frequently go their separate ways in everyday life, meeting each other occasionally for a family meal and going off together on a two-week vacation. Parents raise children in the automobile as they travel from one activity to another. Under these circumstances, it is not unusual for partners to grow apart. The social stigma once attached to divorce no longer keeps a couple together. The advent of the no-fault divorce laws not only gives legal permission for divorce but makes it easier for partners to break up and go their separate ways.

Many consider the idea of unconditional commitment to one person for life to be unreasonable since so much can change over the years. Cartoonists can get laughs with such lines as, "Are you planning a long marriage?" "Will you be my wife for the next couple of years?" Quipsters jest half-seriously, "Watching sports on TV is just something to do between marriages." The problem today is that so many enter marriage without any sense of it being a lifelong commitment. In some circles, divorce is almost expected. A guest on a television talk show tells her host: "If you ever get divorced, call me."

Many other forces in our secular society contrive to wreck marriages. Bruner writes: "Seduction, fornication, and adultery are the erotic engines at the core of the entertainment and advertising industries."[15] These industries also encourage us to be satisfied with nothing but the best and to upgrade

---

14. Constance R. Ahrons, "21st-Century Families: Meeting the Challenges of Change," *Family Therapy News* 3 (October, 1992): 16.

15. Frederick Dale Bruner, *Matthew 13–28* (Dallas: Word, 1990), 674. For a critique of the media's maligning of marriage, see Michael Medved, *Hollywood Vs. America* (San Francisco: HarperCollins, 1992), 122–38.

to new and improved versions. Our culture encourages us to accept better and forget worse (or even average). When a marriage relationship goes through a rocky patch, many decide that they deserve better and leave in search of it.

Despite the changes in our culture, the church needs to take a stand against the rising tide of easy divorce in our society. Christians are not to be conformed to this world—and this includes its indifference toward the marriage vow. But one has to steer between the Scylla of being too lenient on the sin of divorce and the Charybdis of being too harsh. On the one hand, one must be careful to proclaim God's intention for marriage to be a permanent covenant relationship. Marriage is not a temporary, romantic alliance that can be terminated whenever one or both wish. Jesus made radical demands of his disciples and believed that God was working in the world so that they could live up to those demands. Many young people today, however, have never heard in a religious context that divorce is wrong. So many divorced persons sit in the congregation that pastors may want to sidestep the issue lest they offend members and rub salt in old wounds. The church needs to infuse in its youth a deep sense of the sanctity of the marriage commitment to counterbalance all the messages they receive from our culture.

On the other hand, one must also be sensitive not to beat people over the head with the Bible when they are already bruised and broken. While the church should proclaim God's will for marriage and announce God's judgment on sin, we must also proclaim God's forgiveness of sin and acceptance of sinners. Divorce is like an atomic bomb that leaves deep emotional craters and strikes all kinds of innocent bystanders with the fallout. It adds to the explosive chaos and alienation in the world that God has sent his Son to defuse. This is why God hates divorce and why the divorced person usually hates divorce. While God hates divorce, the church must always be mindful that God does not hate the divorced person. God hates sin, but God does not hate the sinner. The church must direct sinners to God's offer of forgiveness and provide a place for them to experience God's healing. Divorce recovery groups may provide an excellent opportunity to minister to people when they need help the most.

It is perhaps more important to ask what the church should be doing to strengthen marriages and prevent divorce than to ask what we should do after a divorce. The church should be sensitive to the pressures on marriage today and ought to do more than make pronouncements about divorce, whether they be words of condemnation or dispensation. It needs to take action to stem the tide of spouse abuse, child abuse, adultery, and divorce in our society. All too often, the church tries to step in after things have reached crisis proportions, when it is often too late for any change to take place. The church therefore needs to be engaged in preventive medicine that will help young people prepare themselves for marriage and help those already married to strengthen their commitment to one another.

John Gottman has isolated warning signs in marriages that if allowed to go unchecked will inevitably lead to a marriage breakup: criticism, contempt, defensiveness, and stonewalling.[16] These issues should be dealt with forthrightly in the church's education program and from the pulpit. People are looking for help in coping with the strains that modern life brings, not only in order to remain married but to have a happy and fulfilling relationship with their spouses. Rather than bemoaning the situation, we must isolate the many causes of divorce and do all in our power to help couples remedy problems and avert pitfalls.

My wife has compared making a marriage to a making a quilt. She thought it would be a fun winter project that would fill a blank kitchen wall that begged for something. Though she had never made a quilt before, she envisioned something beautiful, unlike anything her foremothers had made. How hard was it to cut out simple shapes and sew them together? She plunged into the task by borrowing the children's colored pencils and sketching out a design that picked up the design of the area rug under the table. As she worked on it, she soon realized that the quilt would depart from the original plan. She mismeasured some middle pieces, and the small mistakes in the middle multiplied as she added layer on layer to the edges. She had to patch in extra pieces and change the design to fit the mistakes. The mistakes and midcourse corrections became part of the design. After eight months and far more work than originally anticipated, the quilt was finished and hanging on the wall. It only remotely resembled the original sketch. It refused to hang flat against the wall, and one side was longer than the other. No one will mistake it for a factory-made quilt. Nevertheless, we like it.

In the process of adding more stitches and hoping to persuade it to hang straight, it dawned on her how the quilt was like a good marriage. We start out with a dream that we can make a better marriage than the imperfect one we may think our parents had. We sketch our plans for the future, far underestimating the work it may take to quilt two lives into one pattern. As we busily shape and stitch our lives day by day, we make mistakes and cause hurts. The marriage quilt becomes flawed since it is quilted by two sinful people. We can get discouraged since the pieces do not all fit together as we thought they would. Compromises and patching up have to take place. The original design must be altered, or we will give up and throw it all away. If

---

16. John Gottman, *Why Marriages Succeed or Fail . . . And How You Can Make Yours Last* (New York: Simon & Schuster, 1994).

we persevere, however, we allow God's love to work in and through us. The marriage takes on a unique beauty as love and grace turn flaws into redemption. The hurts and wrongs may not be beautiful, but the love that shapes them into the larger design of God's work can turn them into pictures for the world to see the healing power of God's love.[17]

One needs to convey that the sin of divorce can occur in any marriage, whether there is a legal divorce or not. Many marriages may never end up in divorce court, but they are just as cold and loveless and filled with hate and anger. One unhappy spouse observed, "I am not married, just undivorced." My wife and I concluded previously, "Partners who live in alienation from each other, angry and hurt, and convinced that the other is responsible for the pain in the relationship, are missing the mark as certainly as the couple that legally divorces."[18] Reporters asked a husband celebrating his fiftieth anniversary with his wife if he had ever considered divorce. He replied candidly, "Never divorce. Murder many times, but never divorce."[19]

God is more concerned about the harm that our sins inflict on others than the legal niceties involved. The divorce certificate that finalizes the breakup of a marriage is like the death certificate; it certifies that a death has occurred, but it is not the death. It may also be compared to the accident report written long after colliding automobiles have left casualties strewn on the highway. Consequently, married partners need to confess the failures that can regularly occur within marriage and take measures to correct them before the alienation becomes an insuperable obstacle to overcome.

While proclaiming God's will for marriage, we should recognize that one cannot restore a failed marriage with the prohibition of divorce.[20] Jesus teaches that God does not will divorce, but that does not solve the hardness-of-heart issue. The church in the past has applied Jesus' teaching on the subject of divorce and remarriage with a legalistic rigor that it suspends when it comes to his other sayings.

Jesus here lays down God's intention for marriage, but specific cases always arise that need addressing, as Paul writes in 1 Corinthians 7:10–16. Partners have been yoked together, but what should one do when the marriage becomes a yoke of bondage? If Paul permits divorce in a situation where an unbelieving spouse refuses to continue a marriage with a Christian, can

---

17. Adapted from Diana R. Garland, "Quilting and Marriage Making," *The Western Recorder* (September, 1993), 4.

18. Diana S. Richmond Garland and David E. Garland, *Beyond Companionship: Christians in Marriage* (Philadelphia: Westminster, 1986), 165.

19. Howard J. Clinebell and Charlotte H. Clinebell, *The Intimate Marriage* (New York: Harper & Row, 1970), 154.

20. Wolfgang Schrage, *The Ethics of the New Testament* (Philadelphia: Fortress, 1987), 97.

one insist that a spouse subjected to physical abuse, for example, should continue to hold on to a marriage in a vain attempt to fulfill some ideal that already has been violated? Encouraging an abused spouse to continue the relationship has been shown to promote further abuse rather than to confront the sin and correct it. Sometimes divorce is the best medicine for confronting individuals with the reality of their sin. What should one do when the marriage becomes a legal shell, lacking any personal commitment? Should the quality of the marriage relationship figure into the decision? In addressing these issues we should help people decide which is least evil while not pretending that evil is good.[21]

In treating the issue of divorce, we need to recognize that a broken marriage is no different from any other sin that falls short of God's will, except that it is so public and affects so many—children, the extended family, the community at large. And after one has experienced a broken marriage, then what? What is God's word after a couple has failed to fulfill God's intention for marriage? One cannot turn back the clock, but can the divorced individual have a second chance? Does Jesus' insistence that marriage is indissoluble mean that once a person is divorced, one should never remarry? For some, the answer is clearly yes. Heth and Wenham argue that a second marriage rejects the authority of Christ and cite Archer with approval:

> God has not called us to be happy, but He called us to follow Him, with all integrity and devotion. ... Surely this applies to living with the dismal disappointment and frustration of an unhappy marriage.[22]

In answering this question, however, one should recognize that Jesus was not speaking here to those who had experienced the brokenness of a marriage failure; rather, he was responding to a "test" question of the Pharisees. What he might have said to people in the throes of divorce we can only surmise from what he said to the woman caught in adultery (John 7:53–8:11) and to the Samaritan woman who had five husbands and was living with a man who was not her husband (4:4–29).

How should the church help to put broken lives back together? The principle of salvage and redemption governed Jesus' ministry to people. Peter received more than one chance to start anew after denying his Lord with curses. One may infer that others who commit different kinds of sins also get second chances. The principle that Jesus used regarding Sabbath rules may

---

21. Cranfield, *Mark*, 320.

22. W. A. Heth and G. J. Wenham, *Jesus and Divorce* (Nashville: Nelson, 1984), 96. For a different answer, see Myrna and Robert Kysar, *The Asundered: Biblical Teachings on Divorce and Remarriage* (Atlanta: John Knox, 1978).

also apply. If marriage was made for the blessing of humankind, and not humankind for marriage, then it would seem that one who has failed in marriage should have another opportunity to remarry.[23] This does not mean that the slate is wiped clean, particularly when children are involved. One cannot dismiss the failure of the past, but it need not rule over us or prevent us from beginning anew in the grace of God.

What should the church do with its members who divorce? Is there Christian life after divorce and remarriage? Should churches allow divorced persons to serve in any capacity? Should they be allowed to attend seminary? Should they be ordained? How is one to be faithful to Scripture and also gracious and not legalistic? All these questions become important in applying the Scripture to real-life situations.

This passage should lead us to ask a more important question, however. Jesus commends children to his disciples. They are to extend loving care for them and not to block them off as insignificant. Our attitude toward the value of children surfaces in how we care for the facilities for children in the church, in how much of the budget is designated for their care and training, in how we integrate them into our worship. Do they appear in worship only as cute performers who sing their song and then are shuttled off out of sight and earshot so that they cannot disturb what we regard as more important—our own quiet worship? Worship leaders face a challenge in trying to mix children into the corporate worship of the church so that they feel that they are an important part of Christ's mission and work.

The more desperate challenge, the lack of care for children, continues to plague societies. Children continue to be abused, discarded, and discounted. Young children are enslaved to work in the global economy or are forced into prostitution and have less international protection than endangered species. Christians today must not buy products produced from child labor, must speak out against it, and must use all their political might to stamp it out. In our own culture, we allow advertisers to pose children in sexually suggestive ads for clothing across the page from a story about child molestation. We permit the media to glamorize violence, sex, and drugs in programming targeted for children and adolescents. We allow industries to conduct psychological studies on how to entice children to buy products that have been demonstrated to be addictive and harmful to health. Protecting profit margins is apparently more important than protecting children. We allow parents to skip out on the responsibility of providing financial support for

---

23. Any moral superiority that the undivorced might feel toward the divorced who remarry is undermined by Jesus' claim that everyone who lusts after another is guilty of adultery (Matt. 5:28).

children that they brought into the world, so that the child must cope with poverty as well as the absence of a parent. We have been silent about the sexual and physical abuse of children that occurs in poor, middle-class, rich, and even in Christian homes. We cut programs designed to give impoverished children a chance in an increasingly competitive world so that we can save in taxes.

Few churches offer ministries that try to reach out to children whose parents are not members of the church. These children are at risk, and many have never known unconditional love and acceptance from caring adults. Teenagers are left alone to raise themselves, and the resulting rise in teenage pregnancy that only perpetuates the cycle should not surprise. If, as James Garbarino argues, children are like the canaries in the mine shaft, their plight warns us that we and they live in a toxic environment that desperately needs to be cleaned up.[24] Jesus commits children to our loving protection, and the church must be in the forefront of helping to care for children and helping parents to care for children. Some today may consider children to be liabilities, but the church recognizes that Christ is revealed to us through the child in our midst.

---

24. James Garbarino, *Raising Children in a Socially Toxic Environment* (San Francisco: Jossey-Bass, 1995).

Mark 10:17–31

A S JESUS STARTED on his way, a man ran up to him and fell on his knees before him. "Good teacher," he asked, "what must I do to inherit eternal life?"

18"Why do you call me good?" Jesus answered. "No one is good—except God alone. 19You know the commandments: 'Do not murder, do not commit adultery, do not steal, do not give false testimony, do not defraud, honor your father and mother.'"

20"Teacher," he declared, "all these I have kept since I was a boy."

21Jesus looked at him and loved him. "One thing you lack," he said. "Go, sell everything you have and give to the poor, and you will have treasure in heaven. Then come, follow me."

22At this the man's face fell. He went away sad, because he had great wealth.

23Jesus looked around and said to his disciples, "How hard it is for the rich to enter the kingdom of God!"

24The disciples were amazed at his words. But Jesus said again, "Children, how hard it is to enter the kingdom of God! 25It is easier for a camel to go through the eye of a needle than for a rich man to enter the kingdom of God."

26The disciples were even more amazed, and said to each other, "Who then can be saved?"

27Jesus looked at them and said, "With man this is impossible, but not with God; all things are possible with God."

28Peter said to him, "We have left everything to follow you!"

29"I tell you the truth," Jesus replied, "no one who has left home or brothers or sisters or mother or father or children or fields for me and the gospel 30will fail to receive a hundred times as much in this present age (homes, brothers, sisters, mothers, children and fields—and with them, persecutions) and in the age to come, eternal life. 31But many who are first will be last, and the last first."

WHILE THE PHARISEES seek to test Jesus, others seek his expert opinion on the most advisable course for inheriting eternal life. A man runs up to him and with ingratiating deference kneels before him and addresses him as "Good teacher."[1] This faithful Jew who believed in the life to come must have been taken aback by Jesus' initial response.[2] One would have expected Jesus to respond according to oriental custom with equally exalted language, "Most honored and good sir." Instead, he addresses him with no title and deflects his idle flattery with a reproof for his audacity in thinking that anyone other than God is good.[3]

This brusque response gets to the core issue raised by this encounter. The man's salutation assumes that one can find goodness in human resources and accomplishments. Probably, he identifies himself as "good" as well and asks his question from one good man to another. He wants to know how to ensure that his goodness will pay off in eternal life. He hopes that Jesus can relieve any lingering doubts about his chances and inform him if there is anything in the fine print he needs to worry about. As the scene develops, God's demands turn out to be far more costly than he bargained for, and Jesus' teaching reveals another paradox: Goodness and salvation do not come from our own valiant efforts but only as a gift from God.

After turning aside the greeting, Jesus directs the inquirer to the Ten Commandments, which he already knows. In random order, Jesus reviews those commands that pertain to how humans are to relate to others: murder, adultery, stealing, bearing false witness, defrauding, and honoring your father and mother.[4] These commands are eternally valid and not part of the stuffy

---

1. A comparable incident appears in the rabbinic tradition. "When R. Eliezer fell ill his disciples came to visit him. They said to him, 'Rabbi, teach us the paths that we may merit the life of the world-to-come.' He said to them, 'Be careful about the honour of your colleagues; restrain your sons from studying Greek learning and place them between the knees of the Sages, and when you pray know before whom you stand, and thereby you will merit the life of the world-to-come.'" The man may have expected some kind of similar response from Jesus.

2. He is identified as "young" only in Matt. 19:20 and as a "ruler" only in Luke 18:18.

3. Schweizer (*Mark*, 211) comments: "The church encounters God in the Son because the Son is seeking nothing for himself. He desires that no facet of his life might call attention to himself, but that all may point to One who is greater."

4. Jesus says "Do not defraud" rather than "Do not covet" (Ex. 21:10; Deut. 24:14). The questioner's identity as a rich man may have affected the wording. Many believed in the ancient world that riches could only be attained by defrauding others of their fair share. See Bruce Malina, *The New Testament World: Insights from Cultural Anthropology* (Atlanta: John Knox, 1981), 75–85; "Wealth and Poverty in the New Testament," *Int* 41 (1987): 354–67; G. W. E. Nickelsburg, "Riches in 1 Enoch 92–95," *NTS* 25 (1979): 327.

pedantry that Jesus has previously challenged in his clashes with the Pharisees. He does not undermine the commandments that come from a "good" God (see 1 Cor. 7:19).

Either the man is disappointed to learn nothing new from Jesus or pleased that his hunch about his good prospects in the age to come has been confirmed by a religious specialist. His response, "Teacher . . . all these I have kept since I was a boy," is then either a defensive reaction or a triumphant exclamation.[5] He has been good, and one should no more doubt his sincerity than that of the apostle Paul. Paul claimed that as a zealous Pharisee he was blameless according to the righteousness that comes from obedience to the law (Phil. 3:6).[6]

With an eye for poignant detail, Mark tells us that Jesus looked at the man and loved him (Mark 10:21).[7] Jesus does not sneer at his claims to have obeyed the law. He believes what he says about his obedience; but *because he loves him*, he directly challenges him. He does not try to spare his feelings or avoid offending him but candidly speaks the truth. The man regards himself as respectably good, but being respectably good is not good enough. He lacks one thing. This statement implies that knowing the commandments and faithfully keeping them do not secure eternal life. Jesus does not tell the man specifically what the one thing is but gives him four directives: "Go, sell everything you have and give to the poor. . . . Then come, follow me." These commands stress that if one wants eternal life, everything depends on one's response to Jesus.

The command to sell all sounds quite unreasonable to us, but most in the ancient world would have heard it as radical but sound advice for those who were seriously devout. The Dead Sea Scrolls required adherents to the sect to contribute their possessions to the common treasury. Acts reports that members of the first Christian community in Jerusalem did the same to assist the needs of their fellow believers (see Acts 4:32–37; 5:1–11). Even pagans would have understood the importance, in principle, of renouncing wealth.

The command to honor one's father and mother is out of sequence and listed last for emphasis. Jesus' teaching does not undermine the basic unit of society, the family, which was so important in the context of Roman society. He condemns divorce (Mark 10:1–12) and adultery and insists that parents be honored (7:8–13).

5. He does not address Jesus as "good" a second time.

6. This man may remind one of the Pharisee in Jesus' parable who thanks God that he has not sunk to the depths that others have, the thieves, rogues, adulterers, and toll collectors. He fasts and tithes and comes to the temple regularly to pray (Luke 19:10–12). The parable's conclusion makes the startling declaration that the Pharisee's extraordinary goodness did not make him righteous.

7. See also 3:34; 6:34; 8:33; 9:25; 10:23, 27.

Seneca wrote, "No one is worthy of God unless he despises wealth . . ." (*Letters* 14.18). He also concluded:

> Our soul knows, I tell you, that wealth does not lie where it can be heaped together. It is the soul itself that we ought to fill, not our money-chests. It is the soul that we may set above all other things, and put, god-like, in possession of the universe (*Letters* 92.32–33).

Few followed through on this ideal, and the later rabbis specifically forbade giving away all of one's resources. They limited the maximum that one could give away to 20 percent so that one would not become penniless and a burden to others.[8]

Jesus insists, however, that the wisest investments accrue interest in the treasuries of heaven. In this man's case, it means giving all that he has to support the poor. According to Deuteronomy 32:34, one stores up evil works that God keeps and will one day avenge. James 5:3 contains a warning for the rich who lay up treasure for the last days, which will only bring judgment. Jesus thinks positively of a storehouse of good works that God guards and one day will reward (see Luke 11:33–34). This outlook ran deeply in Jewish piety. Sirach 29:8–13, for example, exhorts people to be generous in this manner:

> Nevertheless, be patient with someone in humble circumstances,
>   and do not keep him waiting for your alms.
> Help the poor for the commandment's sake,
>   and in their need do not send them away empty-handed.
> Lose your silver for the sake of a brother or a friend,
>   and do not let it rust under a stone and be lost [a reference to burying money].
> Lay up your treasure according to the commandments of the Most High,
>   and it will profit you more than gold.
> Store up almsgiving in your treasury,
>   and it will rescue you from every disaster;
> better than a stout shield and a sturdy spear,
>   it will fight for you against the enemy [NRSV].[9]

---

8. *m. 'Arak.* 8:4; *b. Ketub.* 50a; see *b. Ta'an.* 24a.

9. This idea is picked up in later Christian literature. In *Shepherd of Hermas, Similitudes* 1:8–9, one finds the advice: "Therefore instead of lands, purchase afflicted souls, as each is able, and look after widows and orphans and do not despise them, and spend your wealth and all your establishments for such fields and houses as you have received from God. For this reason did the master make you rich, that you should fulfill these ministries for him."

Mark does not introduce the man initially as a rich man. He does not identify him in any way. The reader only finds out that he is rich when Mark reports his disappointment at Jesus' words: "He went away sad, because he had great wealth" (10:22). His unhappy departure reveals that he does not want to enter life under Jesus' guidance. He goes off, presumably in search of a second, more accommodating, opinion. Jesus will not renegotiate the terms, however. One can imagine the disciples standing with mouths agape as they observe this exchange. Jesus lets a good man slip away whose deep pockets could help advance the kingdom cause—or at least their meager treasury. Jesus astounds them further by observing that the rich will have a hard time entering the kingdom of God.

Judaism reflected some ambivalence toward wealth. Some traditions equated prosperity with divine blessing (see Deut. 28:1–14; Job 1:10; 42:10; Ps. 128; Prov. 10:22). The disciples' amazement over Jesus' words presumably stems from this perspective. On the other hand, Jewish writers also warned against wealth. For example, Sirach 31:5–7 states:

> One who loves gold will not be justified;
> one who pursues money will be led astray by it.
> Many have come to ruin because of gold,
> and their destruction has met them face to face.
> It is a stumbling block to those who are avid for it,
> and every fool will be taken captive by it [NRSV].[10]

Jesus shared this negative attitude toward wealth and has nothing good to say about money (Mark 4:19; cf. Matt. 6:19–34; Luke 12:13–32; 16:1–15, 19–31; 19:1–10). He regards possessions as an almost insurmountable obstacle that prevent one from giving oneself completely to God. Wealth is not something neutral but is toxic to the soul. The best thing to do with money is to invest it in heavenly futures by feeding the destitute. One finds a similar perspective in Tobit 4:7–11:

> To all those who practice righteousness give alms from your possessions, and do not let your eye begrudge the gift when you make it. Do

---

10. The attitude in 1 Enoch 97:8–10 is even more harsh:

Woe to you who acquire silver and gold, but not in righteousness, and say, "We have become very rich and have possessions and have acquired everything that we desired. Now let us do what we have planned, for we have gathered silver and filled our storehouses, and as many as water are the husbandmen of our houses." Like water your life will flow away, for riches will not stay with you; they will quickly go up from you, for you acquired everything in wickedness, and you will be given over to a great curse.

not turn your face away from any anyone who is poor, and the face of God will not be turned away from you. If you have many possessions, make your gift from them in proportion; if few, do not be afraid to give according to the little that you have. So you will be laying up a good treasure for yourself against the day of necessity. For almsgiving delivers from death and keeps you from going into the Darkness. Indeed, almsgiving for all who practice it, is an excellent offering in the presence of the Most High [NRSV; see also Ps. 151:1].

Note, however, the difference. Jesus does not say to give "in proportion," but to sell *all* that you have.

The disciples' reaction to Jesus' bombshell about the rich matches many people's reactions: shock and consternation. Even those who know in their heads that money does not buy happiness or heaven still wish in their hearts that they had more. Consequently, Jesus repeats himself to drive home the point. For the first and only time in the Gospel, he addresses the disciples as "children" (10:24), as if to remind them that they must become like children if they are going to enter the kingdom of God (10:15). Children have little concept of the value of money. Adults, however, do because they know how hard money is to come by and all the things that it can acquire. Adults easily fall prey to Mammon and become deceived into thinking that they can find life in wealth and possessions. Many find it hard to give up even a small amount of something so valued, let alone give up all they have, even for the hope of eternal life.

Jesus resorts to colorful hyperbole to reinforce the point that those who are ruled by money cannot be ruled by God. The rich will find entering the kingdom of God (coming under God's rule) more difficult than trying to squeeze a camel through the eye of a needle. The opening of a needle is the smallest thing imaginable, and the camel was the largest animal in Palestine.[11] Shocked by this statement and assuming that the prospects of entering the kingdom of God are hopeless for those who usually get whatever they want in this life, the disciples ask, "Who then can be saved?"

The episode when blind Bartimaeus "is saved [healed]" by his faith (10:52) answers this question more fully. Jesus only affirms here that salvation comes from a divine possibility, not from a human one. He corrects the implicit assumption in the rich man's initial question. The man asked, "What must *I do?*" (10:17) and asserted, "All these *I have kept* since I was a boy" (10:20). He assumed that one could attain eternal life by doing something. Since he

---

11. Compare Matt. 23:24, where camels are contrasted with gnats, and *b. Ber.* 55b and *b. B. Mes.* 38b, which refer to an elephant passing through the eye of a needle. The elephant was the largest animal in Mesopotamia, where the Babylonian Talmud was compiled.

wanted something he could do, Jesus obliged him: Sell all that you have and give it to the poor. The disciples are to learn from this encounter that God requires something more than reverence for Jesus as a good teacher and earnest attempts to obey God's commands (see Rom. 10:2–3). The man has attained conventional respectability with a genteel approach to obedience. But Jesus' demand exposes the man's reluctance to give himself and all he has over to God—to deny himself and all his earthly securities, works, and possessions. He falls short of the one thing the reign of God requires. To enter the kingdom of God one must submit to God's rule so that God reigns over every aspect of life.

Disciples must be prepared to give up everything. Peter quickly reminds Jesus that they have done exactly that. Jesus promises that their sacrifice will not be for naught. Those who have left earthly attachments for the sake of the gospel will receive hundredfold rewards—but *"with ... persecutions"* (10:30). In this age, those who become homeless will have a home among those who receive them (see 6:10).[12] Those who surrender families will become part of a greater family not based on biological kinship (3:33–35).[13] Those who leave fields will be given greater fields of mission opportunity (see Matt. 9:37–38).

At this point many walk away from Jesus, which lays bare the decision of the Twelve and other followers to stick by his side. These others fall away because they are not yet ready to accept the hundredfold persecution that comes with following Christ and with bearing a cross. The first will become last in the end and the last will become first. The disciples need to learn how to make themselves last.

Bridging Contexts

JESUS' RADICAL DEMANDS in this passage can only jar a culture as materialistic as ours. Many will find its radical message difficult to communicate to those who come from the upper socioeconomic strata and to any who share our culture's materialistic values. Most con-

---

12. Stephen G. Barton (*Discipleship and Family Ties in Mark and Matthew* [SNTSMS 80; Cambridge: Cambridge Univ. Press, 1994], 220–21) shows that Jesus' summons to discipleship, which may sever family ties, was not unprecedented, irrational, or arbitrary. It could be found in the strict monotheistic religious tradition of Judaism, which required a proselyte to forsake former relations, and also in the diverse philosophical traditions of the Greco-Roman world. Followers, therefore, could make sense of the demand to subordinate family ties for the sake of a higher good.

13. Walter Wink, *Engaging the Powers: Discernment and Resistance in the World of Domination* (Minneapolis: Fortress, 1992), 119, points out that father is not in the list. The father is one who claims and exerts authority over others. That role is reserved for God alone.

gregants do not want to hear sermons that make them uncomfortable about having material possessions. Pastors also may want to avoid passages that bring up the subject because their congregations might expect them to set the example. The natural temptation is to try to find some cue that Jesus does not make the same demand of us to sell all that we have. Consequently, we must guard against two pitfalls in applying this passage: the desire to whittle away the radical demand to make it more reasonable, and the inclination to make it apply to someone other than us.

Diversionary tactics. Various attempts have been made to dodge the bullet the text aims our way, and some have become well known. Some try to soothe consciences by assuming that what Jesus says applies only to those who are rich. The rich are then assumed to be those who earn more or have more than we do. We always manage to fall below an imaginary "riches danger line," so that we can comfort ourselves that Jesus intended this lesson for someone else. The bid to soften Jesus' demands began quite early, with a textual variant to 10:24 that reads, "How hard it is *for those who trust in riches.*" How easily we convince ourselves that we do not trust in riches and then consider ourselves safe from this danger.

This passage has also been subjected to clever exegetical doctoring that attempts either to reduce the size of the camel or to enlarge the needle's eye. Many people who know hardly anything else about Scripture do know a tradition that the "Needle's Eye" was supposedly the name of a low gate in Jerusalem. Shakespeare reflects knowledge of this view in *Richard III,* referring to the "postern of a needle's eye." Jesus' radical metaphor then becomes an anemic commonplace. A camel can get through the needle's eye if it throws off its burden and gets down on its knees. The lesson becomes practical: Rich persons need not worry if they just are humble. This tradition has no historical basis and looks like the invention of a wealthy church searching for loopholes.[14] A more erudite interpretation claims that "camel" is a mistranslation of a similar Aramaic word for "rope" or a "ship's cable." Why this makes it any easier to thread the needle is hard to see.

One should always be suspicious of exegesis that softens Jesus' radical demands. If one can say after encountering the teaching of Jesus, "all these things I have kept since I was a boy," it probably means that we have met only a watered down version of it. C. S. Lewis vividly captures Jesus' extreme metaphor in a poem:

---

14. Theophylact first suggested this interpretation in the eleventh century; see Paul Minear, "The Needle's Eye. A Study in Form Criticism," *JBL* 61 (1942): 157–69. Mark 10:25 has *raphis,* used especially for a sewing needles, while Luke 18:25 uses *belone.* If such a gate as the "Needle's Eye" ever existed, it would most likely have been identified by the same Greek word.

All things (e.g. a camel's journey through
a needle's eye) are possible, it's true;
But picture how the camel feels, squeezed out
In one long bloody thread from tail to snout.[15]

One can express Jesus' hyperbole similarly in modern imagery: It is easier for a Mercedes (note how one usually picks a car more expensive than one's own) to slip through the night deposit slot at the local bank.[16]

In bridging the contexts, we must be honest in our interpretation even when our conclusions become a stumbling block to us and may offend those whom we do not like to offend—the wealthy who faithfully support the church program. As Mark Twain said: "It ain't those parts of the Bible that I can't understand that bother me, it is the parts that I do understand." We do better if we confess that we are too weak to follow Jesus on his terms than if we try to find loopholes that allow us to continue in our complacency. We also do better to confront congregations with the truth that living a praise-worthy life and always coloring inside the lines do not earn one eternal life, as if salvation were some kind of payoff.

Jesus' confrontation of the rich man expresses true love. Many need to hear his disturbing demand because he casts a spotlight on our everyday values from eternity's angle of vision. From that perspective, our covetousness looks rather silly. Those who invest only in themselves, in their security, and in their own comfort and pleasure need to know that they are making a bad invest-ment. No amount of law observance will turn hearts set on the desire for material things to God. If Jesus advised radical surgery on hands, feet, and eyes so that one can enter life, even if maimed (9:43–48), how much more should we get rid of possessions that anchor the soul to this world and will only fuel the flames of judgment?

How hard it is for the rich to enter the kingdom. Many dismiss Jesus' command to sell all and to give it away as totally unreasonable and out of the question. Their instinct is right; Jesus does not reject having possessions. Many of his first followers did have possessions. Somebody owned the houses in which he retreated with his disciples. The central issue has to do with one's ultimate loyalty. The point of this story is not to drive home the need for all of Jesus' followers to sell their possessions. Jesus did not insist that Zacchaeus sell all his goods and give them to the poor before he would deign to eat with him. Zacchaeus voluntarily offers to give up half of his possessions and to restore fourfold whatever he may have gained by fraud (see

---

15. C. S. Lewis, *Poems* (New York/London: Harcourt Brace Jovanovich, 1964), 134.
16. Adapted from Frederick Buechner, *Wishful Thinking: A Theological ABC* (New York: Harper & Row, 1973), 81.

Ex. 22:1; Lev. 5:16; Num. 5:7). This willingness to make things right evokes Jesus' response, "Today salvation has come to this house" (Luke 19:8–9). Jesus' encounter with this rich man in Mark serves to illustrate how difficult it is for the rich (or any one, for that matter) to do this. Few are willing to risk divesting themselves of whatever provides them security in this life to enter a new quality of life under God's rule.

The text thus raises the question: Is God or Mammon to rule over one's life? Are material possessions to be served or are they to serve?[17] Paul advises the Corinthians to "use the things of the world, as if not engrossed in them. For this world in its present form is passing away" (1 Cor. 7:31). Jesus is calling this man to follow him. He is inviting him to join a community of believers who will take care of one another's material needs. He will not be left destitute and forced to fend for himself.

Jesus' confrontation with the rich man, however, warns our materialistic age that possessions beget hazards even when we are not engrossed in them. Wherever money is at stake, there is danger to life because it is not a neutral or harmless commodity. Wealth possesses high voltage and explosive energy since so many crave it and it strikes such reverence in the heart. No Christian is immune from the danger of Mammon. Covetousness is like a virus that takes residence in the soul and begins slowly to work its destruction. The love of acquisition and an appetite for self-gratification will deaden the instinct for self-sacrifice.

Moreover, the abundance of possessions can easily deceive one into thinking that they offer security and abundant life (see Luke 12:15). Having money beguiles one into believing that everything can be had for a price—even salvation. The rich fool (12:16–21) and the rich man dressed in his fine linen and dining sumptuously while Lazarus lay starving at his gate (16:19–31) serve as two examples of characters in Jesus' parables duped by Mammon. Preachers need to sound the alarm about the danger that a commitment to possessions presents. Those who will save their lives are those who those who are willing to lose their lives for the sake of Jesus and the gospel (Mark 8:35).

A loving confrontation. How are we to communicate this message without watering down Jesus' demands? The mention of Jesus' love for the rich man is a detail that should govern the interpretation of this passage. We may look at those who are rich and envy them for their wealth, hate them for their privileges, or look down on them for their smugness. We may berate them because, unlike us, they are unwilling to give up all that they have to follow Jesus. By contrast, Jesus, who comes from the ranks of the poor and oppressed, loves this man whose wealth gives him opportunities denied

---

17. Robert Guelich, *The Sermon on the Mount* (Waco, Tex.: Word, 1982), 334.

others. The rich man turned his back on Jesus, but Jesus did not turn his back on the rich. He loved them enough to help them see the truth.

It is easy to forget that Jesus loved the righteous as much as the sinner, the up and out as much as the down and out. He does not love this man for the advantage his wealth might bring to him and his movement. He loves him for who he is and therefore tells him exactly what he needs to hear, even if it is not what he wants to hear. Love challenges others for their own good. A good physician prescribes what will bring health to the patient, even when it is unpleasant medicine or radical surgery. This man needs radical surgery to save his life, and to follow Jesus will cost him everything. Our mushier love for someone like this would have demanded far less—only 10 percent perhaps. We would have offered him correct things to do: Write Congress, boycott this, join that organization, contribute to this cause. In the end our approach would have left him with a fatal disease, but we would have felt more comfortable about it and called it love.

Obedience to the law and salvation. This encounter also has implications for understanding the law's role in salvation. God's will demands more than rote obedience to rules, as Jesus' teaching on divorce in the previous section reveals. One must follow Jesus and Jesus' interpretation of the commandments. Via comments, "Laws and rules reveal the kind of concrete issues the will of God is concerned about and in a provisional way show one how one ought to address oneself to these issues."[18] The rich man believed that his obedience was complete and wanted confirmation from a respected teacher, renowned for his preaching about the kingdom of God, to make sure. The disciples learn that salvation is beyond human power to achieve.

This scene thus prepares the reader for Jesus' announcement to his disciples that he will give his life as a ransom for many (10:45). What Jesus offers does not depend on what individuals do for themselves but on what is done for them. This encounter also helps explain the disciples' persistent failure in the story. No one enters the kingdom by dint of his or her own strength.[19] Who can deny himself completely? Who can sell all that she has? Giving oneself completely over to God seems impossible, but Jesus did not need to die on a cross for something that everyone finds easy. Following Jesus, which leads to salvation, does not depend on human ability. It comes from the one who makes all things possible. The impossible becomes possible when divine power infuses a disciple's life through faith (see 11:22–24).

---

18. Via, *Ethics*, 135.

19. This is why all attempts to see the failure of the disciples as some polemical attack on them misread Mark. One can only expect them to fail until the death and resurrection of Christ, which unleashes a new power in their lives.

Those with possessions may find coming under God's rule so hard because they think that they have so much to lose. But God requires the same of everybody—rich and poor, fishermen and toll collectors, prosperous land-holders and destitute day laborers holding up their signs, "Will work for food." All must give up whatever "stands in the way of total commitment to following Jesus and love for the community."[20] The preacher must not shy away from naming these things that stand in our way one by one because people's lives are at stake. A reward beyond our imagining awaits those who do give up all that is dear to them to follow Jesus, but Mark honestly presents our prospects in this fallen world. The reward will come "with . . . persecutions." Are disciples ready to give up even their lives to obey Jesus' call?

 IN OUR AFFLUENT culture, we tend to be more interested in economic success than in excelling religiously. Most Christians do not believe that one should sell all that one has in order to be a disciple; few even tithe to their churches. Many believe that lacking just one thing should be close enough, particularly if God grades on a curve.

Today, people would be more likely to ask Jesus how to get the highest return on their money rather than how they can serve God. Such an attitude sabotages serious commitment and leads many Christians to a dangerous complacency about their faith. More than one minister has turned a blind eye to Jesus' teaching on possessions, and some even use religion to make greedy appeals to fatten their own bank accounts. Advertisements herald newly discovered biblical formulas that show how by giving you can receive a hundredfold more—and ask for hefty contributions to get the secret. They believe that God only requires them to be decent law-abiding citizens. Luccock points out that an edition of Webster's dictionary gave the following as one definition of the word "Christian": "a decent, civilized, or presentable person."[21] The *Random House Dictionary* comes closer to a definition the New Testament would support: "exhibiting a spirit proper to a follower of Jesus Christ, as in having a loving regard for other persons."

The values of our materialistic culture seep in and can undermine that spirit proper to a follower of Jesus. The Roman satirist Juvenal (A.D. 60–140) made a sardonic observation that still holds true today: "Majestic mighty wealth is the holiest of our gods." Many ask, "Why should I give up for others what I worked so hard to get?" They feel deep down, although they may

---

20. Via, *Ethics*, 137.
21. Luccock, "The Gospel According to St. Mark: Exposition," 802.

never say it aloud, that the rich man did the sensible thing in walking away. Religious commitment should cost something but not that much.

We need to confront the materialism of our culture that has infiltrated the church. James Stewart wrote that people will

> always find ways and means of eluding a religion's stern demands while still calling themselves its followers and signing its creeds and continuing to bear its name; they will always be able to convince themselves that, even on the basis of compromise, they have a right to bear its name, and will grow indignant with anyone who challenges that right; they will always regard the half-allegiance they are prepared to give with a wonderful complacency and satisfaction feeling that anyone—even God Himself—might be gratified by the interest they show and the patronage they offer; not realising that attitude, which seems so reasonable and respectable, is dealing religion a blow and doing it damage compared with which all the direct, frontal attacks of its open enemies are a mere nothing.[22]

Jesus said that the rich man in this story lacked one thing, though he did not specify what it was. In applying this passage to our contemporary situation we can imagine that he lacked the very things that we ourselves may lack. First, this man lacked for nothing. He had too much to give up. Money brings people many things (honor, respect, admiration, power, beauty, sex), which is why it is so alluring. Wealth cannot make one holy or purchase eternal life, and it does not offer any deep happiness, even when people get more than their fair share.

David G. Myers points to the statistic that between 1957 and 1990, the per capita income of Americans doubled in real money. Yet the number of Americans who reported being "very happy" remained unchanged at one-third.[23] The explanation? People in our culture have plenty to live on but little to live for. Doubling one's income and having more things does not make for happiness. Many people, both in our congregations and in our world, sense that something vital is missing in their lives. Material success allows them to live in comfort but fails to meet their basic spiritual needs. Their spiritual emptiness becomes a gnawing hunger when they have to confront the reality of death and bereavement, the anxieties and stress of personal relationships, or the tenacious down drag of evil in their own souls. They wonder if there is something more to life and something beyond this life. When

---

22. James S. Stewart, *A Man in Christ: The Vital Elements of Paul's Religion* (London: Holder and Stoughton, 1963), 95–96.

23. David G. Myers, *Pursuit of Happiness: Who Is Happy—and Why* (New York: William Morrow, 1992), 31–46.

confronted by Jesus' invitation to sell all and follow him, however, the world usually counts possessions dearer than the hope of eternal life and a meaningful earthly life. They lack for nothing and, as a result, lack everything.

The second thing this man lacked was trust. God requires something more than simply reverence for Jesus and zealous attempts at obedience. God requires radical trust. Like so many today, this rich man wanted to serve God on his own terms. He obeyed all the commandments that suited him but resisted giving his whole life over to God. He was "afraid to expose himself to the uncertainties and insecurities of the future" or to make himself vulnerable as a child.[24] He accumulated possessions to secure his life in this world, and he accumulated obedience to the commandments to secure his life in the world to come.[25] In a culture that has grown wary of commitment and risk, few want to bet their whole lives on Jesus. They also want to keep a material safety net and refuse to disentangle themselves from something that brings status, influence, and privilege. Few are willing to trust that there will be other brothers and sisters in the faith who will watch over them and care for them, partly because we do not watch out for them. To have life, one must trust God and give up the quest to create one's own security.

Third, this man lacked compassion for others. Origen cites an excerpt from "The Gospel According to the Hebrews":

> But the rich man began to scratch his head, for it did not please him. And the Lord said to him, "How can you say, I have fulfilled the law and the prophets, when it is written in the law: You shall love your neighbor as yourself; and lo, many of your brothers, sons of Abraham, are clothed in filth, dying of hunger, and your house is full of many good things, none of which goes out to them?"[26]

This apocryphal account hits home. Wealth can blind our moral judgment, harden the arteries of compassion, and lead to spiritual bankruptcy. The man was unable to give what he had for the benefit of others because he cared only about himself and nobody else ("What must *I* do to inherit eternal life?"). He was imprisoned in a dungeon of concern only for his own welfare. This attitude contrasts starkly the Son of Man's self-giving love: Jesus had compassion on the crowds and fed them and will eventually give his life for the many (10:45). How can someone like the rich man live in luxury and be complacent about the needs of others, while professing discipleship to one who gave his life for others?

---

24. Waetjen, *Reordering*, 170.
25. Via, *Ethics*, 134–35.
26. Cited by Taylor, *Mark*, 429–30.

Possessions set humans against other humans and against God. A recent survey has revealed that a low but significant percentage of Americans would still buy clothing even if they knew it had been produced by slave labor in a sweatshop. The cheaper cost would override any compassion or justice. Jane Goodall's study of chimpanzees reveals a surprising trait about their communal life, a trait that humans share. The chimps, who were normally placid and cooperative, changed their behavior when she began to give them bananas; they immediately became contentious. The new surplus of food caused the dominant ones to try keep it all for themselves and to chase the others off. The less dominant ones had to come begging. In our own lives we see evidence that the more we have the more we want and the more jealous we become of those who have a little bit more. Jesus tries to free us from these desires to accumulate, which ultimately destroy fellowship and a sense of brotherhood.

Sider argues that we need to distinguish between necessities and luxuries, and we must reject both our desire for the latter and our inclination to blur the distinction. Expenditures for status, pride, staying in fashion, and "keeping up with the Joneses" are wrong.[27] From God's perspective they are foolish.

Annie Dillard tells of the ill-fated Franklin expedition to the Arctic in 1845. That odyssey was a turning point in Arctic exploration because of its well-publicized failure. The preparations made were more suitable for the Royal Navy officer's club in England than for the frigid Arctic. The explorers made room on their ships for a large library, a hand organ, china place settings, cut-glass wine goblets, and sterling silver flatware instead of additional coal for their steam engines. The ornate silver flatware was engraved with the individual officer's initials and family crests. Search parties found clumps of bodies of men who had set off to walk for help when their supplies ran out. One skeleton wore his fine blue cloth uniform edged with silk braid, hardly a match for the bitter arctic cold. Another apparently chose to carry with him the place setting of sterling silver flatware. What must he have been thinking to take sterling silver tableware in a search for help and food?[28] One cannot imagine that any of these sailor adventurers would have said, as they neared death on the frozen landscape, "I wish I had brought more silver place settings." Our hanging on to things that are ultimately useless will look no less foolish. Many cannot envision life without things they cherish. They are in danger of losing the only life that counts.

---

27. Ronald J. Sider, *Rich Christians in an Age of Hunger*, 3d ed. (Dallas: Word, 1990), 159–60.

28. Annie Dillard, *Teaching a Stone to Talk: Expeditions and Encounters* (New York: Harper & Row, 1982), 24–26.

Mark 10:32–45

❧

THEY WERE ON their way up to Jerusalem, with Jesus leading the way, and the disciples were astonished, while those who followed were afraid. Again he took the Twelve aside and told them what was going to happen to him. 33"We are going up to Jerusalem," he said, "and the Son of Man will be betrayed to the chief priests and teachers of the law. They will condemn him to death and will hand him over to the Gentiles, 34who will mock him and spit on him, flog him and kill him. Three days later he will rise."

35Then James and John, the sons of Zebedee, came to him. "Teacher," they said, "we want you to do for us whatever we ask."

36"What do you want me to do for you?" he asked.

37They replied, "Let one of us sit at your right and the other at your left in your glory."

38"You don't know what you are asking," Jesus said. "Can you drink the cup I drink or be baptized with the baptism I am baptized with?"

39"We can," they answered.

Jesus said to them, "You will drink the cup I drink and be baptized with the baptism I am baptized with, 40but to sit at my right or left is not for me to grant. These places belong to those for whom they have been prepared."

41When the ten heard about this, they became indignant with James and John. 42Jesus called them together and said, "You know that those who are regarded as rulers of the Gentiles lord it over them, and their high officials exercise authority over them. 43Not so with you. Instead, whoever wants to become great among you must be your servant, 44and whoever wants to be first must be slave of all. 45For even the Son of Man did not come to be served, but to serve, and to give his life as a ransom for many."

JESUS HAS BEEN going before his disciples on the road, and Mark now identifies their destination as Jerusalem.[1] The disciples and Jesus are marching to Zion. Jesus goes there as the Messiah, who invites all Israel to come under God's mysterious dominion, not just those living in Galilee. Marcus contends that Mark gives the victory procession pictured in Isaiah 35:10 (see also 42:13; 59:20; 62:11) an ironic twist: "The fearful trek of the befuddled, bedraggled little band of disciples *is* the return of Israel to Zion, and Jesus' suffering and death there *are* the prophesied apocalyptic victory of the divine warrior." Jesus goes to Jerusalem not to triumph in a military campaign but to die.[2] He leads his disciples on the way to his Passion, as he will later lead the way to Galilee after the resurrection (14:28; 16:7, where the verb *proago*, "to lead the way," appears again).

Jesus constructs the way of the Lord while the disciples, still worried about the order of procession behind him, trail behind. Mark tells us that they are amazed and afraid. Is it the fear of persecution and suffering that slows their step? If so, it was something that Mark's first readers were well acquainted with. Or is it a sense of awe and amazement directed toward Jesus, who directs his own destiny and theirs?[3] If so, the familiar words from the hymn "Amazing Grace" apply: "Grace has taught my heart to fear, and grace my fears relieved."

Jesus does not allay their fear, however, but predicts for the third time his impending death and subsequent resurrection. He gives more specific details. He will be betrayed to the chief priests and teachers of the law, who will condemn him to death and hand him over to the Gentiles, who in turn will mock him, spit on him, scourge him, and kill him. The Messiah will suffer indignity and a shameful death. Then he will be handed over to God, who will resurrect him.

As Jesus draws nearer to his ordeal, the disciples do not draw nearer to understanding. Each time he speaks to them about his suffering, his words go in one ear and out the other. Immediately after his announcement, James and John come sidling up to him with a special request. The earlier dispute about status and rank among the disciples (9:34) was silenced but not buried. These two act like brazen fortune hunters when they ask Jesus to guarantee that one can sit on his right and the other on his left when he comes into his glory. Jesus responds that the teachers of the law bask in the recognition bestowed on them by others and want the first seats, making clear their

---

1. One always "went up" to the Holy City.
2. Marcus, *The Way of the Lord*, 36.
3. Lane, *Mark*, 374.

honor ranking (12:38). But James and John want even more than that; they want to be crown princes sitting on co-thrones with Jesus. Psalm 110:1 states: "The LORD said to my Lord, 'Sit at my right hand,'" and they are lobbying their Lord for that right-hand seat.

These two are no different from Peter as they envision an earthly kingdom established and run according to human norms (8:33). They still misinterpret what it means for Jesus to be the Messiah and assume that when he ushers in the new age, they as his friends will receive special privileges. The new age they look forward to has all the earmarks of the old age; pork-barrel politics and nepotism still reign supreme. They foresee themselves as the elite of the elite, ruling over others in an earthly empire. Their fantasy differs little from that of the Romans as espoused by Vergil: "For these people I have set no limits, world or time, but make the gift of empire without end, Lords of the world, the toga-bearing Romans" (*Aeneid* I). The kingdom of God will also have no limits, but will be populated by cross-bearing Christians of every nation, who become the servants of the world.

Either Jesus' words about his suffering whistle right by them or they must hope that his travail will only be a temporary setback, quickly reversed. Perhaps all they have heard are Jesus' earlier comments on his coming in glory with the holy angels (8:38). Since they were two of the first called, they want to be first in glory.

What they do not realize is that Jesus' glory will not become fully manifest to all until after great tribulation (13:24, 26). They also do not realize that two bandits will be crucified with Jesus, "one on his right and one on his left" (15:27, the only other place in Mark where these words occur), when he begins his reign from the cross.[4] But the Zebedee brothers are not asking for the honor of being crucified with Jesus. What they really expect is a kingdom for themselves, where they can impose their own will on others. They hope to replace the self-serving oppressive power structure of the Romans with their own self-serving oppressive power structure. Nothing changes except the names of the rulers. Oppressive power gets recycled and new tyrants rise on the scene.[5] The worldly ambition to be at the top and to beat down others still rules.

Jesus responds to their ill-timed and selfish request with grace: "You don't know what you are asking." He informs them that the Father has not placed him in charge of the seating arrangements in the kingdom (nor is he privy

---

4. One can be said "to sit" on a cross because some crosses had a small cleat, called a *sedile*, or a seat for the victim to support himself. See Martin Hengel, *Crucifixion in the Ancient World and the Folly of the Message of the Cross* (Philadelphia: Fortress, 1977), 25.

5. Myers, *Binding*, 343.

to the timing of the end, 13:32). He then asks whether they think they can drink the cup that he drinks and be baptized with the baptism with which he is baptized? The cup is a metaphor for suffering (Isa. 51:17, 22), and baptism is a metaphor for being plunged into calamity (see Pss. 42:7; 69:1). He will not be sprinkled with a bit of suffering; he will be submerged in it. He asks them if they are willing to share his fate (see 8:34) and be doused with the waters of hardship and trial. The point is clear to the reader, if not the disciples: To share his kingdom one has to share his Passion (see Rom. 8:17). No one who enthrones the old values of power without ethics and sacrifice can reign with Jesus.

James and John respond glibly, "We can." They are as self-confident in their own abilities as the rich man was (10:17–22). They believe they can endure a little hardship if Jesus will grant them seats of power and corner offices. They understand faithful discipleship to Jesus as a means to a selfish end; it will help them achieve their goal of having power over others. When Jesus speaks of his cup, they may think in terms of drinking the cup of victory. Their attitude, which expects special favors and advantages, will hardly take up a cross happily. But obedience is learned through suffering, from which even God's Son was not exempt (Heb. 5:8).[6] Jesus cannot promise them cochairs, but he can promise them that they will suffer (see Acts 12:2).

The other disciples become indignant at the brothers' audacity (10:41). They are not livid because James and John have been so insensitive to make such a request after Jesus has bared his heart about his coming suffering and death. They are angry because James and John beat them to the punch and may now have an edge over them for the power slots. Jealousy creates turmoil in the ranks. The disciples would rather bear a grudge than a cross.

The ambitious disciples' misconception prompts Jesus to give final instructions on the nature of true discipleship and his role as Messiah (10:42–45). He tries to channel their desire to be great into humble service: Be great servants of others. Geddert points out that the disciples "are not consigned to 'last' place, they are shown how they can be first; they are not consigned to slavery status, they are shown how to become great."[7] Jesus labels the desire to dominate others as pagan—pagans want seats of power and want to lord it over others.[8] The disciples have taken pagan rulers as their

---

6. Brown, *Death of the Messiah*, 1:170.

7. Geddert, *Watchwords*, 153.

8. From an apocalyptic viewpoint, the real rulers of this world are Satan and his minions, who are being challenged and overcome by God (see 3:22, 24).

models, whereas they need to take Jesus as their model. The way of Jesus is self-giving service. They are not to be on the receiving end of service but on the giving end.

Jesus has told his disciples that he must die, but this is the only passage in Mark that tells us *why* he must die: He "gives his life as a ransom for many." The term *ransom* (*lytron*) was used for compensation for personal injury (Ex. 21:30) or a crime (Num. 35:31–32), for purchasing the freedom of an enslaved relative (Lev. 25:51–52), and for the price paid as an equivalent for the sacrifice of the firstborn (Num. 18:15). In extrabiblical sources, it referred to the amount paid to free a slave or prisoner, redeem a pledge, or reclaim something pawned. Exodus 30:12 connects this word to the annual half-shekel tax that in the time of Jesus went to support the daily temple sacrifices for the people's sins. *Tosepta Seqalim* 1:6 directly connects the half-shekel offering to sin atonement between Israel and God.

The concept of ransom, therefore, is connected to the idea of cost, substitution, and atonement. Isaiah 53:10–12 forms the most likely backdrop here:

> Yet it was the LORD's will to crush him and cause him to suffer,
>   and though the LORD makes his life a guilt offering,
> he will see his offspring and prolong his days,
>   and the will of the LORD will prosper in his hand.
> After the suffering of his soul,
>   he will see the light of life and be satisfied;
> by his knowledge my righteous servant will justify many,
>   and he will bear their iniquities.
> Therefore I will give him a portion among the great,
>   and he will divide the spoils with the strong,
> because he poured out his life unto death,
>   and was numbered with the transgressors.
> For he bore the sin of many,
>   and made intercession for the transgressors.[9]

Jesus thus provides the answer to the question that he asked his disciples earlier, "What can a man give in exchange for his soul?" (8:37). The psalmist asserts that no ransom avails for one's life (Ps. 49:7–9). That is true if we think we can pay the ransom ourselves. But this text affirms that Jesus pays a price for others that they cannot pay themselves.

---

9. See Peter Stuhlmacher, "Vicariously Giving His Life for Many: Mark 10:45 (Matt. 20:28)," in *Reconciliation, Law, and Righteousness: Essays in Biblical Theology* (Philadelphia: Fortress, 1986), 16–29.

The word "many" suggests a select number of recipients of these benefits: many but not all. In Semitic idiom, however, the word "many" can have the inclusive meaning "all" (see 1 Cor. 10:17; 1 Tim. 2:6).[10] The effects of Jesus' sacrifice extend to all who will accept it. But the emphasis falls on the many who need ransoming and on the action of the one who offers his life as that ransom.

MARK SHOWS THE disciples once again competing for first place, trying to outmatch and outmaneuver one another for power and advantage. They want to dominate, not serve. In the Gospel narrative the disciples never understand the significance of suffering and its relationship to vindication and victory. As a result, they fail miserably because the two are so interconnected.

The disciples have displayed a delight in power, glorious achievements, and personal ambition; they want a Messiah who is beyond suffering and death and will then offer them all of their heart's desires. But according to Mark, one can never understand who Jesus is without understanding the necessity of his final destiny of suffering. Suffering distinguishes his role as Messiah and ours as disciples. To know and understand Jesus, therefore, requires us to accept his destiny as a Messiah who dies for others and accept that same destiny for ourselves. All followers must share his self-giving love and service and his fate of suffering before they can share his glory (see Rom. 8:17). The images of baptism and cup recall baptism and the Lord's Supper. All disciples who accept baptism and drink Jesus' cup also pledge themselves to live and die by the pattern of the cross.

Jesus did not choose his disciples because they were brainier or nicer than other people, for they were not. Human nature has not changed over the years, and the influence of the gospel has not eliminated pride and spiritual competition from our midst. We still find people in the church who put meeting their ego needs before meeting their obligations as disciples. The cross is central to discipleship, but many soft sell or neglect that aspect in favor of a more popular brand of discipleship—one that offers fulfillment and satisfies our material needs. That can only feed selfishness and breed competition. This text bridges easily into our culture because it allows us to see our own pettiness mirrored in the pettiness of these disciples. While Jesus is talking about all that he is about to give, the disciples come with a shopping list of all they want to get. The absurdity of this scene brings the

---

10. This saying parallels a text in 4 Ezra 8:3: "Many have been created, but few shall be saved."

judgment of the cross on our selfish ambitions and our maneuvering for position and power.

Mark describes Jesus' going before his disciples as he marches to his fateful death in Jerusalem. While the issue of atonement in 10:45 is vitally important, one should not neglect that Jesus holds himself up as an example to be followed. He does not explain atonement theories so much as show his disciples a way of life. The only way that disciples can possibly live up to Jesus' demands is to realize that he has gone before them, broken through, and cleared the way for others to follow. He is like the man who cut the path through the jungle for days in order to lead a group of prisoners back to freedom and life and then died of exhaustion upon arrival. Such a person would have died "for many," although this would not mean that the many simply had to acknowledge this theoretically or symbolically. They were with him on this march; yet he was the only one who was strong enough to open the way, and he died in doing so.[11]

THIS PASSAGE FORCES Christians to reflect on what it means to have a servant for a Lord. Can they shamelessly seek after glory and honor when our Lord has given his life in a shameful death? It also forces us to reflect on how one defines greatness and to examine how to attain it. Clearly worldly notions of rank, honor, and privilege are out of place in the church that names Jesus as Lord. Self-seeking has no place in a church founded on the ultimate self-giving sacrifice of Jesus Christ. The road to the cross leads in a different direction from the road to success. If one follows Jesus along his road, seeking glory for oneself is out of place.

The passage brings out the danger of overweening ambition. Stott remarks that our world "(and even the church) is full of Jameses and Johns, go-getters and status-seekers, hungry for honour and prestige, measuring life by achievements, and everlastingly dreaming of success."[12] One need not look far to see preachers who do not preach to reach people but preach to reach the top, to become ecclesiastical superstars. They see discipleship to Jesus in terms of rank and privilege. They assume that Jesus is someone who will achieve things for them and give them the status of lords. Thomas à Kempis wrote that "the devil is continually tempting thee to seek high

---

11. Eduard Schweizer, "The Portrayal of the Life of Faith in the Gospel of Mark," in *Interpreting the Gospels*, ed. James Luther Mays (Philadelphia: Fortress, 1981), 176.

12. John R. W. Stott, *The Cross of Christ* (Downers Grove, Ill.: InterVarsity, 1986), 286–87.

things, to go after honors" (*Little Alphabet of Monks*). Bernard of Clairvaux warned against ambition as "a secret poison, the father of livor [spite], and mother of hypocrisy, the moth of holiness, and cause of madness, crucifying and disquieting all that it take hold of" (*Epistle*, 126).

Despite all the warnings in Scripture, pagan values continue to seep into the church and govern its actions. Many ministers still dream of the big church, of the presidency of an institution or of a denomination, or of being acclaimed in national magazines as a mover and a shaker. All too frequently, these people achieve their dreams because of their single-minded purpose to attain them at all costs, regardless of how much suffering they cause others along the way and how much they cause the work of Christ to suffer. The church has had to endure power struggles that make it look no different from the pagan corporate world.

But the church cannot thrive if its leaders are competing with one another for positions of power. That pattern can only lead to anger and hatred. Jotham's scathing parable protesting Abimelech's coronation as king is apt (Judg. 9:7–15). The trees want to anoint a king over themselves, but the productive trees, such as the olive, fig, and vine, all refuse, content in being of service to humankind. The fruitless bramble that catches fire and brings destruction to the other trees is the only one that aspires to power. The church must be cautious of those who hunger for power over others. Such proud ambition usually leads to devastating results. Perhaps it derives from an inferiority complex. The desire to rule over and control others may veil the hidden recognition of an inability to produce anything.

A saying attributed to Genghis Khan maintains that "a man's greatest work is to break his enemies, to drive them before him, to take from them all the things that have been theirs, to hear the weeping of those who cherished them, to take their horses between his knees and to press in his arms the most desirable of their women." This warlike attitude continues to plague our world. It attracts many because it seems to win. Eugene O'Neill aptly describes in the first scene of *The Emperor Jones* how this style of life gets rewarded:

> For de little stealin' dey gits you in jail soon or late. For de big stealin' dey makes you emperor and puts you in de Hall o' Fame when you croaks. If dey's one thing I learns in ten years on de Pullman cars listenin' to de white quality talk, it's dat same fact.

Jesus' life and teaching turns the worldly understanding of greatness and great works on its head. The greatest work ever done was accomplished by one who gave his life for others. Self-giving service is the only greatness recognized by God, and only those who give of themselves for others will be the big winners with God. They are willing "to let life go hang for the sake of another," as Peter de Vries states it.[13] Jesus invites followers to join him in becoming great and doing great things, not the way the world judges "great," but the way God judges it.

Martin Luther King Jr. said that everybody can be great because anybody can serve.

> You don't have to have a college degree to serve. You don't have to make your subject and verb agree to serve. You don't have to know Plato and Aristotle. You don't have to know Einstein's theory of relativity. You don't have to know the second theory of thermodynamics in physics. You only need a heart full of grace. A soul generated by love.[14]

This attitude is illustrated in the character Nancy Mannigoe in William Faulkner's "Requiem for a Nun." She says at the end of her life, "It's all right. I can get low for Jesus too. I can get low for him too." We can check on our own attitude on this score by examining how we respond when given a menial task to perform that we might judge to be beneath our dignity. God truly reigns when Jesus' way of viewing life overthrows this world's destructive ways of living.

This scene with the disciples should also make us reexamine our requests to God. I have heard of people in a prayer group who computerized their entreaties to God, listing the request, the date when it was made, and the date when it was answered. The list of requests included promotions at work, new jobs, fancy new cars, bigger homes, and dates with persons they secretly liked. Would we look like shameless gold diggers if our prayer requests were made public?

Geddes MacGregor describes a typical Sunday morning service in a church following the rites of "Orthodox pretend Christianity." The pastor prays:

> O dear, wonderful Father of our incredibly unbelievable experience, we like to feel assured that we may always come to thee when we feel like it. . . . And now, dear Lord, we want quite naturally and simply and just in a word to ask thee very frankly, to give us our heart's desire. Thou art the Comforter, as the old story puts it, and so thou art our friend, for we are very fond of comfort.[15]

---

13. Peter de Vries, *The Mackeral Plaza* (New York: Little, Brown & Co., 1958), 5.

14. *The Wisdom of Martin Luther King, Jr.*, ed. Alex Ayres (New York: Meridian, 1993), 205.

15. Geddes MacGregor, *From a Christian Ghetto* (London: Longmans Green and Co, 1954), 95–96; cited by Roland Mushat Frye, *Perspective on Man* (Philadelphia: Westminster, 1961), 149.

Looking at James and John is like looking in the mirror. We can see our own selfishness, and Mark hopes that we can see how foolish we look.

Jesus' "ransom" statement uses a metaphor to describe our predicament and his sacrifice. It implies that we are enslaved and that it is impossible for us ever to pay for our own freedom. Someone else must pay. Jesus' death is not a tragic accident or a courageous martyrdom, but a supreme act of sacrifice for all humankind. This image does not exhaust the plight of the human situation and how Jesus' death puts right that situation with God, but it does make clear that atonement is not something we can attain for ourselves. It comes as a gift from God. Jesus has paid with his life the infinite debt owed by humankind. He has delivered us from our captivity to sin.

There is a catch, however. Demosthenes cites the law that the one who was ransomed became the property of the one who freed him.[16] Paul assumes this principle in his admonition to the Corinthians: "You are not your own; you were bought at a price" (1 Cor. 6:19b–20a). Having been ransomed by Christ, we belong entirely to him.

---

16. Cited by Ceslas Spicq, *Theological Lexicon of the New Testament* (Peabody, Mass.: Hendrickson, 1994) 2:427.

Mark 10:46–52

🔥

THEN THEY CAME to Jericho. As Jesus and his disciples, together with a large crowd, were leaving the city, a blind man, Bartimaeus (that is, the Son of Timaeus), was sitting by the roadside begging. ⁴⁷When he heard that it was Jesus of Nazareth, he began to shout, "Jesus, Son of David, have mercy on me!"

⁴⁸Many rebuked him and told him to be quiet, but he shouted all the more, "Son of David, have mercy on me!"

⁴⁹Jesus stopped and said, "Call him."

So they called to the blind man, "Cheer up! On your feet! He's calling you." ⁵⁰Throwing his cloak aside, he jumped to his feet and came to Jesus.

⁵¹"What do you want me to do for you?" Jesus asked him.

The blind man said, "Rabbi, I want to see."

⁵²"Go," said Jesus, "your faith has healed you." Immediately he received his sight and followed Jesus along the road.

Original Meaning

JESUS' LAST HEALING in the Gospel of Mark is set in Jericho on the edge of the wilderness. Galilean Jews on pilgrimage to Jerusalem would detour around the Samaritans' area by passing through Perea on the Jordan's east side. They would cross over the Jordan again at Jericho and then take their journey's final leg up the steep road to Jerusalem. Anticipating the generosity of pilgrims headed toward the Holy City, a blind man reduced to beggary sits by the roadside. Such a man in the ancient world was totally dependent on others for charity and for guidance and protection (see Lev. 19:4). He was one of society's expendables.

That is exactly how the crowd treats him, for they offer him no help. When he cries out to Jesus as the Son of David, they chide him for making a nuisance of himself. They do not bring him to Jesus and beg him to heal him, as the people of Bethsaida did (8:22)—though Mark does not identify the blind man in Bethsaida as a beggar. This crowd must think that so august a figure as Jesus would not want to bother with a helpless, blind mendicant (see David's well-known distaste for the blind, 2 Sam.

5:6–8). Mark, however, gives this beggar dignity by giving his name, Bartimaeus.[1]

The blind man will not be put off by reproaches from the crowd and yells more desperately. Jesus has reached the last stage of his journey to Jerusalem. Despite the shadow of the cross looming ever larger across his path, he can still hear the cries of others in distress. The crowd tries to make the man stop his clamor; Jesus stops for him. The crowd usually gets things wrong. No one is too insignificant to Jesus to command his attention. A leper, a woman with a hemorrhage, little children, and now a blind beggar all received Jesus' care.

Bartimaeus sees with a sixth sense that the man passing by is more than simply a widely acclaimed prophet and miracle worker from Nazareth and cries out to him as the "Son of David" (the only time this title appears in Mark). As Jesus moves closer to Jerusalem and his shameful death, his identity as the Messiah, the Son of David, can be noised abroad. This cry of Bartimaeus thus prepares for Jesus' dramatic entry into Jerusalem (11:1–11). Most associated the title "Son of David" with nationalistic and militaristic visions (see Ps. Sol. 17:21–25). When Jesus arrives on a colt he forces the issue of his messianic identity, and the crowd responds by exulting in the coming kingdom of their father, David (11:9–10). The soldiers know of Jesus' royal pretensions and mock them. Pilate will have him executed as the "King of the Jews." This present episode reveals that as the Son of David, Jesus expresses his royal authority in works of healing and mercy for the despised outcast, not in rounding up recruits for a revolution. This Son of David hears the cries of the oppressed, gives sight to the blind, and brings blessing and peace.

The crowds tell Bartimaeus to keep quiet. Jesus, however, stops and says, "Call him"—further evidence that he came to serve, not to be acclaimed. Jesus answers Bartimaeus's insistent cries for help with an urgent call of his own. The verb "call" (phoneo) is repeated three times in verse 49: Jesus tells the crowd to "call him"; "they called to the blind man," saying, "Cheer up! On your feet! He's calling you."[2] Jesus does not call him to discipleship as he did the fishermen by the sea, but Bartimaeus responds just as rapidly as those first disciples. He springs up to come to Jesus, who then asks him, "What do you want me to do for you?" (10:51).

---

1. Curiously, Mark interprets the meaning of the name Bartimaeus for his audience ("that is, the Son of Timaeus"), while not translating the term "Rabbouni" (10:51, trans. "Rabbi" in the NIV). He may wish to underscore the irony that one whose name means "worthy of honor" is treated so shabbily.

2. Note how the crowd's mood shifts when Jesus takes notice of the man they have been scorning.

This question may seem an odd one to ask a blind man, but Jesus forces him to reflect on what he truly wants from him. His answer, "Rabbouni [lit.], I want to see," demonstrates enough faith to transform him from a blind man begging along the way (10:46; see 4:4, 15) to a person who sees and follows Jesus on the way (10:52).[3] He believes that Jesus is able to fulfill Isaiah 35:5 and give sight to the blind. The whole scene recalls Isaiah's promise in 42:16:

> I will lead the blind by ways they have not known,
>   along unfamiliar paths I will guide them;
> I will turn the darkness into light before them
>   and make the rough places smooth.
> These are the things I will do;
>   I will not forsake them.[4]

Marshall notes that in this healing there is "a conspicuous lack of emphasis on the course of the miracle itself ... no healing word or gesture, no demonstration of the cure, and no choral acclamation."[5] This miracle takes on symbolic significance as it caps the discipleship theme in this section. Jesus has told others he has healed to go (1:44; 2:11; 5:19, 34; 7:29) and that their faith has saved them (see 5:34). Bartimaeus, however, does not choose to go off his own way. With his eyes now open, he decides to follow Jesus as every disciple is called to do (8:34). Like the first disciples Jesus called, he abandons his former way of life and leaves everything. The cloak he leaves behind is not much perhaps, but it is his sole worldly possession and a necessity (Ex. 22:26–27; Deut. 24:12–13). The cloak would have been placed before him to collect alms by day and would have been his source of warmth by night. He will have no encumbrances in following Jesus. Leaving just a garment may seem easier that selling all that one has (10:21), but that is why Jesus indicated how hard it was for those having possessions to enter the kingdom (10:24–25).

---

3. The address, *Rabbouni* ("my teacher," see John 20:17), may express deferential honor to a great teacher or may imply that Jesus bears divine authority by using a title reserved for God (Waetjen, *Reordering*, 178–79).

4. Marcus (*The Way of the Lord*, 34) writes, "The removal of blindness is linked to the picture of the holy highway upon which the redeemed of the Lord return to Zion with exultant singing. Thus, the blooming wilderness, opening eyes of the blind, and the way of the Lord are interrelated themes."

5. Marshall, *Faith As a Theme*, 124.

THE DISCIPLES SHOW themselves to be spiritually blind, and Jesus attempts to open their eyes to God's requirement that he must give his life and to the demand that they must take up their cross and follow him. This scene links the healing of blindness to discipleship issues. Jesus opens the eyes of blind men at the beginning of this large section (8:22–26) and at the end. In interpreting this passage, therefore, one should not simply treat it as another healing miracle but recognize its implications for discipleship.

The parallels with the request of James and John in the preceding incident (10:32–40) help clarify these implications. James and John approach Jesus as they are "on their way" (10:32). Bartimaeus cries out for mercy as he sits "by the roadside [way]" (10:46); and when Jesus restores his sight, he "followed Jesus along the road [way]" (10:52). The "way" (*hodos*) is significant in this section (8:27; 9:33–34; 10:32). Moreover, Jesus asks both the sons of Zebedee and Bartimaeus the same question, "What do you want me to do for you?" (10:36, 51). The disciples' answer to this question is telling: They want to sit on thrones with Jesus and reign with him in triumph. Bartimaeus sits in the dust, makes no demand for glory, but cries out from his wretched poverty: He only wants to see. The disciples see Jesus as a Messiah who will bring them mastery and glory; Bartimaeus sees him as the Son of David who brings him healing and sight. Jesus cannot grant the disciples' request for power, but he can grant a blind man's request for vision.

Jesus can heal physical blindness, but more than that, he wants to heal spiritual blindness. On a literal level, Bartimaeus wants his physical sight and is as optimistic as the leper was (1:40–42) that Jesus, the Son of David, can work a miracle to restore his sight. On a spiritual level, he voices what every disciple should want—to be able to see. The calling and decision of Bartimaeus to follow Jesus reveal that discipleship is opened to all who identify with Jesus in faith and is not just confined to Jesus' specific call to follow.[6] One can become a disciple by putting one's faith in Jesus and choosing to follow him.

THE FAMILIAR LINE from "Amazing Grace"—"I was once lost but now I am found, Was blind, but now I see"—understands conversion as a move from blindness to sight. The healing of Bartimaeus can be a type for the healing of our spiritual blindness today. We will

---

6. Ibid.

look at this incident for what light it sheds on the transformation from blindness to sight in conversion; we will also examine the uncaring attitude of the crowd, who try to hinder the man's pleas for help.

Blindness to sight. Many resonate with this blind man's encounter with Jesus. It matches the healing grace they have received in their own lives. They know what it is like to sit figuratively in the dust, a beggar for grace, calling out desperately for help and shouting all the louder when others would drown out their cries or try to silence them. They know what it is like to learn that Jesus cares—enough to hear the cry above the din of the crowd, to stop, and to extend the call that gladdens the heart.

If we treat this healing as a paradigm for the contemporary restoration of sight, we see several motifs. (1) Healing does not always come easily for those whom Jesus heals. Before Bartimaeus receives healing from Jesus, he must overcome the crowd's determination to throttle his cries for help. He persists in calling out Jesus' name until he hears Jesus call out his own name.

We have seen this dogged determination in the stories of other healings in the Gospel. The Syrophoenician woman will not give up hope that Jesus will heal her daughter even though she is not a Jew and Jesus initially rebuffs her (7:24–30). Jairus must ignore the mockery of the mourners that Jesus can do nothing for his dead child (5:35–43). Friends must force their way through a crowd and a roof to bring their paralyzed companion to Jesus (2:1–12). The leper and the woman with the flow of blood must disregard laws that forbid them from having contact with Jesus to receive his help (1:40–45; 5:25–34). A desperate father must overcome his doubt that Jesus can do anything to help his tormented son when the disciples have already failed (9:14–29). Healing comes to those who are persistent and are not quickly discouraged by whatever hurdles others may place in their way. How many want to see so desperately that they will ignore the put-downs of the crowd to secure that vision?

(2) If healing requires persistence, one must be intentional in coming to Jesus for relief. Bartimaeus does not simply want to meet the famous prophet from Nazareth in some misty-eyed emotionalism. He cries out specifically to Jesus because he believes that he will have mercy on him and can give him his sight.

Jesus' question, "What do you want me to do for you?" might seem dense since the plight of this blind man is obvious. But this query makes perfect sense in the context of Mark 10, where what other characters wanted provides a marked contrast. The Pharisees wanted to outsmart him and trap him (10:2). The rich man wanted eternal security at minimum cost (10:17). James and John wanted to be the top officials in the kingdom bureaucracy (10:35–36). A blind beggar might want only money, but Bartimaeus wants to see again.

"What do you want me to do for you?" is the most important question God ever asks us, and the one to which we most frequently give the wrong answer. We ask for all the wrong things in life. One can think of many examples, but Mark provides two notable ones. Herod asks his dancing step-daughter essentially the same question, "Ask me for anything you want" (6:22). Her answer: "The head of John the Baptist." Pilate asks the crowd the same question (15:9, 12). Their answer: "Barabbas" and "Crucify him!" Our answer to this question will reveal whether we want death or life, whether we want to be healed from our blindness or selfishly want to use God to do our bidding and fulfill our own desires.

(3) The aphorism "He who hesitates is lost" applies in this situation. Bartimaeus cannot hesitate: "Maybe I will wait until Jesus passes this way again in a less crowded, less hectic time." Those who are healed in Mark act decisively and throw pride and caution to the wind to seize the one chance they get when Jesus passes by. Otherwise, the opportunity for healing will be lost.

(4) After being healed, Bartimaeus moves into action. Mark initially describes the blind man as "sitting by the roadside [way]." To sit along the side of the way can be perilous to one's salvation (see 4:15). One cannot sit on the sidelines as a spectator while others lay their lives on the line. When people are healed from a debilitating disease, they usually want to make things right in their life. When one receives sight, one must follow the way behind Jesus.

The crowd's reaction. The crowd's negative reaction to the blind man's cries for help raises the issue of our compassion for those in need. The community may want to silence embarrassing cries that serve to accentuate the helplessness of those whom they have failed to help. Cries of desperation make most people uncomfortable, particularly when they come from our midst. The sad thing is that churches have often turned their backs on those with disabilities, made no effort to reach them, and pretended that they did not exist. Those who are able-bodied sometimes feel uncomfortable around the disabled. Our worry that we might say the wrong thing to such people can cause discomfort. Obviously, this crowd surrounding Bartimaeus does not worry about saying the wrong thing and shows complete insensitivity to his needs until Jesus singles him out as special.

This lesson has not been learned, and those with disabilities are all too frequently shunted aside and ignored today. I heard of a church that had several persons confined to wheelchairs. For the worship service they were wheeled to the front of the sanctuary, where there was the most room and their chairs would not block the aisle. A member actually objected that their presence detracted from his worship, and he thought that it would deter others from joining the church. He argued that the church needed to set up a special place for them where they would not be so prominent—"the first thing you see when you come into the sanctuary."

I have tried to understand the motivation behind this man's objection. Perhaps he did not want the unsettling evidence of others' personal suffering to disturb his worship. Perhaps he did not want to be reminded how fragile life and health are. Maybe he was trying to convince himself that disease, disasters, and disabilities can somehow be avoided in life through religious behavior. The church, if it is to be the church of Jesus Christ, can never be like the crowds that try to repress the urgent yells of those who desperately need help or try to cover up the tragedies that strike people's lives. Like Jesus, we must be willing to listen, to stop, and to respond.

Mark 11:1–11

A S THEY APPROACHED Jerusalem and came to Bethphage and Bethany at the Mount of Olives, Jesus sent two of his disciples, ²saying to them, "Go to the village ahead of you, and just as you enter it, you will find a colt tied there, which no one has ever ridden. Untie it and bring it here. ³If anyone asks you, 'Why are you doing this?' tell him, 'The Lord needs it and will send it back here shortly.'"

⁴They went and found a colt outside in the street, tied at a doorway. As they untied it, ⁵some people standing there asked, "What are you doing, untying that colt?" ⁶They answered as Jesus had told them to, and the people let them go. ⁷When they brought the colt to Jesus and threw their cloaks over it, he sat on it. ⁸Many people spread their cloaks on the road, while others spread branches they had cut in the fields. ⁹Those who went ahead and those who followed shouted,

> "Hosanna! "
> "Blessed is he who comes in the name of the Lord!"
> ¹⁰"Blessed is the coming kingdom of our father David!"
> "Hosanna in the highest!"

¹¹Jesus entered Jerusalem and went to the temple. He looked around at everything, but since it was already late, he went out to Bethany with the Twelve.

Original Meaning

JESUS' ENTRY INTO Jerusalem marks the end of his avoiding crowds and his secrecy and the beginning of open confrontation with opponents in the temple. Day One of his Passion Week begins with the crowd greeting his dramatic arrival on a coronation animal with cheers as they hail the coming of David's kingdom (11:1–10). The scene ends when Jesus makes a brief reconnaissance of the temple (11:11). The next day is given over to his dramatic action in the temple, which is sandwiched by the cursing of a fig tree (11:12–25).

On his third visit to the temple he fends off challenges from various opponents. The high priests ask by what authority he does such things, and Jesus only responds with counterquestions and an ominous parable (11:27–12:27). The Pharisees and Herodians collaborate in trying to trap him with a loaded question, whether he thinks it right for a people belonging to God to pay taxes to Caesar (12:13–17). The Sadducees then pose a mocking question about the resurrection (12:18–27). When he answers them well, a sympathetic teacher of the law questions him about the greatest commandment (12:28–34). Jesus then returns to the theme of David's kingdom, shouted out by excited pilgrims as he entered the city, by offering a riddle about David's Son (12:35–37). To the crowd's delight, he intimates that the Messiah is greater than David and that the Messiah's kingdom will be greater than David's kingdom. He then condemns those teachers of the law who cloak their impiety with holiness and profiteer from the plight of widows (12:38–40). The temple scenes conclude with Jesus' observing a widow who contributes all that she has for her living to the temple coffers (12:41–44).

The episodes centered around the temple begin when Jesus enters the city from the Mount of Olives, east of Jerusalem. He directs his disciples to fetch a colt and shows his supernatural foreknowledge by predicting precisely what they will find: an unridden male colt, tied up, close to where they enter the village. He also warns the disciples that they will be challenged when they try to take the colt. The answer they are to give, "The Lord needs it," is the same justification for David's eating the consecrated bread—"when he and his companions were . . . in need" (2:25). Jesus impresses the animal as a king would who is entitled to whatever he needs; but, unlike plundering kings, Jesus will return the animal immediately.[1] The disciples obey at once, and everything takes place as Jesus said it would.

Jesus orchestrates a grand entrance into Jerusalem that departs significantly from his previous patterns of movement in the Gospel of Mark. He has walked everywhere else in his ministry except for the times he crossed the lake in a boat. The decision to complete this last stage of his journey to Jerusalem riding on an animal "looks like some kind of claim to authority."[2] The animal he chooses has never been ridden, which makes it suitable for a sacred purpose and worthy of a king.[3] The colt that is bound and must be untied (11:2, 4) also alludes to Genesis 49:10–11 and Zechariah 9:9, passages that were interpreted messianically. Jesus enters Jerusalem as Israel's Messiah.

---

1. See G. H. R. Horsley, *New Documents Illustrating Early Christianity* (North Ryde: Macquarie Univ. Press, 1981), 1:36–43.

2. Hooker, *Mark*, 257. Although donkeys were more common in Palestine, the colt could have been a horse or a mule; and kings rode mules (2 Sam. 18:9; 1 Kings 1:33–48).

3. According to *m. Sanh.* 2:5, no one else may ride a king's horse.

This staged arrival in Jerusalem also deviates from Jesus' previous attempts to avoid calling attention to himself. His magnetic power and miracles made his desire to keep a low profile next to impossible. Nevertheless, he consistently tried to elude the starstruck crowds, whose excitement threatened to turn his mission into a carnival. He hushed those who tried to champion his name without fully understanding what he was sent to do. He also dampened the aspirations of those who saw only visions of sugarplums and glory and who could not see that the signs along the way were pointing to Golgotha and death on a cross. What occurs now is a complete reversal: Jesus encourages public rejoicing by his provocative entrance. Myers goes so far as to call it "political street theater."[4] His actions encourage the crowd to blazon his name jubilantly from street corners and rooftops. Passover crowds tended to be expectant during this season that celebrated Israel's deliverance from Egypt, but they will be sadly mistaken if they expect Jesus to mastermind some military coup.

Mark reports that the disciples saddle the animal with their own garments, and the crowd strews the way with their garments (as a crowd did when Jehu was anointed king; 1 Kings 9:12–13). Jesus' followers and those pilgrims caught up in the excitement of the moment also line the streets with leaves and branches (or cut straw) and fill the air with a chorus of "Hosannas" (meaning, "Save us!") and with beatitudes. This street choir chants one of the Hallel (thanksgiving) Psalms (Ps. 118:25–26). Ironically, Jesus enters the city from the Mount of Olives with the Hallel ringing in his ears. He will later depart for the Mount of Olives to pray in torment after he and his disciples have sung a hymn, possibly a Hallel Psalm, at the close of his Last Supper.

The excitement generated by Jesus' arrival ends with somewhat of an anticlimax when he enters the temple, only to look around and leave. Mark raises the readers' expectations that something grand will happen, but nothing does. He tells us that "it was already late" (evening; 11:11). Late for what? Did time run out on Jesus before he could do anything; or is time running out for the temple? This colorless ending to Jesus' dramatic entry into Jerusalem depicts more than meets the eye. It sets the stage for what will happen on the next day, and its true significance can only be filled in by the Old Testament. Jesus does not tour the temple as a tourist, dazzled by its glittering gold, glistening white marble, and gigantic stones.[5] Nor does he visit it out of pious reverence; he offers no prayers or sacrifice. Jesus has identified

---

4. Myers, *Binding*, 294.

5. Mark does not use the verb "to look around" (*periblepomai*) for gawking but for scrutinizing critically (see 3:5, 34; 5:32; 10:23). One may picture Jesus staring reproachfully.

himself as the Lord who requires a mount (11:3). He now enters his temple as prophesied by Malachi 3:1–2, a passage Mark has quoted in the Gospel's prologue (Mark 1:2):

"See, I will send my messenger, who will prepare the way before me. Then suddenly the Lord you are seeking will come to his temple; the messenger of the covenant, whom you desire, will come," says the LORD Almighty.
But who can endure the day of his coming? Who can stand when he appears? For he will be like a refiner's fire or a launderer's soap."

Jesus enters the temple to inspect it, and the next day's events reveal that he comes not to restore it but to pronounce God's judgment on it.

Bridging Contexts

THE JOYFUL ENTHUSIASM and the colorful procession of admirers who greet Jesus as he approaches Jerusalem seem to offer an auspicious beginning to his visit. The reader might hope that Jesus' dire predictions about what will happen to him in Jerusalem are perhaps wrong.[6] The excitement, however, only temporarily screens the looming catastrophe that Mark has prepared the reader to expect. Exuberant joy will turn to bitter weeping; triumphant exultation will turn to cowardly panic.

The crowd is mistaken in their acclaim. They treat Jesus' approach as a triumphal entry and shout nationalist slogans about the restoration of the power and glory of the Davidic kingdom: "Blessed is the coming kingdom of our father David!" They are right that Jesus comes as a king, but they expect a typical monarch, who will establish a temporal empire. Their mistaken presumption that he is entering Jerusalem to purge the nation of foreign domination and to resuscitate the ancient glories of Israel leads to the premature festivity. These false hopes are dashed as he surrenders tamely to those who come to arrest him (see Luke 24:21), but a new and greater hope will be resurrected.

The entry is not triumphal. Jesus does not enter Jerusalem on a white charger. He does not brandish a series of war trophies, and a train of captives does not trail behind him. In fact, within the week, Roman guards will lead him out of the city as a defeated captive. Consequently, Jesus does not share

---

6. In this stirring entry, Mark establishes Jesus' identity as the king of Israel. Bilezikian (*The Liberated Gospel*, 127) shows that the scene also conforms to a dramatic convention. A joyful chorus, dance, or procession, and a lyrical expression of confidence and happiness occur just before the catastrophic climax of the play. The hopes associated with the outburst of joy, however, are not to be realized.

the disciples' earthly fantasies of glory. He appears in the city, as he had forewarned three times, to suffer and die, not to set up a rival kingdom to Caesar. He comes as a king who will be crowned with thorns, enthroned on a cross, and hailed as the chief of fools. His entrance points to a different kind of triumph than the one envisioned by the crowd, one that will be more powerful than any Davidic monarchy and more far-reaching than the narrow borders of Israel or even the Roman empire.

In bridging the contexts, one needs to make clear that while it is appropriate to greet the Messiah with rejoicing, we cannot forget that he has not come to set up some grand earthly kingdom. The crowds hail him without understanding his purpose. While many sermons have been preached on the fickle crowds—hailing him as a king one moment and crying "Crucify him!" the next—it is more likely that Jesus' followers incite the crowd's enthusiasm with their cheering. One should not forget that the disciples are the ones who prove the most fickle. Shouting nationalist slogans is hardly appropriate for what Jesus will accomplish in the next days. The scene portrays the disciples still hoping for a glorious earthly kingdom in which they can reign with their Messiah on thrones.

MANY CHURCHES CELEBRATE Jesus' grand entrance in Jerusalem as Palm Sunday, with children in the congregation excitedly waving palms. The next Sunday Christians celebrate Easter and Jesus' resurrection from the dead. Most of the worshipers in attendance on these days do not come to any special services commemorating the events of Jesus' Passion during the week. Consequently, they miss the suffering in between. They may get the false impression that Christianity moves from one celebration to another or that Easter somehow "erases rather than vindicates the cross."[7] Mark's Gospel, more than any other, brings out Jesus' enormous suffering. The author bears witness to his terrible loneliness amid the deafening applause. If we hail Jesus, we must hail him as the one who comes to die for our sins, not as the one who comes to bring us glory. We must hail him as one who gives his life for the kingdom of God, not as the one who sets up the kingdom of David.

The crowd shouts "Hosanna! Save us!" thinking that Jesus has come to save them from their political enemies. What we need most is for him to save us from ourselves. Human nature and aspirations change little over the years, and this incident reveals that we still need saving from at least three things. (1) We

---

7. Fred B. Craddock, *The Gospels* (Nashville: Abingdon, 1981), 64.

must be saved from a petty nationalism that divides the world into tiny enclaves set over against one another. Jesus does not come to fulfill anyone's political agenda. As our judge, he may condemn it as he did the temple in Jerusalem. Amazingly, people still drape Jesus in nationalist flags and assume that he not only endorses their political slogans but will work to accomplish them. The one who comes to Jerusalem comes as the king of the entire world and dies for all people. His people will not be confined to any one nation and his sacrificial love will reach beyond all national borders and races.

(2) We must also be saved from a mercurial faith that abandons Jesus at the first sign of trouble. Jesus does not welcome cheers from throngs who will not pray with him in dark Gethsemane or go with him to an even darker Golgotha. He can little use those Christians who show up once a year when the cheering starts around Easter. He needs those who will endure to the end, even when faced with unspeakable suffering.

(3) We must be saved from foolish expectations of glory so that we can see God's power truly effected on the cross. God does not win by sending armies into bloody battles but by sending his Son to the cross. As a king who gives his life for others, Jesus reigns with a kind of power that earthly kings cannot match.

Mark 11:12–33

◀

THE NEXT DAY as they were leaving Bethany, Jesus was hungry. ¹³Seeing in the distance a fig tree in leaf, he went to find out if it had any fruit. When he reached it, he found nothing but leaves, because it was not the season for figs. ¹⁴Then he said to the tree, "May no one ever eat fruit from you again." And his disciples heard him say it.

¹⁵On reaching Jerusalem, Jesus entered the temple area and began driving out those who were buying and selling there. He overturned the tables of the money changers and the benches of those selling doves, ¹⁶and would not allow anyone to carry merchandise through the temple courts. ¹⁷And as he taught them, he said, "Is it not written:

> "'My house will be called
> a house of prayer for all nations'?

But you have made it 'a den of robbers.'"

¹⁸The chief priests and the teachers of the law heard this and began looking for a way to kill him, for they feared him, because the whole crowd was amazed at his teaching.

¹⁹When evening came, they went out of the city.

²⁰In the morning, as they went along, they saw the fig tree withered from the roots. ²¹Peter remembered and said to Jesus, "Rabbi, look! The fig tree you cursed has withered!"

²²"Have faith in God," Jesus answered. ²³"I tell you the truth, if anyone says to this mountain, 'Go, throw yourself into the sea,' and does not doubt in his heart but believes that what he says will happen, it will be done for him. ²⁴Therefore I tell you, whatever you ask for in prayer, believe that you have received it, and it will be yours. ²⁵And when you stand praying, if you hold anything against anyone, forgive him, so that your Father in heaven may forgive you your sins. "

²⁷They arrived again in Jerusalem, and while Jesus was walking in the temple courts, the chief priests, the teachers of the law and the elders came to him. ²⁸"By what authority are you doing these things?" they asked. "And who gave you authority to do this?"

²⁹Jesus replied, "I will ask you one question. Answer me, and I will tell you by what authority I am doing these things. ³⁰John's baptism—was it from heaven, or from men? Tell me!"

³¹They discussed it among themselves and said, "If we say, 'From heaven,' he will ask, 'Then why didn't you believe him?' ³²But if we say, 'From men' . . . ." (They feared the people, for everyone held that John really was a prophet.)

³³So they answered Jesus, "We don't know."

Jesus said, "Neither will I tell you by what authority I am doing these things."

JESUS' DEMONSTRATION OF outrage in the temple and at a fruitless fig tree is unexpected and puzzling. Why this sudden violent outburst? Why this withering curse on what seems to be an innocent fig tree that fails to satisfy his hunger? Why does he vent such anger on an inanimate object that fails to produce fruit out of season? Klausner calls it "a gross injustice on a tree which was guilty of no wrong and had but performed its natural function."[1] Manson comments: "It is a tale of miraculous power wasted in the service of ill-temper (for the supernatural energy employed to blast the unfortunate tree might have been more usefully expended in forcing a crop of figs out of season); and as it stands is simply incredible."[2]

Mark's bracketing technique offers a solution to this puzzle and corrects any view that Jesus succumbs to a fit of irrational temper.[3] The fig tree incident sandwiches the temple incident. Interpreting either in isolation from the other leads one in the wrong direction. We will first look at Jesus' actions in the temple and then show how the cursing of the fig tree helps explain what it means. It is common to refer to this event as the temple cleansing. The cursing of the fig tree brings that interpretation into question.

The Temple Action (11:15–19)

JESUS' ACTIONS IN the temple. Many suggestions have been offered to explain Jesus' actions in the temple. Some go so far as to claim that he is engaging in an act of insurgency, striking the first blow in what he hopes will spark an armed revolt. This interpretation has nothing to commend it. The clash is

---

1. Joseph Klausner, *Jesus of Nazareth* (London: George Allen & Unwin, 1925), 269.
2. Cited by Cranfield, *Mark*, 356.
3. See discussion of Mark 3:20–34 for comments on Mark's bracketing technique.

only a modest engagement with the servants of the temple market and is largely symbolic, like his entry into Jerusalem. Otherwise, the temple police or Roman soldiers patrolling from the vantage point of the Fortress Antonia would have been quick to intervene (see Acts 21:27–36). Those involved are probably momentarily stunned by the power of his moral fury and not by any physical means he employs.

Most other interpretations attribute Jesus' ferocity to his righteous indignation over flagrant abuses. They assume that Jesus is acting to reform the temple, but they differ over what precisely he is trying to reform. Some claim that Jesus opposes the buyers and sellers because they impede Gentile worship in the outer court.[4] Who can worship amidst a raucous bazaar where venders haggle to get the highest price? The noisy commerce prevents the temple from being a house of prayer for all nations.

Gundry argues that the audience would think that Jesus is simply reclaiming commercial space for its proper use for prayer.[5] The problem with this view is that the small temple market for cultic provisions was probably located inside the Royal Stoa and not spread out all over the outer court.[6] Also, this outer court was not viewed positively as the place where Gentiles could worship but was regarded instead as the place beyond which Gentiles could not go.[7] Gentiles could not enter the temple proper, and a balustrade surrounding the sanctuary had warning signs cautioning Gentiles against going any further on penalty of death (see Acts 21:27–30).[8] Clearing a quiet place for Gentiles to pray in the forecourt would not remove the barrier that kept them from the sacred place of God's presence. Jesus also could not have expected the area to remain clear simply because of his fierce protest. As

---

4. Eric M. Meyers and James F. Strange (*Archaeology, the Rabbis, and Early Christianity* [London: SCM, 1981], 52) estimate that the entire court could easily hold 75,000 people. This figure could be exceeded when people stood shoulder to shoulder.

5. Gundry, *Mark*, 674, 676.

6. See Jostein Ådna, "The Attitude of Jesus to the Temple," *Mishkan* 17–18 (1992–93): 68; Benjamin Mazar, "The Royal *Stoa* in the Southern Part of the Temple Mount," in *Recent Archaeology in the Land of Israel*, ed. H. Shanks (Washington/Jerusalem: BAS, 1984), 141–47. The Royal Stoa (described by Josephus in *Ant.* 15.11.5 §§ 411–16) was similar to the Caesareum structures and was directly accessible via the steps leading down from "Robinson's arch" to the market below.

7. The outer court was not called "the court of the Gentiles" in the time of Jesus; that is a modern term.

8. Two tablets with the Greek inscriptions have been found. The text of the complete one is cited in Emil Schürer, *The History of the Jewish People in the Age of Jesus Christ*, ed. and trans. Geza Vermes, Fergus Millar, and Matthew Black (Edinburgh: T. & T. Clark, 1979), 2:222, n. 85; 285, n. 57. It reads: "No foreigner is to enter within the forecourt and the balustrade around the sanctuary. Whoever is caught will have himself to blame for his subsequent death."

Hooker admits, "as an act of reforming zeal it would have to be judged a failure: the money changers no doubt soon recovered their coins, and the place was restored to order."[9]

Another view contends that Jesus' concern for the temple's purity prompts his action. He is irate that profane, commercial activity has intruded into the sacred space of the temple precincts (see Zech. 14:21) and desecrated the spiritual purpose of this place of worship. There is little evidence that the forecourt was regarded as sacred space. Schweizer suggests that it was like "the square before a church visited by pilgrims."[10] The market for animals and birds to sacrifice in the temple cult was vital for the operation of the cult and did not desecrate the sanctuary.

The phrase "den of robbers" has influenced the most common view of the causes behind Jesus' action. It assumes that Jesus is protesting because the temple has become a crooked business, defrauding worshipers. The high priestly families did gain wealth from their control of the temple's fiscal affairs, and they were guilty of corruption. Josephus, for example, calls the high priest Ananias the "great procurer of money" (*Ant.* 20.9.2 §205; see 20.8.1. §181; 20.9.2. §§206–7). Jesus may have objected to "the way the financial side of the sacrificial system was run."[11]

While some assume that the crowd responds enthusiastically to Jesus' protest for them, the text only says that they are "amazed at his teaching." The verb "amaze" appears elsewhere in Mark (1:22; 6:2; 7:37; 10:26) and refers to those who were "stupefied" by Jesus. Mark does not describe the crowd as applauding what Jesus has done so much as being baffled by it.

---

9. Hooker, *Mark*, 264–65. She also notes that there is little comparison to what Jesus did and the purification of the temple by Josiah (2 Kings 23) and Judas Maccabeus (1 Macc. 4:36–59).

10. Schweizer, *Mark*, 233. Sanders (*Jesus and Judaism* [Philadelphia: Fortress, 1985], 63) argues: "Those who write about Jesus' desire to return the temple to its 'original,' 'true' purpose, the 'pure' worship of God, seem to forget that the principal function of any temple is to serve as a place of sacrifice, and that sacrifices *require* the supply of suitable animals." See also *Judaism. Practices and Beliefs 63 BCE–66 CE* (Philadelphia: Trinity, 1992), 47–76; *Jewish Law from Jesus to the Mishnah* (Philadelphia: Trinity, 1990), 49–51.

11. Richard Bauckham, "Jesus' Demonstration in the Temple," *Law and Religion: Essays on the Place of the Law in Israel and Early Christianity*, ed. Barnabas Lindars (Cambridge: James Clarke, 1988), 78. The goals of rural religious reformers typically ran counter to the interests of the inhabitants of urban Jerusalem, whose entire population had a direct or indirect stake in the financial well-being of the temple. Jerusalem had no major industry to support the population other than the temple, and no trade routes passed through it. Consequently, the urban Jerusalemites would have been motivated by something more than piety in defending the sanctity of the temple and preserving the status quo. They had a financial interest in protecting the source of their livelihood.

Neusner helps explain why. The tables were set up to receive the annual half-shekel tax that was required of every Jewish male and that funded the daily sacrifices in the temple for the atonement of sin (*t. Seqal.* 1:6). He writes that Jesus' overturning the tables of the money changers

> will have provoked astonishment, since it will have called into question the very simple fact that the daily whole offering effected atonement and brought about expiation for sin, and God had so instructed Moses in the Torah. Accordingly, only someone who rejected the Torah's explicit teaching concerning the daily whole offering could have overturned the tables—or ... someone who had in mind setting up a different table, and for a different purpose: for the action carries the entire message, both negative and positive. Indeed, the money-changers' presence made possible the cultic participation of every Israelite, and it was not a blemish on the cult but its perfection.[12]

Nothing in 11:15–16 suggests that Jesus' ire over dishonest business practices or profiteering provokes his attack on the money changers and animal merchants. He throws out *both* the buyers and sellers.

A key question to ask is why Jesus would attempt to reform or purify something that he predicts, without any great anguish, will soon be destroyed (13:2)? The best answer is that *he does not intend to reform the temple.* Jesus has been acclaimed as a prophet. Prophets do not simply make announcements; they also engage in prophetic actions to communicate.[13] Jesus appears in the temple as a charismatic prophet and graphically acts out God's rejection of the temple cult and its coming destruction. While actions may speak louder than words, they are not always as clear.

Sanders argues that Jesus' actions are designed "to make a point rather than to have a concrete result."[14] His demonstration is a prophetic protest that symbolically stops the activities that contribute to the temple's normal functioning. As the one who comes in the name of the Lord (11:9), he trains his sights on three things: the fiscal foundation of the temple, a vital component of its sacrifices, and a crucial element of its liturgy. If money cannot be exchanged into the holy currency, then monetary support for the temple sacrifices and the priesthood must end. If sacrificial animals cannot be purchased, then sacrifice must end. If no vessel can be carried through the tem-

---

12. Jacob Neusner, "Money-Changers in the Temple: The Mishnah's Explanation," *NTS* 35 (1989): 289; see also "The Absoluteness of Christianity and the Uniqueness of Judaism," *Int* 43 (1989): 25.

13. Examples of prophetic representative actions are recorded in 1 Kings 22:11; Isa. 20:2; Jer. 19:1–15; 28:10–11; Ezek. 4:1–3; Acts 21:11.

14. Sanders, *Jesus and Judaism*, 70.

ple, then all cultic activity must cease.[15] Jesus does not seek to purify current temple worship but symbolically attacks the very function of the temple and heralds its destruction.[16] The temple's glory days are coming to an end. In private, Jesus will predict to his disciples that the temple will be destroyed (13:1–2), and his hostility to the temple emerges as a charge at his trial (14:58) and as a taunt at the cross (15:29).

The interpretation that Jesus gives to his action is crucial for understanding what he intended. This teaching transforms a simple display of protest into an announcement of divine judgment (see 12:9). The disciples and the readers of Mark's Gospel also have the added advantage for understanding this incident because they see the cursing of the fig tree.

The quotation from Isaiah. The passage cited from Isaiah 56:7, "My house will be called a house of prayer for all nations," means that God did not plan for the temple to become a national shrine for Israel. Isaiah 56:1–8 contains God' promise of blessing for all who might think they are excluded from God's salvation: the foreigner who has joined himself to the people (56:3), the eunuch (56:4, who was not allowed to enter the temple, according to the regulations of Deut. 23:1), and the outcasts of Israel (Isa. 56:8). Most assumed that Isaiah 56 spoke of some distant future, but Jesus expects it to be fulfilled now!

During his entire ministry Jesus has been gathering in the impure outcasts and the physically maimed, and has even reached out to Gentiles. He expects the temple to embody this inclusive love. The various purity barriers in the temple, however, have been preventing that. Gentiles were not allowed entry into the temple proper.[17] Would Jesus have envisioned the nations gathered to Mount Zion and then forced to cool their heels in the outer court? Would

---

15. The word *skeuos* ("vessel"; "merchandise," NIV) could be a term used for any object [as in the translation], and some have suggested that Jesus stops people from using the temple as a shortcut to other parts of the city (see Josephus *Ag. Ap.* 2:8; *m. Ber.* 9:5). They do not ask an important question, however: a shortcut to where? The text does not say that Jesus prevents people from using the temple as a shortcut or from carrying anything through the temple but that he prevents anyone from carrying a "vessel through the temple." It is best to translate the word as "vessel," referring to the sacred temple vessels for the showbread, oil for the lamps, and incense censers used in the sacrificial service (see Isa. 52:11). A Gentile audience familiar with the functioning of temples would have assumed that it refers to vessels used in the sacrifice.

16. Jesus' actions have some parallels to the Jesus, son of Ananias, who cried out woes against the city before its destruction (Josephus, *J. W.* 6.1.3 §§ 300–309).

17. Josephus, *Ant.* 15.11.4 § 417; in 4QMMT B 39–42 access is allowed only to Israelites who were ritually pure and physically whole; 4QFlor 3–4 insists that the (ungodly or defiled) Ammonites, Moabites [Deut. 23:3], half-breeds (or bastards) [23:2], aliens, or sojourners will ever enter the house (sanctuary) because God's holy ones are there.

he have condoned segregation—separate and unequal—in God's temple? What kind of beacon is it that would draw the nations to Jerusalem only to partition them from the main body of worshipers in the temple?

In Jesus' day the temple had become a nationalistic symbol that served only to divide Israel from the nations. If it were to become what God intended, "a house of prayer for all nations," walls would have to crumble. Indeed, walls will soon collapse and barriers will be breached. When Jesus dies, the temple veil is split from top to bottom, and a Gentile confesses that he is the Son of God (15:38–39).

The quotation from Jeremiah. By quoting from Jeremiah 7, Jesus reminds the people that something holy can be perverted. He claims that the same abuses that sullied the temple cult in the time of Jeremiah taint it now. The temple, God's house, has been made into "a den of robbers." One needs to read the context of Jeremiah 7:1–15 to understand the allusion.

> This is the word that came to Jeremiah from the LORD: "Stand at the gate of the LORD's house and there proclaim this message:
>
> "'Hear the word of the LORD, all you people of Judah who come through these gates to worship the LORD. This is what the LORD Almighty, the God of Israel, says: Reform your ways and your actions, and I will let you live in this place. Do not trust in deceptive words: and say 'This is the temple of the LORD, the temple of the LORD, the temple of the LORD!' If you really change your ways and your actions and deal with each other justly, if you do not oppress the alien, the fatherless or the widow and do not shed innocent blood in this place, and if you do not follow other gods to your own harm, then I will let you live in this place, in the land I gave your forefathers for ever and ever. But look, you are trusting in deceptive words that are worthless.
>
> "'Will you steal and murder, commit adultery and perjury, burn incense to Baal and follow other gods you have not known, and then come and stand before me in this house, which bears my Name, and say, "We are safe"—safe to do all these detestable things? Has this house, which bears my Name, become a den of robbers to you? But I have been watching! declares the LORD.
>
> "'Go now to the place in Shiloh where I first made a dwelling for my Name, and see what I did to it because of the wickedness of my people Israel. While you were doing all these things, declares the LORD, I spoke to you again and again, but you did not listen; I called you, but you did not answer. Therefore, what I did to Shiloh I will do now to the house the bears my Name, the temple you trust in, the place I gave to you and your fathers. I will thrust you from my presence, just as I did all your brothers, the people of Ephraim.'"

The reference to the "den of robbers" has nothing to do with the trade in the temple. Instead, it denounces the false security that the sacrificial cult breeds.

In other words, the robbers are not swindlers but bandits, and they do not do their robbing in their den. The den is the place where robbers retreat after having committed their crimes. It is their hideout, a place of security and refuge.[18] Calling the temple a robbers' den is therefore not a cry of outrage against any dishonest business practices in the temple. Jesus indirectly attacks them for allowing the temple to degenerate into a safe hiding place where people think that they find forgiveness and fellowship with God no matter how they act on the outside. Jesus' prophetic action and words attack a false trust in the efficacy of the temple sacrificial system. The leaders of the people think that they can rob widows' houses (Mark 12:40) and then perform the prescribed sacrifices according to the prescribed patterns at the prescribed times in the prescribed purity in the prescribed sacred space and then be safe and secure from all alarms. They are wrong. The sacrifice of animals will not enable them to evade the doom that God purposes for those guilty of lying, stealing, violence, and adultery (see 7:21–23).

The sanctuary, supposedly sanctified by God, has become a sanctuary for bandits who think that they are protected from God's judgment. The phrase "I have been watching" (Jer. 7:11) matches the description of Jesus' visit to the temple on the previous day, when he "looked around at everything" (Mark 11:11), turning that visit into an inspection. Jesus shares the purview of God. He has seen what the people are doing and pronounces God's judgment.

The Cursing of the Fig Tree (11:12–14, 20–25)

THE INCIDENT AND *its significance.* The fig tree incident brackets the temple action and interprets it. It reveals more clearly that Jesus does not intend to cleanse the temple. Instead, his actions visually announce its disqualification. The fig tree that has not borne fruit is cursed, not reformed or cleansed. The parable of the tenants of the vineyard (12:1–11) makes the same point. As Jesus seeks fruit from the fig tree, so God, the owner of the vineyard, seeks fruit from the vineyard. When no fruit is to be found or when it is withheld, destruction follows.

---

18. The temple literally became a refuge for bandits during the war with Rome when the Zealots retreated to it. According to Josephus, they committed all manner of vile acts: "For this reason, I think, even God Himself, hating their impiety, turned away from our city, and no longer judging the temple to be a clean house for Him, brought the Romans upon us and a cleansing fire on the city" (*Ant.* 20.8.5 §166). If the original readers were aware of this fact, the reference to the "den of robbers" would have a double meaning.

Mark alone mentions that the tree did not bear anything more than leaves "because it was not the season for figs," and it makes Jesus' action seem even more outlandish. Why curse a fig tree for not bearing figs out of season? Jesus surely knows it is not fig season. This detail is a clue for the reader to look beyond the surface meaning and to see its symbolic meaning.[19] This action is not about a particular unfruitful fig tree; it has to do with the temple. The word "season" (*kairos*) is not the botanical term for the growing season but the religious term found in 1:14–15 denoting the time of the kingdom of God (see 13:33). Moreover, the tenants do not produce the fruits of the vineyard "at harvest time" (12:2; lit., "in season"). The barren fig tree represents the barrenness of temple Judaism that is unprepared to accept Jesus' messianic reign.

As the fig tree's time is barren (cf. Luke 13:6–9), so is the temple's. Time can run out for fruitless tress and prayerless temples. Fruitlessness now when the Messiah has come means fruitlessness forever.[20] It is not the time of the temple's consummation but its consumption. Just as the fig tree was not pruned and manured so that it might bear fruit but cursed so that it died, so the temple was not cleansed so that it could continue in more fitting service to God; rather, it would soon come to an end. The locus of salvation now shifts from the temple to Jesus and his death and resurrection. Faith in him will become the way to God, not the sacrifice of animals in the temple. Thus when Jesus dies, the curtain of the temple is torn from top to bottom.[21]

When Jesus and his disciples pass by the tree on the next day, they confirm the effectiveness of the curse. The fig tree is "withered from the roots." For a fig tree in full leaf to shrivel so completely within a day is a miracle, and it conveys that the temple's condemnation is not a temporary measure. It is everlasting. This event also contrasts the sterility of temple Judaism with the authority and power of Jesus. Jesus is said to "answer" the tree (NIV, "he said," 11:14). What he answers is the tree's false advertising with leaves that hide its fruitlessness. The tree gives the impression that it might have something to eat, just as the temple gives the impression that it is a place dedicated to the service of God. The temple profits only the priestly hierarchy; it profits nothing for God.

Sayings on faith, prayer and forgiveness. The reader may find it surprising that Jesus does not explain to the disciples the significance of what happened to

---

19. The "leafy" fig tree (is it fruitless?) reappears in 13:28–32.

20. Tolbert, *Sowing*, 193.

21. Gundry (*Mark*, 674) argues that this interpretation puts "incredible demands on Mark's audience and imports foreign bodies into the text and context." But Mark puts incredible demands on the reader throughout. The reader, like Jesus' original audience, must listen with care. Hearing, seeing, remembering (11:14, 20–21; see 8:14–21) are crucial to understanding an event.

the tree when they marvel. Instead, he places an emphasis on faith and prayer in 11:22, 24.[22] Some commentators assume that the fig tree incident has been included as a prop to add traditional sayings on the subject of prayer and forgiveness, or that these sayings were added when the original meaning of the cursing of the fig tree as a prophetic sign of God's judgment on the temple was no longer an immediate concern of the church. These sayings, however, are integrally related to context. They reveal the essence of the new order that replaces the old. The new order is based on faith in God (11:22) that overcomes insurmountable odds (11:23), is sustained by grace (11:24), and is characterized by forgiveness (11:25).

We have generalized Jesus' statement, "If anyone says to this mountain . . ." into a proverb about a difficult task, "faith is able to move mountains" (see Matt. 17:20; 1 Cor. 13:2). Jesus does not say "mountains" but specifies "this mountain." In the Markan context he is most likely referring to the temple mount, Mount Zion.[23] Contrary to expectations, the mountain of the Lord's house would not be exalted (Isa. 2:2; Mic. 4:1) but would be cast into the sea, where the demons that infested the pigs drowned (5:13) and those who caused little ones to stumble would be thrown (9:42).[24] In spite of the temple's immense power and holiness, it would be destroyed. In spite of the widespread belief that God's earthly address was the Holy of Holies, the temple, Jerusalem, the Holy Land, the temple would no longer be the focal point of God's presence among the people. God can no more be confined to one spot than Jesus could be contained in a tomb. God's people can function without a holy space or cultic functionaries. The holy place is wherever disciples preach Jesus' gospel and wherever his people, Jews and Gentiles, gather.

Most Jews regarded the temple as the place where prayer was particularly effective.[25] This belief is stated most clearly in 3 Maccabees 2:10 (written sometime between A.D. 30 and 70): "and because you love the house of Israel, you promised that if we should have reverses and tribulation should overtake us, you would listen to our petition when we come to this place and pray"

---

22. Dowd (*Prayer, Power, and the Problem of Suffering*, 96–103) points out that it is faith in God's power. Moving mountains is the work of God alone (Ex. 19:18; Job 9:5–6; Pss. 68:8; 90:2; 97:5; 114:4–7; 144:5; Jer. 4:24; Nah. 1:5), and the leveling of mountains is a characteristic of the eschatological age (Ps. 6:2, 6; Isa. 40:4; 49:11; 54:10; 64:1–3; Ezek. 38:20; Mic. 1:4; Hab. 3:6; Zech. 14:1–4; Judith 16:15; Sir. 16:19; Bar. 5:7).

23. Hooker, *Mark*, 270. The "holy mountain" is mentioned in the opening part of Isa. 56:7; see also Ps. 78:54; Isa. 2:2–3; 10:32; 25:6–7, 10; 27:13.

24. Marshall, *Faith As a Theme*, 168–69.

25. See 1 Sam. 1:1–28; 1 Kings 8:27–30, 31–51, where prayer is offered in or toward the temple; see also 2 Kings 19:14–33; Jonah 2:7; Judith 4:9–15.

(NRSV).[26] This idea continues in later Jewish traditions. A late rabbinic commentary on Psalm 91:7 reads: "When a man prays in Jerusalem, it is as though he prays before the throne of glory, for the gate of heaven is in Jerusalem, and a door is always open for the hearing of prayer, as it is said, 'This is the gate of heaven' (Gen. 28:17)." Other rabbis said:

> From the day on which the Temple was destroyed, the gates of prayer have closed, as it says, "Yea, when I cry for help, He shutteth out my prayer" (Lam. 3:8). ... Since the day that the Temple was destroyed, a wall of iron divides between Israel and their Father in Heaven.[27]

By contrast, Jesus assures his disciples that the effectiveness of prayer has nothing to with the temple or its sacrifices.[28] When he dies on the cross, access to God is not closed off but opened up for all. His death creates a new house of prayer, a temple not made with hands, which will be without barriers or limitations (see John 2:18–22; 1 Cor. 3:16–17; 12:27; 2 Cor. 6:16; Eph. 2:20–22; 1 Peter 2:4–5).

Jesus concludes his explanation with the promise, "And when you stand praying, if you hold anything against anyone, forgive him, so that your Father in heaven may forgive you your sins." Relationship with God is based simply on faith and forgiveness. If one can unleash God's power by faith and find forgiveness through prayer and a forgiving spirit, the temple cultus has been bypassed, and a house of prayer that has become a den of brigands has no more use than a dead fig tree. God's power will become available to those, including Gentiles, who have faith that it can be unleashed apart from the temple. The temple with its priesthood, sacrifices, and taxes is no longer the place of God's presence, where one meets God and where sins are forgiven. By the time Mark writes, the temple is either besieged or already destroyed. He wants to convey to his readers that broken altars do not prejudice atonement with God.

The Reaction of the High Priests (11:18a, 27–33)

THE HIGH PRIESTS and teachers of the law fully understand the implications of Jesus' actions and words and look "for a way to kill him" (11:18). Earlier the Pharisees and Herodians took council "how they might kill Jesus" (3:6); now it is only a question of deciding the right situation. They saw themselves as licensed by heaven to rule over God's temple and now fear losing control

---

26. See Dowd, *Prayer, Power, and the Problem of Suffering*, 47–48.
27. *b. Ber.* 32b.
28. Marshall, *Faith As a Theme*, 162–63; see also S. Hre Kio, "A Prayer Framework in Mark 11," *BibTrans* 37 (1986): 323–28.

of the crowds to this upstart prophet. Jesus, an outsider, is usurping their power. But they must hold off carrying out their plan against him because of his popularity. They are a savvy lot who do not kick people while they are up. To rid themselves of this threat and to debunk his messianic pretensions, they will enlist the help of the Roman governor to sentence him to death— death by crucifixion.

The chief priests (former high priests and priests with permanent duties in the temple), the teachers of the law (learned legal experts), and the elders (laymen drawn from the wealthy aristocracy) are the very ones Jesus predicted would conspire to kill him (8:31). They challenge Jesus to present his credentials: "By what authority are you doing these things?" (11:28). In Mark's context, "these things" have to do with Jesus' actions in the temple, which also include his teaching (cf. John 2:18). The reader knows that Jesus acts by the authority of God. If teachers of the law do not accept his authority to forgive (Mark 2:1–12), however, priests are not likely to accept his authority to condemn the temple.[29]

In Mark, those who approach Jesus with hostility never receive direct answers or incontrovertible proofs from him. To have the kind of faith that Jesus seeks, one has to infer on one's own who has authorized Jesus to do and say what he does. As is his custom, Jesus here fends off his adversaries with his own question. He asks them about John's baptism and twice demands that they "answer" him (11:29, 30). They ask by what authority Jesus could assail the cultic system, and he refers back to the ministry of John the Baptizer. John came preaching a baptism of repentance for the forgiveness of sins that bypassed the temple cult (1:4). It was free; no sacrifice was required except that of a repentant heart. No money exchanged hands. Jesus implicitly aligns himself with the ministry of John, and if John's ministry was from heaven, then the temple has become passé.[30]

The authorities attempt to sidestep the challenge, but the damage is done. They debate the options among themselves and worry that their answer might subvert their own domination. If they answer that John's baptism was "from heaven," they presume that Jesus will score them for not believing. This option reveals they do not care if someone is commissioned by heaven or not; they will do as they please and ignore him. If they answer that his baptism was "from men," they will ignite the ire of the crowds, who esteemed John a prophet, and prophets always increased in authority after their deaths. These corrupt leaders do not want to lose credibility with the crowds or

---

29. Geddert, *Watchwords*, 287, n. 20.

30. Meinrad Limbeck, *Markus-Evangelium* (Stuttgarter Kleiner Kommentar; Stuttgart: Katholisches Bibelwerk, 1984), 170.

alienate them because that may disrupt their scheme to do away with Jesus. Mark's comment that "they feared the people" (11:32) reveals that their authority derives from humans because they do not fear heaven. These leaders only dread losing face before the crowds and will ultimately lose their souls. They may evade Jesus' question, but they cannot evade God's judgment.

Their logic reveals something about Jesus as well as themselves. On the one hand, it underscores how John's and Jesus' destinies intertwine (see 1:14; 2:18; 6:14–29; 9:11–13). The reference to "John's baptism" and the phrase "from heaven" recalls Jesus' own baptism, when the heavens ripped open, the Spirit descended on him, and the voice from heaven announced that he was "my Son." On the other hand, their answer, "We don't know," reveals that they have no understanding of God's working and consequently no authority. They must admit that they cannot tell the difference between what is from God and what is from men (or, for that matter, from Satan; see 3:20–21).

Thus these Jewish leaders cannot recognize the portents of the temple's destruction. Jesus will not answer them directly, only in parables, because they are outsiders. They understand that Jesus' answer in the parable of the wicked tenants contains an implicit threat to their tenancy of the temple, but they do not understand the significance about giving fruit and killing the beloved son.

JESUS' LAST MIRACLE in Mark is the only one that brings death, not life. It raises many questions. Jesus can predict precisely where and how the disciples will find a colt, but he is unable to ascertain from a distance whether a tree has anything edible on it or not. He can read people's thoughts (2:8); why can he not read trees? Why is it that the one who could feed five thousand is stymied by a fig tree? Why does he spitefully take out his frustrations on an inanimate object?

There is a danger for modern readers to shift their sympathy to the tree because they do not appreciate the symbolism. But those at home in the Old Testament know that trees are frequently used as symbols and are portrayed as sensitive to their moral surroundings.[31] Instead of recognizing the guilt of an unproductive tree, modern readers tend to be appalled and embarrassed by Jesus' seemingly irrational and petulant behavior. The cursing of the fig tree is not bizarre, however, if one interprets it as a symbolic action (see

---

31. See Isa. 28:3–4; Jer. 8:13; Hos. 9:10, 16; Joel 1:7, 12; Mic. 7:1; and William R. Telford, *The Barren Temple and the Withered Tree* (JSNTSup 1; Sheffield: JSOT, 1980), 161–62.

Jer. 7:16, 20).[32] What happens to the fig tree parallels what happens to the veil in the temple, ripped from top to bottom. No one feels sorry for the veil or for the temple property and grounds committee. They recognize that this event points to the judgment on the temple and illuminates the significance of Jesus' death. In the same way, the withering of this fig tree to its very root within a day points to God's judgment on this fruitless temple.

One should therefore no longer title this incident "the cleansing of the temple." This is a story about the denunciation of religious corruption that defiles even the most holy things. The temple was the central institution of Israel's religious, political, and economic life. Economically, it dominated more than just the skyline of Jerusalem. It also served as the central bank, the capital building, and Wall Street. For most people living in the city, the temple was their means of employment. Politically, the temple was the power base and source of wealth for the priestly hierarchy, who ruled Judea under the Roman governor. Religiously, the temple marked the separation between the holy and secular, and it became the symbol of God's abiding favor and presence among the people. The Holy of Holies was regarded as a radioactive core of holiness that could fend off and purify the evil that surrounded Israel. As Waetjen puts it well, the temple was "the one place where heaven and earth are united, that absolute point of reference which, like the North Star, serves as a compass and guarantees a divine security in the passage through life."[33]

Later rabbis depict the temple "as the capstone that prevents the abyss from rising again to inundate the world and undo the work of creation."[34] To attack something so important, so holy, so massive took enormous courage and sealed Jesus' fate. The impact of his denunciation of the temple, however, has lost its force two thousand years later. Most dispassionately assume that the temple was corrupt and deserving of God's judgment, and they are unable to imagine how they would have felt about Jesus' actions and words had they witnessed it firsthand. Nothing in our pluralistic culture holds such a dominating place in our lives as the temple did in the lives of Jesus' contemporaries, but sacred cows still exist for different communities and believers.

To bridge the contexts, therefore, one needs to identify and reflect on parallel phenomena in our own religious and political life. This text should cause us to reexamine the institutions we regard as sacrosanct. Is it all show, all

---

32. Victor of Antioch (fifth-century catenist) wrote that it was an acted parable in which Jesus "used the fig tree to set forth the judgment that was about to fall on Jerusalem" (cited by Cranfield, *Mark*, 356).

33. Waetjen, *Reordering*, 185.

34. *b. Sukk.* 53a-b; see Jon D. Levenson, *The Creation and the Persistence of Evil: The Jewish Drama of Divine Omnipotence* (San Francisco: Harper & Row, 1985), 99.

leaves and no fruit? Are the leaders corrupt, intent on furthering their own careers and reputations while feathering their own nests? Does self-interest and popular opinion reign supreme? Does it offer people a false security? Does it allow people to get away with ritual repentance that never affects the heart and how they live? Has it become a source of pride? Is it something that separates us from others and bestows special status only on an elite?

We also have our sacred places, groups, organizations, and ways of doing things. The entire system can become rotten to the core, but the veneer of piety and an aura of holiness make it seem inviolable. It seems a massive mountain, and those who challenge it appear as though they are tilting at windmills. Jesus affirms that for those who have faith, "the world *can* be remade."[35] One should remember, however, that this will not happen without prayer (see 9:29). One should also take heed. If one takes on religious or political corruption, it has its costs. Those invested in such institutions do not sit idly by when someone challenges their hold on power. It cost Jesus his life.

Jesus has been taking the place of the temple during his ministry. He announces forgiveness, heals the sick, and restores persons to society. He replaces the tables of the money changers, where worshipers had to pay for atonement, with the Lord's table, where he announces that his free offering of his life provides forgiveness of sins. The pouring out of his blood will replace once and for all the system of animal sacrifice for atonement. His death is where humankind can be reconciled to God.

JESUS AND THE temple. This incident in Mark 11 should cause us to examine the theological and political ramifications of Jesus' actions and words. (1) Attacking religious corruption is no less dangerous than attacking political corruption. Feelings run deep. People are easily hoodwinked by a show of piety. If one attacked a similar sacred cow today, one could meet with the same results. Martin Luther, in *An Open Letter to Pope Leo X* (September 6, 1520), protested a similar corruption:

> The Roman church, once the holiest of all, has become the most licentious den of thieves, the most shameless of all brothels, the kingdom of sin, death, and hell. It is so bad that even Antichrist himself, if he should come, could think of nothing to add to its wickedness.

(2) Jesus' attack made clear that God's requirements are not ritual but ethical. "I desire mercy, not sacrifice" (Hos. 6:6). Cultic sacrifice is mean-

---

35. Myers, *Binding*, 305.

ingless because everything is a matter of the heart: faith, prayer, and for-giveness of others.

(3) By denouncing the temple, Jesus also denounces the system of dom-ination it represented. Nouwen writes that Jesus' "appearance in our midst has made it undeniably clear that changing the human heart and changing human society are not separate tasks, but are as interconnected as the two beams of the cross."[36] The temple had become the center of power for the nobility who dominated, controlled, indoctrinated, and exploited others who ranked lower on the social scale. The temple preserved the status quo by extending priv-ileges to the few and by resisting the transforming power of the kingdom of God in society. Jesus did not simply help individual poor people; he went to the very source of much of the injustice in society in his day—the temple and its priestly hierarchy.

Myers argues that Jesus attacked the sacrificial accoutrements that com-pounded the oppression of the poor (doves were the sacrifice for those who were poor, Lev. 5:7; 12:8; 14:22, 30). He writes that they

> represented the concrete mechanisms of oppression within a political economy that doubly exploited the poor and unclean. Not only were they considered second-class citizens, but the cult obligated them to make reparation, through sacrifices, for their inferior status—from which the marketers profited. Jesus action here is fully consistent with his first direct action campaign to discredit the socio-symbolic appa-rati that discriminated against the "weak" and the "sinners."[37]

Myers' comments are a helpful pointer to why Jesus may have deplored the sacrificial system. The theology buttressing this system said that you are poor, suffering, and oppressed because you have sinned against God. To be forgiven you must offer sacrifice, which ultimately lined the pockets of those primarily responsible for the oppression of the poor. When Jesus pronounced forgiveness of sins by God (Mark 2:5, 10), he bypassed the sacrificial cult and subverted one of the repressive factors in society. If the church becomes a tool in repressing the people, it needs to be condemned.

(4) The temple system fostered xenophobia and ethnocentrism. The strain between Jew and Gentile, male and female, would never be settled (Gal. 3:28) as long as the temple stood with its series of holy barriers, each saying to a different group, "No entry!" Jesus calls for an end to the exclusivism that allows prayer and sacrifice for only a select group. Schweizer argues, "As a place of prayer the temple should reflect the attitude that man has nothing

---

36. Henri J. M. Nouwen, *The Wounded Healer* (Garden City: Doubleday, 1972), 20.
37. Myers, *Binding*, 301.

to achieve or offer to God, consequently it should be open to all men."[38] God's house accepts one and all, including the outcasts of Israel, lepers, menstruants, blind men, eunuchs, and Gentiles—who all come in a spirit of prayer. If any can say of a church fellowship, "It is easier for a camel to go through the eye of a needle than for some people to be accepted there," it needs to be condemned.

(5) Jesus attacks the merchandising of religion that obstructed the access of others to God. No ministry can legitimately take advantage of the presence of God to make a profit or to give the impression that they are hawking a religious commodity.

The power of prayer. People regarded the temple as the place of prayer. Jesus expected it to be a house of prayer for all nations, though he went on to predict its destruction. In his explanation of the fig tree's withering, Jesus envisioned a future without a temple. But its demise would not bring an end to effective prayer; "there will be a new praying community."[39] As Marshall writes, "The massive, institutionalized power of the existing religious establishment must give way to the kingdom community whose power lies solely in faith-borne prayer."[40] What does prayer look like in this community?

(1) The community needs to pray receptively. Prayer is not imposing our will on God but opening up our lives to God's will. True prayer is not an endeavor to get God to change his will but an endeavor to release that will in our own lives. Prayer is like a boat hook that a boatman uses to pull the craft to its anchoring place. The boatman does not try to pull the shore to the boat, but the other way around. So in prayer we should draw ourselves to God and not try to pull God down to us. Jesus provides an example of this receptive praying in Gethsemane, when he boldly entreats God but concludes: "Not what I will, but what you will" (14:36).

(2) The people are to pray confidently. This text does not invite one to attempt magical miracles. We are not to test our faith by going to a mountain and saying, "Be moved!" We must also guard against treating prayer as if it were a magic wand that allows us to get whatever we want. When Christians pray with confident faith that their prayers will have power, they can, like Jesus, overcome even the greatest oppression. Nothing is impossible. Prayer is not an engine by which we overcome the unwillingness of God. Jesus taught that God is ever ready to grant what is good for us. We do not need to wheedle or to beg God in prayer. The pagans mistakenly believed

---

38. Schweizer, *Mark*, 233.

39. Tom Shepherd, "The Narrative Function of Markan Intercalation," *NTS* 41 (1995): 536.

40. Marshall, *Faith As a Theme*, 176.

that it was the squeaky wheel that would get the grease, and so they plied the diffident gods with extended invocations, sometimes including magical formulae, to solicit their attention (see 1 Kings 18:26–29). Prayer is to be founded on the goodness of God as a loving parent and lays hold on God's benevolence.

When Christians pray in Jesus' name, they may be confident of God's response; but what they ask must be compatible with his teaching, life, and death. Contrast Jesus' promise, "Whatever you ask" (11:24), with Herod's empty boast, "Ask me for anything you want" (6:22). There are some things that Christians should not ask and some things that God will not give. As a parent gives to a child from his or her wisdom what the child needs, so does God. Consequently, we may receive answers we do not want, find things we are not looking for, and have doors open we do not expect. Paul prayed three times (time and again) for the thorn in the flesh to be removed. The answer came back that he would have to live with the thorn: "My grace is sufficient for you, for my power is made perfect in weakness" (2 Cor. 12:9). It was not the answer he wanted, but it was an answer that gave him life.

(3) The new community is to pray expectantly and without discouragement. Our prayers should not only focus on our own small worlds and our immediate futures but should fix our attention on the long term and the large scale. How many times have people offered up the prayer "Your kingdom come" over the centuries? That prayer should never fade from the lips and hearts of Christians. Frequently the church is dumbfounded in the face of liberation.

(4) The community is to pray with a forgiving spirit. We cannot make peace with God if we bear animosity for others.

Mark 12:1–12

H E THEN BEGAN to speak to them in parables: "A man planted a vineyard. He put a wall around it, dug a pit for the winepress and built a watchtower. Then he rented the vineyard to some farmers and went away on a journey. ²At harvest time he sent a servant to the tenants to collect from them some of the fruit of the vineyard. ³But they seized him, beat him and sent him away empty-handed. ⁴Then he sent another servant to them; they struck this man on the head and treated him shamefully. ⁵He sent still another, and that one they killed. He sent many others; some of them they beat, others they killed.

⁶"He had one left to send, a son, whom he loved. He sent him last of all, saying, 'They will respect my son.'

⁷"But the tenants said to one another, 'This is the heir. Come, let's kill him, and the inheritance will be ours.' ⁸So they took him and killed him, and threw him out of the vineyard.

⁹"What then will the owner of the vineyard do? He will come and kill those tenants and give the vineyard to others. ¹⁰Haven't you read this scripture:

> "'The stone the builders rejected
>   has become the capstone;
> ¹¹ the Lord has done this,
>   and it is marvelous in our eyes' ?'"

¹²Then they looked for a way to arrest him because they knew he had spoken the parable against them. But they were afraid of the crowd; so they left him and went away.

Original Meaning

JESUS' ALLEGORY OF the wicked tenants continues his response to the leaders' challenge of his authority (11:27–33) and brings matters to a head. Like the allegory of the sower in 4:1–9, it drives the plot forward and prepares the reader for what follows. What happens to Jesus should come as no surprise, given the leaders' hostility. But the allegory allows us to see these events from the perspective of God's long and turbulent relationship with Israel.

The allegory resembles the clever trap Nathan set for David with his story of the ewe lamb (2 Sam. 12:1–15). Nathan caught David in his web of adultery, murder, and lies with his stern, "You are the man!" Jesus catches the chief priests, teachers of the law, and elders in a similar trap. They were the major landlords in Israel and should naturally sympathize with the plight of the owner in the story.[1] A story about willful and murderous tenants would raise the ire of any landholder—until they realize that Jesus' allegory targets them. They are the vile, incorrigible, deadbeat tenants of God's vineyard.[2] It mirrors the real-life story of their rejection of God's prophets, such as John the Baptizer, and their venomous plotting against God's Son. Like David, they know their guilt—"they knew he had spoken the parable against them" (12:12). Unlike David, they do not repent when confronted with it.

Familiarity with Old Testament images helps one see that the figures in the allegory are transparent metaphors. The vineyard is a symbol of God's relationship to the chosen people Israel, and the description of the building of the vineyard has striking parallels with Isaiah 5:2.[3] Since the hedge, winepress, and tower have no significance in the later development of the story, these details are only included to recall to mind the Isaian context. In Isaiah's allegorical love song, the care lavished by God on the vineyard contrasts with the people's ingratitude and lack of fruitfulness (see Isa. 5:1–7; note how this passage is followed by a series of woes).[4] The friction between the vineyard owner and the tenants may reflect the real world of absentee landlords,[5] but the story is an allegory of God's troubled relationship with Israel that is nearing its climax (see also 3:14; Jer. 12:10).

The later church, from its perspective after Jesus' death and resurrection, quite naturally identified the tenants as Israel or the leaders of Israel. Jesus' original audience, however, would not have made this connection immediately.

---

1. See Martin Goodman, *The Ruling Class of Judea: The Origins of the Jewish Revolt Against Rome A.D. 66–70* (Cambridge: Cambridge Univ. Press, 1987), 55–75. Galilean peasants, on the other hand, would have probably sided with the tenants.

2. More often than not an allegory's biting censure of contemporaries is lost as it is retold in different contexts over the years. Compare Jonathan's Swift's *Gulliver's Travels* and Frank L. Baum's *The Wonderful Wizard of Oz*, which most today read as harmless children's stories.

3. See Klyne Snodgrass, *The Parable of the Wicked Tenants: An Inquiry into Parable Interpretation* (WUNT 27; Tübingen: J. C. B. Mohr [Paul Siebeck] 1983), 76. See also 2 Kings 19:30; Ps. 80:8–9; Song 8:11; Isa. 3:14; 27:6; 37:31; Jer. 2:21; 12:10 (cf. 6:9); Ezek. 15:1, 6; 17:5–10; 19:10; Hos. 10:1 (cf. 14:6–9).

4. In *t. Meʿil.* 1:16 and *t. Sukk.* 3:13 the tower is taken as referring to the temple and the winepress to the altar. See *Tg. Isa* 5:2, 5: God will destroy Israel's sanctuaries.

5. Compare Pliny (*Epistles* 10.8), who describes letting his lands, the time for dressing the vineyards, new tenants, and making abatements in rents because of a bad harvest.

Snodgrass suggests that the first hearers would have initially thought of the Romans as the tenants, whom God was allowing to maintain murderous control over Israel.[6] As the allegory unfolds, they become aware that their initial assumptions are false and must be revised.

The sending of the servants and their callous rejection turn the tide. The word "servant" is a frequent designation in the Old Testament for the prophets whom God sent to the people.[7] Jeremiah 7:25–26, which figures prominently in Jesus' interpretation of his actions in the temple, is an apt commentary:

> From the time your forefathers left Egypt until now, day after day, again and again I sent you my servants the prophets. But they did not listen to me or pay attention. They were stiff-necked and did more evil than their forefathers.

Nehemiah 9:26 also reflects this theme:

> "But they were disobedient and rebelled against you; they put your law behind their backs. They killed your prophets, who had admonished them in order to turn them back to you; they committed awful blasphemies."

And one finds in 2 Chronicles 36:15–16 (cf. 24:18–19) the same argument:

> The LORD, the God of their fathers, sent word to them through his messengers again and again, because he had pity on his people and on his dwelling place. But they mocked God's messengers, despised his words and scoffed at his prophets until the wrath of the LORD was aroused against his people and there was no remedy.

The servants' treatment in the allegory surely called to mind the ill-treatment of the prophets. The abuse of the servants in the allegory becomes progressively worse. The first is beaten and sent away (12:3), the next is struck on the head and treated shamefully (12:4), and the last is killed (12:5). We know the fate of only two relatively insignificant prophets from Scripture—Zechariah son of Jehoida, who was stoned (2 Chron. 24:20–22), and Uriah, who died by the sword (Jer. 26:20). Jeremiah was beaten and put in stocks (Jer. 20:2), but later apocryphal legends about prophets such as Amos, Micah, Isaiah, Jeremiah, Ezekiel, Joel, and Habakkuk had them killed. Popular wisdom in the time of Jesus believed that prophets inevitably were rejected and

---

6. Snodgrass, *The Parable of the Wicked Tenants*, 77–78.

7. See 1 Kings 14:18; 15:29; 18:36; 2 Kings 9:36; 10:10; 14:25; and the phrase "my [your, his] servants the prophets" in Jer. 7:25; Dan. 9:6; Amos 3:7.

suffered a martyr's fate (see Matt. 5:12; 23:31–39; Luke 13:31–33; Acts 7:52; 1 Thess. 2:15; Heb. 11:36–38). The unusual word to describe the fate of one of the servants, the one who is "struck ... on the head" (*kephalioo*, Mark 12:4), may allude to specifically the fate of John the Baptizer, who was beheaded (*apokephalizo*, 6:16, 27). Jesus has just brought up the issue of John's authority and the leaders confess in private their rejection of him (11:30–32).[8]

The allegory reaches its denouement after the servants fail to collect the fruit. The owner has one more card up his sleeve. He will send the son "last of all." He is identified as a "son, whom he loved" (an idiom for an "only son"), which recalls the voice from heaven identifying Jesus as "my Son, whom I love" (1:11; 9:7). The son is on a different level from the servants, and the owner sends him because he assumes that the tenants will "respect him."[9] The son's mission is the same as that of the servants before him. The owner gives the tenants every opportunity to repent and to pay their rent—to give him the required fruits in due season (see Ps. 1:3). Evidence from Qumran (4QFlor 1:11, citing 2 Sam. 7:11, and 1QSa 2:11–12, on Ps. 2:7) suggests the reference to the son could have been understood messianically by the audience.

The tenants recognize the son as the heir and wickedly want his inheritance for themselves (see 15:10; Pilate recognizes the Pharisees' envy of Jesus). Defiance mixed with cunning proves to be their final undoing. They become snared by their own clever plot (Job 5:13; 1 Cor. 3:19). They mistakenly assume that the owner is now dead and foolishly hope that killing the heir will give them sole ownership of the vineyard.[10] After they assassinate the son, they throw his body outside and leave him unburied. To refuse to bury a corpse was an incredible offense in the ancient world.

Jesus concludes the allegory with a pointed question: "What then will the owner of the vineyard do?" He does not wait for their answer but gives it himself. The owner suddenly changes from one who is seemingly impotent to one who can exact revenge. He is now the Lord of the vineyard, who will destroy the tenants who killed his servants and son. But the Lord is not through. He will give the vineyard to others. Although the true heir is rejected and killed, the inheritance still belongs to him and his community. Jesus terminates the confrontation with a citation from Psalm 118:25, the

---

8. In the *Lives of the Prophets* 2, however, Amos was said to have been hit on the head by Amasias, so the reference in v. 4 may only be a general reference.

9. The verb "respect" (*entrepomai*) is used in the Septuagint to refer to people "humbling themselves" before the messengers of God (see Ex. 10:3; Lev. 26:41; 2 Kings 22:19; 2 Chron. 7:14; 12:7, 12; 34:27; 36:12).

10. The phrase, "Come, let's kill him," is the same one used by Joseph's brothers in Gen. 37:20a LXX (see *T. Sim; T. Seb.* 1–5; *T. Dan* 1; *T. Gad* 1–2; *T. Jos.* 1; *T. Ben.* 3).

psalm that the crowd chanted when Jesus entered the city (Mark 11:9–10). This psalm explains that the one who is rejected (the same verb, *apodoki-mazo*, is used in Jesus' first prediction in 8:31) and murdered will be vindicated (12:9–10; cf. Ps. 118:22–23). The block of stone that the builders discarded becomes either the cornerstone or the capstone of a new structure.[11] The image implies a new temple.[12] Mark's readers will understand that Jesus is the stone of stumbling that the psalmist talked about.

The final quotation, "The Lord has done this, and it is marvelous in our eyes" (12:11), attributes Jesus' condemnation of the temple to God's work. The tenants' destruction, the giving of the vineyard to others, and the trans-formation of a rejected stone into the capstone are marvelous to the ones who have eyes to see God's plan. The impotent animal sacrifices in a fruitless, racist, chauvinistic, stone structure will end. The Son whom these leaders will put to death will be raised by God and will become the locus of salvation.

Jesus' allegory is a riddle, but the leaders do not need coaching to see that they are its target. They understand its implications, which only heightens the enormity of their guilt. Jesus has told the disciples that the high priests and teachers of the law in Jerusalem will kill him (9:33). Now he tells the rulers, albeit in an allegory, that they will kill the Son. That they move ahead with their plot means that they carry it out with malice aforethought. They are like the demons who recognize Jesus as a threat who has come to destroy them (1:24), but rather than submit to him they try in vain to destroy him. Jesus' enemies bide their time because they fear the reaction of the fickle crowd more than they fear God (11:18; 12:12). Mark does not present Jesus despised and rejected by the people of Israel but by the leaders of the people.

This allegory has Christological significance. It reflects Jesus' full con-sciousness of his Sonship in relation to the Lord of the vineyard and his full awareness of his impending death at the hands of the authorities.[13] Those who question the authenticity of the allegory tend to question both possibilities.

---

11. The capstone is the central, wedge-shaped stone at the summit of an arch, locking the others into position. In Aramaic, Jesus' statement would feature a play on words between "son" (*ben*) and "stone" (*eben*); see Matthew Black, "The Christological Use of the Old Tes-tament in the New Testament," *NTS* 18 (1971): 11–14. A reference to "the builders of the feeble wall" in CD 4:19; 8:12 suggests that the term "builders" was used in some quarters as an epithet for the temple leadership.

12. Tolbert (*Sowing*, 260) writes " . . . for the rejected stone to become the centerpiece, the buildings presently standing must first be completely dismantled and the tenants presently in control must first be destroyed; only then can the new edifice rise and the faithful tenants be installed."

13. For arguments that the parable originates with Jesus, see James H. Charlesworth, *Jesus Within Judaism* (New York: Doubleday, 1988), 139–43; Snodgrass, *The Parable of the Wicked Tenants*.

Bridging Contexts

IN INTERPRETING THIS allegory one needs to focus on the three key moments. Each is marked by direct discourse: when the frustrated landlord decides to send his son to collect the fruit; when we overhear the tenants ponder their situation and decide to kill the heir; and when Jesus asks, "What then will the owner . . . do?" These three moments unlock the meaning of the allegory.

The owner's forbearance. We listen in on the thought processes of the vineyard owner who has prepared a vineyard but has reaped only insults in the form of battered and murdered servants. He finally decides to send his beloved (= only) son, thinking, "They will respect my son." After the brutal reception of his servants, this action seems imprudent, if not downright foolhardy. Why does the owner think that his son will be treated any differently from his servants? As an allegory about God's relationship with Israel, however, the landlord's musings say something about the nature of God. It recalls the Old Testament theme of God's long-suffering patience and unrequited love, expressed most poignantly in Hosea (Hos. 2:2, 14–20; see also Jer. 3:11–14).[14] Carlston terms it "the blessed idiocy of grace."[15]

The allegory reveals God's continuous pursuit of humans, no matter how often the overtures meet with rejection. The landlord's optimism in sending his son represents God's endless hopefulness and constant effort to bring sinful people to their senses. God fully expects the people to produce fruit and exercises forbearance when they renege on their obligations (Rom. 2:4; 2 Peter 3:9), and what seems to be utter foolishness in sending prophet after prophet and finally a beloved Son to a pack of murderers. What may look like foolishness to worldly wisdom, however (1 Cor. 1:18–25; 3:18–20), reflects the love and wisdom of God.

The tenants' foolishness. The tenants' soliloquy reveals their mental process: "This is the heir. Come, let's kill him, and the inheritance will be ours." Their foolishness reminds us of the wealthy farmer's soliloquy in Luke 12:18–19, who just as vainly says:

> "This is what I'll do. I will tear down my barns and build bigger ones, and there I will store all my grain and my goods. And I'll say to myself, 'You have plenty of good things laid up for many years. Take life easy; eat, drink and be merry.'"

---

14. John R. Donahue, *The Gospel in Parable* (Philadelphia: Fortress, 1988), 55.

15. Charles E. Carlston, *The Parables of the Triple Tradition* (Philadelphia: Fortress, 1975), 185.

Foolish hopes lead to foolhardy behavior. The tenants may stupidly believe that when they kill the heir the vineyard will become ownerless property that they can then commandeer. Like the rich fool, they do not take any account of God.

This aspect of the parable bridges easily into our contemporary setting. It says something about the foolish hubris of those in every age and in every walk of life who think that they can seize control of everything in their lives and push God out of the picture. Did these tenants really believe that by killing the son they could become the owners of the vineyard? Apparently so. Do humans think that by erasing God from their lives they can take control of their earthly and eternal destinies? Apparently so. The allegory reveals the utter foolishness of sinful rebellion against God. It also reminds us that we are only the servants in the vineyard, not its lords or its owners.

The owner's wrath. Jesus' concluding question, "What then will the owner of the vineyard do?" is the climax of the story. The answer to this question is not obvious from what precedes. The owner seems to be rather ineffectual and weak. Perhaps he will do nothing because, as the tenants gambled, he is impotent and can do nothing. It helps to recognize, however, that the owner represents God in this allegory. Obviously, God is not powerless. God has shown inordinate patience, but the conclusion reveals the prophetic warning that God will not be patient forever.

When one interprets this allegory against the backdrop of the larger story of God's relations with Israel, one recalls the biblical axiom that God's kindness is meant to lead to repentance (Rom. 2:4). Isaiah records God's warning, "All day long I have held out my hands to an obstinate people, who walk in ways not good, pursuing their own imaginations—a people who continually provoke me to my very face" (Isa. 65:2–3a). Continual rebellion will meet with certain judgment (65:7). But God will not destroy all Israel; a remnant will be saved (65:8–16). In Jesus' parable the vineyard is not destroyed but given to others. Who those others are is unclear, and this ambiguity leads to the final point to be discussed in bridging the contexts.

The owner's optimism in giving the vineyard to others. One should be careful not to interpret this allegory as explaining the rejection of Israel in favor of a Gentile Christian church. Jesus used this allegory to confront his opponents with their sin and to call them to account, not to put the people of Israel in a bad light. In the same way as Jesus warns Judas at the Last Supper that he knows about his plans to betray him in hopes that Judas might rethink what he is about to do or repent (14:17–21), Jesus warns these chief priests, teachers of the law, and elders. He knows the murderous plans they have hatched in their hearts; perhaps they will repent. In Mark's context, this allegory is not about God's rejection of Israel, but about the defiance of the leaders.

Comparing this allegory with its inspiration in Isaiah 5:1–7 also helps one avoid the pitfall of interpreting it as pointing to the rejection of Israel. In both allegories, God is the owner of the vineyard who fails to receive the fruit that is due. In Isaiah, the owner does not reap a harvest because the vineyard did not produce an adequate one;[16] the vineyard in Jesus' allegory produces fruit, but the wicked tenants withhold it from the owner. In Isaiah, the judgment falls on the vineyard; in Jesus' allegory, judgment falls on the tenants, and the vineyard is given to others.

This comparison reveals that Jesus singles out the tenants, the leaders who comprise the audience, not Israel as a people, for condemnation. We must therefore be careful not to interpret this allegory as a story about evil Israel who rejected the prophets and killed God's Son. Jesus directs it against Israel's *leaders*; and they acknowledge this fact: "Then they looked for a way to arrest him because they knew he had spoken the parable against them" (12:12).

These leaders will not repent and cannot produce the fruit of the kingdom. Instead, they are intent on securing a kingdom for themselves. They have turned the temple, God's house of prayer, into their own personal cash cow. And they will move quickly to eradicate anyone who challenges their prerogatives. These high priests, elders, and teachers of the law are the faithless tenants who rejected prophets such as John and engineer the death of the Son, and they stand in contrast to the naive and vulnerable crowd.

Jesus fills the crowd with awe. But the crowd has no full understanding of who he is and is easily swayed by the unscrupulous masters of the temple. In the Passion narrative, the crowd becomes their unwitting pawns. Violence begets only violence, however, and the wicked tenants will meet destruction. The conclusion from Psalm 118:22 suggests that God will appoint new leaders to tend the vineyard, Israel. The allusive references to "the builders" and the rejected capstone will make more sense after Jesus predicts the temple's demolition: "Not one stone here will be left on another; every one will be thrown down" (13:2). Jesus implies that God will raise a new temple not made with hands, and it will be cemented by a rejected capstone. The quotation has parallels with the classic plot of Cinderella or the Ugly Duckling, except it has divine dimensions. One's response to the Son will be decisive for one's own fate.

Tolbert helpfully points out that "typology by its very nature encourages a more generalized application: any group in power that obstructs the fruitfulness of God's good earth is a manifestation of the evil tenants of the

---

16. Geddert, *Watchwords*, 121.

vineyard."[17] Frequently, one reads parables as making a devastating point about someone else, whereas they may be more applicable to us. Readers and listeners tend to identify with the heroes or "good guys" in a story. Since most have heard the story before, they distance themselves from the guilty parties who stubbornly, maliciously, and selfishly want everything for themselves.

Jesus lulled his first listeners into a trap by relating a story about an absentee landlord's problems with rebellious tenants—something they had to put up with in real life. Then he turned the tables on them so that they realized that they were the evil tenants refusing to yield fruit to God. The parable will be most effective if, in retelling it, it somehow boomerangs back into the face of listeners as they suddenly realize it is speaking about them. Jesus' parables sound so safe, like Nathan's story of the ewe lamb. Then he springs the trap and catches his listeners in their guilt: "You are the man!" This allegory does more than condemn evil leaders who lived some two thousand years ago; it applies to us. The story of God's relationship with a disobedient and rebellious people has not changed much. The judgment that fell on them can fall on us if we, as leaders, fail in our stewardship. We must therefore analyze in what areas we have failed to yield fruit to God, how we may have rejected and mistreated God's servants (3 John 9–10), and how we continue to reject God's Son (Heb. 6:6).

THE WORLD OF the wicked tenants is a world much like ours. It is filled with wanton violence. When threatened, these tenants know no restraint and strike out violently. They stop at nothing to get what they want. It is a world that breaks contracts without blinking. They do not care that they have agreed to fulfill certain obligations; they intend to do whatever they please. It is a world that knows no sense of right and wrong. They believe that whatever achieves their ends is right, no matter what it costs others. Therefore, they greedily seize for themselves what is not theirs. They do not forget who owns the land; they simply intend to take it over for themselves by any means. Their covetousness knows no bounds as they greedily grab more than their share of everything. This unbridled will to power leads them to say, "Mine is the power, the kingdom and the glory."

This story reminds me of what happens every summer when I put up a hummingbird feeder. One hummingbird always attempts to take it over as his

---

17. Tolbert, *Sowing*, 238.

very own private feeder. The bird chases off any other hummingbird that dares to venture near. It requires constant vigilance. It is like watching World War I dogfights as the bird darts back and forth pursuing dozens of trespassers through tree branches and swearing his outrage in hummingbird chirps. The bird only stops when exhausted and rarely takes time to perch and drink at "his" feeder. But it is not "his" feeder. It is mine. I bought it. I prepared the mixture of water, sugar, and red food coloring. I risked my neck hanging it up on a tree branch to draw all the hummingbirds, not just this one.

The imperious hummingbird behaves like many humans do in God's vineyard, only our similar behavior does not cause God much amusement. Covetousness makes humans want what they should not have. It then makes them think that this desire should be fulfilled at all costs. Other persons become things to exploit, and our own desires become our god.

The tenants live in a self-centered, cutthroat world with no awareness of God or God's judgment. They want to establish themselves as the lords of their little world. They reject the reality that they are creatures of God who live in God's vineyard. God, however, stands in the way of their self-absorbed plans. Killing God's messengers sent to remind them of this reality gives them a false sense of security, but their defiance only secures their final destruction.

When they kill the heir, they have not won; they still must deal with God. To many today, God may sometimes seem to be like an absentee landlord, and a foolish one at that—easily betrayed and cheated. The owner in the parable loses his servants, his son, and seemingly his vineyard. People in our world get away with injustice, oppression, and murder. God's messengers continue to be rejected, mocked, beaten, and killed. There seems to be no accountability for sin.

All is not as it seems, however. God sends the servants and the Son in hopes of bringing people to repentance (Rom. 2:4). The rejections and murders reveal God as a tragic figure who suffers with humankind. They also reveal the blind folly of evil. People think that they can get away with it, but God's judgment will inevitably come. Sometimes one can see this judgment clearly manifest in history with the downfall of a nation's evil leaders, sometimes not. The parable assures us that God will win even when it seems that he has lost. Those who reject God's claims on their lives and God's call to repentance will always be the losers even when it seems as if they have won. They sow the seeds of their own destruction.

The parable particularly applies to the church today. Israel was chosen by God to fulfill God's gracious purposes for the whole world. God equipped them specially for the task, but the leaders mistook that assignment as special privilege and wanted to be accountable only to themselves, not to God.

If one asks what fruit God requires from us today, the answer comes from what immediately precedes and follows the parable (12:13–17, 28–34): God requires that our place of worship be a house of prayer for all nations (11:17). God also requires our community to be a forgiving one (11:25). We are to render to God what belongs to God (12:17). We are also to love God with all our heart, soul, mind, and strength (12:30), and our neighbors as ourselves (12:31). In other words, God expects the vineyard, God's people, to be an accepting, prayerful, forgiving, devoted, and loving fellowship built around his Son, the one stone that binds everything together. When it becomes something other than that, it courts God's judgment.

Mark 12:13–17

LATER THEY SENT some of the Pharisees and Herodians to Jesus to catch him in his words. ¹⁴They came to him and said, "Teacher, we know you are a man of integrity. You aren't swayed by men, because you pay no attention to who they are; but you teach the way of God in accordance with the truth. Is it right to pay taxes to Caesar or not? ¹⁵Should we pay or shouldn't we?"

But Jesus knew their hypocrisy. "Why are you trying to trap me?" he asked. "Bring me a denarius and let me look at it." ¹⁶They brought the coin, and he asked them, "Whose portrait is this? And whose inscription?"

"Caesar's," they replied.

¹⁷Then Jesus said to them, "Give to Caesar what is Caesar's and to God what is God's."

And they were amazed at him.

Original Meaning

ALL OF THE questions directed to Jesus in the temple (cf. 11:27) concern "Jewish" issues. Can one pay taxes to Caesar and still honor God? Is the resurrection hope verifiable from the books of Moses? What is the first of all God's commandments? How do you explain the contradiction in Scripture about the Son of David? Jesus' ability to parry these challenges reveals his authority as one "from heaven" (11:30).

The first challenge comes when the triumvirate of chief priests, teachers of the law, and elders send Pharisees and the Herodians to ensnare Jesus in a carefully laid trap (11:27; 12:13). They try to throw him off balance with a fawning approach, praising him for his impartiality. Ironically, they feign sincerity as they affirm Jesus' candor. He does not butter up others or sugarcoat the way of God (see 1:3) when he teaches. They are wrong about one thing, however. Jesus does show partiality and does not give straight answers to those who do not sincerely seek the truth.

These interrogators bait the trap by asking a yes or no question about an explosive issue, taxes. Judea became a Roman province in A.D. 6 after the failed tenure of Herod Archelaus as tetrarch. A census was then taken, from which the Romans levied a head tax, a tax distinct from the one on property and from customs on articles.[1] Its establishment provoked Judas of Galilee to lead a revolt because it placed God's own land at the service of foreigners (Acts 5:37).[2] The question asked of Jesus is loaded because it raises the issue of fidelity to the God of Israel. Can one pay taxes to Caesar and still give allegiance to the God of Israel? Are people traitors to God for supporting Caesar's hegemony over the land?

These opponents probably peg Jesus as an extremist who will flash the same militant zeal as Judas the Galilean. If he openly rejects the head tax, he will be like those diehard rebels who incited revolt and will be subject to arrest for treason. But if he endorses the tax, he will undermine his support among the zealous, who chafe under Roman rule. Almost every resident of Palestine knew someone, even a father or a brother, whom the Romans had victimized. They were sold into slavery (temporarily or permanently), forced off their land when caught in a maelstrom of debt caused by decreasing harvests and increasing tax demands, or executed for rising up against the oppression. Furthermore, a yes answer will also throw into question whether he is really the Christ since the Messiah was expected to depose those who tyrannized God's people and to enforce justice.

Jesus knows his questioners' hypocrisy, adroitly evades their ambush, and sets a trap of his own. By asking for a coin, which he does not possess, he throws them off guard. They must dig through their purses to come up with one while they wonder about his intentions. The head tax was paid by a silver denarius. In Jesus' time, it was probably a Tiberian denarius. Coins in the ancient world were used for propaganda effect, and this coin bore an image of the emperor and proclaimed Roman ideology. The coin's obverse had the effigy of the emperor and the superscription read: "TI[berius] CAESAR DIV[i] AUG[usti] F[ilius] AUGUSTUS" ("Tiberius Caesar, August Son of the Divine Augustus"). The reverse had a female figure seated on a throne, wearing a crown and holding an inverted spear in her right hand and a palm or olive branch in her left. The superscription read: "Pontif[ex] Maxim[us]" ("High Priest"). The woman was either a priestess or Livia, the wife of Augustus and mother of Tiberias, and the coin proclaimed the *pax Romana* that had put all the world in subjection. It was, in effect, a portable idol promulgating pagan ideology.

The opponents produce the coin, and Jesus asks them to identify whose image it bears.[3] When they answer, "Caesar's," Jesus can now answer their

---

1. Mark identifies the tribute with the term "census" (*kensos*).

2. See Josephus, *J. W.* 2.8.1 §§ 117–18; *Ant.* 18.1.1 §§ 1–9.

3. According to *y. Meg.* 1:11, 72b, Nahum is called the most holy because of his scruples about graven images: "he never gazed upon a coin in his entire life." See also *b. Pesah.* 104a.

question. Caesar's coins belong to him. Since they have no qualms about doing business with Caesar's money, they had better pay Caesar's taxes. And since they are able to produce the coin, Jesus also exposes that they have no qualms about bringing an image of Caesar and an emblem of his worldly power and his pretension to deity into God's temple.[4] He makes them look foolish and impious. They already pay a kind of tribute to Caesar by possessing his coin. Therefore, they owe Caesar the tribute he demands from taxes.[5] In effect, Jesus says, "Let Caesar have his idols!"

"Give to Caesar" does not give Caesar a carte blanche. Jesus does more than balance this statement when he tells them to render to God what is God's. God is Caesar's Lord. One may owe Caesar what bears his image and name—money. One owes God what bears God's image and name. Since we are created in the image of God (see Gen. 1:26; Prov. 7:3; Isa. 44:5; Jer. 38:33; cf. Ezek. 18:4) and bear his name as children of God, we owe him our whole selves.[6] Exactly what we owe God becomes clear in Jesus' answer to a certain teacher of the law: We owe God love from all our heart, soul, mind, and strength (12:30, 33).

THIS PASSAGE RAISES the important issue of the relationship between God and the government, which has been debated through the ages. Christians in every generation and society must confront this issue. In this section, I will discuss extreme forms of false alternatives that one must guard against. Then we can discuss the implications of the text for our own situation.

Jesus does not divide life into two realms, the sacred and the secular. "The things that are Caesar's" should not be interpreted to mean that Caesar has control of the political sphere while God keeps control only of the religious sphere. Obviously, Jesus would not regard Caesar and God to be counterparts. There is only one Lord of the world, not two (12:29). The interpretation

---

4. During the war against Rome the rebels minted their own coins with images of the temple and religious festivals.

5. The only tax Jesus specifically rejects is the temple half-shekel dues, but then he recommends paying it to keep from scandalizing others (Matt. 17:24–27; see David E. Garland, *Reading Matthew* [New York: Crossroads, 1993]).

6. Tertullian interpreted this passage to mean: "Render unto Caesar, the image of Caesar, which is on the money, and unto God, the image of God, which is in man; so that thou givest unto Caesar money, unto God thine own self" (*On Idolatry* 15; *Against Marcion* 4.38.3). See Charles H. Giblin, "'The Things of God' in the Question Concerning Tribute to Caesar [Lk. 20:25; Mk 12:17; Mt 22:21]," *CBQ* 33 (1971): 522–23.

given above treats this phrase as a snide word of dismissal. The coin is Caesar's idol, and he can have it back. We therefore must be cautious about building any political theory from this verse.

In the past, however, the church has wanted to exercise sovereign control over Caesar (the state) in the name of God. When the papacy reached the apex of its power, for example, the emperor was considered to be no more than the pope's arm, who enforced the church's will in the secular sphere. Luke 22:35–38 was interpreted allegorically to mean that the pope possessed "two swords," a spiritual and a temporal sword. The papal bull *Unam Sanctum*, issued by Boniface VIII, argued:

> Both swords are thus in the power of the Church, the material and the spiritual, but the former is wielded on behalf of the Church, the latter by the Church; the latter by the hand of the priest, the former by the hand of king or knight, on the word, and with the consent of the priest. It is in fact needful that one sword should be below the other and that the temporal authority should be subject to the spiritual power.[7]

Jesus does not envision that his followers will become the church militant and all powerful. The church of glory and power always loses both its moral compass and its spiritual vigor. It has also done as much harm to God's purposes and God's servants as the satanic state. We cannot imbue the world with Christ's spirit by exercising political force. The view that might makes right is pagan.

Another false alternative wants to place the church under the authority of the state, so that the church becomes a court chaplain. Nazi Germany provided an extreme example of this when its totalitarian rulers attempted to establish a national religion, "the German Christians," under the authority of a *Reichsbishop* with leaders pledged to Nazi Party ideals. The church was expected to obey the dictates of state officials regarding creed, ritual, and discipline. Rosenberg's *Mythus in the Nineteenth Century* argued:

> The religion of Jesus doubtless was a gospel of Love ... but a Germanic religious movement which wants to become a People's Church will have to declare that the love of our fellow men must be subordinated to the idea of National Honor.[8]

We must reject these extreme views regarding the relationship between the church and the state.

---

7. Cited by Joseph Lecler, *The Two Sovereignties* (New York: Philosophical Library, 1952), 60.

8. Cited by Charles Grant Robertson, *Religion and the Totalitarian State* (London: Epworth, 1937), 79.

THE CHURCH HAS always been plagued with self-appointed inquisitors who try to root out suspected heretics with guile and trick questions. The name-calling propaganda and the campaign of dirty tactics in political campaigns are nothing new. Jesus' response to his opponents in this section serves as a model for his followers. These opponents testify that as a man of God Jesus does not curry favor, wheedle, fawn over others, or humor them. Jesus is not concerned with preserving his position. He speaks God's truth with such utter conviction that people will listen.

What are the implications of Jesus' response for our situation? (1) Jesus rejects violence as an alternative. The opponents fully expected such a zealous prophet as Jesus would expose seditionist tendencies when they posed their question. They mistook Jesus the Galilean for another revolutionary, Judas the Galilean (see 14:71), who endorsed subversive action against Rome. Jesus was not intent on supplanting a violent Roman regime with a violent Jewish one, however. That would simply trade one form of oppression for another.

Violent overthrows of oppressive regimes change little. The cartoon character Dick Tracy said, "Violence is golden when it is used to put evil down."[9] The trouble is that evil never stays down, particular when one employs brutal force. It takes something far more revolutionary to make a significant dent in the evil that engulfs our world—a whole transformation of values. Wink observes: "Violent revolution fails because it is not revolutionary enough. It changes the rulers but not the rules, the ends but not the means. Most of the old androcratic values and delusional assumptions remain intact."[10] Jesus, however, offers a whole new way of confronting evil with bold love, turning the other cheek, going the extra mile, forgiving enemies and praying for them, and giving one's life for others.

(2) Jesus rejects militant nationalism but does not propose that his followers drop out completely from society. He does not tell them to have nothing to do with government, nor does he invite them to withdraw to some desert stronghold (as the sectarians at Qumran did). We as Christians may hold citizenship in heaven (Phil. 3:20), but that does not exempt us from being exemplary citizens on earth. Jesus does not call us to disengage from the world, nor does he confer us with special status that allows us to escape its obligations. Christians may be free from the law, but we are not free from civil law designed to promote order.

---

9. Cited by Walter Wink, *Engaging the Powers: Discernment and Resistance in a World of Domination* (Minneapolis: Fortress, 1992), 19.

10. Ibid., 136.

(3) Jesus' statement limits what one owes the government. His answer subverts the pretensions of pagan rulers. There is another Lord over them, and their idolatrous coins are worthless in God's realm. Jesus outwits his opponents and exposes to all that they already acknowledge Caesar's authority by having in their possession a coin bearing his image. If they do business with Caesar, they must play by Caesar's rules. His statement does not grant power to Caesar.

One only owes Caesar those things from which one gains benefits. The early Christians took advantage of the Roman road system and the relative peace and order that Roman power imposed on the world to spread the gospel. If we make use of the state's money and benefit from its highways and sewers, we are bound to pay its taxes. Taxes are a trivial matter compared to what we owe God. The "things" of God are not limited to coins; they are defined in 12:29–31. We owe God all our heart, soul, mind, and strength; and we also owe God a loving concern for our fellow human beings. We may owe Caesar money, but we do not owe Caesar the love that is to be directed only to God.

The problem comes when government oversteps its legitimate bounds and encroaches on the religious allegiances of Christ's followers. States can become idolatrous, and respect for the powers that be can lead to idolatry (see Rev. 13; 17:1–19:10). Jesus was killed by both king and priest. Not only must his followers resist any attempt to make religion a tool of the state, they must also resist any would-be lords who want to be worshiped in some cult, whatever form it might take. God's law prevails over the state's law. The Christian owes Caesar something but not everything. Obedience must be vigilant and discerning because the state is also answerable to God. The demands of God are infinitely greater. We who bear God's image and are inscribed with Jesus' name owe God everything.

(4) The early Christians adopted a positive view of government's role but argued that it derived its authority from God.[11] They advocated submission, but not because of any reverence for Caesar. When one pays taxes to Caesar, one does so out of obedience to Jesus' command, not out of reverence for any earthly ruler.[12] The New Testament proclaims that Jesus is king, which means that Caesar is not (see 1 Tim. 6:14–16). Peter applies Jesus' words in Acts 5:29 when he says, "We must obey God rather than men!" (cf. 4:19–20).

(5) This passage warns against a danger we face in our society, namely, the development of civil religion. Civil religion exists when the state "assumes

---

11. Rom. 13:1–7; 1 Tim. 2:1–2; Titus 3:1–2; 1 Peter 2:13–17; 1 Clem. 61; Pol., *Phil.* 12:3; Justin, *Apology* 1, 17.3; Tertullian, *Apology* 30.

12. Martin Hengel, *Christ and Power* (Philadelphia: Fortress, 1977), 40.

religious dimensions" or religion identifies with or succumbs to the state.[13] Each Christian must know where to draw the line between the things that are Caesar's and those that are God's and to act responsibly and vigilantly to see that it is not crossed. Martin Luther said:

> The church of the New Testament did not attempt to save its existence by making a concordat with Nero and Domitian and Decius in their great persecution, or by stirring up a revolution against these tyrants, or by making an alliance with the Persian empire—but simply confessing the truth of the gospel and building up a truly confessing church whose members were prepared to die for their faith.

An unhealthy union between church and state has been the undoing of both churches and governments throughout history. One must always be cautious about politicizing the church, for that inevitably means that the church becomes involved in power struggles that will detract from its mission, even if its members are fighting for a good cause. The church can become identified solely with political agendas and not the proclamation of the gospel, which transcends society and government. The church must deter politicians from girding their policies and programs with divine authority or branding their opponents as inherently evil or sinful. The church must be far enough removed from the political machine to allow it to speak prophetically.

---

13. Frank Stagg, "Rendering to Caesar What Belongs to Caesar: Christian Engagement with the World," *Journal of Church and State* 18 (1976): 96–97.

Mark 12:18–27

THEN THE SADDUCEES, who say there is no resurrection, came to him with a question. ¹⁹"Teacher," they said, "Moses wrote for us that if a man's brother dies and leaves a wife but no children, the man must marry the widow and have children for his brother. ²⁰Now there were seven brothers. The first one married and died without leaving any children. ²¹The second one married the widow, but he also died, leaving no child. It was the same with the third. ²²In fact, none of the seven left any children. Last of all, the woman died too. ²³At the resurrection whose wife will she be, since the seven were married to her?"

²⁴Jesus replied, "Are you not in error because you do not know the Scriptures or the power of God? ²⁵When the dead rise, they will neither marry nor be given in marriage; they will be like the angels in heaven. ²⁶Now about the dead rising— have you not read in the book of Moses, in the account of the bush, how God said to him, 'I am the God of Abraham, the God of Isaac, and the God of Jacob'? ²⁷He is not the God of the dead, but of the living. You are badly mistaken!"

Original Meaning THE SADDUCEES APPEAR for the first time in this Gospel, and they appear as opponents of Jesus. Mark introduces them as those who do not believe in resurrection. Jesus has predicted his resurrection three times (8:31; 9:31; 10:34). If there is no resurrection, then Jesus will not be vindicated by God.

What little we know about the Sadducees derives almost entirely from their bitter opponents, who preserved memories of conflicts with them. They did not leave a written legacy and did not survive the debacle against Rome. They were a pro-priestly party that considered the five books of Moses alone as binding. Their conservatism led them to reject any theological innovations they regarded as derived from something other than the Pentateuch. The belief in the resurrection fell into that category since the books of Moses never mention it.[1] The Wisdom of Solomon 1:16–2:24 presents the derisive

---

1. See Acts 23:8; Josephus, *Ant.* 18.1.4 §§ 16–17; *J. W.* 2.8.14 §§ 164–65.

worldview of the ungodly; 2:1–5 contains a pessimistic argument against the afterlife. This perspective may accord with that of the Sadducees.

> For they reasoned unsoundly, saying to themselves,
> "Short and sorrowful is our life,
> and there is no remedy when a life comes to its end,
> and no one has been known to return from Hades.
> For we were born by mere chance,
> and hereafter we shall be as though we had never been,
> for the breath in our nostrils is smoke,
> and reason is a spark kindled by the beating of our hearts;
> when it is extinguished, the body will return to ashes,
> and the spirit will dissolve like empty air.
> Our name will be forgotten in time,
> and no one will remember our works;
> our life will pass away like the traces of a cloud,
> and be scattered like mist
> that is chased by the rays of the sun
> and overcome by its heat.
> For our allotted time is the passing of a shadow,
> and there is no return from our death,
> because it is sealed up and no one turns back." (NRSV)

The Sadducees bait Jesus with a teasing conundrum based on the law of levirate marriage, which prescribed what should happen when a man died with no heirs. One of his surviving brothers was to take the widow in marriage to provide the deceased with an heir (Deut. 25:5–10; see Gen. 38:6–26; Ruth 3–4).[2] The law was primarily motivated by the desire to keep the brother's inheritance in the family—"his widow must not marry outside the family" (Deut. 25:5). In the Sadducees' contrived case study, the first brother died with no children to carry on his name. Each of the other brothers married the widow according to the levirate custom and each died childless, until finally the hard-luck widow herself died.[3] With relish, the Sadducees spring the punch line, designed to ridicule belief in the resurrection, "At the resurrection whose wife will she be, since the seven were married to her?" (12:23). Behind this spoof lies a crass assumption that resurrection life will be no different from life as we experience it on earth—except, in this case, more chaotic.

---

2. The term *levirate* is derived from the Latin word for brother, *levir*.

3. Compare the story of Sarah, whose seven husbands had each died on their marriage night (Tobit 3:8; 6:14).

Jesus follows his pattern of dealing with hostile questioners by going on the attack. His response fits a chiastic pattern:

a. You are in error [*planao*].
　b. You do not know the Scriptures.
　　c. You do not know the power of God.
　　c.' [The power of God] raises the dead and they become like angels.
　b.' [Scripture is cited] In the bush passage, the God of Abraham, Isaac, and Jacob is God of the living.
a.' You are badly mistaken [*planao*].

This structure reveals the emphases in Jesus' counterattack that get to the heart of the matter: The Sadducees are deceived because they are ignorant of Scripture and underestimate the power of God.

Jesus first corrects the Sadducees on their view of the resurrection life. They should not compare the resurrection life to life on earth. Resurrection does not mean the continuation of the same thing, only longer. The resurrected are transfigured into a new dimension of life that we have never experienced (see 9:2–3; Rev. 7:9–17).[4]

Jesus then corrects the Sadducees' biblical ignorance by reminding them of the "bush" passage in the Pentateuch that identifies God as the God of Abraham, Isaac, and Jacob (Ex. 3:6).[5] Would God claim to be the God of ghostly shadows or of those who no longer exist? The living God would hardly identify himself as the God of corpses. He does not say, "I was their God," but "I am their God." God remains their God even in death. The Sadducees do not reckon with God's power or God's love to give them life again (see 1 Cor. 6:14). The angel testifies at the conclusion of this Gospel that God is more powerful than death (Mark 16:6; see Rom. 4:17). Jesus' parting shot, "You are badly mistaken," affirms that some truths are not open to debate.

---

4. If the resurrected are "like the angels," Jewish tradition assumed that they do not eat and drink (Tobit 12:19) or marry (1 Enoch 15:6–7; 104:4; 2 Apoc. Bar. 51:9–10).

5. Prior to chapter and verse divisions, one could only cite Scripture by describing a distinguishing feature of the passage; see Rom. 11:2, where Paul uses the phrase "in Elijah" to refer to the passage about Elijah in 1 Kings 19.

Bridging Contexts

MANY PEOPLE IN the ancient world did not believe in an afterlife. Archaeologists have uncovered tombstones inscriptions that were so common they were abbreviated like R.I.P. (Rest in Peace). They read: "I was not. I was. I am not. I do not care." The following are two examples, each including a parting word.

I did not exist, I was born; I existed, I do not exist; so much (for that). If anyone says anything different, he will be lying: I shall not exist. Greetings, if you are a just person.
My child guard yourself lest you trip: the tongue itself is not troubled, indeed, whenever it speaks; but whenever it errs it contributes many evils.[6]

When I had just tasted life fate snatched me, an infant, and I did not see my father's pattern; but I died after enjoying the light of eleven months, then I returned it. I lie in the tomb forever, no longer seeing the light; but you, stranger, read this and weep as you come upon the tomb of Eunoe.[7]

The use of the "I" suggests that the "I don't care" is a faked swagger. They do care and do long to continue after they are dead. But there did not seem to be any reasonable hope. Christianity offered the promise of resurrection, a promise not offered elsewhere.

Many people today do not know what to think about an afterlife. Some take for granted that they will continue in a blessed afterlife with God, no matter how they related to God in this life. Many assume that the human soul is indestructible. Like the black box in an airplane it survives the crash of death. Some believe in reincarnation. Others conjecture nothing and believe nothing. They are consoled by a "maybe" or assume that a total lack of consciousness after death makes the whole issue unimportant. Most persons are so absorbed with life here and now that thought for the future after death never arises.

Jesus appeals only to Scripture and our experience with God to answer the doubters. One should follow his example and resist any attempt to make the case for resurrection from supposed scientific, empirical proof. The

---

6. IG XIV (1890) 1201; cited by G. H. R. Horsley, *New Documents Illustrating Early Christianity 1979* (North Ryde: Macquarie Univ. Press, 1987), 4:42.

7. IG XIV (1890) 1607 + 2171; cited by Horsley, *New Documents Illustrating Early Christianity 1979*, 4:40.

near-death experiences of some, for example, may be shown simply to be the chemical reactions of a brain shutting down. Belief in the resurrection does not derive from what we can prove. Our faith in the resurrection is based on our faith in the power of God and that alone. Our hope cannot be based on human egoism that longs to survive the grave but only in God, who makes alive. The New Testament teaches that the same God who gave us life in the first place will miraculously give us life again. John Baillie wrote:

> If the individual can commune with God, then he must matter to God; and if he matters to God, he must share God's eternity. For if God really rules, He can't be conceived as scrapping what is precious in his sight.[8]

One may guess that death must be something very much like birth. Before birth the child is totally surrounded in what is a safe and warm environment and gets all of his life from his mother. But he does not see his mother. When birth comes, it must be quite a shock to the child. The baby leaves the safe and warm confines of the mother's womb and enters a harsh, bright, cold world. But only after birth is the child able to see its mother and be held and kissed. In life on this earth we are totally surrounded by God, who sustains our lives. But God remains invisible to us. When death comes to each of us, it may be a shock to the system, but then we will see the God who gave us life, nourished us, and gives us life again (1 John 3:2).

JESUS IS NOT interested in carrying on a dialogue with those who disbelieve. Mark does not describe the reaction of the Sadducees to Jesus' argument. He does not say that they were shocked at his answer as the Pharisees and Herodians were (12:17). They probably remained hardened in their skepticism. Most do not come to faith in God's care for each individual and power to raise each one through arguments and proofs. Nevertheless, the church must present its arguments for its faith as Jesus did to counter false views.

The media gives its fantasy version of what happens in death through popular movies. Those images have an enormous subliminal effect on both Christians and non-Christians. The church must give its answer. It needs to proclaim its message clearly to a confused world that is much deceived as the Sadducees were. As Paul recognized, the resurrection is central to our faith. If there is no resurrection from the dead, then we are fools (1 Cor. 15:17–19). Jesus' response to the Sadducees' challenge helps us see what to empha-

---

8. John Baillie, *And the Life Everlasting* (Oxford: Oxford Univ. Press, 1934), 107.

size and what to ignore. He rejects the Sadducees' mistaken earthly images of resurrection life and seizes on an individual's relationship to God. We should avoid attempts to describe what heavenly life is like. Instead, we should highlight the necessity of a close tie to the heavenly Father, who keeps his promises.

One danger in portraying the resurrection life to come is that our image tends to match our wishes for an earthly utopia. The Sadducees derived their illustration from those who painted pictures of the resurrection life in worldly terms. Most envision the resurrection body as a spruced-up version of our physical bodies, and we visualize heaven in earthly terms that suit our own desires. We can see this tendency in contemporary cartoons that depict people floating on clouds, still occupied by the same concerns that they had on earth. Movies also depict ghosts still involving themselves in earthly life, wandering aimlessly about as disembodied spirits, or being summoned from the dead.

Many Christians who believe in the resurrection also view it from a defective anthropocentric point of view. They visualize the afterlife as a great reunion of family and friends—a continuation of life on earth without all the problems that hamper our happiness. Just analyze gospel songs that describe what heaven is like to see the truth of this statement. It is easy to understand why this is so. The family is the place where most experience unconditional love. The problem is that the idea of meeting God takes a backseat. That may be attributable to the failure to have met God while alive on earth. The major danger in trying to portray the resurrection life is that our image more often than not matches our wishes for an earthly utopia, and human beings wind up as the center of this life rather than God.

We should learn from Jesus' reticence in this passage to describe the resurrection life. He says that the Sadducees are quite mistaken in their views, but he does not correct them by giving a more complete picture. In fact, he gives no description of the afterlife, which is understandable. How can we comprehend anything except in earthly images? It would be like trying to explain to persons who lived all their lives isolated on Arctic tundra what a tropical beach is like. Only with difficulty could one describe palm trees, a sandy beach, colorful birds, fish, shells, and coral to someone who has no conception of such things. It would be easier to describe the landscape by telling them what was *not* there: no snow, polar bears, ice floes, freezing winds. The Sadducees pictured the resurrection life in terms of what they were familiar with in earthly life, and it naturally made no sense. Jesus only tells them what is not there: no marriage or giving in marriage.

Jesus' answer to the Sadducees' ridicule of the resurrection scraps their naive view that heaven will be like earth. The resurrection life is like our life on earth in only one way: The relationship that an individual has with God continues beyond death. While relationships among family members and friends, as dear as they are, are severed temporarily by death, nothing, not even death, separates us from God. Being a child of God is therefore not some transitory experience. It lasts forever. The Christian faith affirms that each individual life is important to God, not as a part of some family unit, but as an individual. The same God who gave us life in the first place has the power to raise us to new life. If one does not have a relationship with God in this life, however, one can hardly expect to begin one in the next.

Many today who do not know God believe that dead is dead and that the only thing that lives on is the legacy of one's children and one's notable works. Nietzsche, Marx, and Freud claimed that hope in the resurrection stifles caring about the serious matters of this life. They have been shown wrong by the imposed atheism of governments. There is a direct relation between belief in the life to come and ethical responsibility. A citizen of one of those countries said that the state has taken away belief in the resurrection of the dead, and we have seen a consequent growth in crime and immorality because people have been taught to live only for today and only for themselves. We see the same in nations whose citizens are practical atheists—those who live as if there is no God.

Mark 12:28–44

❦

ONE OF THE teachers of the law came and heard them debating. Noticing that Jesus had given them a good answer, he asked him, "Of all the commandments, which is the most important?"

29"The most important one," answered Jesus, "is this: 'Hear, O Israel, the Lord our God, the Lord is one. 30Love the Lord your God with all your heart and with all your soul and with all your mind and with all your strength.' 31The second is this: 'Love your neighbor as yourself.' There is no commandment greater than these."

32"Well said, teacher," the man replied. "You are right in saying that God is one and there is no other but him. 33To love him with all your heart, with all your understanding and with all your strength, and to love your neighbor as yourself is more important than all burnt offerings and sacrifices."

34When Jesus saw that he had answered wisely, he said to him, "You are not far from the kingdom of God." And from then on no one dared ask him any more questions.

35While Jesus was teaching in the temple courts, he asked, "How is it that the teachers of the law say that the Christ is the son of David? 36David himself, speaking by the Holy Spirit, declared:

"'The Lord said to my Lord:
"Sit at my right hand
until I put your enemies
under your feet." '

37David himself calls him 'Lord.' How then can he be his son?"

The large crowd listened to him with delight.

38As he taught, Jesus said, "Watch out for the teachers of the law. They like to walk around in flowing robes and be greeted in the marketplaces, 39and have the most important seats in the synagogues and the places of honor at banquets. 40They devour widows' houses and for a show make lengthy prayers. Such men will be punished most severely."

41Jesus sat down opposite the place where the offerings were put and watched the crowd putting their money into the temple treasury. Many rich people threw in large amounts. [42]But a poor widow came and put in two very small copper coins, worth only a fraction of a penny.

[43]Calling his disciples to him, Jesus said, "I tell you the truth, this poor widow has put more into the treasury than all the others. [44]They all gave out of their wealth; but she, out of her poverty, put in everything—all she had to live on."

THE DEBATES IN the temple with the enemies of Jesus continue. In this section Jesus answers a question given by a teacher of the law regarding the greatest commandment. Jesus then offers a puzzle of his own about David's Son. This section closes with some words of denunciation from Jesus against the Jewish leaders and his observation concerning a widow's gift in the temple.

The Greatest Commandment (12:28–34)

AFTER JESUS SILENCES the Sadducees with his argument for the resurrection, a teacher of the law, pleased with what Jesus has done, prods him with another issue, "Of all the commandments, which is the most important?" The question assumes a distinction among the various commands found in God's law. Later rabbinic tradition gave the total number of commandments as 613, of which 248 were positive commands and 365 prohibitions. Some were considered to be lighter (smaller) and some weightier (greater).

This teacher is not asking which laws need to be obeyed and which can safely be ignored. He is asking, "What is the fundamental premise of the law on which all the individual commands depend?" Jesus gives an orthodox reply from the daily confession of Israel known as the *Shema*.[1] The confession proclaims that God is the only God, and one is to love him with one's whole being: heart, soul, mind, and strength. But one cannot love God in isolation from one's other relationships in life. For this reason, Jesus couples the command to love God with the command to love one's neighbor as oneself (Lev. 19:18; cf. Rom. 13:10; 15:1–2; Gal. 5:14; James 2:8).

Love is our inner commitment to God that is expressed in all our conduct and relationships. Those who do not show love to others can hardly claim to love God (see 1 John 3:14–18; 4:8, 10–12, 20–22). The statement that

---

1. *Shema* is the Hebrew imperative "to hear." The confession comes from Deut. 6:4–9; 11:13–21; and Num. 15:37–41. The first item discussed in the *Mishnah* concerns the times to recite the *Shema* each day (*m. Ber. 1:1*).

no other command is greater than these two can mean that the other commands simply spell out different ways in which to apply these two primary ones. Or it may be more radical: These are the only two commands that matter. A key passage in the *Mishnah*, *'Abot* 1:2, teaches, "The world rests on three things: the Torah, sacrificial worship, and expressions of love." Jesus does not merely set love above Torah and sacrifice, he ignores them altogether.[2] Paul reflects this radical understanding in Romans 13:8 when he writes that "he who loves his fellowman has fulfilled the law."

The teacher of the law had applauded Jesus' refutation of the Sadducees (12:28) and now affirms that Jesus has answered his question well (12:32). He repeats that answer and adds that these two commands are "more important than all burnt offerings and sacrifices" (12:33).[3] This affirmation occurs in the context of Jesus' prophetic condemnation of the temple worship when he overturned the tables (11:15–17) and before Jesus' announcement of the temple's destruction (13:2). It therefore provides a scribal endorsement of Jesus' own position.

At the time Mark wrote, the temple was inaccessible for worship, either because a brutal war was going on and it was occupied by brigands and besieged by Romans or because the war had ended and the temple was reduced to ashes. The statement by the teacher of the law reinforces for Mark's first readers that the temple cult was irrelevant for fulfilling God's most vital demands. When people truly exude love for God and for others, they have offered the one sacrifice that is well pleasing to God. That affirmation also shows Mark's community that those who believe that Jesus is the Christ do not deviate from the fundamental core of Jewish belief: the hope of the resurrection and God's primary ethical demands.

Jesus only partially affirms what the teacher of the law has said. He had assumed a superior position from which he passed judgment on Jesus' teaching. Jesus puts things in proper perspective as the final arbiter of the interpretation of the law and, what is more important, as the one who knows who is near or far from the kingdom of God. This teacher of the law is not far from the kingdom. He is not in—that is, he has not fully chosen God's rule for himself—but he does not have far to go. This answer effectively silences the teacher. To be "in the kingdom" one must do more than simply approve of Jesus' teaching; one must submit entirely to his authority and person. Can he make the next step and accept Jesus as the Son of David and David's Lord?

---

2. Walter Grundmann, "μέγας," *TDNT*, 4:536.

3. One finds similar sentiments expressed in the Old Testament: 1 Sam. 15:22; Ps. 51:16–17; Isa. 1:11; Jer. 7:21–23; Hos. 6:6.

Jesus' Question About David's Son (12:35–37)

JESUS NOW OFFERS a puzzle of his own about David's Son. Hooker points out that when Jesus teaches publicly in the temple, he "comes closer to revealing his identity than anywhere else."[4] He cites the official scribal position that the Messiah is to be the Son of David.[5] They are correct, but only partially. Their view needs to be supplemented because they do not fully comprehend God's plans for the Messiah.

The teachers of the law represent teaching authority in Israel. Jesus admits they have correct theological answers, but their views always need amending. They taught that Elijah must come first, and Jesus concurs (9:11); but they were unable to recognize Elijah when he came. A teacher knows that the two greatest commands are greater than all burnt offerings and sacrifices, but he remains outside the kingdom of heaven as long as he fails to submit to Jesus' authority (12:28–34). Now we learn that the Jewish leaders teach that the Messiah is the Son of David (12:35). The issue about the Son of David harks back to Bartimaeus's hailing Jesus as the Son of David (10:47, 48) and to the cries of adulation when Jesus entered the city (11:10, "the coming kingdom of our father David"). It also recalls the tenants in the parable, who recognized the son as the heir, and it points forward to the crucial question raised at Jesus' trial by the high priest, "Are you the Christ, the Son of the Blessed One?" (14:61).

Jesus cites Psalm 110:1 to point out a conundrum. If the Messiah is the Son of David, why does David address him "by the Holy Spirit" as Lord? It is hardly customary for fathers to address their sons in this way. One expects quite the reverse. How then can the Messiah be David's Son? Jesus leaves it to his audience to figure out the answer. The reader also must infer that David was referring to someone other than his descendants who built the dynasty after him. He must be referring to someone greater than him and to a regime greater than his.

Mark frequently challenges his readers to understand more of Jesus' full identity by posing questions (see 4:41; 8:29; 11:28). This tantalizer serves to correct the crowd's exultation over "the coming kingdom of our father David." The old "imperial vision" shouted by the crowds needs correcting.[6] Jesus does not wield the political and military authority of David,[7] yet he is greater than the great king of Israel. The kingdom that he brings is greater than that of "our father David"; it is the kingdom of the Father.

---

4. Hooker, *Mark*, 293.

5. See Ps. 18:49–50; Isa. 9:2–7; 11:1–9; Jer. 23:5–6; 33:14–18; Ezek. 34:23–24; 37:24; Amos 9:11–12.

6. Myers, *Binding*, 319.

7. Kingsbury, *The Christology of Mark's Gospel*, 102–14, 248.

Mark reports that the large crowd heard Jesus gladly. This response to his teaching may be less heartening than it seems. The people do not realize that Jesus subverts all of their hopes. The careful reader may remember that Herod also heard John gladly (6:20), but that did not prevent him from beheading this esteemed prophet. A crowd (perhaps composed of different persons) will soon be howling for Jesus' crucifixion (15:13).

The Denunciation of the Teachers of the Law (12:38–40)

AFTER COMMENDING A particular teacher of the law and citing the Jewish theological leaders' opinion about the Son of David, Jesus proceeds to denounce them as a class. First, he chastens them for their desire to wear distinguished dress—they like to parade about in long robes. What precisely these long robes were is not important. Why they wore them is—to set themselves apart from others and to augment their authority. Jesus' authority is connected to his teaching (1:22; 11:27); theirs is connected to their clothing, which also expresses pride that hungers for honors and distinction and arrogance that flaunts its learning and position. What is worse, because they wear flowing robes in the temple, they exalt themselves in the presence of the Lord. An impressive outward appearance hides nothing from Jesus, however (see 13:1–2), and he sees through their pretense.

Jesus also condemns the longing of these teachers of the law for human adulation. They bask in the esteem bestowed on them by those of lesser status, who honor them with formal greetings (contrast 10:18!; see John 5:44; 12:43). He attacks their fight for the first seats in the synagogues and the places of honor at feasts. Jesus demanded the opposite attitude in his disciples when they showed signs of the same egocentrism (9:35; 10:31, 43–44). The longing of the teachers of the law for prestige, however, is coupled with a calloused disregard for the poor. Those who are revered by others mistake that as a license to prey on the weak and vulnerable. They may know what the greatest commands are, but they do not fulfill them. They love recognition more than they love God, and they trample on those who are already crushed.

Jesus accuses the teachers of the law of devouring widows' houses.[8] Widows traditionally symbolized the helpless in the Old Testament, and abusing them was sternly denounced. Isaiah (in Isa. 10:1–4) warned that those who robbed widows would be destroyed.

---

8. The situation may have to do with the dishonest management of the estates of widows, who did not manage their own affairs (J. Duncan M. Derrett, "'Eating Up the Houses of Widows': Jesus' Comment on Lawyers?" *NovT* 14 [1972]: 1–9). Or it may refer to their "sponging off the hospitality of widows" (Gundry, *Mark*, 727).

> Woe to those who make unjust laws,
>> to those who issue oppressive decrees,
> to deprive the poor of their rights
>> and withhold justice from the oppressed of my people,
> making widows their prey
>> and robbing the fatherless.
> What will you do on the day of reckoning,
>> when disaster comes from afar?
> To whom will you run for help?
>> Where will you leave your riches?
> Nothing will remain but to cringe among the captives
>> or fall among the slain.
> Yet for all this, his anger is not turned away,
>> his hand is still upraised.[9]

Finally, Jesus castigates the prayers of these teachers of the law. The temple was supposed to be a place of prayer (11:24), but Jesus attacks the motives behind their "lengthy prayers." Prayers supposedly addressed to God are spoken to win accolades from human eavesdroppers. They do not recognize how despicable their insincerity is and fool themselves into believing that human admiration for their piety accords with God's.

The Widow's Offering (12:41–44)

JESUS' PRESENCE IN the temple began with his condemnation of the buyers and sellers for the animal sacrifices and ends with his commendation of a widow who sacrifices her all for God. He situates himself opposite the treasury— probably a reference to one of thirteen shofar-chests (boxes shaped like a trumpet) that stood around the court of women rather than some special chamber (see John 8:20). The verb "to throw" suggests throwing into a chest. The Mishnaic tractate on the half-shekel dues mentions that shofar-chests were labeled for different types of offerings.[10] The small amount of the widow's contribution suggests that her gift could only go to the free-will offering, which went to the building of the temple (see Ex. 35–36; 1 Chron. 29), or for burnt offerings, from which the priests received the hides (*m. Seqal.* 6:6; *t. Seqal.* 3:8).

---

9. See also Ex. 22:21–23; Deut. 10:17; 24:17; Isa. 1:17, 23; 10:2; Ezek. 22:7.

10. They were designated as "new shekel dues," "old shekel dues" (paid only by males), "bird offerings" (for the purchase of turtle doves), "young birds for whole offerings" (for the purchase of pigeons), "wood" (for burning on the altar), "frankincense," "gold for the mercy seat," and six others as "free-will offerings" (*m. Seqal.* 6:5–6).

Jesus disregards the wealthy donors who throw in large sums that are probably announced by the loud clang they make in the trumpet bell (see Matt. 6:2). The rich were still rich even after a sizable offering. Instead, Jesus singles out a woman whose offering makes only a tiny clink. Mark describes her as "a *poor* widow," not just a widow. Has she been robbed of her house? Her offering is only a pittance—two *lepta*. The *lepton* was the smallest Greek coin (Mark translates it into the smallest Roman coin, the *quadrans*). It had the least value of any in circulation in the time of Jesus.[11] Jesus praises this woman for giving "all she had to live on." While religious leaders may prefer the large gifts, in the divine currency exchange these can swiftly deflate to nothing. God cares not about the money but about the giver's heart. The woman gives God all of her heart, soul, and substance. Jesus is about to make an even greater sacrifice.

The resounding of the trumpet when the rich toss in their silver dwarfs the tinkling of the widow's two coins. But her sacrificial devotion eclipses their perfunctory donations. The rich give from their abundance, but they do not sacrifice their abundance. This poor widow gives all that she has to live on, which is next to nothing. Her unassuming piety sharply contrasts with the conspicuous impiety of the scribes in the preceding denunciation. She shows radical trust in God to provide for her and gives what is surplus for this day to God.

MARK IDENTIFIES JESUS' third questioner as "a teacher of the law." One might expect him to be as hostile as the Pharisees, Herodians, and Sadducees before him, because Mark has told us that the high priests and teachers of the law were seeking how to destroy him (11:18). These teachers have also opposed Jesus before (2:6–7; 3:22), and Jesus' life ends as they, along with the chief priests, taunt him while he suffers on the cross (15:22). But even enemies may be near the kingdom and ready to be instructed.[12] One may find common ground with sworn enemies and should never write them off. The fundamental principles that governed Jesus' ministry—unconditional love of God and neighbor—were not unique to him. They derive from Scripture, and any who honor Scripture can

---

11. It was equivalent to 1/4 of a Roman *as*, which was estimated to be 1/16 of a denarius. It was therefore equal to 1/64 of the wage for the day laborers who work in the vineyard (Matt. 20:2). See D. Sperber, "Mark xii 42 and Its Metrological Background," *NovT* 9 (1967): 178–90.

12. Minear, *Mark*, 114.

recognize this fact. The question is whether they will also recognize that Jesus is the fulfillment of the hopes of Israel detailed in Scripture.

The touching story of the widow and her two copper coins has been used as an example of sacrificial giving. I would not disagree that one can interpret this text beneficially in this way. This woman is a classic example of one who loves God with everything she has. She contrasts with the rich because she is impoverished. She contrasts with the teachers of the law who revel in their mystique as learned and pious. As another victim who has fallen through what safety net there was, she has no honor in this society. She still loves God, however, and will sacrifice all that she has for her whole living in service to God.

One can draw three lessons from her example. (1) Jesus commends those who give because they seek God, not because they seek benefits from God (see 1 Tim. 5:5). (2) So-called little gifts, which count as nothing among humans, may eclipse those gifts that have value into the millions. One cannot build magnificent buildings like this temple with its great stones (13:1) on the meager gifts of widows. But Jesus singles out her offering as the most significant. It reminds us that even the poorest "can make a worthy offering to God."[13] (3) If one assumes that the rich were offering God their tithes, this incident reveals a problem with tithing, which focuses on how much we give and allows us to ignore how much we keep for ourselves. The widow serves as a model for the sacrificial discipleship that Jesus requires (see 10:21). It may cost disciples who live through the woes catalogued in the next discourse their whole livelihood.[14]

One can give this incident a quite different spin, which laments that this widow gives so sacrificially to this den of thieves. The woman is to be praised, but giving sacrificially to a corrupt, spiritually bankrupt, and oppressive temple is to be lamented.[15] She exhibits unquestioning devotion to the temple, a fruitless cause that exploits her. The high priests live in luxury on their cut from the contributions made by the poor. Hers is a misguided gesture, a case of the poor giving to the rich, the victim lining the pockets of the oppressor. The costs to operate this extravagant temple are therefore one of the things that "devour the resources of the poor."[16]

---

13. Hooker, *Mark*, 296.

14. Frederick Danker, "Double-Entendre in Mark XII," *NovT* 10 (1968): 115.

15. See Addison G. Wright, "The Widow's Mites: Praise or Lament?—A Matter of Context?" *CBQ* 44 (1982): 256–65, and the response of Elizabeth Struthers Malbon, "The Poor Widow in Mark and Her Poor Rich Readers," *CBQ* 53 (1991): 589–604, on the problems of context.

16. Myers, *Binding*, 320.

The temple, in other words, has become a place where widows are robbed (see Isa. 1:14–17, where the prophet connects God's rejection of sacrifice to their injustice to widows and orphans). Now that she has given all she has, what will happen to her? Who in the temple hierarchy will help her? What will happen to all the money? Will some of it be used to bribe Judas to betray his master? She throws away her living for the sake of the temple. The temple overlords will throw away Jesus' life to preserve their power base. The new community centered around Jesus places a priority on people rather than cultic rituals and grand edifices that are subject to destruction. What is important is the demonstration of humble faith, sacrificial devotion to God, and care for the poor and needy (1 Tim. 5:16; James 1:27).

OUR LOVE FOR God is a response to God's love for us. Israel confessed that the one true God was the God of Abraham, Isaac, and Jacob, not some generic god. Christians confess that this God is also the one who meets us in Jesus Christ. It is impossible to love with all our heart some New Age principle or some cosmic force. We can, however, give our whole life to a personal God who has first loved us in such dramatic fashion as to send the beloved Son to give his life for us.

God does not love only certain portions of us, but the whole person; therefore, we are to love God with our whole selves. God does not save us by fractions, and we are not to offer to God a mere fraction of ourselves. Jesus warns elsewhere that as the slave cannot serve two masters, so it is impossible to divide our allegiance between two masters, God and Mammon (Matt. 6:24; Luke 16:13). We will be ruled by one or the other. The one who is double-minded will inevitably fall sway to Mammon. One cannot seek power, wealth, empire, and sensual gratification and at the same time be submissive to God's will.

Those who present to God a few moments worship in church once a week while ignoring God in the rest of life—at work, at home, at play—will suffer from a religious schizophrenia. Those who try to straddle the fence by allotting God only token love while maintaining a bosom friendship with the world are doomed to be frustrated in this world and doomed in the world to come. With God, it is all or nothing. Love cannot be tithed like money. Few can honestly sing "All to Jesus I Surrender," but God requires nothing less.

(1) We must love God with *all our heart*. In the Bible, the "heart" is more than a pumping station. It is the command center of the body, where decisions are made and plans are hatched. It is the center of our inner being, which controls our feelings, emotions, desires, and passions. The heart is

where religious commitment takes root. It is in our innermost being, where we decide for or against God. We can give assent with our mind and lips, but it is the telltale heart that betrays our true loyalties (7:6).

The elder brother in Jesus' parable of the prodigal son provides a good example of this. Unlike his younger brother, he stayed home and obeyed his father's every command (Luke 15:29). But his heart was not in it, or else he would not have begrudged his father's joy at the return of a lost son. He performed his duties with the heart of a slave, not as a loving son. Deep within he probably longed to be in the far country too. Jesus said that where our treasure is, there our heart will be (Matt. 6:21), and God expects to be the centerpiece.

Everyone perceived the teachers of the law as models of those who loved God. But Jesus saw through their religious showmanship and examined their hearts. They were in love with themselves, their position, and their financial and religious success. The widow was destitute and without honor, but she showed that she loved God no less for it.

Jesus also taught that what really defiles a person is what comes out of the heart—evil thoughts, evil deeds, and doubt (7:21–22). It is in our hearts where our belief and commitment to God take root. Consequently, the new creation must begin in the heart (Ezek. 11:19). This word is particularly applicable for a generation of persons who ramble aimlessly through life and give their hearts to everything and nothing. Those who give their hearts completely to God have set themselves on a spiritual magnetic north, which will keep them from ever being lost.

(2) We must love God with *all our soul*. God gave breath to the soul of humans. The "soul" is the source of vitality in life. It is the motivating power that brings strength of will. Together with the heart, the soul determines conduct. When we are commanded to love God with all our soul, it refers to the power of our lives. The apostle Paul provides a good example of someone who loved God with all his soul. All of his energies were focused on pursuing God's purposes in his life. He wrote, "But one thing I do" (Phil. 3:13). It was this commitment that drove him to do and suffer all that he did for Christ (see 2 Cor. 11:23–29). His soul was so consumed by God that he was constrained to preach, to press on, and to fight the good fight. Those who love God with all their soul will, like Paul, commit all of their energy and strength to him.

(3) We must love God with *all our mind*. The "mind" is the faculty of perception and reflection that directs our opinions and judgments. Our love for God requires more than an emotional response or a swirl of activity in God's name. We must love God with our intelligence. The statement, "I would rather feel compunction than know how to define it," is on target.

But God does not want us to check our minds in the vestibule when we enter to worship. Thinking about our faith is not something to fear; it is a requirement. God has no use for lazy minds.

What can God do with those who are content to remain forever in spiritual kindergarten and never progress beyond "Now I lay me down to sleep" prayers? The early Christians were tough-minded. They not only outlived and outdied their enemies; the writings of the New Testament testify that they also outthought them. They read, studied, wrote, and served God with all their minds. Christians today should not be conformed to the thinking of this world (Rom. 12:2), but they do little to advance the faith if others can easily dismiss them as ignoramuses.[17] We need to commit our minds to God so that we can offer our society the vital "know why" to all our impressive "know how."

(4) We must love God with *all our strength*. "Strength" refers to one's physical capacities, including one's possessions. The widow provides the best example of this love. She did not come to the temple to recite prayers, she gave all that she had to live on. The rich gave God what they skimmed off the top of their abundance. She gave out of her lack and did not worry about what she would have left over.

(5) We must also *love our neighbors as ourselves*. This command assumes a healthy egoism and encourages an enlightened self-interest. We want others to deal with us according to their highest ideals rather than according to our merits. In the parable of the good Samaritan (Luke 10:25–37), Jesus expands the definition of neighbor to include those whom we would write off as enemies. One can never ask, "Who is my neighbor?" because the question implies that there is such a thing as a non-neighbor. Whoever needs me is my neighbor, and we express love with active compassion and justice.

Loving our neighbor does not mean that we never confront them with their evil. Jesus did not shy away from offending the powerful religious establishment. He attacked their hypocrisy and injustice. Kierkegaard followed that offensive example in calling the Danish priests paid by the state "parasites, quacks, counterfeiters, cannibals, knavish tradesmen."[18] Jesus zeroed in on the contrived authority, the dress for success mentality, and the pomposity of the Jewish leaders. They exulted in the testimonials to their righteousness, which was duly registered by their plaques and medals.

---

17. See discussion in Mark A. Noll, *The Scandal of the Evangelical Mind* (Grand Rapids: Eerdmans, 1994).

18. David McCracken, *The Scandal of the Gospels: Jesus, Story and Offense* (New York/Oxford: Oxford Univ. Press, 1994), 64.

Paul Minear asks, "Is there any society which does not grant these recognitions, or which does not encourage the desire for them?"[19] Jesus would answer that the church should not. James also condemns this dangerous attitude (James 2:1–7). When Mr. Goldfinger comes to the assembly, he is given special treatment, flattery, perks such as special valet parking, and a special couch to sit on. This is the way one may expect to be treated at an expensive boutique, but not in a church. The reason people fawn over the rich and honorable is not because they love them but because they want to win their favor. The poor, on the other hand, are treated with contempt because people ask themselves, "What can they ever contribute to us?" Jesus looked at things from God's vantage point. The gleaming reputations of the pious and wealthy were stained by a mean-spirited oppression of the helpless poor. The widow, however, was rich in faith, the only thing that counts with God. She had the only honor worth striving for.

Jesus therefore concludes his stint in the temple with one last public protest against hypocritical worship and social abuses. Howard Thurman points out that many Negro spirituals were protest songs. One such protest song is familiar.

> I got shoes, you got shoes
> All God's chillun got shoes.
> When we get to Heaven
> We're goin' to put on our shoes
> An' shout all over God's Heaven

Thurman writes that before the next line these slaves, who many times did not have shoes and had no freedom to shout or walk all over God's earth, would look up at the big house where the master lived and sing:

> But everybody talking about Heaven
> Ain't going there.[20]

19. Minear, *Mark*, 115.

20. Howard Thurman, *Deep River: Reflections on the Religious Insight of Certain Negro Spirituals* (New York: Harper, 1955), 44.

Mark 13:1–37

✤

AS HE WAS leaving the temple, one of his disciples said to him, "Look, Teacher! What massive stones! What magnificent buildings!"

²"Do you see all these great buildings?" replied Jesus. "Not one stone here will be left on another; every one will be thrown down."

³As Jesus was sitting on the Mount of Olives opposite the temple, Peter, James, John and Andrew asked him privately, ⁴"Tell us, when will these things happen? And what will be the sign that they are all about to be fulfilled?"

⁵Jesus said to them: "Watch out that no one deceives you. ⁶Many will come in my name, claiming, 'I am he,' and will deceive many. ⁷When you hear of wars and rumors of wars, do not be alarmed. Such things must happen, but the end is still to come. ⁸Nation will rise against nation, and kingdom against kingdom. There will be earthquakes in various places, and famines. These are the beginning of birth pains.

⁹"You must be on your guard. You will be handed over to the local councils and flogged in the synagogues. On account of me you will stand before governors and kings as witnesses to them. ¹⁰And the gospel must first be preached to all nations. ¹¹Whenever you are arrested and brought to trial, do not worry beforehand about what to say. Just say whatever is given you at the time, for it is not you speaking, but the Holy Spirit.

¹²"Brother will betray brother to death, and a father his child. Children will rebel against their parents and have them put to death. ¹³All men will hate you because of me, but he who stands firm to the end will be saved.

¹⁴"When you see 'the abomination that causes desolation' standing where it does not belong—let the reader understand—then let those who are in Judea flee to the mountains. ¹⁵Let no one on the roof of his house go down or enter the house to take anything out. ¹⁶Let no one in the field go back to get his cloak. ¹⁷How dreadful it will be in those days for pregnant women and nursing mothers! ¹⁸Pray that this will not take place in winter, ¹⁹because those will be days of

distress unequaled from the beginning, when God created the world, until now—and never to be equaled again. ²⁰If the Lord had not cut short those days, no one would survive. But for the sake of the elect, whom he has chosen, he has shortened them. ²¹At that time if anyone says to you, 'Look, here is the Christ!' or, 'Look, there he is!' do not believe it. ²²For false Christs and false prophets will appear and perform signs and miracles to deceive the elect—if that were possible. ²³So be on your guard; I have told you everything ahead of time.

²⁴"But in those days, following that distress,

"'the sun will be darkened,
    and the moon will not give its light;
²⁵ the stars will fall from the sky,
    and the heavenly bodies will be shaken.'

²⁶"At that time men will see the Son of Man coming in clouds with great power and glory. ²⁷And he will send his angels and gather his elect from the four winds, from the ends of the earth to the ends of the heavens.

²⁸"Now learn this lesson from the fig tree: As soon as its twigs get tender and its leaves come out, you know that summer is near. ²⁹Even so, when you see these things happening, you know that it is near, right at the door. ³⁰I tell you the truth, this generation will certainly not pass away until all these things have happened. ³¹Heaven and earth will pass away, but my words will never pass away.

³²"No one knows about that day or hour, not even the angels in heaven, nor the Son, but only the Father. ³³Be on guard! Be alert! You do not know when that time will come. ³⁴It's like a man going away: He leaves his house and puts his servants in charge, each with his assigned task, and tells the one at the door to keep watch.

³⁵"Therefore keep watch because you do not know when the owner of the house will come back—whether in the evening, or at midnight, or when the rooster crows, or at dawn. ³⁶If he comes suddenly, do not let him find you sleeping. ³⁷What I say to you, I say to everyone: 'Watch!'"

Original Meaning

TENSION HAS BEEN building from Jesus' confrontations with opponents in the temple, but the action is suspended for his second lengthy discourse in Mark. The hostile examiners retreat into the background, and Jesus leaves the temple, never to return. On the eve of his own suffering, he predicts the suffering of his disciples, linking the two.[1] In the parable discourse in chapter 4, the theme was "hearing"; in this Olivet discourse the theme is "watching." Jesus' disciples must watch because evil will materialize in proud nationalism, false religion, and sacrilegious symbols that will threaten the elect. But Jesus confidently assures his disciples that ultimate victory falls hard on the heels of great tragedy and a full measure of suffering. Even when they are torn by Satan, the elect will be gathered by God.

After the introduction, where Jesus predicts the destruction of the temple (13:1–4), the discourse divides into three units. A double warning to watch out for false prophets and false messiahs brackets the first unit (13:5–23).[2] Jesus gives his disciples three temporal signposts of things that will happen: "when you hear of wars and rumors of wars" (13:7); "whenever you are arrested and brought to trial" (13:11); and "when you see 'the abomination that causes desolation'" (13:14). The charge not to be alarmed accompanies the first two warnings (13:7, 11); the third signals the time for them to flee from Judea (13:14). These signs, however, *are not* harbingers of the end. The disciples should not allow themselves to become entangled in false hopes or be paralyzed by false fears. This first unit forms a chiasm.

A. Deceivers (13:5–6, Watch!)
   B. International wars (13:7–8, When you hear . . .)
      C. Persecution of Christians (13:9–13, Watch!)
   B'. War in Judea (13:14–20, When you see . . .)
A'. Deceivers (13:21–23, Watch!)[3]

The second unit deals with the coming of the Son of Man (13:24–27). It will be unmistakable, but it will not be preceded by any premonitory signs to help one prepare for it. Cosmological upheaval will occur (13:24–25); "at that time" they will see him coming (13:26), and he will then send angels to gather the elect (13:27).

---

1. Francis Watson, "The Social Function of Mark's Secrecy Theme," *JSNT* 24 (1985): 61.

2. The command to "look!" (*blepete*, trans. "watch out" in 13:5 and "be on your guard" in 13:23) and the warning about being deceived (*planao, apoplanao*) appear at the beginning and the end of the unit (13:5–6 and 13:22–23).

3. The disciples initiate the discourse by asking, "Tell us . . . [about all] these things" (13:4a), and Jesus responds at the end of this unit, "I have told you everything ahead of time" (13:23).

The third unit concludes with the parables of the budding fig tree (13:28–29) and the watchful and indifferent doorkeepers (13:33–37). These parables surround Jesus' solemn declaration that no one, not even the Son, knows the hour (13:30–32).

Introduction (13:1–4)

AS JESUS DEPARTS the temple, the disciples are overawed by its magnificence. Anyone who has seen reconstructed models of the temple or read descriptions of it can understand why. Just as marvels of engineering prowess in our towns or cities kindle pride in us, so this imposing structure glistening in the sun inspired the disciples' awe. Josephus described its grandeur:

> Now the outward face of the temple in its front wanted nothing that was likely to surprise either men's mind or their eyes: for it was covered all over with plates of gold of great weight, and, at the first rising of the sun, reflected back a very fiery splendor, and made those who forced themselves to look upon it to turn their eyes away, just as they would have done at the suns' own rays. But this Temple appeared to strangers, when they were at a distance, like a mountain covered with snow; for, as to those parts of it that were not gilt, they were exceedingly white. . . . Of its stones, some of them were forty-five cubits in length, five in height and six in breadth.[4]

The temple also gave the Jews a sense of security because it was the place where God lived ("my resting place for ever and ever," Ps. 132:14). How could God ever abandon this beautiful house or allow it to be destroyed?

As the great harlot of Babylon mesmerized John (Rev. 17:6), the temple's awesome majesty electrifies the disciples, who are too much charmed by size, beauty, and economic might. Jesus reproaches them for their reverence and wonder, "Do you see all these great buildings?" When he tells them to look, he means more than take another good look at the great stones and buildings. "To see" means to look with perception. Jesus bids them to see through all the glitzy religiosity. What they do not yet see is the temple's barrenness. What they do not know is that this temple's overlords are preparing to exert all their power to destroy the disciples' teacher and that they will later train their sights on them. They do not see that the present splendor disguises the future devastation, when these great stones will soon become a pile of rubble.

The prophet Haggai recited the rallying cry—"Consider how things were before one stone was laid on another in the LORD's temple"—to spark

---

4. *J. W.* 5.5.6 §5.

a turning point in the rebuilding project (Hag. 2:15). If they built it, he said, God would come and bless the people.[5] Jesus makes exactly the opposite observation: God no longer blesses this temple, and stone upon stone will be cast down. What has been implicit in Jesus' actions in the temple now becomes explicit. He openly prophecies its complete destruction.[6] The temple belongs to an old order, whose builders will reject the stone that will become central to God's new temple. This temple has become obsolete, and God will allow it to be utterly destroyed.

Jesus abandons the temple and crosses over to the Mount of Olives, where he sits magisterially (see 4:1; 14:62).[7] When he earlier predicted his death and resurrection, the disciples never asked when it would happen; but talk of the temple's destruction temple sends off alarm bells in their heads. They clearly connect the temple's destruction to the end time, for they still see it as the center of their narrow universe. Peter, James, John, and now Andrew want to know exactly when this will occur and what is *the* sign so that they can prepare themselves for the catastrophe and perhaps escape its terrors (cf. Dan. 12:6–7; 4 Ezra 6:7).

Jesus gives them no single sign (see 8:11–12) but instead a flustering hodgepodge of signs, some true and some false, but none useful for predicting the time of the end. The true signs of the end come so fast that they will provide no warning at all (13:24–27). He therefore does not give them the confidential information they want. But he does give them *what they need*: instructions on how to discern the signs of the times so they will not be disheartened by persecution, panicked by wars, fooled by appearances, or led to apostasy by false prophets during uncertain and trying days. They need discernment to distinguish between what has to do with the end of their own little worlds and what has to do with the end of the world.

Warnings About the Destruction of the Temple (13:5–23)

HAVING PREDICTED THE destruction of the temple, Jesus now gives his disciples clues about what will happen, leading up to its demise. The central theme is that they should not be deceived by events or by false prophets. These things must happen before the end comes, but they do not augur the end. They need to heed Jesus' warnings to prevent being beguiled by end-time fervor. Terrible events will occur, but they only mean that one must

---

5. Noted by Lane, *Mark*, 452.

6. Compare Ps. 74:3–7; Jer. 7:14; 26:6–9; Mic. 3:9–12.

7. The Mount of Olives is where the glory of Yahweh withdraws from a corrupt Jerusalem: "The glory of the LORD went up from within city and stopped above the mountain east of it" (Ezek. 11:23).

break with the temple and flee from its domain. These events should not cause undue dread or hysteria or distract them from their calling.

Warning about deceivers who feed false hopes (13:5–6). Rather than giving his disciples "the sign," Jesus tells them what are not signs. He warns that they must "watch," though this command does not mean simply to "be on your guard." The word *blepo* in Mark calls for "discernment concerning realities which lie beyond the observations of the physical senses."[8] False prophets will come, who will feed false hopes (see Jer. 14:14–16; 23:21–25; 29:8–9). The disciples will need uncommon spiritual acumen to be able to withstand the deceivers and to weather the storms of persecution. They will need to keep their wits so that they will not be led astray in the midst of crises and cries of confusion.

The deceivers who come claiming "I am he" do not hail from Christian circles or come as representatives of Jesus. They usurp the name and lay claim for themselves divine authority that rightfully belongs only to Jesus. These messianic pretenders easily dupe their followers with dramatic gestures and daring declarations. Humans are free to choose for or against God, but that choice is made even more difficult by those who vest themselves with divine authority and tie themselves to divinely commissioned institutions. Ironically, Jesus announces, "I am he" (14:62; see 6:50), but he is not believed. The messianic frauds say, "I am he," and sweep many off their feet.[9] Since there will be a ceaseless parade of impostors, pretenders, and glory hounds, their appearance cannot be a sign of the end.[10] The disciples must steel themselves to see through these impostors and not be caught up in the excited delusions of the crowd.

Warning about wars and earthquakes that feed false fears (13:7–8). Jesus also warns about international commotions and natural disasters. These also should not cause excessive alarm. They are not a sign of the end or even that the end is near. Some thought the end of the world would be preceded by a great bloodbath, and when war threatened, many panicked that the last battle was about to begin. Jesus' warning seeks to correct the penchant to read current events and disasters as heralds of the end. When one stands in the middle of history, one can easily misjudge the importance of events on God's scale. Earthquakes, warfare, and famines are always happening somewhere. By say-

---

8. Geddert, *Watchwords*, 60, 146.

9. Hooker, *Mark*, 306.

10. Josephus castigates a group whom he claims were worse than the violent revolutionaries: "Cheats and deceivers, claiming inspiration, they schemed to bring about revolutionary changes by inducing the mob to act as if possessed and by leading them out into the wild country on the pretence that there God would give them signs of approaching freedom" (*J. W.* 2.13.4 §§ 258–60).

ing that wars "must happen" (13:7), Jesus assures his disciples that this mayhem is not out of the sovereign control of God. But wars bring death, not the
kingdom of God. They signify nothing more than human sinfulness.[11]

Jesus identifies these things as the "beginning of the birth pains"—a time
of suffering.[12] When the world is collapsing around them, Christians may
impatiently yearn for deliverance from their present distress. They must prepare themselves for the long haul, however. The suffering only marks the
beginning. One cannot know how long the labor will be, only that it will be
a hard delivery. What Jesus calls the "beginning of the birth pains" will
embrace him and covers "the entirety of the period during which Jesus' disciples bear witness, suffer persecution, and stand in danger of deception,
however long or short that period may turn out to be."[13] By comparing the
travail in history to the birth process, where the pain gets worse just before
delivery, however, Jesus conveys that things are not hopeless. The end is
certain,[14] and the torment will result in God's deliverance of the elect.

Warning about persecutions that can break resolve (13:9—13). The warning translated "You must be on your guard" (13:9) literally reads, "Watch yourselves."
The disciples are to attend to the personal implications of what will happen
to them during "the birth pains" and not to fix all their attention on cosmic
signs or international strife. Jesus gives these warnings so that they will not
be surprised and can respond appropriately when suffering overtakes them.[15]
They must grasp what it means to be persecuted as a Christian. These persecutions are of a different order than the preceding calamities. The disasters described in 13:5—8 overwhelm everyone in the path of the armies or
situated on geological fault lines. The persecutions sketched in 13:9—13,
however, specifically target Christians because they are Christians. They
will be singled out for persecution because they faithfully follow their Lord
(see 4:17).

Suffering and hatred come to Christ's followers because they preach the
gospel faithfully. They are not the sign of the end. Christians will be handed

---

11. Seneca wrote: "Man, naturally the gentlest class of being, is not ashamed to revel in
the blood of others, to wage war, and to entrust the waging of war to his sons, when even
dumb beasts and wild beasts keep peace with one another" (*Epistles to Lucilium*, 95.30—31).

12. For the image see, Isa. 26:17; 66:8—9; Jer. 22:23; Hos. 13:13; Mic. 4:9—10.

13. Gundry, *Mark*, 739.

14. See 4 Ezra 4:40—43: "Go ask a pregnant woman whether, when her nine months have
been completed, her womb can keep the fetus within her any longer. . . . No, Lord, it cannot."

15. Morna Hooker, "Trial and Tribulation in Mark XIII," *BJRL* 65 (1982): 86. Beasley-
Murray (*Jesus and the Last Days*, 404) comments, "Mark would call his starry-eyed fellow
Christians to cease gazing into heaven for intimations of the parousia and to further the wit-
ness to Christ in a world that continues to be hostile to the gospel."

over to "local councils" (lit., "sanhedrins"), flogged in synagogues, and brought before kings and governors. They will be loathed by everyone (13:13). Tacitus's account of how Nero tried to pin the guilt for the devastating fire in Rome on the Christians describes them as "a class hated for their abominations ... by the populace."[16] The "abomination" was their devotion to Jesus' name. The antagonism will be so intense that family members will even turn on other family members because they passionately hate the gospel or are desperate to escape persecution themselves.

When these things happen, astute disciples will realize they are suffering precisely what their Lord has prophesied. They also suffer what he himself endured. Jesus was betrayed by an initiate (14:43–45), was handed over to the Sanhedrin (14:55), was brought before the governor (15:1–5), was the victim of false testimony (14:59), was savagely mocked (14:64–65; 15:11–14, 19–20, 29–32), and was killed. He hopes that his disciples will understand that through their suffering the kingdom of God silently advances as they proclaim the gospel in the midst of trial and tribulation.[17]

The central issue that Jesus addresses is not how disciples can learn the timing of the end from external events but what they will do when they are handed over. Will they wilt under pressure? Will they succumb to temptation and renounce Christ to save their earthly lives? Jesus gives them assurance. They need not worry what to say. They may be uneducated in the art of rhetorical persuasion, but they will receive divine help (see Ex. 4:10–12). This assurance assumes that when they stand before the mighty in the halls of power as defendants, they need only worry about what to say that might convict their accusers of the truth. They will not have to worry about proving their innocence or escaping any judgment. Jesus promises only that they will receive divine help to preach, not divine deliverance, which comes only after death and after his final coming in glory.

In the midst of this bleak landscape of wars, starvation, atrocities, earthquakes, persecutions, and treachery, the one bright light is God's intention to get the word of the gospel out to all (13:10). It is necessary for the gospel to be preached first to the whole world. Tolbert interprets this statement to mean "The sooner the gospel is preached to all nations, the sooner the kingdom will arrive and all suffering will cease." Preaching is "the one human act that can expedite the demise of this present evil, oppressive, and suffering-filled existence."[18] This inference is mistaken. The timing of the end depends entirely on God, not on any human activity, including our preaching.

---

16. Tacitus, *Annals* 15.44.2, 4.
17. Geddert, *Watchwords*, 217.
18. Tolbert, *Sowing*, 265.

There is in fact nothing humans can do to hasten the end. Jesus only emphasizes the urgency of the evangelization of the world and warns that it will occur under the cloud of persecution. He assures his disciples that hatred and persecution will not silence their testimony. This prophecy that the gospel will be preached to the whole world also assures the reader that the pre-Easter cowardice of the disciples will somehow be transformed into bravery. It makes clear that the empty tomb is not the end of the gospel, only the beginning (1:1).

Warning about the war in Judea (13:14–20). The warning in these verses applies specifically to the first and second generation of Jesus' disciples, who will witness the war in Judea that will result in the destruction of the temple. What meaning can the command to flee Judea have for someone who does not live there? In other words, Jesus is not referring to the end time, which will affect the entire world, not just Judea. Who would be anxious to retrieve their garments or valuables if it were the end of the world? What difference would it make if it were winter or not, whether one was pregnant or not? The sympathy for the plight of those trying to flee when travel is difficult or impossible only makes sense if they are trying to evade the savagery of an advancing army.

The cue to take flight comes when they see the "abomination that causes desolation" (13:14), which refers to what is detestable and rejected by God and causes horror and destruction among humankind.[19] The term derives from Daniel 11:31, "His armed forces will rise up to desecrate the temple fortress and will abolish the daily sacrifice. Then they will set up the abomination that causes desolation" (cf. Dan. 8:13; 9:27; 12:11; also Jer. 7:30–34). In 168 B.C., Israel had already experienced what the author of 1 Maccabees (1 Macc. 1:54–56) identifies as an abomination of desolation, under the tyranny of Antiochus Epiphanes:

> Now on the fifteenth day of Chislev, in the one hundred forty-fifth year, they erected a desolating sacrilege on the altar of burnt offering. They also built altars in the surrounding towns of Judah, and offered incense at the doors of the houses and in the streets. The books of the law that they found they tore to pieces and burned with fire. (NRSV)

Since Jesus specifically mentions Judea and uses a phrase from Daniel referring to an enemy's desecration of the sanctuary, he is predicting some horrifying event in the temple. Therefore it applies to a time when the temple was still standing.

The masculine participle ("standing") modifying a neuter noun ("the abomination that causes desolation") suggests a reference to a person rather than

---

19. Beasley-Murray, *Jesus and the Last Days*, 411, 416.

some idolatrous object (see 2 Thess. 2:3–4, "the man of lawlessness ... [who] sets himself up in God's temple"). This grammatical irregularity may explain the admonition, "Let the reader understand." Modern Christians possess individual Bibles and study them privately, and we naturally assume that this aside advises an individual reader poring over the Gospel of Mark to take a hint (see Dan. 12:9–10).

But a hint about what? In contrast to the leads John gives in Revelation 13:11–18 to help identify the second beast, Mark offers no clues about what the reader is supposed to understand. Because we view Bible reading as something done mostly in private, most modern readers would not consider the possibility that Mark included this narrative aside for the one who publicly read the Gospel to the assembly (see Rev. 1:3). Individual copies of Scripture were rare, and it is more likely that this note instructs the one reading in Greek not to correct the masculine participle with a neuter noun out of some mistaken grammatical sensitivity. What Mark has written, he has written deliberately. The masculine participle makes "the abomination" refer to a person.[20] Best likens it to our modern *sic* that is placed after a word that seems odd or misspelled: "But when you see that thing, the abomination of desolation, standing where he [*sic*] should not be. ..."[21]

This dreadful atrocity in the temple could refer to something that occurs before the war against Rome, during that debacle, or after the defeat and the destruction of the temple. The chief candidate for something that occurred before the war is the directive from the emperor Gaius Caligula to have his statue erected in the temple in A.D. 40.[22] The problem with this option is that his order created only a temporary crisis and was never carried out. Knowing that this mandate would precipitate a violent uprising by the Jews, the legate of Syria, Petronius, stalled as long as he could. The emperor was assassinated before he could discipline his commander.

If it refers to something during the war, the heinous crimes of the Zealots who occupied the temple precincts during the last years of the war are prime candidates.[23] Josephus writes:

> For there was an ancient saying of inspired men that the city would
> be taken and the sanctuary burned to the ground by right of war,
> when it should be visited by sedition and native hands should be the

20. Ernest Best, "The Gospel of Mark: Who Is the Reader?" *Irish Biblical Studies* 11 (1989): 124–32.

21. Ibid., 129.

22. See Josephus, *J. W.* 2.10.1 §§ 184–203; *Ant.* 18.8.2–9 §§ 257–309; Philo, *Embassy to Gaius*; Tacitus *Histories.* 5.9.

23. Josephus *J. W.* 4.3.6–10 §§ 147–92; 4.5.4 §§ 334–44.

first to defile God's sacred precincts. This saying the Zealots did not disbelieve; yet they lent themselves as instruments of its accomplishments.[24]

Jesus could also be referring to something that occurred after the destruction of the temple. Josephus reports that after the capture of Jerusalem the Roman soldiers set up their standards in the temple and sacrificed to them. The problem with this view is that when this happened, it was already too late to flee the city.[25]

The allusion remains inside information that the original audience of the Gospel understood, but we are left only with guesses. In my opinion, it refers to some specific first-century phenomenon related to the war against Rome when it made sense to flee Jerusalem. It would be useless to flee to some mountain redoubt at the end of the ages. Whatever that abomination was, Mark intended the audience to understand it as a fulfillment of Daniel's prophecy and another sign of the beginning of the birth pains.

Jesus does not lament here over the temple's desecration, but he does express compassion for those caught in the cataclysm. During the Jewish war, many people fled *to* the temple fortress for refuge (cf. Jer. 4:6). Jesus counsels flight *away* from the temple (cf. Jer. 6:1; Rev. 18:4). Jerusalem will not be a stronghold of saving help but will become a dragon's lair, where people find only death and divine judgment. To stay in the vicinity because of some deceived allegiance to the temple or some mistaken belief that it will offer divine protection is to court disaster.

When this event occurs, there will be no time for the refugees to retrieve precious possessions or even such essentials as cloaks. Those who are slowed in their flight by the need to care for children will be particularly vulnerable. If it occurs in the cold of winter, escape without provisions over flooded rivers and dangerous mountain passes will be precarious. Josephus reports an incident when Gadarene refugees seeking shelter in Jericho could not cross the swollen Jordan and were slain by the Romans.[26] Unlike the time of Joshua, when the soles of the priests' feet touched the water and the Jordan River ceased flowing so that they could pass over on dry ground (Josh. 3:13–17), the rivers will not part for them.

Geddert argues persuasively that Jesus' concern for his disciples' personal safety in this critical moment does not motivate his call for their flight. If that were so, he would have warned them to skip town at the first sign of trouble.

---

24. Ibid., *J. W.* 4.6.3 § 388.
25. Ibid., 6.6.1 § 316.
26. Ibid., 4.7.5 §§ 433–36.

The elect can only be spared by God's intervention (13:20), not by their flight. Presumably, they stay as long as possible to proclaim the gospel. Their abandonment of the city testifies that they do not owe allegiance to temple Judaism and do not consider it to be the basis of their security. Beasley-Murray comments that martyrdom for the sake of the gospel is one thing, but being slaughtered for the sake of the temple is another.[27]

The temple no longer symbolizes God's abiding favor and protection, since God will allow it to be desecrated and destroyed. Any reverence of the temple and its cherished heritage or belief that its sanctity still ensures God's blessing is more than simply mistaken devotion to a lost cause. The Roman historian Dio describes just such a deluded allegiance. He was amazed at the Jewish resistance to the very end of the war when obviously everything was lost.

> The Jews resisted [Titus] with more ardor than ever, as if it were a kind of windfall [an unexpected piece of luck] to fall fighting against a foe far outnumbering them, they were not overcome until a part of the Temple had caught fire. Then some impaled themselves voluntarily on the swords of the Romans, others slew each other, others did away with themselves or leaped into the flames. They all believed, especially the last, that it was not a disaster but victory, salvation, and happiness to perish together with the Temple.[28]

To reverence the temple means to disavow trust in Jesus and his commands. His followers should not allow themselves to become entangled in the fate of the doomed nation and its temple.[29] Geddert concludes:

> The disciples are to flee, not because they fear what the enemy will do, but because God desires them to absent themselves when everything stands poised for the divine judgment to fall. When the judgment falls, all who will trust in themselves, their might, their leaders, their election or their temple will be judged along with the religious system they represent. All who take their stand with Jesus will leave the temple and the city to its fate.[30]

---

27. Beasley-Murray, *Jesus and the Last Days*, 14, 74.

28. Dio, *History*, 66.6.2–3. Sadly the Jewish people fought three wars against Rome, in 66–70 (74), 115–17, 132–5, with the same fierce devotion to their nationalistic hopes centered on the temple, with the result that all Jews were eventually expelled from Jerusalem entirely.

29. Geddert, *Watchwords*, 218.

30. Ibid., 219.

Walls, fortifications, and weapons are useless (see Jer. 38:2) if God is not on their side. Jesus makes it plain that God will not be on their side in this conflict. Get out![31]

Jesus also warns that this conflict will result in unprecedented suffering (Mark 13:19; see Ex. 9:18; Dan. 12:1; Joel 2:2). Josephus gives gruesome accounts of famine, cannibalism, and wholesale slaughter during the Roman siege of Jerusalem. Jesus' warning, however, serves as a source of comfort because he affirms that even this terrible affliction is not outside the control or will of God, who can shorten the days (see 2 Sam. 24:16; Isa. 45:8). The phrase "no one would survive" (13:20) means that no one will be "left alive" (see 4 Ezra 6:25; 7:27).[32] Beasley-Murray interprets it as a reference to God's mercy on the people of Israel.[33]

Warning about deceivers (13:21–23). This unit about the war in Judea concludes as it began—with a warning about deceivers. False prophets will arise, who will exploit catastrophes for their own ends and add to the miseries of the people. Both deceivers and the deceived will perish. Josephus records that a large crowd met their deaths from giving heed to just such a charlatan:

> They owed their destruction to a false prophet, who had on that day proclaimed to the people in the city that God commanded them to go up to the temple court, to receive there the tokens of their deliverance. Numerous prophets, indeed, were at this period suborned by the tyrants to delude the people by bidding them to await help from God, in order that desertions might be checked and that those who were above fear and precaution might be encouraged by hope. In adversity man is quickly persuaded; but when the deceiver actually pictures release from prevailing horrors, the sufferer wholly abandons himself to expectation.[34]

"Signs and miracles" are things associated with false prophets. However compelling the signs and portents and however persuasive their interpretations, disciples must ever keep on their toes to resist their lures. They must

---

31. Eusebius (*Ecclesiastical History* 3.5.3) records the escape of Christians before the war:

The people of the Church of Jerusalem were bidden in an oracle given by revelation to men worthy of it to depart from the city and to dwell in a city of Perea called Pella. To it those who believed in Christ migrated from Jerusalem. Once the holy men had completely left the Jews and all Judea, the justice of God at last overtook them, since they had committed such transgressions against Christ and all his apostles. Divine justice completely blotted out that impious generation among men.

32. Hooker, *Mark*, 316.
33. Beasley-Murray, *Jesus and the Last Days*, 420.
34. Josephus, *J. W.* 6.5.1. §§ 285–86.

guard against religious leaders who appeal to false hopes and want to exalt themselves and expand their influence. They must not allow the yearning for God to deliver them to cause them to embrace mirages, fantasies, and errors. Jesus urges them to hold fast to the certainty that God's Messiah has already come and is hidden in heaven, not on earth. He will not come to save the temple from its fate.

The Coming of the Son of Man (13:24–27)

THE HOPE OF Jesus' coming enables Christians to endure any affliction, but Jesus gives no precise timetable about how long it will take for the end to come after the temple's destruction. Two things are clear: The end of the temple must happen before the end of time, but it does not denote the end. Jesus is silent about what might lie between the two events. He simply says, "But in those days, following that distress."

How long following that distress? Geddert contends that because Jesus neither affirms nor denies that there is a time gap between the destruction of the temple and the end in 13:24–27, he wants to prevent his followers from trying to nail down a specific chronology of end-time events.[35] Anything is possible. The ambiguity is deliberate, and Jesus does not intend for us to try to unravel it. Otherwise, he would have given more definite clues. He expects his disciples to be ready for anything anytime. Busying oneself with calculations about dates is thus a fruitless exercise that can only distract from the mission that God has called the church to do—to preach the gospel. God does not require a studious deciphering of international threats and natural disasters but spiritual vigilance that makes one ready for Christ's return whenever he comes.

One knows that the end is certain, and the cosmic tumult will make it obvious to all. There will be no secret appearances so that people need to search here and there. Only in the Parousia will the veil that cloaks the Son of Man in mystery be completely lifted for all to see. The clouds of his coming unveil his glory as the one who shares in the majesty and power of God, who also comes in clouds.

The images of the sun darkening, the moon not giving its light, the stars falling, and the powers in the heaven shaking are woven together from the Old Testament (Isa. 13:10; Joel 2:10; 3:4, 20). Beasley-Murray contends that they do not describe the dissolution of the cosmos but picture it "in terror and confusion before the overwhelming might of the Lord of Hosts when he steps forth into the world to act in judgment and salvation."[36] "The elements

---

35. Geddert, *Watchwords*, 234–35.
36. Beasley-Murray, *Jesus and the Last Days*, 425.

of creation go into confusion and fear *because* he appears, not as a sign that he is about to do so (see, e.g., Judg. 5:4–5; Pss. 77:14–16; 114:1–8; Amos 1:2; Hab. 3:3–6, 10–11)." No preliminary sign warns of his coming. The imagery, therefore, highlights "the glory of that event."[37]

Jesus' coming means salvation for the elect as angels are sent out to gather them (see Deut. 30:4 (LXX); Isa. 11:11–12; 43:5–6; 66:8; Jer. 23:3; 32:37; Ezek. 34:12–13; 36:24). The elect are those who have faithfully responded to the gospel. The gospel begins with the one who is faithful to the very end and is raised up by God; it will close with the gathering of the many elect who remain faithful to the end.

Final Warnings To Watch (13:28–37)

THE FINAL WARNINGS come in the veiled form of parables wrapped around Jesus' earnest announcement that no one knows the timing of the end. Jesus concludes from the first parable, however, that one can know something: "When you see these things happening, you know that it is near, right at the door" (13:29). He concludes from the second parable, "You do not know when [that time will come]" (13:35). I take "these things" in 13:29 to be a reference to the events leading up to the abomination of desolation, not the coming of the Son of Man (see 13:4, 8). This helps explain the statement in 13:30, "This generation will certainly not pass away until all these things have happened" (see 13:23). Throughout Mark "this generation" refers to Jesus' evil contemporaries (8:12, 38; 9:19). If one interprets "all these things" to refer to the coming of the Son of Man, Jesus was either mistaken or one has to redefine the meaning of "this generation."[38] If one interprets "all these things" to refer to the events leading up to the temple's destruction, however, Jesus' prophecy was fulfilled. His contemporaries did not escape doom when the Romans laid waste Jerusalem in A.D. 70.

The second parable about the doorkeeper applies to the coming of the Son of Man and illustrates Jesus' declaration that no one knows the hour.

---

37. Ibid.

38. George Beasley-Murray (in "Jesus' Apocalyptic Discourse," *RevExp* 57 [1960]: 160) offers one possible explanation for Jesus' misunderstanding. "Intensity and certainty of prophetic convictions express themselves in terms of a *speedy* fulfillment. . . . The very intensity and sharpness of the vision of the end vouchsafed to Jesus added to the naturalness of his reckoning with nothing else in time but it alone, just as in clear atmosphere mountains appear far closer than they do on a dull day." Another image suggests that a prophet's vision is foreshortened and two-dimensional. Viewing things from the top of a mountain one cannot always perceive the amount of space in between one mountain top and the next. As a prophet, Jesus can only see the coming of the end, which looks near, and cannot see the space of history that will unfold before the end comes.

Therefore, one can know the portents leading to the war in Judea and the destruction of the temple, but one cannot know when the end will come.

The lesson from the fig tree (13:28–32). The fig tree is one of the few deciduous trees in Palestine. Jesus uses it to illustrate another lesson. Its leafing out is a harbinger of summer. Does summer refer literally to the summertime, summer fruit-bearing, or summer harvest? Is it an image of judgment or harvest (Joel 3:13; Amos 8:1–2; Rev. 14:14–15; see Mark 4:26–29)? Does it simply imply that as the fig tree goes through the cycle of budding to summer harvest, so God's judgment is working its way through this current generation? Is the leafing fig tree a counterpoint to the withered fig tree (11:21)?[39] If so, does it refer to the revival of Israel, as Hooker contends? "The dormant tree, apparently dead, bursts into new life, and its young leaves are a promise of coming summer: hope, and not destruction, is the final word."[40] Or, does it refer to the replacement of the old temple with a new community gathered around Jesus?[41] If Jesus refers to the return of the Son of Man, could he have been mistaken? Does one need to redefine what "this generation" means?

So many questions, and even more answers have been proposed. For me, the simplest explanation is to take the fig tree parable and the statement that all these things will come upon this generation as a reference to the woes preceding the destruction of the temple (13:5–23). It sums up Jesus' warning in this unit. One can see the evidence of the coming destruction of Jerusalem as surely as one can tell that a budding fig tree means summer is near. Jesus' predictions about the temple's destruction will come true. Those things that humans may believe are the center of the universe may disappear from the face of the earth.

Only Jesus' words abide. They are "the firm ground upon which the church can dare to live and to meet courageously all the terrors which are coming before the end."[42] One cannot, however, see the warning signs that tell you that the coming of the Son of Man is near. Jesus' next statement and the parable about the doorkeeper make this plain (13:32–37). There is, in other words, a qualitative difference between "all these things," which refer to the temple's destruction, and "that day or hour," which refers to the coming of the Son of Man.

The unknown time of the end (13:32). Jesus affirms that the time of the end is hidden from all humans, the angels in heaven, and even the Son. Nothing can be clearer. No one knows how the seed grows (4:27); no one knows when the end will come. The timing of the final day belongs to the power

---

39. Telford, *The Barren Temple and the Withered Fig Tree,* 216–17.
40. Hooker, *Mark,* 320.
41. Geddert, *Watchwords,* 251–52.
42. Schweizer, *Mark,* 282.

of God alone (see Acts 1:7: "The Father has set [the times and dates] by his own authority"). Just as it is not in Jesus' power to grant to anyone to sit at his right hand or left, so Jesus must be obedient to the sovereign will of God, who determines the time. No apocalyptic calculations beforehand can violate that sovereignty. The end comes without any warning. No one will have time for last-second preparations.

The parable of the doorkeeper (13:33–37). This parable of the doorkeeper applies to the coming of the Son of Man. Its key element is that the servants have no advance warning when the master of the house will return. The doorkeeper must keep alert throughout the watches of the night. One moment's sleep might give an intruder the opportunity to sneak in, or the master might return and charge him with dereliction of duty. He must endure the test of absence and uncertainty. What kind of servant is it that requires a master to look constantly over his shoulder to make sure he does his job faithfully and properly? How can the doorkeeper fulfill his duties if he spends his time computing how long the delay will last? Jesus' warnings affirm that only those who are valiant under fire and vigilant during the delay will be vindicated in the end. We are to work faithfully because the Master will return; we are to work with assurance because it is the Master who returns.

The discourse began privately with four close friends; it ends addressed to all (13:37). The end comes suddenly to both believer and unbeliever. It catches the unbelievers unaware because they are blind to the spiritual realities that govern events. Disciples, however, understand the nature of the trials and are able to endure so as not to be shaken (1 Thess. 3:2–5).

Bridging Contexts

THE DIRE PREDICTIONS of troubles in this discourse resemble Tacitus's rueful description of the time when Mark wrote:

The history on which I am entering is that of a period rich in disasters, terrible with battles, torn by civil struggles, horrible even in peace. Four emperors fell by the sword; there were three civil wars, more foreign wars, and often both at the same time. ... Italy was distressed by disasters unknown before or returning after the lapse of the ages. ...

Beside the manifold misfortunes that befell mankind there were prodigies in the sky and on the earth, warnings given by thunderbolts, and prophecies of the future, both joyful and gloomy, uncertain and clear.[43]

---

43. Tacitus, *Histories* 1.2–3.

Mark wrote his Gospel at a time when the whole world was falling apart—particularly if one was a Jewish Christian. Jesus' warnings served as a guide to help make sense of what was happening.

One also has to be mindful that Jesus uses apocalyptic language. This discourse contains much of the terminology and many of the issues that one finds in Jewish apocalyptic works. These issues include the question, "When will this be?" and the references to the end (13:7, 13), the birth pains (13:8), the tribulation (13:19, 24), the things that must happen before the end (13:7), and cosmic portents (13:24–25). The discourse has striking parallels with Daniel's reference to a desolating sacrilege (13:14; cf. Dan. 9:27; 11:31; 12:11; see 1 Macc 1:54), a great tribulation (Mark 13:19; cf. Dan. 12:1), and the coming of the Son of Man (Mark 13:26; cf. Dan. 7:13).

But Jesus' discourse differs significantly from what one normally finds in apocalyptic writings. It contains no tour of heaven or hell guided by an angel, no bizarre imagery, no division of history into different epochs to show the outworking of God's plan, no reference to a last great battle or war, no last-ditch demonic assault, a complete refusal to identify the time of the end, and no description of what happens after the Parousia. Jesus says nothing about the last judgment, where the righteous are rewarded and the wicked punished. Jesus did not intend his words to be used as a palette for painting end-time scenarios.

In bridging the contexts, however, one must be sensitive to how confusing this language is and how it excites some today while turning off others. The latter regard apocalyptic discussions as strange and disturbing—the province of crackpots and fanatics. Every generation knows of some deluded leader who persuades credulous followers that Armageddon is just around the corner. They become the object of local or even national media scrutiny and wind up being exposed as fools or destroyed in a fiery holocaust. Many are therefore much more comfortable with Jesus' more serene Farewell Discourse in the Upper Room in John 14–16. It contains all the same themes—persecution by the synagogue, hatred from the world, martyrdom, birth pains, prayer, endurance, the Holy Spirit's working in the disciples, Jesus' coming to gather his own—without all the enigmatic references to the abomination of desolation and the cosmic fireworks.[44]

Others, however, are overly fascinated with eschatology. A series of sermons predicting the timing of the end and the identity of the Antichrist will probably draw far more interest than one on Jesus' ethical demands in the Sermon on the Mount. Such messages also may be wedded to certain views of the end, and those who adhere to these teachings will become bitterly hos-

---

44. Noted by Gundry, *Mark*, 750.

tile to any who disagree with them. By contrast, I believe Mark 13 was intended to dampen apocalyptic fervor. One misunderstands and misuses this discourse *or* ignores it at one's peril.

The problem with this discourse is that it contains far more puzzles than answers. The number of questions raised in the original meaning section may be frustrating because the answers are not always forthcoming. The ambiguities and mystifying features in this chapter have occupied commentators for a long time. Some explain them away by accusing Mark of being a clumsy editor who failed to integrate fully his supposed source, some apocalyptic fly sheet. Geddert, however, argues persuasively that Mark deliberately promoted a paradoxical perspective. He was not careless but subtle. Geddert contends that Mark is more concerned "to teach his readers *how* to know than *what* to know." Consequently, interpreting Mark 13 does not mean that we must explain or remove all of its ambiguities so much as to explain their implications.[45]

Jesus did not intend to remove the veil of secrecy surrounding the timing of the end for his disciples when they asked him. We should not try to do so either. Mark's message is more subtle than to give us events to enter on our end-of-time charts. The message is simply this: God's way, God's Christ, and God's people will be vindicated in a conclusive manner that all will recognize. That time is not yet. Geddert concludes, "The disciple is not called to *eliminate* his ignorance of the timing of the End, he is called to *cope* with it, and respond to it appropriately."[46] The question the text addresses is, "How does one live in difficult times?" The eschatological drama will run its course, scene by scene. But the actors on the stage have only vague clues about where they are precisely in the play. Only the stage director knows. He has given the actors instructions about what to do and what to say when they see certain things happen. But that is it. They know how the play ends, but they do not know when the curtain will fall.

If Mark does not record this discourse to provide a horoscope of the future, what is its purpose and how can it be applied? (1) Mark uses it to exhort his readers. It contains seventeen imperatives. Christians need to be forewarned so that they can be forearmed. They will face adversity, harrowing persecution, false alarms, and the ruin of nations, even their own. He wants to "inspire faith, endurance, and hope in the face of the impending sufferings of the church and of the Jewish nation."[47] He also wants to assure the fainthearted. Persecution should not take them by surprise. When

---

45. Geddert, *Watchwords*, 25–26.
46. Ibid., 283, n. 53.
47. Beasley-Murray, *Jesus and the Last Days*, 442.

one lives in the midst of a firestorm of persecution, one cannot always perceive how God's purposes are being accomplished in the world. Mark helps readers see that the persecutions they suffer must be suffered. Things may look bleak and all hope seem lost, but God is still fully in control and God's purposes will triumph. They may not understand why they suffer, but they can take comfort in knowing that they follow the steps of their Lord.

It is easiest to understand this section when we find ourselves in a similar situation of persecution and social upheaval that is turning the world upside down. Those who suffer to the limits of their endurance better appreciate the message of hope. Most people, however, experience some form of pressure and uncertainty in their lives. Jesus warns that they can expect to be assaulted by the powers, which take many guises. As Wink notes, "The Powers that had crucified Jesus had an equal stake in crushing this new movement."[48] Jesus' warnings, assurance, and exhortation apply to any troubled situation Christians may face.

Humans may imperfectly grasp what is happening and why; they may be puzzled by it all—"Why do bad things happen to good people?" Jesus offers no explanation except to say that Christians may rest assured that all is within the scope of God's grand design. In trying times, they need not be unduly alarmed and should guard against being swept up in nationalistic movements that return evil for evil or being deceived by charismatic leaders who offer only delusional hopes.

(2) This discourse also serves as a warning. On the one extreme, there are the eschatological enthusiasts, who are in danger of losing their heads as they look for all kinds of menacing signs in the highly charged atmosphere of end-time excitement. The earth is usually overrun by enough troubles to make believable excited claims that the Messiah is about to come. On the other extreme, there are the eschatological nonchalant, who, during the interim period of delay, become unconcerned, inattentive, and even derisively skeptical.

Mark 13 cautions the first group that too much attention on end-time speculation diverts their gaze from Christ, distracts them from their duties, and deceives them into thinking that they can decipher the times. In the first century, most Christians believed Christ's return was imminent. With some, however, that expectation became so overheated that it disrupted the life of the church. One can see the effect of an excessive end-time fever among the Thessalonians. Paul warns the enthusiasts "not to become easily unsettled or alarmed by some prophecy, report or letter supposed to have come from us,

---

48. Walter Wink, *Engaging the Powers: Discernment and Resistance in a World of Domination* (Minneapolis: Fortress, 1992), 316.

saying that the day of the Lord has already come" (2 Thess. 2:2). The Thessalonian church mistook Paul's assurances that God's purposes were being worked out in certain events as an indication that the church's suffering was over and that they could now plot Christ's return (see 1 Thess. 5:2–5).

Jesus forewarns his disciples in his teaching that Christians will not escape danger until the end of the age and they must bear their crosses to the bitter end. He also forewarns that all this eschatological fervor only fritters away the opportunity for mission. Guesses about how current events relate to the end time are useless. Spiritual vigilance and prudence, whether in the midst of crisis or calm, are the only things that matter. Christians can be assured of two things: that the coming of the Lord is certain and that it will occur someday. Looking for premonitory signs can only agitate Christians, sidetrack them from the important business at hand, or become simply a cerebral amusement.

Mark 13 also serves as a warning to the eschatological skeptics not to fall asleep, lose interest, faith, or concentration. Many may say to themselves, "Why bother to watch when almost two thousand years have gone by since Jesus spoke these words?" This attitude is confronted in 2 Peter 3:3–4 (cf. vv. 1–10):

> First of all, you must understand that in the last days scoffers will come, scoffing and following their own evil desires. They will say, "Where is this 'coming' he promised? Ever since our fathers died, everything goes on as it has since the beginning of creation."

If one loses any sense of expectation one becomes like the doorkeeper who falls asleep on the job.

(3) I have interpreted 13:5–23 to refer to a specific situation in the first century that directly affected the lives of those first disciples—the destruction of Jerusalem and the temple. The warning for those in Judea to flee to the mountains is therefore not directly applicable to us. Within human history, however, new abominations arise. When we try to bridge the contexts, the exhortation to flee applies in our setting as a general principle. When Jesus tells his disciples to flee, he is not advising them to head for cover whenever the going gets rough but to dissociate themselves from a false ideology. In their first-century context, he warns them to dissociate themselves from the rebel cause.

The principle undergirding this instruction is that Christianity is not tied to any national identity. One's loyalty is owed entirely to Christ, not some religio-nationalist ideology. It is hard for us to grasp how shattering the fall of the temple must have been for many Jews. Maybe we can understand from recent twentieth-century history. How hard was it for Christians in Nazi

Germany to see the evil of Hitler and flee when he was winning battles with ease, instilling patriotic pride, and restoring the fortunes of the nation? How hard was it for Christians in the American South to see through the inculturated racism that was given a biblical rationale? When Jesus calls for vigilance, we must examine ourselves to see where we may be placing false hopes.

JESUS TELLS HIS followers what must happen before the end comes, but he does not tell them what they long to know—the precise dates and signs. The reason is that God has not revealed it even to the Son (13:32). One must conclude that God does not deem it vital for us to know such things. Juel aptly comments, "If Jesus is uncertain of God's timing, there is good reason to be suspicious of other forecasters boasting knowledge of matters received for God alone."[49]

Nevertheless, Christians today continue to ask the same question about the end that those first disciples asked: "Tell us, when will these things happen? And what will be the sign that they are all about to be fulfilled?" They want Jesus to give them a crib sheet to help them identify precisely when the end will come. In spite of Jesus' disclaimer in 13:32, some today claim to have decoded the mystery and to speak for God. Obviously, they think they comprehend more than Jesus and can arrange all events on a timetable.

Although history is riddled with vain predictions about the timing of the end, such speculation continues. Without any embarrassment, people revise their calculations for the dates of the rapture and Christ's merciful return again and again. Some compile a "Rapture Index," toting up all the earthquakes, wars, and other disasters to gauge the probabilities that the time will be soon. Christians are bombarded with paperback-book prophets, both secular and religious, who have produced libraries of books that forecast an era of war, nuclear holocaust, famine, ecological disaster, economic ruin, and pestilence just around the corner.

Religious authors identify the Antichrist as any number of persons they do not like, and they assure their audience that he is set to pounce and devour his prey. Most know of some extremist group that makes the news when they quit their jobs, turn their backs on their neighbors, and put on white ascension robes, waiting for the appointed time for Jesus to sweep them away from their earthly cares. The fiery death of David Koresh, along with many of the Branch Davidians, is the most recent tragedy connected to such apocalyptic delusions. Their foolhardiness holds the Christian faith up to public ridicule.

---

49. Juel, *Mark*, 184.

Jesus specifically warns against such eschatological hysteria. He deliberately gives no information helpful for fixing any date. Yet false prophets continue to arise and reduce Christianity to simplistic answers. They exploit the fears and weaknesses of the poor and uneducated while frequently making a handsome profit. The preacher who can crack the code to what is advertised as God's best-kept secret is empowered as a revealer and arbiter of the truth. His audience is also empowered as those who now are in the know.[50] They capitalize on our craving to escape what Cranfield calls "the painful paradoxes and tensions and indirectness of faith into the comfortable security of sight."[51]

Some preachers may intend to bolster faith by focusing on such issues, but they undermine it. With such a key Christians will not have to bother with the laborious task of "watching" (being faithful under pressure) in the meantime. I was intrigued to watch a television preacher run through a long list of fulfilled prophecies and confidently describe what was supposed to happen next on the world scene. Not once did he mention what the viewer was supposed to do except to send in money to receive more prophecies. No ethical implications for how this affects the way we live our lives were ever mentioned. Were the viewers only supposed to be entertained by all this?

I have interpreted Mark 13 to mean that the last great act of history will come when God chooses, without any preliminary warnings or signs. Jesus does say that certain things must happen. Elijah must come first (9:11–13); he has. The Son of Man must suffer many things and be raised (8:31; 9:31; 10:32–34); he has. The temple will be destroyed; it has. The disciples will face persecution; they have. The gospel must be preached to all nations; it is. After these things, the seed grows into the full ear, and it is only a matter of time before the reaper comes to harvest. How long this will be, we cannot know. We can only prepare ourselves for his coming by being constantly prepared.

The most important thing that Christians have been called to do is to preach the gospel to all the nations (13:10). When the Son of Man comes, he will not quiz people to see whose predictions on the date were accurate. He will want to know what we were doing. Were we proclaiming the gospel to all the nations? Were we enduring suffering faithfully? Were we fulfilling the assigned tasks? Those who have been asleep on the job or buried in the task of trying to map out the times rather than carrying out the mission will be more than just embarrassed; they will be judged. That is why Jesus warns his disciples to be on their guard (13:9).

---

50. Barry Brummett, *Contemporary Apocalyptic Rhetoric* (New York/Westport, Conn./London: Praeger, 1991), 124.
51. Cranfield, *Mark*, 405.

In a Jules Feiffer cartoon a man is looking up in the sky when another asks him what he is doing. He responds, "I am waiting for him to come back; that's what I'm doing." The other responds, "But that's silly; he won't come back from up there." "You can find him in ordinary life—in loving your neighbor, doing good to those who hate you, in suffering for the truth." The man replies, "Did you say suffering for the truth?" The last panel shows them both looking up into the sky, and the first man says, "I find this position more comfortable." We may live in times of persecution and natural disasters, or relative comfort and peace. Whichever it is, Jesus requires unceasing vigilance so that we are spiritually alert even when everything seems to indicate "peace and safety" (see 1 Thess. 5:2).

An explanation for suffering. Jesus' words help us understand what it means to be a persecuted Christian. What Jesus predicted about the war in Judea applies to every generation of Christians before the end. In each generation, there will be Christians who must undergo severe trials and tribulations. Jesus declares that the advancement of the kingdom of God and the suffering of God's elect are mysteriously bound together. Those who would be heirs to God's glory and gathered with the elect must embrace the affliction that precedes it.

In Revelation 1:9, John identifies himself as "your brother and companion in the suffering and kingdom and patient endurance that are ours in Jesus." Paul and Barnabas returned to congregations they had founded on their missionary journeys to strengthen them, to exhort them to continue in the faith, and to emphasize that "through many hardships [we must] enter the kingdom of God" (Acts 14:22). Geddert employs a helpful analogy to capture this idea:

> Mark's theology of the advancing kingdom is much more like a relay race in which persecution for the sake of the Gospel is the baton passed on from each runner to the next as they take their round on the track . . . or (to stick closer to Mark's imagery), it is the cross passed on from shoulder to shoulder as new recruits travel the "way" from Galilee to Jerusalem.[52]

The baton passes from John the Baptizer to Jesus, to his disciples, to us. We are in the next leg of the race. We do not know if we run the last leg or not, and it should make no difference how we run the race. Running in a race requires giving it one's all.

This image is also found in John Bunyan's *Pilgrim's Progress*. When Mr. Valiant-for-Truth is summoned to cross over the river, he says:

---

52. Geddert, *Watchwords*, 150.

"I am going to my Father's; and though with great difficulty I have got hither, yet now I do not repent of all the trouble I have been at to arrive where I am. My sword I give to him that shall succeed me in my pilgrimage, and my courage and skill to him that can get it. My marks and scars I carry with me, to be a witness for me that I have fought His battles who will now be my rewarder."

George Orwell wrote in *Nineteen Eighty-Four*: "If you want a picture of the future, imagine a boot stamping on the human face—forever."[53] Jesus also saw the boot, but he assures his disciples that the "forever" part is false. The Son of Man will come and send his angels to gather his elect who have held fast to the end. Despite their suffering, the future belongs to God's people, because God will intervene in the world to destroy evil forever. One cannot place one's hope in any imaginary societal progress but only on God's merciful intercession.

Preaching under fire. When persons are arrested in the United States, they are supposed to be read their rights: "You have the right to remain silent." Christians do not have that right. They have the obligation, which is also a privilege, to proclaim even to their persecutors the liberating love of Jesus. Jesus predicts that his disciples will live under a cloud of persecution, but they cannot allow persecution to stop proclamation. The preaching does not relieve the distress. In fact, it may only increase it. Jesus promises that the gospel will be preached to all the nations, but he offers no assurances that they will believe it and respond warmly. The message of the cross teaches that as God's cause thrives, it creates an even greater resistance from the powers of evil until, in the end, that power is spent and God ultimately triumphs.

In Acts, the disciples always preached in the face of bitter opposition. Peter and John stood before the Sanhedrin that condemned their Lord to death (Acts 4:8–12; 5:27–32). Stephen turned the prisoner's dock into a pulpit (7:1–53). Paul faced a Jerusalem mob (22:1–21), a raucous Sanhedrin (23:1–11), and corrupt governors (Felix, 24:10–21; Festus, 25:13–26:23) and kings (Agrippa, 26:1–23). Five times, he says, he was flogged in the synagogues (2 Cor. 11:24). But the beatings did not stop their hearts from beating with the love of Christ. After every pounding, the Christians got up again to preach the same things; or if they did not get up again, others showed up to take their place. Persecution led to more proclamation. Paul, writing from prison to the worried Philippians, explained that his imprisonment was not a setback for the gospel but something that led to its advancement. The

---

53. George Orwell, *Nineteen Eighty-Four* (New York: Harcourt, Brace, 1949), 271.

whole palace guard now knew about Christ and believers had become emboldened to proclaim it without fear (Phil. 1:12–14).

Caird compares the resistance to Christian proclamation to the resistance a supersonic jet encounters. As the jet "meets growing resistance until the breaking point at the sound barrier, God's purpose by its very success evokes a cumulative opposition, which reaches its height only at the crack of doom. The devil has come down to you in great wrath, because he knows that his time is short' (Rev. 12:12)."[54] One may despair of salvation even as Moses despaired that God would deliver Israel from Pharaoh (Ex. 5:23). God only responds: "Now you will see" (6:1). The new world order will not come from human prospects and potential. It can only come from God's direct intervention.

The danger is that we want to be popular and accepted by society. We do not want to be treated as outcasts or dismissed as fools for our faith. Few relish being castigated and hated by all. We will therefore be tempted to trim the message to win the favor of others rather than to convert them to God's reign. We will be enticed to conform to societal norms rather than to confront them.

Will Campbell tells the story of an Anabaptist woman who lived in Antwerp. She had been arrested a few days earlier for proclaiming the gospel of Christ as she understood it from her personal reading of the Scripture and from study and discussion with others of like faith. She underwent the inquisition of the clerics for heresy and the bodily torture of the civil authorities, but she would not buckle under to their pressure. After six months, she would not promise to stop preaching the word from her own reading of the Bible. So the authorities did what they thought they had to do: They sentenced her to death on October 5, 1573. Included in the sentence was the stipulation to the executioner that her tongue be screwed fast to the roof of her mouth so that she might not testify along the way as they took her to the stake where she was to be burned.

That day her teenage son, Adriaen, took his youngest brother, three-year-old Hans Mattheus, and they stood near the stake so that her first and last issue might be near her at her moment of death. Three other women and a man were to die that day for the same terrible offense—unauthorized preaching of the gospel. When the flames were lit, Adriaen fainted. He could not witness the horror. But when it was all over and the ashes had cooled, he sifted through them until he found the screw that had silenced his mother's tongue. It would not silence his.[55]

---

54. G. B. Caird and L. D. Hurst, *New Testament Theology* (Oxford: Clarendon, 1994), 115.
55. Will D. Campbell, "On Silencing Our Finest," *Christianity and Crisis* 45 (1985): 340.

Mark 14:1–11

NOW THE PASSOVER and the Feast of Unleavened Bread were only two days away, and the chief priests and the teachers of the law were looking for some sly way to arrest Jesus and kill him. ²"But not during the Feast," they said, "or the people may riot."

³While he was in Bethany, reclining at the table in the home of a man known as Simon the Leper, a woman came with an alabaster jar of very expensive perfume, made of pure nard. She broke the jar and poured the perfume on his head.

⁴Some of those present were saying indignantly to one another, "Why this waste of perfume? ⁵It could have been sold for more than a year's wages and the money given to the poor." And they rebuked her harshly.

⁶"Leave her alone," said Jesus. "Why are you bothering her? She has done a beautiful thing to me. ⁷The poor you will always have with you, and you can help them any time you want. But you will not always have me. ⁸She did what she could. She poured perfume on my body beforehand to prepare for my burial. ⁹I tell you the truth, wherever the gospel is preached throughout the world, what she has done will also be told, in memory of her."

¹⁰Then Judas Iscariot, one of the Twelve, went to the chief priests to betray Jesus to them. ¹¹They were delighted to hear this and promised to give him money. So he watched for an opportunity to hand him over.

MARK BEGINS THE countdown to Jesus' death by telling us that the Passover will arrive "after two days" (lit.). In Jewish time reckoning, this could mean "the next day" (today counts as one day, the next day as the second day; see 8:31); and everything that Mark narrates could be compressed into a forty-eight-hour time span. The NIV chooses a better option and has the anointing take place two days before the Passover. Jesus is killed on the third day after the plot and his anointing.

During the Passover festival, an estimated 85,000 to 300,000 pilgrims flocked to the city of Jerusalem, which had a population estimated at 60,000 to 120,000.[1] The sounds and smells of hordes of people and animals filled the city. The story of Jesus' being left behind by his parents in the temple (Luke 2:41–44) shows the chaos that resulted from the crush of people. Most of these pilgrims slept in tents or boarded in the towns of the surrounding countryside. The atmosphere may have been much like a state fair.

The celebration of appointed times reminded Israel of its inheritance. Passover commemorated the liberation of the nation from Egypt, when God sent a plague that took the lives of the Egyptians' firstborn. The Israelites were spared by dabbing their doorways with the blood of a slaughtered lamb. Many in Jesus' day saw this first deliverance as the model for their final liberation. Pilgrims came to commemorate this event filled with hopes and expectations that the Messiah would eventually come to deliver Israel from foreign oppression and economic misery during the night of Passover.[2]

It was a particularly nervous time for the high priests and their police force since the chance for an outbreak of riots increased dramatically during this time. The Roman governor usually moved to Jerusalem from his headquarters in Caesarea on the Mediterranean coast to monitor the volatile mobs of fervent pilgrims. The slightest provocation could set them off, and Josephus duly records the disturbances that broke out during a festival.

Each scene in this section—the plotting by the Jewish leaders, the anointing, and the betrayal contract—foreshadows Jesus' death. The Jewish leaders, identified by Mark as the chief priests and the teachers of the law, are agitated both by Jesus' threatening actions in the temple and the acclamation from the crowd. They begin to make good on their determination to do away with a dangerous rabble-rouser (11:18; 12:12; see 3:6), who menaces the temple and their priestly class. Because of his popularity, they plot to arrest him by stealth and to kill him.[3]

The conspirators do not want to kill Jesus "in the feast" (lit.). The word "feast" can have two different meanings. It may refer to the festival crowd (see

---

1. Wolfgang Reinhardt, "The Population Size of Jerusalem and the Numerical Growth of the Jerusalem Church," in *The Book of Acts in Its First Century Setting: Volume 4. Palestinian Setting*, ed. Richard Bauckham (Grand Rapids: William B. Eerdmans, 1995), 237–65.

2. One does not find this eschatological expectation in the discussion of the Passover in rabbinic literature. One reason for its absence is that the *Mishnah* was compiled long after the second and third revolts against Rome had ended again in utter disaster. The last revolt resulted in the martyrdom of many leading rabbis at the hands of the Romans, and Jerusalem became a forbidden city to Jews. After the last catastrophe in A.D. 135, the surviving rabbis frowned on any messianic fervor since, in their minds, it brought about Israel's sorry state.

3. For those sensitive to Old Testament allusions, this intrigue echoes the plight of the innocent victim (Pss. 10:7–11; 31:13; 54:3; 71:10; 86:14) and the terror all around that Jeremiah faced (Jer. 6:25; 11:19; 20:3, 10).

John 7:11) or the time of Passover. If it means the former, then the leaders fear seizing Jesus before all the people because it might precipitate a riot (see Luke 22:6). If they are going to retain their position of power as puppets of the Romans, they need to keep the streets peaceful and to suppress quickly any disturbances. That is why they arrest Jesus in the dead of night in the more secluded Gethsemane. If "in the feast" means "during the Feast of the Passover," then the authorities do not want to kill Jesus at this season. Judas's treachery, however, causes them to change their minds and expedite Jesus' arrest.

Either way, the furtive plotting of the temple leaders on how best to handle the Jesus problem is filled with irony. If they do not want to seize Jesus during the Feast, then the very thing they desire to prevent happens, for Jesus is executed during the Feast.[4] His death transforms the meaning of Passover for Christians, for they do not remember Passover as the time when God struck down the firstborn in the land of Egypt and liberated Israel from the bondage. Instead, they associate it with God's beloved Son being struck down to deliver all humankind from the bondage to Satan and sin.

If these Machiavellian masterminds have plotted to seize Jesus apart from the excitable festal crowd, they succeed. They arrest him as he prays in private and thus successfully avoid any tumult. The web of intrigue proves ultimately futile, however. Everything goes according to plan, but little do they know that "killing Jesus was like trying to destroy a dandelion seed-head by blowing on it."[5] They may attribute their failure to the law of unintended consequences, but the reader knows that divine forces are working unseen. The Jewish leaders may think that they are in control; but God's will, not theirs, is being accomplished.

The next scene finds Jesus dining at the home of Simon the leper. Mark gives no details about who this Simon is or how Jesus happens to be in his house. He is only interested in what happens when an anonymous woman breaks into the company of men and pours precious perfume over Jesus' head. She breaks a costly jar containing pure nard, and the even more costly perfume streams out.[6] Mark pegs its value at three hundred denarii, almost a year's wage for a day laborer (see Matt. 20:4, 10). According to Mark 6:37, two hundred denarii would have been sufficient to provide a meal for five thousand people.

---

4. As John the Baptizer was murdered at Herod's birthday party, Jesus will be executed during the Feast.

5. Walter Wink, *Engaging the Powers* (Minneapolis: Fortress, 1992), 143.

6. Nard was an expensive perfume from two plants, nadala, imported from Nepal, and spike; it is sometimes called spikenard.

This woman's act of extraordinary adoration is sandwiched between extraordinary malice and betrayal. We have already noted the machinations of the temple hierarchy, "looking for some sly way to arrest Jesus and kill him" (14:1). Immediately after the anointing, we learn of Judas's duplicity as he offers to betray Jesus to the chief priests: "So he watched for an opportunity to hand him over" (14:11). Traps have been set for Jesus, whose doom is sealed.

This woman's devotion stands in stark contrast to Judas's disloyalty. Except for a kiss from Judas in Gethsemane, Jesus receives no other expression of love from anyone else during his Passion. Judas is looking for the appropriate opportunity (*eukairos*, 14:11) to betray Jesus, and his treachery will never be forgotten.[7] He is willing to sacrifice Jesus to obtain material rewards for himself. The woman, on the other hand, seizes an opportunity to show love to Jesus and sacrifices her precious gift for him. Her act will never be forgotten either.

What is going on in this woman's mind as she pours out the precious contents of the jar on Jesus' head? Anointing was common at feasts in the ancient world.[8] Is she extending to him customary courtesy with uncustomary extravagance? Or does she think she is anointing a Messiah (the anointed one) with the oil of crowning to set him apart for his office? In the Old Testament, kings were anointed in private, and it sometimes signaled a revolt (see 1 Sam. 10:1; 16:12–13; 1 Kings 1:38–39, 45; 2 Kings 9:1–13; 11:12). Maybe she hopes it is time for God to intervene in the affairs of Israel with this king. If this is her intention, how ironic the situation is. A woman, not a priest or an authorized prophet, anoints Jesus in the home of a leper.

In any case, Jesus must gently correct the woman and declare that her action prepares him for burial. He is not a king who will ascend a temporal throne and crush his enemies by temporal means. She anoints a king who is going to die, and he is the true Anointed One of God precisely because he is going to die. Some contend that this woman is the only follower of Jesus who understands the implications of his teaching. She knows that he is destined to die and seizes this last opportunity to express her love.

We may not know what this woman was thinking, but Mark does tell us exactly what is going on in the minds of the bystanders who witness this scene. They complain about the waste of something so expensive. "They rebuked her harshly" translates *embrimaomai* (14:5), a verb that means to snort

---

7. Cf. 6:21, where Herodias was looking for "an opportune time" (*eukairos*) to have John the Baptizer killed.

8. In Luke 7:46, Jesus chides his host, "You did not put oil on my head." See Deut. 28:40; Ruth 3:3; Ps. 23:5; Eccl. 9:7–8; Ezek. 16:9; Dan. 6:15; Mic. 6:15.

or roar and is used, for example, of horses. Caring for the poor was central in Judaism, and it was customary to remember the poor on holy days (Neh. 8:12; Est. 9:22). The complainers, as pious Jews, naturally think that giving something so valuable to care for the poor would be far better than pouring it down the drain; moreover, it would earn one a reward from God (Prov. 19:17; see Luke 14:14).

But Jesus cherishes this woman's devotion and defends her as having done "a beautiful thing" (lit., a "good work"). Daube has suggested that the phrase "good work" has a technical sense here, referring to what the later rabbis listed as good works: almsgiving, putting up strangers, visiting the sick, and burying the dead.[9] In rabbinic logic, almsgiving was considered to be less praiseworthy than burying the dead because the former was done to the living while the latter was extended to the dead.[10] Almsgiving could be done any time; preparing a body for burial had to be done when the need arose. Therefore, one can conclude that what this woman did was better than almsgiving because it was done to one who was as good as dead.

After Jesus' death, where are these complaining followers when he needs to be buried? Unlike the disciples of John the Baptizer, who claimed his body after his execution and buried it (6:29), Jesus' disciples are missing in action. According to Mark, Jesus is hurriedly buried by a stranger in a borrowed tomb, with no mention of any anointing of the corpse. This anointing before his death will have to suffice. The later attempt by other women to anoint the body after Jesus' burial (16:1) is not realized because he receives a greater anointing from God.

The anointing reveals that Jesus has prophetic knowledge both of his death and of his ultimate triumph. Good news pierces through the tragedy. Jesus announces that this woman's devotion will be remembered wherever the gospel is preached in the whole world. People will understand more clearly what her act of pouring out precious perfume on Jesus' head means when they recognize that he poured out his blood for the many (14:24). Jesus' announcement also affirms that the gospel will be preached to all the nations (14:9; see 13:10). In other words, this story is not a tragedy; it is good news. Faithful and loving actions toward Jesus will not be forgotten; for that matter, neither will acts of foul play. Humans will scheme to deliver him up, but they do not know that God also delivers him up (14:21). They deliver him up to death; God will deliver him up from the grave.

---

9. David Daube, *The New Testament and Rabbinic Judaism* (New York: Arno, 1973; orig. 1956), 315.

10. See *t. Pe'a* 4:9; *b. Sukk.* 49b.

Bridging Contexts

A SIMILAR ANOINTING scene is found in Luke 7:36–50, in the house of Simon the Pharisee, earlier in Jesus' ministry. One must be careful not to import details from that scene into this anointing in the house of Simon the leper. Ancient custom suggests that Jesus would have been anointed more than once as a guest. The most dramatic instances were remembered and recorded. There is no indication that the woman in Mark 14:3–9 is a sinner plying her trade in the city and that her act of love is a sign of repentance. All attention is drawn away from her circumstances to focus on her extravagance, the bystanders' disapproval, and Jesus' interpretation of her action in terms of his death and vindication.

The woman's extravagant devotion exhorts devotion and love for Christ. Her gesture displays the proper personal devotion of the disciple toward Jesus, and he comes to her defense. The text prompts us to ask: How much is too much devotion to Christ? A little oil, even expensive perfume, is fine; but to break open a whole jar seems too extravagant.

Comparing this incident with the widow and her two copper coins (12:41–44) may help clarify things. The NIV translates the beginning of verse 8: "She did what she could." Literally, it reads, "What she had she did." The parallels between the two women become clearer by translating it literally. The widow threw everything she had (lit., "all things whatsoever she has, the whole of her living," 12:44) into the treasury. Now this woman pours out everything she has on Jesus. Both women stand in contrast with men. The widow is an antithesis to the teachers of the law, who plunder widows' houses, and the prosperous, who give only from their abundance (12:39–44). The anonymous woman is the antithesis of the disciple who will betray his master for whatever money the priests will give him and those tightfisted bystanders who mouth pious clichés about giving to the poor but take no action.

Both women serve as examples of total commitment that holds nothing back. Their deeds do not bring them fame. Their names have been lost in the mists of time. We only "memorialize the anonymity of loving kindness."[11] The bystanders might have commended the widow who sacrificed her whole living had they witnessed her donation. It was just a pittance, although it was all she had. But they sneer at the misuse of something valuable: "Why this waste?" This reflects a crass utilitarian concern over the waste of something precious that can be turned into cash.

The disciples in Mark have been very adept at counting the cost of things. In 6:37, when Jesus tells them to feed the crowd, their mental cash registers

---

11. Tolbert, *Sowing*, 274.

ring up two hundred denarii worth of bread. Here they see three hundred denarii going down the drain and a royal opportunity to do a good work wasted. They do not understand, however, that if anything was a waste, it was the widow's copper coins donated to the bulging coffers of a flourishing but spiritually destitute temple. The widow's gift ultimately lined the pockets of the rich temple hierarchy. The woman who anoints Jesus sacrifices her wealth to do service to one who is poor.

Mark's readers can understand the indignant question, "Why the waste?" (lit., "To what purpose this destruction?"), in a different sense. Something of great value was poured out in 14:3. Jesus ties this act to his upcoming death. In 14:24, in the words of institution, Jesus says that his blood is poured out for the many. It is of inestimable value; no price can be put on it. In other words, the woman's pouring out of costly perfume foreshadows the costliness of the pouring out of Jesus' blood. Why waste Jesus on a cross? The answer to this question is to be found in the very attitudes of the indignant grumblers, the treacherous leaders of the nation, and the traitorous false disciple. The world needs saving. The text resounds with the affirmation that neither the pure nard poured out for Jesus nor his blood poured for the many is a waste. It is all connected to the good news that will be preached to the whole world.

The story places an emphasis on love and adoration of Christ and may seem to downplay the significance of almsgiving. One can easily misinterpret Jesus' statement, "The poor you will always have with you," to mean that there is nothing that can be done about the poor. One rabbi interpreted Deuteronomy 15:11, "There will always be poor people in the land," to mean what it says—always. Consequently, he concluded, "there is no difference between this world and the world of the Messiah except that there will be no bondage of foreign powers" (*b. Ber.* 34b).

In quoting from Deuteronomy, however, Jesus does not subscribe to a view that poverty is somehow divinely ordained to continue forever. Jesus was not implying that nothing could be done to eliminate poverty, even though calloused interpreters may misinterpret his words to justify their neglect of the poor. Jesus himself felt a deep concern for the poor and exploited (see 10:21). No Christian blessed with this world's goods may tell others to accept their poverty as inevitable, as God's will, or as their own fault (see James 2:15–16; 1 John 3:17). If the shoe were on the other foot, we would find it much harder to accept our condition as God's will. The gospel calls Christians to help those in need; it also calls for unrestrained adoration of Christ.

The text underscores the need for total devotion to Jesus. But if we respond to Jesus properly, we will take care of the poor. Remember that this woman does not anoint just any individual; she anoints the Son of God, who demands total commitment. Had she done this for any other person it would have been wrong.

It is possible to read Jesus' statement about the poor as an ironic rebuke. In the context of Deuteronomy 15:11, God commanded Israel about the sabbatic release of debts and said that if they obeyed, there would be no poor in the land:

> However, there should be no poor among you, for in the land the LORD your God is giving you to possess as your inheritance, he will richly bless you, if only you fully obey the LORD your God and are careful to follow all these commands I am giving you today. (Deut. 15:4–5)

God admonished the Israelites that if they hardened their hearts, their eyes became stingy, and greed and selfishness consumed them, there would indeed be poor among them. Jesus' citation of Deuteronomy 15:11, then, is perhaps not a candid perception about the way things are and always will be but is a rebuke. If God's people were obedient to God, there would be no poor. The presence of the poor is an indictment of all. It is not enough to talk about what can be done for the poor (by others). We need to take concrete action ourselves. But those willing to take such actions are those who are ready to make radical sacrifices for Jesus.

Three of Jesus' statements confirm this interpretation. Jesus says, "You can help [the poor] any time you want" (14:7). Our generosity need not be confined to certain seasons of the year; it depends simply on our willingness. Those who will not wish to help people in need will not do much for Jesus either (see Matt. 25:31–46). If one translates Jesus' response in 14:8 literally, "What she had she did," one can infer that helping the poor does not depend on having an abundance. The woman gave all that was in her power to give. Those who will hold back on the poor will hold back on what they will offer to Jesus (10:21–22). Finally, Jesus connects her action to "wherever the gospel is preached" (14:9). What is the gospel if not good news for the poor (see Matt. 5:3, 11:5; Luke 4:17–19)?

THE MALICIOUS SCHEMING against Jesus surrounding the act of sacrificial love reveals that people did not come pouring out of the saloons and peep shows to kill Jesus. It was the religious politicos and one of Jesus' intimates who did him in. The church tends to look for threats from without and to ignore the threats from within. Those who hold the reins of power may honestly believe that what they are doing is in the best interests of God's cause on earth. They may convince themselves that the end justifies the means. They may never see that self-interest motivates their words and actions and that it leads them into their greatest guilt.

Jesus' commendation of this anonymous woman also reveals that one can never be fully aware of one's own significance or role in God's kingdom. The woman had no idea of the worldwide significance of her action, nor did the high priests, Judas, or Pontius Pilate. Albert Einstein said, "It is a tragic mistake for those in power to think that they are in control." It is also a mistake for us to think that our sacrificial devotion is wasteful or insignificant. Who knows how God will use it?

Caring for the Poor. This text also forces us to decide what is the proper focus of lavish giving to Christ. How do we best show our love for Jesus? Pope Nicholas V advised his successors on his deathbed in 1455 that people's faith needed to be inspired and strengthened by "majestic buildings, imperishable memorials, and witnesses seemingly planted by the Hand of God." Mee, who cites this quote, comments acidly: "God's majesty being, of course, infinite, there was no end of inspiring to be done and no end of the money needed to do it."[12] Elaborate buildings built to the glory of God at sacrificial cost to members may not be appropriate gifts to God. We may be doing these things to feed our own pride. There are times that one should give this money to missions or to help the poor, or at least to open our doors to offer them meals.

Jesus says that what this woman did was good because she was anointing him for his burial. Since Jesus has died and risen again, such gifts should now be directed to the poor. We must remember Jesus' words from another Gospel, "I tell you the truth, whatever you did for one of the least of these brothers of mine, you did for me" (Matt. 25:40). As we relate to the poor, we relate to our Savior. Giving statistics, however, suggest that many in the church do not wrestle with how to use material resources to show their devotion to Christ. According to the *International Bulletin of Missionary Research*, the total worldwide income of Christians recently was $10.1 trillion dollars, and gifts to Christian causes was $17 billion—less than 2 percent.

Judas's Betrayal. Modern readers usually want to know more why Judas betrayed Jesus than why the woman was so generous. Mark offers no motive at all for the betrayal. Luke tells us that Satan entered Judas (Luke 22:3). According to Matthew, greed was the chief motive—Judas was the one who introduced the issue of money by asking, "What are you willing to give me if I hand him over to you?" (Matt. 26:15). In John's Gospel, Judas is identified as a thief concerned about money (John 12:6) and as one in league with Satan (13:2).

---

12. Charles L. Mee, *White Robe, Black Robe* (New York: Putnam, 1972), 42–43.

But scholars have not been satisfied with these answers and propose others. Some have contended that Judas was a devoted disciple whose ardor for Jesus cooled for various reasons. The most popular one imagines that Judas was attracted by the objectives of the Zealots and became disillusioned as time went by. He could accept the harsh realities of discipleship since ousting the heathen empire of Rome required sacrifice. But he grew more uneasy when Jesus remained spinelessly inactive and implied he would make a tame surrender without putting up a fight. When Jesus purged the temple instead of the Gentiles and kept military spending down to two swords (Luke 22:38), that was the final straw. Judas had been ready to commit his life to holy war. Jesus turned out to be a charlatan, and Judas took revenge on him for causing his disappointment. Or perhaps he even contacted Jewish authorities in hopes that their action against him would force Jesus finally to set kingdom events in motion. If so, he may have fooled himself into thinking that he was helping God, not betraying Jesus. It is also possible that Judas was cowed by the certain reprisal of the temple power structure. He switched to what he believed was the winning side to save himself from any retaliation.

If one sticks only to the Gospel of Mark, Mark gives no clear motive for the betrayal. This lack of motive has significant implications. If Judas, one of the Twelve, could, without any discernible reason, become the one who betrayed his Master, then every disciple is potentially another Judas.[13] Dostoevsky writes in *The Idiot*: "The causes of human actions are usually immeasurably more complex than are our subsequent explanations of them, and can rarely be distinctly discerned."[14] Attempts to find *the* reason or reasons to explain why Judas did what he did are diversions that prevent us from looking at our own potential betrayal. If we convince ourselves that Judas acted for this or that reason, we can also convince ourselves that we would not succumb to such perfidy. If no specific reason can be given except greed or Satan, then we all are susceptible. We too can betray Jesus for all the temptations in life that may snare us.

---

13. Augustin Stock, *Call to Discipleship* (Wilmington: Michael Glazier, 1984), 195.
14. Cited in W. H. Vanstone, *The Stature of Waiting* (New York: Seabury, 1983), 2.

Mark 14:12–31

N THE FIRST day of the Feast of Unleavened Bread, when it was customary to sacrifice the Passover lamb, Jesus' disciples asked him, "Where do you want us to go and make preparations for you to eat the Passover?"

¹³So he sent two of his disciples, telling them, "Go into the city, and a man carrying a jar of water will meet you. Follow him. ¹⁴Say to the owner of the house he enters, 'The Teacher asks: Where is my guest room, where I may eat the Passover with my disciples?' ¹⁵He will show you a large upper room, furnished and ready. Make preparations for us there."

¹⁶The disciples left, went into the city and found things just as Jesus had told them. So they prepared the Passover.

¹⁷When evening came, Jesus arrived with the Twelve. ¹⁸While they were reclining at the table eating, he said, "I tell you the truth, one of you will betray me—one who is eating with me."

¹⁹They were saddened, and one by one they said to him, "Surely not I?"

²⁰"It is one of the Twelve," he replied, "one who dips bread into the bowl with me. ²¹The Son of Man will go just as it is written about him. But woe to that man who betrays the Son of Man! It would be better for him if he had not been born."

²²While they were eating, Jesus took bread, gave thanks and broke it, and gave it to his disciples, saying, "Take it; this is my body."

²³Then he took the cup, gave thanks and offered it to them, and they all drank from it.

²⁴"This is my blood of the covenant, which is poured out for many," he said to them. ²⁵"I tell you the truth, I will not drink again of the fruit of the vine until that day when I drink it anew in the kingdom of God."

²⁶When they had sung a hymn, they went out to the Mount of Olives.

²⁷"You will all fall away," Jesus told them, "for it is written:

"'I will strike the shepherd,
    and the sheep will be scattered.'

²⁸But after I have risen, I will go ahead of you into Galilee."

²⁹Peter declared, "Even if all fall away, I will not."

³⁰"I tell you the truth," Jesus answered, "today—yes, tonight—before the rooster crows twice you yourself will disown me three times."

³¹But Peter insisted emphatically, "Even if I have to die with you, I will never disown you." And all the others said the same.

THIS PASSAGE BREAKS into three scenes: the preparations for Jesus' Passover meal with his disciples (14:12–16), the Last Supper (14:17–25), and the departure for the Mount of Olives (14:26–31). A single theme runs through each scene: Jesus' foreknowledge of events.

Preparations for the Passover Meal (14:12–16)

MARK NOTES THAT the disciples are anxious to make preparations for the Passover meal.[1] On the eve of Passover, 14 Nisan, work normally ceased at noon and the ritual slaughter of the Passover lambs began around 3:00 P.M. as the heads of the household brought their animals to the temple (see Jub. 49:10–12). The priests sprinkled the blood against the base of the altar and offered the fat on the altar. The animals were dressed with the legs unbroken and the head still attached to the carcass and returned to the worshipers. Because of the great number of people, the slaughter had to be separated from the place of eating. The only stipulation was that the lamb had to be eaten in Jerusalem, whose borders were expanded to accommodate the crowds. Worshipers returned to their homes or wherever they could find a nook or a cranny to spit the lamb on a stick for the late evening meal. This took place in the evening (after sunset) on 15 Nisan, strictly speaking, the first day of Unleavened Bread.

Jesus gives the disciples directions that may reflect some secret arrangement on his part with coded signs. A man carrying a water jar would have been an unusual spectacle since women normally fetched water. Finding the

---

1. Mark tells us that it was the first day of Unleavened Bread when the Passover was sacrificed. Actually the first day of Unleavened Bread began after Passover day (see Lev. 23:5–6; Num. 28:16–17), but Jews in the first century referred to the two feasts in combination (see 2 Chron. 35:17). The confusion between the two days stems from the fact that leaven was removed in a ceremonial search of the dwelling on the morning the Passover lambs were sacrificed, and it could be thought of as the first day of Unleavened Bread.

room is so similar to finding the donkey in 11:1–6, however, that the scene may be intended to show that Jesus knows everything in advance and has total control of the situation (see 14:8).[2] The emphasis falls on the conclusion: "The disciples ... found things just as Jesus had told them" (14:16). Owners of homes in Jerusalem were obligated to provide space for pilgrims to eat their Passover lambs within the city.

The disciples secure such a room by identifying Jesus only as "the teacher." His authority as "the teacher" (see 1:22; 12:14) makes him deserving of special honor. The wording in the account also stresses that it is Jesus' Passover. The disciples ask Jesus where to go to "make preparations *for you* to eat the Passover" (14:12). Jesus responds that they are to go to "*my* guest room, where *I* may eat the Passover with my disciples" (14:14).

The Last Supper (14:17–25)

THE UPPER ROOM was, as Barclay aptly describes it, "a smaller box on top of a bigger box."[3] It was used as a guest room, storeroom, and place of retreat. According to later rabbinic tradition, the sages met their students in upper rooms to teach (*m. Sabb.* 1:14; *b. Menah.* 41b; see Acts 1:13; 20:8).

Most popular paintings of the Last Supper depict the disciples sitting serenely around the table. Judas is usually identifiable as dark and shifty-eyed. Mark's depiction of this meal differs significantly from these portraits. The most appropriate portrait of his portrayal of the Last Supper would paint each disciple's face with a look of horror. They eat and drink in an atmosphere of sorrow and worry. The central question preoccupying their minds is not the fate of Jesus but who might be the one to betray him.

Jesus serves as host, and the scene begins with his grave announcement that one of them will betray him, "one who is eating with me" (14:18). All the disciples ask him one by one, "Surely not I?" (14:19). This translation captures the force of the Greek *meti*, which expects a negative answer: "It is not I, is it?" (see 4:21). Jesus reassures no one but gives only an ambiguous response to their questioning that essentially repeats his first declaration: "It is one of the Twelve ... one who dips bread into the bowl with me" (14:20).[4] This statement adds no new information but reiterates that the betrayer has infiltrated their midst and is eating with him.

The horror for Mark is that "one who is eating with me" (14:18), "one of the Twelve" (14:20a), "one who dips bread into the bowl with me" (14:20b) will hand Jesus over. Eating bread with someone barred one from hostile

---

2. Hooker, *Mark*, 335.

3. William Barclay, *The Gospel of Mark* (Philadelphia: Westminster, 1956), 347–48.

4. We should probably picture a common bowl.

acts against that person. Table fellowship had more significance for Jews than simply a social gathering. Eating together was evidence of peace, trust, forgiveness, and brotherhood.[5] To betray the one who had given you his bread was a horrendous act (see Ps. 41:9; John 13:18). Jesus had hosted another meal for sinners (see 2:15), but this time he utters a bitter woe for a betrayer: "Woe to that man who betrays the Son of Man! It would be better for him if he had not been born" (14:21). Only then does Jesus take the bread and the wine.

Mark does not record this meal simply because it was Jesus' last meal with his disciples, but because "he did and said something memorable."[6] He connects the elements of the meal to his coming suffering and death. Jesus has fully anticipated his death. It would be a violent death, as the imagery of broken bread and blood poured out implies. He interprets it as an atoning death (10:45). The visible union between himself and his disciples will dissolve at his death, but Jesus provides a symbol by which that visible union will be replaced by an invisible one.

The head of a family took bread eaten at every meal, lifted it up, and said, "Praise be Thou, O Lord our God, King of the Universe, who causes bread to come forth from the earth." After the Amen response, the bread was broken and distributed, mediating the blessing to each one who ate. The same was true over the wine (see *m. Ber.* 6:1 on the blessing over "the fruit of the vine"). Jesus gives the traditional blessing of the bread a new twist by saying, "This is my body." In effect, he says, "This is myself." To a Semite, the body encompasses the whole person, not just the physical part of oneself.

Jesus' words are symbolic and akin to what Jeremiah did when he took a long-necked pottery jar outside the gates of Jerusalem and smashed it in the presence of selected leaders (Jer. 19:1–15). Jeremiah could have said, "This is you." When Jesus breaks the bread and distributes it to the disciples, it means that what has happened to this bread will happen to him. The broken bread given to the disciples also symbolizes that his Passion will benefit them and is an acted-out parable of his offering up his life for the many.

What is significant is that Jesus uses an article of food so simple and so universal that the disciples can never again recline at a meal, take bread, bless it, and break it without thinking of the last night that they were together

---

5. Covenants were sealed by a meal—for example, Abimelech and Isaac (Gen. 26:26–31), Laban and Jacob (31:51–54), and Jehoiachin and the king of Babylon (2 Kings 25:27–29; Jer. 52:31–33).

6. Hooker, *Mark*, 338. On the Lord's Supper, see Joachim Jeremias, *The Eucharistic Words of Jesus* (London: SCM, 1966); I. Howard Marshall, *Last Supper and Lord's Supper* (Grand Rapids: Eerdmans, 1980).

with their Lord. Just as our memories are triggered by something that reminds us of the last moments we spent with a departed loved one, these disciples can never eat another meal without thinking about what Jesus did for them on the cross.

The disciples have failed to understand about bread throughout Jesus' ministry. In the Last Supper, the reader can put the various pieces of the puzzle together. In 6:36, they implored Jesus to send the crowds away so that they could go and buy themselves something to eat. But Jesus told them to give them something to eat. Their incredulous response was, "That would take eight months of a man's wages! Are we to go and spend that much on bread and give it to them to eat?" (6:37). No, Jesus will supply the bread. He commanded them to sit in platoons and *blessed* the bread, *broke* it, and *gave* it to the disciples to divide among the people (6:41). They ate and were filled with twelve baskets left over—reminiscent of the twelve tribes of Israel that would be gathered on the day of salvation. Later that night when Jesus came walking to them on the sea, they were terrified. Mark explains that were terrified because "they had not understood about the loaves; their hearts were hardened" (6:52).

The second feeding miracle occurred across the lake in Gentile territory and followed the same pattern. Jesus would not send the crowd away hungry. When he asked the disciples to feed the crowd, they exclaimed, "But where in this remote place can anyone get enough bread to feed them?" (8:4). Jesus took their meager supply of loaves, seven, *blessed* them, *broke* them, and *gave* them to the disciples to set before the people. Seven baskets of leftovers were gathered up (8:8), which indicated completion or universality of Jesus' mission.

Jesus had now fed both Jew and Gentile miraculously. In 8:14, the disciples had forgotten to bring bread except that they had one loaf with them in the boat. That one loaf with them in the boat was Jesus. The disciples did not understand, as evidenced by their lament, "We have no bread" (8:16). Jesus broke up the quarrel by asking, "Why are you talking about having no bread? Do you still not see or understand? Are your hearts hardened? Do you have eyes but fail to see, and ears but fail to hear? And don't you remember?" (8:17–18).

Bread has become a symbol of Jesus' mission, and the disciples do not understand.[7] When they take bread again after Jesus' resurrection, they will remember that they have bread of a most unusual nature. Combined with the statement, "This is my blood," Jesus' presence is made possible by his death, by which God makes a new covenant.

---

7. Senior, *The Passion of Jesus*, 58.

After the blessing of the cup, Jesus gives it to them. Mark reports that *after* they have all drunk from the cup, Jesus announces, "This is my blood of the covenant, which is poured out for many" (14:24). Years of taking communion have so conditioned us that we hardly blink an eye over this statement. Think of what that might have meant to a Jew in the first century. You have drunk from the cup, and the host says, "This is my blood." Jewish aversion to blood is notorious. Genesis 9:4 forbade the consumption of blood, which was enjoined on all persons and was therefore more universal than the Decalogue (see Acts 15:20, 29). The law forbade the drinking of blood because it was "the life" and because it had been ordained of God as a means of atonement. Any animals killed for human consumption had to be drained of all blood before being eaten.[8] Therefore, to drink blood was not only to break a universal commandment but to desecrate something that was holy.[9] Consequently, Jewish scholars have argued that this word would have been impossible on the lips of a Jew.[10]

Taylor responded to this objection by arguing that Jesus was no ordinary Jew but one who believed himself to be the Son of Man, destined to suffer for the many. Furthermore, his words often aroused a sense of religious horror and intense opposition. And the disciples had long been in the school of Christ learning that the Son of Man had to suffer, and throughout the Gospel it had been hard for them to swallow.[11]

What do Jesus' statements, "This is my body. . . . This is my blood" imply? (1) Wine was considered to be the blood of the grape, plucked from the vine and crushed. The blood of the sacrificial animals was poured out by the priests on the altar as a sin offering to atone for the sins of the people (Lev. 4:17, 18, 25, 30, 34). When Jesus makes his statements, he is saying that *his* death is a new sacrifice offered to God. No more sacrificial victims need be killed, only bread broken and shared, wine poured out and shared.

(2) Mark makes it clear that they all drank from the one cup rather than from individual cups, as was customary (14:23). Drinking the cup of someone meant entering into a communion relationship with that person, to the point that one shared that person's destiny, good or ill (see Ps. 16:4–5, which suggests that the Lord is one's chosen portion and my cup, not other gods). Jesus had asked James and John if they were able to drink the cup that he would drink and then assured them that they would (10:38–39). Not only

---

8. Hooker, *Mark*, 342.

9. See Lev. 3:17; 7:26; Deut. 12:16, 23–25; 15:23; 1 Sam. 14:32; 1 Chron. 11:15–19.

10. Claude Montefiore, *The Synoptic Gospels* (London: Macmillan, 1927), 1:332; Joseph Klausner, *Jesus of Nazareth* (London: George Allen & Unwin, 1925), 329; see also Hooker, *Mark*, 342.

11. Vincent Taylor, *Jesus and His Sacrifice* (London: Macmillan, 1937), 134.

did all the disciples have to overcome the offense of a suffering Messiah and begin to understand his death as an atoning death for the many, they also had to overcome the offense that they were to follow in the way of their Master and accept his destiny of suffering for themselves.

(3) Blood sealed or inaugurated a covenant. In Exodus 24:3–8, 11, Moses took the blood and sprinkled it over the people saying, "This is the blood of the covenant that the LORD has made with you in accordance with all these words" (24:8; see Zech. 9:11; Heb. 9:19–20). Jesus' sacrificial death is also a covenant-making event. It marks a new act of redemption and begins a new relationship between God and the people—one that supersedes the old. It creates a new community gathered around his table. It is probable, although debated, that Isaiah 53:12 also forms the backdrop of Jesus' statement about his blood poured out for the "many": "he poured out his life unto death, and was numbered with the transgressors. For he bore the sin of many,[12] and made intercession for the transgressors."

Gloom predominates the Last Supper in Mark. But whenever Jesus speaks of his death, he combines it with a positive note of his vindication. A glimmer of joy emerges when Jesus speaks of drinking the fruit of the vine anew in the kingdom of God. The supper that begins on such a sad note ends on a note of joy. In the face of death, duplicity, and desertion, Jesus exudes confidence that ultimately he will be vindicated by God's reign (14:28; see 8:31; 9:31; 10:33–34).

To the Mount of Olives (14:26–31)[13]

JESUS HAS BEEN able to foresee all that will take place related to his Passion (e.g., the animal to commandeer, the man carrying the water jar, and the betrayal). Now he predicts that all the disciples will scatter to the winds, but he will regather them. The verb *skandalizo* ("scandalize"; NIV, "you will . . . fall away") first appeared in the parable of the soils in 4:17. The rocky soil responds with superficial zeal but has no depth. When persecution arises on account of the word, they are scandalized and fall away. Jesus predicts, in other words, that all of the disciples are going to be like the rocky soil, and Peter will have the rockiest time of all.

---

12. "Many" in the biblical idiom means "all" (see Rom. 5:19, "many were made sinners"; 1 Cor. 15:22).

13. The REB translates that they left the Upper Room after they sang "the Passover hymn." But *hymneo* need not refer to the Hallel hymns (Pss. 115–18), sung after the Passover meal. Brown (*The Death of the Messiah*, 1:122–23) argues that it conveys the "prayerful context as the meal closed," and the first readers would have connected it to hymns they were familiar with singing in their worship.

Jews were expecting the nations to be scattered by mighty whacks from the Messiah; instead, Jesus predicts, his disciples will be routed when he as the Messiah is struck. Jesus has worked hard all through Mark's narrative and now at the end has little to show for it. Even his small band will be thrown into confusion and fly in all directions. The citation from Zechariah reveals, however, that what happens is all in God's control. This prediction seals that the disciples will fail but puts it in a biblical context of eschatological hope.

The Last Supper scene contains many allusions to Zechariah 9–14: my blood of the covenant (Mark 14:24/Zech. 9:11); that day, the kingdom of God (Mark 14:25/Zech. 14:4, 9); the Mount of Olives (Mark 14:26/Zech. 14:4); strike the shepherd (Mark 14:27/Zech. 13:7); resurrection and restoration of the sheep (Mark 14:28/Zech. 13:8–9). Marcus concludes from these allusions that Mark portrays Jesus' last night on earth as the time of eschatological testing spoken of by Zechariah. God's shepherd will be struck, and his people "will be tested to the breaking point."[14] The use of "I" ("*I* will strike the shepherd") underscores the divine initiative behind Jesus' death. What happens is not a travesty of justice outside God's sovereign control. This blow lays on him the iniquity of us all (Isa. 53:6b) and initially has a devastating effect on the flock. Some will perish, but the remnant will be refined, purified, and restored as God's people (Zech. 13:9). Jesus will reverse the breakup by regathering them.

Jesus again gives them a cheering promise, "After I have risen, I will go ahead of you into Galilee." For the fifth time in the Gospel Jesus predicts his resurrection (8:31; 9:9; 9:31; 10:34). The future of Jesus' movement depends entirely on God's direct intervention, not on the disciples' individual bravery.[15] As Mark presents the story, the disciples cannot stand on their own strength until God has accomplished his purpose in Christ. Jesus therefore must go it alone. Only after his death on the cross and his resurrection by God will disciples have strength enough to take up their own cross and follow him.

Jesus will "go ahead of" them, which does not mean that he will arrive first in Galilee or walk ahead of them on the road (see 10:32). It implies that he will resume his shepherding role, leading them and calling them together.[16] This promise is the key for understanding the ending of this Gospel (16:8). Readers can read in the Gospel how Jesus' prophecy of the disciples' failures proved true. They also learn from the angel's announcement at the empty tomb that Jesus' prophecy of his triumph over death is fulfilled. I would con-

---

14. Marcus, *The Way of the Lord*, 157–59.
15. Juel, *Mark*, 195.
16. Brown, *The Death of the Messiah*, 1:130.

tend that the first readers of Mark's Gospel also must have known that Jesus' reconciliation with his disciples occurred as Jesus promised even though Mark does not narrate it in his text.[17] All readers can infer that Jesus' resurrection not only defeats the powers of death but can also overcome human failure. It heralds the chance for all to begin anew.

When Jesus speaks again of his death, Peter and the other disciples remain confident of their ability to remain faithful. Jesus is confident only in God's faithfulness to raise him up when he is struck down. The disciples' protest of loyalty (14:29–31) makes it clear that they are still unseeing and unready. Earlier, Peter protested Jesus' announcement that the Son of Man *must* suffer according to the divine plan (8:31–33). Now, he does not shrink from contradicting Jesus' citation from Scripture that they will all fail.[18] He will prove Jesus to be a false prophet and inveighs against any suggestion that he will wilt under pressure. Peter disputes Jesus' word in a spirit of rivalry and must regard himself as a Triton among minnows. He insists that he will prove himself *more* trustworthy than the rest, who, he implies, probably will fall away.

This competitive egotism, "Even if all fall away, I will not," will never go willingly to a cross. Consequently, Peter's failure at the crucial moment will be immortalized. Jesus does not call him to undergo the death of a valiant bodyguard, cut down in a heroic last stand. He must take up his cross and put to death the selfish ambition and self-centered purpose, no matter how sincere and noble it might appear. The scattering of the disciples, therefore, already begins when Peter speaks for himself and not for the others. He relies on his own power. The other disciples follow Peter's lead and join in protest that they will never be false to Jesus. Tolbert perceptively observes, "If they are not sure whether or not they will betray him, how can they possibly swear faithfulness to death?"[19] The problem is that their pledge of loyalty is premature and swells with vanity. They do not yet fully realize that a cross will really be involved.

Jesus now prophesies that Peter will deny him three times before the cock crows twice. The cock crow may refer to a rooster crowing or to the bugle call of the *gallicinium*, which signaled the beginning of the fourth watch. The second cock crow was connected to the dawn or rising sun. Jesus may simply mean "before the next dawn."[20] Peter's head must be spinning. In 8:32–34, Jesus rebuked him because he would not accept his suffering. Now

17. See below, p. 622.
18. Brown, *The Death of the Messiah*, 1:134. Peter's protest, "Yet not I," is not unlike the high priest's concern, "not during the Feast."
19. Tolbert, *Sowing*, 212.
20. Brown, *The Death of the Messiah*, 1:137.

he is willing to accept the fact that Jesus must suffer and is willing to suffer with him. He is even willing to die with Jesus (14:31). To die with Jesus *is* necessary, but Jesus does not need knight errants to defend him. The word "to die with" (*synapothnesko*) occurs in Pauline literature to refer to our participation in the saving death of Jesus (see 2 Cor. 7:3; 2 Tim. 2:11; also Rom. 6:8; Col. 2:20). This statement then is grandly ironic and reflects Peter's continued ignorance of the significance of Jesus' death.

O'COLLINS HAS OBSERVED that "the rise of biblical criticism led some writers to minimize drastically Jesus' expectations about his coming death. At times they even declared his death to be something that overtook him without being accepted and interpreted in advance."[21] He cites Bultmann's claim that we cannot know how Jesus understood his death and that his crucifixion was not an inherent and necessary consequence of his activity.

> Rather it took place because his activity was misconstrued as political activity. In that case it would have been a meaningless fate. We cannot tell whether or how Jesus found meaning in it. We may not veil from ourselves the possibility that he suffered collapse.[22]

Bultmann and others may be criticized for ignoring the Last Supper and Gethsemane and for making a false dichotomy between the political realm and the religious. Küng asks:

> Would he have been so naive as not to have any presentiment of what finally happened to him? ... No supernatural knowledge was required to recognize the danger of a violent end, only a sober view of reality. His radical message raised doubts about the pious self-reliance of individuals and of society and about the traditional religious system as a whole, and created opposition from the very beginning. Consequently, Jesus was bound to expect serious conflicts and violent reaction on the part of the religious and perhaps also the political authorities, particularly at the center of power.[23]

---

21. Gerald O'Collins, *Interpreting Jesus* (London: Geoffrey Chapman, 1983), 80.

22. Rudolf Bultmann, *Historical Jesus and Kerygmatic Christ*, eds. Carl E. Braaten and Roy A. Harrisville (New York/Nashville: Abingdon, 1964), 23; cited by O'Collins, *Interpreting Jesus*, 82.

23. Hans Küng, *On Being a Christian* (London/New York: Collins, 1977), 320; cited by O'Collins, *Interpreting Jesus*, 84.

Jesus firmly believed that his death was not a stroke of fate but that its purpose lay deep within the providence of God. He viewed this death as a representative death for the many. It was something that they were unable to supply for themselves but which he supplies for them, standing alone in the breach. He views his death positively, as part of his vocation, and connects it closely with the kingdom of God, which brings salvation to humans.

There is a trend in some churches today to have a Passover seder the Thursday evening of Holy Week. To my mind, this desire is misdirected and misunderstands the thrust of Mark's presentation of the Last Supper. Aside from the fact that scholars debate whether Jesus' Last Supper was a Passover meal,[24] the Passover elements are ignored in Mark's recounting of the meal. Mark makes no mention of the paschal lamb, the stewed fruit, the bitter herbs, the unleavened bread, or the deliverance from Egypt. Because the Passover of Israel is fulfilled in Jesus, the disciples will never need a ritual lamb again.[25] The Lord's Supper was not celebrated in the early church as an annual ritual, but each Lord's day. Passover became a metaphor for Christ's sacrifice (cf. 1 Cor. 5:7). For Christians to celebrate Passover subtly undermines the significance of Christ's death and the meaning he attached to this meal. In the same way as Jesus' death abrogated the animal sacrifices in the temple, so the Lord's Supper has become the festal celebration of all God's people, both Jews and Gentiles, which transcends the old.

Passover	Lord's Supper
In the old age of law	In the new age of the kingdom
The great festival meal celebrating the birth of God's people	The new celebratory meal of the birth of God's people
Participants associated themselves with deliverance and the old covenant	Participants associate themselves with redemption and the new covenant
Looks back to the Exodus and forward to God's salvation	Looks back to the cross, which brings salvation, and forward to the final realization of God's kingdom

---

24. For the complex arguments, see Joachim Jeremias, *The Eucharistic Words of Jesus* (London: SCM, 1966), 1–88; Brown, *Death of the Messiah*, 2:1350–78.

25. Xavier Léon-Dufour, *Sharing the Eucharistic Bread: The Witness of the New Testament* (New York/Mahwah: Paulist, 1987), 193.

THE PASSOVER WAS not intended to be a gratifying memento of God's past deliverance of Israel. The celebration was meant to place each generation in touch with that event and make it a present reality. It celebrates what "the Lord did for *me*" (cf. Ex. 13:8–9). In the same way, the Lord's Supper is not a memorial of something past and gone but reminds us of what the Lord has done for us and makes his death and his presence a living reality. Hunter points out that "remembering" in the biblical idiom "is not to entertain a pallid idea of a past event in one's mind, but to make the event present again so that it controls the will and becomes potent in our lives for good or ill."[26]

The Lord's Supper works for good. It reminds us who we are, what our story is, what our values are, and who claims us as his own. In the Lord's Supper, the gospel confronts all five of our physical senses. We see, hear, taste, smell, and touch what it meant for Christ to die for us. It also binds the past, present, and future together. We look back to Jesus' Last Supper and experience the beginning of the new covenant with God. We experience Jesus' death for us and the power of our sins being forgiven in the present. We look forward to the future celebration in God's kingdom, when all will acknowledge Jesus as Lord. When Jesus distributes the wine to his disciples, he solemnly assures that he will be vindicated by God and will drink it anew in the kingdom of God. His words contain an implicit promise that those "who shared His table in the time of His obscurity, would also share it in the time of His glory."[27]

Eating the bread and drinking the cup of wine is not some magic ritual, however. It brings no automatic guarantee of salvation. One does not become a beneficiary of Jesus' redemptive death through participation in any rite. Did Judas partake of the bread and drink the cup? If he did, it had no salvific effect (Acts 1:25). Even Jesus' stern warning has no immediate effect. Jesus lets Judas know that he is on to his conspiracy and thereby gives him one last chance to turn from his course. Jesus went as it was written of him in Scripture; but Judas was under no divine necessity to betray his Master. He voluntarily chose to ignore Jesus' alarm and apparently left to fulfill his bargain with the priests, still unsuspected by the other disciples.

If Judas participated with the other disciples in the meal, and there is no indication in the text that he did not, then eating the bread and drinking the cup must be internalized for it to be saving. The new covenant must be writ-

---

26. A. M. Hunter, *Jesus—Lord and Saviour* (Grand Rapids: Eerdmans, 1976), 140.

27. Albert Schweitzer, *The Quest for the Historical Jesus: A Critical Study of Its Progress from Reimarus to Wrede* (New York: Macmillan, 1968), 376.

ten on the hearts of God's people (Jer. 31:31–34). This sacramental aspect of the Lord's Supper was misconstrued at Corinth. They thought that it was the food of immortality that enabled them to participate in the glorification of the Lord, which in turn made them immune from suffering and from God's judgment (see 1 Cor. 10:3–5). Paul had to remind them that when they ate this bread and drank this cup, they proclaimed the Lord's death until he returned (11:26). They participated in his death. The implication was that one might not partake of the Lord's Supper and take life easy or not make sacrifices.

Mark does not present the Last Supper as a sacrament that brings blessing and assurance. The scene, filled with high tension, sweaty palms, lumps in throats, and nervous anxiety, serves as a warning to readers. They are to examine themselves in precisely the same way as these first disciples did. One of them would betray Jesus. The gathered disciples did not immediately single out Judas as the guilty party. They looked to themselves. Today, each must ask himself or herself, as these disciples did, "Surely not I?"

When the Lord's Supper is served at the end of a worship service, people may examine their watches more than their hearts and may be worried more about dinner than how they have betrayed Jesus in the previous week or how they might betray him in the next. Mark's account of the Last Supper should jolt us awake. Each should contemplate his or her own life and confess all the ways, big and small, that he or she has betrayed the Lord and acknowledge such weaknesses. We should all be humbly aware that if one of the Twelve could betray Jesus, every Christian has that potential. This idea of self-examination, as opposed to cross-examination, is preserved in Paul's comments on the Lord's Supper (1 Cor. 11:27–29), along with the idea of eating worthily. We are worthy of the Lord's Supper when we recognize how unworthy we are. We feel its power when we also recognize that Jesus died for us and accepts us in spite of our unworthiness.

One should note, however, the danger of egocentricity that can permeate those gathered around the Lord's table. When Jesus announces that a betrayer is in their midst, each disciple hopes Jesus will assure him that he is not the one. When he gets that assurance, he can presumably breathe a sigh of relief; he would never betray his Master. None of the disciples expresses any concern that Jesus will be betrayed; none expresses any concern for the traitor. Each focuses only on himself, wanting reassurance from Jesus that he is in the clear, and then each one wants to reassure Jesus that he would never be guilty of such a crime.

But one of those gathered at the table will be guilty of heinous treason. Judas, with ice water in his veins, bluffs his way through the meal with the rest of the disciples. But none of the disciples will be above reproach. Each will show himself to be an unfaithful servant. The contrast is striking. Jesus gives his life for others and only laments the miserable fate of the betrayer. The disciples' response shows that they are concerned only about themselves. This same egocentricity can surface in our celebration of the Lord's Supper, where our rupture, separation, and isolation from each other stands revealed. This Supper calls us to imitate Christ's self-sacrificing love and should be a moment when we can heal our broken relationships.[28]

Throughout church history, the Lord's Supper has been a flashpoint that proclaims the rift among Christians rather than a sign of peace that proclaims the reconciling effects of the Lord's death. Christians even within the same confessional tradition continue to argue about the mode of observance, how it should be served, how often it should be observed, who may officiate, and who may participate. Much of the division among denominations stems from edicts and decisions that have nothing to do with the New Testament text.

Problems began when the Lord's Supper was treated as a sacramental rite separated from the context of a meal and when church offices developed, which led to restrictions on who could preside at the celebration. If we want to capture the meaning of the Lord's Supper as Jesus' last meal with his disciples, in which he declared symbolically the meaning of his death and offered his assurance for the future, we should celebrate in the context of a meal in which the two, the rite and the meal, are integrated (see Acts 2:42, 46; 6:1–2; 21:7, 11).[29] The action unfolds "while they were eating" (Mark 14:22).

But dangers lurk here also. The Corinthians' celebration of the Lord's Supper in a meal setting was also beset by schisms (1 Cor. 11:18). They apparently followed the pattern that Paul delineates from the tradition: Jesus gave thanks and broke bread, and *after the supper* he took the cup (11:23–25). The abuses arose during the Supper. According to Paul Winter's reconstruction, the supper began with the breaking of bread, in which all participated. The wealthier Corinthians and those attached to a household then selfishly devoured their meals and filled themselves while the "have-nots," who did not

---

28. Theodore E. Dobson, *Say But the Word: How the Lord's Supper Can Transform Your Life* (New York/Ramsey, N.J.: Paulist, 1984), 5.

29. Hans Lietzmann (*Mass and Lord's Supper* [Leiden: Brill, 1953], 204–8) argued that the early Christians developed two distinct Supper observances: (1) the Jerusalem type, which grew out of Jesus' table fellowship with his disciples and was a joyous meal celebrating Jesus' spiritual presence and looking forward to his return; (2) the Pauline type, which was a memorial to Jesus' death and stressed its meaning for salvation. Paul, however, argues that he passed on the tradition he had received, which went back to Jesus' last meal with his disciples (1 Cor. 11:23). The case for two distinct types of Lord's Supper observances has not been established.

have the security of belonging to a household, went hungry (11:21).[30] The poor then joined their fellow Christians in the cup after the meal.

Paul contrasts the Corinthians' selfish taking (*prolambano*, 11:21) with Jesus' taking bread (*lambano*, 11:23). Both take. The Corinthians took on their own behalf; Jesus took bread on others' behalf. The Corinthians acted selfishly; Jesus gave to others. The Corinthians stood condemned because they showed no concern for another's hunger or honor (11:22). They may have revered the body on the table but they did not discern the body *at* the table (11:29). Paul asks them to overcome their selfishness and "receive one another" (11:33), which entails sharing with those who have not.[31] Winter concludes that the Corinthians could only declare their love for God by demonstrating love for their needy brothers and sisters.

> To refuse to receive at the Lord's Dinner (*deipnon*) in the fullest sense of the word, those whom Christ has unreservedly received, both denies the reality of the gospel to break down all barriers, and brings to light in the banquet of the new age those socio-economic divisions that belong to the age that is passing away.[32]

How could things have gone so awry in Corinth? The dinner conventions of the ancient world would have accustomed them to have servants stand around as they ate, and so it was easier for them to overlook the fact that some had nothing to eat. But human egocentricity again lay at the root of the calamity in Corinth, which passed under the guise of the Lord's Supper.

The same problem can also infiltrate our Supper, particularly when we emphasize that it has to do only with individuals who have communion with the risen Christ. The presence of Christ's saving power in the Eucharist manifests itself when we recognize our common union with one another. Churches should compare their ecclesiastical tradition regarding the Lord's Supper critically with the New Testament witness. Perhaps they will discover that they need to develop ways to convey the presence of Christ's saving power in new and different ways. Perhaps this can be communicated best if we return to the practice of the New Testament in observing the Lord's Supper at a shared meal. We can celebrate our fellowship with the Lord and with one another.

---

30. Paul Winter, "The Lord's Supper at Corinth: An Alternative Reconstruction," *RTR* 37 (1978): 73–82.

31. Ibid., 79. Winter argues that the verb *ekdechomai* does not mean "wait for one another" in the semantic context of a meal but welcome one another, implying that they share with them.

32. Ibid., 81.

Mark 14:32–52

🌿

THEY WENT TO a place called Gethsemane, and Jesus said to his disciples, "Sit here while I pray." 33He took Peter, James and John along with him, and he began to be deeply distressed and troubled. 34"My soul is overwhelmed with sorrow to the point of death," he said to them. "Stay here and keep watch."

35Going a little farther, he fell to the ground and prayed that if possible the hour might pass from him. 36"Abba, Father," he said, "everything is possible for you. Take this cup from me. Yet not what I will, but what you will."

37Then he returned to his disciples and found them sleeping. "Simon," he said to Peter, "are you asleep? Could you not keep watch for one hour? 38Watch and pray so that you will not fall into temptation. The spirit is willing, but the body is weak."

39Once more he went away and prayed the same thing. 40When he came back, he again found them sleeping, because their eyes were heavy. They did not know what to say to him.

41Returning the third time, he said to them, "Are you still sleeping and resting? Enough! The hour has come. Look, the Son of Man is betrayed into the hands of sinners. 42Rise! Let us go! Here comes my betrayer!"

43Just as he was speaking, Judas, one of the Twelve, appeared. With him was a crowd armed with swords and clubs, sent from the chief priests, the teachers of the law, and the elders.

44Now the betrayer had arranged a signal with them: "The one I kiss is the man; arrest him and lead him away under guard." 45Going at once to Jesus, Judas said, "Rabbi!" and kissed him. 46The men seized Jesus and arrested him. 47Then one of those standing near drew his sword and struck the servant of the high priest, cutting off his ear.

48"Am I leading a rebellion," said Jesus, "that you have come out with swords and clubs to capture me? 49Every day I was with you, teaching in the temple courts, and you did not arrest me. But the Scriptures must be fulfilled. 50Then everyone deserted him and fled. 51A young man, wearing nothing but a linen garment, was following Jesus. When they seized him, 52he fled naked, leaving his garment behind.

Original Meaning

JESUS RETIRES AFTER the Last Supper to a place on the Mount of Olives identified as Gethsemane, a word that word means "oil press."[1] Jesus separates Peter, James, and John from the rest of the group to go with him as he prays. Peter has just boasted that he would stand firm with Jesus through his trials even if they lead to death (14:29). James and John promised that they could be baptized with his baptism and could drink his cup (10:39). Jesus gives them a chance to back up their words. These three disciples have witnessed his raising of Jairus's daughter and his glorious transfiguration (5:37; 9:2). Now they must witness his agony. Jesus' suffering is as important as these other two events.[2] One can divide the treatment of this incident into two parts: the Gethsemane experience of Jesus and the Gethsemane experience of the disciples. From there we will discuss Jesus' arrest.

The Gethsemane of Jesus (14:32–36)

ALTHOUGH JESUS WANTS the support and prayer of Peter, James, and John, he knows that even these three disciples will be of no help to him now and goes off a little farther alone. Mark uses a word to suggest the greatest possible degree of horror and suffering (*ekthambeo*) in 14:33. He boldly allows us to see Jesus suffering psychological anguish before his physical suffering. Jesus is in the grip of a shuddering horror as he faces the dreadful prospect before him.[3]

Jesus tells the disciples that he is grieved with a sorrow unto death, a phrase describing the extent of his sorrow.[4] It drives him to prayer. The prayer is also startling. Jesus does not enter his suffering stoically but biblically, with loud lament.[5] Mark also reports that Jesus falls on the ground (14:35). Normally, one lifted one's hands toward heaven and prayed aloud in a standing posture. But if a person was in particular distress, he might lie prostrate and pray face down (see 2 Sam. 12:16).

---

1. The slopes of the Mount of Olives were filled with olive groves before the Romans cut down huge numbers to build their siege works during the war of A.D. 66–70.

2. Urs Sommer, *Die Passionsgeschichte des Markusevangeliums* (WUNT 2/58; Tübingen: J. C. B. Mohr [Paul Siebeck], 1993), 105.

3. Cranfield, *Mark*, 431.

4. Sir. 37:1–2 describes a grief unto death when one's friend and companion turns to enmity. Jesus is not burdened down by a sorrow that could kill (see Pss. 42:5, 6, 11; 43:5; 116:3) or a sorrow so great that death would be preferable (see the laments of the drained prophets, Num. 11:14–15 [Moses]; 1 Kings 19:4 [Elijah]; Jer. 20:14–18; Jonah 4:3–9).

5. Schweizer, *Mark*, 311; for example, see Ps. 55:4–6; Sir. 51:6–10.

Jesus' prayer of lament follows a well-known pattern of lament found in the Psalms (see Pss. 13:1–3; 22:1–21; 31:1–24; 40:11–13; 42:5, 9–11; 43:1–2, 5; 55:4–8; 61:1–3; 116:3–4). In the Jewish lament, Senior notes that one's prayer is not "fully controlled, or strained with politeness. In a rush of emotion, complaint, and even recrimination, the believers pour out their hearts to God."[6] Prayers asking God to have a change of mind are not considered insubordinate but actually exude trust that God listens to prayer and grants requests that can be reconciled "with overall Providence."[7]

This trusting relationship is reflected in Jesus' familiar address of God as *Abba*. Jews addressed God as "Father" in prayer. Years ago, Gustav Dalman declared that the view that the Jews did not understand God as Father and that an intimate relationship with him was unknown until the revelation of the New Testament is incorrect. He wrote: "It was therefore nothing novel when the Fatherly relation of God was also applied within the Jewish community to the individual."[8] One prayed to a loving parent eager to listen. But no Jew used this familiar address (*Abba*) in prayer. Jesus shatters pious custom with this childlike address of "Daddy."[9] He expresses his intimacy with his Father as well as his confidence in his nearness and loving care.

Jesus knows God as Father in ways that others do not and cannot. One should not forget, however, that "to the Jew the first connotation of the fatherhood of God is the right to obedience."[10] Jesus trusts completely in God as his Father and is completely obedient. He also confesses God's omnipotence in his prayer to be spared suffering. His prayer does not try to run counter to the Father's purpose but explores the limits of the purpose without trying to burst its bounds.[11] Might there be another way? Might he escape the horrifying cup?

The cup may represent God's wrathful judgment, the awful consequences of God's judgment on sinful humanity (Pss. 11:6; 16:5; 23:5; 75:8–9; 116:13; Isa. 51:17–23; Jer. 16:7; 25:15–18; 27:46, 51; 49:12; 51:7; Ezek. 23:31–34; Lam. 2:13; 4:21; Hab. 2:15–16; Zech. 12:2; Rev. 14:10; 16:19; 17:4; 18:3, 6). On the other hand, the cup may simply refer to Jesus' death and the suffering he must endure. Jesus uses the cup and baptism as symbols of his redemptive death (Mark 10:38, 45). He connects the cup to the hour in 14:35; and

---

6. Senior, *The Passion of Jesus*, 76.

7. Brown, *The Death of the Messiah*, 1:167.

8. Gustav Dalman, *The Words of Jesus* (Edinburgh: T. & T. Clark, 1902), 189.

9. See Georg Schelbert, "Sprachgeschichtliches zu 'abba,'" *Mélanges Dominique Barthélemy*, eds. P Casetti, et al. (Orbis Biblicus et Orientalis 38; Göttingen: Vandenhoeck & Ruprecht, 1981), 395–447.

10. G. B. Caird and L. D. Hurst, *New Testament Theology* (Oxford: Clarendon, 1994), 401.

11. Richard T. France, *Matthew* (TNTC; Grand Rapids: Eerdmans, 1985), 373.

in 14:41, Jesus says that the hour has come when he is handed over to sinners. Jesus prays to be delivered *from* death; instead, he will be delivered *through* death and glorified by the resurrection.[12]

In Gethsemane, Jesus meets the dreadful silence of heaven. There is no reassuring voice from heaven proclaiming, "This is my Son, whom I love." No dove descends; no ministering angels come to serve him. God has already spoken, and his Son must obey. Jesus overcomes the silence, fights off the human temptation to do as he wills, and through prayer acquiesces to God's will. He will not try to evade the cup either by slipping away in the dark or by resorting to violence. He will accept the nails of the cross as he accepted the stones of the desert.

The Gethsemane of the Disciples (14:37–42)

MARK SHOWS JESUS in three moments of prayer. This does not indicate an evolving process of struggle as he finally makes the supreme decision to accept the will of God. Since Jesus comes three times to find drowsy disciples, his own wrestling with God's will is then only one dimension of the story. Mark reports the content of Jesus' prayer only once but reports what Jesus says to his disciples when he finds them asleep each time (14:37–38, 40, 41). The emphasis therefore falls on the return to the disciples (14:37, 40, 41), not his return to prayer.

One can interpret his checking on the disciples both positively and negatively. On the one hand, Jesus returns to them as the Good Shepherd (14:27), who, confronted with the threat of the destruction of the flock, returns repeatedly to look after it (see 6:34).[13] On the other hand, Mark underscores the failure of the disciples at this most crucial point. Jesus initially tells the disciples, "Stay here and keep watch" (14:34; *gregoreite*; a present imperative and stronger than "keep awake"). He is not telling them to scout out the enemy or to post lookouts to sound the alarm if any of the enemy approach. It recalls Jesus' last warning to them when they were with him on the Mount of Olives (13:36).

Three times, however, Jesus discovers them sleeping after strongly bidding them to keep watch (14:37–41). Jesus had slept through their crisis during the storm at sea, which was no real crisis (4:37–41); they sleep through his crisis, which is a real crisis. Their drowsiness at this crucial moment is due to their failure to realize how crucial this moment is.

---

12. Austin Farrer, *The Triple Victory: Christ's Temptation According to St. Matthew* (London: Faith, 1965), 94.

13. So David M. Stanley, *Jesus in Gethsemane: The Early Church Reflects on the Suffering of Jesus* (New York/Ramsey, N.J.: Paulist, 1980), 139.

In Gethsemane, the hour has come (14:35, 41)—not the last hour, but the hour of the Son of Man—and the disciples are caught napping (14:37, 40, 41). Jesus' admonitions emphasize their grave failure at this momentous hour and foreshadow Peter's three denials. (1) When he first finds them sleeping, he addresses Peter as "Simon" (14:37). Simon is not his apostolic name (3:16). He is identified as Peter everywhere in Mark except in 1:16, 29, 30, 36 (before his nickname is mentioned in 3:16), and here in Gethsemane. Peter is not strong enough to watch even one hour. But those who are strong have no need of a physician (2:17).

(2) On his second trip Jesus finds them again sleeping (14:40). Mark adds the explanation that "their eyes were heavy" and "they did not know what to say to him." Heavy eyes are tokens of the frailty of the flesh (compare Jacob's eyes, heavy with age, Gen. 48:10). On a literal level, their sleep may be caused by physical exhaustion. On a spiritual level, however, they have had a bad case of heavy eyes, along with hardened hearts for some time. Jesus has already accused them of having eyes that do not see (8:18). The disciples do not know how to respond to this chastisement. Not knowing what to say is how Mark has described Peter's reaction to the Transfiguration (9:6). These disciples were dumb in the face of Jesus' glory and now are numb in the face of his anguish. It reflects their complete lack of understanding about him.

By contrast, Jesus goes into his Passion with his eyes open. His disciples have closed their eyes to what is happening, and they let it slip by and would have failed even if they had had forty cups of coffee instead of four cups of wine (if it was a Passover meal). They were not watching spiritually, the kind of watching that can spy buds sprouting on a fig tree. These disciples have been looking at the wrong things. They have not prayed, the kind of praying that can exorcise the demonic (see 9:28–29) and shield the flesh from Satan's onslaughts.

(3) Jesus catches them asleep a third time and gives them one last sad reproach, "Are you still sleeping and resting?" (14:41). Their sleep during Jesus' struggle reveals, as Juel puts it, that watching and praying lies "beyond their strength." "The disciples, like others, require redemption and liberation."[14]

Jesus' agonizing lament and submission to God's will contrast sharply with the oblivious stupor of his three disciples. Despite his predicting his own suffering and death, the betrayal by one of the Twelve, the desertion of the disciples, and the denials by Peter, the disciples take no heed and are led astray. While Jesus prays fervently in trembling horror, the weakness of the "flesh" (*sarx*; NIV, "body," 14:38) overtakes them, and they slumber peace-

---

14. Juel, *Mark*, 197.

fully. The flesh is the bridgehead "through which Satan moves to distract people from God's plan; it represents the vulnerability of the human being."[15] The weak flesh is up against the Strong Man. It requires constant vigilance and prayer for fortification.

Jesus' reproach should remind the reader of the closing words of his last discourse on the Mount of Olives (13:35–37):

> Therefore keep watch because you do not know when the owner of the house will come back—whether in the evening, or at midnight, or when the rooster crows, or at dawn. If he comes suddenly, do not let him find you sleeping. What I say to you, I say to everyone: "Watch!"

The hour has come, and the disciples are found snoozing. They fail miserably in their responsibilities. A nameless woman anoints Jesus for his burial over the objections of his friends. A bystander carries his cross. A pagan centurion who supervises his execution makes the public confession that he is the Son of God. A council member who probably participated in his condemnation obtains the body and buries it in his tomb. Women followers watch him die on the cross and go later to anoint the body. By contrast, the male disciples doze while he shudders in horror, betray him, flee for their lives when he is hauled away, and deny him while he is being condemned to death. They do not keep watch but fall asleep.

Summing up the connection to 13:35, in the *evening*, when the Lord comes with his disciples for what will be his Last Supper with them, one of the Twelve at his table chooses to play into the hands of his enemies and betray him. At *midnight*, all the disciples flee into the darkness—one stark naked and each deserting his Lord to the enemy. At *cockcrow*, Peter disowns his Lord three times with curses. In the *morning*, Jesus is left alone—abandoned by all, condemned to death, and delivered into the hands of the Gentiles, just as he prophesied.

Jesus' prayer in Gethsemane ends when he senses that the hour has come. The verb translated, "Enough!" (*apechei*, 14:41) is difficult. Jesus seems to refer to the disciples' sleep, but little evidence supports this usage of *apechei*. More frequently, the verb is used in a commercial sense, to mean "paid in full," "the account is closed" (see Matt. 6:2, 5, 16; Luke 6:24; Phil. 4:18). Some therefore argue that Judas is the verb's subject, and Jesus announces that he has his money (14:9) and comes to fulfill his part of the bargain.[16]

---

15. Brown, *Death of the Messiah*, 1:199.

16. Among the many other proposals, some have argued that the subject is impersonal and means, "It is paid up," that is, "The time is up." Some manuscripts add the words "the end." It could be punctuated as a question addressed to the disciples, "Is the end far off?" as your sleep suggests. Jesus then answers his own question, "No, the hour has come!"

The immediate context, however, should govern how one interprets *apechei*. The disciples know nothing about what Judas is doing or his devilish pact with the high priests. If Jesus is referring to Judas's receiving his payoff, he is speaking aloud to himself. Yet Jesus is speaking to his disciples; and, in the context, he has found them dozing three times after imploring them to watch. The hour has come when they must rise from sleep and go. The context therefore suggests that Jesus responds to the disciples with exasperation: "Are you still sleeping and resting? Enough! The hour has come." The hour for prayer (or sleep) has ended; the hour of the power of darkness (Luke 23:53) has begun.

Jesus knows that he will not be delivered from the cup but will be delivered into the hands of sinners. He has freely accepted God's will for himself and through prayer has steeled himself for what lies ahead. By contrast, the disciples have squandered the opportunity for prayer by sleeping. Consequently, they will fold under pressure. Jesus then gives two sharp commands to rouse them from sleep and to get them ready to encounter the hour that comes with the traitor and the thugs: "Rise! Let us go!" The command echoes the first words Jesus spoke to them, "Come, follow me!" (1:17). It also recalls the words he spoke to them during the halcyon days of his first great success in Galilee, "Let us go. . . . That is why I have come" (1:38).

These are the last words Jesus speaks directly to his disciples in the Gospel of Mark, but they will hear the same command again after his resurrection. The angel at the tomb instructs the women to tell the disciples that they must go on to Galilee, where Jesus goes before them (16:7). The Gethsemane scene clarifies that when the time comes for going, only prayer enables one to answer the call. The disciples slept instead of praying; and when they finally rise, they go off in every direction but the one that Jesus leads, trying to save their own lives.

Jesus' Arrest (14:43–50)

A GRIM REALISM stamps Mark's account of Jesus' arrest. A misguided rabble, deputized by the temple officials, invades Gethsemane with swords and clubs (14:43). They come out armed to the teeth, as if Jesus were some terrorist bandit bent on revolutionary upheaval. To them, it might have seemed a wise precaution. To the reader, they only look foolish. Jesus is a nonviolent teacher with no weapons and nothing to hide. He has taught daily in the temple under their noses, hardly the activity of someone bent on fomenting revolution. Justifiably, he condemns their violent ways (14:48). Ironically, Jesus castigated the temple for being a robber's den instead of a house of prayer for all nations (11:17). Now temple goons arrest him in the middle of his prayer, as if he is a robber.

The sad performance of Jesus' disciples in this crucial moment dominates this scene. First, Judas, one of the Twelve, leads the posse to Jesus' secluded place of prayer, where the temple representatives can arrest him with the least amount of commotion. Judas has given the armed band an agreed-upon sign, "The one I kiss is the man, arrest him and lead him away under guard [lit., securely]." Judas wants them to make sure that they place Jesus under tight restraint. Did he so misunderstand Jesus to think that his former Master would try to escape? Jesus' willing submission shows all human devices and intrigues to be ridiculous.[17]

The sign of the kiss reflects the normal greeting one gave a respected teacher. One kissed the hand out of deference or the cheek if one considered oneself an equal (see Luke 7:45, "You did not give me a kiss"). Judas addresses Jesus with the honorific title, "Rabbi," and kisses him. The word Mark uses (*kataphileo*) can picture Judas kissing him affectionately (see Luke 15:20, where the father kisses his returning prodigal son as a sign of reconciliation; Acts 20:37, where the Ephesian elders give a kiss to the departing Paul). Or it can indicate that he kisses him deferentially on the hand or even the foot (see Luke 7:38, 45). Whichever it is, Judas gives Jesus no sign that their fellowship has been broken. He wants everything to appear normal up to the last second, when guards rush to capture him. He turns him over to a certain death with a warm gesture of love or the customary greeting of respect, turning a sign of intimacy and goodwill into a sign of infamy and death. Note the biblical precedent for this treachery in 2 Samuel 20:9–10:

> Joab said to Amasa, "How are you, my brother?" Then Joab took Amasa by the beard with his right hand to kiss him. Amasa was not on his guard against the dagger in Joab's hand, and Joab plunged it into his belly, and his intestines spilled out on the ground. Without being stabbed again, Amasa died.

Mark does not record any response from Jesus; Judas vanishes from the story, though not from memory as the one guilty of vile treachery.

In spite of the well-laid plans to avoid any ruckus, "one of those standing near" drew his sword and struck. Mark does not identify the individual. If we ignore the accounts from the other Gospels—which specifically identify the culprit as "one of Jesus' companions" (Matt. 26:51), as "one of them" (Luke 22:49–50), and as "Peter" (John 18:10)—Mark may intend to picture a violent mob scene. An edgy member of the gang of rowdies who rush in with swords and clubs to arrest Jesus could have struck in the passion of the moment. The scene's structure suggests the swashbuckler to be one from the

---

17. Schweizer, *Mark*, 318.

crowd of ruffians. It begins with the action of Judas (Mark 14:43–45), then shifts to the arresting mob (vv. 46–47), then focuses on the response of Jesus (vv. 48–49), and closes with the scattering of the disciples (vv. 50–52). One can imagine swordplay on both sides in the midst of the bedlam.

Whether by accident or intentionally, the high priest's servant has his ear cut off.[18] In Matthew, Jesus utters an aphorism renouncing violence, that "all who draw the sword will die by the sword" (Matt. 26:52). In Luke, Jesus condemns even more strongly the violent ways of his sympathizers, and he heals the slave's ear, the only miracle recorded in the Passion narrative (Luke 22:51). Jesus condemns only the violent demeanor of the arresting party in Mark's account and then announces that the Scriptures are being fulfilled (Mark 14:49).

The disciples have awakened sufficiently by this time to make their shameless getaway. They all forsake him (*aphiemi*) and flee (14:50), but not before the announcement about the fulfillment of the Scriptures. The reference to the Scriptures undoubtedly refers to Jesus' citation of Zechariah 13:7 as the group made their way to the Mount of Olives: "I will strike the shepherd, and the sheep will be scattered" (14:27). Jesus' arrest, however, sets in motion a whole range of Scriptures that will be fulfilled. This explains why the one who has exhibited so much power throughout the Gospel willingly submits to this mob. The Son of Man is handed over in accordance with God's will as attested by Scripture.

This mob, however, does not understand the Scriptures and has no inkling of the significance of what is about to happen. The high priests have fooled themselves into thinking that they are cleverly accomplishing their purposes with their covert plots, secret signs, and high-powered weaponry to ensure that they can lead him away securely (14:44). Jesus, however, affirms that God's purposes are being accomplished, and God does not use swords and clubs. God's power is made manifest through weakness. Jesus has eaten with sinners, extending God's mercy and forgiveness to them (2:15–17); now he will be killed by sinners. His death, however, again presents God's offer of mercy and forgiveness to sinners.

Previously, Peter reminded Jesus that they had forsaken family, livelihood, and all things that they might follow Jesus (1:18, 20; 10:28–30). Now, they disavow their discipleship as they beat a hasty retreat. In the last scene where they appear together as a group, they break up and flee in every direction. The future spread of the gospel depends on them, and things look hopeless. But Mark reminds us that, in spite of appearances, God's will is

---

18. Luke and John identify it as the right ear, and John gives the victim's name as Malchus.

being fulfilled, and the reader should remember Jesus' promise that they are to rendezvous with Jesus in Galilee after the resurrection (14:28).

The Young Man's Flight (14:51–52)

MARK ALONE INCLUDES the account of a young man, identified only as one who was following Jesus, being grabbed by the arresting party and wriggling free from their grasp. He runs away into the darkness naked (14:51–52). Taylor asks, "Why insert so trivial a detail into so solemn a narrative?"[19] This incident fascinates many, but what is it intended to convey?

Since only Mark records it, many have speculated that the Evangelist injects his own intimate memory of the scene. Some regard it as Mark's remorseful signature, akin to Alfred Hitchcock's fleeting appearances in his own films.[20] On the other hand, the desperate flight may allude to Amos 2:16, which refers to flight on the Day of the Lord: "'Even the bravest warriors will flee naked on that day,' declares the LORD." If the bravest warrior will turn tail and run, what will happen to those less stout of heart? Jesus did warn that when people saw the desolating sacrilege, those in Judea were to flee to the mountains. They were not go back into the house, and those in the fields were not to fetch their mantle (13:14–16). This man, however, has fled at the wrong time.

Another interpretation attaches significance to the linen garment (*sindon*) the man leaves behind. Jesus' body was wrapped for burial in a linen cloth (*sindon*, 15:46), and a "young man" clothed in a white robe greets the women at the tomb and relays the message about the resurrection (16:5). From these slender connections, some interpreters contend that this young man's flight symbolizes the resurrection. As this young man escapes the clutches of his would-be captors in the garden, leaving behind his linen garment, so Jesus escapes the clutches of his would-be captor, death, leaving behind his linen burial cloth (cf. John 20:6).

A similar interpretation suggests that this scene reflects the later baptismal practice of taking off one's garment before immersion and putting on a white one afterward. This interpretation comes to grief over two details. First, the young man sheds his garment at the point of failure, not upon his confession, and he does not die with Jesus. Second, Jesus is the one who is wrapped in a linen cloth (15:46).

---

19. Taylor, *Mark*, 561–62.

20. Some go so far as to imagine that the Upper Room in the house of Mary, the mother of John Mark, was the place where the Last Supper was eaten (Acts 12:12; 1:13). John Mark thus followed the disciples into the night, hastily clad in a linen sheet.

One recent scholar labels such allegorization as "imaginative flights of fancy,"[21] which miss the obvious emphasis on cowardly flight. The young man's escape reflects the "every man for himself, save yourself if you can" mindset that swept through the followers of Jesus (cf. Acts 19:16). The disciples had the chance to make good their boasts: James and John to drink the cup with Jesus (Mark 10:38–39), and Peter and the others to die with Jesus (14:31). They break down completely, just as Jesus had prophesied they would (14:28). The arresting party strips away their last shred of resolve to follow Jesus. Their mad dash to safety consequently exposes the nakedness of their empty pledges. Leviticus 26:36–37 is apropos:

> As for those of you who are left, I will make their hearts so fearful in the lands of their enemies that the sound of a windblown leaf will put them to flight. They will run as though fleeing from the sword, and they will fall, even though no one is pursuing them. They will stumble over one another as though fleeing from the sword, even though no one is pursuing them. So you will not be able to stand before your enemies.

The disciples' panicked flight sharply contrasts with the quiet dignity of Jesus, who has kept watch and is ready. Jesus now will become increasingly alone and must face the horror of his death without any human support. The craven fear of this young man who is seized and stripped and escapes into the darkness compares badly with the courage of Jesus, who is seized and stripped and does not escape but is crucified in the darkness.

MARK'S GETHSEMANE SCENE is darkest of the four Gospels. He boldly presents Jesus' emotion; some have said so boldly that it could come only from the recollection of an eyewitness. Some have thought it too bold. Watson points out that "Christian piety, both ancient and modern, has tended to find these passages offensive and distasteful."[22] The grim picture of Jesus' mental state has been attenuated somewhat by Matthew, who simply describes Jesus as grieving (*lypeo*, Matt. 26:37) rather than as being deeply distressed (*ekthambeo*). Luke omits all reference to Jesus' grief (cf. John 12:27).

Jesus' suffering was even more of an embarrassment to a later theology that believed Jesus must have been free from any internal turmoil (see Ignatius,

---

21. Brown, *The Death of the Messiah*, 1:299.

22. Francis Watson, "Ambiguity in the Marcan Narrative," *Kings Theological Review* 10 (1987): 14.

Polycarp 3:2, who describes Jesus as one "who cannot suffer"). Modern readers might also worry that Jesus suffered from a shameful eleventh hour failure of nerve. Did he grovel before God in tears and lamentations? Watson declares, "Mark's account is utterly stark and comfortless, and we should not allow its impact to be blunted by the modifications of it in other gospels."[23] If one does try to relieve the scandalous impact of this scene, one is preaching something different from Mark's text.

Mark's bleak presentation of Jesus' mental anguish cries for an explanation. Jesus' mental anguish during the period of waiting presented a real test. The flogging, the nails, the fire, or whatever it might be are only a physical ordeal. The anxiety of waiting can make one fall to pieces. Jesus' distress drove him from his disciples to pray and to seek peace from his Father. Celsus fastened on almost every word in the Gethsemane incident to discredit Christian claims about Jesus' divinity. Why did Jesus challenge James and John to drink his cup (10:38) when he now shrinks from it himself? Could even the Son of God experience the dread of suffering?

The answer is yes. Orthodox Christians confess Jesus to be fully human and fully divine. Mark's scene makes it clear that Jesus experienced a full range of human emotions. The author of Hebrews states it just as boldly, "During the days of Jesus' life on earth, he offered up prayers and petitions with loud cries and tears to the one who could save him from death, and he was heard because of his reverent submission" (Heb. 5:7). Swete comments that Jesus' human soul shrank from the cross, and that fact adds to the sense of greatness of his sacrifice.[24]

But modern readers want to know what it was that caused him to shrink from death. Kelber has warned, "The exegesis of Jesus' state at Gethsemane is habitually attended with the danger of being seduced into a psychological reading of the mind of Jesus."[25] Many explanations have been offered to try to explain exactly what was going on in Jesus' mind to explain such trembling horror. Some argue that Jesus thought of all the sins of the world that would be laid upon him (2 Cor. 5:21), but Mark does not hint of this in the text.

Others argue that knowing that he would die an accursed death, hanging on a tree (Gal. 3:13), may have afflicted his soul.

Still others contend that Jesus shuddered at the thought that his suffering and death would cause his disciples to lose faith and to scatter, just as he predicted. This last fragment of his public ministry's success would be

---

23. Ibid., 15.

24. Swete, *Mark*, 343–44.

25. Werner Kelber, "Mark 14,32: Gethsemane. Passion Christology and Discipleship Failure," *ZNW* 63 (1972): 177.

destroyed. Jesus was willing to accept God's will for himself, but he recoiled at the prospect of the dissolution of the little band of believers. The very thought of his disciples denying him and being scattered was enough to kill him. He did not wish to acquiesce in the complete failure of his ministry. But note that the prediction of their failure was counterbalanced by the prediction that they would be regathered (14:28). Jesus exuded optimism about the disciples' restoration.

Others have suggested that Jesus was plagued by a fear that his disciples were too ill-prepared to assume responsibility for preaching the kingdom of God. They did not understand and might never understand. Jesus may also have quaked at the thought that God might foreclose upon the spiritual bankruptcy of Israel's leaders.

Hypothetical psychologizing about what might have been passing through Jesus' mind is presumptuous on our part. All we can safely say is that in Gethsemane Jesus was following his own teaching. He taught the disciples to pray, "Lead us not into temptation [testing], but deliver us from the evil one" (Matt. 6:13), and he practiced what he taught. When the text is silent on such matters, it is best that we admit our ignorance and ask what we can learn from this. What does Mark want to teach in this scene?

Looking at the significance of an interior monologue in other ancient literature helps shed some light on how Mark's first readers would have understood the scene. Tolbert notes that monologues in ancient literature "are not basically psychological but rather rhetorical."[26] The monologues typically occur at crucial points, such as when a character is on the verge of battle or some other risky venture: "Why does my own heart dispute with me thus?" (see Homer, *Iliad* 11.402 [Odysseus]; 17.97 [Menials]; 21.562 [Agenor]; 22.122 [Hector]). Tolbert observes that monologues appear in those critical moments when "a character seems to be giving way to the promptings of his *thymos* [heart or mind] but pulls himself together in the formulaic mind . . . and proceeds to do the right thing." [27]

Thus, when Mark allows the reader to hear Jesus' prayer at a moment of great crisis when the hour has come upon him, it strikes a chord in his audience. They can identify with Jesus' pain, which makes him an example. Jesus could hardly be an example if he were above temptation and above the fray. Satan battles for the heart of every human, and all humans are hardwired to try to save their own lives. The disciples serve as a negative example of this instinct. Judas switches allegiance to what he believes is the

---

26. Tolbert, *Sowing*, 215; following R. Scholes and R. Kellogg, *The Nature of Narrative* (London: Oxford Univ. Press, 1966), 177–94.

27. Ibid., citing Scholes and Kellogg, *The Nature of Narrative*, 180.

winning side. The others run for their lives. Another, under pressure, denies any association with his Master. Jesus, however, heroically resolves the struggle over the great sacrifice God requires of him and obediently submits to God's will.

What does the reader then learn from this struggle? (1) Jesus' grappling with God's will reveals that he is not "a joyful martyr bent on self destruction, not an unwilling pawn forced into sacrifice . . . he is a courageous hero who knows what dangers lie ahead and resolves to do the will of God (see 3:35)."[28] The cross is God's decision for him. It comes to him as a cup that needs to be drunk. He must be obedient, but he does not relish the conflict or the prospect of death. Jesus does not eagerly embrace suffering but accepts it under a sense of ought. Jesus has told his disciples to take up their crosses and follow him, but he does not exalt martyrdom. Death is not something that one should eagerly seek out. One can and should pray for release. One should know, however, that some things that one prays and asks for with faith (11:22–24) cannot be given. If it is not in God's will, then one must accept what comes with prayer and courage. As Dowd states it, one prays "expecting power, accepting suffering."[29]

(2) Jesus' intense distress is overcome by intense prayer. Jesus accepts God's will the same way we must—through prayer. James Montgomery's hymn captures this idea:

> Go to Dark Gethsemane,
> Ye who feel the tempter's pow'r;
> Your Redeemer's conflict see;
> Watch with him one bitter hour;
> Turn not from his griefs away;
> Learn of Jesus Christ to pray.

We learn how to pray from his intimate address to God, from his confidence in God's omnipotence, from his plea to be spared testing, and from his obedient submission to God's will. Jesus came to terms with the necessity of drinking the cup through painful lament. Brown comments:

> As Mark's readers face their trial and find it too much, emboldened by knowing that all things are possible with God, they may find themselves, despite all their previous commitments, asking that this cup be taken away. And they can do that in Jesus' name provided that they add as he did, "But not what I will but what you (will)."[30]

---

28. Tolbert, *Sowing*, 216.
29. Dowd, *Prayer, Power, and the Problem of Suffering*, 33.
30. Brown, *The Death of the Messiah*, 1:178.

Because David prayed: "Test me, O LORD, and try me; examine my heart and my mind" (Ps. 26:2), some rabbis thought it was proper to place oneself in temptation, where our faith and obedience are put to the test, in order to overcome it (*b. Abod Zar* 17ab). Temptations were viewed as spiritual muscle-builders for the faithful. Jesus does not take this view. We should pray, ever mindful of the weakness of the flesh, for the cup to be removed. We are weak; and if we are not strengthened by God's power, we will always fail.

The flight of the disciples exposes their grave failure. Mark's vivid portrayal of it helped his first readers to understand "its own lapses in following Jesus during periods of suffering (and perhaps persecution), especially since there was also the implicit promise that those who failed could be gathered once more into the flock of Jesus (Mark 14:28; 16:7)."[31] To get sidetracked by curiosity over the identity of the young man who streaks into the darkness naked prevents the interpreter from wrestling with the issue that is so central to Mark. Followers of Jesus who do not pray and try to follow on their own power will collapse. The scene should compel readers to imagine what they would have done under the circumstances. It compels each one "to ponder the tenacity of his or her own commitment."[32] One person lingers, but when he too is seized, he fails the test and hightails it out of there. Trying to identify who this young man is diverts us from asking the more important question, Why does he flee? It keeps us from asking ourselves, What would we do when angry mobs wave swords or guns in our faces? Would we flee?

FREDERIC L. KNOWLES'S poem "Grief and Joy" captures the poignancy of Mark's Gethsemane scene:

> Joy is a partnership,
> Grief weeps alone;
> Many guests had Cana
> Gethsemane had one.

Jesus is alone and grieving over what confronts him and his disciples, but through prayer he comes to a resolution. Peck writes, "Once suffering is completely accepted, it ceases in a sense to be suffering."[33] It is the time of waiting that can do us in.

---

31. Ibid., 1:309.
32. Senior, *The Passion of Jesus*, 85.
33. M. Scott Peck, *The Road Less Travelled* (New York: Simon & Schuster, 1979), 75.

Vanstone perceptively observes:

> Waiting can be the most intense and poignant of all human expe-
> riences—the experiences which, above all others, strips us of affecta-
> tion and self-deception and reveals to us the reality of our needs, our
> values and ourselves. Waiting is at its most intense and wearing when
> it takes one or other of two particular forms. Sometimes we wait with
> dread for the onset of or occurrence of something which, with our
> rational faculties, we know to be necessary or appropriate or even
> beneficial to ourselves. So a nervous actor may wait for the curtain to
> rise or a paratrooper for the moment when he must make his first
> jump: so many of us wait in the dentist's room. We dread the immi-
> nent onset of strain or danger or pain, but we know with our rational
> faculties that what lies ahead is "for the best." Usually rational con-
> siderations overcome dread and we do not "run away." We count it
> weakness or cowardice if we do; and we also count it weakness if, as
> we wait, we find ourselves hoping or praying that which lies ahead—
> that which is "for the best"—may not happen: that the performance
> on the stage may be cancelled, that bad weather may prevent the
> parachute jump, that the dentist may find himself too busy to see us.
> There is weakness—pardonable weakness but nevertheless weak-
> ness—in hoping or praying to be "spared" that which we know to be
> for the best. Air-crews about to embark on a particularly dangerous
> mission in war-time may sometimes hope or pray that their allotted air-
> craft may prove unserviceable; but few if any would admit at the time
> to doing so.[34]

In Gethsemane Jesus must wait. Wait for the hour to come upon him, wait
for the betrayer to come at any moment. Some interpretations of Jesus' struggle in Gethsemane claim that he shows a flash of weakness while he is waiting. He knows what God's purpose is and what is necessary, and he prays to
escape. But Vanstone shows that "there is another form of peculiarly intense
and poignant waiting."

> It is the manner of waiting in which the prisoner in the dock—or
> the prisoner's wife or mother—waits for the jury to announce their
> verdict; the manner in which an intelligent man waits for the surgeon's
> report on a biopsy of his liver; the manner in which, after an explosion
> in a coalmine, a wife waits at the pit-head to hear if her own man is safe.
> One waits at such moments in an agonizing tension between hope

---

34. W. H. Vanstone, *The Stature of Waiting* (New York: Seabury, 1983), 83–85.

and dread, stretched and almost torn apart between two dramatically different anticipations. A wise person will then steel and prepare himself for the worst; but the very tension in which he waits shows that hope is still present, and that hope will often express itself in unbelievers, in the urgent and secret prayer, "O God, let it be all right." In such hope and prayer there is no weakness, no failure of nerve: torn between rational hope and rational dread one may properly pray for the best while still prepared for the worst.[35]

Vanstone suggests, I think correctly, that Jesus waited and prayed in such a way. He had already handed himself over to death when he acted and taught as he did in the temple. He had brought his proclamation of God's reign to the seat of human power. Now he must change from the one who acts to the one who waits and is acted upon. This change is one of the hardest things to accept in life—to become passive after a life of active involvement, to be at the mercy of others. Mark's readers need not shy from crying to God to be spared from their own cross that they must bear, but they can learn from Jesus to accept God's plan through prayer.

"That Jesus went through pain is a continuing source of comfort and courage to pain-stricken people."[36] We can learn to handle pain and suffering from Jesus. Many blanche at Jesus' boldness in addressing God in such familiar terms as "Daddy." If a person prayed to God this way in church, the majority would think that proper religious decorum had been overstepped. If one complained loudly to God in lament as the psalmist and Jesus do, again the majority would think it too brazen. Our hesitancy to do anything like this perhaps reflects our distance from God. Jesus was on such intimate terms with God that he did not shy away from vociferously laying bare his thoughts—like a hurting child crying to a loving parent. His prayer shows that we can express our feelings honestly to God.

Jesus models what he means when he tells disciples to watch in 13:33–37. Watching is not what we might first think it is. Jesus does not tell them to watch for the end of all things. Geddert writes, "Because Jesus had modelled faithful 'watching,' he was prepared for the arrival of The Hour, and *therefore* recognized its advent."[37] The disciples expected cosmic upheaval that would come with plenty of warning, with sirens blaring, swords flashing, and angels descending. They did not recognize that we fight against demonic powers and not just the powers of flesh and blood (Eph. 6:10–18). Watching has nothing to do with scouting out the enemy or watching for portents

---

35. Ibid., 85.
36. Ibid., 69.
37. Geddert, *Watchwords*, 99.

but "with faithful discipleship in a time of crisis."[38] The trouble is that we never know when the crisis will come. Minear writes, "No one set of actions can be objectively labeled as watching, because it refers to the internal orientation of servants of their absent and returning Lord."[39] It has to do with their present state.

The disciples serve as negative examples because they sleep, a basic Christian term for infidelity.[40] In John Bunyan's *Pilgrim's Progress*, when Pilgrim finally releases his burden at the foot of the cross and goes a little further, he finds three men fast asleep with fetters on their legs. The name of one was Simple, the second Sloth, and the third Presumption. He awoke them and they spoke. Simple said, "I see no danger"; Sloth said, "Yet a little more sleep"; and Presumption said, "Every tub must stand on its own bottom." Spiritual drowsiness is dangerous and will prove the Christian's undoing.

(1) To sleep is to stop praying. We often do not pray because we are unaware that we are in the midst of trial. Although the disciples have been explicitly warned (13:23), they remain spiritually groggy. To watch and be prepared, we must pray continually. When crunch time comes, Jesus tells disciples to rise and go. They go, but they go in the wrong direction. Disciples must first learn how to remain in prayer (14:34, "Stay here and keep watch") before they can ever get up and go the way Jesus leads. Adversity brings out the worst in us while requiring the most of us. The only way we can ready ourselves to bear up under pressure is through fervent prayer.

(2) To sleep is to be unable to recognize the onset of trial or to accept it as God's will. The disciples heard only what they wanted to hear and tuned out Jesus' teaching on the necessity of suffering and the requirement of taking up a cross. They are like bad students who intend to quiz the professor about what is going to be on the exam and plan to study only the night before the exam. They are totally unprepared for the pop quiz.

(3) To sleep is to presume that the Spirit is willing without being mindful of the weakness of the flesh. Jesus does not want bravado from his disciples. Their bravado only masked their weakness and kept them from asking for God's help. Consequently, they lacked strength for the battle within. The battlefield that counts is within each person's heart, and the foe is not easily dispatched—and certainly not with swords. One must be ever mindful how close we are to falling. The good news, however, is that failure in times of crisis is not permanent.

---

38. Ibid., 98.
39. Paul Minear, *The Commands of Christ* (Nashville: Abingdon, 1972), 178.
40. Ibid., 159.

(4) To sleep is to assume that we have arrived (see Phil. 3:12–16). Leo Tolstoy's short story "Father Sergius" portrays a man who took up the monastic life and quickly excelled all others. He regarded the spiritual life as a checklist of tasks and goals to be accomplished. He reached the point where he believed he had accomplished all his goals. He had "learnt all there was to learn and had attained all there was to attain, there was nothing more to do."[41] The sudden arrival of the hour of trial can be a cruel reminder how mistaken false confidence in past spiritual achievements is.

---

41. Leo Tolstoy, *Great Short Works of Leo Tolstoy*, trans. Louis and Aylmer Maude (New York: Harper & Row, 1967), 512; cited by Caroline J. Simon, "Evil, Tragedy and Hope: Reflections on Tolstoy' 'Father Sergius,'" *Christian Scholar's Review* 24 (1995): 292.

Mark 14:53–72

❧

THEY TOOK JESUS to the high priest, and all the chief priests, elders and teachers of the law came together. ⁵⁴Peter followed him at a distance, right into the courtyard of the high priest. There he sat with the guards and warmed himself at the fire.

⁵⁵The chief priests and the whole Sanhedrin were looking for evidence against Jesus so that they could put him to death, but they did not find any. ⁵⁶Many testified falsely against him, but their statements did not agree. ⁵⁷Then some stood up and gave this false testimony against him: ⁵⁸"We heard him say, 'I will destroy this man-made temple and in three days will build another, not made by man.'" ⁵⁹Yet even then their testimony did not agree.

⁶⁰Then the high priest stood up before them and asked Jesus, "Are you not going to answer? What is this testimony that these men are bringing against you?" ⁶¹But Jesus remained silent and gave no answer.

Again the high priest asked him, "Are you the Christ, the Son of the Blessed One?"

⁶²"I am," said Jesus. "And you will see the Son of Man sitting at the right hand of the Mighty One and coming on the clouds of heaven."

⁶³The high priest tore his clothes. "Why do we need any more witnesses?" he asked. ⁶⁴"You have heard the blasphemy. What do you think?"

They all condemned him as worthy of death. ⁶⁵Then some began to spit at him; they blindfolded him, struck him with their fists, and said, "Prophesy!" And the guards took him and beat him.

⁶⁶While Peter was below in the courtyard, one of the servant girls of the high priest came by. ⁶⁷When she saw Peter warming himself, she looked closely at him.

"You also were with that Nazarene, Jesus," she said.

⁶⁸But he denied it. "I don't know or understand what you're talking about," he said, and went out into the entryway.

⁶⁹When the servant girl saw him there, she said again to those standing around, "This fellow is one of them." ⁷⁰Again he denied it.

After a little while, those standing near said to Peter, "Surely you are one of them, for you are a Galilean.

[71]He began to call down curses on himself, and he swore to them, "I don't know this man you're talking about."

[72]Immediately the rooster crowed the second time. Then Peter remembered the word Jesus had spoken to him: "Before the rooster crows twice you will disown me three times." And he broke down and wept.

OLIVETTE GENEST'S STUDY reveals interesting structural parallels in Mark's presentation of Jesus' hearing before the Sanhedrin (14:53–72), his trial before Pilate (15:1–22), his crucifixion (15:23–33), and his death and burial (15:34–47).[1] In each scene, the first element focuses on Jesus. The second element interprets who Jesus is and highlights a Christological title. The mockery ironically expresses some truth about Jesus: Jesus is a prophet, the King of the Jews, the Messiah, and the Savior of others. But he is more. In the last scene, the centurion correctly identifies him as the Son of God. The third element depicts the stance or response of others to Jesus, and each scene concludes with an exit or interlude that leads into the next.

1. The Hearing Before the Sanhedrin (14:53–73)
   a. Jesus led to the high priest for the hearing (14:53–64)
   b. Mockery of Jesus as a prophet (14:65)
   c. Peter denies Jesus (14:66–72a)
   d. Exit (4:72b)
2. The Trial Before Pilate (15:1–22)
   a. Jesus led to Pilate for trial (15:1–15)
   b. Mockery of Jesus as the King of the Jews (15:16–20)
   c. Simon of Cyrene carries Jesus' cross (15:21)
   d. Exit (15:22)
3. The Crucifixion (15:23–33)
   a. Jesus' crucifixion (15:23–27)
   b. Mockery of Jesus as Savior, Messiah, and King of Israel (15:29–32a)
   c. The ones crucified with him revile him (15:32b)
   d. Darkness covers the whole land (15:33)

---

1. Olivette Genest, *Le Christ de la passion—Perspective structurale: Analyse de Marc 14,53–15,47, des parallèles bibliques et extra bibliques* (Recherches 21; Montreal: Belarmin, 1978), 116.

4. The Death and Burial (15:34–47)
   a. Jesus' death (15:34–38)
   b. The centurion confesses Jesus to be the Son of God (15:39)
   c. The women watch from afar (15:40–41)
   d. The burial of Jesus (15:42–47)

The Hearing Before the Sanhedrin (14:53–65)

MARK'S TRIAL SCENE pins the primary responsibility and initiative for Jesus' death on the high priest and his Sanhedrin. Though Mark tells us that "all" the Sanhedrin has gathered (14:53), we should not assume that it consisted of the seventy-one members dictated by the later rabbinic tractate on the Sanhedrin (*m. Sanh.* 1:6).[2] In the first century, it was not "a fixed body regularly in session."[3] Presumably the high priest convenes a council of whatever members he can gather at this late hour of the night. Nocturnal trials were abnormal (see Acts 4:3–5) and were later forbidden under rabbinic law. A hearing in the middle of the night suggests the kangaroo justice of a lynch mob dressed in hooded sheets, but it also shows that these leaders are under time constraints.

These proceedings form a preparatory investigation before the Sanhedrin delivers Jesus to the Roman governor for final deliberation. A debate continues among scholars, but the evidence strongly suggests that the Jewish leaders did not have the power of capital punishment (John 18:31).[4]

---

2. The Mishnaic tradition was compiled around A.D. 200, in another era and circumstance. Some scholars, however, have appealed to the laws in *Mishnah Sanhedrin* regarding capital cases to argue that Mark invented the trial before the Sanhedrin to shift blame from the Romans to the Jews. But the laws for the Sanhedrin are idealized and theoretical. The rabbis who compiled the oral tradition were driven by wishful thinking, and the idealistic regulations regarding the Sanhedrin may never have been operative. For example, the tractate *Sanhedrin* treats the council as if it were an all-powerful body, not subject to any other external power. It is assumed to have the authority to judge the king and the high priest, to set boundary lines, and to declare war (*m. Sanh.* 1:5). That is what the compilers of the tradition thought should be the case, but it certainly was not the way it was in the first century. They have provided prescription, not description. Consequently, one should be cautious in using this Mishnaic tractate to judge the historicity of Mark's account of Jesus' trial.

3. Brown, *The Death of the Messiah*, 1:348–49.

4. Jerusalem was anything but a free city, and the nation consisted of anything but loyal subjects to Rome. The Jews were allowed to follow their own peculiar customs as far as religious matters were concerned, and the local authorities had police powers. But they could not sentence offenders to death as they pleased. Turbulent Judea is the last place in the empire where one would expect the Romans to make such extraordinary concessions. The high priest was a political appointee of the Romans; the council did not have the right to convene without the governor's permission (Josephus, *Ant.* 20.9.1 § 202), and they did not

Apparently, it is not enough to arrest and flog Jesus, which was in their power; the ruling priests want him dead and disgraced before the crowds. They presume his guilt, because he is a threat. The hearing will serve to convince anyone with misgivings that he is worthy of death and will fix the charge they will present to the Roman governor.

Josephus reports a similar case concerning a peasant prophet named Jesus, son of Ananias (*J. W.* 6.5.1 § 300–309). Just before the outbreak of the war against Rome this prophet stood in the temple and denounced the city and the sanctuary with piercing and unrelenting woes. The leading citizens, incensed by his cries, arrested and beat him. When he continued his cries day and night, the magistrates brought him before the Roman governor, Albinus, for more severe punishment. He had him flayed to the bone; but when he continued his dirge, the governor pronounced him a maniac and let him go. The governor presently in charge in Judea, Pontius Pilate, is no rubber stamp, and the ruling priests know they need to present a convincing case so that the Roman governor will not just scourge him and then let him go.

Mark has told us that the high priests, teachers of the law, and elders have been "looking for a way to kill him" (11:18), "for a way to arrest him" (12:12), and "for some sly way to arrest Jesus and kill him" (14:1). Now that they have arrested him, they "are looking for evidence against Jesus" (14:55) that will put a noose around his neck. The law allowed the condemnation of an accused person only on the evidence of two or more witnesses who agreed (Num. 35:30; Deut. 17:6; 19:15–21; see Sus. 51–61). Mark relates that many volunteer testimony against Jesus, and he fastens on one particular charge. Certain ones testify that Jesus said, "I will destroy this man-made temple and in three days will build another, not made by man" (14:58).[5]

The Targum on Isaiah 53:5 and the Targum on Zechariah 6:5 specified that the Messiah would build the new temple. These traditions were compiled at a later time, but they may preserve a popular expectation in the first century. If so, the accusers may obliquely be denouncing Jesus for claiming

---

even have the right to keep custody of the high priest's vestments and ornaments. They were stored in the Antonia fortress under Roman guard until Pilate was recalled and Vitellius granted them the right to keep them again in the temple (Josephus, *Ant.* 15 § 403–8; 18.4.3 § 90–95; 20 § 6–9). If Mark is writing to a Roman audience, he does not have to explain why the Jewish court did not put Jesus to death in a manner prescribed by Jewish law. It would have been taken for granted that they did not have this power. See further the discussion in Brown, *The Death of the Messiah*, 1:357–72.

5. Something made with hands is of purely human origin and opposed to God. In Old Testament usage it is associated with idolatry and pagan gods (Ps. 115:4, Isa. 46:6; Wis. 13:10).

to be the Messiah. It makes sense of the high priest's frustrated question when he asks him point-blank if he is the Christ (14:61).

Mark reports twice, however, that the witnesses cannot agree (14:56, 59) and that their testimony is false (14:56–57). In other words, false witnesses try to frame Jesus. But the reader knows that Jesus has indeed made menacing noises against this man-made temple with his daring protest against the money changers and dove sellers. He also predicted privately to his disciples that the vast temple complex would be destroyed (13:1–2). Since what the witnesses say about Jesus' stance toward the temple seems close to the truth, and since this charge resurfaces when passersby taunt him with it while he hangs from the cross (15:29), how is their testimony false?

Mark may consider the testimony to be false because any witness against Jesus has to be a false witness, particularly if he is trumping up charges against him (see Pss. 27:12; 35:11; 109:2). Perhaps Mark regards their testimony to be false because of a technicality.[6] Jesus never explicitly said that *he* would destroy the temple and rebuild it. He only implied that God had judged it and would allow it to be destroyed. Most likely, however, Mark emphasizes that the testimony of the witnesses is false primarily because of the second element in the charge. His first readers may have held out hopes that Jesus as the Messiah would build another temple. Since Scripture mentions that David's offspring would build a house for God's name, some probably assumed that Jesus would do that (2 Sam. 7:13). Mark therefore makes it clear that Jesus never claimed he would build another earthly temple, and thus no one should expect any kind of earthly temple. In Mark's view, the temple was destroyed when Jesus died, making its atonement sacrifices superfluous. The temple where God now lives has nothing to do with buildings (see Acts 7:48; 17:24).

Like the Suffering Servant and the Righteous One of the Psalms, Jesus remains silent before his false accusers (Pss. 38:12–15; 39:9; Isa. 53:7).[7] His silence shows defiant contempt for their opportunism and lack of principle. False witnesses who cannot get their stories straight provide no help, and they do not pursue the charge of speaking against the temple further. The high priest takes charge and asks Jesus directly, "Are you the Christ, the son of the

---

6. The witnesses also use the word *naos*, which refers to the sanctuary of God's presence (14:58; see 15:29, 38). Mark, however, consistently uses the word *hieron* to refer to the entire temple complex (11:11, 15, 16, 17; 12:35; 13:1, 3; 14:49). If Mark makes a distinction between the two words, the testimony of the witnesses is only partially true because Jesus did not say or intimate that he would destroy the sanctuary of God's presence. See Donald Juel, *Messiah and Temple*, 127–28.

7. His quiet deportment makes an interesting contrast with Herod the Great's defiant belligerence, which cowered the Sanhedrin (Josephus, *Ant.* 14.9.4 §§ 168–76).

Blessed One?" (14:61). He piously avoids God's name with a circumlocution while using underhanded means to get rid of an enemy.

For the first time in the Gospel, "the Son of God" title (cf. 1:1) appears on the lips of a human character in the story. Only demons (3:11; 5:7) and the voice from the cloud (1:11; 9:7) have uttered it until now. Also for the first time in the Gospel (see 1:34; 3:11–12; 8:30; 9:9, 30–31), Jesus publicly accepts that he is the Messiah, with his reply: "I am." The title of this Gospel is "the beginning of the gospel about Jesus Christ, the Son of God" (1:1); Jesus now himself affirms his identity before the high priest and his council and continues with, "And you will see the Son of Man sitting at the right hand of the Mighty One [lit., Power] and coming on the clouds of heaven."[8]

The drama heightens as the high priest labels his response "blasphemy" and tears his garment to underscore his judgment. This gesture was an ancient way of expressing distress, mourning, or outrage (see Josh. 7:6; 2 Sam. 1:11; 2 Kings 18:37; 19:1; Isa. 37:1; Jer. 36:24; Joel 2:13; Acts 14:14) and is a fitting response to perceived blasphemy, but it also may be a grandstanding display to get others to see things his way. To the high priest, the evidence is conclusive: Jesus has incriminated himself, and the council unanimously condemns him. They judge him to be worthy of death (see 3:29).

What is blasphemous about the answer in 14:62?[9] We must not allow technical definitions of blasphemy (see Lev. 24:16) to govern our answer. What different persons regard as blasphemous rarely fits any technical definition. Some argue that Jesus' open admission that he is the Messiah is considered blasphemous since he presumes on God's prerogative to name the Messiah. But the high priest's reaction follows Jesus' complete statement that they will see the Son of Man sitting at the right hand of God. This answer combines a messianic tradition from Psalm 110 with an apocalyptic tradition from Daniel 7.

The result is radical. In the messianic tradition the king of Israel was invited to take his seat at the right hand of God. The seating symbolized the king's temporal sharing of God's power. The king was established on Zion and occupied the throne of God's kingship over Israel as God's representative on earth (1 Chron. 28:5; 29:23; 2 Chron. 9:8). This passage was interpreted messianically, but no Old Testament passage explicitly conferred on the Messiah full equality with God on a heavenly plane. Jesus earlier appealed to Psalm 110:1 to question how the Christ is David's son if David called him

---

8. That the crucified Jesus has been exalted at the right hand of God is a central confession in the New Testament (Acts 2:33; 5:31; 7:55; Rom. 8:34; Eph. 1:20; Col. 3:1; Heb. 1:3).

9. See Joel Marcus, "Mark 14:61: 'Are You the Messiah-Son-of-God?'" *NovT* 31 (1989): 125–41.

Lord (Mark 12:35–37). That question suggests that as far as Jesus is concerned, the Christ is something more than simply the Son of David, an earthly ruler. Jesus extends that image here with the allusion to Daniel 7:13, "coming with the clouds of heaven."

The vision of Daniel 7 takes place in the clouds of heaven, on the divine level. "One like a son of man" comes to the Ancient of Days and receives divine power (Dan. 7:14). The vision never specifically identifies who this "son of man" is, however. Is he a real person or an abstraction? In 7:18, he represents the saints of the Most High; is he their angel or only a symbol of them? Is he a human or some divine being? Daniel 7 has no royal messianic overtones, and the "one like a son of man" does not share the throne. Jesus' answer combines these two different traditions so that they interpret each other. On the one hand, the "one like a son of man" is no longer some mysterious apparition but a real human being, a descendant of David in whom the messianic prophecies are realized. On the other hand, the sitting down at God's right hand is no longer simply a symbol of royal dignity. It represents divine power exercised on the heavenly plane.[10]

In other words, Jesus claims to be more than the Christ, the Son of the Blessed One. He understands his Sonship to be on a higher plane than that implied in Psalm 2:7 and 2 Samuel 7:14 for the Davidic king. His affirmation far surpasses any current conception about the Messiah, because he implies that he has divine authority, and they will one day see it. This implication would be blasphemy if it proved to be wrong.[11] Either the high priest is correct that Jesus is a deluded blasphemer, or Jesus is correct and the high priest is the deluded blasphemer. The high priest is shocked, for Jesus' confession confirms his suspicions that Jesus is guilty of *hybris* against God, not only claiming to be the Messiah, the Son of God, but also claiming the divine right of judgment at the end time. The reader may be shocked that this Son of Man is now certain to die.

Hooker comments: "In contrast to the claims of the false messiahs proclaiming 'I am' (13:6), Jesus' words will be substantiated."[12] Jesus assures his

---

10. A. Vanhoye, *Structure and Theology of the Accounts of the Passion in the Synoptic Gospels* (Collegeville, Minn.: Liturgical Press, 1967), 25–27.

11. A passage in the Talmud deals with the heresies of those who see God as more than one being on the basis of the phrase from Daniel 7:9, "till thrones were placed." "One [throne] was for Himself and one for David [the Messiah]. Even as it has been taught: One was for Himself and one for David: this is R. Akiba's view. R. Jose protested to him: Akiba, how long wilt thou profane the Shechinah? [note: by asserting that a human sits beside him] Rather, one [throne] for justice, and the other for mercy" (*b. Sanh.* 38b; cited by Donald Juel, *Messianic Exegesis: Christological Interpretation of the Old Testament in Early Christianity* [Philadelphia: Fortress, 1988], 137–38).

12. Hooker, *Mark*, 361.

---

captors that they will see it. "Seeing" relates to witnessing his vindication (see Isa. 40:5; Wis. 2:21–3:4; 5:1–2), when a higher court will overturn the decision of this lower court.[13] Jesus has told his disciples that some of them would see the kingdom coming with power (Mark 9:1). All these leaders can see now is a rustic from Galilee, who was easily captured when one of his own followers betrayed him. The rest of his small band vanished harmlessly into the darkness. To imagine this man as God's Messiah, let alone as the one who exercises the power of God, must have seemed laughable to them if it were not so offensive. Those who gather around Jesus' cross can see nothing either. They demand to see something dramatic (15:32, 35, 36), but nothing seems to happen. They can see nothing this side of the cross. But others will see something after his death. A Gentile centurion who watches him die blurts out his confession (15:39). For the disciples, the seeing will take place in Galilee, after the resurrection (14:28; 16:7).

The two charges that emerge from this hearing are religious in nature and have to do with the temple (14:57–58) and the Messiah (14:61–62).[14] They will resurface as two taunts at the cross: 15:29–30: "So! You who are going to destroy the temple and build it in three days, come down from the cross and save yourself!" and 15:32: "Let this Christ, this King of Israel, come down now from the cross, that we may see and believe." Two events occur at Jesus' death that parallel these taunts. The temple veil is torn from top to bottom (15:38), and a Roman centurion confesses, "Surely this man was the Son of God" (15:39).

The hearing before the Sanhedrin, which has made a mockery of justice, concludes with callous mockery of Jesus. Certain people spit on Jesus as a sign of repudiation (Num. 12:14; Deut. 25:9), slap him around, cover his face, and taunt him to prophesy. In the parallels in Matthew 26:68 and Luke 22:64, the taunt becomes a question, "Who struck you?" Mark has only the mocking command to prophesy. They may be playing a childish game of blind man's bluff, or these brutal assailants want Jesus to predict something since many believed that the Messiah was supposed to have a prophetic gift (see Isa. 11:2–4).[15]

---

13. Geddert, *Watchwords*, 212. See 1 Enoch 62:3–5: "On the day of judgment, all the kings, the governors, the high officials and the landlords shall see and recognize him—how he sits on the throne of his glory, and righteousness is judged before him. . . . They shall be terrified and dejected; and pain shall seize them when they see that Son of man sitting on the throne of his glory. . . ."

14. See Juel, *Messiah and Temple*.

15. A passage from the Talmud, citing Isa. 11:2–4, asserts that the Messiah is able to judge by smell. Bar Koziba (perhaps "son of lies," a name given to Bar Kochba) was the leader of the third revolt, A.D. 132–135. He "reigned two and a half years and said to the rabbis,

The reader can see the irony of all this. Three of Jesus' prophecies have been fulfilled or are being fulfilled at this very moment. Jesus has told his disciples that the Son of Man "will be betrayed to the chief priests and teachers of the law. They will condemn him to death and will hand him over to the Gentiles, who will mock him and spit on him, flog him and kill him. Three days later he will rise" (10:33–34). That prophecy forms a precise outline of what is happening in Mark's Passion narrative. He was betrayed to the high priests (14:10–52) and condemned to death (14:53–64). He is about to be handed over to the Gentiles (15:1–20), who will mock him, scourge him, and finally kill him (15:21–47). After three days, he will be raised (16:1–8).

Besides this key prophecy, Jesus also predicted that the disciples would be scattered when the shepherd was struck (14:27), and this prophecy was sadly fulfilled (14:50). He also prophesied that Peter would deny him three times this very night before the rooster crowed twice (14:30). Peter's denials are occurring at this very moment, and only Mark notes that the rooster crowed a second time when Peter had denied him the third time (14:72), fulfilling that prophecy to the letter.

All of these negative prophecies are being fulfilled, but Jesus has just uttered another prophecy in this scene that is of a greater magnitude: They will see the Son of Man sitting on the right hand of Power, coming with the clouds of heaven (14:62; see 8:38; 13:26). Having seen Jesus' prophecies fulfilled to the letter, the reader knows that this prophecy is neither blasphemous nor ridiculous and can trust that it also will be fulfilled. Jesus will be vindicated in his resurrection and will judge his oppressors. The blindfolded Jesus is therefore the only one who sees, while his tormentors are blinded by their hatred.

Peter's Denial (14:53–54, 66–72)

MARK INTRODUCES THE setting for Peter's denial of Jesus in 14:54, immediately after introducing the setting for Jesus' hearing before the Sanhedrin (14:53), in order to show that both take place simultaneously. While Jesus undergoes interrogation, Peter waits outside in the courtyard.[16] Jesus' examination is his final and climactic encounter with the hostile authorities. He

---

'I am the Messiah.' They answered, 'Of the Messiah it is written that he smells and judges: let us see whether he can do so.' When they saw that he was unable to judge by scent, they slew him" (b. *Sanh.* 93b).

16. The courtyard (*aule*, 14:66) was the open space around which rooms were arranged; the *proaulion* (14:68) was the vestibule leading to the courtyard.

openly acknowledges his identity (14:61–62), which results in his condemnation, mockery, and beating. The scene then shifts back to Peter, warming himself by the fire (lit., "the light"). While Jesus boldly confesses before the high priest, Peter denies before one of the high priest's servant girls that he ever knew Jesus.

If Mark were simply interested in giving a factual report about what Peter did during the trial of Jesus, he leaves us with many loose ends. The report of Peter's denials ends abruptly (14:72), with no indication of what happens to him after his wretched exit. We are left with questions such as: Why was Peter not arrested when he was identified? How did he escape? What did he do next? The conclusion of the incident contains an enigmatic reference to Peter's breaking down in tears. Does this mean that he repented? Mark does not tell us, and Peter drops out of the narrative the same way that he drops out of Acts (Acts 12:17), with many questions left up in the air.

Mark is not interested, however, in solely reporting what happened to Peter; rather, he wants to draw the reader into what Peter's denial means by connecting it to Jesus' trial. Peter's trial in the courtyard is a parody of his Lord's. He may have remembered his rash pledge to die with Jesus and tries to follow through, but he only trails from a safe distance (Mark 14:54) after Jesus' arrest. He then sits with Jesus' captors. While Jesus is under fire inside, Peter warms himself by the fire outside (14:54, 66). As Jesus confesses under immense pressure and hostility that seals his fate, Peter capitulates under the gentlest of pressure and lies to save himself.

Peter's threefold denial matches his threefold failure to watch with Jesus in Gethsemane, and it shows him to be much like the shallow rocky ground in the parable of the sower. When tribulation comes, the word that has been received with joy begins to wilt under persecution's scorching heat, and people fall away (4:16–17). He is accused of having been "with ... Jesus" (14:67). As the scene develops, we see that he would rather be "with" the crowd, cozying up to the warm fire. But the waiting mob will not accept this outsider in their group, even when he tries to join in their rancor against his Master.

In the first denial Peter's courage disintegrates before the private suspicions of a female servant. He responds to her initial query with evasion, "I don't know or understand what you're talking about" (14:68). He says more than he intends. The phrase "know and/or understand" is a loaded one (see 4:12–13; 6:52; 8:17–18; 9:32). The disciples have repeatedly displayed their failure to know and understand; Peter's repudiation of Jesus is the culmination of this process.

Peter moves away from the light into the vestibule. The pressure increases, however, as the female servant voices her suspicions about Peter to others. "This fellow is one of them" (14:69). Peter keeps on denying (imperfect tense) and betrays his Galilean accent. They then say, "Surely you are one of them, for you are a Galilean!" Galileans would probably stand out like a sore thumb in the high priest's courtyard. Anyone with access to the high priest's palace probably held the prejudice that all Galileans were alike, a bunch of rebellious riffraff.

In his third denial, Peter invokes a curse. The verb "call down curses" has no object in the Greek text. It may be that he calls down curses on himself, as the NIV translates it. He denies Jesus under oath and curses himself if he is lying. Or he may have pronounced a curse on Jesus.[17] The younger Pliny reported to the emperor Trajan as special commissioner to Pontus-Bithynia (ca. 110) that when he interrogated suspected Christians, he asked the prisoner three times, "Are you a Christian?" with threats of punishment. The accused proved his or her innocence by cursing Jesus—something, Pliny insists, "those who are really Christians cannot be made to do" (*Epistles* 10.96.3, 10.96.5). This curse was proof enough to the authorities that the person was not a Christian. In the *Martyrdom of Polycarp* 9:3, the proconsul tells the bishop, "Swear and I will release you." Polycarp replies, "Eighty-six years I have served him, and he had done me no wrong. How can I blaspheme my King who has saved me?" According to Justin Martyr, the Jewish rebel leader Bar Kochba (132–135) gave Christians the choice between death and cursing Christ (*1 Apol.* 31.6). Cursing Christ therefore was proof that one was not a Christian. In my opinion, Mark implies that Peter commits this blasphemy. This would make Peter's fall all the more dreadful and his restoration all the more remarkable.

Things happen exactly as Jesus said that they would: Peter would deny him three times before the rooster crowed twice. Mark now tells us that the rooster crowed a second time.[18] That implies that the first crowing gave Peter early warning, yet he persisted in his denial of Jesus. A textual variant in 14:68 after Peter's first denial has the rooster crowing the first time. It is ironic that a rooster, renowned for its foolish pride, reminds Peter of Jesus' prediction that he would deny him three times (14:30). The king of the chicken coop rules the roost and struts around, thinking that he is king of the

---

17. See G. W. H. Lampe, "St. Peter's Denial and the Treatment of the Lapsi," in *The Heritage of the Early Church: Essays in Honor of G. V. Florovsky* (Orientalia Christiana Analecta 195; Rome: Pontifical Oriental Institute, 1973), 113–33.

18. Some have argued from later rabbinic tradition that fowl were forbidden in Jerusalem (*m. B. Qam.* 7:7; but see the contradictory evidence in *m. Ed.* 6:1). They conclude that the rooster crowing refers to the third watch of the night (12:00–3:00 A.M.) according to Roman reckoning (see 13:35, where the four watches of the night are listed). It was sounded by the blowing of a horn at the end of the watch. Mark, however, clearly understands a rooster to be somewhere in the vicinity because he assumes it crows a second time.

world. The rooster fits perfectly Peter's cocky boastfulness in 14:29, but it is the crowing of the rooster that snaps him to awareness of what he has just done. This belongs to a common biblical theme, where human beings are rebuked by the so-called lower creation (see Balaam's ass and Jonah's worm).[19]

Peter's flight into the darkness comes too late now to save him from his shame. The violence of his sorrow is emphasized by the verb *epiballo*, but it is hard to translate.[20] It means "to throw over" or "to cast upon." Perhaps "he threw himself down," or "he broke down and wept" (NIV, NRSV), or "he dashed outside" (see Matt. 26:75; Luke 22:62). He does not rend his garments as the high priest did, but he does rend his heart (cf. Joel 2:12–13) over his great sin. When Peter confessed Jesus as the Christ (Mark 8:29), Jesus admonished his disciples, "If anyone is ashamed of me and my words in this adulterous and sinful generation, the Son of Man will be ashamed of him when he comes in his Father's glory with the holy angels" (8:38). Billows of shame now wash over Peter because he was ashamed to be associated with Jesus.

Bridging Contexts

PETER'S DENIALS BRIDGE easily into our contemporary setting; two other issues in the trial scene, however, need special attention. The first has to do with how a figure associated with power and glory, the Son of Man, could be connected to suffering and death. The second has to do with the Christian penchant throughout history to blame the Jewish people for Jesus' death.

The Son of Man: Power Blended with Suffering

THE MEANING OF the term *son of man* in the Judaism of Jesus' day is an elusive subject, which emerges again in Jesus' dramatic answer to the high priest. In Daniel 7 and in the popular apocalyptic work 1 Enoch, this enigmatic figure is associated with power, glory, heavenly exaltation, and judgment, and he is distinct from the righteous community in that he does not suffer what the community does. Collins concludes that he is a supernatural being in Daniel:

> The fact that he is preserved from their sufferings makes him a figure of pure power and glory and an ideal embodiment of the hopes of the persecuted righteous. The efficaciousness of the "Son of Man" fig-

---

19. Note Job 12:7: "The animals . . . will teach you, or the birds of the air . . . will tell you."

20. Brown (*The Death of the Messiah*, 1:609–10) lists nine options for translating it.

ure requires that he be conceived as other than the community, since he must possess the power and exultation which they lack.[21]

In Mark, we see the Son of Man associated with power that is blended with suffering and weakness. Jesus openly declares that he is the Messiah only when there is no possibility that crowds will rise up to crown him king. His admission seals the case against him and ensures that he will die. If Jesus is the Son of Man who will sit on the right hand of Power and come in the clouds of heaven, one must completely rethink what one believes about the Messiah and about power. Jesus as the Messiah is far less than many people hoped, because he never raises a finger against anyone and passively submits to death. As the Messiah, he is far more than anyone hoped, because he divinely exercises the power of God. God's power is revealed in weakness, however. Anyone looking for mighty displays of force, miraculous feats, or startling prophecies will see nothing. In bridging the contexts, we should examine our expectations of where and how we will see God's power working in our world.

Assigning Guilt

THE JEWISH HEARING before the high priest has become a sensitive issue for scholars in recent years. Some scholars have accused Mark of concocting this hearing before the council in a devious attempt to curry favor with Roman officialdom by shifting the blame for Jesus' death to the Jews. This interpretation has convinced many, not so much because it is based on sound historical arguments, but because it exonerates the Jews from guilt. For centuries they have been cursed as the murderers of God, and this charge has been used as a pretext for horrendous evil committed against them.

Paul Winter, for example, has carefully developed the argument that the Roman governor initiated Jesus' arrest and that the Jewish leaders were uninvolved in his condemnation. Life experiences affect what one looks for and one's analysis of evidence. Winter himself was a Jew who barely escaped from Czechoslovakia before the Nazis took over. At the end of the war he was a senior liaison officer charged with care of persons liberated from concentration and forced labor camps. He learned that his mother, sister, and other close relations died in the extermination camps. I believe his research, which he conducted at great cost to himself, is seriously flawed, but his concerns to remove the onus of guilt for the death of Jesus from his people is legitimate.

---

21. John J. Collins, *The Apocalyptic Imagination* (New York: Crossroad, 1987), 150; cited by Marcus, *The Way of the Lord,* 170.

We must be sensitive not to single out one group of people as responsible for Jesus' death. Those who were specifically guilty of orchestrating his death were the Jewish *priestly leaders*. In the trial before Pilate, they incite the crowd to call for Jesus' crucifixion (15:11). They represent the "rulers of this age," who have been seized by evil (1 Cor. 2:8; Col. 2:15), and this is not a category of persons limited to any one race or nation. The same kinds of people have plotted evil against others in back rooms from time immemorial. These leaders are little different from the Nazi officials who gathered at Wahnsee and planned the "final solution" to eradicate Jews from Europe. Mark's account of Jesus' trial and crucifixion has nothing to do with the guilt of the Jewish people. It has everything to do with persons who abuse power for their own ends and cloak their evil with religiosity, thinking that their ends justify the means.

The guilt for Jesus' death, therefore, is not to be apportioned to any one group. The trustees of Israel's national religious shrine bear the greatest responsibility for taking the initiative to put Jesus to death. But Pilate bears responsibility for taking no responsibility. To the shame of Christians, the stress on Jewish corporate guilt for this crime has been too easily transferred into the social, economic, and political realms, with horrendous consequences in this very century. Claude Montefiore, commenting on Matthew 27:25, wrote that it was "a terrible verse; a horrible mention . . . one of those phrases which have been responsible for oceans of human blood and a ceaseless stream of misery and desolation."[22] He wrote before World War II. The result of Christian persecution of Jews means that the cross does not represent the forgiving love of God to most Jews but the age-old charge of deicide and justification for the pogrom.

I doubt that we would have done much differently had we been in their position. Anyone who has ever dealt with persons in positions of power, whether in the religious world or the secular world, knows that they are just as capable of doing the same things as these ruling priests did. They scheme to destroy people's lives, shamelessly lie, manipulate crowds, and try to cover up their dirty work with slick propaganda. This is nothing new, and this violence continues today. Innocent victims are made scapegoats and are framed, tortured, and eliminated. Few voices cry out for justice. We may feel more comfortable finding a scapegoat to blame for the great evil perpetrated against God's Son, but we cannot evade our own guilt. We do not become saints by establishing the culpability of others. The cross reveals that *all* humankind is guilty. We must look to ourselves and our leaders, who would crucify Jesus afresh.

---

22. Claude Montefiore, *The Synoptic Gospels* (London: Macmillan, 1927), 2:342.

MARK SHOWS THAT Jesus suffered the greatest injustice. He was the victim of lies and innuendo, frame-ups, and a rigged jury. What makes this worse is that Jesus' condemnation was not done in a fit of mindless passion. Those who were supposedly the wisest and the holiest in the land had Jesus killed after deliberate proceedings, coldly and rationally.[23] We cannot help but abhor these leaders for their malicious corruption. But we must see that those who hate revolutionary ideas and feel responsible to God for keeping intact their vision of the American way of life, for example, would probably have acted in exactly the same way.

The traditional aristocracy, charged with the preservation of law and order and the Jewish way of life, carried out what they thought were the best interests of the country. These interests just happened to coincide with their best interests. The high priest's speech in John 11:50, although interpreted theologically, provides a clear motivation for their actions: They were removing a troublemaker who posed a grave danger to the whole nation if he roused the crowds. The Romans would step in to quell the movement with their normal heavy-handed brutality. The Romans charged these leaders with keeping the peace; if the peace was not kept, their power was in jeopardy. They were not unlike the men who tried to set up Martin Luther King, Jr., and did not shed a tear when he was shot. Jesus was killed by self-serving religious leaders in control of the temple, who were intent on preserving their power.

The king in John Steinbeck's novel *The Short Reign of Pippin IV* says: "Power does not corrupt. Fear corrupts, perhaps the fear of a loss of power."[24] The Jewish leaders feared what the Romans might do to them, not what God might do. They were swollen with ecclesiastical pride and filled with professional jealousy at the success of a true religious leader. They were embedded in a prosperous and mighty institution, and institutions can forget their original purpose and become concerned only with self-preservation. Even institutions dedicated to God can become taken over by evil and can try to thwart God's will rather than serving as an agent of God's will. Jesus confronted a corrupt institution and threatened its existence. What happened next should not surprise us. Confront them today and see what happens. Wink writes:

> What killed Jesus was not irreligion, but religion itself; not lawlessness, but precisely the law; not anarchy, but the upholders of order.

---

23. Schweizer, *Mark*, 331.
24. John Steinbeck, *The Short Reign of Pippin IV* (New York: Viking, 1957), 102.

It was not the bestial but those considered best who crucified the one in whom the divine Wisdom was visibly incarnate. And because he was not only innocent, but the very embodiment of true religion, true law, and true order, this victim exposed their violence for what it was: not the defense of society, but an attack against God.[25]

Jesus was innocent of the charges. The Jewish leaders were guilty, but we cannot blackball the whole lot. Every group of religious people has in its midst the wily and unscrupulous ecclesiastical politician, the fanatically righteous headhunter, the spineless toady who stands up for nothing, the turncoat who will switch to whatever he thinks will be the winning side to further his career, and the pious who are intent on mercy and justice. These first-century Jewish religionists are not the only ones who were guilty. They embody the universal guilt of all religious people. Pilate was also guilty, and he embodies the universal guilt of an idolatrous state. Judas too was guilty; he betrayed his Master.

I find it interesting in examining scholarly treatises and hearing sermons that we try to get different ones of these perpetrators off the hook. Some want to exonerate the Jewish leaders because the Jewish people have endured centuries' worth of undeserved blame. Gentiles now feel guilty over what has been done to the Jews in the name of Christianity and try to rid them of any connection at all in the death of Jesus. It was all Pilate's doing; no Jews were involved. Those in the pew more commonly absolve Pilate of guilt and regard him as a sad victim of circumstance. All kinds of justifications for Judas's betrayal have been proposed.

I am convinced that such attempts to excuse these original miscreants are ultimately attempts to excuse ourselves. Nobody is guilty. It was all God's plan, so that leaves only God to take responsibility. Schweizer rings the bell when he concludes: "Whoever is conscious of his own negligence in obedience, of his own failure to love, of the lethargy of his own heart in the midst of the demands of everyday life, cannot escape from his responsibility before God for Jesus' death by fixing the blame upon some other person."[26] When we read this account, we must see how easily we can become a crafty high priest, a devious Judas, a lying false witness, a cowardly Peter, a wishy-washy governor, a mindless member of a hate-filled crowd, a coarse soldier, and an absent disciple hidden for fear. Then we realize that it is we who are on trial before Jesus and not vice versa.

The sad plight of Peter, the rock who disintegrates into a pile of sand, evokes our horror and sympathy. We understand how tempting it is to with-

---

25. Walter Wink, *Engaging the Powers* (Minneapolis: Fortress, 1992), 139–40.
26. Schweizer, *Mark*, 322.

draw from others who get into difficulty with the authorities. In private we may say, "We are behind you all the way." And we usually are—way behind. We can learn from examples of bravery, including Jesus himself, who fearlessly confessed and then withstood the withering assault from those who hated him. The examples of the many martyrs of the faith throughout the centuries who bravely resisted unto death can inspire us. Yet the vivid portrayal of Peter's abject failure perhaps teaches us best. The account of his dismal collapse could only have come from his own testimony, which he told to help others. The readers of Mark's Gospel certainly know that his repudiation of Christ was not the end for Peter, that he was restored (16:7), that he went on to preach boldly the gospel, and that his faith cost him his life. The poignancy of his denials in an hour of crisis becomes both a warning and a solace to others.

Sins of omission lead to sins of commission.[27] Three times Peter failed to understand Jesus' announcement of his suffering. Three times he did not heed Jesus' urgent appeal to watch, stay awake, and pray. Three times he denied Jesus. The sin of boastful rivalry led him to think that he was different from all the others—"I will not" (14:29). He relied on his own strength and fell farther than the other disciples. Paul's warning to the Corinthians is apropos: "So, if you think you are standing firm, be careful that you don't fall!" (1 Cor. 10:12). The sin of spiritual complacency kept Peter from watching as his Lord commanded. In 1 Peter 1:7, Peter speaks of being tested by fire and warns about a fiery ordeal of suffering that will come on Christians (4:7). We never know when our faith or allegiance might be tested, however. Fiery ordeals might slip up on us while we warm ourselves by comfortable fires, as Peter did (Mark 14:54, 67).

Many Christians today do not face the fierce persecution that engulfed the first Christians. Few today are forced to choose between Christ and imprisonment or execution. Consequently, our denials of Christ may take more subtle forms, such as timid silence. We may not want to be identified as Christians. We do not speak out against those who sarcastically dismiss Christianity as a fantasy. We try to blend into the crowd of our Master's enemies because we do not want to be jeered by others or to rock any boats.

The Christian faith calls for us to stand out from others. When the Hall of Fame baseball player Mickey Mantle was on the verge of death after years of abusing his body with alcohol, his many friends gathered around his hospital bed to say their farewells. One former teammate who came to his bedside was Bobby Richardson. As a Christian he had not joined the wild partying of his mates and had become a minister after his retirement from the

---

27. Mitton, *Mark*, 122.

game. Mickey Mantle used to make fun of him as "the milk drinker"; but as his life ebbed away, he most wanted to talk with Bobby Richardson. The testimony of Bobby's life amid the jeers had made its impact.

One can also take solace from the account of Peter's denials. Peter was the most prominent of Jesus' disciples, yet he was still a sinner in need of God's mercy. He thought he would die for Jesus, but he needed Jesus to die for him. His failure reveals the truth of Jesus' statement in Mark 2:17: "It is not the healthy who need a doctor, but the sick. I have not come to call the righteous, but sinners." Mark is the Gospel of the second chance. The angel's command in 16:7, "Go, tell his disciples *and* Peter," holds the promise of his restoration. There were probably members in Mark's church who already had betrayed and denied their Lord. If Peter could be restored after denying his Lord and even cursing him, then there was hope for others who might be guilty of the same or worse.[28] Peter's tears of remorse mark the beginning of that restoration.

---

28. R. W. Herron, *Mark's Account of Peter's Denial of Jesus: A History of Its Interpretation* (Lanham, Md.: Univ. Press of America, 1992), 143.

Mark 15:1–20

ιϕ

VERY EARLY IN the morning, the chief priests, with the elders, the teachers of the law and the whole Sanhedrin, reached a decision. They bound Jesus, led him away and handed him over to Pilate.

²"Are you the king of the Jews?" asked Pilate.

"Yes, it is as you say," Jesus replied.

³The chief priests accused him of many things. ⁴So again Pilate asked him, "Aren't you going to answer? See how many things they are accusing you of."

⁵But Jesus still made no reply, and Pilate was amazed.

⁶Now it was the custom at the Feast to release a prisoner whom the people requested. ⁷A man called Barabbas was in prison with the insurrectionists who had committed murder in the uprising. ⁸The crowd came up and asked Pilate to do for them what he usually did.

⁹"Do you want me to release to you the king of the Jews?" asked Pilate, ¹⁰knowing it was out of envy that the chief priests had handed Jesus over to him. ¹¹But the chief priests stirred up the crowd to have Pilate release Barabbas instead.

¹²"What shall I do, then, with the one you call the king of the Jews?" Pilate asked them.

¹³"Crucify him!" they shouted.

¹⁴"Why? What crime has he committed?" asked Pilate.

But they shouted all the louder, "Crucify him!"

¹⁵Wanting to satisfy the crowd, Pilate released Barabbas to them. He had Jesus flogged, and handed him over to be crucified.

¹⁶The soldiers led Jesus away into the palace (that is, the Praetorium) and called together the whole company of soldiers. ¹⁷They put a purple robe on him, then twisted together a crown of thorns and set it on him. ¹⁸And they began to call out to him, "Hail, king of the Jews!" ¹⁹Again and again they struck him on the head with a staff and spit on him. Falling on their knees, they paid homage to him. ²⁰And when they had mocked him, they took off the purple robe and put his own clothes on him. Then they led him out to crucify him.

MARK 15:1 FORMS a bridge from the high priest's proceedings against Jesus to his delivery to the Roman governor, Pontius Pilate. It moves the reader from the courtyard, where Peter has denied his Lord for the third time and darted away, back inside the chamber, where the council has finished its deliberations. Mark does not intend to suggest that the council reassembled early in the morning for a second meeting to rehash their earlier decision. He simply recaps the ruling they reached (14:64) during Peter's denials outside the chamber.[1] It is the "whole Sanhedrin" against one, and they bind him securely before sending him off to the governor. Such extreme measures—sending an arresting party with swords and clubs and orders to seize him securely, and now tying him up with trusses to transfer him to Pilate—seem ludicrous for a peaceful, nonviolent prophet. They fulfill what Jesus predicted would happen to him, however (10:33).

The Charge Against Jesus

THE ROMANS DID not interfere in local politics any more than necessary to maintain order. They favored the ruling oligarchies in the cities. Since Pilate was an equestrian (knight), he had no assistants of a similar rank and little bureaucracy to handle all of the administrative matters. A large part of the everyday chores of government and administration, therefore, was carried out by the local councils and magistrates. They had the power to arrest, to take evidence, and to make a preliminary examination for the purpose of presenting a prosecution case before the governor for a formal trial. The prosecution's case was normally brought by private parties, usually consisting of no more than two to three spokesmen (see Acts 24:1–9). The legal system of the Roman empire served the interests of the wealthy and the governing class. The high priest, Caiaphas (unnamed in Mark), was in office during the entire tenure of Pilate, and one can hardly expect a fair verdict when the accusers are powerful men and have had a long working relationship with the judge.[2] Jesus could make no appeal to Caesar, only to God.

The Roman prefect (called a procurator only after A.D. 44) had the power of life and death over all the inhabitants of his province who were not Roman citizens. No criminal code existed for a malefactor who was a non-Roman citizen tried in the provinces. The governor was free in such cases to make his own rules and judgments as he saw fit, to accept or reject charges, and to fash-

---

1. So Brown, *The Death of the Messiah*, 1:629–32.
2. Paul found himself in a similar situation and escaped the leaders' vendetta against him only because he was a Roman citizen (Acts 22:22–30; 24:1–23).

ion, within reason, whatever penalties he chose. Tacitus and Pliny record almost forty trials of malfeasance on the part of provincial governors from the time of Augustus to Trajan,[3] suggesting that many governors took unfair advantage of their discretionary powers. Josephus and Philo register bitter complaints against Pilate for his arbitrary actions and cruelty.[4]

A Roman governor would not have put a native Jew on trial for his life simply because he had violated Jewish religious regulations. That is, a religious charge of blasphemy (i.e., Jesus' declaring himself to be the Messiah) would not suffice for Pilate to take action (Acts 18:14–17), although the Romans would not have been indifferent to threats against temples. The governor could have cared less as long as matters religious did not become matters political. Thus, the high priests reformulate the charge against Jesus in a way that the Roman governor will understand and have to take seriously. Since Pilate's first question is, "Are you the king of the Jews?" (15:2), presumably this is the official charge against Jesus (cf. also 15:12, "the one you call the king of the Jews"). If Jesus claims to be a king, he is guilty of a crime against the sovereign power of Rome. Sending him to Pilate in tethers also insinuates that he is a threat to public order.

Mark has emphasized Jesus' greater authority throughout the Gospel. Not surprisingly, Pilate suspects almost immediately that the high priests have handed him over because of their "envy" (15:10). Accused prisoners had opportunity to defend themselves against their charges. If one chose to

---

3. Colin Wells, *The Roman Empire* (Stanford: Stanford Univ. Press, 1984), 146–47.

4. See Josephus, *J. W.* 2.9.2–4 §§ 169–77; *Ant.* 18.2.2. § 35; 18.3.1–2 §§ 55–62; 18.4.1 §§ 85–89; Philo, *Embassy to Gaius*, 299–305. Pilate remained in office for ten years (A.D. 26 or 27 to 37). According to Josephus (*Ant.* 18.6.5 §§ 174–78), Tiberias explained why he left governors in place with a wry illustration.

Once a man lay wounded, and a swarm of flies hovered about his wounds. A passer-by took pity on his evil plight and, in the belief that he did not raise a hand because he could not, was about to step up and shoo them off. The wounded man, however, begged him to think no more of doing anything about it. At this the man spoke up and asked him why he was not interested in escaping from his wretched condition, "Why," said he, "you would put me in a worse condition if you drove them off. For since these flies have already had their fill of blood, they no longer feel such pressing need to annoy me but are in some measure slack. But if others were to come with fresh appetite, they would take over my now weakened body and that would indeed be the death of me." He too, he said, for the same reason took the precaution of not dispatching governors continually to the subject peoples who had been brought to ruin by so many thieves; for the governors would harry them utterly like flies. Their natural appetite for plunder would be reinforced by their expectation of being speedily deprived of that pleasure. The record of Tiberias' acts will bear out my account of his humor in such matters. For during the twenty-two years that he was emperor he sent altogether two men, Gratus and Pilate, his successor, to govern the Jewish nation.

remain silent, he was directly questioned three times so that he might change his mind before his case was allowed to go by default.

Much to Pilate's consternation, Jesus chooses to answer the charge enigmatically and then to remain silent (15:2–5). Jesus responds to the question, "Are you king of the Jews?" with (lit.) "You say." This phrase can have a variety of meanings, depending on the inflection. The NIV translation, "Yes, it is as you say," is possible; but it is more likely that Jesus' answer is less direct, "You say so," or "Whatever you say." Jesus refuses to defend himself and implicate his fellow Jews in a Gentile's court. His silence before such charges evokes Pilate's amazement. The governor may want to release Jesus, but he cannot release someone who refuses to deny such a serious charge. Jesus leaves it to God to provide the answer to the charges and to the evil massed against him. Even after God acts, many will be blind to truth.

Barabbas

ROMAN TRIALS FREQUENTLY took place in public, and it was not unusual for crowds to clamor with judges for and against prisoners. Magistrates were frequently confronted with a unified uproar. The Judeans customarily confronted the Roman governor with large and boisterous crowds.[5] Mark records that a crowd now approaches Pilate to remind him of "the custom at the Feast" to release a prisoner to them. The Gospels provide the only evidence for this practice, and some scholars have argued that it is a fiction. The governor, however, had the privilege to do whatever he liked; and the release of a prisoner once a year to appease the people is not improbable.[6] Pilate is perplexed, however, that the crowd cries for the release of the murderous Barabbas instead of the harmless Jesus. Mark offers no reason why they choose Barabbas and call for the crucifixion of Jesus except that the high priests have stirred them up. Crowds, of course, can be easily manipulated. The crowd that these leaders so feared (11:32; 12:37) has now become their willing pawn, and things turn ugly.

Barabbas had been arrested for committing murder in an insurrection.[7] Mark does not describe the nature of the uprising or riot in which he was

---

5. Acts 24:1; Josephus, *J. W.* 2.9.4 § 175.

6. Evidence may exist in a passage from the Mishnah: "they may slaughter [the Passover lamb] for one ... whom they have promised to bring out of prison ..." (*m. Pesaḥ.* 8:6). A papyrus document records judicial proceedings where the governor of Egypt, G. Septimus Vegetus, allowed the crowd to decide a verdict: "You deserve to be scourged ... but I will deal more humanely with you and will give you to the people" (PFlor 61).

7. See Richard A. Horsley and J. S. Hanson, *Bandits, Prophets, and Messiahs* (New York: Winston, 1985); see also Richard A. Horsley, *Jesus and the Spiral of Violence: Popular Jewish Resistance in Roman Palestine* (San Francisco: Harper & Row, 1987) on banditry in Palestine.

involved. Barabbas may have been a right-wing extremist fighting to deliver Israel from the pollution of Roman rule, or he may have simply been a bandit. Social banditry plagued many parts of the empire. In Palestine, some of the peasants forced off their land when they were caught in the maelstrom of debt chose the path of outlawry rather than meek submission as tenant farmers or day laborers. Their victims were usually the rich landlords and their retainers. The bandits operated in the countryside and retreated to their strongholds in the hills.

Josephus, who wrote from the biased perspective of the urban elite, reports that Galilee was a haven for bandits, who were guilty of "habitual malpractices, theft, robbery, and rapine."[8] He also reports that many were caught and duly crucified. The rich man's terrorist, however, is frequently the poor man's Robin Hood. The impoverished common people, from whose ranks the bandits came, looked to them as heroic figures who justly exacted vengeance against their oppressors. They openly sympathized with them and frequently offered them protection at great cost to themselves when the Romans punished them severely for complicity. Barabbas may have been a hero in the eyes of the crowd, which explains their choice.

Even though the crowd wants amnesty for Barabbas, that fact does not make Jesus guilty. Pilate cedes his responsibility as judge to the crowd by asking them what he should do with Jesus. Not only do they choose Barabbas over Jesus, they choose crucifixion for Jesus. When Pilate asks, "Why?" they only raise the volume of their screams.

The crowd's choice is ironic. Jesus, who had no interest in causing sedition or social upheaval, will be crucified between two brigands. Barabbas, a brigand guilty of murder, will go free because Jesus has taken his place on the cross intended for him. The crowd chooses the one who takes the lives of others to achieve his own selfish ends and condemns the one who gives his life for others in obedience to God. They want a king who will be comfortable with murder and mayhem, not one who refuses to resist evil with violence. It is a fatal preference. The violence of renegades like Barabbas continued to spiral until it eventually erupted in war against Rome. The outcome was inevitable: Rome destroyed Jerusalem, its temple, and most of the inhabitants in a brutal siege. The chief priests fear Jesus because he is a threat to the temple, their power base. In turn, they urge the release of one whose violent ways will eventually rain down terror and destruction on the land.

Mark gives us no insight into the workings of Pilate's mind except that he "want[ed] to satisfy the crowd." He will give them their prisoner and their

---

8. *J. W.* 2:10.7 § 581.

victim. Though it is obvious to him that the high priests are driven by envy (15:10) and that Jesus has done no evil (15:14), Pilate is indifferent to his responsibility to carry out justice.

The Scourging and Mockery of Jesus

PILATE HANDS JESUS over to be crucified, and scourging was a customary preliminary. Prisoners to be flogged were bound to a pillar or post and given strokes with a *flagellum*. This lash was different from the simple whip. It consisted of leather thongs plaited with pieces of bone, lead, or bronze. It was fittingly called a scorpion. There were no prescribed number of lashes, and sometimes the scourging itself was fatal. The balls (sometimes having hooks) would cause deep contusions as the flesh was literally ripped into bloody ribbons. Significant blood loss could also occur, critically weakening the victim. It was so horrible that Suetonius claimed even the cruel emperor Domitian was appalled by it.[9]

Mark reports that the whole company of soldiers (around six hundred in a cohort) joins in the mockery of Jesus in the courtyard of Pilate's Praetorium.[10] Jesus' Jewish captors derided him as a false messiah. The Roman soldiers now deride him as a false king. They deck him out in royal purple (15:17; see 1 Macc. 14:43–44) and plait a crown of thorns (Mark 15:17b), which may or may not have been intended as the instrument of torture depicted in Christian art. The soldiers had to improvise and would have grabbed whatever was at hand. A variety of thorny plants were available in Jerusalem. The thorns may have come from a type of palm tree common to Jerusalem, a dwarf date palm or thorn palm, which grew as an ornamental plant and had formidable spikes. The leaves could have been easily woven into a wreath and the long spikes from the date palm inserted to make a radiate crown.[11] Evidence for this type of crown is found in the seals from the Roman camp in Jerusalem. The crown may also have been simply a clump of thorns heaped together.

The soldiers' mock homage climaxes the masquerade. They hail him as "King of the Jews" and bow down before him (15:18–19). Their ridicule probably expresses as much contempt for the Jews as it does for Jesus. Officially, the Jews had had no king after the death of Herod the Great. The mockery implies that this pitiful, weak figure is the kind of king they deserve.

---

9. Suetonius, *Domitian* 11.

10. Pilate had probably taken over the former palace of Herod the Great when he traveled to Jerusalem to attend to business there.

11. H. St. J. Hart, "The Crown of Thorns in John 19:2–5," *JTS* 3 (1952): 66–75.

The recognition of Jesus in Mark's Passion narrative is almost complete. A woman had lovingly anointed him in the home of a leper, but he announced that it was for his burial (14:3–9). The high priest asked if he was the Christ, the Son of the Blessed One, and he responded with a yes. Pilate called him the king of the Jews (15:17–19), and the soldiers mockingly saluted him as a king (15:16–19). While on earth, Jesus was a different type of king, as ruffians anointed him with spit, crowned him with thorns, and prepared to enthrone him on a cross.[12] At this point, everyone has abandoned Jesus, and now only God can deliver him.

FROM EARLY ON, Pilate has come off well in Christian tradition as a sympathetic figure. In the apocryphal *Gospel of Peter*, Pilate does not pronounce the death sentence; Herod does; and Pilate later begs for Jesus' body from Herod. Tertullian speaks of a full report of the trial that Pilate sent to the emperor and hints that he was a Christian at heart (*1 Apol.* 21.24). In the apocryphal *Acts of Pilate*, Pilate puts up a more forceful defense on behalf of Jesus, and his eventual conversion is recorded. A letter claiming to be from Pontius Pilate maintains that he sent two thousand troops to try to stop the crucifixion. In the Ethiopic and Coptic churches Pilate has been canonized. Many today consider Pilate to have been an innocent, bewildered bystander, caught in an impossible situation.

We should be cautious about imaginative reconstructions of Pilate's state of mind and his later life. We should also be cautious not to present him as a sympathetic figure. Mark certainly did not consider him so. Pilate represents a state concerned only with preserving order, regardless of the injustice suffered by others. His guilt is no greater and no less than that of anyone else in the story, but he is clearly guilty. His investigation is marked by indecision. Is he in charge or not? He asks the crowd, "Do you want me to release to you the king of the Jews?" (15.9), and, "What shall I do, then, with the one you call the king of the Jews?" (15:12). He puts up only a feeble protest when they call for Jesus' death: "Why? What crime has he committed?" (15:14). Finally, he caves in to moral cowardice. He is the governor who can do as he wishes but he ends up serving the wishes of the Jewish leaders and their crowd (15:15).

The soldiers' mockery of Jesus reveals the evil that bursts forth from human hearts. It also reflects the human idea of what a king ought to be. The

---

12. Camery-Hoggatt, *Irony*, 170–71.

kings the soldiers have served are those who lord it over others and exercise authority, who maintain the illusions of power at the expense of others (10:42–45). Jesus does not fit any royal category known to them. People frequently take refuge in mocking what they cannot comprehend rather than trying to take it seriously. To bow down before such a king must have seemed to them both amusing and absurd. Jesus had no army. His frail followers deserted him. He was totally powerless to save himself.

As Juel points out, however, these soldiers ironically "testify to a truth that is quite hidden from them." That is, Jesus "is a king, not one who foments rebellion against Rome and who restores Israel to its national splendor as a rival empire, but one who endures mockery willingly and who obediently chooses the path that will lead to his death."[13] Rarely does a king put himself last, take the role of a slave, and willingly suffer death—even death on the cross—and isolation on behalf of his people. But here is the king before whom every knee will bow and whom every tongue will confess (Phil. 2:11). God will turn the mockery into reality. Marcus writes: "So powerful is the kingdom that it reaches down even into the hate-filled minds and venomous lips of its foes, drawing unwitting testimony from those who look without seeing."[14]

Contemporary Significance

PEOPLE WITH NO moral compass and no moral backbone ask, What am I to do? The answer they usually get is to satisfy the crowd. In doing so, Pilate cedes his responsibility, acquiesces to injustice, and refuses to risk anything for another. He is the type of leader who forever has his finger in the wind to see which way it is blowing and does something for others as long as it costs him nothing. He will not pursue truth or justice. He only wants to satisfy the crowd, whose intentions he knows are less than honorable, and allows them to make his decisions. Pilate did ask the right question, "What shall I do, then, with [Jesus]?" but came up with the wrong answer.

Many today are like Pilate. They prefer Jesus to the envious, malicious high priests and the violent Barabbas, but that is as far as it goes. They see no harm in him, but they see nothing else, and therefore they see no reason to risk anything for him. They regard Jesus as simply "the king of the Jews" and do not recognize that he is the "King of kings" (cf. Rev. 19:16).

As far as Pilate is concerned, this crucial moment in God's dealing with our sinful world is only another day in his long tenure of dealing with trou-

---

13. Juel, *Messiah and Temple*, 28.
14. Marcus, *Mystery*, 117.

blesome Jews. Anatole France, in his tale *The Procurator of Judea*, imagines that Pilate, when asked to recall the trial of one Jesus of Nazareth, cannot do so. Great evil comes from moral indifference. In this text we can see evil at work in the cunning chief priests, who manipulate crowds to their end; in the mercurial crowds, who allow themselves to be manipulated and cry for blood; and in boorish thugs, who carry out orders with sadistic pleasure. But a reluctant governor unconcerned with justice allows this evil to be unleashed. This attitude continues to allow others to be victims of false arrest, mob justice, and brutal treatment. Many turn away their eyes so they can pretend not to know. Few stand up and say, "Stop!"

The choice of Barabbas represents the human preference for the one who represents our narrow personal hopes—in this particular case, a perverted nationalism. He appeals to our basic instinct to protect our interests, with violence if necessary. In contemporary culture, we have been indoctrinated to prefer the violent answer over the peaceful one. Most Western children are bombarded with television shows and movies where the hero is pushed to the limit by oppressors until he can take no more and strikes back with a vengeance. Usually, the plot pits one man against many, and he always resorts to violence to win the day—the more spectacular the violence, the better the ratings or the box office returns. The subliminal lesson learned is that the only way to handle the evil of others is to blow them away. Our heroes become the Barabbases of the world, who take matters into their own hands and dispatch the enemy with brute force or clever trickery. If the vote came today, then, Barabbas would likely win again, hands down. We are more comfortable with the violent machismo of the knight-errant than with the passive suffering of a seemingly powerless savior who submits to beatings and mockery.

In other words, we have learned little since the day the crowd hailed Barabbas and called for Jesus to be crucified. Barabbas's way only doles out more violence in a never-ending cycle. Jesus' way soaks up the injustice, evil, and oppression like the venom of a sting and unleashes a far more powerful force of love and forgiveness. God's way responds to evil redemptively and short-circuits it. On the cross, Jesus took the sting of death and absorbed all the poison. Our failure to choose this way stems from our failure to trust God. We may trust God to take care of the afterlife, but we do not trust God enough to let go of too much control of the here and now. If we have to suffer, we would rather put our trust in the Barabbases of this world, who fight back and murder enemies. We have yet to see that this way only leads to more death and tragedy.

The suffering of Jesus has made a vivid impact on Christians throughout the centuries. It is especially meaningful to those who have suffered in the same way. One person who endured persecution in a South American torture cellar reported that all the intricacies of Christian doctrine disappeared. The only thing that sustained him was knowing that Jesus had also been on the wrong side of a whip and that Jesus was with him. The same was true of many who suffered in the concentration camps of Hitler. Chuck Colson tells of one man who took courage from the suffering of Christ. Father Maximilian Kolbe, a Polish priest, was sentenced to Auschwitz for refusing to cave in to the Nazi demands "to keep the Poles quiet, stupid and dull-witted." In a moment of great courage he stepped out of line (in more ways than one) to volunteer to die in the place of someone else who had been arbitrarily chosen for death with nine others because a prisoner from their barracks had successfully escaped. The startled and contemptuous commandant consented to this rash offer. Father Kolbe joined the line of condemned men being herded to their death. They were ordered to take off their clothes. *"Christ died on a cross naked,* Father Kolbe thought as he took off his pants and thin shirt, *It is only fitting that I suffer as he suffered."*[15]

Jesus also took the place of a condemned man. He did not volunteer to die specifically for Barabbas, but he was chosen by God to die for all sinful humanity. He accepted the bitter cup of judgment and took the place of a murderous Barabbas and all guilty humans.

To fall into the hands of malicious rulers and to be at their mercy is difficult for anyone, but it is particularly difficult for one who has been active in bringing good to other people's lives. Vanstone hits upon an interesting feature of Jesus' Passion—his passivity. It is a dramatic turnabout from his ministry:

> As He moves about He leaves behind him a trail of transformed scenes and changed situations—fishermen no longer at their nets, sick people restored to health, critics confounded, a storm stilled, hunger assuaged, a dead girl raised to life. Jesus' presence is an active and instantly transforming presence: He is never the mere observer of the scene or the one who waits upon events but always the transformer of the scene and the initiator of events.[16]

All this changes in Mark's Passion narrative. Jesus is no longer the one who initiates the action; he is the subject of others' actions (the subject of nine verbs, and the object of fifty-six).[17] He is silent, answering nothing, taking nothing—except the lashes from their scourges. We can learn of him how to endure suffering with peace and grace, trusting in God to deliver us.

---

15. Charles Colson with Ellen Santini Vaughn, *The Body* (Dallas: Word, 1992), 318–27.
16. W. H. Vanstone, *The Stature of Waiting* (New York: Seabury, 1983), 17–18.
17. Ibid., 22.

❧

ACERTAIN MAN from Cyrene, Simon, the father of Alexander and Rufus, was passing by on his way in from the country, and they forced him to carry the cross. ²²They brought Jesus to the place called Golgotha (which means The Place of the Skull). ²³Then they offered him wine mixed with myrrh, but he did not take it. ²⁴And they crucified him. Dividing up his clothes, they cast lots to see what each would get.

²⁵It was the third hour when they crucified him. ²⁶The written notice of the charge against him read: THE KING OF THE JEWS. ²⁷They crucified two robbers with him, one on his right and one on his left. ²⁹Those who passed by hurled insults at him, shaking their heads and saying, "So! You who are going to destroy the temple and build it in three days, ³⁰come down from the cross and save yourself!"

³¹In the same way the chief priests and the teachers of the law mocked him among themselves. "He saved others," they said, "but he can't save himself! ³²Let this Christ, this King of Israel, come down now from the cross, that we may see and believe." Those crucified with him also heaped insults on him.

³³At the sixth hour darkness came over the whole land until the ninth hour. ³⁴And at the ninth hour Jesus cried out in a loud voice, "Eloi, Eloi, lama sabachthani?"—which means, "My God, my God, why have you forsaken me?"

³⁵When some of those standing near heard this, they said, "Listen, he's calling Elijah."

³⁶One man ran, filled a sponge with wine vinegar, put it on a stick, and offered it to Jesus to drink. "Now leave him alone. Let's see if Elijah comes to take him down," he said.

³⁷With a loud cry, Jesus breathed his last.

³⁸The curtain of the temple was torn in two from top to bottom. ³⁹And when the centurion, who stood there in front of Jesus, heard his cry and saw how he died, he said, "Surely this man was the Son of God!"

⁴⁰Some women were watching from a distance. Among them were Mary Magdalene, Mary the mother of James the younger and of Joses, and Salome. ⁴¹In Galilee these women

had followed him and cared for his needs. Many other women who had come up with him to Jerusalem were also there.

⁴²It was Preparation Day (that is, the day before the Sabbath). So as evening approached, ⁴³Joseph of Arimathea, a prominent member of the Council, who was himself waiting for the kingdom of God, went boldly to Pilate and asked for Jesus' body. ⁴⁴Pilate was surprised to hear that he was already dead. Summoning the centurion, he asked him if Jesus had already died. ⁴⁵When he learned from the centurion that it was so, he gave the body to Joseph. ⁴⁶So Joseph bought some linen cloth, took down the body, wrapped it in the linen, and placed it in a tomb cut out of rock. Then he rolled a stone against the entrance of the tomb. ⁴⁷Mary Magdalene and Mary the mother of Joses saw where he was laid.

EXECUTION OF CONDEMNED criminals was a public affair. Wells comments: "The Romans had a highly developed and theatrical sense of the public ceremonial."[1] The triumph was one aspect of it, and the soldiers have given Jesus a mock triumph. Crucifixion was another facet of it. This horrible means of execution served two purposes. (1) It punished the criminal by prolonging the pain for as long as possible. Victims could linger on crosses for days as they slowly died from asphyxiation from muscle fatigue.

(2) The public exposure served also as a warning and a deterrent. The victim was paraded through the streets with a placard announcing the crime and was then hanged on a cross strategically placed beside well-traveled roads. His torment would then strike fear into the hearts of those who happened to pass by. During the first revolt against Rome, those caught by the Romans trying to sneak away from the besieged Jerusalem to forage for food were crucified next to the walls of the city. According to Josephus, the Roman general Titus

hoped that the spectacle might perhaps induce the Jews to surrender, for fear that continued resistance might involve them in a similar fate. The soldiers out of rage and hatred amused themselves by nailing their prisoners in different postures; and so great was their number, that space could not be found for the crosses nor crosses for the bodies.[2]

---

1. Colin Wells, *The Roman Empire* (Stanford: Stanford Univ. Press, 1984), 53.
2. *J. W.* 5.11.1 §§ 449–51.

To Golgotha

NORMALLY, A CONDEMNED man carried the *patibulum*, the crossbeam, to the site of his crucifixion, where it was fastened to the *stipes*, the vertical beam already firmly embedded into the ground. Dionysius of Halicarnassus describes barbarous preliminaries to an execution:

> A Roman citizen of no obscure station, having ordered one of his slaves to be put to death, delivered him to his fellow-slaves to be led away, and in order that his punishment might be witnessed by all, directed them to drag him through the Forum and every conspicuous part of the city as they whipped him. . . . The men ordered to lead the slave to his punishment, having stretched out both his arms and fastened them to a piece of wood which extended across his breast and shoulders as far as his wrists, followed him, tearing his naked body with whips. The culprit, overcome by such cruelty, not only uttered ill-omened cries, forced from him by the pain, but also made indecent movements under the blows.[3]

Mark does not tell why Jesus does not carry his own cross, but it is easy to guess. He is either too weak or too slow from the severe lashing, and the soldiers must conscript an innocent onlooker to carry the crossbar.[4] Gill comments: "One of the profound paradoxes of Christianity is to be found in the fact that the one who was not able to carry his own cross (15:21) is the one who enables us to carry ours."[5]

Simon is "passing by" just as Jesus was passing by when he called the first disciples (1:16) and Levi (2:14). Simon comes from the country or the field into the city; he must reverse direction as the guards take Jesus outside the city to execute him. Mark identifies Simon as from Cyrene in North Africa and as the father of Rufus and Alexander.[6] Most likely, his name is remembered because he later became a Christian. Mark mentions the names of his two sons (who do not figure in the plot) because they were known to the first readers of this Gospel. Paul mentions a Rufus in Romans 16:13 (see also Polycarp's *Letter to the Philippians* 9:1). The names Simon, Rufus, and Alexander are Hebrew,

---

3. *Roman Antiquities* 7.69.1–2.

4. "Forced" (*angareuo*) is a technical term for commandeering a person or property (see Matt. 5:41).

5. Athol Gill, *Life on the Road: The Gospel Basis for a Messianic Lifestyle* (Scottdale, Pa.: Herald, 1992), 63.

6. Simon may have had some connection with the synagogue of Cyrenians that later instigated the arrest and death of Stephen (Acts 6:8–15). Was he the Simon who was called Niger, who is mentioned in Acts 13:1? Mark tells the story of Jesus, not of Simon and his family, and all conjecture about them is just that—conjecture.

Latin, and Greek names, respectively, and hint at the universality of the gospel, which will reach across cultures to the ends of the earth.

The procession ends at a place called Golgotha, which Mark interprets for his Greek-speaking readers as "The Place of the Skull."[7] The name could refer to the shape of the outcropping of rock that resembled a skull, the discovery of a skull or skulls in this place, or the fact that it was the location for executions. Mark does not describe the details of Jesus' crucifixion—how he was fastened to the cross, what type of cross was used, or how excruciating (this word is derived from the Latin *excruciatus*, which means "out of the cross") the pain was. Nearly everyone in the ancient world knew what crucifixion was like, and it served no purpose to sketch its horrors.[8] The details Mark does isolate have theological significance.

"They"—presumably the same "they" as those who led him out (15:22)—offer Jesus wine mixed with myrrh, which had a narcotic property (15:23). This act may have been a compassionate attempt to relieve somewhat the pain.[9] It is unlikely, however, that the executioners are now showing Jesus charity after mocking and scourging him. They may only have wanted to give their exhausted victim a spurt of energy so that he would last longer and suffer more. One can surmise why Jesus rejects the offer of wine. He had made a vow of abstinence at the Last Supper not to drink from the fruit of the vine until he would drink it anew in the kingdom of God (14:25). He has been destined to drink the cup of God (10:38; 14:36), not of men,[10] and he wishes to remain fully conscious to the bitter end as he accepts his suffering. Jesus is not going to sleep on the cross as the disciples slept in Gethsemane.

It was customary for executioners to share out the minor personal belongings of the person being executed.[11] This detail would not have been mentioned by Mark if it had not been recognized that the division of garments also appears in Psalm 22:18. The linkage helps the reader see that this moment of absolute humiliation for Jesus is fully consonant with God's will. Jesus' garments have been mentioned before in the Gospel.[12] They were

---

7. The familiar term "Calvary" derives from the Latin *calvaria*, which means skull.

8. See the discussion in Martin Hengel, *Crucifixion in the Ancient World and the Folly of the Message of the Cross* (Philadelphia: Fortress, 1977); Brown, *The Death of the Messiah*, 2:945–52; Pierre Barbet, *A Doctor at Calvary* (New York: P. J. Kennedy & Sons, 1953).

9. According to later rabbinic tradition (*b. Sanh.* 43a), the women of Jerusalem, motivated by Prov. 31:6–7, offered a narcotic drink to those who were condemned to death in order to alleviate the pain of execution, but it refers to wine and frankincense.

10. Frank J. Matera, *Passion Narratives and Gospel Theologies* (New York/Mahwah, N.J.: Paulist, 1986), 42.

11. Justinian, *Digest*, 48.20.6.

12. See Tolbert, *Sowing*, 280; Gundry, *Mark*, 945.

emblematic of his great power to heal people when they touched the hem (6:56; see 5:27–31). In the Transfiguration, his garments became white beyond the power of any human fuller to make white (9:3) and were emblematic of his future glory as God's Son. The soldiers mocked him as a bogus king by taking his garments from him and giving him purple to wear (15:16–20)—a scene portraying a humiliated king. Now his garments are taken from him again and are raffled off at the foot of his cross. It reveals his utter degradation. The powerful healer and transfigured Son of God dies as a publicly humiliated human being.

Jesus the Messiah resisted all political overtones during his ministry in Galilee and probably disappointed many followers because of his reserve. Ironically, he is executed as a political messiah. The inscription placed on the cross announces to all Jesus' crime: He is the King of the Jews. The posse came out to arrest Jesus as if he were a brigand; now they crucify him between two brigands. The reader can now understand more clearly why Jesus told James and John that they did not know what they were asking when they requested to sit on his right and his left when he came into his glory (10:37). That dubious honor has been reserved for others. Jesus had spent his life in the company of sinners; it is fitting that he dies between two sinners.[13]

Mark tells the hours during the crucifixion. It is the third hour (9:00 A.M.) when they crucify him. Darkness covers the land at the sixth hour (high noon); and Jesus cries out in a loud voice at the ninth hour, the Jewish hour of prayer (15:34–35). Some suggest that these three-hour periods dividing the day point to a regularity following a divine plan.[14]

The Derision (15:28–33)

THE VICTIM OF crucifixion customarily became the butt of contemptuous abuse. For some perverse reason, certain people relish witnessing the agony of others and enjoy adding to it.[15] Individuals from all walks of life heap insults on Jesus, from the low criminals who are crucified with him to the high priests gathered to gloat over their triumph. The "Aha" (NIV "So!") appears as a derisive cry in certain psalms (Pss. 35:21; 40:15; 70:3). Wagging the head is also a gesture of contempt (2 Kings 19:21; Job 16:4; Pss. 22:7; 109:25; Isa.

---

13. A textual variant highlights this fact by inserting a quotation from Isa. 53:12 (Mark 15:28).

14. Matera, *Passion Narratives,* 42.

15. A rabbinic story tells of a wicked man who taunted his uncle when he was crucified. He rode by on a horse, though it was the Sabbath, and mocked: "Behold my horse which my master lets me ride and thy horse which thy Master [God] makes thee sit" (*Gen. Rab.* 65:22).

37:22; Jer. 18:16; Lam. 2:15). As they see Jesus hanging helplessly on his cross, he looks wholly defeated, and his enemies think they have won. The scene drips with irony as these scoffers spout their derision from their own blind point of view and unknowingly proclaim the truth about Jesus.

The passersby "hurled insults at him." Mark may use this verb (*blasphemeo*) to mean simply "to deride," but he may also intend an ironic contrast with the blasphemy charge leveled by the high priest against Jesus at the conclusion of his initial interrogation (14:64). He condemned Jesus for making a mockery of God's power by claiming to be God's Messiah, the Son of the Blessed One, when, in his view, Jesus was only a pitiful wretch. The reader must decide who is the real blasphemer—Jesus or the spectators (see 2:7; 3:29). The reader knows that Jesus is obedient to God's will. The passersby unknowingly challenge him to thwart God's will by coming down from the cross.[16] Jesus called Peter "Satan" when he attempted to deflect him from the course God laid out for him. The tormentors do not realize that their taunt borders on a satanic blasphemy.

The scoffing aimed Jesus' way recalls the charges raised before the high priest and his council. They taunt him as the one who would destroy the colossal temple and rebuild it in three days (15:29–30; see 14:58). Seeing this feeble and exhausted figure strung up on a cross naturally makes such a boast seem laughable. Their mockery, however, testifies to a truth beyond their range of vision. Jesus' death does destroy the temple made with hands and builds a new one not made with hands. This new temple has no ties to any geographical location. It consists of a new community of worshipers who believe that in his death Jesus bore the sins of a jeering and murderous world and that God vindicated him by raising him from the dead. His death abolishes the need for any more temple sacrifices, and God will soon build a temple without walls through Jesus' resurrection.

The chief priests and the teachers of the law join the fray next. They scoff that he saved others but cannot save himself. The reference to saving others recalls the verb used in Jesus' healings (*sozo*; cf. 3:4; 5:23, 34; 6:56). These leaders therefore admit what Peter later preached, that he "went around doing good and healing all who were under the power of the devil" (Acts 10:38). They refuse to acknowledge, however, that God anointed him "with the Holy Spirit and power," and that he saved others "because God was with him" (10:38). This impotent object of scorn was without form or comeliness and looked absurd as a savior. They could hardly see how God could be with someone so abandoned and tormented on a cross. By their reasoning, if he were a savior, he ought to be able to save himself.

---

16. Matera, *Passion Narratives*, 44.

Their jeers underscore Mark's point. He saved others—the disciples in the midst of a sea storm; the woman with a hemorrhage—and he truly cannot save himself. Were he to save himself, he could not save others from something more deadly than storms or illnesses. The nails do not hold him fast to the cross; the love of God constrains him. He himself taught that whoever wants to save his own life will ultimately lose it (8:35). His detractors cannot understand this way of looking at life. They cannot see that he dies as a ransom for many (10:45) or that his body is being broken and his blood is poured out for the many (14:22–25).

Because they cannot see they, they next demand a miracle. They want him to come down from the cross so that they can see and believe. They claim that some miraculous display of power or a miraculous escape will finally convince them, but they are only taunting his helplessness. The mockery reveals something about their shriveled theology. As Marshall states it, "They evaluate divine power purely in human, self-serving terms, according to their own standards of practice" (see 11:18; 12:1–9; 14:43, 48–49).[17] That is what they would have done if they had that power. Jesus taught his disciples to "take up" the cross, not to "come down" from one. A miraculous rescue would have proven only that he was a superman, not the Messiah, the Son of God. Those who want tangible proof of the divine presence will never see anything.

Darkness shrouds the whole land for the next three hours, from the sixth to the ninth hour (noon until 3:00 P.M.). The darkness occurring at such a critical moment can signify a number of things.[18] (1) Darkness was associated in antiquity with mourning (Jer. 4:27–28; 2 Apoc. Bar. 10:12). This is how it is interpreted in the Pseudo-Clementine *Recognitions* 1:41: "While he was suffering, all the world suffered with him, for the sun was darkened." That is, the darkness can mean that Jesus' death brought the sun to lamentation. (2) Darkness was also associated with the death of great men. Both Gentile and Jewish readers could understand darkness as a cosmic sign that accompanied the death of a king.[19] (3) In addition, darkness was a sign of God's judgment (see Ex. 10:21–23; Isa. 13:9–13; Jer. 13:16; 15:19; Joel 2:10; 3:14–15; Amos 5:18, 20). Amos declares in Amos 8:9–10:

"In that day," declares the Sovereign LORD,
"I will make the sun go down at noon

---

17. Marshall, *Faith As a Theme*, 206.

18. See Dale C. Allison, Jr., *The End of the Ages Has Come: An Early Interpretation of the Passion and Resurrection of Jesus* (Philadelphia: Fortress, 1985), 27–30.

19. Virgil writes: " . . . the Sun will give you signs. Who dare say the Sun is false? Nay, he oft warns us that dark uprisings threaten, that treachery and hidden wars are upswelling. Nay, he had pity for Rome when, after Caesar sank from sight, he veiled his shining face in dusky gloom, and a godless age feared everlasting night" (*Georgics* 1.463–68).

and darken the earth in broad daylight.
I will turn your religious feasts into mourning
and all your singing into weeping.
I will make all of you wear sackcloth
and shave your heads.
I will make that time like mourning for an only son
and the end of it like a bitter day."

(4) Jesus said that darkness would announce the great day of the Lord (Mark 13:24). The darkness that settles on the land may thus signify that the day has dawned with a new beginning (Gen. 1:2, Job 38:17; Ps. 74:12–20).[20] (5) Note that darkness does *not* indicate God's absence. The Scriptures reveal that God works even in the darkness. He chose to dwell in thick darkness (1 Kings 8:12; 2 Chron. 6:1) and gave the law in darkness: "Moses approached the thick darkness where God was" (Ex. 20:21). God descended for battle in darkness (2 Sam. 22:10; Ps. 18:9–11).

All these images may form the backdrop for understanding Jesus' crucifixion in darkness. The Pharisees earlier demanded a sign from heaven, and Jesus refused by saying (lit.), "If a sign be given this generation" (8:12). This curse formula was left uncompleted. Normally, it would be finished with something like, "May God strike me dead." Belatedly, the leaders do receive a sign from heaven, but it is not the kind they want or that they can read.

Jesus' Cry from the Cross (15:34–37)

AT THE NINTH hour, Jesus cries out from the cross with a great voice. The only other time that Mark uses the verb "to cry" (*boao*) is in the opening lines of the Gospel. Isaiah's prophecy is applied to John the Baptizer, the voice of one "calling" in the desert to prepare the way of the Lord (1:3). Now the paths have been made straight, and Jesus cries out.

Jesus' ghastly cry, "My God, my God, why have you forsaken me?" which are the last words he speaks in this Gospel, continue to perplex Christians.[21] It has summoned many explanations, and interpreters are divided whether to consider only the words written (which come from Psalm 22:1) or to weigh them against the entire psalm, a lament that ends with a triumphant

---

20. Gundry (*Mark*, 947, 964) adds another suggestion. The darkness veils the shame of the crucifixion: "God hides the Son from the blasphemer's leering." Jesus, however, has been open to view for three hours.

21. We find a completely different atmosphere in Luke and John. In Luke, we hear a cry of resignation to the will and protection of God (23:46). In John, we hear a victor's shout of triumph (19:30). The apocryphal *Gospel of Peter* drastically altered the cry to "My power, my power, why hast thou abandoned me?"

hope of vindication. (The options will be discussed in bridging the contexts.) However one interprets this death cry, Jesus' death forms a striking contrast to that of the dying Hercules in Seneca's *Hercules Oetaeus*. After completing the twelve tasks assigned to him, he bitterly faces death and announces the collapse of the universe, which will shake Jove's sovereignty:

> "Yea, father [*genitor*], thy whole realm of air will my death put to hazard. Then ere thou art utterly despoiled of heaven, bury me father, 'neath the whole ruined world. Shatter the skies which thou art doomed to lose" (1148–1150).[22]

Jesus' death establishes the sovereignty of God, who sends his beloved Son to give his life as a ransom for many.

When Jesus was arrested, he said (lit.), "But in order that the Scriptures be fulfilled" (14:49); he leaves the sentence incomplete. One can only overcome the scandal of the cross and see how God's will is at work in Jesus' death by understanding that it fulfills the Scriptures. Jesus' end is not a tragic failure but the glorious fulfillment of the destiny God assigned him as the Messiah. Marcus outlines how allusions to the psalms of the righteous sufferer form a prominent backdrop for understanding Mark's Passion narrative.[23]

Mark	Psalms
14:1—to kill him by cunning	10:7–8
14:18—the one eating with me	41:9
14:34—very sad	42:5, 11; 43:5
14:41—delivered to the hands of sinners	140:8
14:55—sought to put him to death	37:32; 54:3
14:57—false witnesses rising up	27:12; 35:11
14:61—silence before accusers	38:13–15; 39:9
15:4–5—silence before accuser	38:13–15; 39:9
15:24—division of garments	22:18
15:27—robbers are encircled by evildoers	22:16
15:29—mockery, head wagging	22:7
15:30–31—Save yourself!	22:8
15:32—reviling	22:6
15:34—cry of forsakenness	22:1 (11, 19–21)
15:36—vinegar to drink	69:21
15:40—looking on from a distance	38:11

---

22. Cited by Bilezikian, *The Liberated Gospel*, 129.
23. Marcus, *The Way of the Lord*, 174.

Marcus also shows how Mark's narrative from 15:20b to the end of the Gospel follows the course of Psalm 22 in many significant details.[24]

Psalm 22	Mark 15–16
vv. 1–21—suffering	15:20b–27—Jesus' crucifixion
v. 27—the Gentiles' worship	15:39—the centurion's confession
v. 28—the kingdom of God	15:43—Joseph is one looking for the kingdom
vv. 29–30—resurrection	16:6—Jesus' resurrection
vv. 30–31—proclamation to God's people	16:7—command to tell the disciples

The scoffers either misunderstand Jesus' final prayer or deliberately distort his words as a final jest. They think he is calling for Elijah, presumably to rescue him from the cross. Elijah was believed to be, among other things, an aid to people in crisis, a patron saint of lost causes. Someone in the crowd runs to fill a sponge with sharp wine. Is it intended to give Jesus a burst of energy to enable him to hold off death until Elijah arrives? Medical discussions of the effects of crucifixion on the body argue that drinking only served to hasten the process of death by suffocation.

Others stop this man and mockingly wait for a miraculous deliverance from Elijah, who was himself taken up in a chariot of fire (2 Kings 2:11). Their jeer, "Let's see if Elijah comes to take him down," turns his cry of desperation into a heartless joke; but the joke is filled with irony. After all, the reader knows that Elijah has already come, and they did to him as it was written concerning him (9:12–13). Elijah (i.e., John the Baptizer) has already been put to death and will not return to rescue Jesus. Moreover, these scoffers want to see something, but they reveal themselves to be those who can *see* nothing.

With this last taunt, Jesus lets out a great voice and "breathed his last" (*ekpneuo*), a euphemism for death. The loud cry is unusual since crucified victims normally died of exhaustion and lack of breath. Gundry suggests that it expresses superhuman strength[25] and causes the events that follow.

---

24. Ibid., 182. Matera (*The Kingship of Jesus*, 130) argues that the use of Ps. 22:22 in Heb. 2:12, Ps. 22:18 in Rev. 11:15, and Ps. 22:23 in Rev. 19:5 from the viewpoint of the risen Christ means that it "was an apt vehicle for describing God's eschatological victory as well as the sufferings of Jesus."

25. Gundry, *Mark*, 947–48.

The Tearing of Temple Veil and the Centurion's Confession (15:38–39)

MARK NARRATES VISUAL theology by reporting that the temple veil rips from top to bottom at Jesus' death. The veil screened the Holy Place from the Most Holy Place (Ex. 26:31–35; 27:16, 21; 30:6; 40:21; Lev. 4:17; 16:2, 12–15; 21:23; 24:3; Josephus, *Ant.* 8.3.3 §§ 71–72).

This closing scene of Jesus' life parallels the opening scene of his baptism (Mark 1:9–11). (1) In Jesus' baptism, John appears in the garb of Elijah (1:6) and is later identified with Elijah (9:13). In the crucifixion, bystanders think that Jesus is calling for Elijah to rescue him.

(2) Both incidents also record the rending of a holy place (the verb "torn" [*schizo*] appears only in these two scenes in Mark).[26] When Jesus ascended from the waters at his baptism, he saw the heavens, which Isaiah likens to a curtain (Isa. 40:22), "torn open." The temple veil was also likened to the heavens. Josephus describes the tabernacle for his Greco-Roman readers as divided into three equal parts. The court and the Holy Place are likened to the land and the sea, which are accessible to humanity; the third area, the Holy of Holies, represents heaven, which is accessible to God alone.[27] He describes the veil as eighty feet high, a "Babylonian tapestry with embroidery of blue and fine linen, of scarlet also and purple, wrought with marvelous skill. Nor was the mixture of materials without its mystic meaning: it typified the universe." It was embroidered with "the whole panorama of the heavens," excluding the signs of the Zodiac.[28]

(3) The divine presence descends on Jesus like a dove at his baptism and a voice sounds forth from heaven announcing, "You are my Son, whom I love" (1:11). The centurion echoes that voice from heaven: "Surely this man was the Son of God" (15:39).

(4) While the tearing of the fabric of the heavens at the baptism scene was a private revelation for Jesus—only "he saw" (*eiden*, 1:10)—the crucifixion is a public revelation for all to see. For the first time human beings can fully see what God intends to reveal.

When Jesus dies so ignominiously, one can imagine that the high priests and teachers of the law consider his death to be the proof that his claims are bogus (see Wis. 2:17–20). The events confirm their prejudice that God did not send Jesus, for God would never have allowed the Messiah to die in this way. The confession from the leader of the death squad therefore comes as

---

26. David Ulansey, "The Heavenly Torn Veil: Mark's Cosmic *Inclusio*," *JBL* 110 (1991): 123–25.

27. Josephus, *Ant.* 3.6.4 § 123; 3.7.7 § 181.

28. Josephus, *J. W.* 5.5.4 §§ 212–14.

a surprise. As a centurion, he is a battle-hardened campaigner promoted from the ranks, who had no reason to be sympathetic toward Jesus. Mark tells us, however, that he saw "how he died"—a powerless death but with a powerful cry—and acknowledges, "Surely this man was the Son of God" (15:39).[29] The confession means that Jesus' full identity is inseparably linked to his death. It marks the beginning of the fulfillment of Psalm 22:27, "All the families of the nations will bow down before him." With Jesus' death, the reader begins to see a new temple, which will be "a house of prayer for all nations" (11:17), becoming a reality.

The Burial (15:40–47)

A SOMBER CLUTCH of grieving women who have followed Jesus from Galilee look on at the execution of Jesus from a distance (15:40) and witness his burial (15:47).[30] Unlike the disciples, they have not vanished from the scene, but they are not close by to give testimony to their love and support. Standing at a distance may show delicacy; they do not gaze at his nakedness at close hand. Their stance, however, parallels that of Peter, who followed Jesus "at a distance" so that he might disguise his discipleship (14:54). They witness his death but do not confess as the centurion does. Mark commends their past service. They followed in Galilee, "cared for [Jesus'] needs," and went up with him to Jerusalem. The only ones who cared for his needs are the angels (1:13), Peter's mother-in-law (1:31), and these women, who will also serve his needs in death.

Joseph of Arimathea (presumably from Ramathaim, east of Joppa, 1 Sam. 1:1) takes the initiative in securing Jesus' body for burial. He is the third exceptional character to emerge from the enemies' camp. First came the teacher of the law whom Jesus commended as not far from the kingdom (12:28–34), then the centurion who confessed that Jesus was the Son of God (15:39). Now Joseph of Arimathea courageously asks for Jesus' body and buries it at his own expense (see Acts 8:2; 13:29). A stranger, Simon, took up Jesus' cross for his execution; another stranger takes down his body from the cross for his burial.

---

29. "Son of God" is anarthrous (without a definite article) and could mean simply that he was a divine man, but the same anarthrous usage appears in 1:1 and clearly means "the Son of God." See the evidence compiled by Gundry, *Mark*, 951.

30. Mary was a common name. The Mary named in 15:40 could refer to one woman who is the wife, mother, or daughter of James the younger and the mother of Joses, or to two women named Mary—one the wife, mother, or daughter of James the younger, and the other the mother of Joses. The best option seems to be that it refers to one woman: "Mary the mother of James the younger and of Joses."

Mark describes Joseph as "a prominent member of the Council." He could be a member of his village council, but the reader would naturally identify him as a member of the council that condemned Jesus for blasphemy (14:64). Mark also describes him with emphasis as one who was "waiting for the kingdom of God." This phrase identifies him as a pious man (see Simeon and Anna in Luke 2:25, 38), which may explain his motivation for claiming the body. Risk is involved because Mark tells us that he "dares" ("went boldly," NIV) to ask Pilate for the corpse. The Romans felt no qualms about leaving victims on their crosses for days. Horace refers to one who says to a slave, "You'll hang on the cross to feed crows."[31]

Deuteronomy 21:23 was the basis for Jewish belief that one was obligated to bury the body of criminals and even enemies on the day of their death. Philo interprets the text freely to apply to murderers who are crucified and paraphrases it: "Let not the sun go down upon the crucified but let them be buried in the earth before sundown."[32] Ordinarily, the family or friends would summon courage to request the body (see the disciples of John the Baptizer, Mark 6:29), but Jesus' family and friends do not do this.

To ask for the body of someone executed for high treason could be looked upon as sympathizing and could earn one the same fate. But as a member of the Council who condemned Jesus to death, Joseph is above suspicion. Pilate's only concern is to ascertain that Jesus is already dead. The centurion who confessed Jesus as the Son of God affirms that Jesus is really dead. Jesus' quick death (15:44) amazes Pilate as much as his silence before his accusers (15:5). That Pilate readily grants the body to Joseph either confirms that he did not seriously consider Jesus guilty of treason or suggests that he willingly accedes to Jewish sensibilities.

Mark has been tolling the watches as they tick by during the Passion and the hours during the crucifixion. The Passion began in the evening when Jesus came with his disciples for his Last Supper (14:17); it now ends in the evening with his burial. The statement in 15:42 that it was already the evening of Preparation Day (the day before the Sabbath) gives the motivation behind Joseph's actions. The body must not be allowed to hang beyond sundown so as not to defile the land (Deut. 21:23). But a burial on the Sabbath, which began with the shining of the first star, would have been prohibited. Mark says that Joseph (presumably with the help of servants) wraps Jesus' body up in a newly bought linen cloth and buries him in a tomb carved in rock.

---

31. *Epistles* 1.16.48.
32. *On the Special Laws* 3.151–52.

Bridging Contexts

THE ACCOUNT OF Jesus' crucifixion as portrayed by Mark is as gloomy as the darkness that covered the land until the ninth hour. Jesus went to his death in utter loneliness, betrayed, deserted, and denied by his followers. He was rejected by his own people, who clamored for his death. After being mocked, beaten, and spat upon, Jesus faced an excruciating death alone, isolated from the human race. No "good thief" spoke to relieve the oppression; no close friends or relatives stood close by to watch. A handful of women followers were there, faithful in the face of despair, but they looked on from a distance. Jesus did not serenely pray, "Father, into your hands I commit my spirit" (Luke 23:46); nor did he sound the final note of victory, "It is finished" (John 19:30). Instead of a voice from a cloud affirming him as the Son, we have a tormented shout from the cross asking why he has been abandoned. Evil engulfed Jesus on the cross, and we should not try to relieve this stark picture with any misguided sentimentality.

This is the climax of human blindness and iniquity spilling over in brutal outrage against God's Son; it shows a world that has gone topsy-turvy. Jesus is a king who died an outlaw's death. Jesus is the Messiah, who was rejected by the people he came to deliver. Jesus is the mighty Son of God, who did not use his power for himself but died a seemingly powerless death. All traditional symbols have been reversed. Weakness is a sign of power. Death is the means to life. Godforsakenness leads to reconciliation with God. The perpetrators who executed Jesus did not realize that they were executing God's will (14:36) and that Jesus submitted willingly as God's obedient Son (10:45). They also did not realize that this death would not be the end of him. Instead, it meant the end of their whole order. They could not fathom how such a powerless death disclosed the character and power of God.

Three theological issues emerge from this section: the meaning of Jesus' cry, the splitting of the temple veil, and the centurion's confession. We will take each in order.

Jesus' Cry on the Cross

MANY DIVIDE OVER the meaning of Jesus' cry of forsakenness. We should first admit that we may never fathom the mystery behind this cry, but we can probe the major options.

Those who insist that we should only interpret the words that Mark cites and ignore the context of Psalm 22 disagree over what those words mean. Some explain the cry from the perspective of God's holy wrath and the character of sin that cuts the sinner off from God (see Isa. 59:2). Jesus drank the bitter cup of God's wrath on the cross and took our place, just as he had taken

Barabbas's place to face the judgment on sin that was deservedly ours. Paul writes, "God made him who had no sin to be sin for us, so that in him we might become the righteousness of God" (2 Cor. 5:21; see also Gal. 3:13). The darkness that crept over the land signifies the judgment of God, and Jesus was on the wrong end of it. As a substitute for sinners, he bore the punishment that was due us, and his cry expressed profound horror at his separation from God. He encountered the evil within and without the soul of humans and cried out when he sensed God's turning away from that evil as he died on the wood of the cross (Deut. 21:23; Gal. 3:13). In that fearful hour, Jesus bore in his own consciousness the utmost penalty and cried out as one abandoned by God to the terrible abyss. Calvin reasoned: "If Christ had died only a bodily death, it would have been ineffectual. ... Unless his soul shared in the punishment, he would have been the Redeemer of bodies alone."[33]

Many question this interpretation as "inconsistent with the love of God and the oneness of purpose with the Father manifest in the atoning ministry of Jesus."[34] If one cites 2 Corinthians 5:21 one can also cite 5:19: "God was reconciling the world to himself in Christ." Some find it difficult to accept that Jesus, who had been betrayed, abandoned, denounced, denied, denuded, and derided by humans, was also abandoned by God in his hour of need. We have clear indications that the Son of Man would suffer utter degradation, but this did not entail utter abandonment by God. Nowhere in Mark do we have any hint that God's holy wrath required that God had to turn away from sin. Others therefore interpret Jesus' words as a human cry of despair in the face of defeat and estrangement. The confidence that Jesus had maintained throughout his ministry in the coming of the kingdom of God suddenly failed him.

Albert Schweitzer interpreted Jesus' death precisely this way, writing that Jesus expected the kingdom of God to come and laid

> hold of the wheel of the world to set it moving on that last revolution which is to bring all ordinary history to a close. It refuses to turn, and He throws Himself upon it. Then it does turn; and crushes Him.[35]

Consequently, he contended that Jesus died on the cross "with a loud cry, despairing of bringing in the new heaven and the new earth."[36] The darkness that had beset the land now penetrated his own heart.

---

33. John Calvin, *Institutes*, 2.16.10 and 12; cited by John R. W. Stott, *The Cross of Christ* (Downers Grove, Ill.: InterVarsity, 1986), 81.

34. Taylor, *Mark*, 594.

35. Albert Schweitzer, *The Quest for the Historical Jesus: A Critical Study of Its Progress from Reimarus to Wrede* (New York: Macmillan, 1968), 370–71.

36. Ibid., 255, 285.

Others contend that Jesus may have believed that God had failed him or that he had failed God in some way. The kingdom had not come, and he felt forsaken as his agony obscured his sense of communion with the Father. Jesus felt utterly abandoned by God, but he refused to let go and cried out, "My God." Broadus writes:

> If it be asked how he could feel himself to be forsaken, we must remember that a human soul as well as a human body was here suffering, a human soul thinking and feeling within human limitations (Mark 13:32), not psychologically unlike the action of other devout souls when in some great and overwhelming sorrow.[37]

Amid human hatred and violence, God may seem to be absent; but never was God more fully and forcefully present than when Jesus died on the cross. God is not an abandoning God.

Watson goes further and challenges attempts to mitigate Jesus' existential despair—that Jesus only felt abandoned. He argues that the crucifixion in Mark shatters the naive view of the world upheld with loving care by a heavenly Father. He writes:

> The God who was once gladly addressed as "Abba" has incomprehensibly turned away and hidden his face. In a moment of both bewilderment and insight, the reality of God-forsakenness as a characteristic of the world is recognized. No resolution to the problem is offered: only the question, "Why. . . ?", and the equally eloquent though wordless "loud cry" with which Jesus dies.[38]

For Watson, the cry means that "God-forsakenness" is "an inescapable aspect of reality." "Here, the story of Jesus makes the same point as the older story of Job: the world does not point unambiguously to a rational and loving providential care, and we must honestly accept this fact."

Hooker comments that "these words provide a profound theological comment on the oneness of Jesus with humanity, and on the meaning of his death, which shares human despair to the full."[39] The first readers, who also were experiencing insecurity and a sense of abandonment, would identify with this desperation. Tolbert argues:

> The content of Jesus' cry from the cross, his expression of abandonment by God, stands as an assurance to his followers that the worst

---

37. John A. Broadus, *The Gospel of Matthew* (Philadelphia: The American Baptist Publication Society, 1886), 574.

38. Francis Watson, "Ambiguity in the Marcan Narrative," *Kings Theological Review* 10 (1987): 15.

39. Hooker, *Mark*, 375.

desolation imaginable, cosmic isolation, can be endured faithfully. What is separation from family and betrayal or denial by friends in comparison to that timeless moment of nothingness when God's Son is deserted by God?[40]

Other interpreters emphasize that Jesus' last words were not formed by Jesus himself but by the psalmist (Ps. 22:1). If this were only an existential cry of personal distress, why did Jesus not use *Abba* as he did in the Gethsemane? One answer might be that he felt estrangement from *Abba*, who did not answer his prayer. A more probable answer is that Jesus' intimate familiarity with Scripture led him to this particular lament, which was a classic expression of anguish.

I find it probable that Jesus, who lived by Scripture and believed that he was fulfilling Scripture (14:49), would turn to Scripture for solace when he was in desperate straits. Mark tells us that when Jesus cried out, it was the ninth hour, the Jewish hour of prayer (cf. Acts 3:1), and Jesus prayed the prayer of the righteous sufferer, who trusts fully in God's protection. Psalm 22 naturally came to mind because he was mocked (Ps. 22:7–9), his strength was dried up (22:15–16), his hands and feet were pierced (22:16), and his garments were divided (22:18). Jesus therefore did not simply let out an anguished wail of pain but deliberately quoted this lament, which moves from an expression of pain to confidence in God's deliverance. Why would Jesus cry out to an absent God unless he believed that God was indeed there to hear and able to deliver him? Senior argues:

> These words are, in effect, the final version of the prayer in Gethsemane where, also in a "lament," Jesus affirmed his unbroken trust in his Father while feeling the full horror of approaching death (14:32–42).[41]

Some ask, reasonably, why Jesus should have quoted the beginning of Psalm 22 if he was alluding to its end? One could not expect a crucifixion victim, painfully struggling for every breath, to recite the entire psalm. Without chapter and verse divisions in the Hebrew Scriptures, specific passages were cited often by the first verse or key phrases. One can see an example of this practice in Mark 12:26, when Jesus referred to a specific passage as from "the book of Moses, in the account of the bush." This particular passage is indicated by referring to a key phrase. Jews in Jesus' day were immersed in the Scripture the way moderns are immersed in television and the movies, and they would know that Psalm 22 begins with despair but ends on a triumphant note.

---

40. Tolbert, *Sowing*, 286–87.
41. Senior, *The Passion of Jesus*, 124.

In other words, by using Psalm 22, Jesus chose to complain stridently about his suffering and tragedy but to look beyond it to express his faith in the God who vindicates the righteous. He identifies himself with the righteous sufferer, who feels the pain of his testing but whose intimacy with God allows him to voice his complaint bluntly and to demand rescue. He accepts his suffering, trusting that God's intervention will come in his death. If one understands this cry as a prayer, God immediately answers it. The darkness lasting from the sixth to the ninth hour lifts, and the following events reveal in overwhelming fashion that his confident hope in God's vindication has not been misplaced. "For he has not despised or disdained the suffering of the afflicted one; he has not hidden his face from him but has listened to his cry for help" (Ps. 22:24).

Mark presents Jesus' deportment during his Passion as a model for followers to emulate. When faced with severe trial, Jesus prayed. When dragged before authorities and put on trial for his life, he gave his fearless testimony. When beaten and taunted, he endured suffering without reviling. We should also expect to learn how to face death and suffering from the way he died. Mark therefore does not present Jesus' death simply as a transaction. He certainly does not want his readers to think that Jesus' faith faltered at the end and that he died in surprised despair. Jesus castigated his disciples for their lack of faith (4:40) and encouraged others to have faith in the midst of woe (9:23) and when facing insurmountable odds (11:23–24). The centurion did not confess "because he saw a man die in utter abandonment."[42] Jesus painfully accepted God's will that the cup must be drunk. Unlike the disciples, he fully comprehended the necessity of the cross and did not expect something else from God.

Mark's first readers knew trial and tribulation. They faced the literal possibility of taking up their cross and dying the same way their Lord did. What they could see from the description of Jesus' death was one who was obedient unto death because he trusted God. But he also could voice loudly his lament. When painful ordeals roar into our lives, God does not call for us to be stoic, unmoved by grief, or to take our medicine "like a man." We learn that we can vent our feelings and complain vociferously to God. Many other texts in the New Testament may be used to instruct listeners about views of the atonement. This text is best used to help those who are undergoing agonizing suffering and loss and acutely feel God's distance in their own lives.

---

42. Matera, *The Kingship of Jesus*, 137.

The Rending of the Temple Veil

MARK DOES NOT report that the temple veil rips from top to bottom out of any antiquarian interest. "The torn curtain unveils something of the mystery of the dying Christ."[43] Modern listeners may need help with a diagram of the temple layout to appreciate that significance fully, but even then how Mark understood this event is not obvious. Geddert lists some thirty views under four basic categories.[44] Several of these interpretations are not mutually exclusive and deserve reflection. Matera allows that the tearing of the temple curtain "is a rich image with both positive and negative poles."[45] When the veil rips, something is destroyed but also something that was previously hidden opens up to view. The positive and negative images of a torn veil suggest that Jesus' death has both a positive and a negative impact.

On the positive side, the torn veil symbolizes a new revelation. The veil that shielded the holiest part of the temple where God's glory resided was torn away. The veil of secrecy lifted, and all could see the face of God and the love of God in Jesus' death. Humans can now know and confess what was already announced from heaven (1:11; 9:7) and was known only to demons: Jesus is God's Son, who was obedient unto death, even death on a cross. Even a rough centurion, a spokesman from the Gentile world, could recognize this fact. Toward the end of the movie *The Wizard of Oz*, the curtain hiding the feared wizard is torn away to reveal an impotent fraud, desperately pulling levers. His vaunted power was nothing but smoke and mirrors. By contrast, when Jesus died on the cross, the curtain torn in two reveals an all-powerful, all-loving God.

A second view understands that the torn veil lets something out. God's glory cannot be confined to a national shrine of frozen stone but now floods the world. Just as the heavens ripped open and the Spirit descended on Jesus at his baptism, one can imagine that something breaks forth from the Holy of Holies to fill the world. God's protecting presence is no longer limited to a chamber that only a high priest may briefly visit once a year.

A third view contends that the tearing of the veil signifies that the barrier between God and humanity has been torn away. It vividly reveals the at-one-ment now available between God and humanity. Priests can no longer rope God off from others. This idea is expressed in prose by the author of Hebrews (Heb. 6:19–20; 9:3, 7–8, 12, 24–28; 10:19–20). The tearing of the veil therefore implies that all now have direct access to a gracious God, who has allowed his Son to die on behalf of the many. Even Gentiles, formerly

---

43. Gérard Rossé, *The Cry of Jesus on the Cross* (New York /Mahwah: Paulist, 1987), 20.

44. Geddert, *Watchwords*, 141–43.

45. Matera, *The Kingship of Jesus*, 139.

barred access even to the sanctuary, may now enter into the Holy of Holies. The confession by a Gentile centurion signals that Gentiles will also be included in the salvation offered by Jesus' death.

A fourth view understands that the torn veil marks the end of the old order. The veil is not opened but ripped in two, from top to bottom, indicating its destruction. Tearing "from top to bottom" may picture God unleashing judgment from heaven and represents divine condemnation of the temple cultus. The temple and its sacrificial system are now redundant and unnecessary. Ultimately, God forsakes this temple, not Jesus. Jesus will be raised; the temple will be razed (Mark 13:2), its service judged and abolished. There is nothing holy about this grand building. The rending of the veil therefore provides confirmation for Jesus' words against the temple (13:1–2; 14:58; 15:29).

The Centurion's Confession

AS JESUS DIED on the cross, he daringly asked God "Why? [For what reason?]" (15:34). The centurion's confession offers one answer: His death will transform others and bring them to faith.[46] The Gentile soldier heard the same great cry as the bystanders; why did he confess and not mock with the others? He never saw Jesus' miracles, never heard his interpretation of what his death meant, but only witnessed the mockery and his death. If such a one could believe that Jesus is the Son of God only by witnessing how he died, then anyone can believe. Jesus' death means that Caesar and all the values that Caesar's world is built on are endangered. It reveals to Mark's first readers and to today's readers that faithful obedience unto death, not wondrous works of power, can convert even the executioner. Christians can win the world, not by winning over them with violence but by winning them over through love and obedience to God.

To make this confession, the centurion must have changed his perception of the basic things that governed his entire life. As a centurion he has sworn allegiance to the emperor, and he represents Roman imperial power. For the Romans, "the notion of power was central to the definition of deity,"[47] and the title "Son of God" properly belonged only to the emperor, who embodied Rome's majesty. Remarkably, this soldier bestows the title on a Jew who has just been executed. He must have changed his mind not only about Jesus but also about what it meant to be a son of God. Divinity was no longer associated with the splendor and military might of an empire. It resided where there was no apparent splendor or might.[48]

---

46. Geddert, *Watchwords*, 302, n. 103.

47. J. R. Fears, "Rome: The Ideology of Imperial Power," *Thought* 55 (1980): 106.

48. Lightfoot, *The Gospel Message of St. Mark*, 58.

The centurion therefore stands in stark contrast to those who wanted to see some great power demonstration. To refuse to believe unless God provides an obvious demonstration that meets their worldly criteria is the opposite of faith. The attitude that says, "Show us and we will believe," never believes no matter how much is shown to them. "Faith is not a matter of seeing in order to believe, but of trusting to the point of death."[49] One must be able to see that precisely here in the obscurity, lowliness, humiliation, and powerlessness of the cross, not in any miraculous display, God demonstrates power over the demonic and humankind.

To make his confession, the centurion also must have completely revised his understanding of power. The power that Rome represented was coercive. It forced others to submit or else. Jesus' powerless death exerts a different kind of power from what the centurion had served and used on others. He recognized that true power, which was revealed in the cross, is not coercive, exploitative, or manipulative. The power he served crushed others and transformed life into death. The power of the cross gives itself for others and transforms death into life.

One thing about Jesus' death did not require the centurion to change his mind but could only reinforce his preconceived views. As a soldier, he understood and appreciated the necessity of absolute obedience (see Matt. 8:9). He saw in Jesus' death someone who had been faithful in carrying out his mission. We should lead modern bystanders to revise their false view of the nature of divinity and power and reinforce their understanding of obedience.

MARK'S PICTURE OF Jesus' suffering on the cross is bleak but avoids sensationalism. His sober and concise report carries enormous power, although he provides no graphic description of Jesus' physical agony. His account avoids sentimentality but also does not rouse hatred for the perpetrators. Something more profound was happening than just another gruesome execution, and Mark focuses on the theological significance of Jesus' death. The cross is the point at which the blind rage of humanity against God is unleashed with a horrible intensity and is shown for what it is. The Gospel story depicts many of the sins that put Jesus on this cross: pride, envy, jealousy, betrayal, cruelty, greed, indifference, cowardice, and murder. We need only add our own many sins to complete the list.

The scene at the cross shows both the religious and irreligious inflicting their wounds on the heart of God. Jerusalem's highest religious officials

---

49. Matera, *Passion Narratives,* 44.

converged at the cross to add insult to injury with bitter vindictiveness. Soldiers ignored what was happening before them and concentrated on their lottery for his possessions. They cared only about gaining some extra profit from the day's work. This kind of petty greed has not been driven from the human heart. One need only remember pictures of the piles of jewelry, clothes, and hair that the death camp workers collected from their doomed Jewish prisoners.

The two bandits did not recognize that Jesus was giving his life for sinners, and they joined in reviling him. Others gathered at the cross to make sport. They thought that the verdict was already in, and Jesus came up the big loser. These persons could not see why anyone would want to save anything other than himself or herself. The old spiritual, "Were you there when they crucified my Lord?" must be answered, "Yes." We were not there as loyal supporters to sing hymns, however. Human beings still need saving from evil's clench. When we look around our world, we see that "justice is still perverted, truth still on the scaffold, and wrong upon the throne. The protest of good men is dumb on their lips; few stand by the cross fearlessly."[50]

(1) The cross reveals the truth about humankind but also about God's incredible power. God's power takes the venomous mockery spit out at Jesus and turns it into the proclamation of the gospel: "He saved others ... but he can't save himself." If there were to be a tombstone, this taunt would have made a fitting epitaph. God's power absorbs the toxin of human sin and hatred and turns it into salvation for all who put their trust in a God who loves this much and who works in this way. The gospel is the only thing that makes sense of a world so ugly and so beautiful. After the horrors of the holocaust, a Jewish skeptic said that the only God that he could believe in was one who knows firsthand what it is like to be a Jewish child buried alive and knows what it is like to be a Jewish mother watching her child die. The cross reveals that God has indeed witnessed this tragedy firsthand and uses it to save the world from itself. Who would believe that such a horrifying death could bring such blessing to the world?

(2) The cross reveals God's incredible love. We truly see who God is when we see the Son of God crying out from the cross and then raised in glory, and when we hear the offer of forgiveness of sins ring out ever more loudly. In Kipling's poem "Cold Iron," a baron who rebelled against his king boasts of his arsenal, "Iron, cold iron is the master of men all." When he was defeated, the triumphant king set before him a banquet instead of inflicting revenge.

---

50. E. M. Blaiklock, *The Young Man Mark* (Exeter: Paternoster, 1963), 19.

He took the wine and blessed it. He blessed and brake the Bread.
With His own Hands He served Them, and presently He said:
See! These Hands they pierced with nails, outside My city wall.
Show Iron—Cold Iron to be master of men all.

The poem concludes, "Iron—Cold Iron—is the master of men all, The iron nails of Calvary are master of men all."[51]

(3) The cross reveals that things are never what they seem in our world. It seems as if God is absent. But Henri Nouwen writes: "Where God's absence was most loudly expressed, God's presence was most profoundly revealed."[52] It seems as if the high priests have won. Jesus is dead and buried, and they have averted a tumult among the people (14:2) that might unleash Roman wrath. Those today who exult in their political triumphs through clever ploys may think that they have won, like the wicked tenants thought they had taken possession of the vineyard by killing the son. In truth, these corrupt leaders failed. Jesus did not stay dead and buried, and they could do nothing to quash the power of God unleashed by his resurrection or the Spirit-led movement of those who believe in him. They also could do nothing to prevent the ill-fated rebellion against the Roman juggernaut that resulted in the leveling of the temple, their base of power. God remains in control and accomplishes God's purposes, planned from creation.

(4) The cross reveals that God's love and power can win those one might never have dreamed would respond. The actions of the centurion who put Jesus to death and of Joseph, the respected and wealthy council member who condemned Jesus to death, mean that one can never write off an enemy. The power of the gospel is so great that even those who persecute Christians may be won to the faith. The centurion may or may not have won the lottery for Jesus' pitiful belongings, but he took away from this execution something infinitely more precious. He did not say that Jesus was innocent or that he did not deserve such a terrible fate. He made the confession that is the rock on which the church is built. Joseph was looking for the kingdom. One can only assume that he found it when he learned of Jesus' resurrection.

(5) The cross also reveals the pain of the human situation. The Son of God took on our humanity and absorbed all the bitter suffering and anguish of the world. When cornered by evil, he prayed. According to a Jewish tradition, prayer has ten names. The first on the list is "cry."[53] The cries come when we see no indication whatsoever that God is on our side, when we feel

---

51. Rudyard Kipling, *Complete Verse* (New York: Doubleday, 1989), 507–8.

52. Henri J. M. Nouwen, *Reaching Out: The Three Movements of the Spiritual Life* (Garden City, N.Y.: Doubleday, 1975), 91.

53. *Sipre Deut* 3:23 § 26, noted by Brown, *The Death of the Messiah*, 2:1044, n. 34.

that God is silent. No one can go through life and not feel this isolation from humans and from God at times. What should we do when we are overwhelmed by inconsolable grief, when we feel completely forsaken? Defeat may tempt us to give up faith in God, but Jesus' cry on the cross reveals a faith that will not let go of God even when deluged by the greatest of all suffering. He makes lament.

The biblical lament begins by invoking God's name in a cry of distress and a frank expression of grievance against him. The mourner outlines the distress, expresses perplexity at the apparent triumph of enemies, and urgently prays for relief. The lament concludes with an expression of trust, thanksgiving, and confidence that God has heard. Many Christians today shy away from ever crying aloud to God or making an outcry of reproach when they are not rescued. Some do not feel that they can lay bare their true emotions to God, including their anger. They feel that such honesty reflects a deficiency of faith or blasphemous gall. This timidity may in fact reflect a sense of distance and alienation from God, because they fear that God might reject them if they are too complaining in an hour of trial. But notice how small children do not hesitate to make their complaints known to their parents. Only when they have been abused do they try to hold in their pain because they feel that their parents do not care. The cry of despair to God when overcome by evil and pain is a sign of great intimacy with God and a robust faith.

While it may sound scandalous to our ears, Jesus' prayer would not shock those attuned to the Old Testament. Wink observes that "biblical prayer is impertinent, persistent, shameless, indecorous. It is more like haggling in an oriental bazaar than the polite monologues of the churches."[54] Moses, for example, cried out to God (Ex. 5:22—23):

> O Lord, why have you brought trouble upon this people? Is this why you sent me? Ever since I went to Pharaoh to speak in your name, he has brought trouble upon this people, and you have not rescued your people at all.

Joshua complained (Josh. 7:7—9):

> Ah, Sovereign LORD, why did you ever bring this people across the Jordan to deliver us into the hands of the Amorites to destroy us? If only we had been content to stay on the other side of the Jordan! O Lord, what can I say, now that Israel has been routed by its enemies? The Canaanites and the other people of the country will hear about this

---

54. Walter Wink, *Engaging the Powers: Discernment and Resistance in a World of Domination* (Minneapolis: Fortress, 1992), 301.

and they will surround us and wipe out our name from the earth. What then will you do for your own great name?

Gideon protested: "But sir . . . if the LORD is with us, why has all this happened to us? Where are all his wonders that our fathers told us about when they said, 'Did not the LORD bring us up out of Egypt?' But now the LORD has abandoned us and put us into the hand of Midian" (Judg. 6:13).

Job lamented bitterly to God that he had been abandoned (see Job 29–31).

And Jeremiah accused God of deceiving the people (Jer. 4:10), lamenting (14:8–9):

O Hope of Israel,
  its Savior in times of distress,
why are you like a stranger in the land,
  like a traveler who stays only a night?
Why are you like a man taken by surprise,
  like a warrior powerless to save?
You are among us, O LORD,
  and we bear your name;
  do not forsake us!

Such laments, which were a central part of the worship of Israel, have disappeared from our prayer and worship. We cannot obscure the hurtful side of life. It might be helpful in giving pastoral care to those suffering from enormous grief to teach them about biblical lamentation that cries out boldly to God. We do not cry out from the depths simply to cry out. We cry out because God is the only one who can deliver us and can answer the question "Why?"

(6) The cross reveals a new way of life. Those who taunted Jesus assumed that anyone with power would use it to extricate himself from a personal life-threatening situation. The disciples heeded the call to save themselves when they fled into the night. Peter heeded it when he denied Jesus three times. The high priest heeded it when he moved quickly to eliminate this threatening prophetic figure. Pilate heeded it when he refused to take a stand for justice. Jesus lives out his teaching. The one who tries to save his life will lose it. The one who gives up his or her life will gain it and will give life to others.

Mark 16:1–8

W HEN THE SABBATH was over, Mary Magdalene,
Mary the mother of James, and Salome bought
spices so that they might go to anoint Jesus' body.
²Very early on the first day of the week, just after sunrise, they
were on their way to the tomb ³and they asked each other,
"Who will roll the stone away from the entrance of the tomb?"

⁴But when they looked up, they saw that the stone, which
was very large, had been rolled away. ⁵As they entered the
tomb, they saw a young man dressed in a white robe sitting on
the right side, and they were alarmed.

⁶"Don't be alarmed," he said. "You are looking for Jesus the
Nazarene, who was crucified. He has risen! He is not here.
See the place where they laid him. ⁷But go, tell his disciples
and Peter, 'He is going ahead of you into Galilee. There you
will see him, just as he told you.'"

⁸Trembling and bewildered, the women went out and fled
from the tomb. They said nothing to anyone, because they
were afraid.

THE WOMEN FOLLOWERS of Jesus rise to unexpected prominence at the very end of the story.
Prior to Jesus' crucifixion and burial, there has
been no indication in the Gospel that Jesus had
any women followers. Now they surface as the prime witnesses to the events
that are the foundation of Christian belief: that Jesus died, was buried, and
was raised (1 Cor. 15:3–4). Their emergence as the key witnesses oddly
attests to the truth of what Mark reports since it is highly unlikely that the
church would have invented a small group of women to furnish evidence for
such events.¹

---

1. Later Jewish law required two male witnesses to verify the truth of something except
in exceptional circumstances (*m. Yebam.* 16:7; *m. Ketub.* 2:5; *m. 'Ed.* 3:6), and it is reasonable
to conclude that this rule was applicable in the first century. For an event so critical to the
faith, one would want the testimony of reputable persons who were considered to be reliable (compare Acts 4:13).

Mark inconsistently lists their names in 15:40; 47; and 16:1. The differences may be
attributable to stylistic variation to avoid "monotonous repetition" (so Adela Yarbro Collins,

Mark's Passion narrative began with a woman lavishly anointing Jesus to express her deep devotion, and he interpreted it as the preparation for his burial. It ends with women no less loving and devoted seeking to anoint Jesus after his burial. They come with their articles of death, expecting to apply their unguents on a brutalized corpse. They are drawn to the tomb by their loyalty to Jesus, determined to render one last service to their Master, just as Peter was drawn to the courtyard of the high priest. They bolt from the tomb, however, seized by fear, just as Peter dashed into the night, seized by grief. Their true loyalty is thrown into question because Mark reports that they ignore the angel's command to "go, tell." They say nothing to anyone.

The account of the women's arrival of the women at the tomb parallels the account of Jesus' burial. Each scene begins with a time reference, and they form a chiasm:

Time reference: When evening had come on the Day of Preparation, before the Sabbath (15:42).
  A. Joseph, a respected Council member who was awaiting the kingdom of heaven, comes to Pilate and dares to ask for the body of Jesus (15:43).
    B. Pilate marvels that Jesus is already dead, confirms it with the centurion (15:44), and grants the body to Joseph (15:45).
      C. Joseph purchases a linen shroud, wraps Jesus in it, lays him in a tomb hewn from rock, and rolls a stone before the door of the tomb (15:46).
        D. Mary Magdalene and Mary [the mother] of Joses observe where Jesus is laid (15:47).

Time reference: After the Sabbath had passed . . . very early at sunrise on the first day of the week (16:1–2).
        D'. Mary Magdalene and Mary [the mother] of James (16:1) decide to head to the tomb.
      C'. They purchase spices to anoint the body, go to the tomb, and worry, "Who will roll the stone from the entrance of the tomb?" (16:3).
    B'. They discover that the large stone has been rolled back (16:4) and marvel at a young man who informs them that

---

The Beginning of the Gospel: Probings of Mark in Context [Minneapolis: Fortress, 1992], 130). Only the second name varies. In the first reference (15:40), she is described fully as the mother of James the younger and of Joses. The second reference shortens it to a reference to Joses (15:47); the third (16:1), to James.

Jesus the Nazarene, who was crucified, is not dead but has been raised (16:5–6).

A'. The women flee in fear and trembling and do not relay the instructions to the disciples that Jesus goes before them to Galilee, for they are afraid (they do not dare).

The Report of Jesus' Resurrection

THE TIME NOTICES—"PREPARATION Day (that is, the day before the Sabbath)" (15:42) and "when the Sabbath was over" (16:1)—explain why the women do not try to anoint Jesus sooner. They cannot purchase spices or travel about on the Sabbath, but they move into action as soon as they can. They obviously do not anticipate Jesus' resurrection and do not go to the tomb to check if his prediction that he will be raised on the third day might be fulfilled. Mark makes it plain that they go on the third day because they cannot come earlier.

The rising of the sun dispels the darkness that covered the whole land during the crucifixion (16:2). The beginning of this week marks the dawning of a new beginning for humanity. In Scripture, God's help comes to the afflicted especially in the morning: "Weeping may remain for a night, but rejoicing comes in the morning" (Ps 30:5; see 59:16; 90:14; 143:8).[2]

The women must still be grief-stricken because they give no thought to how they will move the stone before they set out. Their anxiety about the stone, however, allows the narrator to emphasize its great size. It cannot easily be rolled back; only a miracle can move it. The women do not come to the tomb with any sense of hope, and their fretting about the stone creates dramatic tension. When "they look up," they realize that they have been anxious about entering a tomb already open.[3] Even when they discover the stone removed, they are still unprepared for the news about what it means. They come to the tomb wondering how the stone can *be* moved; they leave wondering how the stone could *have been* moved. They come to the tomb to anoint the body of Jesus; they learn that he has received a higher anointing from God.

Mark is not interested in telling the story of how the stone was moved. The tomb is open so that the women can enter and see that Jesus is not there. But the tomb is not empty. Looking into the tomb, the women find a young man clothed in a white robe sitting on the right, the favorable side that bodes well. The readers are essentially left to guess for themselves who this

---

2. Gnilka, *Markus*, 2:341.

3. For the design of rock tombs, see R. H. Smith, "The Tomb of Jesus," *Biblical Archaeologist* 30 (1967): 80–90.

young man is, but recent interpretations that try to connect this young man to the young man who fled in the garden leaving behind his linen cloth are unwarranted.[4] He is an angelic figure, who gives a typical angelic reassurance, "Don't be alarmed" (16:6; cf. Dan. 8:17–18; 10:8–12).[5] Christian art has led us to imagine angels with expansive wings and halos. This angel is not like the fantastical "four living creatures" who came to Ezekiel in a stormy wind with brightness and fire flashing forth (Ezek. 1:4–14). The biblical description of other angels depicts them as quite humanlike (Gen. 18:2; 19:1–11; Dan. 8:15–16; 9:21; 10:5).[6]

Mark's Gospel began with God's messenger announcing what God was about to do (1:2–8); it closes with God's messenger announcing what God has done. The clothes of both messengers are described. The rough hair shirt of the prophet contrasts with the white robe of the angel. The "way" figures in both scenes: In the opening scene, the way is to be prepared; in the last, the way has been prepared and disciples are to follow, going to Galilee, where Jesus has gone before them.

The angel's message in chapter 16, however, is more momentous than that of the prophet John. Only a divine being can disclose divine truth that is beyond ordinary human experience and knowledge, and the angel explains the meaning of the empty tomb. He comes also to steer the women to a new quest. As Minear puts it well, "God does not disclose the Resurrection fact except to enlist people in a task."[7] His greeting assures them that they are at the right tomb: "See the place where they laid him." They have not

---

4. For example, Robin Scroggs and Kent I. Groff ("Baptism in Mark: Dying and Rising with Christ," *JBL* 92 [1973]: 542) identify the young man as the Christian initiate in baptism who has laid aside his garments, descends into the water naked, and emerges clothed with a white garment. The young man who was stripped of everything is now restored, radiantly dressed and seated at the right hand, a fulfillment of Isa. 40:30–31. This interpretation is a case of extreme allegorization.

5. The white robe is the customary attire of heavenly beings. See Dan. 7:9; 2 Macc. 11:8–10; Acts 1:10; 10:30; Rev. 4:4; and the description of Jesus' garments in the Transfiguration (Mark 9:3).

6. Only the seraphim had wings, and they numbered six (Isa. 6:2). The cherubim had animal and human features. In 2 Macc. 3:26, 33, angels are described as "two other young men remarkably strong, strikingly beautiful, and splendidly attired." In Tob. 5:4–21, the angel Raphael appears as a man. According to *Bib. Ant.* 9:10, "a man in a linen garment" appeared to Miriam in a dream. And in 64:6, when Saul asked the witch of Endor about the appearance of Samuel, she responds that Saul is asking her about divine beings: "for behold his appearance is not the appearance of a man. For he is clothed in a white robe with a mantle placed over it, and two angels are leading him." Josephus describes the angel who appears to the wife of Manoah in Judg. 13:13 as being in the likeness of a beautiful youth (*Ant.* 5.8.2 § 277).

7. Minear, *Mark*, 134.

made a mistake. The angel also identifies the one they seek as "Jesus the Nazarene" (see 1:24; 10:47; 14:67), the crucified and risen one. His terse announcement of Jesus' resurrection, "he has risen," is similar to Mark's description of his execution: "and they crucified him" (15:24). The resurrection erases the disdain associated with the name "Nazarene" and the dishonor connected to being crucified. God reverses Jesus' miserable earthly fate, fulfilling his predictions that he would rise again (8:31; 9:31; 10:34).

Throughout the Gospel, Jesus has been on the move; nothing changes after his resurrection. He is not in the tomb for the women to cling to and embrace. Yet the story cannot end with a joyful reunion because the resurrection is only the beginning of the gospel that must be proclaimed throughout the world. The women must go to the disciples, who must in turn go to Galilee. This command is the first time that Jesus' followers are told to tell something about him. The crucifixion and the resurrection, therefore, mark a turning point. There is no need for silence or secrets now (see 9:9). As Marcus points out, "Whereas before those events Jesus commanded secrecy and open proclamation was disobedience, now Jesus commands open proclamation and secrecy is disobedience."[8]

Peter is especially singled out in the command, and this last reference to him forms a kind of inclusio. He is the first and last disciple mentioned in the Gospel (1:16; 16:7). The resurrection revokes death and destruction, and it also revokes sin. This special nod to Peter hints at his full restoration despite his extraordinary breach of faith. Jesus does not give up on his disciples, no matter how great their failure or how many their faults.

The announcement that "he is going ahead of you" is as important as the word that "he is not here." The verb used here (*proago*) does not simply mean that Jesus has gone on ahead of his disciples. Thucydides uses the verb for leading troops forward, and Polybius uses it for a commander making an advance.[9] Earlier, Jesus connected the promise that he would go before them to Galilee to the image of shepherd (14:27–28). Jesus has fed his flock (6:34) and has laid down his life for them, which caused them to be scattered. As the risen Lord, he will regather them into the fold. Just as the earthly Jesus led his frightened disciples to Jerusalem by going before them (10:32), so the risen Jesus goes ahead of them still, leading the church.

What is the significance of going back to Galilee? Many understand this reference as theological as well as literal geography. Some take it to be a symbolic summons to the Gentile mission. Mark, however, never refers to

---

8. Joel Marcus, "Mark 4:10–12 and Marcan Epistemology," *JBL* 103 (1984): 573.

9. Thucydides, *Hist.* 7.6.2; Polybius, *Hist.* 3.60.13; 3.72.8; 4.80.3; 5.7.6; 5.13.9; 5.48.12; 5.57.6; 5.70.12; 9.18.7; 11.20.4; 12.17.3; 27.16.3; 31.17.5.

Galilee as the "Galilee of the Gentiles," as Matthew does (Matt. 4:15). If anything symbolizes the Gentile mission in Mark, it is Jesus' forays *outside* Galilee. Others interpret the verb "to see" ("there you will see him") to refer to the Parousia rather than the resurrection (see Mark 13:26; 14:62). They explain this command to mean that the disciples (and Mark's readers) are to assemble in Galilee to await the eschatological climax. But Mark does not associate Galilee with the Parousia either. The reference to Galilee in 14:28 explicitly connects it with Jesus' resurrection ("after I have risen"), not his Parousia. The verb "to see," therefore, refers to seeing the risen Lord (see John 20:18, 25, 29; 1 Cor. 9:1).

The command to go to Galilee does make one thing clear: Jerusalem is not the center of God's movement. The disciples' future lies elsewhere. Jerusalem has become the city of the fruitless and doomed temple, the stronghold of hostility to the gospel, and the place of Jesus' savage execution. In the Gospel, Galilee has been the place of calling, faith, compassion, healing power, and authority. By going back to Galilee where Jesus will be, the disciples go back to the promising birth of their call to discipleship. There they can regroup and begin again the journey of discipleship.

In Galilee the disciples will physically see Jesus, but "seeing" also has to do with spiritual perception (2:5; 4:12; 8:18; 15:39)—something that has eluded the disciples more often than not in the narrative. They will also see him "in the sense of gaining true insight into his identity."[10] Jesus will heal them of their blindness so that they will understand fully who he is, what his life and death mean, and how they must now follow him. The disciples' shabby performance during the last week of Jesus' life has exposed them as sinners. Now Jesus will regather them as a new people who take up their cross, following after him and proclaiming God's triumph over Satan, sin, and death. Their eyes and ears will be open; they will know more about where the road leads.

The Conclusion to the Gospel

IN THE EARLIEST and most reliable manuscripts, Mark's Gospel ends with verse 8. Such an abrupt ending has perplexed readers for centuries. Many argue that Mark would not have left the narrative hanging and must have continued with a fuller picture of what happened next. They point to several problems with this ending. (1) It seems unusual, if not impossible in Greek, to end a paragraph, let alone a book, with the conjunction "for" (*ephobounto gar*, "for they were afraid"). (2) It seems unusual to end the story

---

10. Marshall, *Faith As a Theme*, 40.

with the women paralyzed by fear and failing to carry out what the angel commissioned them to do. (3) It seems peculiar that Mark would not include some account of Jesus' meeting his disciples in Galilee since the resurrection appearances were a basic element of Christian preaching from the beginning (see 1 Cor. 15:5).

These objections do not carry the verdict, however. The grammar may be thought graceless, like ending an English sentence with a preposition; but Mark is not known for his elegant style, and verse 8 is a complete thought.[11] The shorter and longer endings to Mark have the women informing the disciples about what they have seen, which appears to contradict the statement that "they said nothing to anyone." As for this final gap in the narrative, Hooker notes that Mark's method throughout the Gospel has been "to leave his readers to make the crucial step of faith."[12] The restoration of the "scattered disciples" occurs beyond the narrative of the Gospel.

Convincing arguments tell against the longer ending (16:9–20) as the original ending to Mark. The two oldest Greek manuscripts omit it, along with many versions, and early church fathers show no knowledge of its existence. The longer ending's vocabulary and style differ strikingly from that found in the rest of Mark and are immediately recognizable. The transition between 16:8 and 16:9 is also awkward. In 16:8, the women are the subject. The subject suddenly switches to Jesus in 16:9,[13] when he appears to Mary Magdalene, completely ignoring the other two women. Mary Magdalene is specifically identified as the one from whom Jesus had cast out seven demons (see Luke 8:2), although she had already been introduced in 15:40, 47 and 16:1 without any such description. Why would the fourth mention of Mary Magdalene suddenly introduce this background? It serves as a tip-off that a later scribe, drawing on other traditions, has added this section.

Moreover, all of the material in 16:9–20 appears to be garnered from accounts found in the other three Gospels: the appearance to Mary Magdalene (16:9–11; cf. John 20:14–18); the appearance to two disappointed disciples in the country (Mark 16:12–13; cf. Luke 24:13–35); the commissioning of the disciples (Mark 16:14–16; cf. Matt. 28:16–20); speaking in tongues (Mark 16:17; cf. Acts 2:4–11; 10:46; 19:6); handling snakes (Mark 16:18a; cf.

---

11. Many scholars have found examples where sentences end in *gar*; see Peter W. van der Horst, "Can a Book End with *gar*?" *JTS* 23 (1972): 121–24. See also Mark's use of *gar*: "for they were fishermen" (1:16); "for she was twelve years" (5:42); "for they were exceedingly afraid" (9:6); "for they feared him" (11:18); "for it was very large" (16:4). See also Gen. 18:15 (LXX), where Sarah denied that she had laughed, "for she was afraid."

12. Hooker, *Mark*, 392.

13. Contrary to the NIV, the name "Jesus" is not mentioned. We only know Jesus must be the subject of the verb because the participle *anastas* is masculine.

Luke 10:19; Acts 28:3–6); laying on hands (Mark 16:18b; cf. Acts 3:1–10; 5:12–16; 9:12, 17–18; James 5:14–15); the ascension of Jesus (Mark 16:19; cf. Luke 24:50–53; Acts 1:9–11). That a later scribe compiled these excerpts from the other Gospels to provide an orthodox and more satisfactory conclusion to Mark's Gospel is the most likely explanation. Even the longer ending has been subject to tinkering. Sixteen lines of text that describe Jesus' upbraiding of his disciples and his outlining an eschatological scheme have been appended to 16:14 in one ancient fragment.

The existence of a shorter ending suggests that other scribes tried their hand at tying up the loose ends of what was considered a ragged and inconclusive finale. This text appears in only a handful of later manuscripts. The phrase "the sacred and imperishable proclamation of eternal salvation" clearly smacks of the vocabulary and style of a later era.

The two main extant endings to Mark testify that some early readers did not appreciate an ending that left everything in the air. One naturally wants to bring a sense of closure to the story and to pad it with something more uplifting and reassuring. Both variants, in my opinion, are examples of a less-skilled hand trying to fix what the Master had not made explicit or had made too explicit, like the later artists who tried to fix Michelangelo's masterpiece in the Sistine Chapel by painting clothes on naked figures.

Some scholars who judge these surviving endings to the Gospel to be spurious surmise that the Evangelist never completed the Gospel for some reason.[14] Various imaginative explanations have been proposed. Perhaps Mark was martyred before finishing the task. The Gospel's ending was possibly damaged in some way and lost. A column or two at the end of the scroll could have been accidentally torn off or tattered from frequent use. If it were a codex, one could imagine that the first leaf would have also been damaged. The Gospel of Mark begins no less abruptly than it ends. Perhaps a birth narrative has disappeared as well as the resurrection narrative. If the ending were lost, presumably from constant use, however, it would have been in use long enough for someone to restore the ending from memory or for other copies to exist. Otherwise, the loss must have occurred almost immediately.

Against such speculation, Hooker observes that it is "remarkable ... that an accidental break should have occurred at a point where a case can at least be made for arguing that Mark intended to stop."[15] Many today have discerned literary genius in the sudden ending to the Gospel and appreciate its artistic effect. It is unlikely that the Gospel would fortuitously break off at

---

14. So Cranfield, *Mark*, 471; Schweizer, *Mark*, 366; Gundry, *Mark*, 1009–12.
15. Hooker, *Mark*, 383.

precisely the right word,[16] and the great textual critic Kurt Aland character-izes attempts to recover the lost ending as fascinating but "will of the wisp."[17] In my opinion, Mark fully intended to end his Gospel with the startling dis-closure that the women spoke to no one because they were afraid. If we want to understand Mark, we must grapple with this awkward conclusion no matter how unsatisfying it might be.

The abrupt ending both surprises and creates suspense. Mark may have felt no need to relate resurrection appearances to readers who had heard them so often. Magness argues that it was standard literary practice in the ancient world to allude to well-known events that occurred after those being narrated in a text without actually narrating those events.[18] Peterson makes a distinction between "story time" and "plotted time."[19] The ancient stylist Demetrius advises leaving gaps in narratives: "Some things seem to be more significant when not expressed," and those omissions "will make an expres-sion more forcible."[20]

In sum, the ending goads the reader to react. We must assume that the dis-ciples reunite with Jesus in story time, though not in the plotted time of the Gospel; otherwise this Gospel would never have been written. We must now become participants because we are forced to fill in the unnarrated events from the clues Mark has offered thus far. When presented with this ending, we must ask, "What happened? What will happen?" We must also go to Jesus and not only tell about his resurrection but tell the entire story from the beginning.

The Women's Fear

THIS CONCLUSION ABOUT Mark's ending raises questions about the women's departure from the tomb and the nature of their fear. One might expect them to run quickly from the tomb with fear and great joy and tell his dis-ciples (so Matt. 28:8), but Mark reports that they dash away in incoherent silence. Are their flight and silence to be attributed to faintheartedness and disobedience or to urgency and awe? Is one to understand their silence as only temporary incapacity because of the breathtaking nature of the news or as another sad example of abject failure by Jesus' followers?

---

16. Bilezikian (*The Liberated Gospel*, 136) argues: "In artistic endeavors serendipity is the result of diligence, not chance."

17. Kurt Aland, "Die wiedergefundene Markusschluss," *ZTK* 67 (1970): 3–13.

18. J. L. Magness, *Sense and Absence* (Semeia Studies; Atlanta: Scholars, 1986), 30–31.

19. Norman R. Peterson, *Literary Criticism for New Testament Critics* (Philadelphia: Fortress, 1978), 49–80.

20. *On Style*, 119–20; cited by Gerd Theissen, *The Miracles Stories of the Early Christian Tra-dition* (Philadelphia: Fortress, 1983), 167.

Some contend that the women's silence depicts the effects of a frightening encounter with divine power. Jesus told his disciples, "The secret of the kingdom of God has been given to you" (4:11), but sometimes the mystery's staggering nature is too much to comprehend. The women's fear may be interpreted as awe that befalls one who stands before God's presence and action (see Ps. 2:11)—an explanation that makes Mark's conclusion less grim. Jesus' resurrection from the dead is so astounding that one cannot grasp it all, and the women need time to collect their thoughts. When they flee the tomb, their sense of urgency causes them to speak to no one on the way (see Luke 10:4; cf. 2 Kings 4:29). Minear's poetic conclusion to his commentary on Mark best summarizes this interpretation of the women's flight.

> The amazement of the women (vs. 5) turns into trembling, astonishment, fear, flight, silence. All of these are considered in the Bible to be appropriate and normal human responses to the appearance of God, to a messenger from God, to an event in which God's power is released. The prophets all knew this fear and trembling (for example, Isa. 6). They all knew the unutterable weakness of those who receive God's call. Fear stresses the reality of the divine power and glory. Flight (very different from the flight at Jesus' arrest) accents the unbearable character of the presence of God. Silence is appropriate to God's speaking, and to the stupendous impact of God's word. Who can stand when he appears? Who can speak when he speaks? Who can remain calm when he gives a commission? At least the women could not, and presumably neither could the disciples when the message from the women had been delivered, starting them on their new work.[21]

But this is not the only possible interpretation. People respond with fear throughout Mark. The disciples were awestruck when confronted with Jesus' overwhelming power to calm the sea (4:41). The Gerasenes feared Jesus' power to drive out a legion of demons and to restore a man to his right mind (5:15). A woman feared when her plague was healed by simply touching his garments (5:33). The disciples were filled with fear when they saw Jesus walk on the sea (6:50), appear transfigured (9:6), and march undaunted toward his destiny on a cross (10:32). Humans have been deaf and dumb to God's glory throughout the story. Why should we not expect this same reaction when these women meet with the most powerful divine act of all, Jesus' resurrection from the dead?

---

21. Minear, *Mark*, 136.

Juel points out a "great irony" here: "When followers are finally told to speak about Jesus, they say nothing to anyone."[22] It is absurd, however, to think that something this incredible can be kept quiet for long. That these women say nothing immediately does not mean that they never speak anything for decades. Their silence will only be limited.[23] Throughout the Gospel it has been impossible to keep silent the stupendous miracles of Christ. Something this remarkable cannot be kept hidden.

On the other hand, one can interpret the women's fear as an improper reaction and their silent stupor as disobedience.[24] Peter's wrong response to the Transfiguration is connected to fear: "He did not know what to say, they were so frightened" (9:6). The disciples' fear in following Jesus to Jerusalem is a sign of their weakness and incomprehension in spite of the private tutorials (9:32; 10:32). Just as the disciples failed when they beat a retreat at Jesus' arrest (14:50–52), followed him from a distance (14:54), and denied him before others (14:66–72), so the women failed by standing at a distance during his crucifixion (15:40), not confessing at his death; and they fail again as they flee from the tomb, not telling the good tidings.

It is not a closed-minded disbelief that muzzles their voices; that would drain the power of the gospel (see 6:3–5). Rather, the cause is pure and simple fear. Fear surfaces among Jesus' followers both before the cross and after the resurrection. The resurrection does not mean that all now is set right and that everyone will live happily ever after. The flesh is still weak (14:38). The discourse on the Mount of Olives makes it clear that after the resurrection, Jesus' followers will be living in a period of woes. There will be wars (13:7), persecution (13:9), betrayal (13:12–13), tribulation (13:19), and deception (13:21–22). If they proclaim the good news, Jesus has promised that they will be hated by all (13:13). Many will suffer the same fear as the women and will try to take cover in silence. Disciples need to learn to lose their lives to save them, which means losing their fear.

The beginning of the Gospel also matches the end in that there is no closure to the story of the temptation. The reader is not told the outcome. Jesus is left in the desert and served by angels. The scene beginning the next section shows him in Galilee, proclaiming the gospel. The reader is therefore subconsciously prepared for the ending. Jesus has battled the forces of evil on the cross and has conquered death through the empty tomb. The next scene assumes that there will be a rendezvous in Galilee, where again the

---

22. Juel, *Mark*, 45.

23. Samuel was afraid to tell the of his vision to Eli (1 Sam. 3:15) but eventually did. As Daniel kept silent about the visions in his head but eventually made them known (Dan. 7:28) (noted by Pesch, *Das Markusevangelium*, 2:536).

24. Andrew Lincoln, "The Promise and the Failure: Mark 16:7,8," *JBL* 108 (1989): 286–87.

good news of victory will ring out, only this time it will be of an even greater and decisive victory.

Bridging Contexts

NO CANONICAL GOSPEL narrates a description of the resurrection. It is only prophesied in advance, foreshadowed in the Transfiguration, and announced after the fact. Mark does not answer the prying questions that both the skeptical and pious might raise today: When did he arise? By what means? In what form? By what evidence may we be sure?[25] The resurrection is something off the map of what we can know through our primitive historical and scientific methods. Mark also does not present the empty tomb as proof of the resurrection. He does not argue that because the grave is empty, Jesus must be resurrected.

Without question, the tomb was empty, but others in the first century drew quite different conclusions from that fact. Matthew reports that the leaders began to spread a rumor that the disciples came at night and stole the body (Matt. 28:11–13). An empty tomb therefore provides no conclusive proof. Instead, Mark argues: Jesus has been resurrected; therefore he is not here.[26] Jesus has promised that God will raise him from the dead, and the angel announces that God has done so. Faith rests on the proclamation of the resurrection and going to see him. This leads us to the more important questions: Where is he? and, How can we find him?

Mark's Gospel ends on a puzzling note: an empty tomb, a mysterious young man declaring that Jesus has been raised but offering no proof, a promise of Jesus' going ahead of his disciples (or leading them) to Galilee, and women too scared to say anything. This strange, dissatisfying ending does not seem an appropriate one for a story supposed to be good news. Instead of triumph and joy, we encounter confusion and terror. We expect that something good is going to happen when the women find the large stone rolled away, but it does not. The angel does not announce, "Surprise! Here he is!" but "He is not here!" The women go from the tomb, but they do not go and tell as the angel instructed them. The angel does not track them down to reassure them again and spur them on to complete the task.

---

25. Minear, *Mark*, 134.

26. A. Lindemann, "Die Osterbotschaft des Markus. Zur theologischen Interpretation von Mark 16:1–8," *NTS* 26 (1980): 305. See William Lane Craig, "Did Jesus Rise from the Dead?" in *Jesus Under Fire: Modern Scholarship Reinvents the Historical Jesus*, eds. Michael J. Wilkins and J. P. Moreland (Grand Rapids: Zondervan, 1995), 141–76, for an excellent assessment of the evidence for the resurrection of Jesus. For a more popular treatment, see Murray J. Harris, *Three Critical Questions About Jesus* (Grand Rapids: Baker, 1994), 31–64.

In other words, Mark's ending seems to lead to a dead end. Since Mark does not record Jesus' rendezvous with his disciples in Galilee, the last words he speaks in this Gospel are: "My God, my God, why have you forsaken me?" (15:34). We readers may feel a little forsaken at this point. Any anticipation of a grand, triumphant reunion with the remnant of faithful disciples, of more proofs of the verity of Jesus' resurrection, and of more specific instructions and assurances is smashed by this abrupt ending.

It is not as if no one will learn or can find out what happened next. We can assume that this Gospel's first auditors were familiar with the account of the postresurrection appearances since they were so well known at Corinth (1 Cor. 15:3–10). Mark's ending, in fact, conforms to the creedal formula in 1 Corinthians 15:3–5:

1 Corinthians 15	Mark 16
Christ died for our sins (v. 3).	You are looking for Jesus the Nazarene, who was crucified (v. 6).
He was buried (v. 4).	See the place where they laid him (v. 6).
He was raised on the third day (v. 4).	He has risen! He is not here (16:6).
He appeared to Cephas, and then to the Twelve (v. 5)	Tell his disciples and Peter, "He is going ahead of you into Galilee. There you will see him, just as he told you" (v. 7).

One is left to speculate why Mark does not supply all the details of the resurrection appearances. Did he want to emphasize Jesus' humanity and consequently shrink from reporting his appearances as a resurrected heavenly being? The first auditors were not hoping for a private appearance of Jesus to a select few but the consummation of the age, when Jesus would become manifest to all as the Son of God and before whom every knee would bow. Did Mark want to stress that the next time disciples would see him was when he returned in the clouds with great power and glory and dispatched his angels to gather his elect from the four winds (13:26–27)?

Recent reader response criticism offers perhaps the best explanation for this hanging conclusion. Mark wants to draw the reader into this account. He writes for Christians who are already acquainted with the account of Jesus' resurrection. They do not fret, "Oh, those foolish women, who never told the good news! Now no one will ever know what happened!" They know that the news has been proclaimed. Readers can deduce this from the text. How else could the report of the Transfiguration, witnessed only by Peter, James, and John, have been made known? Jesus commanded them not to tell what happened *"until [he] had risen from the dead"* (9:9).

A secular literary critic has commented on Mark's ending: "The conclusion is either intolerably clumsy; or it is incredibly subtle."[27] I would argue that it is incredibly subtle and consequently incredibly powerful. It forces us back into the narrative to fill the gaps, and we see that Jesus' words have been fulfilled to the letter in everything that has happened to this point. We know that Jesus' word is trustworthy, and his promises will come true. Jesus promised his disciples that they would be scattered and he would go before them to Galilee (14:28). We know that they did from accounts beyond this narrative, but the Gospel ends like one of Jesus' parables and forces us to work things out for ourselves.[28] This incomplete ending, therefore, has Christ still waiting symbolically in Galilee for his followers to come and forces us to ask whether we will go to meet him there as well. It also prompts us to reflect on our own fear and silence.

We expect more from the end of this Gospel because modern readers are familiar with the more extensive endings of the other Gospels. Since preachers frequently choose the texts they use for Easter worship, many prefer to preach the resurrection accounts from one of the other Gospels or to use the long ending of Mark, so familiar to people raised on the KJV. They may regard Mark's stopping point as intolerably clumsy, completely inadequate, or deeply unsatisfying. This ending does not quite fit the Easter hymns with their alleluias. Its incredible subtlety and power, therefore, goes untapped. It comes as a jolt, but one can profit greatly from reflecting on what this abrupt ending means.

(1) "He is not here. See the place where they laid him." There is no reunion with the familiar earthly form of Jesus, with tears of joy and hugs all around. Jesus cannot be held by death, let alone by a stone. He is free from death, transformed from this earthly existence and unleashed on the world. One cannot meet him at the place where they laid him. His grave is not to become a shrine like David's tomb (Acts 2:29), the dressed-up tombs of the prophets (Matt. 23:29–31), or the tombs of modern-day leaders. The God who raises the dead has no use for earthly memorials. The tombstone is not to become a wailing wall. God is not the God of the dead, entombed in shrines, but of the living.

(2) When we read accounts of Jesus' resurrection, we look for confirmation that what we believe about Jesus' resurrection is completely trustworthy rather than being presented with more disturbing questions. Mark disappoints us. He opened his Gospel with a voice from heaven authenticating Jesus' identity, mission, and authority. At the end, we have only the testimony

---

27. Frank Kermode, *The Genesis of Secrecy* (Cambridge, Mass.: Harvard, 1979), 68.
28. Best, *The Gospel as Story*, 132–33.

of a young man, whom we can identify as an angel, and the witness of women whose testimony was considered to be invalid—and they keep mum. The resurrection, as Mark presents it, is not formally verifiable according to scientific rules of evidence. Mark offers no evidence that the young man's message is true, except that he reiterates precisely what Jesus said would happen (14:28). The reader is therefore left in suspense with the bare word of Jesus' promise.

We may want from Mark what Acts reports: "He showed himself to these men and gave many convincing proofs that he was alive" (Acts 1:3). Today, however, one cannot prove scientifically beyond a shadow of a doubt that the resurrection occurred. Belief that the resurrection did happen is a logical inference. When other messianic figures, such as Bar Kochba, died, their followers did not solve the problem of their disappointing deaths by inventing stories of their resurrection. They reacted the same way the disciples on the Emmaus road did after the crucifixion: "We had hoped that he was the one who was going to redeem Israel," but we were wrong (Luke 24:21). One does not logically infer resurrection from crucifixion. The first Christians' firm belief that God raised Jesus from the dead can only stem from the fact that something actually happened.

The Gospels, however, do not offer proof for those who say, in effect, "Show us and we will believe" (Mark 15:32). When we proclaim the text from Mark, we should not try to supplement the account by amassing other convincing proofs. All we have is the news that Jesus has been raised. If any want to see Jesus for themselves, they must leave the tomb and go where he leads—to Galilee, back to the beginning, where one must learn to follow him again. If we ask where the Christ is, Mark's answer is that he is always on ahead of us, leading us on to new lands. Jesus is to be found today in obedience to his command.

(3) Mark does not dwell on the theological significance of the resurrection. The reader can see that Jesus' resurrection reverses the humiliation and degradation of his scandalous crucifixion. The God who brought Israel up out of the sea (Isa. 63:11) has brought Jesus up from the grave. His resurrection sets the stage for his exaltation to the right hand of Power, where he now reigns and will return to judge (Mark 8:38; 14:62) and to gather the elect (13:26–27). The reader can surmise that Jesus' resurrection is qualitatively different from the raising of Jairus's daughter. His resurrection not only permanently exalts him as the firstborn of those raised from the dead, but becomes a saving event for all those who confess him as the Son of God and follow him in obedience. God has decisively answered the women's question, "Who will roll the stone away?"—not only from Jesus' grave but also from ours. Jesus' resurrection destroys the power of death over human beings,

which seems to be a huge stone that no one can ever roll it away. The message of Jesus' resurrection transforms a hopeless end into an endless hope.

(1) MARK'S ENDING teaches us that Christians after the resurrection must still live with ambiguity. We want the Gospel to conclude on a note of victory and good cheer, but that was not Mark's situation. The ache of death is not so easily assuaged. Mark writes for those who never will experience Jesus' physical presence. He writes for those who may feel like the disciples, struggling against the wind in a tiny skiff during the dark hours of the night and feeling acute anguish because Jesus is not physically there to be touched or to give a word of assurance. In a setting of withering persecution, things can look ambiguous. The risen Jesus does not materialize bodily in our midst. Angels do not descend to give reassuring reports. We have to believe in Jesus' resurrection based on hearsay evidence—the same report that the women heard: "He has risen." Lincoln writes: "Even after God's revelation has taken place in Jesus' resurrection, mystery, fear, and failure remain."[29]

Confusion also reigns in the other Gospels when news of Jesus' resurrection breaks. In Matthew, some doubt when Jesus appears to the Eleven (Matt. 28:17); Jesus dispels that doubt by his word of command (Matt. 28:19–20). On the Emmaus road, two friends mistake the risen Jesus for a stranger (Luke 24:13–21); their eyes are opened only after Jesus breaks bread with them. In the Fourth Gospel, Mary Magdalene confuses the resurrected Jesus for the gardener (John 20:11–18); her despair is allayed when Jesus calls her name. The resurrection has not completely changed people's cloudy vision or their sinfulness. People will still tell lies about him, and his messengers will still be beaten and killed. Followers will still experience confusion. Only at the end of time, when the Son of Man is manifest in all his glory, will all ambiguity be eliminated.

Like the first auditors of this Gospel, we have only the reports from the eyewitnesses to confirm the resurrection, no scientific proof. How will we know for sure that what they say is true? Will we be willing to stake our lives on that truth? Will we demand something more from God before we will make a commitment? Mark's ending shows that the historical question, "Was it real?" ignores the more crucial question, "Is it real?" Something other than a pious dropping by the tomb once every Easter and looking in to see that it is empty is required to spark faith.

---

29. Lincoln, "The Promise and the Failure," 298.

(2) The ending of this Gospel means that the last scene in which Jesus speaks is from the cross. In Mark one sees most vividly the power of God working in the crucifixion. The ending therefore means that one cannot proclaim the glories of the resurrection to the neglect of the suffering of the cross. The confession, "Surely this man was the Son of God!" (15:39), comes when Jesus dies on the cross, not at the empty tomb.

(3) The ending touches on the problem that fallible humans must live with failure. The way of discipleship is not a triumphant procession through the world, like a hot knife cutting through butter. It is a way pocked by personal failure after personal failure. It may seem that the Gospel ends on a pessimistic note because Mark does not report that the women successfully fulfill their commission. Mark's story, however, is not about the disciples' foolishness and failure. The gospel is about the power of God, which overcomes human dysfunction and disaster. We know that Jesus' resurrection was proclaimed and is being proclaimed throughout the world, just as Jesus said it would. This means that God's will and Jesus' promise have been fulfilled *despite* human disobedience. Jesus promised his disciples that he would go before them to Galilee in 14:28, and the angel reiterates that promise in 16:7. Mark only recorded the promise in 16:7 because he knew it took place, though he has chosen not to tell us the details. Lane perceptively comments, "The focus upon human inadequacy, lack of understanding and weakness throws into bold relief the action of God and its meaning."[30]

Mark's ending, therefore, reveals that the "successful conclusion of the story" cannot be "dependent upon human performance."[31] McDonald rightly sees that this ending "conveys the continued power and presence of God in human weakness, and therefore hope and expectation for the future."[32] Though these women appear to be more faithful and stronger than the men, watching at the cross and coming to tend his body, their nerve fails them in the end. Consequently, the divine promise is wreathed by human weakness. The reader, who knows that the promise was fulfilled, can only assume that it came to pass because God overruled human failure and disobedience.[33] We thus learn that with God our failure is not fatal. But we cannot jump for joy and give one another high fives as members of winning sports teams do. We consistently fail. We must humbly and consistently turn to God for help and can give only God the glory when failure turns into victory by divine power.

---

30. Lane, *Mark*, 592.

31. Juel, *Mark*, 234.

32. J. I. H. McDonald, *The Resurrection Narrative and Belief* (London: SPCK, 1989), 52.

33. Lincoln, "The Promise and the Failure," 292–93.

The fulfillment of this promise to go to Galilee suggests to us that Jesus' other promises will come true as well.

- John prophesied that the one coming after him would baptize with the Holy Spirit (1:8). Mark does not narrate the fulfillment of this prophecy, but the auditors know it has come true because they have experienced this baptism for themselves.
- Jesus promised Peter and Andrew that he would make them fishers of men (1:15).
- He promised Peter that those who have made sacrifices to follow him will receive a hundredfold more and in the age to come, eternal life (10:29–30).
- He promised James and John that they would be baptized with his baptism and would drink his cup (10:39).
- He promised that before the end comes, the gospel will be preached to all the nations (13:10).
- He promised that the woman's extravagant anointing of him for his burial will be remembered wherever the gospel is preached in the whole world (14:9).
- He promised his disciples that some would not taste death before they saw the kingdom of God come with power (9:1).
- He assured his disciples that he will drink from the fruit of the vine anew in the kingdom of God (14:25).
- He promised the high priest and his council that they would see the Son of Man sitting at the right hand of the Mighty One and coming on the clouds of heaven (14:62).

Because Jesus' foreknowledge of what was to come has been proven, we can trust that what he says will come true despite human muddling and satanic opposition, not only in the lives of his first disciples, but also in the lives of persons today.

The last word, therefore, ultimately belongs to God, who will accomplish all things. Like the seed that grows, the farmer knows not how (4:27), Jesus' promises will be fulfilled and we know not how. As Geddert states it well:

> Whether Jesus is walking on water (6:49), or on the dusty road from Galilee to Jerusalem (10:32)—whether Jesus is sharing a loaf with twelve companions (14:22), or a lunch with five thousand (6:39–44)—whether he rises early to spend the morning in prayer (1:35), or to spend eternity as the resurrected Lord (16:1–8)—the kingdom is secretly advancing. We only know that their fulfillment depends upon God's power, not on human capacity to carry out orders effectively.

The hidden potency of God's kingdom will burst forth in full proclamation.[34]

This truth puts in a new light the disciples' failures in this Gospel to understand (6:52; 8:17–18), to exorcise demons (9:14–29), to stand with Jesus during the fiery test, and to herald the resurrection. Failure does not mean the end of discipleship or the defeat of God's purposes. The words of Jesus will not fail, and his promise will overcome the disciples' bungling and dereliction of duty.

Brown writes that Mark and his readers probably held Peter and his disciples as "saintly witnesses." He goes on to say:

> But Mark uses the Gospel to stress that such witness to Jesus did not come easily or under the disciples' own impetus. .... Mark is offering a pedagogy of hope based on the initial failure of the most famous followers of Jesus and a second chance for them. He may have in mind readers who failed initially or became discouraged by the thought of the cross. He is issuing parenetic warnings against the danger of being scandalized or falling away from faith and against overconfidence.[35]

Consequently, Mark presents no model disciples. All of Jesus' followers, male and female, falter. Achtemeier observes:

> If the disciples were unfaithful because they could not come to terms with Jesus' death, the women proved unfaithful precisely because they had come to terms with it: it was the news that he was no longer dead that proved unsettling to them. They in their turn were unable to come to terms with his life.[36]

Discipleship is established by Jesus' call and can only be sustained by God's mercy and power alone. We can take comfort from this fact when we also fail in our commission, as we inevitably will. Everything depends on God, not us. When we do succeed, we can therefore only give credit to God.

(4) This ending fits the title of Mark's Gospel: "The beginning of the gospel about Jesus Christ, the Son of God" (1:1). The burial of Jesus and the news of his resurrection bring the narrative to a close, but the resurrection is not the end of the story, only the beginning. How does one end such a story? Juel comments that "just as the tomb will not contain Jesus, neither can

---

34. Geddert, *Watchwords*, 202.
35. Brown, *The Death of the Messiah*, 1:141.
36. Achtemeier, "Mark," 4:556.

Mark's story."[37] The resurrection sets in motion a new story that is not yet finished or resolved. It will not be completed until the elect are gathered from the ends of the earth (13:27). What happens next, then, is up to us as believers.

We cannot allow the resurrection account to become a faded if cherished memory that is to be placed in a photo album and taken out once a year and admired. The ending forces us to enter the story. We are the next chapter. What would we have done if we were those first women let in on the tremendous news? The question then becomes not what will the women do—how long will they keep silent?—but what will we do now that we have been let in on the news? Will we flee in fear and become silent? Will the story die with us? Will we obediently follow Jesus to Galilee or try to hunker down in our safe cocoons?

The Gospel of Mark leaves us with unfinished business to preach the gospel to the ends of the earth. The ending (which is not an ending) becomes a never-ending story as the baton passes on to us to join in the race and spread the news. Mark's stunning ending raises the question, Who will tell the story? His Gospel is the account of the beginning of the gospel; will we now join in its continuation?

Many will hear news during Easter Sunday worship that Jesus has been raised and will sing hymns praising God. All too many will then go home quietly to an Easter dinner and go back to the routines of their lives, largely unaffected by the news. They are neither filled with awe nor compelled to tell anyone about what they know. Will the story be told by anyone other than the Evangelist? What stops it from being told? We are no less susceptible to fear than the disciples when they were caught off guard by a violent posse in Gethsemane, than Peter when he was surrounded by a hostile crowd in enemy territory, than these women when they were confronted by this surprising news and told to go and tell in a death-filled world. Jesus goes on ahead, but we may remain frozen in our tracks, struck by a fear that makes us mute.

At the outset of God's great work, humans frequently recoil in fear. The command, "Do not be afraid," reverberates throughout Scripture. We must hear these words again and again because God is always doing what is unexpected and leading people where they may least want to go. Beginning from the time that God established a covenant with Abraham (Gen. 15:1), God has grand plans for Abraham's seed. He tells Jacob not to be afraid to go down to Egypt (46:3); he has grand plans to make a great nation. God promises through Isaiah that the enemies will vanish: "Do not fear; I will help you" (Isa. 41:13); "Fear not, for I have redeemed you" (43:2).

---

37. Juel, *Mark* 235.

Peter asks, "Who is going to harm you if you are eager to do good?" (1 Peter 3:13). The answer in the first century was, "Plenty." Enemies were everywhere, and their threats naturally elicited fear and inhibited witness. The kinds of people who killed Jesus are still out there, ready to kill his followers. No one enjoys being hated or hunted down. It is safer to remain silent, to treasure all these things in our hearts (Luke 2:51) rather than to bare our hearts to others. One might understand why those facing the persecution might be reticent to speak, but what excuse do those have who enjoy all the comforts of life and freedom of worship?

Scripture Index

Subject Index

Subject Index

We want to hear from you. Please send your comments about this book to us in care of the address below. Thank you.

GRAND RAPIDS, MICHIGAN 49530

www.zondervan.com